AIA

S
T
U
D
Y

T
E
X
T

PAPER 13
FINANCIAL ACCOUNTING 3

In this 2020 edition

- A **user-friendly format** for easy navigation
- **Exam-centred topic coverage**, directly linked to AIA's syllabus
- **Exam focus points** showing you what the examiner will want you to do
- Regular **fast forward** summaries emphasising the key points in each chapter
- **Questions** and **quick quizzes** to test your understanding
- **Exam question bank** containing further exam standard questions with answers
- **2 Mock exams** for real exam practice using the November 2017 and May 2018 exams
- A full index

FOR EXAMS IN 2020

BPP LEARNING MEDIA

First edition 2007
Thirteenth edition January 2020

ISBN 9781 5097 8728 9
(Previous ISBN 9781 5097 2511 3)

eISBN 9781 5097 2937 1
(Previous eISBN 9781 5097 2578 6)

British Library Cataloguing-in-Publication Data
A catalogue record for this book is available from the British Library

Published by

BPP Learning Media Ltd
BPP House, Aldine Place
142-144 Uxbridge Road
London W12 8AA

www.bpp.com/learningmedia

Printed in the United Kingdom

Your learning materials, published by BPP Learning Media Ltd, are printed on paper obtained from traceable sustainable sources.

All rights reserved. No part of this publication may be reproduced, stored in a retrieval system or transmitted in any form or by any means, electronic, mechanical, photocopying, recording or otherwise, without the prior written permission of BPP Learning Media.

The contents of this book are intended as a guide and not professional advice. Although every effort has been made to ensure that the contents of this book are correct at the time of going to press, BPP Learning Media makes no warranty that the information in this book is accurate or complete and accept no liability for any loss or damage suffered by any person acting or refraining from acting as a result of the material in this book.

We are grateful to the Association of International Accountants for permission to reproduce past examination questions. The suggested solutions in the exam answer bank have been prepared by BPP Learning Media Ltd.

BPP Learning Media is grateful to the IASB for permission to reproduce extracts from the International Financial Reporting Standards including all International Accounting Standards, SIC and IFRIC Interpretations (the Standards). The Standards together with their accompanying documents are issued by:

The International Accounting Standards Board (IASB) 30 Cannon Street, London, EC4M 6XH, United Kingdom. Email: info@ifrs.org Web: www.ifrs.org

Disclaimer: The IASB, the International Financial Reporting Standards (IFRS) Foundation, the authors and the publishers do not accept responsibility for any loss caused by acting or refraining from acting in reliance on the material in this publication, whether such loss is caused by negligence or otherwise to the maximum extent permitted by law.

©
BPP Learning Media Ltd
2020

A note about copyright

Dear Customer

What does the little © mean and why does it matter?

Your market-leading BPP books, course materials and e-learning materials do not write and update themselves. People write them on their own behalf or as employees of an organisation that invests in this activity. Copyright law protects their livelihoods. It does so by creating rights over the use of the content.

Breach of copyright is a form of theft – as well as being a criminal offence in some jurisdictions, it is potentially a serious breach of professional ethics.

With current technology, things might seem a bit hazy but, basically, without the express permission of BPP Learning Media:

- Photocopying our materials is a breach of copyright
- Scanning, ripcasting or conversion of our digital materials into different file formats, uploading them to facebook or e-mailing them to your friends is a breach of copyright

You can, of course, sell your books, in the form in which you have bought them – once you have finished with them. (Is this fair to your fellow students? We update for a reason.) Please note the e-products are sold on a single user licence basis: we do not supply 'unlock' codes to people who have bought them secondhand.

And what about outside the UK? BPP Learning Media strives to make our materials available at prices students can afford by local printing arrangements, pricing policies and partnerships which are clearly listed on our website. A tiny minority ignore this and indulge in criminal activity by illegally photocopying our material or supporting organisations that do. If they act illegally and unethically in one area, can you really trust them?

Copyright © IFRS Foundation

All rights reserved. Reproduction and use rights are strictly limited. No part of this publication may be translated, reprinted or reproduced or utilised in any form either in whole or in part or by any electronic, mechanical or other means, now known or hereafter invented, including photocopying and recording, or in any information storage and retrieval system, without prior permission in writing from the IFRS Foundation. Contact the IFRS Foundation for further details.

The IFRS Foundation logo, the IASB logo, the IFRS for SMEs logo, the "Hexagon Device", "IFRS Foundation", "eIFRS", "IAS", "IASB", "IFRS for SMEs", "IASs", "IFRS", "IFRSs", "International Accounting Standards" and "International Financial Reporting Standards", "IFRIC" "SIC" and "IFRS Taxonomy" are **Trade Marks** of the IFRS Foundation.

Further details of the Trade Marks including details of countries where the Trade Marks are registered or applied for are available from the Licensor on request.

Contents

Page

Introduction

The introduction pages contain lots of valuable advice and information. They include tips on studying for and passing the exam, also the content of the syllabus and what has been examined.

How the BPP Learning Media Study Text can help you pass – Help yourself study for your AIA exams – Syllabus – AIA List of examinable Standards – Command words and learning outcomes – The exam paper

Part A Contemporary issues
1. Current thought and practice 3
2. Presentation of published financial statements 27
3. Environmental and social reporting 51
4. Ethics and regulation of corporate financial reporting 71
5. Reporting for specialised entities 85

Part B Business combinations and group financial statements
6. Revision of basic groups 105
7. Complex groups 153
8. Changes in group structures 179
9. Foreign currency translation 207
10. Group statements of cash flows 233

Part C Accounting and reporting techniques
11. Interim reporting, first-time adoption and fair values 263
12. Tangible non-current assets and inventory 283
13. Intangible non-current assets 319
14. Financial instruments 339
15. Leasing contracts 377
16. Employee benefits 397
17. Taxation 421
18. Reporting financial performance 453
19. Provisions, contingencies and events after the reporting period 493
20. Related parties and share-based payment 507
21. Revenue recognition 525
22. IFRS for SMEs 551
23. Ratio and trend analysis 577

Answers to end of chapter questions 597

Exam question bank 633

Exam answer bank 675

Mock exam 1 759

Mock exam 2 777

Index 807

INTRODUCTION

How the BPP Learning Media Study Text can help you pass

> It provides you with the knowledge and understanding, skills and application techniques that you need to be successful in your exams

This Study Text has been targeted at the **Financial Accounting 3** syllabus.

- It is **comprehensive**. It covers the syllabus content. No more, no less.
- It is written at the **right level**. Each chapter is written with AIA's syllabus in mind.
- It is aimed at the **exam**. We have taken account of recent exams, guidance the examiner has given and the assessment methodology.

> It allows you to study in the way that best suits your learning style and the time you have available, by following your personal Study Plan (see page vi)

You may be studying at home on your own or you may be attending a course. You may like to read every word, or you may prefer to do a fast read through and learn through doing practise questions the rest of the time. However you study, you will find the BPP Learning Media Study Text meets your needs in designing and following your personal Study Plan.

Help yourself study for your AIA exams

Exams for professional bodies such as AIA are very different from those you have taken at college or university. You will be under **greater time pressure before** the exam – as you may be combining your study with work. Here are some hints and tips.

The right approach

1 **Develop the right attitude**

Believe in yourself	Yes, there is a lot to learn. But thousands have succeeded before and you can too.
Remember why you're doing it	You are studying for a good reason: to advance your career.

2 **Focus on the exam**

Read through the Syllabus	This tells you what you are expected to know and is supplemented by **Exam focus points** in the text.
Study the Exam paper section	Past papers are likely to be good guides to what you should expect in the exam.

3 **The right method**

See the whole picture	Keeping in mind how all the detail you need to know fits into the whole picture will help you understand it better. • The **Introduction** of each chapter puts the material in context. • The **Syllabus content** and **Exam focus points** show you what you need to **grasp**.
Use your own words	To absorb the information (and to practise your written communication skills), you need to **put it into your own words**. • Take **notes**. • Answer the **questions** in each chapter. • Draw **mindmaps**. • Try **'teaching' a subject** to a colleague or friend.
Give yourself cues to jog your memory	The Study Text uses **bold** to **highlight key points**. • Try **colour coding** with a highlighter pen. • Write **key points** on cards.

4 **The right recap**

Review, review, review	Regularly reviewing a topic in summary form can **fix it in your memory**. The Study Text helps you review in many ways. • **Chapter roundups** summarise the 'Fast forward' key points in each chapter. Use them to recap each study session. • The **Quick quiz** actively tests your grasp of the essentials. • Go through the **Examples** in each chapter a second or third time.

Developing your personal Study Plan

BPP recommends you follow a study plan. Planning and sticking to the plan are key elements of learning successfully.

There are five steps you should work through.

Step 1 **How do you learn?**

What types of intelligence do you display when learning? You might be advised to brush up on certain study skills before launching into this Study Text, but refer to the 'tackling your studies' section below which will help.

Step 2 **What do you prefer to do first?**

If you prefer to get to grips with a theory before seeing how it is applied, we suggest you concentrate first on the explanations we give in each chapter before looking at the examples and case studies. If you prefer to see first how things work in practice, read through the detail in each chapter, and concentrate on the examples and case studies, before supplementing your understanding by reading the detail.

Step 3 **How much time do you have?**

Work out the time you have available per week, given the following.

- The standard you have set yourself
- The other exam(s) you are sitting
- Practical matters such as work, travel, exercise, sleep and social life

Note your time available in box A.   A [Hours]

Step 4 **Allocate your time**

- Take the time you have available per week for this Study Text shown in box A, multiply it by the number of weeks available and insert the result in box B.   B [   ]

- Divide the figure in box B by the number of chapters in this text and insert the result in box C.   C [   ]

Remember that this is only a rough guide. Some of the chapters in this book are longer and more complicated than others, and you will find some subjects easier to understand than others.

Step 5 **Implement**

Set about studying each chapter in the time shown in box C, following the key study steps in the order suggested by your particular learning style.

This is your personal **Study Plan**. You should try to combine it with the study sequence outlined below. You may want to modify the sequence to adapt it to your **personal style**.

Tackling your studies

The best way to approach this Study Text is to tackle the chapters in order. Taking into account your individual learning style, you could follow this sequence for each chapter.

Key study steps	Activity
Step 1 **Topic list**	This topic list helps you navigate each chapter; each numbered topic is a numbered section in the chapter.
Step 2 **Introduction**	This sets your objectives for study by giving you the big picture in terms of the context of the chapter. The content is referenced to the syllabus, and Exam guidance shows how the topic is likely to be examined. The Introduction tells you **why** the topics covered in the chapter need to be studied.
Step 3 **Knowledge brought forward boxes**	These highlight information and techniques that it is assumed you have 'brought forward' with you from your earlier studies. Remember that you may be tested on these areas in the exam. If you are unsure of these areas, you should consider revising your more detailed study material from earlier papers.
Step 4 **Fast forward**	Fast forward boxes give you a quick summary of the content of each of the main chapter sections. They are listed together in the roundup at the end of each chapter to help you review each chapter quickly.
Step 5 **Explanations**	Proceed methodically through each chapter, particularly focusing on areas highlighted as significant in the chapter introduction, or areas that are frequently examined.
Step 6 **Key terms and Exam focus points**	• Key terms can often earn you **easy marks** if you state them clearly and correctly in an exam answer. They are highlighted in the index at the back of this text. • Exam focus points state how the topic has been or may be examined, difficulties that can occur in questions about the topic, and examiner feedback on common weaknesses in answers.
Step 7 **Note taking**	Take brief notes, if you wish. Don't copy out too much. Remember that being able to record something yourself is a sign of being able to understand it. Your notes can be in whatever format you find most helpful; lists, diagrams, mindmaps.
Step 8 **Examples**	Work through the examples very carefully as they illustrate key knowledge and techniques.
Step 9 **Case studies**	Study each one, and try to add flesh to them from your own experience. They are designed to show how the topics you are studying come alive in the real world.
Step 10 **Questions**	Attempt each one, as they will illustrate how well you've understood what you've read.
Step 11 **Answers**	Check yours against ours, and make sure you understand any discrepancies.
Step 12 **Chapter roundup**	Review it carefully, to make sure you have grasped the significance of all the important points in the chapter.
Step 13 **Quick quiz**	Use the Quick quiz to check how much you have remembered of the topics covered and to practise questions in a variety of formats.
Step 14 **Question practice**	Attempt the Question suggested at the very end of the chapter. These are all AIA past exam questions, so provide an excellent indication of the type and standard of question that you can expect in your real exam. Some of these questions cover more than one subject area, which is a common feature of exam questions.

AIA Achieve

AIA provides an interactive course of study AIA Achieve, which offers students the tools, resources and learning environment to study for the exams. The study tools include a course of study e-book, marked practice questions, marked mock exam paper and feedback and technical advice via an e-Tutor. Contact the Study Support team at: Achieve@aiaworldwide.com.

Moving on...

When you are ready to start revising, you should still refer back to this Study Text.

- As a source of **reference** (you should find the index particularly helpful for this)
- As a way to **review** (the Fast forwards, Exam focus points, Chapter roundups and Quick quizzes help you here)

Syllabus

Aims

The aim of the paper is to examine a candidate's ability to:

- Critically evaluate current thought and developments in international financial accounting and reporting

- Apply knowledge and professional judgement in an assessment of the requirements of international financial reporting standards and other reporting requirements

- Ability to prepare and assess a wide variety of accounting and financial statements in a wide variety of business contexts

The examination paper will be set within the context of financial accounting and reporting in accordance with the standards and other output of the International Accounting Standards Board and other related bodies such as the International Federation of Accountants (IFAC).

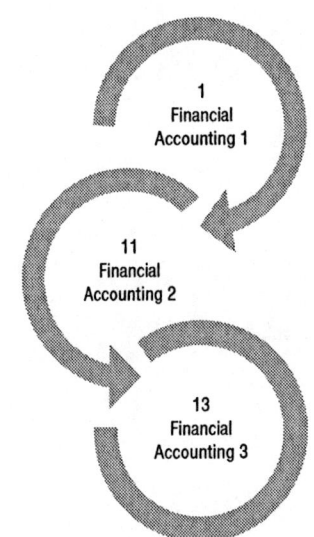

FIG. 13 INTER-RELATIONSHIP OF UNITS

Descriptors

In order to successfully complete this paper a candidate should be able to:

- Demonstrate through discussion and/or application of knowledge, a critical evaluation of current thought and developments in international financial accounting and reporting, including the ethical and professional responsibilities of an accountant, the *Conceptual Framework* and accounting regulation and specialised entities

- Demonstrate that he/she can apply and critically analyse and discuss current international reporting requirements and regulations

- Prepare and interpret a wide variety of corporate accounting and reporting statements including the financial statements of groups in accordance with appropriate international financial reporting standards

- Prepare and assess reports and other communications which aim to offer to users, professional advice on a group entity's financial performance and position

Structure of the Paper

Overall, the paper examines a candidate's ability to act in a professional capacity in the area of international financial accounting and reporting.

Assessment is by a three-hour 15 minute exam consisting of five questions. Section A will contain a compulsory scenario based question worth 40 marks which will involve the preparation of consolidated financial statements and the consideration of related financial reporting issues. Section B will be primarily case study based and will contain four questions which could concern any part of the syllabus. Each of Section B's questions will be worth 20 marks and students must attempt three.

Normally approximately 70% of the paper will be computational. The remainder (approximately 30%) will be essay based. Individual questions may have both computational and essay elements, so that the final ratio of computational to essay work produced by a candidate may vary with his/her choice of questions.

Syllabus

13.1 Contemporary Issues

Topic Weighting   15%

The development and application of international reporting practice, including:

- The development and application of international financial reporting standards including first-time adoption of IFRS and implications for an entity's accounting systems
- The IASB's *The Conceptual Framework for Financial Reporting*, including:
  - Its contribution in helping financial statements to meet the needs of users, including its role in the IASB's promulgation of the 'balance sheet method of income determination' and 'fair value'.
  - Implications of the convergence project for national standard-setters and their reporting requirements, including reasons for international differences in accounting practice
  - Exposure Drafts (EDs), Discussion Papers (DPs) and Interpretations by the IFRS Interpretations Committee as follows:
    - ED/2017/1 Annual Improvements to IFRSs (2015–2017 Cycle)
    - ED/2017/2 Improvements to IFRS 8 *Operating Segments* (Proposed amendments to IFRS 8 and IAS 34)
    - ED/2017/3 Prepayment Features with Negative Compensation (Proposed amendments to IFRS 9)
- Corporate environmental and social reporting
- The development of integrated reporting
- The management commentary

The ethical and professional responsibilities of accountants in a business context.

The application of knowledge from other parts of the syllabus to the financial reporting needs of not-for-profit organizations and small to medium-sized entities (SMEs).

13.2 The Financial Statements of Groups

Topic Weighting   45%

The preparation, presentation and assessment of financial statements of groups, including:

- Statements of comprehensive income, financial position, cash flow and changes in equity
- The identification and treatment of subsidiaries, associated companies, joint arrangements and foreign entities in complex groups
- Acquisitions and disposals, including piecemeal acquisitions and disposals and conversion of passive investments and/or associates into subsidiaries and vice versa; and measurement of goodwill and non-controlling interests using the fair value method
- Exclusion of subsidiaries from group accounts and exemptions from preparing group accounts
- Continuing and discontinued operations
- Reporting within hyperinflationary economies

INTRODUCTION

- Assessment of particular consolidation techniques and strategies including their impact on key performance indicators (KPIs). Impact on KPIs could include an assessment of ratios relevant to profit, profitability, liquidity, funds management and investment (including trend analysis) and could include consideration of the difficulties of international financial analysis.

13.3 Business Combinations

Topic Weighting   10%

Specific accounting and corporate reporting issues relating to business combinations and reconstructions including:

- Conceptual differences, including identification of control
- Acquisition accounting, including the determination of cost of acquisition and the recognition and measurement of identifiable net assets and goodwill and non-controlling interests
- Equity accounting versus proportional consolidation
- Assessment of an entity's going concern status, including accounting for a reconstruction
- Separate financial statements
- Joint arrangements

13.4 Accounting and Reporting Techniques

Topic Weighting   30%

Particular accounting and reporting issues involving the reporting of financial performance within the context of all types of proprietorship organisations, including:

- Accounting policies, changes in accounting estimates and errors
- Accounting for non-current assets, including tangible and intangible assets, investment properties, fair value measurement, impairments, revaluations and non-current assets held for sale
- Events after the reporting period
- Income taxes including deferred taxation
- Revenue recognition
- Borrowing costs
- Related party disclosures
- Financial instruments, including recognition and measurement of financial assets, financial liabilities, equity and compound instruments; impairment of financial assets and hedge accounting
- Earnings per share (basic and diluted)
- Effects of changes in foreign exchange rates
- Interim financial reporting
- Provisions, contingent liabilities and contingent assets
- Segmental reporting
- Leases (lessee and lessor accounting)

INTRODUCTION

- Employee benefits, including pension fund reporting and share-based payments
- Inventories
- Accounting for government grants

All extant International Standards on Auditing and all International Financial Reporting Standards/ International Accounting Standards are examinable, subject to the six month rule defined under New Legislation. For RPQ (statutory auditor qualification) students the relevant UK standards are Financial Reporting Standards (FRS) and Statements of Standard Accounting Practice (SSAP) issued by the FRC. In respect of auditing, the relevant UK standards are all current Auditing Standards (ISAs (UK and Ireland)) issued by the FRC.

Relationship to overall syllabus

Financial Accounting 3 builds upon the knowledge required for the preceding Financial Accounting papers in the Professional 1 and Foundation level examinations. Candidates will also be expected to relate the topics covered in this paper to those in Paper 15 Professional Practice.

Ethics

Students are advised that the standards outlined in The Code of Ethics for Professional Accountants issued by the International Ethics Standards Board for Accountants (IESBA Code) are implicit in, and examinable throughout, the AIA syllabus. In this paper a brief question relating to ethics could be included in any of the five questions but will typically be included as part of compulsory question 1. The Code can be accessed via the AIA website at www.aiaworldwide.com

Recommended Reading

AIA Magazine – International Accountant

ISSN: 1465 – 5144

AIA Text Book

Paper 13 Financial Accounting 3

Publisher: BPP Learning Media
ISBN: 9781 5097 8728 9

The e-Book is available at: exams@aiaworldwide.com

Contact our publisher BPP for information on purchasing a hard copy of the text book at: https://www.bpp.com/learning-media-listing/lmlist/6293

You can purchase any of the books listed below quickly and easily through the publisher's website or link stated below. The following is a list of suggested readings which students may consult to supplement the above text.

International GAAP 2019

Authors: Ernst & Young
Publisher: John Wiley & Sons Ltd
ISBN: 97811195577760
Website: https://www.wiley.com/en-gb/International+GAAP+2019-p-9781119557760

Financial Accounting and Reporting with (MyAccountinglab) (18th Edition)

Authors: Elliot, B. and Elliot, J
Publisher: Pearson Education Limited
ISBN: 9781292162409
Website: http://www.pearsoned.co.uk/bookshop/detail.asp?item=100000000632055

International Financial Reporting and Analysis (7th Edition)

Authors: Alexander, D, Britton, A, and Jorissen, A, Hoogendorn, M, Van Mourik, C
Publisher: Cengage Learning
ISBN: 9781473725454
Website: http://edu.cengage.co.uk/catalogue/product.aspx?isbn=1473725453

Free website providing comprehensive information about IFRS:

www.iasplus.com/en

INTRODUCTION

AIA List of examinable Standards

All extant International Standards on Auditing, International Standards on Quality Control, International Financial Reporting Standards/International Accounting Standards are examinable, subject to the six months rule (refer to New Legislation).

The depth of knowledge of the standards required for the different levels can be defined as:

- **Foundation** – Students should be aware of the standard and be familiar with the basic concepts involved.

- **Professional 1** – Students should be aware of all major requirements of the standard and be able to apply it to straight forward situations. Students should be able to recognise some of the pitfalls and issues associated with the standard.

- **Professional 2** – Students must be fully cognisant of the standard and know how to apply it to specialized situations. They must also be fully aware of the important issues, contemporary thinking and criticisms related to the standard.

For RPQ (statutory auditor qualification) students the relevant UK standards are Financial Reporting Standards (FRS) and The International Standards on Auditing (UK) (ISAs (UK)) and International Standard on Quality Control (UK) (ISQC (UK)), issued by the Financial Reporting Council (FRC). In respect of auditing, the relevant UK standards are: https://www.frc.org.uk/Our-Work/Audit/Audit-and-assurance/Standards-and-guidance/Standards-and-guidance-for-auditors/2016-Auditing-Standards.aspx

IASs and IFRSs

In Paper 1 Financial Accounting 1 candidates are required to have studied a limited number of IASs and IFRSs, however in Paper 11 Financial Accounting 2 the bulk of IASs and IFRSs are examinable. There are still some exclusions and these will be covered in Paper 13 Financial Accounting 3.

A list of currently examinable IASs and IFRSs is given below.

International Accountings Standards (IASs)		Examinable in Paper						
No	Title	1	3	5	7	11	13	15
1	Presentation of Financial Statements	✓		✓	✓	✓	✓	✓
2	Inventories	✓	✓	✓	✓	✓	✓	✓
7	Statements of Cash Flows	✓		✓	✓	✓	✓	✓
8	Accounting Policies, Changes in Accounting Estimates and Errors					✓	✓	✓
10	Events After the Reporting Period	✓		✓	✓	✓	✓	✓
12	Income Taxes					✓	✓	✓
16	Property, Plant and Equipment	✓		✓	✓	✓	✓	✓
19	Employee Benefits						✓	✓
20	Accounting for Governments Grants and Disclosure of Government Assistance					✓	✓	✓
21	The Effects of Changes in Foreign Exchange Rates						✓	✓
23	Borrowing Costs					✓	✓	✓
24	Related Party Disclosures					✓	✓	✓
27	Separate Financial Statements					✓	✓	✓
28	Investment in Associates and Joint Ventures					✓	✓	✓
29	Financial Reporting in Hyperinflationary Economies						✓	✓
32	Financial Instruments: Presentation					✓	✓	✓

INTRODUCTION

International Accountings Standards (IASs)		Examinable in Paper						
No	Title	1	3	5	7	11	13	15
33	Earnings per Share					✓	✓	✓
34	Interim Financial Reporting					✓	✓	✓
36	Impairment of Assets					✓	✓	✓
37	Provisions, Contingent Liabilities and Contingent Assets	✓		✓	✓	✓	✓	✓
38	Intangible Assets	✓		✓	✓	✓	✓	✓
40	Investment Property					✓	✓	✓

International Financial Reporting Standards (IFRS)		Examinable in Paper					
No	Title	1	5	7	11	13	15
1	First-time Adoption of International Financial Reporting Standards				✓	✓	✓
2	Share-based Payment					✓	✓
3	Business Combinations				✓	✓	✓
5	Non-current Assets Held for Sale and Discontinued Operations				✓	✓	✓
7	Financial Instruments: Disclosures				✓	✓	✓
8	Operating Segments				✓	✓	✓
9	Financial Instruments				✓	✓	✓
10	Consolidated Financial Statements				✓	✓	✓
11	Joint Arrangements					✓	✓
12	Disclosure of Interests in Other Entities				✓	✓	✓
13	Fair Value Measurement					✓	✓
14	Regulatory Deferral Accounts					✓	✓
15	Revenue from Contracts with Customers	✓	✓	✓	✓	✓	✓
16	Leases				✓	✓	✓
IFRS for SMEs	IFRS for Small and Medium-sized Entities					✓	✓

Exposure drafts, discussion papers and IFRICs are not examinable at Paper 1 and Paper 11. Those still current (ie they have not been superseded by other publications) are examinable in Paper 13 but only an understanding of their basic principles is required.

Command words and learning outcomes

The following list contains active command words and generic learning outcomes appropriate for use at each stage of the AIA qualification. Reference to the learning outcomes and use of the command words is essential to understanding how the assessment is applied in AIA exams.

Professional Level 2 Command Words

Word	Definition
ADVISE	To inform or notify
APPRAISE	To evaluate and conclude on the basis of arguments for and against, synthesize, argue, develop a view, balance, provide evidence, and identify patterns
ASSESS	Determine the strength, weakness and significance
CALCULATE	Work out a value mathematically
CRITIQUE/ CRITICALLY ANALYSE	Examine in detail using arguments for and against
EVALUATE	Determine the value in light of arguments for and against
EXPLORE	To examine or investigate, in a systematic way
FORMULATE	Plan or describe precisely and clearly
JUSTIFY	Defend an action as being appropriate
RECOMMEND	Advise the appropriate action in terms the recipient will understand
REPORT	Give an account of the results of the investigation

Please note:

1. The word 'Calculate' may be used at all levels of the syllabus

    CALCULATE — Select the appropriate method and techniques and apply your knowledge and understanding to work out and show how figures were arrived at.

2. The word 'Advise' may be used at all levels of the syllabus

    ADVISE — Notify or inform

3. For the Professional Level 1 exams, examiners may include a command word from the Foundation Level providing it is linked to another command word selected from the Professional 1 list. For example:

    '… prepare and discuss a set of accounts…'

4. For the Professional Level 2 exams, examiners may include a command word from the Foundation and Professional Level 1 providing it is linked to another command word from the Professional 2 list. For example:

    '…recommend the appropriate action and prepare a memo…'

The exam paper

Analysis of past papers

The analysis below shows the topics which were examined in all sittings of the current syllabus so far. (Note that IAS 11, IAS 17, IAS 18, IAS 39 and IAS 41 are no longer examinable).

May 2018

1. Consolidated statement of financial position (IFRS 3, IFRS 10), borrowing limits, financial instruments presentation, ethical implications of changing presentation of items relevant to borrowing limits.
2. Employee share options (IFRS 2), retirement benefits (IAS 19), recognition of intangible assets (IAS 38, IFRS 3), deferred taxation (IAS 12).
3. Leases (IFRS 16), effect of applying IFRS 16.
4. Revenue (IFRS 15), compound financial instruments (IAS 32, IFRS 9), Foreign currency transactions (IAS 21).
5. Consolidated statement of changes in equity with disposal (IFRS 10), integrated reporting.

November 2017

1. Consolidated statement of financial position (IFRS 3, IFRS 10), including identification of a subsidiary's associate and changes in group structure.
2. Fair value measurement (IFRS 13), employee share options (IFRS 2).
3. Ethical implications of dealing with financial distress.
4. Financial instruments and hedge accounting (IFRS 9).
5. Accounting for business combinations (IFRS 3, IFRS 12).

May 2017

1. Consolidated statement of financial position (IFRS 3) including determining whether or not an investment is an associate, dealing with the ethical implications of misclassification and dealing with intercompany transactions.
2. Acquisition of a subsidiary and determining the cost of obtaining control, including measuring consideration transferred (IFRS 3).
3. Leases (IFRS 16), effect of applying IFRS 16, early application and ethical issues.
4. Impairment of assets (IAS 36), responsibilities and role of an accountant.
5. Segmental reporting (IFRS 8), pensions (IAS 19).

November 2016

1. Consolidated statement of financial position (IFRS 3), changes in group structure, financial instruments (IFRS 9), leases, employee benefits (IAS 19).
2. Measurement of inventory and land using fair values (IFRS 13), prudence.
3. Segmental reporting (IFRS 8) and disposal of an asset in exchange for shares.
4. Presentation of income and expense items in profit or loss or other comprehensive income (IAS 1).
5. Joint arrangements (IFRS 11, IAS 28).

May 2016

1. Consolidated statement of financial position – business combination achieved in stages, customer contract (IAS 38), contingent consideration (IFRS 3), joint venture, lease. Related parties scenario.
2. Subsidiary acquired with a view to resale (IFRS 10), restructuring (IAS 37), service contracts (IFRS 5), leases, research and development (IAS 38), financial asset (IFRS 9). Discuss exclusion from consolidation.
3. EPS (IAS 33). Disclosure of non-GAAP earnings. Discussion of Integrated Reporting Framework.
4. Safety equipment and decommissioning liability (IAS 37), benefits of environmental report.
5. Treatment of transactions under IFRS 5. Treatment of associate in consolidated financial statements.

November 2015

1. Consolidated statement of profit or loss and other comprehensive income with disposals and application of IFRS 3, IFRS 10, IAS 37, IFRS 9, IAS 16, IAS 12, IAS 38, IFRS 2. Discussion of treating workforce as intangible asset.
2. Defined benefit pension scheme, share options, termination of operation – IAS 19, IFRS 2, IAS 37. Treatment of employee share options.
3. Calculation of restructuring provision, treatment of environmental clean-up costs (IAS 37).
4. Impairment loss, property held for sale (IAS 36, IFRS 5). Application of IFRS 11.
5. Contingent consideration (IFRS 3), brand name (IAS 38), partial disposal (IFRS 10). Applying definition of control.

May 2015

1. Consolidated statement of profit or loss and other comprehensive income and application of IFRS 9, IFRS 5, IFRS 3, IAS 16, IAS 19.
2. Revenue (IAS 18 and ED of IFRS 115), foreign currency (IAS 21), borrowing costs (IAS 23).
3. Changes in accounting policy and application of IAS 16, IAS 8, IFRS 13. Discussion of impact of ED on leases.
4. Share for share exchange and discussion of proportional consolidation, including application of IFRS 3, IFRS 11 and IAS 28. EPS calculation (IAS 33).
5. Assets held for sale (IFRS 5) and performance measurement.

November 2014

1. Consolidated statement of cash flows, including application of IAS 7, IAS 2, IAS 12, IAS 38, IAS 19, IAS 40. Consideration of ethical practice.
2. Goodwill and deferred consideration, including application of IFRS 3, the IFRS for SMEs and IAS 40.
3. Foreign currency (IAS 21) and application of IFRS 10 and IFRS 13.
4. Assessment of control (IFRS 10), asset recognition and development costs (IAS 38) Financial instruments (IFRS 9 and IAS 39) and leases.

May 2014

1. Consolidated statement of financial position and application of IFRS 3, IFRS 11, leases, IAS 36.
2. Provisions and contingent liabilities (IAS 37).
3. Foreign currency consolidation (IAS 21) and discussion of reporting financial performance.
4. Reporting acquisitions, including piecemeal acquisitions and calculations of goodwill after changes to estimates (IFRS 3).
5. Fair value measurement (IFRS 13), deferred tax (IAS 12), events after the reporting period (provision for decommissioning) (IAS 10).

November 2013

1. Consolidated statement of financial position and application of IFRS 3, IFRS 11, IAS 16, IAS 36, IAS 39, accounting for a sale and repurchase transaction.
2. Accounting for joint operations (IFRS 11).
3. Leasing (IAS 17) and pensions (IAS 19).
4. Deferred tax (IAS 12).
5. Foreign currency consolidation (IAS 21), discontinued operations (IFRS 5).

May 2013

1. Consolidated statement of financial position and application of IFRS 3, IAS 37, IAS 39, IFRS 9, IAS 19.
2. Share valuation incorporating IAS 38, IFRS 2, IAS 16, IFRS 5, IAS 37.
3. Leasing.
4. Segmental reporting (IFRS 8).
5. Fair value measurement (IFRS 13), provision for decommissioning (IAS 37).

November 2012

1. Consolidated statement of financial position and application of IFRS 9, IFRS 2, IFRS 3, IAS 38 and IAS 21.
2. Accounting treatment of joint arrangements, IAS 31 and IFRS 11 (ED9).
3. Accounting for a customer loyalty programme, application of IFRS 9, IAS 33 and the *Conceptual Framework*.
4. Deferred tax implications of transactions, application of IAS 24, interim financial reporting.
5. Regulation of corporate financial reporting, first time adoption of IFRS.

May 2012

1. Consolidated statement of cash flows; ethics.
2. Application of IAS 37 and IAS 16; calculation of goodwill.
3. Cash-settled share-based payment schemes; reorganisation of capital.
4. Accounting for a sale and leaseback transaction; interaction of IAS 17 leasing standards and the *Conceptual Framework*.
5. Application of IFRS 5.

November 2011

1. Consolidated statement of comprehensive income (statement of profit or loss and other comprehensive income); ethics.
2. Loyalty points and money off vouchers; IAS 18; IAS 11; deferred revenue.
3. Earnings per share.
4. IFRS 8.
5. Share valuation; intangible assets; fair values; sale and leaseback.

May 2011

1. Consolidated statement of financial position with step acquisition and disposal and ethics.
2. Accounting treatment of investment and foreign currency goodwill.
3. Application of IFRS 2 to share options and SARs.
4. Application of IAS 1, IAS 8, IAS 21, IAS 16, IAS 40 and IAS 39.
5. First time adoption and application of IAS 38.

November 2010

1. Consolidated statement of financial position, financial reporting of not-for-profit organisation and ethics.
2. Corporate, environmental and social reporting, subsidiary held-for-sale and non-consolidation of subsidiaries.
3. Application of IAS 18, IAS 37, IFRS 3 and the effect on deferred tax.
4. Application of IFRS 3, IAS 32, IAS 27, IAS 37 and IAS 10.
5. Application of IAS 16, IAS 20, IAS 23 and IAS 19.

May 2010

1. Consolidated statement of cash flows and ethics.
2. Consolidated statement of financial position (simple group) and disposal of subsidiary.
3. Current thought and practice: globalisation of IFRS and IAS 29.
4. Developments in lease accounting.
5. Application of IAS 24.

November 2009

1. Consolidated income statement (statement of profit or loss), application of IAS 37 and ethics.
2. Application of IAS 16, IAS 23, financial instruments and convergence.
3. Full and part disposal of a subsidiary: impact on the consolidated financial statements.
4. Valuation of shares.
5. Application of IAS 18, IAS 10, IAS 8 and IAS 41.

May 2009

1. Consolidated income statement (statement of profit or loss); IFRS 5; IAS 36; and IAS 18.
2. Consolidated statement of financial position (simple group).
3. Application of IAS 37 *Provisions, Contingent Liabilities and Contingent Assets*.
4. Application of IAS 21 and IAS 29.
5. Analysis of summarised financial data; ethics.

November 2008

1. Consolidated financial statements and IAS 33.
2. IFRS 3 (goodwill, non-controlling interests and reverse acquisitions).
3. Foreign currency translation; groups; functional and presentation currency.
4. Application of IAS 10, IAS 23, and IAS 41.
5. Interpretation of cash flow statement.

May 2008

1. Consolidated balance sheet (statement of financial position).
2. Application of lease accounting, IAS 19 and IFRS 5.
3. IAS 19 *Employee Benefits*.
4. Financial instruments.
5. Analysis of financial information.

November 2007

1. Summarised income statement (statement of profit or loss) and balance sheet (statement of financial position) with foreign currency, statement of cash flows.
2. Segment reporting.
3. Consolidated income statement (statement of profit or loss) using IAS 28 and IAS 31.
4. Application of IAS 16, IAS 36, IAS 37 and IFRS 3.
5. Consolidated balance sheet (statement of financial position).
6. Application of IFRS 2 *Share-based Payment* and IAS 18 *Revenue*.

May 2007

1. Consolidated statement of changes in equity.
2. Consolidated income statement (statement of profit or loss) using IAS 21, IAS 31 and IAS 33.
3. IAS 37 Provisions.
4. Consolidated balance sheet (statement of financial position).
5. Lease accounting.
6. Historic cost, current cost and current purchasing power.

November 2006

1. Preparation and analysis of segment report.
2. Business valuation using NRV and future earnings.
3. Consolidated balance sheet (statement of financial position) with foreign currency.
4. Calculation of basic and diluted earnings per share.
5. Accounting issues including non-current assets, agriculture, leases and investment property.
6. Consolidated income statement (statement of profit or loss).

May 2006

1. Revenue.
2. Disposal of shares and consolidated balance sheet (statement of financial position).
3. IAS 36 Impairment.
4. Measurement bases.
5. Measuring and reporting in financial statements.
6. Segment reporting.

November 2005

1. Earnings per share.
2. IFRS 5 *Non-current Assets Held for Sale and Discontinued Operations*.
3. Consolidated income statement (statement of profit or loss).
4. IAS 8 *Accounting Policies, Changes in Accounting Estimates and Errors* and IAS 39 *Financial Instruments*.
5. Consolidated balance sheet (statement of financial position).
6. Historical cost and current purchasing power.

May 2005

1. IFRS 3 and treatment of goodwill.
2. Acquisition and consolidated balance sheet (statement of financial position).
3. IAS 21 *The Effects of Changes in Foreign Exchange Rates*.
4. Consolidated income statement (statement of profit or loss) using IAS 27, IAS 28, Joint arrangements.
5. Consolidated balance sheet (statement of financial position).
6. Assessing financial performance.

November 2004

1. Acquisition.
2. Consolidated profit and loss plus analysis.
3. Consolidated balance sheet (statement of financial position).
4. Earnings per share.
5. Interpreting accounting standards.
6. Construction contracts.

May 2004

1. Impact of adopting International Accounting Standards.
2. Application of various accounting standards: IAS 27, IAS 28, construction contracts, IFRS 1, IAS 38.
3. Consolidated income statement (statement of profit or loss).
4. Capital instruments.
5. Consolidated balance sheet (statement of financial position).
6. Current cost accounting.

PART A

Contemporary issues

Current thought and practice

Topic list	Syllabus reference
1 The regulatory system of accounting	13.1
2 The IFRS Foundation and the International Accounting Standards Board (IASB)	13.1
3 Development of IASC/IASB	13.1
4 *Conceptual Framework*	13.1
5 Harmonisation and international differences	13.1

Introduction

Welcome to the Financial Accounting 3 paper using International Financial Reporting Standards (IFRS). This paper is about thinking and applying your knowledge of IFRS. Most of the standards and topics have been covered in your earlier studies. However, at this level, you need to think critically about them and show an understanding of topical issues. In the exam, you will need to put yourself in the role of an adviser to a business entity, using your knowledge to give practical advice.

PART A CONTEMPORARY ISSUES

1 The regulatory system of accounting

> **FAST FORWARD**
>
> Various national factors will affect the regulatory framework of entities, but our concern in this text is with international matters, particularly the **IASB** and **IAS/IFRS**.

1.1 Introduction

This section revises material from your earlier studies. If necessary, refer back to your Financial Accounting 2 studies.

1.1.1 Factors which have shaped financial accounting

- National/local legislation
- Accounting concepts and individual judgement
- Accounting standards
- Other international influences
- Generally accepted accounting principles (GAAP)
- True and fair view (or fair presentation)

1.2 National/local legislation

Limited liability companies may be **required by law** to prepare and publish financial statements annually. The form and content of the statements may be regulated primarily by national legislation, but must also comply with International Financial Reporting Standards (IFRS).

1.3 Accounting concepts and individual judgement

Financial statements are prepared on the basis of a number of **fundamental accounting assumptions and conventions**. However, accountants still have to use judgement in putting these assumptions into practice.

Using the same data, different accountants are likely to produce very different financial statements. If the exercise of judgement is completely unfettered, any **comparability** between the financial statements of different organisations will disappear. In addition, deliberate manipulation can occur in order to present statements in the most favourable light.

1.4 Accounting standards

1.4.1 Financial reporting (accounting) standards

Financial reporting (accounting) standards attempt to deal with some of the subjectivity, and to achieve comparability between different organisations. Standards are developed at both a **national level** (in most countries) and an **international level**.

1.4.2 International financial reporting/accounting standards

Until 1 April 2001, International Accounting Standards (IAS) were produced by the **International Accounting Standards Committee (IASC)**. From 1 April 2001, the **International Accounting Standards Board (IASB)** took over standard-setting responsibilities from the IASC and began to issue International Financial Reporting Standards (IFRS). The IASB also adopted those IASs and SICs in issue at 1 April 2001.

1.4.3 Interpretations

The IFRS Interpretations Committee (IFRSIC) (sometimes referred to by its previous name, IFRIC) is responsible for preparing interpretations of IAS and IFRS. Once these have been approved by the IASB, they have the same standing as IAS/IFRS.

The IFRIC deals with issues of reasonably widespread importance, not issues of concern to only a small number of entities.

The interpretations cover both:

- Mature issues (areas where there is unsatisfactory practice within the scope of existing IAS/IFRS)
- Emerging issues (new topics relating to an existing IAS/IFRS but not considered when the Standard was developed).

The IASB publishes a report on IFRIC recommendations immediately after each IFRIC meeting. This report is made available (in electronic format) as soon as possible to subscribers and, subsequently, posted to the IASB website.

1.5 Other international influences

These include the EC, the UN, the IFAC and the OECD.

1.5.1 European Commission (EC)

The EC regulations form one part of a broader programme for the harmonisation of company law in member states. The Commission is uniquely the only organisation to produce international standards of accounting practice which are legally enforceable, in the form of **directives** which must be included in the national legislation of member states.

However, the EC has also **acknowledged the role of the IASB** in harmonising world-wide accounting rules and it promotes the use of IFRS worldwide.

Since 2005, the EC has required all listed companies in member states to use those IFRS, as endorsed by the European Financial Reporting Advisory Group (EFRAG) for their consolidated financial statements. There are occasionally differences between IFRS as issued by the IASB and IFRS as endorsed by EFRAG (and used within the EU). These differences are either (i) arising from the timing of implementation of new and revised IFRS (for example, when there is a delay, even if short, between the issue of a new IFRS and its endorsement by EFRAG or (ii) a refusal by EFRAG to endorse fully a new IFRS (for example, there is an EU version of IAS 39 which omits certain paragraphs).

1.5.2 United Nations (UN)

Various bodies working under the umbrella United Nations Conference on Trade and Development (UNCTAD) gather information concerning the activities and reporting of multinational companies. The UN processes are highly **political** and probably reflect the attitudes of the governments of developing countries to multinationals.

1.5.3 International Federation of Accountants (IFAC)

IFAC is the global organisation for the accountancy profession. IFAC identifies its objective as serving the public interest by strengthening the profession and contributing to the development of strong international economies. IFAC has over 175 members and associates in 130 countries and jurisdictions, representing approximately 2.5 million accountants. (Source: http:www.ifac.org)

1.5.4 Organisation for Economic Co-operation and Development (OECD)

The OECD supports the work of the IASB but also undertakes its **own research** into accounting standards via *ad hoc* working groups. For example, in 1976 the OECD issued guidelines for multinational companies on financial reporting and non-financial disclosures. The OECD appears to work on behalf of developed countries to protect them from extreme proposals of the UN. The OECD has also entered the debate on corporate governance.

1.6 Generally Accepted Accounting Principles (GAAP)

We also need to consider some important terms which you will meet in your financial accounting studies. GAAP, as a term, has sprung up in recent years and may or may not have statutory or legal authority or definition, depending on the country involved. GAAP is in fact a **dynamic concept** and changes constantly as circumstances alter through new legislation, standards and practice It signifies **all the rules, from whatever source, which govern accounting**.

- Local (national) company legislation
- National and international accounting standards
- Statutory requirements in other countries (particularly the US)
- Stock exchange requirements

1.7 True and fair view (or fair presentation)

It is a requirement of both national legislation (in some countries eg the UK) and International Standards on Auditing that the financial statements should give a true and fair view of (or present fairly) the assets, liabilities, financial position and profit or loss of the entity.

1.7.1 Fair presentation and compliance with IFRS

The terms 'present fairly' and 'true and fair view' are not defined in accounting or auditing standards. But under IAS 1 *Presentation of Financial Statements* the application of IFRS is presumed to result in fair presentation. Non-compliance with IFRS is only permitted when compliance would be so misleading as to conflict with the objective of financial statements set out in the IASB's *Conceptual Framework for Financial Reporting* (See IAS 1 paragraphs 19 – 23).

2 The IFRS Foundation and the International Accounting Standards Board (IASB)

> **FAST FORWARD**
>
> You should be able to describe the **organisation of the IFRS Foundation and the IASB** and their relationships with intergovernmental bodies, professional accountancy bodies, national standard-setting bodies and IOSCO.

2.1 Background

The IFRS Foundation is an oversight body of the IASB and includes governance, oversight and support operations.

The primary mission of the IFRS Foundation is to develop, in the public interest, a single set of high quality, understandable, enforceable and globally accepted financial reporting standards based upon clearly articulated principles.

The IASB is the independent standard-setting body of the IFRS Foundation, including technical staff and experts advisors.

The principal objectives of the IFRS Foundation are:

- To develop these International Financial Reporting Standards (IFRS) through its standard-setting body, the International Accounting Standards Board (IASB);

- To promote the use and rigorous application of those Standards;

- To take account of the financial reporting needs of emerging economies and small and medium-sized entities (SMEs); and

- To promote and facilitate adoption of IFRS, being the Standards and Interpretations issued by the IASB, through the convergence of national accounting standards and IFRS.

(Source: http://www.ifrs.org)

2.2 Scope and authority of IFRS

The IASB achieves its objectives primarily by developing and publishing IFRS and promoting the use of those standards in **general purpose financial statements** and other financial reporting.

IFRS set out **recognition, measurement, presentation** and **disclosure requirements** dealing with transactions and events that are important in general purpose financial statements. IFRS are based on the IASB's *Conceptual Framework for Financial Reporting,* which:

- Addresses the **concepts** underlying the information presented in general purpose financial statements
- Facilitates the **consistent** and logical formulation of IFRS
- Provides a **basis for the use of judgement** in resolving accounting issues

IFRS are designed to apply to the general purpose financial statements and other financial reporting of all profit-oriented entities. Profit-oriented entities include those engaged in commercial, industrial, financial and similar activities, whether organised in **corporate or in other forms.**

General purpose financial statements are primarily directed towards the **information needs** of current and potential investors, lenders and other creditors. However other parties may also find them useful, for example employees, regulators and the public at large. The objective of financial statements is to provide information about economic resources and claims and changes in those resources and claims.

A complete set of financial statements comprises:

- A statement of financial position (balance sheet)
- A statement of profit or loss and other comprehensive income
- A statement of changes in equity
- A statement of cash flows
- Notes, comprising a summary of significant accounting policies and other explanatory information
- Comparative information

The term 'financial statements' includes a complete set of financial statements prepared for an interim or annual period, and condensed financial statements for an interim period.

In the interest of timeliness and cost considerations and to avoid repeating information previously reported, an entity may provide less information in its **interim financial statements** than in its annual financial statements. **IAS 34** *Interim Financial Reporting* **prescribes** the **minimum content** of complete or condensed financial statements for an interim period.

The old IASC sometimes permitted a regime of **'benchmark treatments'** and **'allowed alternative treatments'**. The **IASB's objective** is to require **like transactions** and events to be accounted for and **reported in a like way** and unlike transactions and events to be accounted for and reported differently, both within an entity over time and among entities. Consequently, the **IASB,** with very few exceptions, **does not permit choices in accounting treatment**. Also, the IASB has reconsidered, and will continue to reconsider, those transactions and events for which IAS permit a choice of accounting treatment, with the objective of **reducing the number of those choices.**

Any limitation of scope of an IFRS will be made clear in the standard.

2.3 IFRS due process

IFRS are developed through an international **due process** that involves accountants, financial analysts and other users of financial statements, the business community, stock exchanges, regulatory and legal authorities, academics and other interested individuals and organisations from around the world. The IASB consults the IFRS Advisory Council (previously the Standards Advisory Council) in public meetings on major projects, agenda decisions and work priorities, and discusses technical matters in meetings that are open to public observation.

PART A   CONTEMPORARY ISSUES

The IASB's standard-setting process comprises six stages:

1. **Setting the agenda**

    Staff work to **identify, review and raise issues** that might warrant the IASB's attention. The IASB evaluates the merits of adding a potential item to its agenda, mainly by reference to the needs of investors.

2. **Planning the project**

    When adding an item to its agenda, the IASB decides whether to conduct the project **alone** or with **another** (national) **standard-setter.** A working group may be established at this stage and a project plan is drawn up.

3. **Developing and publishing a discussion paper**

    A discussion paper is not mandatory, however the IASB normally publishes it as its first publication on any major new topic in order to explain the issue and solicit early comment from constituents.

4. **Developing and publishing an exposure draft**

    Publication of an exposure draft (ED) is a mandatory step in due process. An ED sets out the proposed new standard (or amendment to an existing standard). IASB staff draft the ED after resolving issues and, when the draft is complete, the IASB is balloted on it and publishes it for public comment.

5. **Developing and publishing an IFRS**

    The development of an IFRS is carried out during IASB meetings when the IASB considers the comments received on the ED. After resolving issues arising from the ED, the IASB decides whether a topic should be re-exposed ie a second ED published. When the IASB is satisfied that it has reached a conclusion on the issues arising from the ED, staff draft the IFRS. When the IASB members have balloted in favour of publication, the IFRS is issued.

6. **After a standard is issued**

    After an IFRS is issued, the IASB holds meetings with interested parties to help understand unanticipated issues related to the practical implementation and impact of the Standard. In time this feedback may result in a review of the standard.

2.4 IFRIC due process

Interpretations of IFRS are developed through an **international due process** that involves accountants, financial analysts and other users of financial statements, the business community, stock exchanges, regulatory and legal authorities, the business community, stock exchanges, regulatory and legal authorities, academics and other interested individuals and organisations from around the world. The IFRIC discusses technical matters in meetings that are open to public observations. The due process for each project normally, but not necessarily, involves the following seven steps:

1. **Identification of issues**

    Preparers, auditors and others are encouraged to refer issues to the IFRIC when they believe that divergent practices have emerged or when there is doubt about appropriate accounting treatment.

2. **Setting the agenda**

    The IFRIC decides after debate in a public meeting whether to add an issue to the agenda. Where an issue is not added to the agenda, the draft reason for this is published in a tentative rejection notice and there is a comment period. The issue is then be re-debated and may be added to the agenda at a later stage.

3. **IFRIC meetings and voting**

    The IFRIC meets publicly to debate matters on the agenda. Ten voting members constitute a quorum and each Committee member has one vote.

1: CURRENT THOUGHT AND PRACTICE

4. **Development of a draft interpretation**

    An agenda paper is developed for the IFRIC's consideration after a thorough review of accounting literature and possible alternatives. A draft interpretation is then developed on which the IFRIC vote. Consensus is achieved when no more than 4 members have voted against a proposal.

5. **The IASB's role in the issue of an interpretation**

    When the IFRIC has reached a consensus on an interpretation, the interpretation is put to the IASB for ratification. This requires the approval of at least 9 members of the IASB, the same as for an IFRS.

6. **Comment period and deliberation**

    Draft interpretations are then available for public comment for not less than 90 days. All comments received are considered by the IFRIC before an interpretation is finalised. If a proposed interpretation is changed significantly, it may be re-exposed.

2.5 Comment periods

The Board issues each Exposure Draft of a Standard and discussion documents for public comment, with a normal comment period of **120 days**. For a major project, or one that is controversial, this period may be extended. In certain circumstances, the Board may expose proposals for a much shorter period. However, such limited periods would be used only in extreme circumstances.

2.6 The consultation process

The development of an IFRS involves an **open, public process of debating technical issues** and evaluating input sought through several mechanisms. Opportunities for interested parties to participate in the development of IFRS would include, depending on the nature of the project:

(a) Participation in the development of views as a member of the **IFRS Advisory Council**
(b) Participation in **advisory groups**
(c) Submission of a **comment letter** in response to a **discussion document**
(d) Submission of a **comment letter** in response to an **Exposure Draft**
(e) Participation in **public hearings**
(f) Participation **in field visits and field tests**

The IASB publishes an annual report on its activities during the past year and priorities for next year. This report provides a basis and opportunity for comment by interested parties.

IASB reports on its technical projects on its website. IASB publishes a report on IASB decisions immediately after each IASB meeting in its newsletter *IASB Update*. Do visit the IASB website on a regular basis.

2.7 Current position

The IASB has now been in existence for some years and has issued 17 new standards (IFRSs), as well as revising many of the standards previously issued by the IASC (IASs).

The list of IASB's current accounting standards is as follows:

IAS 1 *Presentation of Financial Statements*

IAS 2 *Inventories*

IAS 7 *Statement of Cash Flows*

IAS 8 *Accounting Policies, Changes in Accounting Estimates and Errors*

IAS 10 *Events after the Reporting Period*

IAS 12 *Income Taxes*

IAS 16 *Property, Plant and Equipment*

PART A CONTEMPORARY ISSUES

IAS 19 *Employee Benefits*

IAS 20 *Accounting for Government Grants and Disclosure of Government Assistance*

IAS 21 *The Effects of Changes in Foreign Exchange Rates*

IAS 23 *Borrowing Costs*

IAS 24 *Related Party Disclosures*

IAS 26 *Accounting and Reporting by Retirement Benefit Plans*

IAS 27 *Separate Financial Statements*

IAS 28 *Investments in Associates and Joint Ventures*

IAS 29 *Financial Reporting in Hyperinflationary Economies*

IAS 32 *Financial Instruments: Presentation*

IAS 33 *Earnings per Share*

IAS 34 *Interim Financial Reporting*

IAS 36 *Impairment of Assets*

IAS 37 *Provisions, Contingent Liabilities and Contingent Assets*

IAS 38 *Intangible Assets*

IAS 40 *Investment Property*

IAS 41 *Agriculture*

IFRS 1 *First-time Adoption of International Financial Reporting Standards*

IFRS 2 *Share-based Payment*

IFRS 3 *Business Combinations*

IFRS 4 *Insurance Contracts*

IFRS 5 *Non-current Assets Held for Sale and Discontinued Operations*

IFRS 6 *Exploration for and Evaluation of Mineral Resources*

IFRS 7 *Financial Instruments: Disclosures*

IFRS 8 *Operating Segments*

IFRS 9 *Financial Instruments*

IFRS 10 *Consolidated Financial Statements*

IFRS 11 *Joint Arrangements*

IFRS 12 *Disclosure of Interest in Other Entities*

IFRS 13 *Fair Value Measurement*

IFRS 14 *Regulatory Deferral Accounts*

IFRS 15 *Revenue from Contracts with Customers*

IFRS 16 *Leases*

IFRS 17 *Insurance Contracts*

Note that the following standards do not form part of your syllabus: IAS 26, IAS 41, IFRS 4, IFRS 6 and IFRS 17.

An understanding of the basic principles of the Exposure Drafts, Discussion Papers and IFRICs listed on page x of the Introduction to this Study Text is also required at Paper 13 level.

Exam focus point

> Remember that the examiner is likely to concentrate on controversial areas in the exam. This means questions are likely on new or controversial standards.

In addition, the IASB has an extensive work plan for the continued development and improvement of international accounting standards. The following are the issues that are being dealt with by the IASB. In addition the IASB operates an annual improvements process through which minor changes and enhancements are made to existing IFRS.

Hot topic	Where to find it
Recent changes	
Conceptual Framework	Chapter 1
Insurance contracts	not in syllabus
Rate-regulated activities	Chapter 5
IFRS for SMEs	Chapter 22
Financial instruments	Chapter 14
Revenue	Chapter 21
Leases	Chapter 15
Narrow scope amendments and annual improvements	see below

Other projects are covered in the relevant chapters of the Study Text.

2.7.1 Annual improvements

The annual improvements process is implemented by the IASB in order to clarify and make minor changes to existing standards and interpretations. Each project cycle lasts two years such that changes are identified, proposed in an 'omnibus' exposure draft and finally incorporated into the relevant standards in the following year.

The last annual improvement cycle to be completed was 2015-2017. The 2016-2017 cycle includes only clarifications rather than substantive changes as follows:

IAS 12 *Income Taxes* — clarify recognition and presentation of the income tax consequences of dividends

IAS 23 *Borrowing Costs* — clarify the borrowing costs eligible for capitalisation

IAS 28 *Investments in Associates and Joint Ventures* — clarify that an entity applies IFRS 9 *Financial Instruments* to long-term interests in an associate or joint venture that form part of the net investment in the associate or joint venture but to which the equity method is not applied.

The 2018-2020 improvement cycle is ongoing.

3 Development of IASC/IASB

3.1 History

The IASC was set up in 1973 to formulate International Accounting Standards until its functions were assumed by the IASB in 2001.

Difficulties in agreeing how the standards should be used in practice led to the setting up of the Standing Interpretations Committee (SIC) in 1997.

During its existence, the IASC published 41 IAS, including revised standards.

In May 2000, the Presidents Committee of the International Organisation of Securities Commissions (IOSCO) recommended that IOSCO members permit incoming multi-national issuers to use the IASC core standards to prepare their financial statements for cross-border offerings and listings (ie when a company in one country wishes to list its shares on another country's stock exchange). The core standards include all IAS except for IAS 26, IAS 40 and 41.

As the use of IAS grew, the role of the IASC expanded and as a result, the member bodies approved the restructuring of the IASC.

In March 2001 the IASC Foundation was formed as a not-for-profit corporation incorporated in the USA. The IASC Foundation is the parent entity of the IASB.

From April 2001 the IASB assumed accounting standard setting responsibilities from its predecessor body, the International Accounting Standards Committee (IASC). This restructuring was based upon the recommendations made in the report *Recommendations on Shaping IASC for the Future.* All existing IAS and SICs were adopted by the IASB.

In March 2010 the IASCF was renamed the International Financial Reporting Standards Foundation (IFRS Foundation). Its remit is, however, unchanged.

A substantial number of multinational companies prepare financial statements in accordance with IFRS. IAS and IFRS are also endorsed by many countries as their own standards, either unchanged or with minor amendments.

3.2 Structure of the IASB

The structure of the IASB has the following main features:

(a)   The IFRS Foundation is an independent corporation having two main bodies – the Trustees and the IASB.

(b)   The IFRS Foundation trustees appoint the IASB members, exercise oversight and raise the funds needed.

(c)   A Monitoring Board provides a formal link between the Trustees and public authorities. (This Board is described in more detail in Section 3.4 below.)

(d)   The IASB has sole responsibility for setting IFRS.

(e)   There are also two further bodies, the IFRS Advisory Council (known as the Standards Advisory Council or SAC until March 2010) and the IFRS Interpretations Committee (known as the International Financial Reporting Interpretations Committee until March 2010).

The structure can be illustrated as follows:

- IFRS Foundation Monitoring Board — 3. Public accountability
- IFRS Foundation Trustees — 2. Governance and oversight
- IFRS Foundation
  - International Accounting Standards Board
  - IFRS Interpretations Committee
- IFRS Advisory Council (left side)
- ASAF* (right side) — 1. Independent standard-setting and related activities

(Source: http://www.ifrs.org)

Trustees. The Trustees comprise a group of 22 individuals, with diverse geographic and functional backgrounds. The Trustees appoint the members of the IASB, the IFRIC and the IFRS Advisory Council. In addition to monitoring the IFRS Foundation's effectiveness and raising its funds, the Trustees approve the IFRS Foundation's budget and have responsibility for constitutional changes. Trustees are appointed so that there are six from North America, six from Europe, six from Asia/Oceania, one from Africa, one from South America and two others from the rest of the world.

IFRS Advisory Council. The IFRS Advisory Council provides a formal vehicle for further groups and individuals with diverse geographic and functional backgrounds to give advice to the Board and, at times, to advise the Trustees.

IFRS Interpretations Committee. The IFRS Interpretations Committee provides timely guidance on the application and interpretation of International Financial Reporting Standards.

4 Conceptual Framework

FAST FORWARD

IFRS are based on the IASB's *Conceptual Framework for Financial Reporting*.

4.1 The principle of a *Conceptual Framework*

Key term

A *Conceptual Framework*, in the field we are concerned with, is a statement of generally accepted theoretical principles which form the frame of reference for financial reporting. These theoretical principles provide the basis for the development of new accounting standards and the evaluation of those already in existence.

The financial reporting process is concerned with providing information that is useful in the business and economic decision-making process. Therefore, a *Conceptual Framework* will form the **theoretical basis** for determining which events should be accounted for, how they should be measured and how they should be communicated to the user. Although it is theoretical in nature, a *Conceptual Framework* for financial reporting has highly practical final aims.

PART A   CONTEMPORARY ISSUES

The **danger of not having a** *Conceptual Framework* is demonstrated in the way some countries' standards have developed over recent years; standards tend to be produced in a **haphazard and fire-fighting approach**. Where an agreed framework exists, the standard-setting body act as an architect or designer, rather than a fire-fighter, building accounting rules on the foundation of sound, agreed basic principles.

The lack of a *Conceptual Framework* also means that fundamental principles are tackled more than once in different standards, thereby producing contradictions and inconsistencies in basic concepts. This leads to ambiguity and this affects the true and fair concept of financial reporting.

Another problem with the lack of a *Conceptual Framework* has become apparent in the USA. The large number of **highly detailed standards** produced by the Financial Accounting Standards Board (FASB) has created a financial reporting environment governed by specific rules rather than general principles. This would be avoided if a cohesive set of principles were in place.

A *Conceptual Framework* can also bolster standard setters against political pressure from various 'lobby groups' and interested parties. Such pressure would only prevail if it was acceptable under the *Conceptual Framework*.

4.2 Advantages of a *Conceptual Framework*

The **advantages** arising from using a *Conceptual Framework* may be summarised as follows:

(a) The situation is **avoided** whereby standards are developed on a **patchwork** basis, where a particular accounting problem is recognised as having emerged, and resources are then channelled into **standardising accounting practice** in that area, without regard to whether that particular issue is necessarily the most important issue remaining at that time without standardisation. It facilitates consistency of standards.

(b) As stated above, the development of certain standards (particularly national standards) have been subject to considerable political interference from interested parties. Where there is a conflict of interest between user groups on which policies to choose, policies deriving from a *Conceptual Framework* will be **less open to criticism** that the standard-setter buckled to **external pressure**.

4.3 Counter-argument

A counter-argument might be as follows:

(a) Financial statements are intended for a **variety of users**, and it is not certain that a single *Conceptual Framework* can be devised which will suit all users.

(b) Given the diversity of user requirements, there may be a need for a variety of accounting standards, each produced for a **different purpose** (and with different concepts as a basis).

(c) It is not clear that a *Conceptual Framework* makes the task of **preparing and then implementing** standards any easier than without a framework.

Before we look at the IASB's attempt to produce a *Conceptual Framework,* we need to consider another term of importance to this debate: Generally Accepted Accounting Principles, or GAAP.

4.4 Generally Accepted Accounting Principles (GAAP)

This term has sprung up in recent years and it signifies all the rules, from whatever source, which govern accounting. In individual countries this is seen primarily as a combination of:

- National corporate law
- National accounting standards
- Local stock exchange requirements

Although those sources are the basis for the GAAP of individual countries, the concept also includes the effects of **non-mandatory sources** such as:

- International accounting standards
- Statutory requirements in other countries

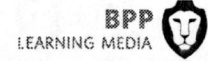

In many countries, like the UK, GAAP does not have any statutory or regulatory authority or definition, unlike other countries, such as the USA. The term is mentioned rarely in legislation, and only then in fairly limited terms.

There are different views of GAAP in different countries. The UK position can be explained in the following extracts from *UK GAAP* (Davies, Paterson & Wilson, Ernst & Young, 5th edition).

> 'Our view is that GAAP is a dynamic concept which requires constant review, adaptation and reaction to changing circumstances. We believe that use of the term "principle" gives GAAP an unjustified and inappropriate degree of permanence. GAAP changes in response to changing business and economic needs and developments. As circumstances alter, accounting practices are modified or developed accordingly... We believe that GAAP goes far beyond mere rules and principles, and encompasses contemporary permissible accounting **practice**.'

> 'It is often argued that the term "generally accepted" implies that a high degree of practical application of a particular accounting practice must exist. However, this interpretation raises certain practical difficulties. For example, what about new areas of accounting which have not, as yet, been generally applied? What about different accounting treatments for similar items – are they all generally accepted?'

> 'It is our view that "generally accepted" does **not** mean "generally adopted or used". We believe that, in the UK context, GAAP refers to accounting practices which are regarded as permissible by the accounting profession. The extent to which a particular practice has been adopted is, in our opinion, not the overriding consideration. Any accounting practice which is legitimate in the circumstances under which it has been applied should be regarded as GAAP. The decision as to whether or not a particular practice is permissible or legitimate would depend on one or more of the following factors:

> (a) Is the practice addressed either in the accounting standards, statute or other official pronouncements?

> (b) If the practice is not addressed in UK accounting standards, is it dealt with in International Accounting Standards, or the standards of other countries such as the US?

> (c) Is the practice consistent with the needs of users and the objectives of financial reporting?

> (d) Does the practice have authoritative support in the accounting literature?

> (e) Is the practice being applied by other companies in similar situations?

> (f) Is the practice consistent with the fundamental concept of "true and fair"?'

This view is not held in all countries, however. In the USA particularly, the equivalent of a 'true and fair view' is 'fair presentation in accordance with GAAP'. Generally accepted accounting principles are defined as those principles which have 'substantial authoritative support'. Therefore financial statements prepared in accordance with accounting principles for which there is not substantial authoritative support are presumed to be misleading or inaccurate.

The effect here is that 'new' or 'different' accounting principles are not acceptable unless they have been adopted by the mainstream accounting profession, usually the standard-setting bodies and/or professional accountancy bodies. This is much more rigid than the UK view expressed above.

4.5 GAAP and a *Conceptual Framework*

A *Conceptual Framework* for financial reporting can be defined as an attempt to codify existing GAAP in order to reappraise current accounting standards and to produce new standards.

4.6 The IASB'S *Conceptual Framework*

In July 1989 the IASB produced a document, *Framework for the preparation and presentation of financial statements* ('*Framework*'). The *Framework* acted as a framework upon which all IAS/IFRS were based and hence it determined the content of financial statements.

Subsequent versions of the *Conceptual Framework* were produced in 2010 and 2018. The rest of this section is based on the 2018 *Conceptual Framework*.

4.6.1 *Conceptual Framework* project

The *Conceptual Framework* project was initially undertaken jointly between the IASB and the FASB with the aim of providing the best common foundation for developing principles-based and converged standards.

Phase A (Objective and qualitative characteristics) was completed 28 in September 2010.

During late 2010, the IASB deferred further work until other more urgent convergence projects were finalised. The project was reactivated in September 2012 as an IASB-only project. The revised *Conceptual Framework* was issued in March 2018. It is the 2018 version that you are expected to be aware of for exams in 2020.

4.6.2 Purpose and status

The purpose of the *Conceptual Framework* is to:

(a) Assist the International Accounting Standards Board (Board) to develop IFRS Standards (Standards) that are based on consistent concepts;

(b) Assist preparers to develop consistent accounting policies when no standard applies to a particular transaction or other event, or when a standard allows a choice of accounting policy; and

(c) Assist all parties to understand and interpret the standards.

(*Conceptual Framework*, para. SP1)

The *Conceptual Framework* is not a standard and so does not overrule any individual IFRS. In the (rare) case of conflict between an IFRS and the *Conceptual Framework*, the **IFRS will prevail**.

4.6.3 The objective of general purpose financial reporting

The objective of general purpose financial reporting is to provide financial information about the reporting entity that is useful to existing and potential **investors, lenders and other creditors** in making **decisions relating to providing resources** to the entity.

Those decisions involve decisions about:

(a) Buying, selling or holding equity and debt instruments;

(b) Providing or settling loans and other forms of credit; or

(c) Exercising rights to vote on, or otherwise influence, management's actions that affect the use of the entity's resources.

(*Conceptual Framework*, para.1.2)

For example, providers of capital need to make decisions about whether to buy, sell or hold equity and debt instruments, or whether to provide or settle loans and other forms of credit.

The **focus therefore is on capital providers** (investors in the form of equity capital and lenders, and other creditors in the form of debt capital) as the primary users of financial statements. Financial reporting is aimed at users who provide resources to an entity but are not able to compel the entity to provide them with the information that they need in order to make decisions. Although the *Conceptual Framework* acknowledges that other parties, such as regulators and members of the public, may also find general purpose financial reports useful, it states that those reports are not primarily directed to these other groups.

The revised *Conceptual Framework* explains that existing and potential investors, lenders and other creditors may make decisions about buying, selling or holding shares or debt instruments, or providing or settling loans (para. 1.2).

To make these decisions, the primary users need information about:

(a) The **economic resources of the entity**;

(b) **Claims against the entity**;

(c) Changes in the entity's **economic resources and claims**; and

(d) How efficiently and effectively the entity's management and governing board have discharged their responsibilities to use the entity's economic resources.

(Conceptual Framework, para. 1.4)

The *Conceptual Framework* requires that financial performance is reflected by the application of **accrual accounting**. Accrual accounting is important because information about a reporting entity's economic resources and claims and changes in its economic resources and claims during a period provides a better basis for assessing the entity's past and future performance than information solely about cash receipts and payments during that period.

4.6.4 Qualitative characteristics of useful financial information

Chapter 3 considers the qualities that make financial information useful. It distinguishes between fundamental qualitative characteristics and enhancing qualitative characteristics.

The **fundamental qualitative characteristics** are:

(a) **Relevance**: Information is relevant if it is capable of **making a difference** in the decisions made by users. Information may be capable of making a difference in a decision even if some users choose not to take advantage of it or are already aware of it. Financial information is capable of making a difference in decisions if it has predictive value, confirmatory value, or both.

Materiality is an entity specific **aspect of relevance**. Information is material if omitting, misstating, or obscuring it could be reasonably expected to influence the decisions that users make on the basis of financial information about a specific reporting entity. Information can be material by its nature, magnitude or both.

(b) **Faithful representation**: To be useful, financial information must not only represent relevant phenomena but it must also **faithfully represent** the phenomena that it purports to represent. A perfectly faithful representation is **complete, neutral** and **free from error**.

Information must be both relevant and faithfully represented if it is to be useful. In practice there must be a balance between the two.

The **enhancing qualitative characteristics** are:

(a) **Comparability**: This enables users to identify and understand similarities in, and differences among, items. **Consistency** (use of the same methods for the same items) is not the same as comparability, although it helps to achieve comparability.

(b) **Verifiability**: This helps assure users that information faithfully represents the economic phenomena it purports to represent. It means that different knowledgeable and independent observers could reach consensus, although not necessarily complete agreement, that a particular depiction is a faithful representation.

(c) **Timeliness**: This means having information available to decision-makers in time to be capable of influencing their decisions.

(d) **Understandability**: For users who have a reasonable knowledge of business and economic activities and who review and analyse the information diligently.

Cost is a pervasive **constraint** on the reporting entity's ability to provide useful financial information. It is important that the costs of reporting financial information are justified by the benefits.

4.6.5 Key points from the remainder of the *Conceptual Framework*

The main points of the remaining text are revised below.

> **Knowledge brought forward from earlier studies**

Underlying assumption

- The financial statements are normally prepared on the assumption that the entity is a going concern.

The elements of financial statements

- **Asset**. A present economic resource controlled by the entity as a result of past events. An economic resource is a right that has the potential to produce economic benefits.
- **Liability**. A present obligation of the entity to transfer an economic resource as a result of past events.
- **Equity**. The residual interest in the assets of the entity after deducting all its liabilities.
- **Income**. Increases in assets, or decreases in liabilities, that result in increases in equity, other than those relating to contributions from equity participants.
- **Expenses**. Decreases in assets, or increases in liabilities, that result in decreases in equity, other than those relating to distributions to equity participants.

Recognition of the elements of financial statements

- Items which meet the definition of assets or liabilities may still not be recognised in financial statements because they must also meet certain recognition criteria.

Definition

Recognition. Recognition is the process of capturing for inclusion in the statement of financial position, or the statement(s) of financial performance, an item that meets the definition of one of the elements of financial statements.

An item should be recognised in the financial statements if:

(a) The item meets the definition of an **element** (asset, liability, income, expense or equity); and

(b) Recognition of that element provides users of the financial statements with information that is **useful**, ie with:
- **Relevant** information about the element
- A **faithful representation** of the element

Items may still qualify for recognition at a later date due to changes in circumstances or subsequent events.

Measurement of the elements of financial statements

Measurement is the process of determining the monetary amounts at which the elements of the financial statements are to be recognised and carried in the statement of financial position and statement of profit or loss and other comprehensive income.

Definitions

Historical cost. Historical cost measures provide monetary information about assets, liabilities and related income and expenses, using information derived, at least in part, from the price of the transaction or other event that gave rise to them.

Current value. Current value measures provide monetary information about assets, liabilities and related income and expenses, using information updated to reflect conditions at the measurement date.

> The *Conceptual Framework* recognises four current value measurement bases:
> - Fair value
> - Value in use for assets/fulfilment value for liabilities
> - Current cost
>
> **Historical cost** is the most commonly adopted measurement basis, but this is usually combined with other bases, eg inventory is carried at the lower of cost and net realisable value.

5 Harmonisation and international differences

Before we look at any countries in particular, we must consider what barriers there are to international harmonisation and why harmonisation is considered so desirable, before looking at comparative accounting systems.

5.1 Barriers to harmonisation

There are undoubtedly many barriers to international harmonisation. If there were not then greater progress would probably have been made by now. The main problems are as follows:

(a) **Different purposes of financial reporting**. In some countries the purpose is solely for tax assessment, while in others it is for investor decision making.

(b) **Different legal systems**. These prevent the development of certain accounting practices and restrict the options available.

(c) **Different user groups**. Countries have different ideas about who the relevant user groups are and their respective importance. In the USA and UK investor and creditor groups are given prominence, while in continental Europe employees enjoy a higher profile.

(d) **Needs of developing countries**. Developing countries are obviously behind in the standard-setting process and they need to develop the basic standards and principles already in place in most developed countries.

(e) **Nationalism** is demonstrated in an unwillingness to accept another country's standard.

(f) **Cultural differences** result in objectives for accounting systems differing from country to country.

(g) **Unique circumstances**. Some countries may be experiencing unusual circumstances which affect all aspects of everyday life, including the ability of companies to produce proper reports, eg hyperinflation, civil war, currency restriction.

(h) **The lack of strong accountancy bodies**. Many countries do not have strong independent accountancy or business bodies, which would press for better standards and greater harmonisation.

(i) **Inertia and cost**. There is often a national resistance to change reinforced by cost considerations.

5.2 Advantages of global harmonisation

In spite of all these difficulties, why is harmonisation perceived as so desirable? The advantages are based on the benefits to users and preparers of financial statements.

PART A CONTEMPORARY ISSUES

Globalisation

Suggest reasons why harmonisation is seen as desirable on a global basis.

Answer

(a) **Investors**, both individual and corporate, would like to be able to compare the financial results of different companies internationally (as well as nationally) in making investment decisions. Differences in accounting practice and reporting can be a barrier to such cross-border analysis. There is a growing amount of international investment across borders, but there are few financial analysts experienced in international markets. For example, an analyst familiar with UK accounting principles finds it difficult to analyse the financial statements of a Dutch or German company. Harmonisation would aid these analysts.

(b) **Multinational companies** would benefit from harmonisation for many reasons.

- Better access to foreign investor funds
- Aid internal communication of financial information
- Easier appraisal of foreign entities for take-overs and mergers
- Easier to comply with reporting requirements of overseas stock exchanges
- Easier consolidation of foreign subsidiaries and associated companies
- Possible reduction in audit costs
- Easier to transfer of accounting staff across national borders

(c) **Governments of developing countries** would save time and money by adopting international standards. If these were used internally, governments of developing countries could control the activities of foreign multinational companies within their own country, as these companies could not 'hide' behind foreign accounting practices which are difficult to understand.

(d) **Tax authorities**. It would be easier to calculate the tax liability of investors, including multinationals who receive income from overseas sources.

(e) **Regional economic groups** usually promote trade within a specific geographical region. This would be aided by common accounting practices within the region.

(f) **Large international accounting firms** would benefit as accounting and auditing would be much easier if similar accounting practices existed throughout the world.

5.3 Progress with harmonisation to date

The barriers to harmonisation may be daunting but some progress has been made. There are various bodies which are working on different aspects of harmonisation and these are discussed below. The most important of these bodies, in the light of recent developments, are the IASB and the UK Financial Reporting Council (FRC).

5.3.1 UK Financial Reporting Council and international standards

The UK FRC considers the development of international standards of **fundamental importance**. In addition, the UK FRC meets on a formal and regular basis with standard-setters around the world.

5.4 The EC regulation

FAST FORWARD The EC has required that **since 2005** consolidated financial statements of all listed companies should **comply with IFRS**.

As we have already seen, the EC regulations form one part of a broader programme for the harmonisation of company law in member states. The commission is uniquely the only organisation to produce **international** standards of accounting practice which are legally enforceable, in the form of directives which must be included in the national legislation of member states. The directives have been criticised as they might become constraints on the application of world-wide standards and bring accounting standardisation and harmonisation into the political arena.

The EC adopted a regulation stating that **from 2005 consolidated financial statements of listed companies have been required to comply with international accounting standards.** The implications of this proposal are far reaching.

Many commentators believe that, in the light of the above, it is only a matter of time before national standard setting bodies like the UK Financial Reporting Council are, in effect, replaced by the IASB and national standards fall into disuse.

5.5 IFRS and UK GAAP

The FRC issued a new standard, FRS 100 *Application of Financial Reporting Requirements* in November 2012 which lays out the future of UK GAAP and provides rules and guidance on how to select the appropriate accounting framework for a particular entity or group.

From January 2015, UK companies will be required to follow one of four sets of accounting requirements, depending on factors such as their size and whether they are listed:

- Full IFRS
- IFRS together with FRS 101 *Reduced Disclosure Framework*. FRS 101 makes minor amendments to IFRS in order to achieve compliance with the UK Companies Act and reduces IFRS disclosures significantly for qualifying entities, such as subsidiaries of groups reporting their individual entity financial statements under EU adopted IFRS.
- FRS 102 *The Financial Reporting Standard Applicable in the UK and Republic of Ireland*, a new single UK standard based on the *IFRS for Small and Medium-sized Entities*, which will replace existing UK accounting standards. FRS 102 adopts an IFRS-based framework, amended to ensure compliance with company law and improves accounting for financial instruments. It is intended for all UK entities other than those applying the FRSSE, or listed companies preparing group financial statements, who are already required to report under full IFRS. Such companies will still be allowed to apply FRS 101 or FRS 102 in preparing their individual entity financial statements.
- FRSSE – the *Financial Reporting Standard for Smaller Entities*.

The issue of FRS 101 ensures that IFRS become more accessible to unlisted companies in the UK which have, to date, been allowed to adopt full IFRS, but are, in many cases reluctant to do so due to the onerous disclosure requirements.

5.6 Convergence with US GAAP

FAST FORWARD

In recent years, the IASB has worked very closely with the US FASB. As a result, **IFRS has moved closer to US GAAP.**

5.6.1 Norwalk agreement

In October 2002, the IASB reached an agreement with the US FASB (Financial Accounting Standards Board) (the **'Norwalk' agreement**) to undertake a short-term convergence project aimed at removing a variety of individual differences between US GAAP and IFRS. The first standard resulting from this project was IFRS 5 *Non-current Assets Held for Sale and Discontinued Operations* (published March 2004).

5.6.2 Principles-based approach

In March 2003, an 'identical style and wording' approach was agreed for standards issued by FASB and the IASB on joint projects. Revised business combinations standards were issued as a result of this approach in January 2008, and most recently, IFRS 10–13 in May 2011.

The FASB also recognised the need to follow a **'principles-based' approach** to standard-setting (as the IASB has always done) in the light of recent corporate failures and scandals which have led to criticism of the 'rules-based' approach.

5.6.3 Common *Conceptual Framework*

In October 2004 the IASB and FASB agreed to develop a **common *Conceptual Framework*** which would be a significant step towards harmonisation of future standards (discussed earlier in this chapter). Together the IASB and FASB worked on the objective and qualitative characteristics of financial reporting; however, the remainder of the project was completed by the IASB working alone.

5.6.4 Memorandum of understanding

In February 2006, the two Boards signed a **'Memorandum of Understanding' (MoU)**. This laid down a 'roadmap of convergence' between IFRS and US GAAP in the period 2006-2008, identifying short-term and longer-term convergence projects that would bring the most significant improvements to IFRS and US GAAP.

In June 2010 the convergence strategy documented in the Memorandum of Understanding was modified. The modified work plan retained a target completion date of June 2011 or earlier for the MoU projects for which 'the need for improvement of both IFRS and US GAAP is the most urgent'. However it deferred less important work until after this date.

In April 2012, the IASB and FASB issued an update note stating that:

- Most short-term projects were now complete or close to completion
- Several longer-term projects were complete, with three – those on leases, revenue recognition and financial instruments – yet to be finalised.

The Boards continue to work on the incomplete longer-term projects, however work is being taken at a pace that enables thorough consultation. A final standard on revenue recognition was issued in May 2014 and IFRS 9 *Financial Instruments* was issued in July 2014, but the project on leasing is being redeliberated.

5.6.5 Adoption of IFRS in the USA

The initial aim of the convergence project was to remove by 2009 the requirement for foreign companies reporting under IFRS listed on a US stock exchange to have to prepare a reconciliation to US GAAP.

Events moved faster than expected, and in November 2007 the US Securities and Exchange Commission (SEC) decided to allow non-US filers to report under IFRS for years ended after 15 November 2007 with no reconciliation to US GAAP.

Consultation is also underway on the possibility of the use of IFRS by US filers. In November 2008, the SEC published a proposal, titled *Roadmap for the Potential Use of Financial Statements Prepared in Accordance with International Financial Reporting Standards by U.S. Issuers*. The Commission formally met again to discuss IFRS in 2010 and issued a statement expressing its strong commitment to the development of a single set of high-quality globally accepted accounting standards. It further clarified that upon completion of the MoU modified work plan, the Commission would be in a position to determine whether to incorporate IFRS into the US financial reporting system.

In July 2012, the SEC published its final report on its IFRS work plan. The report does not include a final policy decision or recommendation as to whether IFRS should be incorporated into the US financial reporting system. It concludes that there is limited support for the adoption of IFRS as authoritative guidance in US capital markets, and that such adoption would not be consistent with the methods of incorporation adopted by other major capital markets (such as the endorsement process followed by the EC). However, there is substantial support for exploring other methods of incorporating IFRS that demonstrate US commitment to the objective of a single-set of globally accepted accounting standards.

5.7 Dialogue with other key standard setters

The IASB maintains a policy of dialogue with other key standard-setters around the world, in the interest of harmonising standards across the globe.

National standard-setters are often involved in the development of Discussion Papers and Exposure Drafts on new areas.

5.7.1 China and Japan

In February 2006, China officially released a new set of Chinese Accounting Standards (CASs also known as Accounting Standards for Business Enterprises (ASBEs)) which are substantially converged with IFRS, and reaffirmed its commitment to international convergence.

In June 2009 a road map for the adoption of IFRS in Japan was approved, which proposed mandatory adoption of IFRS by 2016. As a result, in 2010 the Financial Services Authority of Japan allowed certain Japanese public companies to start using IFRS on a voluntary basis. In June 2011, however, the plan for mandatory adoption by 2016 was abandoned on the basis that Japanese companies were suffering enough financial hardship as a result of the 2011 tsunami, without being required to invest in IFRS implementation. As it stands, the government have not made a decision on whether to continue with the planned mandatory adoption of IFRS, and in the event that adoption does go ahead, there will be a transition period of five to seven years.

5.8 The situation today and in the future

Many organisations committed to global harmonisation have done a great deal of work towards this goal. It is the case at present, however, that fundamental disagreements exist between countries and organisations about the way forward. One of the major gulfs is between the reporting requirements in developed countries and those in non-developed countries. It will be some time before these difficulties can be overcome. The IASB is likely to be the lead body in attempting to do so, as discussed above.

PART A   CONTEMPORARY ISSUES

Chapter roundup

- Various national factors will affect the regulatory framework of entities, but our concern in this text is with international matters, particularly the **IASB** and **IAS/IFRS**.

- You should be able to describe the **organisation of the IFRS Foundation and the IASB** and its relationships with intergovernmental bodies, professional accountancy bodies, national standard-setting bodies and IOSCO.

- IFRS are based on the IASB's *Conceptual Framework for Financial Reporting*.

- The EC has required that **since 2005** consolidated financial statements of all listed companies should **comply with IFRS**.

- In recent years, the IASB has worked very closely with the US FASB. As a result, **IFRS has moved closer to US GAAP**.

Quick quiz

1. Which of the following factors govern the regulatory system of accounting over entities? Circle all that apply.

   (a) National legislation
   (b) Local legislation
   (c) IAS
   (d) Accounting systems
   (e) IFRS
   (f) Auditing systems
   (g) FBI

2. What are the objectives of the IFRS Foundation and the IASB?

3. Which are the most recent IFRS?

Answers to quick quiz

1. (a), (b), (c) and (e)
2. See Section 2.1
3. IFRS 14 *Regulatory Deferral Accounts*

    IFRS 15 *Revenue from Contracts with Customers*

    IFRS 16 *Leases*

    IFRS 17 *Insurance Contracts*

End of chapter question

IASB

'A major achievement of the IASB has been the development of its *Conceptual Framework*. However, it is too theoretical to be applied to accounting standards.'

Critically analyse this statement, considering what the merits of the *Conceptual Framework* are and whether you agree with the criticism that it is too theoretical.

(10 marks)

PART A CONTEMPORARY ISSUES

Presentation of published financial statements

Topic list	Syllabus reference
1 Limited liability	13.1
2 IAS 1 (revised) *Presentation of Financial Statements*	13.1
3 Statement of financial position	13.1
4 The current/non-current distinction	13.1
5 Statement of profit or loss and other comprehensive income	13.1
6 Statement of profit or loss (income statement)	13.1
7 Changes in equity	13.1
8 Notes to the financial statements	13.1

Introduction

The bulk of this Study Text looks at the accounts of limited liability companies, either single companies or groups of companies.

In this chapter we look at the overall **content and format** of company financial statements. These are governed by IAS 1 *Presentation of Financial Statements*.

1 Limited liability

> Limited liability offers various advantages to companies, although there are disadvantages as well.

1.1 Fundamental differences

There are some fundamental differences in the financial statements of limited liability companies **compared to sole traders or partnerships**, of which the following are perhaps the most significant.

(a) The **national legislation** governing the activities of limited liability companies tends to be very extensive. Among other things such legislation may define certain minimum accounting records which must be maintained by companies; it may specify that the annual financial statements of a company must be filed with a government bureau and so available for public inspection; and often contains detailed requirements on the minimum information which must be disclosed in a company's financial statements. Businesses which are not limited liability companies (non-incorporated businesses) often enjoy comparative freedom from statutory regulation.

(b) The **owners of a company** (its members or shareholders) may be very numerous. Their capital is shown differently from that of a sole trader; and similarly the 'appropriation account' of a company is different.

1.2 Limited liability

You may be able to recognise the relative **advantages and disadvantages** of limited liability. Sole traders and partnerships are, with some significant exceptions, generally fairly small concerns. The amount of capital involved may be modest, and the proprietors of the business usually participate in managing it. Their liability for the debts of the business is unlimited, which means that if the business runs up debts that it is unable to pay, the proprietors will become personally liable for the unpaid debts, and would be required, if necessary, to sell their private possessions in order to repay them. For example, if a sole trader has some capital in his business, but the business now owes $40,000 which it cannot repay, the trader might have to sell his house to raise the money to pay off his business debts.

Limited liability companies offer **limited liability to their owners**. This means that the maximum amount that an owner stands to lose in the event that the company becomes insolvent and cannot pay off its debts is his share of the capital in the business. Thus limited liability is a major advantage of turning a business into a limited liability company. However, in practice, banks or other lenders will normally seek personal guarantees from shareholders before making loans or granting an overdraft facility and so the advantage of limited liability is lost to a small owner managed business.

There are also disadvantages to limited liability:

(a) Compliance with national legislation
(b) Compliance with national accounting standards and/or IFRS
(c) Any formation and annual registration costs

As a business grows, it needs **more capital** to finance its operations, and significantly more than the people currently managing the business can provide themselves. One way of obtaining more capital is to invite investors from outside the business to invest in the ownership or equity of the business. These new co-owners would not usually be expected to help with managing the business. To such investors, limited liability is very attractive.

Investments are always risky undertakings, but with limited liability the investor knows the maximum amount that he stands to lose when he puts some capital into a company.

1.3 The accounting records of limited liability companies

There is almost always a **national legal requirement** for companies to keep accounting records which are sufficient to show and explain the company's transactions. The records will probably:

(a) Disclose the company's current financial position at any time

(b) Contain:

    (i) Day-to-day entries of money received and spent

    (ii) A record of the company's assets and liabilities

    (iii) Where the company deals in goods:

        (1) A statement of inventories held at the year end, and supporting inventory count records

        (2) With the exception of retail sales, statements of goods bought and sold which identify the sellers and buyers of those goods

(c) Enable the managers of the company to ensure that the **final financial statements** of the company give a true and fair view of the company's profit or loss and statement of financial position.

The detailed requirements of accounting records which must be maintained will vary from country to country.

Question — Regulation

How are limited liability companies regulated in your country?

2 IAS 1 (revised) *Presentation of Financial Statements*

FAST FORWARD

IAS 1 covers the **form and content** of financial statements, which comprise:

- Statement of financial position
- Statement of profit or loss and other comprehensive income
- Statement of changes in equity
- Statement of cash flows
- Notes to the financial statements, comprising significant accounting policies and other explanatory information
- Comparative information in respect of the preceding period

IAS 1 *Presentation of Financial Statements* gives substantial guidance on the form and content of published financial statements. It was revised in September 2007 with a narrow scope amendment made as part of the disclosure initiative in December 2014. The standard looks at the statement of financial position and statement of profit or loss and other comprehensive income (the statement of cash flows is covered by IAS 7). First of all, some general points are made about financial statements.

2.1 Profit or loss for the period

The statement of profit or loss and other comprehensive income is the most significant indicator of a company's financial performance. So it is important to ensure that it is not misleading.

IAS 1 stipulates that all items of income and expense recognised in a period shall be included in profit or loss unless a **Standard** or an **Interpretation** requires otherwise.

Circumstances where items may be excluded from profit or loss for the current year include the correction of errors and the effect of changes in accounting policies. These are covered in IAS 8.

2.2 How items are disclosed

IAS 1 specifies disclosures of certain items in certain ways.

- Some items must appear in the statement of financial position or statement of profit or loss and other comprehensive income
- Other items can appear in a **note to the financial statements** instead
- **Recommended formats** are given which entities may or may not follow, depending on their circumstances

Obviously, disclosures specified by **other standards** must also be made, and we will mention the necessary disclosures when we cover each standard in turn. Disclosures in both IAS 1 and other standards must be made either in the statement or in the notes unless otherwise stated, ie disclosures cannot be made in an accompanying commentary or report.

2.3 Identification of financial statements

As a result of the above point, it is most important that entities **distinguish the financial statements** very clearly from any other information published with them. This is because all IFRS apply **only** to the financial statements (ie the main statements and related notes), so readers of the annual report must be able to differentiate between the parts of the report which are prepared under IFRS, and other parts which are not.

The entity should **identify each** financial statement and the notes very clearly. IAS 1 also requires disclosure of the following information in a prominent position. If necessary it should be repeated wherever it is felt to be of use to the reader in his understanding of the information presented.

- **Name** of the reporting entity (or other means of identification)
- Whether the financial statements cover the **single entity** only or a group of entities
- The **date of the end of the reporting period** or the period covered by the financial statements (as appropriate)
- The **presentation currency**
- The **level of rounding** used in presenting amounts in the financial statements

Judgement must be used to determine the best method of presenting this information. In particular, the standard suggests that the approach to this will be very different when the financial statements are communicated electronically.

The **level of rounding** is important, as presenting figures in thousands or millions of units makes the figures more understandable. The level of rounding must be disclosed, however, and it should not obscure necessary details or make the information less relevant.

2.4 Reporting period

It is normal for entities to present financial statements **annually** and IAS 1 states that they should be prepared at least as often as this. If (unusually) the end of an entity's reporting period is changed, for whatever reason, the period for which the statements are presented will be less or more than one year. In such cases the entity should also disclose:

(a) The **reason(s) why** a period other than one year is used; and
(b) The fact that the comparative figures given **are not in fact comparable**.

For practical purposes, some entities prefer to use a period which **approximates to a year**, eg 52 weeks, and the IAS allows this approach as it will produce statements not materially different from those produced on an annual basis.

3 Statement of financial position

FAST FORWARD

IAS 1 suggests a **format** for the statement of financial position. Certain items are specified for **disclosure in the financial statements**.

IAS 1 discusses the distinction between current and non-current items in some detail, as we shall see in the next section. First of all we can look at the **suggested format** of the statement of financial position (given in an appendix to the standard) and then look at further disclosures required.

3.1 Example: Statement of financial position

The example given by IAS 1 revised is as follows:

XYZ GROUP – STATEMENT OF FINANCIAL POSITION AT 31 DECEMBER

	20X7 $'000	20X6 $'000
Assets		
Non-current assets		
Property, plant and equipment	350,700	360,020
Goodwill	80,800	91,200
Other intangible assets	227,470	227,470
Investments in associates	100,150	110,770
Financial assets	142,500	156,000
	901,620	945,460
Current assets		
Inventories	135,230	132,500
Trade receivables	91,600	110,800
Other current assets	25,650	12,540
Cash and cash equivalents	312,400	322,900
	564,880	578,740
Total assets	1,466,500	1,524,200
Equity and liabilities		
Equity attributable to owners of the parent		
Share capital	650,000	600,000
Retained earnings	243,500	161,700
Other components of equity	10,200	21,200
	903,700	782,900
Non-controlling interest	70,050	48,600
Total equity	973,750	831,500
Non-current liabilities		
Long-term borrowings	120,000	160,000
Deferred tax	28,800	26,040
Long-term provisions	28,850	52,240
Total non-current liabilities	117,650	238,280
Current liabilities		
Trade and other payables	115,100	187,620
Short-term borrowings	150,000	200,000
Current portion of long-term borrowings	10,000	20,000
Current tax payable	35,000	42,000
Short-term provisions	5,000	4,800
Total current liabilities	315,100	454,420
Total liabilities	492,750	92,700
Total equity and liabilities	1,466,500	1,524,200

IAS 1 (revised) specifies various items which must appear in the **statement of financial position**.

(a) Property, plant and equipment
(b) Investment property
(c) Intangible assets
(d) Financial assets (excluding amounts shown under (e), (h) and (i))
(e) Investments accounted for using the equity method
(f) Biological assets
(g) Inventories
(h) Trade and other receivables
(i) Cash and cash equivalents
(j) Assets classified as held for sale under IFRS 5
(k) Trade and other payables
(l) Provisions
(m) Financial liabilities (other than (j) and (k))
(n) Current tax liabilities and assets as in IAS 12
(o) Deferred tax liabilities and assets
(p) Liabilities included in disposal groups under IFRS 5
(q) Non-controlling interests
(r) Issued capital and reserves

Any **other line items**, headings or sub-totals should be shown in the statement of financial position when it is necessary for an understanding of the entity's financial position.

The example shown above is for illustration only (although we will follow the format in this Study Text). The IAS, however, does not prescribe the order or format in which the items listed should be presented. It simply states that they **must be presented separately** because they are so different in nature or function from each other.

Whether additional items are presented separately depends on judgements based on the assessment of the following factors:

(a) **Nature and liquidity of assets and their materiality**. Thus goodwill and assets arising from development expenditure will be presented separately, as will monetary/non-monetary assets and current/non-current assets.

(b) **Function within the entity**. Operating and financial assets, inventories, receivables and cash and cash equivalents are therefore shown separately.

(c) **Amounts, nature and timing of liabilities**. Interest-bearing and non-interest-bearing liabilities and provisions will be shown separately, classified as current or non-current as appropriate.

The standard also requires separate presentation where **different measurement bases** are used for assets and liabilities which differ in nature or function. According to IAS 16, for example, it is permitted to measure certain items of property, plant and equipment at cost or at a revalued amount.

3.2 Information presented in the statement of financial position or the notes

Further **sub-classification** of the line items listed above should be disclosed either in the statement of financial position or in the notes. The classification will depend upon the nature of the entity's operations. As well as each item being sub-classified by its nature, any amounts payable to or receivable from any **group company or other related party** should also be disclosed separately.

The sub-classification details will in part depend on the requirements of IFRS. The size, nature and function of the amounts involved will also be important and the factors listed above should be considered. **Disclosures** will vary from item to item and IAS 1 gives the following examples.

(a) **Property, plant and equipment** are classified by class as described in IAS 16, *Property, Plant and Equipment*

(b) **Receivables** are analysed between amounts receivable from trade customers, other members of the group, receivables from related parties, prepayments and other amounts

(c) **Inventories** are sub-classified, in accordance with IAS 2 *Inventories,* into classifications such as merchandise, production supplies, materials, work in progress and finished goods

(d) **Provisions** are analysed showing separately provisions for employee benefit costs and any other items classified in a manner appropriate to the entity's operations

(e) **Equity capital and reserves** are analysed showing separately the various classes of paid in capital, share premium and reserves

The standard then lists some **specific disclosures** which must be made, either in the statement of financial position or in the related notes.

(a) **Share capital disclosures** (for each class of share capital)
   (i) Number of shares authorised
   (ii) Number of shares issued and fully paid, and issued but not fully paid
   (iii) Par value per share, or that the shares have no par value
   (iv) Reconciliation of the number of shares outstanding at the beginning and at the end of the year
   (v) Rights, preferences and restrictions attaching to that class including restrictions on the distribution of dividends and the repayment of capital
   (vi) Shares in the entity held by the entity itself or by related group companies
   (vii) Shares reserved for issuance under options and sales contracts, including the terms and amounts

(b) Description of the nature and purpose of **each reserve** within owners' equity

Some types of entity have no share capital, eg partnerships. Such entities should disclose information which is **equivalent** to that listed above. This means disclosing the movement during the period in each category of equity interest and any rights, preferences or restrictions attached to each category of equity interest.

4 The current/non-current distinction

FAST FORWARD

You should appreciate the distinction between **current** and **non-current** assets and liabilities and their different treatments.

4.1 The current/non-current distinction

An entity must present **current** and **non-current** assets as separate classifications in the statement of financial position. A presentation based on liquidity should only be used where it provides more relevant and reliable information, in which case all assets and liabilities must be presented broadly **in order of liquidity**.

In either case, the entity should disclose any portion of an asset or liability which is expected to be recovered or settled **after more than 12 months**. For example, for an amount receivable which is due in instalments over 18 months, the portion due after more than 12 months must be disclosed.

The IAS emphasises how helpful information on the **operating cycle** is to users of financial statements. Where there is a clearly defined operating cycle within which the entity supplies goods or services, then information disclosing those net assets that are continuously circulating as **working capital** is useful.

This distinguishes them from those net assets used in the long-term operations of the entity. Assets that are expected to be realised and liabilities that are due for settlement within the operating cycle are therefore highlighted.

The liquidity and solvency of an entity is also indicated by information about the **maturity dates** of assets and liabilities. As we will see later, IFRS 7 *Financial Instruments: Disclosures* requires disclosure of maturity dates of both financial assets and financial liabilities. (Financial assets include trade and other receivables; financial liabilities include trade and other payables.) In the case of non-monetary assets, eg inventories, such information is also useful.

4.2 Current assets

Key term

An asset should be classified as a **current asset** when it:

- The entity expects to realise the asset, or intends to sell or consume it, in its normal operating cycle; or
- The asset is held primarily for trading purposes; or
- The asset is expected to be realised within 12 months of the end of the reporting period; or
- The asset is cash or a cash equivalent asset which is not restricted in its use.

All other assets should be classified as non-current assets. (IAS 1)

Non-current assets includes tangible, intangible, operating and financial assets of a long-term nature. Other terms with the same meaning can be used (eg 'fixed', 'long-term').

The term 'operating cycle' has been used several times above and the standard defines it as follows.

Key term

The **operating cycle** of an entity is the time between the acquisition of assets for processing and their realisation in cash or cash equivalents. (IAS 1)

Current assets therefore include inventories and trade receivables that are sold, consumed and realised as part of the normal operating cycle. **This is the case even where they are not expected to be realised within 12 months.**

Current assets will also include **marketable securities** if they are expected to be realised within 12 months after the reporting period. If expected to be realised later, they should be included in non-current assets.

4.3 Current liabilities

Key term

A liability should be classified as a **current liability** when it:

- The entity expects to settle the liability in its normal operating cycle; or
- The liability is held primarily for the purpose of trading; or
- The liability is due to be settled within 12 months after the reporting period; or
- The entity does not have an unconditional right to defer settlement of the liability for at least 12 months after the reporting period.

All other liabilities should be classified as non-current liabilities. (IAS 1)

The categorisation of current liabilities is very similar to that of current assets. Thus, some current liabilities are part of the **working capital** used in the normal operating cycle of the business (ie trade payables and accruals for employee and other operating costs). Such items will be classed as current liabilities **even where they are due to be settled more than 12 months after the end of the reporting period**.

There are also current liabilities which are not settled as part of the normal operating cycle, but which are due to be settled within 12 months of the end of the reporting period. These include bank overdrafts, income taxes, other non-trade payables and the current portion of interest-bearing liabilities. Any interest-bearing liabilities that are used to finance working capital on a long-term basis, and that are not due for settlement within 12 months, should be classed as **non-current liabilities**.

A **non-current financial liability** due to be **settled within 12 months** of the end of the reporting period should be classified as a **current liability**, even if an agreement to refinance, or to reschedule payments, on a long-term basis is completed after the end of the reporting period and before the financial statements are authorised for issue.

End of the reporting period	Agreement to refinance on long-term basis	Date financial statements authorised for issue	Settlement date <12 months after end of the reporting period therefore current liability

A **non-current financial liability** that is payable on **demand** because the entity **breached** a **condition** of its loan agreement should be classified as **current** at the end of the reporting period even if the **lender** has agreed **after the end of the reporting period**, and **before** the financial statements are **authorised for issue**, **not** to **demand payment** as a consequence of the breach.

Condition of loan agreement breached. Non-current liability becomes payable on demand	End of the reporting period	Lender agrees not to enforce payment resulting from breach	Date financial statements are authorised for issue. Loan shown as current liability

However, if the **lender** has **agreed** by the **end of the reporting period** to provide a **period of grace** ending **at least 12 months after the end of the reporting period** within which the entity can rectify the breach and during that time the lender cannot demand immediate repayment, the liability is classified as **non-current**.

5 Statement of profit or loss and other comprehensive income

FAST FORWARD

IAS 1 (revised) requires all items of income and expense in a period to be shown in a **statement of profit or loss and other comprehensive income**.

The revision of IAS 1 in 2007 introduced a new statement, the **statement of comprehensive income**. This shows both income and expense items (profit or loss) and unrealised items known as other comprehensive income. An amendment to IAS 1 in 2011 changed the name of the statement to 'Statement of profit or loss and other comprehensive income', however allows alternative titles to be used.

5.1 Statement of profit or loss and other comprehensive income – format

IAS 1 (revised) allows income and expense items to be presented either:

(a) In a single statement of profit or loss and other comprehensive income; or

(b) In two statements: a separate statement of profit and loss (or income statement) and a statement of profit or loss and other comprehensive income.

Exam focus point

In the examinations, generally 'Statement of profit or loss and other comprehensive income' will be referred to and this will usually relate to the single statement format. If 'Income Statements' or 'Statements of Profit or Loss' are referred to, this normally relates to the statement from 'Revenue' to 'Profit for the year'. Where we have used 'statement of profit or loss' in this text, this can be taken to refer to the section of the statement of profit or loss and other comprehensive income as far as profit, or separate statement or profit or loss.

XYZ GROUP – STATEMENT OF PROFIT OR LOSS AND OTHER COMPREHENSIVE INCOME FOR THE YEAR ENDED 31 DECEMBER 20X7

	20X7 $'000	20X6 $'000
Revenue	39,000	355,000
Cost of sales	(245,000)	(230,000)
Gross profit	145,000	125,000
Other income	20,667	11,300
Distribution costs	(9,000)	(8,700)
Administrative expenses	(20,000)	(21,000)
Other expenses	(2,100)	(1,200)
Finance costs	(8,000)	(7,500)
Share of profit of associates	35,100	30,100
Profit before tax	161,667	128,000
Income tax expense	(40,417)	(32,000)
Profit for the year from continuing operations	121,250	96,000
Loss for the year from discontinued operations	–	(30,500)
Profit for the year	121,250	65,500
Other comprehensive income:		
Items that will not be reclassified to profit or loss:		
Gains on property revaluation	933	3,367
Remeasurements of defined benefit pension plans	(667)	1,333
Share of gain on property revaluation of associates	400	(700)
Income tax relating to items that will not be reclassified	(166)	(1,000)
	500	3,000
Items that may be reclassified subsequently to profit or loss		
Exchange differences on translating foreign operations	5,334	10,667
Financial assets held at fair value through other comprehensive income	(24,000)	26,667
Cash flow hedges	(667)	(4,000)
Income tax relating to items that may be reclassified	4,833	(8,334)
	(14,500)	25,000
Other comprehensive income for the year, net of tax	(14,000)	28,000
Total comprehensive income for the year	107,250	93,500
Profit attributable to:		
Owners of the parent	97,000	52,400
Non-controlling interest	24,250	13,100
	121,250	65,500
Total comprehensive income attributable to		
Owners of the parent	85,800	74,800
Non-controlling interest	21,450	18,700
	107,250	93,500
Earnings per share (in currency units)	0.46	0.30

Companies are given the option of presenting this information in two statements as follows:

XYZ GROUP – STATEMENT OF PROFIT OR LOSS AND OTHER COMPREHENSIVE INCOME FOR THE YEAR ENDED 31 DECEMBER 20X7:

	20X7	20X6
	$'000	$'000
Revenue	39,000	355,000
Cost of sales	(245,000)	(230,000)
Gross profit	145,000	125,000
Other income	20,667	11,300
Distribution costs	(9,000)	(8,700)
Administrative expenses	(20,000)	(21,000)
Other expenses	(2,100)	(1,200)
Finance costs	(8,000)	(7,500)
Share of profit of associates	35,100	30,100
Profit before tax	161,667	128,000
Income tax expense	(40,417)	(32,000)
Profit for the year from continuing operations	121,250	96,000
Loss for the year from discontinued operations	–	(30,500)
Profit for the year	121,250	65,500
Profit attributable to:		
Owners of the parent	97,000	52,400
Non-controlling interest	24,250	13,100
	121,250	65,500

XYZ GROUP STATEMENT OF PROFIT OR LOSS AND OTHER COMPREHENSIVE INCOME FOR THE YEAR ENDED 31 DECEMBER 20X7

	20X7	20X6
	$'000	$'000
Profit for the year	121,250	65,500
Other comprehensive income:		
Items that will not be reclassified to profit or loss		
Gains on property revaluation	933	3,367
Remeasurements of defined benefit pension plans	(667)	1,333
Share of gain on property revaluation of associates	400	(700)
Income tax relating to items that will not be reclassified	(166)	(1,000)
	500	3,000
Items that may be reclassified subsequently to profit or loss		
Exchange differences on translating foreign operations	5,334	10,667
Financial assets at fair value through other comprehensive income	(24,000)	26,667
Cash flow hedges	(667)	(4,000)
Income tax relating to items that may be reclassified	4,833	(8,334)
	(14,500)	25,000
Other comprehensive income for the year, net of tax	(14,000)	28,000
Total comprehensive income for the year	107,250	93,500
Total comprehensive income attributable to		
Owners of the parent	85,800	74,800
Non-controlling interest	21,450	18,700
	107,250	93,500

5.2 Presentation of other comprehensive income

An amendment to IAS 1 in 2011 requires that regardless of whether a one or two statement presentation is adopted, other comprehensive income must be grouped into amounts which, in accordance with other IFRS:

(a) Will not be reclassified subsequently to profit or loss; and
(b) May be reclassified subsequently to profit or loss if specific conditions are met.

A similar disclosure must be made for the share of the comprehensive income of associates and joint ventures that are accounted for using the equity method. Items of other comprehensive income may be presented either net of related tax effects or before related tax effects. If the second approach is adopted, the aggregate amount of income tax relating to items of other comprehensive income must be disclosed and this must be split according to whether the other comprehensive income may be reclassified to profit or loss.

This method of presentation is shown in the examples in Section 5.1 above.

6 Statement of profit or loss (income statement)

IAS 1 offers **two** possible formats for the statement of profit or loss section or separate statement of profit or loss – by function or by nature. Classification by function is more common.

6.1 Example: Statements of profit or loss

XYZ GROUP
STATEMENT OF PROFIT OR LOSS FOR THE YEAR ENDED 31 DECEMBER 20X8

Illustrating the classification of expenses by **function**

	20X8 $'000	20X7 $'000
Revenue	X	X
Cost of sales	(X)	(X)
Gross profit	X	X
Other income	X	X
Distribution costs	(X)	(X)
Administrative expenses	(X)	(X)
Other expenses	(X)	(X)
Finance costs	(X)	(X)
Share of profit of associates	X	X
Profit before tax	X	X
Income tax expense	(X)	(X)
Profit for the year	X	X
Attributable to:		
Owners of the parent	X	X
Non-controlling interest	X	X
	X	X

Illustrating the classification of expenses by **nature**

	20X8 $'000	20X7 $'000
Revenue	X	X
Other operating income	X	X
Changes in inventories of finished goods and work in progress	(X)	X
Work performed by the entity and capitalised	X	X
Raw material and consumables used	(X)	(X)
Employee benefits expense	(X)	(X)

	20X8	20X7
	$'000	$'000
Depreciation and amortisation expense	(X)	(X)
Impairment of property, plant and equipment	(X)	(X)
Other expenses	(X)	(X)
Finance costs	(X)	(X)
Share of profit of associates	X	X
Profit before tax	X	X
Income tax expense	(X)	(X)
Profit for the year	X	X
Attributable to:		
Owners of the parent	X	X
Non-controlling interest	X	X
	X	X

Note. The usual method of presentation is expenses by function and this is the format likely to appear in your exam.

6.2 Information presented in the profit or loss section or separate statement of profit or loss

The standard lists the following as the **minimum** to be disclosed in the statement of profit or loss:

(a) Revenue
(b) Finance costs
(c) Share of profits and losses of associates and joint ventures accounted for using the equity method
(d) Tax expense
(e) A single amount for the total of discontinued operations

The following items must be disclosed in the statement of profit or loss as allocations of profit or loss for the period.

(a) Profit or loss attributable to non-controlling interest
(b) Profit or loss attributable to owners of the parent

The allocated amounts must not be presented as items of income or expense. (These relate to group financial statements, covered later in this text.)

Income and expense items can only be **offset** when, and only when:

(a) It is permitted or required by an IFRS; or
(b) Gains, losses and related expenses arising from the same or similar transactions and events are immaterial, in which case they can be aggregated.

6.3 Information presented either in the statement or in the notes

An analysis of expenses must be shown either in the statement of profit or loss section (as above, which is encouraged by the standard) or by note, using a classification based on **either** the nature of the expenses or their function. This **sub-classification of expenses** indicates a range of components of financial performance; these may differ in terms of stability, potential for gain or loss and predictability.

6.3.1 Nature of expense method

Expenses are not reallocated amongst various functions within the entity, but are aggregated in the statement of profit or loss **according to their nature** (eg purchase of materials, depreciation, wages and salaries, transport costs). This is by far the easiest method, especially for smaller entities.

6.3.2 Function of expense/cost of sales method

You are likely to be more familiar with this method. Expenses are classified according to their function as part of cost of sales, distribution or administrative activities. This method often gives **more relevant information** for users, but the allocation of expenses by function requires the use of judgement and can be arbitrary. Consequently, perhaps, when this method is used, entities should disclose **additional information** on the nature of expenses, including staff costs, and depreciation and amortisation expenses.

Which of the above methods is chosen by an entity will depend on **historical and industry factors**, and also the **nature of the organisation**. Under each method, there should be given an indication of costs which are likely to vary (directly or indirectly) with the level of sales or production. The choice of method should fairly reflect the main elements of the entity's performance.

6.4 Further points

(a) IAS 1 also requires disclosure of the amount of **dividends** (both in total and per share) recognised in the period covered by the financial statements. This may be shown either in the statement of changes in equity or in the notes. Dividends are not disclosed in the statement of profit or loss and other comprehensive income.

(b) An entity must disclose, in its significant accounting policies and/or other notes, the **judgements** made by management in **applying** the **accounting policies** that have the **most significant effect** on the amounts of items recognised in the financial statements.

(c) An entity must disclose in the notes information regarding **key assumptions** about the **future**, and other sources of **measurement uncertainty**, that have a significant **risk of** causing a **material adjustment** to the carrying amounts of assets and liabilities within the **next financial year**.

The figure in the statement of financial position for capital and reserves therefore bears **no relationship** to the market value of shares. Market values are the product of a large number of factors, including general economic conditions, alternative investment returns (eg interest rates), likely future profits and dividends and, not least, market sentiment.

7 Changes in equity

> **FAST FORWARD**
>
> IAS 1 requires a statement of changes in equity. This shows the movement in the equity section of the statement of financial position.

7.1 Format

This is the format of the statement of changes in equity as per IAS 1 (revised).

XYZ GROUP – STATEMENT OF CHANGES IN EQUITY FOR THE YEAR ENDED 31 DECEMBER 20X7

2: PRESENTATION OF PUBLISHED FINANCIAL STATEMENTS

	Share capital $'000	Retained earnings $'000	Equity instruments at FVTOCI $'000	Revaluation surplus $'000	Total $'000	Non-controlling interest $'000	Total equity $'000
Balance at 1 January 20X6	600,000	118,100	1,600	–	719,700	29,800	749,500
Changes in accounting policy	–	400	–	–	400	100	500
Restated balance	600,000	118,500	1,600	–	720,100	29,900	750,000
Changes in equity							
Dividends	–	(10,000)	–	–	(10,000)	–	(10,000)
Total comprehensive income for the year	–	53,200	16,000	1,600	70,800	18,700	89,500
Balance at 31 December	600,000	161,700	17,600	1,600	780,900	48,600	829,500
Changes in equity for 20X7							
Issue of share capital	50,000	–	–	–	50,000	–	50,000
Dividends	–	(15,000)	–	–	(15,000)	–	(15,000)
Total comprehensive income for the year	–	96,600	(14,400)	800	83,000	21,450	104,450
Transfer to retained earnings	–	200	–	(200)	–	–	–
Bal at 31 December 20X7	650,000	243,500	3,200	2,200	898,900	70,050	968,950

Note that where there has been a change of accounting policy necessitating a retrospective restatement, the adjustment is disclosed for each period. So, rather than just showing an adjustment to the balance b/f on 1.1.X7, the balances for 20X6 are restated.

8 Notes to the financial statements

FAST FORWARD

Some items need to be disclosed by way of note.

8.1 Contents of notes

The notes to the financial statements will **amplify** the information given in the statement of financial position, statement of profit or loss and other comprehensive income and statement of changes in equity. To some extent, then, the contents of the notes will be determined by the level of detail shown in **the statements**.

8.2 Structure

The notes to the financial statements should perform the following functions:

(a) Provide information about the **basis on which the financial statements were prepared** and which **specific accounting policies** were chosen and applied to significant transactions/events

(b) Disclose any information, not shown elsewhere in the financial statements, which is **required by IFRS**

(c) Show any additional information that is relevant to understanding which is not shown elsewhere in the financial statements

The way the notes are presented is important. They should be given in a **systematic manner** and **cross referenced** back to the related figure(s) in the statement of financial position, statement of profit or loss and other comprehensive income or statement of cash flows.

A systematic manner may be achieved by giving prominence to the most important items, grouping together information about similar items, or following the order of the items in the primary statements.

Notes to the financial statements will amplify the information shown therein by giving the following:

(a) More **detailed analysis** or breakdowns of figures in the statements
(b) **Narrative information** explaining figures in the statements
(c) **Additional information**, eg contingent liabilities and commitments

IAS 1 suggests a **certain order** for notes to the financial statements. This will assist users when comparing the statements of different entities.

(a) Statement of **compliance** with IFRS

(b) Statement of the **measurement basis** (bases) and accounting policies applied

(c) **Supporting information** for items presented in each financial statement in the same order as each line item and each financial statement is presented

(d) Other disclosures, eg:

    (i) Contingent liabilities, commitments and other financial disclosures
    (ii) Non-financial disclosures

The order of specific items may have to be varied occasionally, but a systematic structure is still required.

8.3 Presentation of accounting policies

The accounting policies section should describe the following:

(a) The **measurement basis** (or bases) used in preparing the financial statements

(b) The **other accounting policies** used, as required for a proper understanding of the financial statements

This information may be shown in the notes or sometimes as a **separate component** of the financial statements.

The information on measurement bases used is obviously fundamental to an understanding of the financial statements. Where **more than one basis is used**, it should be stated to which assets or liabilities each basis has been applied.

8.4 Other disclosures

An entity must disclose in the notes:

(a) The amount of dividends proposed or declared before the financial statements were authorised for issue but not recognised as a distribution to owners during the period, and the amount per share

(b) The amount of any cumulative preference dividends not recognised

IAS 1 ends by listing some **specific disclosures** which will always be required if they are not shown elsewhere in the financial statements:

(a) The domicile and legal form of the entity, its country of incorporation and the address of the registered office (or, if different, principal place of business)

(b) A description of the nature of the entity's operations and its principal activities

(c) The name of the parent entity and the ultimate parent entity of the group

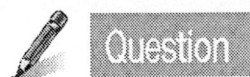

Financial statements

The accountant of Wislon Co has prepared the following list of account balances as at 31 December 20X7.

	$'000
50c ordinary shares (fully paid)	450
10% debentures (secured)	200
Retained earnings 1.1.X7	242
General reserve 1.1.X7	171
Land and buildings 1.1.X7 (cost)	430
Plant and machinery 1.1.X7 (cost)	830
Accumulated depreciation	
Buildings 1.1.X7	20
Plant and machinery 1.1.X7	222
Inventory 1.1.X7	190
Sales	2,695
Purchases	2,152
Ordinary dividend	15
Debenture interest	10
Wages and salaries	254
Light and heat	31
Sundry expenses	113
Suspense account	135
Trade receivables	179
Trade payables	195
Cash	126

Notes:

(a) Sundry expenses include $9,000 paid in respect of insurance for the year ending 1 September 20X8. Light and heat does not include an invoice of $3,000 for electricity for the three months ending 2 January 20X8, which was paid in February 20X8. Light and heat also includes $20,000 relating to salesmen's commission.

(b) The suspense account is in respect of the following items.

	$'000
Proceeds from the issue of 100,000 ordinary shares	120
Proceeds from the sale of plant	300
	420
Less consideration for the acquisition of Mary & Co	285
	135

(c) The net assets of Mary & Co were purchased on 3 March 20X7. Assets were valued as follows:

	$'000
Financial assets	231
Inventory	34
	265

All the inventory acquired was sold during 20X7. The financial assets are held at fair value and this remains unchanged at 31.12.X7. Goodwill has not been impaired in value.

(d) The property was acquired some years ago. The buildings element of the cost was estimated at $100,000 and the estimated useful life of the assets was 50 years at the time of purchase. As at 31 December 20X7 the property is to be revalued at $800,000.

(e) The plant was sold on 1.1.X7. It had cost $350,000 and had a carrying amount of $274,000 at the date of disposal. $36,000 depreciation is to be charged on plant and machinery for 20X7.

PART A CONTEMPORARY ISSUES

(f) The management wish to provide for:
   (i) Debenture interest due
   (ii) A transfer to general reserve of $16,000
   (iii) Audit fees of $4,000

(g) Inventory as at 31 December 20X7 was valued at $220,000 (cost).

(h) Taxation is to be ignored.

Required

Prepare the financial statements of Wislon Co as at 31 December 20X7. You do not need to produce notes to the statements.

Answer

(a) Normal adjustments are needed for accruals and prepayments (insurance, light and heat, debenture interest and audit fees). The debenture interest accrued is calculated as follows.

	$'000
Charge needed in profit or loss (10% × $200,000)	20
Amount paid so far, as shown in list of account balances	10
Accrual: presumably six months' interest now payable	10

The accrued expenses shown in the statement of financial position comprise:

	$'000
Debenture interest	10
Light and heat	3
Audit fee	4
	17

(b) The misposting of $20,000 to light and heat is also adjusted, by reducing the light and heat expense, but charging $20,000 to salesmen's commission.

(c) Depreciation on the building is calculated as $\frac{\$100,000}{50} = \$2,000$.

The carrying amount of the property is then $430,000 – $20,000 – $2,000 = $408,000 at the end of the year. When the property is revalued a revaluation surplus of $800,000 – $408,000 = $392,000 should be recognised.

(d) The profit on disposal of plant is calculated as proceeds $300,000 (per suspense account) less carrying amount $274,000, ie $26,000. The cost of the remaining plant is calculated at $830,000 – $350,000 = $480,000. The depreciation provision at the year end is:

	$'000
Balance 1.1.X7	222
Charge for 20X7	36
Less depreciation on disposals (350 – 274)	(76)
	182

(e) Goodwill arising on the purchase of Mary & Co is:

	$'000
Consideration (per suspense account)	285
Assets at valuation	265
Goodwill	20

This is shown as an asset in the statement of financial position. The financial assets, being owned by Wislon at the year end, are also shown on the statement of financial position, whereas Mary's inventory, acquired and then sold, is added to the purchases figure for the year.

(f) The other item in the suspense account is dealt with as follows:

	$'000
Proceeds of issue of 100,000 ordinary shares	120
Less nominal value 100,000 × 50c	50
Excess of consideration over par value (= share premium)	70

(g) The transfer to general reserve increases it to $171,000 + $16,000 = $187,000.

We can now prepare the financial statements.

WISLON CO
STATEMENT OF PROFIT OR LOSS AND OTHER COMPREHENSIVE INCOME FOR THE YEAR ENDED 31 DECEMBER 20X7

	$'000
Revenue	2,695
Cost of sales (W1)	(2,156)
Gross profit	539
Other income (profit on disposal of plant)	26
Administrative expenses (W2)	(437)
Finance costs	(20)
Profit for the year	108
Items which will not be reclassified to profit or loss	
Gain on property revaluation	392
Total comprehensive income for the year	500

Note.
The only item of 'other comprehensive income' for the year was the revaluation gain. If there had been no revaluation gain, only an income statement or statement of profit or loss would have been required.

Workings

1 *Cost of sales*

	$'000
Opening inventory	190
Purchases (2,152 + 34 re Mary)	2,186
Closing inventory	(220)
	2,156

2 *Administrative expenses*

	$'000
Wages, salaries and commission (254 + 20)	274
Sundry expenses (113 − (9 × 9/12))	107
Light and heat (31 − 20 + 3)	14
Depreciation: buildings	2
Plant	36
Audit fees	4
	437

WISLON CO
STATEMENT OF FINANCIAL POSITION AS AT 31 DECEMBER 20X7

	$'000	$'000
Assets		
Non-current assets		
Property, plant and equipment		
Property at valuation		800
Plant: Cost	480	
Accumulated depreciation	(182)	
		298
Goodwill		20
Financial assets		231

	$'000	$'000
Current assets		1,349
Inventory	220	
Trade receivables	179	
Prepayments	6	
Cash	126	
		531
Total assets		1,880
Equity and liabilities		
Equity		
50c ordinary shares	500	
Share premium	70	
Revaluation surplus	392	
General reserve	187	
Retained earnings	319	
		1,468
Non-current liabilities		
10% loan stock (secured)		200
Current liabilities		
Trade payables	195	
Accrued expenses	17	
		212
Total equity and liabilities		1,880

WISLON CO
STATEMENT OF CHANGES IN EQUITY
FOR THE YEAR ENDED 31 DECEMBER 20X7

	Share capital $'000	Share premium $'000	Retained earnings $'000	General reserve $'000	Revaluation surplus $'000	Total $'000
Balance at 1.1.X7	450	–	242	171	–	863
Issue of share capital	50	70				120
Dividends			(15)			(15)
Total comprehensive income for the year			108		392	500
Transfer to reserve			(16)	16		–
Balance at 31.12.X7	500	70	319	187	392	1,468

Note that the total comprehensive income is analysed into its components.

Chapter roundup

- **Limited liability** offers various advantages to companies, although there are disadvantages as well.
- IAS 1 covers the **form and content of** financial statements, which comprise:
    - Statement of financial position
    - Statement of profit or loss and other comprehensive income
    - Statement of changes in equity
    - Statement of cash flows
    - Notes to the financial statements, comprising significant accounting policies and other explanatory information
    - Comparative information in respect of the preceding period
- IAS 1 suggests a **format** for the statement of financial position. Certain items are specified for **disclosure in the financial statements**.
- You should appreciate the distinction between **current and non-current** assets and liabilities and their different treatments.
- IAS 1 (revised) requires all items of income and expense in a period to be shown in a **statement of profit or loss and other comprehensive income**.
- IAS 1 offers **two** possible formats for the statement of profit or loss section or separate statement of profit or loss – by function or by nature. Classification by function is more common.
- IAS 1 requires a statement of changes in equity. This shows the movement in the equity section of the statement of financial position.
- Some items need to be disclosed by way of note.

Quick quiz

1. Limited liability means that the shareholders of a company are not legally accountable.

    True ☐   False ☐

2. Which of the following are examples of current assets?

    (a) Property, plant and equipment
    (b) Prepayments
    (c) Cash equivalents
    (d) Manufacturing licences
    (e) Retained earnings

3. Provisions must be disclosed in the statement of financial position.

    True ☐   False ☐

4. Which of the following must be disclosed in the statement of profit or loss?

    (a) Tax expense
    (b) Analysis of expenses
    (c) Profit or loss for the period.

PART A CONTEMPORARY ISSUES

5   *Fill in the blanks.*

The accounting policies section of the notes describes:

The .... used in preparing the financial statements and...................................... required for a proper understanding of the financial statements.

Answers to quick quiz

1   False. It means that if the company becomes insolvent, the maximum that an owner stands to lose is his share capital in the business.
2   (b) and (c) only
3   True
4   (a) only
5   Measurement basis (or bases)
    Specific accounting policies

End of chapter question

Polymer

The following list of account balances has been prepared by Polymer Co, plastics manufacturers, on 31 May 20X8, which is the end of the company's accounting period.

	$	$
Authorised and issued 300,000 ordinary shares of $1 each		300,000
100,000 8.4% cumulative redeemable preference shares of $1 each		100,000
Revaluation surplus		50,000
Share premium		100,000
General reserve		50,000
Retained earnings – 31 May 20X7		283,500
Patents and trademarks	215,500	
Freehold land at cost	250,000	
Leasehold property at cost	75,000	
Amortisation of leasehold property – 31 May 20X7		15,000
Factory plant and equipment at cost	150,000	
Accumulated depreciation – plant and equipment – 31 May 20X7		68,500
Furniture and fixtures at cost	50,000	
Accumulated depreciation – furniture and fixtures – 31 May 20X7		15,750
Motor vehicles at cost	75,000	
Accumulated depreciation – motor vehicles – 31 May 20X7		25,000
10% loan notes (20Y0 – 20Y5)		100,000
Trade receivables/ trade payables	177,630	97,500
Bank overdraft		51,250
Inventories – raw materials at cost – 31 May 20X7	108,400	
Purchases – raw materials	750,600	
Carriage inwards – raw materials	10,500	
Manufacturing wages	250,000	
Manufacturing overheads	125,000	
Cash	5,120	
Work in progress – 31 May 20X7	32,750	
Sales		1,526,750
Administrative expenses	158,100	
Selling and distribution expenses	116,800	
Legal and professional expenses	54,100	
Allowance for receivables – 31 May 20X8		5,750
Inventories – finished goods – 31 May 20X7	184,500	
	2,789,000	2,789,000

Additional information:

(1) Inventories at 31 May 20X8 were:

	$
Raw materials	112,600
Finished goods	275,350
Work in progress	37,800

(2) Depreciation for the year is to be charged as follows:
Plant and equipment 8% on cost – charged to production
Furniture and fixtures 10% on cost – charged to admin
Motor vehicles   20% on reducing value   – 25% admin
                                              – 75% selling and distribution

PART A CONTEMPORARY ISSUES

(3) Financial, legal and professional expenses include:

	$
Solicitors' fees for purchase of freehold land during year	5,000

(4) An accrual should be recognised for a full year's interest on the loan notes.

(5) Income tax on the profits for the year is estimated at $40,000 and is due for payment on 28 February 20X9.

(6) The directors recommended on 30 June 20X8 that a dividend of 3.5c per share be paid on the ordinary share capital. No ordinary dividend was paid during the year ended 31 May 20X7.

(7) The leasehold land and buildings are held on a 50 year lease, acquired ten years ago.

Required

From the information given above, prepare the statement of profit or loss of Polymer Co for the year to 31 May 20X8 and a statement of financial position at that date for publication in accordance with International Financial Reporting Standards.

Notes to the financial statements are not required. **(25 marks)**

Environmental and social reporting

Topic list	Syllabus reference
1 Environmental reporting	13.1
2 Sustainability	13.1
3 Social responsibility	13.1
4 Human resource accounting	13.1

Introduction

Environmental issues are very topical. Just because these topics are discursive does not mean that you can 'waffle'. Environmental reporting also comes under current developments as this is an area that is changing.

PART A CONTEMPORARY ISSUES

1 Environmental reporting

FAST FORWARD

Although not compulsory, **environmental reports** are becoming increasingly important. You should distinguish between:

- Items that affect the financial statements (eg IAS 37)
- Items that affect the environmental report

Exam focus point

This topic could be tested as a current issue, or as an aspect of the limitations of conventional financial statements, or alternatively in the context of provisions, covered in Chapter 19.

At the end of the 1980s there were perhaps only two or three companies in the world issuing environmental reports. Now most listed companies produce them. Worldwide there are around 20 award schemes for environmental reporting. This section looks at environmental reporting mainly under three headings:

- The effect of environmental matters on management information and accounting
- External reporting and auditing
- Possible future developments

Let us consider the major areas of impact on (any) accountant's job caused by consideration of environmental matters.

(a) **Management accountant**

  (i) Investment appraisal: evaluation of environmental costs and benefits.
  (ii) Incorporating new costs, capital expenditure and so on, into budgets and business plans.
  (iii) Undertaking cost/benefit analysis of any environmental improvements.

(b) **Financial accountant**

  (i) The effect of revenue costs: site clean up costs, waste disposal or waste treatment costs and so on, which will affect profit or loss.
  (ii) Gauging impacts on the statement of financial position, particularly liabilities, contingencies, provisions **and** valuation of assets.
  (iii) The effect of environmental matters, and particularly potential liabilities, on a company's relationship with bankers, insurers and major shareholders (institutional shareholders).
  (iv) Environmental performance evaluation in annual reports.

(c) **Project accountant**

  (i) Environmental audit of proposed takeovers, mergers and other planning matters.
  (ii) Investment appraisal.

(d) **Internal auditor**: environmental audit.

(e) **Systems accountant**: effect on, and required changes to, management and financial information systems.

1.1 What is environmental accounting?

The following list encompasses the major aspects of environmental accounting.

(a) 'Recognising and seeking to mitigate the negative environmental effects of conventional accounting practice.
(b) Separately **identifying environmentally related costs and revenues** within the conventional accounting systems.
(c) Devising new forms of financial and non-financial accounting systems, information systems and control systems to **encourage more environmentally benign management decisions**.

(d) Developing new forms of **performance measurement**, reporting and appraisal for both internal and external purposes.

(e) Identifying, examining and seeking to **rectify** areas in which conventional (financial) criteria and environmental criteria are in **conflict**.

(f) Experimenting with ways in which, **sustainability** may be assessed and incorporated into organisational orthodoxy.'

Accounting for the Environment by Rob Gray (with Jan Bebbington and Diane Walters)

The whole environmental agenda is **constantly changing** and businesses therefore need to monitor the situation closely. Most businesses, certainly those in the UK, have generally ignored environmental matters in the past. How long will they be able to do so?

1.2 Management information and accounting

The means of codifying a company's attitude towards the environment is often the creation of a published **environmental policy document** or charter. This may be internally generated or it may be adopted from a standard environmental charter, such as the **CERES Principles**.

The CERES Principles

We adopt, support and will implement the principles of:

1. Protection of the biosphere
2. Sustainable use of natural resources
3. Reduction and disposal of waste
4. Wise use of energy
5. Risk reduction
6. Marketing of safe products and services
7. Damage compensation
8. Disclosure
9. Environmental directors and managers
10. Assessment and annual audit

The problem here, as with other similar principles or charters, is that the commitment required from companies is generally too high and the fear exists that the principles may have legal status which could have a severe effect on a company's liability. Other documents available are:

- The International Chamber of Commerce Business Charter for Sustainable Developments
- The Chemical Industries Association Responsible Care Programme
- Local Government guides on to how to write an environmental policy
- International Federation of Accountants *International Guidance Document: Environmental Management Accounting*

Adopting such a charter is one thing; implementing and monitoring it are more important and generally more difficult to achieve.

1.3 Environmental audit

Environmental auditing is exactly what is says: auditing a business to assess its impact on the environment, or as the CBI expressed it 'the systematic examination of the interactions between any business operation and its surroundings'.

The audit will cover a range of areas and will involve the performance of different types of testing. The scope of the audit must be determined and this will depend on each individual organisation. There are, however, some aspects of the approach to environmental auditing which are worth mentioning.

(a) **Environmental Impact Assessments (EIAs)** are required, under EU directive, for all major projects which require planning permission and have a material effect on the environment. The EIA process can be incorporated into any environmental auditing strategy.

(b) **Environmental surveys** are a good way of starting the audit process, by looking at the organisation as a whole in environmental terms. This helps to identify areas for further development, problems, potential hazards and so forth.

(c) **Environmental SWOT analysis.** A 'strengths, weaknesses, opportunities, threats' analysis is useful as the environmental audit strategy is being developed. This can only be done later in the process, when the organisation has been examined in much more detail.

(d) **Environmental Quality Management (EQM).** This is seen as part of TQM (Total Quality Management) and it should be built in to an environmental management system. Such a strategy has been adopted by companies such as IBM, Dow Chemicals and by the Rhone-Poulenc Environmental Index which has indices for levels of water, air and other waste products.

(e) **Eco-audit.** The European Commission has adopted a proposal for a regulation for a voluntary community environmental auditing scheme, known as the eco-audit scheme. The scheme aims to promote improvements in company environmental performance and to provide the public with information about these improvements. Once registered, a company will have to comply with certain on-going obligations involving disclosure and audit.

(f) **Eco-labelling.** Developed in Germany, this voluntary scheme will indicate those EC products which meet the highest environmental standards, probably as the result of an EQM system. It is suggested that eco-audit **must** come before an eco-label can be given.

(g) **BS 7750 Environmental Management Systems.** BS 7750 also ties in with eco-audits and eco-labelling and with the quality BSI standard BS 5750. Achieving BS 7750 is likely to be a first step in the eco-audit process.

(h) **Supplier audits**, to ensure that goods and services bought in by an organisation meet the standards applied by that organisation.

Case Study

In June 1999 BP Amoco commissioned KPMG to conduct an independent audit of its greenhouse gas emissions in the first ever environmental audit.

1.4 Financial reporting

There are **no disclosure requirements relating to environmental matters under IFRS**, so any disclosures tend to be **voluntary** unless environmental matters happen to fall under standard accounting principles (eg recognising liabilities).

(a) In most cases disclosure is descriptive and unquantified.

(b) There is little motivation to produce environmental information and many reasons for not doing so, including secrecy.

(c) The main factor seems to be apathy on the part of businesses but more particularly on the part of shareholders and investors. The information is not demanded, so it is not provided.

Environmental matters may be reported in the financial statements of companies in the following areas.

- Contingent liabilities
- Exceptional charges
- Operating and financial review comments
- Profit and capital expenditure forecasts

The voluntary approach contrasts with the position in the United States, where the SEC/FASB accounting standards are obligatory.

While nothing is compulsory, there are a number of **published guidelines** and **codes of practice**, including:

- The Confederation of British Industry's guideline *Introducing Environmental Reporting*
- The Association of Chartered Certified Accountants' *Guide to Environment and Energy Reporting*
- The Coalition of Environmentally Responsible Economies (CERES) formats for environmental reports
- CERES' *The 21st Century Corporation: The Ceres Roadmap to Sustainability*
- CERES' Sustainability Reporting Guidance
- DEFRA Environmental Reporting Guidelines and Environmental KPIs
- The Eco Management and Audit Scheme Code of Practice

1.5 Example: environmental liabilities

You have met IAS 37 *Provisions, Contingent Liabilities and Contingent Assets* in your earlier studies. IAS 37 deals with the issue of whether environmental liabilities should be provided for.

Question — Contamination

During the year a number of situations have arisen in a company and the board is to meet soon to determine an appropriate treatment.

Site A
This site is occupied by a small refinery. The site and some adjacent land has been contaminated by chemical spillages. The cost of remedying the contamination is $20m, but under local laws there is no requirement to clean up the site.

Site B
Similar contamination has arisen but the local government, and a neighbouring land owner, require the contamination to be remedied soon. The cost of cleaning up the site is $15m, but an extra $5m could be spent to raise the standard of the operation in line with undertakings given to the local community ten years ago.

Site C
Considerable contamination needs to be remedied, but the managing director is arguing that no provision is required this year since the amount concerned cannot be estimated with accuracy.

Site D
Spillage of chemicals has reduced the value of the site from $25m, its carrying amount, to $10m, its current realisable value. By spending $5m on rectification, the site value will be increased to $20m. The spillage has seeped into a local river and fines of $3m are now payable.

Required

Determine the appropriate treatment in the financial statements for the above situations.

Answer

Site A
The mere existence of contamination does not establish an obligation on the part of the company and without an obligation there is no need for a provision.

Site B
An obligation does exist which the local government and a neighbour can prove in court. At least $15m must be provided, but there may be a constructive obligation, wider than a legal obligation, to spend an

extra $5m to raise the standard of rectification. Concern for its long term reputation may influence the company to honour its undertaking given to the local community.

Site C

Whilst the exact amount of the expenditure may not be known with certainty, it should be possible to arrive at a realistic and prudent estimate. It is not acceptable to omit a liability on the grounds that its amount is not known with certainty – this would be a distortion.

Site D

The fines of $3m are a current cost to be charged to the statement of profit or loss and other comprehensive income. The spillage has impaired the value of the site, which must be written down to its net realisable value in its current state (see Chapter 12) of $10m after rectification. The cost of the write-down ($15m) is charged to profit or loss. The site is now carried in the books at its recoverable amount.

Exam focus point

You will need to distinguish between:

(a) Transactions that affect the financial statements, for example provisions that need to be made under IAS 37; and

(b) Information to be disclosed elsewhere, for example in the operating and financial review (management commentary), or in a separate environmental report.

1.6 Example: environmental report

A good example of an environmental report is the Royal Dutch Shell plc report for 2014 (http://www.shell.com/global/aboutshell/media/reports-publications.html). This was published as part of a separate sustainability report consisting of 60 pages. Abridged extracts from the pages of the report covering the environment are reproduced below to give you a feel for it. Note that the report is based around 'key performance indicators'. These are monitored against targets. We emphasise that this is not the only possible approach to environmental reporting.

ENVIRONMENT

'We carefully consider the potential environmental impact of our activities and how local communities might be affected, both before projects begin and during operations.

Our environmental standards focus on key areas such as managing emissions, reducing our energy use, flaring less gas produced with oil, preventing spills and leaks, minimising our use of fresh water and conserving biodiversity. We work to manage and minimise environmental impact from our operations.

We use energy-efficiency technologies and processes to reduce our carbon dioxide (CO_2) emissions and are also working to advance carbon capture and storage (CCS) technologies which could reduce cumulative global CO_2 emissions by around 15% by 2050.

ENVIRONMENTAL PERFORMANCE

We improved our environmental performance in most areas. The main exception has been our flaring performance which also led to an increase in our overall greenhouse gas (GHG) emissions. We have a series of projects underway to reduce our flaring.

SPILLS

Shell has clear requirements and procedures to prevent operational spills. We have ongoing programmes in place to maintain and improve our facilities and pipelines. However, spills still occur for reasons such as operational failure, accidents or unusual corrosion.

In 2014, we achieved our lowest level of recorded operational spills. The volume of operational spills of oil and oil products amounted to 0.7 thousand tonnes, down from 0.9 thousand tonnes in 2013. The number of operational oil spills also decreased in 2014 to 153, down from 174 in 2013. We continue to investigate and learn from all spills to improve our performance. We continue to invest in improving the reliability and maintenance of our facilities to help reduce operational spills.

> **ENERGY EFFICIENCY**
>
> One of the ways we can manage our direct GHG emissions is to work on improving the energy efficiency of the facilities we operate. The main metric that we use to measure our energy efficiency is energy intensity (the amount of energy consumed for every unit of output).
>
> In 2014, the overall energy intensity for the production of oil and gas in our Upstream business (excluding oil sands and gas-to-liquids (GTL)) slightly improved compared with 2013, partially driven by increased production in Brazil, Iraq and Nigeria.
>
> **AIR EMISSIONS**
>
> We track air emissions released to the atmosphere from our upstream and downstream operations including routine and non-routine activities:
>
> **Greenhouse gas emissions**
>
> The direct GHG emissions from facilities we operate were 76 million tonnes on a carbon dioxide (CO_2) equivalent basis in 2014, which is higher than 73 million tonnes of CO2 equivalent reported in 2013.'

2 Sustainability

2.1 What is sustainability?

Pressure is mounting for companies to **widen** their **scope for corporate public accountability**. Many companies are responding by measuring and disclosing their social impacts.

Examples of social measures include: philanthropic donations, employee satisfaction levels and remuneration issues, community support, and stakeholder consultation information.

The next step beyond environmental and social reporting is sustainability reporting which includes the economic element of sustainability (such as wages, taxes and core financial statistics) and involves integrating environmental, social and economic performance data and measures.

2.2 The Global Reporting Initiative (GRI)

> **FAST FORWARD**
>
> The Global Reporting Initiative arose from the need to **address the failure of the current governance structures to respond to changes in the global economy.**

It is 'a long-term, multi-stakeholder, international undertaking whose mission is to develop and disseminate globally applicable Sustainability Reporting Guidelines for voluntary use by organisations reporting on the economic, environmental and social dimensions of their activities, products and services'.

2.3 GRI Guidelines

The GRI published revised Sustainability Reporting Guidelines ('G3.1') in March 2011.

The Guidelines state that a sustainability report should provide a balanced and reasonable representation of the sustainability performance of a reporting organisation – including both positive and negative contributions.

They provide the following reporting principles which determine the content of a sustainability report:

- Materiality, such that information contained within a report covers significant topics which would substantively influence the assessments and decisions of users
- Stakeholder inclusiveness, meaning that a reporting organisation should identify its stakeholders and explain in the report how it has responded to their reasonable expectations and interests
- Sustainability context, ie the report should present the organisation's performance in the wider context of sustainability
- Completeness, such that significant economic, environmental and social impacts are reflected and the reporting organisation's performance can be assessed based on coverage of topics presented

The Guidelines also provide principles which define the quality of information presented:
- Balance (of positive and negative elements of performance)
- Comparability (achieved by the consistent selection, compilation and reporting of topics)
- Accuracy
- Timeliness (the presentation of information in time for stakeholders to make informed decisions)
- Clarity (ie information should be presented in an understandable and accessible manner)
- Reliability (the information contained within a report should be supported by internal controls or documentation)

In addition, the Guidelines set out the framework of a sustainability report. It consists of five sections:

	GRI Report content	Detail of GRI requirements
1	Strategy and Analysis	Provides a high-level, strategic view of the organisation's relationship to sustainability in order to provide context for subsequent and more detailed reporting, including a statement from the CEO.
2	Organisational Profile	The organisation's structure including brands, location of operations, geographical markets served and size of operations.
3	Report Parameters	The reporting period, materiality, report boundaries (eg countries), data measurement techniques and a GRI Content Index.
4	Governance, Commitments and Engagement	Governance structure of the organisation, commitments to external initiatives and how the organisation engages the stakeholders in its business.
5	Management Approach and Performance Indicators	Organised by economic, environmental, and social categories. Each category includes a Disclosure on Management Approach and a corresponding set of Core and Additional Performance Indicators.

2.4 Indicators in the GRI framework

GRI structures key performance indicators according to a hierarchy of category, aspect and indicator. Indicators are grouped in terms of the three dimensions of the conventional definition of sustainability – economic, environmental, and social.

	CATEGORY	ASPECT
Economic	Economic	Economic performance Market presence Indirect economic impacts
Environmental	Environmental	Materials Energy Water Biodiversity Emissions, effluents, and waste Products and services Compliance Transport Overall

CATEGORY		ASPECT
Social	Labour Practices and Decent Work	Employment
		Labour/management relations
		Occupational health and safety
		Training and education
		Diversity and equal opportunity
		Equal remuneration for women and men
	Human Rights	Investment and procurement practices
		Non-discrimination
		Freedom of association and collective bargaining
		Child labour
		Forced and compulsory labour
		Security practices
		Indigenous rights
		Assessment
		Remediation
	Society	Local communities
		Corruption
		Public policy
		Anti-competitive behaviour
		Compliance
	Product Responsibility	Customer health and safety
		Product and service labelling
		Marketing communications
		Customer privacy
		Compliance

2.5 Influence of GRI

There is a trend to report on broader sustainability issues and to include **social and economic information** alongside environmental disclosures.

An increasing number of companies, including BT, Vauxhall Motors Ltd, British Airways and Shell are following the GRI guidelines in their reporting. GRI provides these companies with a service whereby it checks the extent to which its guidelines have been applied, and awards an application level of between A – C with A+ being the highest.

2.6 Example: Royal Dutch Shell

Royal Dutch Shell plc began producing sustainability reports in 1997 and released its 2014 report in 2015. This includes economic, social and environmental information (see Section 1.6 above) provided in narrative, graphic and tabular formats. GRI has confirmed an A+ application level of its Reporting Guidelines. The report describes how the company is meeting energy demand through technology and innovation applied in the right way: with respect for communities and the environment.

For the seventh successive year, an independent External Review Committee has reviewed and assessed the Report's balance, completeness and responsiveness. The Committee's assessment is included in the Report.

PART A CONTEMPORARY ISSUES

Extracts from the social section of the report

> **SOCIAL PERFORMANCE**
>
> Social performance involves working with communities to reduce the impact of our operations and share the benefits of our activities. We respectfully engage with relevant parties, evaluate impacts, plan mitigation strategies and find opportunities to support communities, such as helping to build local economies through the creation of jobs and business opportunities.
>
> Shell requires all major assets where we are the operator to have effective community feedback mechanisms (CFMs): more than 100 locations have working CFMs in place. From 2013 to 2014, the number of locations with effectively run CFMs increased by 25%. To further improve in 2015, we will be increasing the frequency of the reporting of CFM data within Shell as well as introducing new parameters. This will help us to better assess the quality and speed of our responses to complaints.
>
> We have management systems in place that set out our social performance requirements for activities such as engagement and impact assessment, and are aligned with international standards. In 2014, we made improvements in defining social risks by developing and using specific tools. Each year, we review the extent to which our operations, as well as our contractors and suppliers, have processes in place to prevent violations of human rights, such as the use of child or forced labour. In 2014, we trained 481 (441 in 2013) employees in our social performance requirements.
>
> **SOCIAL INVESTMENT**
>
> Across our operations we invest in projects that benefit communities. Our intention is to help the project become sustainable in the long term. In 2014, we successfully completed the first round of global reporting on the projects' impact. Social investment programme managers have been measuring the output and are beginning to capture longer-term social and business outcomes. Also in 2014, we spent around $160 million on voluntary social investments worldwide, compared with $159 million in 2013. These figures do not include investments that are part of contractual agreements or legal requirements with host governments, which is in excess of $100 million.
>
> We spent around $39 million on our three global strategic themes of enterprise development, road safety and energy access. Around $121 million was spent on our locally tailored programmes covering community development, disaster relief, education, health and biodiversity. We estimate that almost $70 million of our spend in 2014 was in countries that are part of the UNDP Human Development Index 2013 defined as having a gross domestic product of less than $15,000 a year per person. Significant support is also provided by voluntary work by Shell employees and donations of equipment.
>
> **LOCAL PROCUREMENT**
>
> Where it makes overall business sense, we buy goods and services from local suppliers and help support local businesses and skills development. In 2014, we spent more than $67.1 billion on goods and services worldwide. Around 61% of this was spent in Canada, the Netherlands, Nigeria, the UK and the USA. We estimate around $13.7 billion was spent in countries that have a gross domestic product of less than $15,000 a year per person, according to the UNDP Human Development Index 2013. In these countries, Shell companies spent more than 69% ($9.5 billion) with local companies.
>
> We check that our suppliers are complying with key sustainability criteria, including good working conditions. In 2014, we conducted 92 rigorous assessments of suppliers in Africa and the Middle East, 132 in the Americas, 394 in the Asia-Pacific region, and 456 in Europe to check compliance against our Supplier Principles. These principles include areas such as human rights, labour practices such as the prohibition of child and forced labour, and business integrity.

2.7 Integrated reporting

In addition to existing GRI guidance, the International Integrated Reporting Council (IIRC) (previously the International Integrated Reporting Committee) was formed in August 2010 and aims to create a globally accepted framework for accounting for sustainability, bringing together financial, environmental, social and governance information in an "integrated" format. The IIRC's stated objective was to develop an internationally accepted Integrated Reporting Framework by 2014.

3: ENVIRONMENTAL AND SOCIAL REPORTING

In December 2013, the IIRC published the *International Integrated Reporting Framework*. The Framework refers to an organisation's resources as 'capitals'. Capitals are used to assess value creation. Increases or decreases in these capitals indicate the level of value created or lost over a period. Capitals cover various types of resources found in a standard organisation. These may include financial capitals, such as the entity's financial reserves through to its intellectual capital which is concerned with intellectual property and staff knowledge.

2.7.1 Types of capital

The integrated reporting framework classifies the capitals as:

Capital	Comment
Financial capital	The pool of funds that is: • Available to an organisation for use in the production of goods or the provision of services • Obtained through financing, such as debt, equity or grants, or generated through operations or investments
Manufactured capital	Manufactured physical objects (as distinct from natural physical objects) that are available to an organisation for use in the production of goods or the provision of services, including: • Buildings • Equipment Infrastructure (such as roads, ports, bridges and waste and water treatment plants) Manufactured capital is often created by other organisations, but includes assets manufactured by the reporting organisation for sale or when they are retained for its own use.
Intellectual capital	Organisational knowledge-based intangibles, including: • Intellectual property, such as patents, copyrights, software, rights and Licences • Organisational capital' such as tacit knowledge, systems, procedures and protocols
Human capital	People's competencies, capabilities and experience, and their motivations to innovate, including their: • Alignment with and support for an organisations governance framework, risk management approach and ethical values • Ability to understand, develop and implement an organisation's strategy • Loyalties and motivations for improving processes, goods and services, including their ability to lead, manage and collaborate
Natural	Input to goods and services and what activities impact: • Water, land, minerals and forests • Biodiversity and eco-system health

Capital	Comment
Social and relationship capital	The institutions and the relationships within and between communities, groups of stakeholders and other networks, and the ability to share information to enhance individual and collective well-being. Social and relationship capital includes: • Shared norms and common values and behaviours • Key stakeholder relationships and the trust and willingness to engage that an organisation developed and strives to build and protect with external stakeholders • Intangibles associated with the brand and reputation that an organisation has developed • An organisations social licence to operate

Source: *The International Integrated Reporting Framework*, www.theiirc.org

2.7.2 Interaction of capitals

Capitals continually interact with one another, an increase in one will result in a decrease another. For example, a decision to purchase a new IT system would improve an entity's 'manufactured' capital while decreasing its financial capital in the form of its cash reserves.

At present adopting integrated reporting is voluntary, as a result organisations are free to report only on those 'capitals' felt to be most relevant in communicating performance.

2.7.3 Short term v long term

Integrated reporting forces management to balance the organisation's short term objectives against its longer term plans. Business decisions which are solely dedicated to the pursuit of increasing profit (financial capital) at the expense of building good relations with key stakeholders such as customers (social capital) is likely to hinder value creation in the longer term. It is thought that by producing a holistic view of organisational performance that this will lead to improved management decision making, ensuring that decisions are not taken in isolation.

2.7.4 Monetary values

Integrated reporting is not aimed at attaching a monetary value to every aspect of the organisations operations. It is fundamentally concerned with evaluating value creation through the communication of qualitative and quantitative performance measures. Key performance indicators are effective in communicating performance.

For example when providing detail on customer satisfaction this can be communicated as the number of customers retained compared to the previous year. Best practice in integrated reporting requires organisations to report on both positive and negative movements in 'capital' to avoid only providing half the story.

2.7.5 Materiality

When preparing an integrated report management should disclose matters which are likely to impact on an organisations ability to create value. The inclusion of both internal and external threats regarded as being materially important are evaluated and quantified. This provides users with an indication of how management intend to combat risks should they materialise.

2.7.6 Implications of introducing integrated reporting

Implications	Comment
IT costs	The introduction of integrated reporting will most likely require significant upgrades to be made to the organisation's IT and information system infrastructure. Such developments will be needed to capture KPI data. Due to the broad range of business activities reported on using integrated reporting (customer, supplier relations, finance and human resources) it is highly likely the costs of improving the infrastructure will be significant.
Time/ staff costs	The process of gathering and collating the data for inclusion in the report is likely to require a significant amount of staff time. This may serve to decrease staff morale if they are expected to undertake this work in addition to existing duties. This may require additional staff to be employed.
Consultancy costs	Organisations producing their first integrated report may seek external guidance from an organisation which provides specialist consultancy on integrated reporting. Consultancy fees are likely to be significant.
Disclosure	There is a danger that organisations may volunteer more information about their operational performance than intended. Disclosure of planned strategies and key performance measures are likely to be picked up by competitors.

3 Social responsibility

> **FAST FORWARD**
>
> The **stakeholder** view holds that there are many groups in society with an interest in the organisation's activities. Some firms have objectives for these issues. Some argue, however, that a business's only objective should be to make money: the state, representing the public interest, can levy taxes to spend on socially desirable projects or can regulate organisational activities.

Not only does the environment have a significant influence on the structure and behaviour of organisations, but also organisations have some influence on their environment.

Since organisations have an effect on their environment, it is arguable that they should act in a way which shows **social awareness and responsibility**.

> 'A society, awakened and vocal with respect to the urgency of social problems, is asking the managers of all kinds of organisations, particularly those at the top, what they are doing to discharge their social responsibilities and why they are not doing more.'
>
> *Koontz, O'Donnell and Weihrich*

Social responsibility is expected from all types of organisation.

(a) **Local government** is expected to provide services to the local community, and to preserve or improve the character of that community, but at an acceptable cost to the ratepayers.

(b) **Businesses** are expected to provide goods and services, which reflect the needs of users and society as a whole. These needs may not be in harmony – arguably, the development of the Concorde aeroplane and supersonic passenger travel did not contribute to the public interest, and caused considerable inconvenience to residents near airports who suffer from excessive aircraft noise. A business should also be expected to anticipate the future needs of society; examples of socially useful products might be energy-saving devices and alternative sources of power.

(c) **Pollution control** is a particularly important example of social responsibility by industrial organisations, and some progress has been made in the development of commercial processes for recycling waste material. British Coal attempts to restore the environment by planting on old slag heaps.

(d) **Universities and schools** are expected to produce students whose abilities and qualifications will prove beneficial to society. A currently popular view of education is that greater emphasis should be placed on vocational training for students.

(e) In some cases, **legislation** may be required to enforce social need, for example to regulate the materials used to make crash helmets for motor cyclists, or to regulate safety standards in motor cars and furniture. Ideally, however, organisations should avoid the need for legislation by taking **earlier self-regulating action**.

3.1 Social responsibility and businesses

Arguably, institutions like hospitals, schools and so forth exist because health care and education are seen to be desirable social objectives by government at large, if they can be afforded.

However, where does this leave businesses? How far is it reasonable, or even appropriate, for businesses to exercise 'social responsibility' by giving to charities, voluntarily imposing strict environmental objectives on themselves and so forth?

One school of thought would argue that **the management of a business has only one social responsibility, which is to maximise wealth for its shareholders**. There are two reasons to support this argument:

(a) If the business is owned by the shareholders the assets of the company are, ultimately, the shareholders' property. Management has no moral right to dispose of business assets (like cash) on non-business objectives, as this has the effect of reducing the return available to shareholders. The shareholders might, for example, disagree with management's choice of beneficiary. Anyhow, it is for the shareholders to determine how their money should be spent.

(b) A second justification for this view is that management's job is to maximise wealth, as this is the best way that society can benefit from a business's activities.

   (i) Maximising wealth has the effect of increasing the tax revenues available to the state to disburse on socially desirable objectives.

   (ii) Maximising wealth for the few is sometimes held to have a 'trickle down' effect on the disadvantaged members of society.

   (iii) Many company shares are owned by pension funds, whose ultimate beneficiaries may not be the wealthy anyway.

This argument rests on certain assumptions.

(a) The first assumption is, in effect, the opposite of the stakeholder view. In other words, it is held that the **rights** of legal ownership are paramount over all other **interests** in a business: while other stakeholders have an interest, they have few legal or moral rights over the wealth created.

(b) The second assumption is that a business's **only** relationship with the wider social environment is an economic one. After all, that is what businesses exist for, and any other activities are the role of the state.

(c) The defining purpose of business organisations is the maximisation of the wealth of their owners.

Henry Mintzberg (in *Power In and Around Organisations*) suggests that simply viewing organisations as vehicles for shareholder investment is inadequate.

(a) In practice, he says, organisations are rarely controlled effectively by shareholders. Most shareholders are passive investors.

(b) Large corporations can manipulate markets. Social responsibility, forced or voluntary, is a way of recognising this.

(c) Moreover, businesses do receive a lot of government support. The public pays for roads, infrastructure, education and health, all of which benefits businesses. Although businesses pay tax, the public ultimately pays, perhaps through higher prices.

(d) Strategic decisions by businesses always have wider social consequences. In other words, says Mintzberg, the firm produces two outputs: **goods and services** and the **social consequences of its activities** (eg pollution).

3.1.1 Externalities

If it is accepted that businesses do not bear the total social cost of their activities, then the exercise of social responsibility is a way of compensating for this.

An example is given by the environment. Industrial pollution is injurious to health: if someone is made ill by industrial pollution, then arguably the polluter should pay the sick person, as damages or in compensation, in the same way as if the business's builders had accidentally bulldozed somebody's house.

In practice, of course, while it is relatively easy to identify statistical relationships between pollution levels and certain illnesses, mapping out the chain of cause and effect from an individual's wheezing cough to the dust particles emitted by Factory X, as opposed to Factory Y, is quite a different matter.

Of course, it could be argued that these external costs are met out of general taxation: but this has the effect of spreading the cost amongst other individuals and businesses. Moreover, the tax revenue may be spent on curing the disease, rather than stopping it at its source. Pollution control equipment may be the fairest way of dealing with this problem. Thus advocates of social responsibility in business would argue that business's responsibilities then do not rest with paying taxes.

However, is there any justification for social responsibility outside remedying the effects of a business's direct activities? For example, should businesses give to charity or sponsor the arts? There are several reasons why they should:

(a) If the **stakeholder concept** of a business is held, then the public is a stakeholder in the business. A business only succeeds because it is part of a wider society. Giving to charity is one way of encouraging a relationship.

(b) Charitable donations and artistic sponsorship are a useful medium of **public relations** and can reflect well on the business. It can be regarded, then, as another form of promotion, which like advertising, serves to enhance consumer awareness of the business, while not encouraging the sale of a particular brand.

The arguments for and against social responsibility of business are complex ones. However, ultimately they can be traced to different assumptions about society and the relationships between the individuals and organisations within it.

Question — Ethics

The Heritage Carpet Company is a London-based retailer which imports carpets from Turkey, Iran and India. The company was founded by two Europeans who travelled independently through these countries in the 1970s. The company is the sole customer for carpets made in a number of villages in each of the source countries. The carpets are hand woven. Indeed, they are so finely woven that the process requires that children be used to do the weaving, thanks to their small fingers. The company believes that it is preserving a 'craft', and the directors believe that this is a justifiable social objective. Recently a UK television company has reported unfavourably on child exploitation in the carpet weaving industry. There were reports of children working 12 hour shifts in poorly lit sheds and cramped conditions, with consequent deterioration in eyesight, muscular disorders and a complete absence of education. The examples cited bear no relation to the Heritage Carpet Company's suppliers although children are used in the labour force, but there has been a spate of media attention. The regions in which the Heritage Carpet Company's supplier villages are found are soon expected to enjoy rapid economic growth.

What boundary management issues are raised for the Heritage Carpet Company?

Answer

Many. This is a case partly about boundary management and partly about enlightened self-interest and business ethics. The adverse publicity, although not about the Heritage Carpet Company's own suppliers, could rebound badly. Potential customers might be put off. Economic growth in the area may also mean that parents will prefer to send their children to school. The Heritage Carpet Company as well as promoting itself as preserving a craft could reinvest some of its profits in the villages (eg by funding a school), or by enforcing limits on the hours children worked. It could also pay a decent wage. It could advertise this in a 'code of ethics' so that customers are reassured that the children are not simply being exploited. Alternatively, it could not import child-made carpets at all. (This policy, however, would be unlikely to help communities in which child labour is an economic necessity. Children already living on the margins of subsistence might end up even more exploited, in begging or prostitution.)

4 Human resource accounting

Human resource accounting is an approach which regards **people as assets**.

4.1 Introduction

Human resource accounting has at its core the principle that **employees are assets.** Competitive advantage is largely gained by **effective use of people**.

4.2 Implications of regarding people as organisational assets

(a) **People are a resource** which needs to be carefully and efficiently managed with overriding concern for organisational objectives.

(b) The organisation needs to **protect its investment** by retaining, safeguarding and developing its human assets.

(c) **Deterioration in the attitudes and motivation** of employees, increases in labour turnover (followed by costs of hiring and training replacements) are **costs to the company** – even though a 'liquidation' of human assets, brought about by certain managerial styles, may produce short-term increases in profit.

(d) A concept developed some time ago was that of **human asset accounting** (the inclusion of human assets in the financial reporting system of the organisation).

Case Study

There are difficulties in isolating and measuring human resources, and it is also hard to forecast the time period (and area of business) over which benefits will be received from expenditure on human assets. *Texas Instruments* uses a system which identifies potential replacement costs for groups of people, taking into account the learning time required by the replacement, and the individual's salary during that period.

4.3 Intellectual assets

FAST FORWARD There are **problems in putting a value on people** which traditional accounting has yet to overcome.

Because of the difficulties found in both theory and practice, the concept of **human assets was broadened and became intellectual assets.** Intellectual assets, or 'intellectual capital' as they are sometimes called, can be divided into three main types.

(a) **External assets.** These include the reputation of brands and franchises and the strength of customer relationships.

(b) **Internal assets.** These include patents, trademarks and information held in customer databases.

(c) **Competencies.** These reflect the capabilities and skills of individuals.

'Intellectual assets' thus includes 'human assets'.

The value of intellectual assets will continue to rise and will represent an increasing proportion of the value of most companies. Whether or not traditional accounting will be able to measure them, remains to be seen.

PART A CONTEMPORARY ISSUES

Chapter roundup

- Although not compulsory, **environmental reports** are becoming increasingly important. You should distinguish between:
  - Items that affect the financial statements (eg IAS 37)
  - Items that affect the environmental report

- The Global Reporting Initiative arose from the need to **address the failure of the current governance structures to respond to changes in the global economy.**

- The **stakeholder** view holds that there are many groups in society with an interest in the organisation's activities. Some firms have objectives for these issues. Some argue, however, that a business's only objective should be to make money: the state, representing the public interest, can levy taxes to spend on socially desirable projects or can regulate organisational activities.

- **Human resource accounting** is an approach which regards **people as assets.**

- There are **problems in putting a value on people** which traditional accounting has yet to overcome.

Quick quiz

1. Give an example of an environmental audit.
2. Name four areas of company financial statements where environmental matters may be reported.
3. If a site is contaminated, a provision must always be made.

    True ☐
    False ☐

4. What objectives might a company have in relation to wider society?
5. To whom might management have responsibilities, and what are some of these responsibilities?
6. Why does Mintzberg say that the profit motive is not enough?
7. What is the basic principle of human resource accounting?
8. Give three examples of intellectual assets.

Answers to quick quiz

1. In 1999 KPMG conducted an audit of the greenhouse gas emissions of BP Amoco.

2. Contingent liabilities
   Exceptional charges
   Operating and financial review comments
   Profit and capital expenditure forecasts

3. False. There must also be an obligation to rectify the contamination.

4. Protection of the environment, support for good causes, a responsible attitude to product safety.

5. Managers of businesses are responsible to the owners for economic performance and to wider society for the externalities related to their business operations.

6. Large businesses are rarely controlled by their shareholders; they receive a lot of support from public funds; and their activities have wider consequences.

7. Employees are assets.

8.
   - External assets
   - Internal assets
   - Competencies

End of chapter question

Schrattenbach (AIA May 2006)

You are a trainee accountant working for Schrattenbach AG.

The managing director of Schrattenbach AG is proud of the fact that his company operates ethically. The company has adopted environmentally friendly operating procedures and contributes resources to local, national and international arts and charity organisations.

The managing director does not feel the conventional financial statements of the company adequately inform stakeholders about these activities and would like to know how best to quantify and present this information in the company's corporate report.

Required

Advise the managing director on how this information could be presented effectively in the corporate report. **(5 marks)**

PART A CONTEMPORARY ISSUES

Ethics and regulation of corporate financial reporting

Topic list	Syllabus reference
1 The case for regulation	13.1
2 Impact of changes in accounting standards and policies	13.1
3 Accounting theory and practice	13.1
4 Principles and guidance on professional ethics	13.1
5 Practical situations	13.1

Introduction

This chapter looks at two important issues which are related: regulation of financial reporting; and professional ethics.

The first part of the chapter focuses on changes in accounting standards and accounting policies and the implications for reporting entities.

The second part of the chapter introduces the IESBA Code which you will be required to observe when you become a member of the AIA. Ethics are an important aspect of the AIA qualification. They need to be applied in all aspects of managerial behaviour. An attempt to massage profit figures, or non-disclosure of a close relationship may amount to unethical behaviour.

PART A   CONTEMPORARY ISSUES

1 The case for regulation

1.1 Introduction

The regulatory framework is the most important element in ensuring relevant and reliable financial reporting and thus meeting the needs of shareholders and other users.

Without a single body overall responsible for producing financial reporting standards (the IASB) and a framework of general principles within which they can be produced (the *Conceptual Framework*), there would be no means of enforcing compliance with GAAP. Also, GAAP would be unable to evolve in any structured way in response to changes in economic conditions.

1.2 Principles-based versus rules-based systems

> **FAST FORWARD**
>
> A principles-based system works within a set of laid down principles. A rules-based system regulates for issues as they arise. Both of these have advantages and disadvantages.

The *Conceptual Framework* provides the background of principles within which standards can be developed. This system is intended to ensure that standards are not produced which are in conflict with each other and also that any departure from a standard can be judged on the basis of whether or not it is in keeping with the principles set out in the *Conceptual Framework*. This is a **principles-based** system.

In the absence of a reporting framework, a more **rules-based** approach has to be adopted. This leads to a large mass of regulation designed to cover every eventuality, as in the US. As we have seen over the past few years, a large volume of regulatory measures does not always detect or prevent financial irregularity. Rules can be evaded by means of 'creative accounting'. This is the deliberate manipulation of figures in the financial statements to give a biased impression of an entity's performance while still complying with accounting standards.

However, management may need to use judgement in applying principles. It can be argued that principles-based standards are also open to abuse.

In practice, current IAS and IFRS are a mixture of rules and principles. For example, most of the standards relating to non-current assets are based on the fundamental principles in the *Conceptual Framework*, although the definition of assets and the recognition criteria under the revised *Conceptual Framework* 2018 has resulted in some differences between the terminology and criteria used in the standards and that in the *Conceptual Framework*. In contrast, the standards on financial instruments have been influenced by US reporting practice and are extremely detailed, with many definitions and rules.

1.3 The 'free market' versus accounting regulation

> **FAST FORWARD**
>
> There are many convincing arguments in favour of regulation of corporate financial reporting.

Some economists advocate a 'free market' approach to accounting regulation. Supporters of the 'free market' approach argue that accounting information is like any other good. If there is a demand for that information it will be supplied. Regulation of the market (by means of accounting standards) leads to the supply of non-optimal information.

However, the absence of effective regulation has been blamed for many failures in accounting; such as the Wall Street Crash in 1929, the GEC/AEI debacle of the 1960s, the WorldCom and Enron catastrophes and more recently the downfall of Lehman Brothers.

There are many convincing arguments in favour of regulation:

(a)   Regulation leads to uniformity (or at least standardisation) which in turn provides for greater comparability between entities.

(b)   A 'free' market for information cannot be efficient and such inefficiencies lead to the provision of information which may therefore not be the best available.

(c) Without adequate regulation there is no way of knowing whether the information investors are using is in any way fraudulent. Investors and other users need to be able to have faith in the information.

(d) Regulation is needed to protect those who have less power (to demand information) than others.

2 Impact of changes in accounting standards and policies

FAST FORWARD

> Accounting policies may be adopted for the purpose of **manipulation**.
>
> **Changes in accounting standards** can have a significant impact on the financial statements.

We discussed the disclosure of accounting policies in your earlier studies. The choice of accounting policy and the effect of its implementation are almost as important as its disclosure in that the results of a company can be altered significantly by the choice of accounting policy.

2.1 The effect of choice of accounting policies

Where accounting standards allow alternative treatment of items in the financial statements, then the accounting policy note should declare which policy has been chosen. It should then be applied consistently.

Consider, though, the **effects produced by the different treatment of some items**.

An example is the treatment of investment properties, which may be measured under either the cost model or the fair value model. Under the cost model, investment properties are measured at historic cost less depreciation, in accordance with IAS 16 *Property, Plant and Equipment*. Under the fair value model, investment properties are measured at fair value with gains or losses arising from a change in fair value recognised in profit or loss. (We will be covering investment properties in Chapter 12.)

You should be able to think of other examples of how the choice of accounting policy can affect the financial statements.

2.2 Changes in accounting policy

The effect of a change of accounting policy is treated as a retrospective adjustment to the opening balance of each affected component of equity, as if the accounting policy had always applied.

IAS 8 *Accounting Policies, Changes in Accounting Estimates and Errors* states that changes in accounting policies are rare, and only allowed if **required by statute** or if the change results in **relevant and more reliable information.**

There is still some scope for directors to **manipulate the results** through change(s) of accounting policies. This would be done to avoid the effect of an old accounting policy or gain the effect of a new one. It is likely to be done in a sensitive period, perhaps when the company's profits are low or the company is about to announce a rights issue. The management would have to convince the auditors that the new policy was more appropriate, but it is not difficult to produce reasons in such cases.

The effect of such a change is **very short-term**. Most analysts and sophisticated users will discount its effect immediately, except to the extent that it will affect any dividend (because of the effect on distributable profits). It may help to avoid breaches of banking covenants because of the effect on certain ratios.

Obviously, the accounting policy for any item in the financial statements could only be changed once in quite a long period of time. No auditors would allow another change, even back to the old policy, unless there was a wholly exceptional reason.

The managers of a company can choose accounting policies **initially** to suit the company or the type of results they want to get. Any changes in accounting policy must be justified, but some managers might try to change accounting policies just to manipulate the results.

2.3 Changes in accounting standards

> **FAST FORWARD**
>
> You may be asked to **advise the directors** on the implication of a change in accounting standards, or on the effect of using the correct accounting treatment.

The effect of a change of accounting standard can be far reaching. For example when IFRS 11 *Joint Arrangements* was brought in, and IAS 28 revised to become *Investments in Associates and Joint Ventures*, the option to proportionately consolidate a joint venture was removed. This treatment required the investor's share of assets, liabilities, income and expenses to be consolidated on a line by line basis. Instead, equity accounting must be applied to all joint ventures. Under this, the investor's share of the joint venture's profits is included as one line in the consolidated statement of profit or loss and other comprehensive income and the investor's share of the joint venture's net assets is included as one line in the consolidated statement of financial position.

Exam focus point

The Paper 13 Examiner has said that this topic is likely to be examined by a written question, possibly including a small calculation.

Usually you will be in the position of advising the directors. You are very likely to be asked to explain the significance of a proposed change in accounting standards. The Examiner has also said that you may be asked to consider ethics. If the directors, in adopting certain accounting treatments, are acting unethically, you may need to discuss this.

3 Accounting theory and practice

3.1 The nature of profit

During your earlier studies you have seen that accounting 'profit' is an arbitrary figure, subject to the whims and biases of accountants and the variety of treatments in accounting standards. We will be covering individual IFRS in detail in later chapters, but you can probably remember the examples that we give below.

3.1.1 IAS 2 *Inventories*

Companies are allowed to use different methods of valuing inventory under IAS 2, which means that the final inventory figure in the statement of financial position will be different under each method. Profit will be affected by the closing inventory valuation, particularly where the level of inventory fluctuates to a great extent.

3.1.2 IAS 16 *Property, plant and equipment*

As with IAS 2, IAS 16 allows different accounting bases for depreciation. Choosing to use the reducing balance method rather than the straight-line method can front-load the depreciation charge for assets. It is also the case that the subjectivity surrounding the estimated economic lives of assets can lead to manipulation of profits.

3.2 Other problems with financial statement information

You will have already studied ratio analysis and possibly other techniques used in analysing financial statements. So you will already know that while these techniques are useful, they have some serious limitations.

Two frequent problems affecting financial analysis (the interpretation of financial statements) are discussed here.

- Seasonal fluctuations
- Window dressing

3.2.1 Seasonal fluctuations

Many companies are located in industries where trade is seasonal. For example:

- Swimwear manufacturers
- Ice cream makers
- Umbrella manufacturers
- Gas companies
- Travel agents
- Flower suppliers and deliverers
- Football clubs

Year on year the seasonal fluctuations affecting such companies does not matter; a year end has to be chosen and as long as the fluctuations are at roughly the same time every year, then there should be no problem. Occasionally a perverse sense of humour will cause a company to choose an accounting period ending in the middle of the busy season: this may affect the cut off because the busy season might be slightly early or late.

A major difficulty can arise if companies affected by seasonal fluctuations change their accounting date. A shorter period (normally) may encompass part, all or none of the busy season. Whatever happens, the figures will be distorted and the comparatives will be meaningless. Analysts would not know how to extrapolate the figures from the shorter period to produce a comparison for the previous year. Weightings could be used, but these are likely to be inaccurate.

Case Study

An example of the problems this can cause occurred when the UK company British Gas plc changed its accounting period to 31 December from 31 March. The company published two reports and financial statements.

- For the year to 31 March 1991
- For the year to 31 December 1991

Thus including the first three months of the calendar year in both reports. As a note to the later financial statements, the company produced a profit and loss account for the last nine months of the calendar year.

Although the British Gas auditors did not qualify the audit report, the Review Panel was not very happy about this double counting of results. The nine month profit and loss account did not meet the provisions of the Companies Act 1985, which then applied, 'either as to its location or its contents, nor did it contain the relevant earnings per share figure'. British Gas had to promise that, in their 1992 results, the 1991 comparative would be for the nine months period only.

The effect here is obvious. The first three months of the calendar year are when British Gas earns a high proportion of its profits (winter!). If the 1991 results had covered the period from 1 April only, then the profits would have been reduced by more than an average loss of three months' profit. By using a 12 month period, British Gas avoided the risk of the period's results looking too bad.

3.2.2 Window dressing

Window dressing transactions were made largely redundant by IAS 10 *Events After the Reporting Period*. Note that window dressing transactions were not outlawed, but full disclosure would render such transactions useless.

One example of window dressing is a situation where a large cheque is written against one group company's positive bank balance in favour of another group company with a large overdraft. The cheque is put through at the year end and then cancelled at the beginning of the next year, thus concealing the overdraft in the consolidated statement of financial position (where positive and negative bank balances cannot be netted off).

You may be able to think of other examples of window dressing and you should look for any potential examples which come up in examination questions.

3.2.3 Summary of limitations of financial analysis

(a) Information problems:

    (i) The base information is often out of date, so timeliness of information leads to problems of interpretation.

    (ii) Historical cost information may not be the most appropriate information for the decision for which the analysis is being undertaken.

    (iii) Information in published financial statements is generally summarised information and detailed information may be needed.

    (iv) Analysis of accounting information only identifies symptoms not causes and thus is of limited use.

(b) Comparison problems: inter-temporal

    (i) Effects of price changes make comparisons difficult unless adjustments are made.

    (ii) Impacts of changes in technology on the price of assets, the likely return and the future markets.

    (iii) Impacts of a changing environment on the results reflected in the accounting information.

    (iv) Potential effects of changes in accounting policies on the reported results.

    (v) Problems associated with establishing a normal base year to compare other years with.

(c) Comparison problems: inter-firm

    (i) Selection of industry norms and the usefulness of norms based on averages.

    (ii) Different firms having different financial and business risk profiles and the impact on analysis.

    (iii) Different firms using different accounting policies.

    (iv) Impacts of the size of the business and its comparators on risk, structure and returns.

    (v) Impacts of different environments on results, for example different countries or home-based versus multinational firms.

We will be looking at interpretation of financial statements again in a later chapter.

4 Principles and guidance on professional ethics

> The AIA has adopted the *Code of Ethics for Professional Accountants issued by IESBA (the IESBA Code).*

4.1 The public interest

> Organisations sometimes issue **codes of conduct** to employees. Many employees are bound by professional codes of conduct.

The International Federation of Accountants (IFAC) sets international standards of ethics through the International Ethics Standards Board for Accountants (IESBA). Its *Code of Ethics for Professional Accountants (the IESBA Code)* gives the key reason why accountancy bodies produce ethical guidance: the public interest.

> 'A distinguishing mark of the accountancy profession is its acceptance of the responsibility to act in the public interest. Therefore, a professional accountant's responsibility is not exclusively to satisfy the needs of an individual client or employer.
>
> **The public interest** is considered to be the collective well-being of the community of people and institutions the professional accountant serves, including clients, lenders, governments, employers, employees, investors, the business and financial community and others who rely on the work of professional accountants.'

The **key reason** that **accountants need** to have an **ethical code** is that **people rely on them and their expertise**.

Accountants deal with a range of issues on behalf of clients. They often have access to confidential and sensitive information. Auditors claim to give an independent view. It is therefore critical that accountants, and particularly auditors, are, and are seen to be, independent.

The AIA has adopted the IESBA Code. All AIA members are bound by the AIA's Constitution to observe this Code.

The Code consists of fundamental principles, specific guidance and explanatory notes. It can be downloaded from the AIA website: www.aiaworldwide.com/Ethics.

4.2 The fundamental principles

IESBA
• **Integrity**. A professional accountant should be **straightforward** and **honest** in all professional and business relationships.
• **Objectivity**. A professional accountant **should not allow bias, conflict of interest or undue influence of others** to override professional or business judgements.
• **Professional Competence and Due Care**. A professional accountant has a continuing duty to maintain professional knowledge and skill at a level required to ensure that a client or employer receives the advantage of competent professional service based on current developments in practice, legislation and techniques. A professional accountant should act diligently and in accordance with applicable technical and professional standards when providing professional services.
• **Confidentiality**. A professional accountant should respect the confidentiality of information acquired as a result of professional or business relationships **and should not disclose** any such information to third parties without proper and specific authority **unless there is a legal or professional right or duty to disclose**. Confidential information acquired as a result of professional and business relationships should not be used for the personal advantage of the professional accountant or third parties.
• **Professional Behaviour**. A professional accountant should **comply with relevant laws and regulations and should avoid any action that discredits the profession.**

4.3 Ethical framework

The ethical guidance discussed above is in the form of a **framework, rather than a set of rules**. There are a number of advantages of a framework over a system of ethical rules. These are outlined in the table below.

Advantages of an ethical framework over a rules based system
A framework of guidance places the onus on the accountant to **actively consider** independence for every given situation, rather than just agreeing a checklist of forbidden items. It also requires him or her to **demonstrate** that a responsible conclusion has been reached about ethical issues.

PART A CONTEMPORARY ISSUES

Advantages of an ethical framework over a rules based system
The framework **prevents accountants interpreting legalistic requirements narrowly** to get around the ethical requirements. There is an extent to which rules engender deception, whereas principles encourage compliance.
A framework **allows for** the variations that are found in every **individual situation**. Each situation is likely to be different.
A framework can accommodate a **rapidly changing environment**, such as the one that auditors are constantly in.
A **framework can contain prohibitions** where these are necessary because safeguards are not feasible.

5 Practical situations

FAST FORWARD

Exam questions may ask you to think about what should be done if breaches of laws, regulations or ethical guidelines occur. **Close relationships** between the parties or other **conflicts of interest** are often a complication.

Exam focus point

Ethics is most likely to be tested as part of a larger question. The AIA has said that it could be included in any of the five questions but will typically be included as part of the compulsory question 1.

5.1 The problem

Examination questions will expect you to be able to apply your understanding of ethical issues to practical problems arising in organisations. The exam may present you with a scenario, typically containing an array of detail much of which is potentially relevant. The problem, however, will be one or other of two basic types.

(a) A wishes B to do C which is in breach of D

where

    A = a situation, person, group of people, institution or the like

    B = you/a management accountant, the person with the ethical dilemma

    C = acting, or refraining from acting, in a certain way

    D = an ethical principle, quite possibly one of the IESBA Code fundamental principles

(b) Alternatively, the problem may be that A has done C, B has become aware of it and D requires some kind of response from B.

5.2 Example: The problem

An accountant joined a manufacturing company as its Finance Director. The company had acquired land on which it built industrial units. Before he had started at the company, the Finance Director discovered that one of the units had been sold and the selling price was significantly larger than the amount which appeared in the company's records. The difference had been siphoned off to another company – one in which his boss, the Managing Director, was a major shareholder. Furthermore, the Managing Director had kept his relationship with the second company a secret from the rest of the board.

The Finance Director confronted the Managing Director and asked him to reveal his position to the board. However, the Managing Director refused to disclose his position to anyone else. The secret profits on the sale of the unit had been used, he said, to reward the people who had secured the sale. Without their help, he added, the manufacturing company would be in a worse position financially.

The Finance Director then told the Managing Director that unless he reported to the board he would have to inform the board members himself. The Managing Director still refused. The Finance Director disclosed the full position to the board.

The problem is of the **second basic type. B** is of course the easiest party to identify. Here it is the **Finance Director. A** is clear, as well: it is the **Managing Director. C** is the **MD's breach of his directorial duties** regarding related party transactions not to obtain any personal advantage from his position of director without the consent of the company for whatever gain or profit he has obtained. **D** is the **principle that requires B not to be a party to an illegal act.** (Note that we distinguish between ethical and legal obligations. B has legal obligations as a director of the company. He has ethical obligations not to ignore his legal obligations. In **this** case the two amount to the same thing.)

5.3 Relationships

You may have a feeling that the resolution of the problem described above is just too easy, and you would be right. This is because A, B, C and D are either people, or else situations involving people, who stand in certain relationships to each other.

- A may be B's boss, B's subordinate, B's equal in the organisational hierarchy, B's husband, B's friend.

- B may be new to the organisation, or well-established and waiting for promotion, or ignorant of some knowledge relevant to the situation that A possesses or that the people affected by C possess.

- C or D, as already indicated, may involve some person(s) with whom B or A have a relationship – for example the action may be to misrepresent something to a senior manager who controls the fate of B or A (or both) in the organisation.

Question — Relationships

Identify the relationships in the scenario above. What are the possible problems arising from these relationships?

Answer

The MD is the Finance Director's boss. He is also a member of the board and is longer established as such than B the Finance Director.

In outline the problems arising are that **by acting ethically the Finance Director will alienate the MD**. Even if the problem were to be resolved the episode would sour all future dealings between these two parties. Also, **the board may not be sympathetic to the accusations of a newcomer**. The Finance Director may find that he is ignored or even dismissed.

Relationships should never be permitted to affect ethical judgement. If you knew that your best friend at work had committed a major fraud, for example, **integrity** would demand that **in the last resort** you would have to bring it to the attention of somebody in authority. But note that this is only in the last resort. Try to imagine what you would do in practice in this situation.

Surely your **first course** would be to try to **persuade your friend** that what he or she had done was wrong, and that he or she had an ethical responsibility to own up. Your **second option**, if this failed, might be to try to get **somebody** (perhaps somebody outside the organisation) that you knew could **exert pressure** on your friend to persuade him or her to own up.

There is obviously a limit to how far you can take this. The important point is that just because you are dealing with a situation that involves ethical issues, this **does not mean that all the normal principles of good human relations and good management have to be suspended**. In fact this is the time when such business principles are most important.

5.4 Consequences

Actions have consequences and the consequences themselves are quite likely to have their own ethical implications.

In the example given above, we can identify the following further issues:

(a) The MD's secret transaction appears to have been made in order to secure the sale of an asset the proceeds of which are helping to prop up the company financially. Disclosure of the truth behind the sale may mean that the company is pursued for compensation by the buyer of the site. The **survival of the company** as a whole may be jeopardised.

(b) If the truth behind the transaction becomes public knowledge this could be highly damaging for the company's **reputation**, even if it can show that only one black sheep was involved.

(c) The board may simply rubber stamp the MD's actions and so the Finance Director may still find that he is expected to be party to dishonesty. (This assumes that the **company as a whole is amoral** in its approach to ethical issues. In fact the MD's refusal to disclose the matter to the board suggests otherwise.)

In the last case we are back to square one. In the first two cases, the Finance Director has to consider the ethicality or otherwise of taking action that could lead to the collapse of the company, extensive redundancies, unpaid creditors and shareholders and so on.

5.5 Actions

In spite of the difficulties, your aim will usually be to reach a satisfactory resolution to the problem. **The actions that you recommend** will often include the following.

- **Informal discussions** with the parties involved.
- **Further investigation** to establish the full facts of the matter. What extra information is needed?
- The **tightening up of controls or the introduction of new ones**, if the situation arose due to laxity in this area. This will often be the case and the principles of professional competence and due care and of technical standards will usually be relevant.
- **Attention to organisational matters** such as changes in the management structure, improving communication channels, attempting to change attitudes.

Question — Cunning plan

Your finance director has asked you to join a team planning a takeover of one of your company's suppliers. An old school friend works as an accountant for the company concerned, the finance director knows this, and has asked you to try and find out 'anything that might help the takeover succeed, but it must remain secret'.

Answer

There are three issues here. Firstly you have a **conflict of interest** as the finance director wants you to keep the takeover a secret, but you probably feel that you should tell your friend what is happening as it may affect their job.

Second, the finance director is asking you to deceive your friend. Deception is unprofessional behaviour and will break your ethical guidelines. Therefore the situation is presenting you with **two conflicting demands**. It is worth remembering that no employer should ask you to break your ethical rules.

Finally, the request to break your own ethical guidelines constitutes **unprofessional behaviour** by the finance director. You should consider reporting him to their relevant body.

Question — Manipulation

Carrow's directors are concerned about the results for the year in the statement of profit or loss and other comprehensive income and the subsequent effect on the statement of cash flows. During the year the company has sold several items of property, plant and equipment and the directors have suggested that the sale proceeds should be included in 'cash generated from operations'. They are afraid of an adverse market reaction to their results and are very aware of the importance of meeting targets in order to ensure job security, and feel that the adjustments for the proceeds would enhance the 'cash health' of the business.

Discuss the ethical responsibility of the company accountant in ensuring that manipulation of the statement of cash flows, such as that suggested by the directors, does not occur.

Answer

Directors may, particularly in times of falling profit and cash flow, wish to **present a company's results in a favourable light.** This may involve manipulation by creative accounting techniques such as window dressing, or, as is proposed here, an **inaccurate classification.**

If the proceeds of the sale of property, plant and equipment are presented in the cash flow statement as part of 'cash generated from operations', the picture is **misleading**. Operating cash flow is crucial, in the long term, for the survival of the company, because it derives from trading activities, which is what the company is there to do. **Sales of non-current assets generate short term cash flow,** and cannot be repeated year-on-year, unless there are to be no assets left to generate trading profits with.

As **a professional, the accountant has a duty** not only to the company he works for, but to his professional body, stakeholders in the company, and to **the principles of independence and fair presentation of financial statements.**

It is essential that the accountant **tries to persuade the directors not to proceed with the adjustments**, which he or she must know violates IFRS and may well go against the requirements of local legislation. If, despite his protests, the directors insist on the misleading presentation, then the accountant has a duty to **bring this to the attention of the auditors.**

Exam focus point

In an internal company role, ethical problems could be in the following forms.

- Discovering an illegal act or fraud perpetrated by the company (ie its directors)
- Discovering a fraud or illegal act perpetrated by another employee
- Pressure from superiors to take certain viewpoints, for example towards budgets (pessimistic/optimistic etc) or not to report unfavourable findings
- Breaches or potential breaches of confidentiality

PART A   CONTEMPORARY ISSUES

Chapter roundup

- A principles-based system works within a set of laid down principles. A rules-based system regulates for issues as they arise. Both of these have advantages and disadvantages.
- There are many convincing arguments in favour of regulation of corporate financial reporting.
- Accounting policies may be adopted for the purposes of **manipulation**.
- **Changes in accounting standards** can have a significant impact on the financial statements.
- You may be asked to **advise the directors** on the implication of a change in accounting standards, or on the effect of using the correct accounting treatment.
- The AIA has adopted the *Code of Ethics for Professional Accountants issued by IESBA (The IESBA Code)*.
- Organisations sometimes issue **codes of conduct** to employees. Many employees are bound by professional codes of conduct.
- Exam questions may ask you to think about what should be done if breaches of laws, regulations or ethical guidelines occur. **Close relationships** between the parties or other **conflicts of interest** are often a complication.

Quick quiz

1   Give an example of a recent change to IFRS which will have a significant impact on the financial statements.

2   Match the fundamental principle to the characteristic.

   Fundamental principle: (a)   Integrity
   　　　　　　　　　　　　(b)   Objectivity

   Characteristic: (i)   Members should be straightforward and honest in all professional and business relationships.

   　　　　　　　　(ii) Members should not allow bias, conflict or interest or undue influence of others to override professional or business judgements.

Answers to quick quiz

1 The issue of IFRS 11 *Joint Arrangements* and revision to IAS 28 *Investments in Associates and Joint Ventures*

2 (a) (i)
   (b) (ii)

End of chapter question

Mancroft

Mancroft is considering selling its subsidiary, Hungate. Just prior to the year end, Hungate sold inventory to Mancroft at a price of $3 million. The carrying amount of the inventory in the financial records of Hungate was $1 million. The cash was received before the year end, and as a result the bank overdraft of Hungate was virtually eliminated. After the year end the transaction was reversed, and it was agreed that this type of transaction would be carried out again when the interim financial statements were produced for Hungate, if the company had not been sold by that date.

Required

Explore how the manipulation of financial statements by company accountants is inconsistent with their responsibilities as members of the accounting profession, setting out the distinguishing features of a profession and the privileges that society gives to a profession. (Your answer should include reference to the sale of the inventory and should suggest the correct treatment of this transaction.)

PART A CONTEMPORARY ISSUES

Reporting for specialised entities

Topic list	Syllabus reference
1 The not-for-profit sector: Primary aims	13.1
2 The not-for-profit sector: Regulatory framework	13.1
3 The not-for-profit sector: Performance measurement	13.1
4 Smaller entities	13.1
5 Other specialised entities	13.1
6 Rate-regulated entities	13.1

Introduction

You should be aware that not-for-profit entities and smaller entities may have different accounting needs from the larger profit-making entities that you are used to. This chapter gives you the background you need to set you thinking about whether a one-size-fits-all set of standards is adequate.

PART A   CONTEMPORARY ISSUES

1 The not-for-profit sector: Primary aims

Exam focus point

A question could feature a not-for-profit organisation, a small or medium-sized entity (SME) or (possibly) some other kind of specialised entity. You might be asked to apply your knowledge of IFRS to a transaction or event or to discuss more theoretical issues, such as the information needs of the users of the financial statements of (say) a charity or a local authority.

FAST FORWARD

The not-for-profit sector includes **public sector entities** and **private** not-for-profit entities such as charities.

Not-for-profit entities have **different goals** from profit making entities, but they still need to be **properly managed** and their financial statements need to present the information fairly.

What organisations do we have in mind when we refer to **not-for-profit and public sector entities**? These are the most obvious examples:

(a) Central government departments and agencies
(b) Local or federal government departments
(c) Publicly-funded bodies providing healthcare (in the UK this would be the NHS) and social housing
(d) Further and higher education institutions
(e) Charitable bodies

The first four are **public sector entities**. Charities are **private** not-for-profit entities.

Not-for-profit entities have different goals and purposes to profit-making entities and are responsible to different stakeholders. However, they may be dealing in very large sums of money and it is important that they are properly managed and that their financial statements present fairly the results of their operations.

Traditionally, public sector organisations have used a cash-based accounting system. This system does not, however, provide information necessary for efficient and effective financial operations and a growing number of countries are moving to some form of accruals-based accounting within the public sector.

1.1 *Conceptual Framework* for not-for profit entities

The *Conceptual Framework* focuses only on business entities in the private sector. There was an earlier monitoring group in respect of the development of the *Conceptual Framework* which made the following points:

(a) Not-for-profit entities have different objectives, different operating environments and other different characteristics to private sector businesses.

(b) The following issues exist regarding application of the proposals to not-for-profit entities:

- Insufficient emphasis on accountability/stewardship
- A need to broaden the definition of users and user groups
- The emphasis on future cash flows is inappropriate to not-for-profit entities
- Insufficient emphasis on budgeting

1.2 Accountability/stewardship

Not-for-profit entities are not reporting to shareholders, but it is very important that they can account for funds received and show how they have been spent. In some cases, resources may be contributed for specific purposes and management is required to show that they have been utilised for that purpose. Perhaps most importantly, taxpayers are entitled to see how the government is spending their money.

1.3 Users and user groups

The primary user group for not-for-profit entities is the providers of funds. In the case of public bodies, such as government departments, this primary group will consist of taxpayers. In the case of private bodies such as charities it will be financial supporters, and also potential future financial supporters. There is also a case for saying that a second primary user group should be recognised, being the recipients of the goods and services provided by the not-for-profit entity.

1.4 Cash flow focus

Not-for-profit entities need to generate cash flows, but other aspects of financial information are generally more significant – for instance, the resources the entity has available to deliver future goods and services, the cost and effectiveness of those it has delivered in the past and the degree to which it is meeting its objectives.

1.5 Budgeting

Budgets and variance analyses are very important to not-for-profit entities. In some cases, funding is supplied on the basis of a formal, published budget.

2 The not-for-profit sector: Regulatory framework

FAST FORWARD

> The International Public Sector Accounting Standards Board (IPSASB) is developing a set of **International Public Sector Accounting Standards** based on IFRS. In the UK, consideration has been given to public benefit entities in the development of FRS 102, a new single standard which has replaced other UK accounting standards for unlisted companies.

Regulation of public not-for-profit entities, principally local and national governments and governmental agencies, is by the International Public Sector Accounting Standards Board (IPSASB), which comes under the International Federation of Accountants (IFAC).

2.1 International public sector accounting standards

The IPSASB is developing a set of International Public Sector Accounting Standards (IPSASs), based on IFRS. To date 38 IPSASs have been issued.

Exam focus point

You don't need to know these – skim over for background only.

1. Presentation of financial statements
2. Cash flow statements
3. Accounting policies, changes in accounting estimates and errors
4. The effect of changes in foreign exchange rates
5. Borrowing costs
6. Consolidated and separate financial statements
7. Investments in associates
8. Interests in joint ventures
9. Revenue from exchange transactions
10. Financial reporting in hyperinflationary economies
11. Construction contracts
12. Inventories
13. Leases
14. Events after the reporting date
15. Financial instruments: disclosure and presentation – superseded by IPSAS 28 and IPSAS 30
16. Investment property
17. Property, plant and equipment
18. Segment reporting
19. Provisions, contingent liabilities and contingent assets
20. Related party disclosures
21. Impairment of non-cash-generating assets
22. Disclosure of financial information about the general government sector

	23	Revenue from non-exchange transactions (taxes and transfers)
	24	Presentation of budget information in financial statements
	25	Employee benefits
	26	Impairment of cash-generating assets
	27	Agriculture
	28	Financial Instruments: presentation
	29	Financial Instruments: recognition and measurement
	30	Financial Instruments: disclosures
	31	Intangible assets
	32	Service Concession Arrangements: Grantor
	33	First-time adoption of accrual basis IPSASs
	34	Separate financial statements
	35	Consolidated financial statements
	36	Investments in associates and joint ventures
	37	Joint arrangements
	38	Disclosure of interests in other entities

Cash basis IPSAS – Financial reporting under the cash basis of accounting

You are not required to remember this list of IPSASs, or know any of their detailed provisions, but you can see that they closely mirror IFRS and each one is based on the relevant IFRS.

These IPSAS are mainly based on the accrual method of accounting and one of the aims of the IPSASB is to move public sector organisations from the cash to the accruals basis of accounting.

2.1.1 Use of IPSAS

IPSAS have been adopted by a number of countries, such as South Africa, Russia and Switzerland, whilst others, such as France incorporate IPSAS within their public sector accounting framework.

2.1.2 Regulatory framework in the UK

In the UK, a major change to public sector accounting has recently taken place with central government and the health sector preparing their financial statements under EU-adopted IFRS from 2009/2010 onwards. The change was extended to local government in 2010/2011.

The new governance framework for UK government entities formalises a common accounting standards setting hierarchy. EU-adopted IFRS are at the top of the hierarchy; next, in a supportive role and providing additional public-sector specific guidance, are IPSAS, and finally UK standards.

At the same time as the introduction of IFRS was taking place in the central and local government and the health sector, the UK Financial Reporting Council (FRC) was considering two issues:

1   The development of an FRS for Public Benefit Entities (FRSPBE)
2   The future of UK GAAP

A draft FRSPBE was issued in 2011, however the second issue, the future of UK GAAP, quickly gathered momentum and as a result of broader developments in UK reporting, the FRSPBE will now not be issued. Instead, FRS 102, the new (May 2013) UK standard designed to replace all existing UK standards, incorporates the special considerations for PBEs. Certain paragraphs apply solely to PBEs and these will are identified by the prefix 'PBE'.

2.2 Characteristics of not-for-profit entities

As part of its preliminary report on the revised *Conceptual Framework* (2018), the IASB set out some of the characteristics of not-for-profit entities as follows:

2.2.1 Private Sector

Not-for-profit entities in the private sector have the following characteristics:

- Their objective is to provide goods and services to various recipients and not to make a profit

- They are generally characterised by the absence of defined ownership interests (shares) that can be sold, transferred or redeemed
- They may have a wide group of stakeholders to consider (including the public at large in some cases)
- Their revenues generally arise from contributions (donations or membership dues) rather than sales
- Their capital assets are typically acquired and held to deliver services without the intention of earning a return on them

2.2.2 Public Sector

Not-for-profit entities in the public sector have similar key characteristics to those in the private sector. They are typically established by legislation and:

- Their objective is to provide goods and services to various recipients or to develop or implement policy on behalf of governments and not to make a profit
- They are characterised by the absence of defined ownership interests that can be sold, transferred or redeemed
- They typically have a wide group of stakeholders to consider (including the public at large)
- Their revenues are generally derived from taxes or other similar contributions obtained through the exercise of coercive powers
- Their capital assets are typically acquired and held to deliver services without the intention of earning a return on them

2.3 Not-for-profit entities – specific issues

While the general trend is to get not-for-profit entities producing financial statements which are based as far as possible on accruals accounting and the provisions of IFRS and which are generally comparable to those produced for profit-making entities, there are two issues which have yet to be resolved.

2.3.1 Cost of transition

While there has been a general assumption that for public sector entities the move to the accruals basis will result in more relevant and better quality financial reporting, no actual cost-benefit analysis has been undertaken on this.

One of the arguments in favour of the adoption of the accruals basis is that it will be possible to compare the cost of providing a service against the same cost in the private sector. It will then be possible to see how goods and services can be most cheaply sourced.

However, it is questionable whether governments get a good deal anyway when they involve themselves with the private sector and the move to accruals accounting has not gained universal acceptance. The main issue is the huge cost involved in terms of the number of qualified accountants required. For developing countries this cost is considered to be prohibitive.

2.3.2 Definition of a liability

The IASB's *Conceptual Framework* defines a liability as 'a present obligation of the entity to transfer an economic resource as a result of past events. An obligation is a duty or responsibility that an entity has no practical ability to avoid.' A liability is recognised when the transaction meets the definition of an element and its recognition provides information that is useful to the primary users of financial information.

Public benefit entities are subject to a commitment to provide public benefits, but there is an issue to be resolved over whether this commitment meets the definition of a liability. In this situation there has been no 'exchange'. The entity has not received any goods or services for which it is required to make 'settlement'. A distinction can be drawn between 'general commitments to provide public benefits' and 'specific commitments to provide public benefits'. The specific commitment can be regarded as a 'present obligation', but it can be argued that the obligation only arises when the entity formally undertakes to provide something such as a non-performance-related grant. (If the grant were performance-related, the entity would be able to withdraw from the agreement if the performance targets were not reached.)

There is also the issue of 'reliable measurement'. Governments in particular often find themselves funding projects which go a long way over budget, suggesting that reliable measurement was not obtained at the outset.

This issue has been considered by the IPSASB, and in November 2012, it issued an Exposure Draft entitled '*Conceptual Framework for General Purpose Financial Reporting by Public Sector Entities: Measurement of Assets and Liabilities in Financial Statements*'. Final guidance was issued by the IPSAB in November 2014. Since the ED the definitions of elements have been aligned more closely with those in the IASB's *Conceptual Framework*.

The issue is of major importance in the financial reporting of the social policies of governments.

2.4 Charities

Charities are regulated by accounting standards, charity law, relevant company law and best practice. This will vary from country to country. Here we are taking the UK as a typical example.

2.4.1 Statement of financial activities

In addition to a statement of financial position, charities also produce a Statement of Financial Activities (SoFA), an Annual Report to the Charity Commission and sometimes an income and expenditure account. The SoFA is the primary statement showing the results of the charity's activities for the period.

The SoFA shows incoming resources, resources expended, and the resultant net movement in funds. Under incoming resources, income from all sources of funds are listed. These can include:

- Subscription or membership fees
- Public donations
- Donations from patrons
- Government grants
- Income from sale of goods
- Investment income
- Publication sales
- Royalties

The resources expended will show the amount spent directly in furtherance of the charity's objects. It will also show items which form part of any statement of profit or loss (income statement), such as salaries, depreciation, travelling and entertaining, audit and other professional fees. These items can be very substantial.

Charities, especially the larger charities, now operate very much in the way that profit-making entities do. They run high-profile campaigns which cost money and they employ professional people who have to be paid. At the same time, their stakeholders will want to see that most of their donation is going towards achieving the aims for which funds were donated, not on the running of the business.

One of the problems charities experience is that, even although the accruals basis is being applied, they will still have income and expenditure recognised in different periods, due to the difficulty of correlating them. The extreme example is a campaign to persuade people to leave money to the charity in their will. The costs will have to be recognised, but there is no way to predict when the income will arise.

Exam focus point

The Paper 13 Examiner has said that candidates need to have only a basic awareness of the special requirements of not-for-profit organisations. Candidates also need to be aware of the issues concerning the appropriateness of applying IFRS to their performance measures and statements of financial position. This topic will almost certainly be tested by means of an essay question.

Question — Conceptual Framework and not-for-profit organisations

Should the *Conceptual Framework* apply equally to profit-oriented and non profit-oriented entities or just to profit-oriented entities?

Answer

Arguments for applying the *Conceptual Framework* to not-for-profit organisations:

- There is evidence that some national standard setters consider non profit–oriented entities to be just as important as profit-oriented entities as their *Conceptual Frameworks* cater for both. So the idea is not totally without support around the world.

- One of the main features of the last 20 years or so has been the introduction of performance based accountability into both profit-oriented and non profit-oriented sectors. The financial position of both sectors is also of growing concern. It would follow from this that common concepts and principles could be developed.

- Many public sector bodies use IFRS for reporting purposes; eg concerning the recognition of liabilities.

- If the above development continues then it may be best to develop a framework that applies to both sectors from the beginning. If a framework develops which concentrates on one rather than the other then costly and disruptive changes may have to be made in future.

Arguments against applying the *Conceptual Framework* to not-for-profit organisations:

- The performance of a non profit-oriented entity is likely to be measured in terms of the quality of its contribution to society. The performance of a profit-oriented entity is not measured in this way. It is measured in terms of the returns it makes and in an assessment of its future cash flow potential. This focus on returns and the future cash flows therefore colours the type of information it produces. Concepts and principles to reflect this will therefore be very different to that for a non profit-oriented entity.

- Risk is assessed in very different ways. A profit-oriented entity has shareholders whose risk is assessed and measured in a different way to those interested in the affairs of a non profit-oriented entity whose stakeholders may be interested more in environmental or employment risk than in financial risk. Objectives of financial reporting would therefore vary greatly.

- The IASB's activities are in accordance with the constitution of its overseeing body, the IFRS Foundation, which seeks to develop financial statements and other financial reporting to aid economic decision making in the world's capital markets. This is a major statement which focuses on, although undefined, profit-oriented entities.

3 The not-for-profit sector: Performance measurement

Not-for-profit and public sector entities produce financial statements in the same way as profit-making entities do but, while they are expected to remain solvent, their performance cannot be measured simply by the bottom line.

A public sector entity is not expected to show a profit or to underspend its budget. In practice, central government and local government departments know that if they underspend the budget, next year's allocation will be correspondingly reduced. This leads to a rash of digging up the roads and other expenditure just before the end of the financial year as councils strive to spend any remaining funds.

Private and public sector entities are judged principally on the basis of what they have achieved, not how much or how little they have spent in achieving it. So how is performance measured?

3.1 Public sector entities

These will have performance measures laid down by government. The emphasis is on economy, efficiency and effectiveness. Departments and local councils have to show how they have spent public money and what level of service they have achieved. Performance measurement will be based on Key Performance Indicators (KPIs). Examples of these for a local council could be:

- Number of homeless people rehoused
- % of rubbish collections made on time
- Number of children in care adopted

Public sector entities use the services of outside contractors for a variety of functions. They then have to be able to show that they have obtained the best possible value for what they have spent on outside services. This principle is usually referred to as Value For Money (VFM). In the UK, local authorities are required to report under a system known as Best Value. They have to show that they applied 'fair competition' in awarding contracts.

Best Value is based on the principle of the 'four Cs':

1. **Challenging** why, how and by whom a service is provided
2. **Comparing** performance against other local authorities
3. **Consulting** service users, the local community etc
4. Using fair **Competition** to secure efficient and effective services

3.2 Charities

While charities must demonstrate that they have made proper use of whatever funds they have received, their stakeholders will be more interested in what they have achieved in terms of their stated mission. People who donate money to a relief fund for earthquake victims will want to know what help has been given to survivors, before enquiring how well the organisation has managed its funds. Although it must be said that any mismanagement of funds by a charity is taken very seriously by the donating public.

Some charities produce 'impact reports' which highlight what the charity set out to achieve, what it has achieved and what it has yet to do. Stakeholders should know what the organisation is aiming to achieve and how it is succeeding. Each charity will have its own performance indicators which enable it to measure this.

Question   Charity performance indicators

Choose a charity with which you are familiar and produce a possible set of performance indicators for it.

4 Smaller entities

The IASB has addressed the **Big GAAP/Little GAAP** debate by issuing an *IFRS for SMEs*.

4.1 Background

Within each individual country **local regulations** govern, to a greater or lesser degree, the issue of financial statements. These local regulations include accounting standards issued by the national regulatory bodies and/or professional accountancy bodies in the country concerned. In some cases they also include IFRS.

IFRS do not override local regulations on financial statements. Entities should simply disclose the fact where IFRS are complied with in all material respects. Members of the IASB in individual counties will attempt to persuade local authorities, where current regulations deviate from IFRS, that the benefits of harmonisation make local change worthwhile.

4.2 Application of IFRS to smaller entities

> **Exam focus point**
>
> The Paper 13 Examiner has said that candidates need to be aware of the 'Big GAAP vs. Little GAAP' debate.

In most countries the majority of companies or other types of entity are **very small**. They are generally owned and managed by one person or a family. The owners have invested their own money in the business and there are no outside shareholders to protect.

Large entities, by contrast, particularly companies listed on a stock exchange, may have shareholders who have invested their money, possibly through a pension fund, with no knowledge whatever of the company. These shareholders need protection and the regulations for such companies need to be more stringent.

It could therefore be argued that company financial statements should be of two types:

(a) 'Simple' ones for small companies with fewer regulations and disclosure requirements
(b) 'Complicated' ones for larger companies with extensive and detailed requirements

This is sometimes called the **big GAAP/little GAAP divide**.

Some standards may simply not apply to a smaller entity. For example, a company with equity not quoted on a stock exchange has no need to comply with IAS 33 *Earnings per Share*. Also an entity with a small local market may find IFRS 8 *Operating Segments* to be superfluous.

It is certainly the case that there are several IFRS which very rarely have any bearing on small company financial statements, whereas others almost always have an impact. In particular, almost all small companies will be affected by the standards on:

- Property, plant and equipment
- Impairment
- Inventories
- Presentation of financial statements
- Events after the reporting period
- Taxes on income
- Revenue
- Provisions and contingencies

Although these standards are relevant, their application can cause small entities problems and burden them with additional costs. For example, impairment reviews can be time consuming and a smaller entity may not have sufficient staff to spare to carry out these reviews.

These problems historically resulted in calls to take one of two approaches to the issue of small entity reporting:

- Exclude small entities from the scope of certain more complex IFRS, such that only 'core' standards remain applicable; or
- Provide smaller entities with a new IFRS containing all requirements relevant to them.

The IASB has taken the second of these approaches, and in 2009 issued the IFRS for SMEs.

4.3 IFRS for small and medium-sized entities

In July 2009, the IASB published an International Financial Reporting Standard for small and medium-sized entities (IFRS for SMEs). The standard consists of the fundamental requirements drawn from existing full IFRS, organised by topic. Topics not relevant to SMEs (for example, segment reporting and earnings per share) have been omitted. The requirements regarding recognition and measurement have been simplified in certain cases (for example, those relating to financial instruments and intangible assets). Disclosure requirements have also been simplified.

The IFRS for SMEs is intended to be a 'stand alone' document. If an entity undertakes a transaction that is not covered by the standard, management can refer to full IFRS, but this is not mandatory. Management is expected to refer to guidance on similar issues elsewhere in the standard. The definitions and recognition criteria for assets, liabilities, income and expenses taken from the IASB's 2010 *Conceptual Framework* have also been included in the SME standard. There is inconsistency in the definitions since the revision to the *Conceptual Framework* in 2018.

SMEs are not defined by size, but in terms of accountability. An SME does not have public accountability. An entity is publicly accountable if it has issued debt or equity securities in a public market or is a business (such as a bank, an insurance company or a pension fund) which hold these assets in a fiduciary capacity for a broad group of outsiders. Individual countries are free to set size limits and/or to impose other restrictions on the use of the standard.

The accounting requirements of the IFRS for SMEs are covered in detail in Chapter 23.

4.3.1 How the standard might be applied

The IFRS for SMEs has largely been welcomed. It is considerably shorter and simpler than full IFRS (it runs to approximately 250 pages as opposed to 2,500!). However, there are concerns that the new standard will apply to a very wide range of entities and will still be too onerous for the very smallest companies. (The IASB originally began the project by focusing on the transactions likely to be undertaken by a 'typical' company with around 50 employees; a much larger entity than many small companies.) Individual countries will now have the option of allowing or requiring some or all SMEs to apply the IFRS for SMEs as an alternative to full IFRS or local GAAP. Developing countries may find this particularly useful. For some countries, the existence of the new standard may be a further incentive to move away from local GAAP.

It is possible that some countries may use the IFRS for SMEs, or a standard based on it, as a kind of half way house between full IFRS and local GAAP.

4.4 Small Business Enterprise and Employment Act

The Act was passed in 2015 and applies to businesses in the UK. The Act is designed to make the United Kingdom a more attractive place to start, finance and grow a business and reduce the barriers faced by many small businesses. It deals with a number of issues including access to finance, regulatory reform, company filing requirements, insolvency and employment regulations.

The main provisions dealing with company reporting and qualification of directors are:

- Companies need to keep a register of people with significant control (PSCs). These are people to whom one or more of the following apply:
    - Hold more than 25% of shares
    - Hold more than 25% of voting rights
    - Can appoint or remove a majority of directors
    - Are able to, or do, exercise significant influence or control.
- The statement of capital is simplified – no need to set it out in full if there have been no changes during the year.
- An accelerated strike-off procedure for companies no longer trading – reduced from three months to two months.
- The date of birth of directors will no longer appear on the public record.

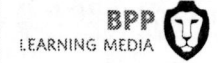

5: REPORTING FOR SPECIALISED ENTITIES

- Newly-appointed officers must have consented to act – if they did not consent they can apply to have the notification of their appointment removed.
- Directors can now be disqualified for certain convictions obtained abroad and for instructing another unfit director.
- Bearer shares are abolished.
- A procedure is set out for dealing with registered office disputes.
- The annual return filed with Companies House is replaced with a 'confirmation statement' to be submitted at least once a year. This statement contains information relating to the company's registered office, directors and shareholders.

5 Other specialised entities

Exam focus point

> You may be asked to apply current accounting standards to a particular transaction or event in an 'unusual' entity.

5.1 Approaching specialised entity questions

Examiners use unusual situations in order to test whether you are flexible enough to apply your knowledge and understanding of accounting standards in a fresh context. Below are some typical questions.

5.1.1 An agricultural college

An agricultural college is not the kind of setting you are used to encountering in your accountancy studies. It doesn't manufacture or trade in goods. But there are issues that it will have in common with companies that do.

Question — Agricultural college

Swindale Agricultural College derives its income from a variety of sources. It receives a grant from central government, further subsidies from the European Union and money from the local council tax. In addition, students pay fees.

The Diploma in Agriculture course lasts nine months – from October till the end of June. The College's accounting year end is 31 December 20X8. Students pay $3,000 subsidised tuition fees. As at 1 October 20X8, twenty students have enrolled, each paying a non-refundable deposit of $1,200. The balance of $1,800 per student is to be paid in nine monthly instalments of $200.

The College Bursar argues that because the deposit is non-refundable, the fee income should be recognised on a cash receipt basis.

Required

Advise the College Bursar on the correct accounting treatment for the fee income. Show the journal entries for this treatment.

Answer

This question deals with revenue recognition, specifically in the context of the provision of a service.

Total fee income from students for this course (deposits and instalments) will be:

(20 × $1,200) + (20 × $200 × 9) = $60,000

Currently it is proposed to recognise revenue on the basis of cash received, which, as at 31 December 20X8, is the deposit plus three monthly instalments:

(20 × $1,200) + (20 × $200 × 3) = $36,000

PART A CONTEMPORARY ISSUES

This is wrong, as it does not take account of the accrual concept. As at 31 December 20X8, only one third of the course (three out of nine months) has been delivered, so only one third of the total fee income should be recognised. Income recognised should be $20,000.

There is an element of deferred income. As this is over months, rather than years, it will not be necessary to discount to arrive at the fair value of the consideration. The excess of the $36,000 cash received over the $20,000 revenue recognised should be regarded as deferred income. These deposits are non-refundable, but they create an obligation to complete the contract. Accordingly they should be a liability in the statement of financial position.

The journal entries are as follows:

DEBIT	Cash	$36,000	
CREDIT	Fee income (recognised)		$20,000
CREDIT	Deferred income (received in advance of delivery of services)		$16,000

5.1.2 A football club

You do not need any specialist knowledge of the football club finance sector to answer this question, which is basically about accounting for assets. The principles are exactly the same as when accounting for assets held by any other entity.

We will be revising the relevant accounting standards later in the text, but you should be able to remember enough of your earlier studies to make a reasonable attempt at this question.

Question — Football club

United Wanderers is a famous football club but has significant cash flow problems. The directors and shareholders wish to take steps to improve the club's financial position. The following proposals had been drafted in an attempt to improve the cash flow of the club. However, the directors need advice upon their implications.

(a) **Player registrations**

The club capitalises the unconditional amounts (transfer fees) paid to acquire players.

The club proposes to amortise the cost of the transfer fees over ten years instead of the current practice which is to amortise the cost over the duration of the player's contract. The club has sold most of its valuable players during the current financial year but still has two valuable players under contract.

Player	Transfer fee capitalised $m	Amortisation to 31 December 20X6 $m	Contract commenced	Contract expires
Headham	20	4	1 January 20X6	31 December 20Y0
Meadows	15	10	1 January 20X5	31 December 20X7

If United Wanderers wins the national football league, then a further $5 million will be payable to the two players' former clubs. United Wanderers is currently performing very poorly in the league.

(b) **Player trading**

Another proposal is for the club to sell its two valuable players, Headham and Meadows. It is thought that it will receive a total of $16 million for both players. The players are to be offered for sale at the end of the current football season on 1 May 20X7.

Required

Discuss how the above proposals would be dealt with in the financial statement of United Wanderers for the year ending 31 December 20X6, setting out their accounting treatment and appropriateness in helping the football club's cash flow problems.

Answer

(a) **Player registrations**

The player registrations are **capitalised** by the club as intangible non-current assets under IAS 38 *Intangible Assets*. This is an **acceptable** accounting treatment; the transfer fees should be classified as assets as it is probable that expected future benefits will flow to the club as a result of the contracts and the cost can be measured reliably at the amount of the transfer fees actually paid.

According to IAS 38, intangible non-current assets which are capitalised should be **amortised over their useful life**. Therefore on the face of it claiming a useful life of 10 years might be acceptable. However IAS 38 recommends that amortisation reflects the useful life of the assets and the pattern of economic benefits. Therefore the proposal to amortise the transfer fees over a period of **10 years is not acceptable as the contracts are only for 5 years and 3 years**.

In terms of **cash flow** this proposal regarding the amortisation would have **no effect** at all. It would simply be a bookkeeping entry which would reduce the amortisation charge to the statement of profit or loss and other comprehensive income.

The potential payment to the two players' former clubs of $5 million would **not** appear to be **probable** due to the current form of the club. Therefore under IAS 37 *Provisions, Contingent Liabilities and Contingent Assets* no provision would be recognised for this amount. However, the possible payment does fall within the IAS 37 definition of a contingent liability which is a possible obligation arising out of past events whose existence will be confirmed only by the occurrence or non-occurrence of one or more uncertain future events not wholly within the control of the entity. Therefore as a contingent liability the amount and details would be **disclosed** in the notes to the financial statements.

(b) **Player trading**

In accounting terms there is no issue to deal with at 31 December 20X6 as the potential sale of the players will not fall to be classified as 'held for sale' non-current assets under IFRS 5 *Non-current Assets Held for Sale and Discontinued Operations*. In order for these players to be classified as held for sale they would need to be available for immediate sale which they are not.

However, the club must consider carrying out an **impairment review** of these assets at 31 December 20X6. If the players are sold for the anticipated figure of $16 million then the following loss will be incurred:

	$m
Carrying amount at 1 May 20X7	
Headham ($20m − ($4m + (4/12 × $4m))	14.7
Meadows ($15m − ($10 + (4/12 × $5))	3.3
	18.0
Potential sales value	16.0
Potential loss	2.0

This potential loss of $2 million on the sale of these players may be evidence of impairment and a review should be carried out at 31 December 20X6 and the **players' value written down to recoverable amount** if necessary.

In terms of cash flow, the sale of the players would **provide much needed cash**. However, as the club is performing poorly currently the sale of the two best players **may lead to even worse performance** which is likely to have a detrimental affect on ticket sales and the liquidity of the club in future.

5.2 Other possibilities

The possibilities are wide ranging, and you need to apply common sense. Suppose, for example, the question relates to a property dealer, who was trying to classify his properties as investment properties? This would not be permitted, because the properties are for sale and not held for investment potential.

6 Rate-regulated entities

Exam focus point

IFRS 14 *Regulatory Deferral Accounts* is new to the syllabus.

FAST FORWARD

IFRS 14 *Regulatory Deferral Accounts* is designed as a limited scope standard to provide an interim, short-term solution for rate-regulated entities that have not yet adopted International Financial Reporting Standards (IFRS).

The standard allows entities adopting IFRS for the first-time to avoid changes in accounting policies in respect of regulatory deferral accounts until the IASB has completed the current project on rate regulated activities.

6.1 Introduction of IFRS 14

IFRS 14 applies only to entities whose business includes rate regulated activities and who are adopting IFRS for the first time.

The IASB is currently engaged in a comprehensive review of accounting for rate regulated activities and this standard is an interim measure designed to avoid forcing accounting policy changes onto entities adopting IFRS for the first time.

6.2 Regulatory deferral balances

Rate regulation refers to a framework for establishing the prices that can be charged to customers for goods or services (IFRS 14). Such frameworks exist to protect consumers from price increases where goods or services are provided by a monopoly or where the government decides for political or social reasons to limit price increases.

Examples of such price regulation are common in industries such as power supply.

A **regulatory deferral account balance** is the balance of any expense or income account that would not be recognised as an asset or a liability in accordance with other Standards, but that is included by the rate regulator in establishing the rate(s) that can be charged to customers (IFRS 14).

IFRS 14 gives examples of the types of costs that rate regulators might allow in rate-setting decisions and that an entity might, therefore, recognise in regulatory deferral account balances:

- Volume or purchase price variances;
- Costs of approved 'green energy' initiatives (in excess of amounts that are capitalised as part of the cost of property, plant and equipment in accordance with IAS 16 *Property, Plant and Equipment*);
- Non-directly-attributable overhead costs that are treated as capital costs for rate regulation purposes (but are not permitted, in accordance with IAS 16, to be included in the cost of an item of property, plant and equipment);
- Project cancellation costs;
- Storm damage costs; and
- Deemed interest (including amounts allowed for funds that are used during construction that provide the entity with a return on the owner's equity capital as well as borrowings).

For example, an entity may recognise account balances as assets, even when IFRS would normally proscribe such recognition, on the grounds that the entity expects to generate economic benefit (in the form of permitted price increase ultimately resulting in higher revenue)

Items of expense and income that are outside the regulated rate(s) because, for example, the amounts are not expected to be accepted by the rate regulator or because they are not within the scope of the **rate regulation**. are recognised as income or expense as incurred, unless another standard permits or requires them to be included in the carrying amount of an asset or liability.

6.3 Presentation and Disclosure

The net movement in all regulatory deferral account balances should be shown as separate line items in profit or loss or other comprehensive income as appropriate.

The following disclosures must be made:

- Information about the nature of, and the risks associated with, the rate regulation
- The effects of that rate regulation on financial position, financial performance and cash flows
- Explanations of activities subject to rate regulation
- Explanations of recognised amounts

PART A   CONTEMPORARY ISSUES

Chapter roundup

- The not-for-profit sector includes **public sector entities** and **private** not-for-profit entities such as charities.

    Not-for-profit entities have **different goals** from profit making entities, but they still need to be **properly managed** and their financial statements need to present the information fairly.

- The International Public Sector Accounting Standards Board (IPSASB) is developing a set of **International Public Sector Accounting Standards** based on IFRS. In the UK, consideration has been given to public benefit entities in the development of FRS 102, a new single standard which has replaced other UK accounting standards for unlisted companies.

- The IASB has addressed the **Big GAAP/Little GAAP debate** by issuing an *IFRS for SMEs*.

- IFRS 14 *Regulatory Deferral Accounts* is designed as a limited scope Standard to provide an interim, short-term solution for rate-regulated entities that have not yet adopted International Financial Reporting Standards (IFRS).

- The standard allows entities adopting IFRS for the first-time to avoid changes in accounting policies in respect of regulatory deferral accounts until the IASB has completed the current project on rate regulated activities.

Quick quiz

1   Charities are public sector entities. True or false?

2   Why do not-for-profit entities need to prepare financial statements if they are not reporting to shareholders?

3   Are there any special reporting standards for the public sector?

4   Are there any special IFRS for small companies?

Answers to quick quiz

1. False. Charities are private not-for-profit profit entities.
2. They often deal in large sums of money.
3. Yes, the IPSASB is developing a set of International Public Sector Accounting Standards; in the UK public benefit entities are considered within FRS 102.
4. Yes, the *IFRS for Small and Medium-sized Entities (SMEs)* was published in 2009.

End of chapter question

Small and medium-sized entities

In July 2009, the IASB issued the *International Financial Reporting Standard for Small and Medium-sized Entities* (IFRS for SMEs). The aim of the new standard is to provide a simplified, self-contained set of accounting principles for smaller companies. The resulting standard reduces the volume of accounting guidance applicable to SMEs by more than 85% when compared to a full set of IFRS.

Required

Assess the advantages and disadvantages of having a separate IFRS for SMEs as opposed to requiring compliance with full IFRS. **(10 marks)**

PART A CONTEMPORARY ISSUES

Business combinations and group financial statements

Revision of basic groups

Topic list	Syllabus reference
1 Introduction	13.2
2 Types of investment	13.2, 13.3
3 IFRS 3 *Business Combinations*	13.2, 13.3
4 IFRS 10 *Consolidated Financial Statements*	13.2, 13.3
5 IFRS 3 – further issues	13.2, 13.3
6 Associates	13.2, 13.3
7 Joint arrangements	13.2, 13.3
8 Disclosure of interests in other entities	13.2, 13.3
9 Separate financial statements of investor	13.2, 13.3
10 Current developments	13.1

Introduction

Basic groups were covered in your earlier studies. In this paper, the emphasis is likely to be on the **more complex** aspects of consolidation. In this chapter, you will revise briefly the main principles of consolidation and consider the changes as a result of the new package of consolidation standards issued in 2011. You will also meet other types of group investments, namely associates and joint arrangements and consider the accounting treatment applied to such investments.

Note. Throughout Part B, all entities are limited liability companies, unless otherwise stated. However, you should bear in mind that IFRS 10 includes unincorporated entities such as partnerships within the definition of subsidiary.

Note. The term 'statement of profit or loss and other comprehensive income' is used. Examiners will normally use this term or may use 'statement of profit or loss' where the last line of the statement is 'profit for the year'.

PART B   BUSINESS COMBINATIONS AND GROUP FINANCIAL STATEMENTS

1 Introduction

Exam focus point

You are unlikely to be examined just on the basic principles. However, you will gain marks for knowing the basic principles in a more complex consolidation.

In traditional accounting terminology, a **group of companies** consists of a **parent company** and one or more **subsidiary companies** which are controlled by the parent company. A group may also have investments in associates and joint arrangements.

The guidance in respect of group accounting is found in six accounting standards, five of which were issued or revised in 2011, in culmination of the IASB's Consolidation project:

FAST FORWARD

- IAS 27 *Separate Financial Statements*
- IAS 28 *Investments in Associates and Joint Ventures*
- IFRS 3 *Business Combinations*
- IFRS 10 *Consolidated Financial Statements*
- IFRS 11 *Joint Arrangements*
- IFRS 12 *Disclosure of Interests in Other Entities*

It is possible that you previously studied the 'old' consolidation standards, IAS 27 (2008) *Consolidated and Separate Financial Statements,* IAS 28 (2003) *Investments in Associates* and IAS 31 *Interests in Joint Ventures.* In many cases the accounting treatment and consolidation procedures required by the new IFRS are the same as those required by the 'old' consolidation standards. There are, however, some differences, particularly in terms of definitions, and these are highlighted throughout the chapter.

1.1 Definitions

Exam focus point

All the definitions relating to group financial statements are extremely important. You must **learn them** and **understand** their meaning and application.

Definitions are very important when looking at group financial statements.

The definitions listed below include some which you have met before in your previous studies. Other, definitions are new and will be explained in the relevant sections of the chapter.

Key terms

Consolidated financial statements. The financial statements of a group in which the assets, liabilities, equity, income, expenses and cash flows of the parent and its subsidiaries are presented as those of a single economic entity. (IAS 27 [2011], IAS 28 [2011], IFRS 10)

Subsidiary. An entity that is controlled by another entity. (IFRS 3 [revised], IFRS 10)

Parent. An entity that controls one or more entities. (IFRS 3 [revised], IFRS 10)

Group. A parent and its subsidiaries. (IFRS 10)

Control. An investor controls an investee when the investor is exposed to, or has rights to, variable returns from its involvement with the investee and has the ability to affect those returns through its power over the investee. (IFRS 10)

Power. Existing rights that give the current ability to direct the relevant activities (IFRS 10)

Relevant activities. Activities of the investee that significantly affect the investee's return (IFRS 10)

Associate. An entity, over which the investor has significant influence (IAS 28 [2003])

Significant influence is the power to participate in the financial and operating policy decisions of an investee or an economic activity but is not control or joint control over those policies. (IAS 28 [2003])

Joint arrangement. An arrangement of which two or more parties have joint control. (IFRS 11)

Key terms (cont'd)

Joint control. The contractually agreed sharing of control of an arrangement, which exists only when decisions about the relevant activities require the unanimous consent of the parties sharing control (IFRS 11)

Joint operation. A joint arrangement whereby the parties that have joint control of the arrangement have rights to the assets and obligations for the liabilities relating to the arrangement. (IFRS 11)

Joint venture. A joint arrangement whereby the parties that have joint control of the arrangement have rights to the net assets of the arrangement. (IFRS 11)

The Equity method is a method of accounting whereby the investment is initially recognised at cost and adjusted thereafter for the post-acquisition change in the investor's share of the investee's net assets. The investor's profit or loss includes its share of the investee's profit or loss and the investor's other comprehensive income includes its share of the investee's other comprehensive income. (IAS 28 [2003])

Acquiree. The business or businesses that the **acquirer** obtains control of in a **business combination**. (IFRS 3)

Acquirer. The entity that obtains control of the **acquiree**. (IFRS 3)

Business combination. A transaction or other event in which an **acquirer** obtains control of one or more **businesses**. (IFRS 3)

Contingent consideration. Usually, an obligation of the **acquirer** to transfer additional assets or **equity interests** to the former owners of an **acquiree** as part of the exchange for **control** of the **acquiree** if specified future events occur or conditions are met. (IFRS 3)

Fair value. The price that would be received to sell an asset or paid to transfer a liability in an orderly transaction between market participants at the measurement date. (IFRS 3)

Non-controlling interest. The equity in a subsidiary not attributable, directly or indirectly, to a parent. (IFRS 3, IFRS 10)

2 Types of investment

FAST FORWARD

Investments are classified as subsidiaries, associates, joint arrangements or financial asset investments. The accounting treatment applied differs depending on the type of investment.

Investments may be classified as subsidiaries, associates, joint arrangements or financial asset investments. The guidance on how an investment is classified is found in:

- IFRS 10 *Consolidated Financial Statements* in the case of subsidiaries;
- IAS 28 (2011) *Investments in Associates and Joint Ventures* in the case of associates; and
- IFRS 11 *Joint Arrangements* in the case of joint arrangements.

Before going into the detailed accounting requirements, we shall consider each of the types of investment in turn.

2.1 Investment in subsidiaries

One entity is a subsidiary of another where it is **controlled** by that entity.

You will previously have studied the definition of control given in IAS 27 (2008), that is 'the power to govern the financial and operating policies of an entity so as to obtain benefits from its activities'.

IFRS 10, issued in 2011 provides an amended definition, and identifies three separate elements of control. It states that an investor controls an investee if and only if it has all of the following:

(i) Power over the investee;
(ii) Exposure, or rights, to variable returns from its involvement with the investee; and
(iii) The ability to use its power over the investee to affect the amount of the investor's returns.

Each of these elements is considered in turn below:

2.1.1 Power

Power is defined as existing rights that give the current ability to direct the relevant activities of the investee. There is no requirement for that power to have been exercised.

Relevant activities may include selling and purchasing goods or services; managing financial assets; selecting, acquiring and disposing of assets; researching and developing new products and processes and determining a funding structure or obtaining funding.

In some cases assessing power is straightforward, for example, where power is obtained directly and solely from having the **majority of voting rights** or potential voting rights, and as a result the ability to direct relevant activities.

In other cases, assessment is more complex and more than one factor must be considered. IFRS 10 gives the following examples of **rights**, other than voting or potential voting rights, which individually, or alone, can give an investor power:

- Rights to appoint, reassign or remove key management personnel who can direct the relevant activities
- Rights to appoint or remove another entity that directs the relevant activities
- Rights to direct the investee to enter into, or veto changes to transactions for the benefit of the investor
- Other rights, such as those specified in a management contract
- An investor can have power over an investee even where other entities have significant influence or other ability to participate in the direction of relevant activities

2.1.2 Variable returns

An investor must have exposure, or rights, to variable returns from its involvement with the investee in order to establish control.

This is the case where the investor's returns from its involvement have the potential to vary as a result of the investee's performance.

Returns may include:

- Dividends
- Remuneration for servicing an investee's assets or liabilities
- Fees and exposure to loss from providing credit support
- Returns as a result of achieving synergies or economies of scale through an investor combining use of their assets with use of the investee's assets

2.1.3 Ability to use power to affect returns

In order to establish control, an investor must be able to use its power to affect its returns from its involvement with the investee.

Exam focus point

You should learn the definition of control as you may be asked to apply it in the exam.

2.1.4 Accounting treatment in group financial statements

IFRS 10 requires a parent to present consolidated financial statements, in which the financial statements of the parent and subsidiary (or subsidiaries) are combined and presented **as a single entity**. This process is **consolidation.** We shall cover the detailed accounting requirements in Sections 3–5 of this chapter.

2.2 Investments in associates

This type of investment is something less than a subsidiary, but more than a simple investment (nor is it a joint venture). The key criterion here is **significant influence**. This is defined as the 'power to participate', but **not** to 'control' (which would make the investment a subsidiary).

Significant influence can be determined by the holding of voting rights (usually attached to shares) in the entity. IAS 28 (2011) states that if an investor holds **20% or more** of the voting power of the investee, it is presumed that the investor has significant influence over the investee, **unless** it can be clearly shown that this is not the case.

Significant influence is presumed **not** to exist if the investor holds **less than 20%** of the voting power of the investee, unless it can be demonstrated otherwise.

The **existence of significant influence** is evidenced in one or more of the following ways.

(a) Representation on the **board of directors** (or equivalent) of the investee
(b) Participation in the **policy making process**
(c) **Material transactions** between investor and investee
(d) Interchange of **management personnel**
(e) Provision of **essential technical information**

2.2.1 Accounting treatment in group financial statements

IAS 28 (2003) requires the use of the **equity method** of accounting for investments in associates. This method will be explained in detail in Section 6 of this chapter.

2.3 Investments in joint arrangements

IFRS 11 defines a joint arrangement as an arrangement of which two or more parties have joint control. The joint arrangement may be either a joint operation or a joint venture depending on the rights of the parties with joint control.

2.3.1 Accounting treatment in group financial statements

IFRS 11 requires that:

- Equity accounting is applied in the case of joint ventures
- The parties with joint control recognise their share of joint items

The identification and classification of joint arrangements and relevant accounting treatment is discussed in more detail in Section 7 of this chapter.

2.4 Other investments

Investments which do not meet the definitions of any of the above are financial assets and should be accounted in accordance with IFRS 9 *Financial Instruments*. Financial instruments are covered in Chapter 14.

2.5 Summary of types of investments

We can summarise the different levels of investment **and** the required accounting treatment as follows.

Investment	Criteria	Required treatment in group financial statements
Subsidiary	Control	Full consolidation
Associate	Significant influence	Equity accounting
Joint venture	Joint control	Equity accounting
Joint operation	Joint control	Recognise share of joint items
Investment which is none of the above	Asset held for accretion of wealth	Financial asset accounting per IFRS 9

The remainder of the chapter will consider each of these levels of investment in more detail. Firstly, however, we shall recap the basic requirements of IFRS 3 *Business Combinations*. A business combination is a transaction where an acquirer obtains **control** of one or more businesses. It is therefore relevant to accounting for **subsidiaries.**

3 IFRS 3 *Business Combinations*

You should have studied IFRS 3 *Business Combinations* for Paper 11. Here is a re-cap of the basic calculation of goodwill.

3.1 Objective of IFRS 3

The objective of IFRS 3 is to improve the relevance, reliability and comparability of the information that a reporting entity provides in its financial statements about a business combination and its effects. To accomplish that, IFRS 3 establishes principles and requirements for how the acquirer:

(a) Recognises and measures in its financial statements the identifiable assets acquired, the liabilities assumed and any non-controlling interest in the acquiree.

(b) Recognises and measures the goodwill acquired in the business combination or a gain from a bargain purchase.

(c) Determines what information to disclose to enable users of the financial statements to evaluate the nature and financial effects of the business combination.

3.2 Identifying a business combination

IFRS 3 requires entities to determine whether a transaction or other event is a business combination by applying the definition in the IFRS. As we saw earlier, a business combination is defined as 'a transaction or other event in which an acquirer obtains control of one or more businesses'.

3.3 The acquisition method

Entities must account for each business combination by applying the **acquisition method.** This requires:

(a) **Identifying the acquirer.** This is generally the party that obtains control.

(b) **Determining the acquisition date.** This is generally the date the consideration is legally transferred, but it may be another date if control is obtained on that date.

(c) Recognising and measuring the **identifiable assets acquired, the liabilities assumed** and any non-controlling interest in the acquiree (see below).

(d) Recognising and measuring goodwill or a gain from a bargain purchase (see below and Chapter 13).

The recognition and measurement of identifiable assets acquired and liabilities assumed other than the non-controlling interest is dealt with in Section 3. Below we deal with the cost of the acquisition, the consideration transferred, the goodwill and the non-controlling interest, as these treatments have recently changed.

3.4 Acquisition-related costs

Under IFRS 3, **costs relating to the acquisition must be recognised as an expense** at the time of the acquisition. They are not regarded as an asset. (Costs of issuing debt or equity are to be accounted for under the rules of IFRS 9.)

3.5 Contingent consideration

IFRS 3 defines contingent consideration as:

> 'Usually, an obligation of the acquirer to transfer additional assets or equity interests to the former owners of an acquiree as part of the exchange for control of the acquiree if specified future events occur or conditions are met. However, contingent consideration also may give the acquirer the right to the return of previously transferred consideration if specified conditions are met.'

3.5.1 IFRS 3

IFRS 3 requires recognition of contingent consideration, measured at fair value, at the acquisition date.

IFRS 3 is based on the principle that, by entering into an acquisition, the acquirer becomes obliged to make additional payments. Not recognising that obligation means that the consideration recognised at the acquisition date is not fairly stated.

IFRS 3 therefore **requires recognition of contingent consideration, measured at fair value, at the acquisition date.** This is, arguably, consistent with how other forms of consideration are fair valued.

The acquirer may be required to pay contingent consideration in the form of equity or of a debt instrument or cash. Debt instruments are presented in accordance with IAS 32 *Financial Instruments: Presentation*. Contingent consideration may occasionally be an asset, for example if the consideration has already been transferred and the acquirer has the right to the return of part of it, an asset may occasionally be recognised in respect of that right.

3.5.2 Post acquisition changes in the fair value of the contingent consideration

The treatment depends on the circumstances:

(a) If the change in fair value is due to additional information obtained that affects the position at the acquisition date, goodwill should be re-measured.

(b) If the change is due to events which took place after the acquisition date, for example, meeting earnings targets:

    (i) Account for under IFRS 9 if the consideration is in the form of a financial instrument, for example loan notes.

    (ii) Account for under IAS 37 *Provisions, Contingent Liabilities and Contingent Assets* if the consideration is in the form of cash.

    (iii) An equity instrument is not remeasured.

3.6 Goodwill and the non-controlling interest

IFRS 3 views the group as an economic entity. This means that it treats all providers of equity – including non-controlling interests – as shareholders in the group, even if they are not shareholders of the parent. Thus goodwill attributable to the non-controlling interest may be recognised.

We will come back to this point below, but first we need to consider how IFRS 3 sets out the calculation for goodwill.

3.6.1 IFRS 3 goodwill calculation

In words, IFRS 3 states:

> Fair value of consideration paid by parent + non-controlling interest − fair value of the subsidiary's net identifiable assets = consolidated goodwill

3.6.2 BPP proforma goodwill calculation

The proforma goodwill calculation could be set out like this:

	$
Consideration transferred	X
Amount of any non-controlling interests	X
	X
Less net acquisition-date fair value of identifiable assets acquired and liabilities assumed	(X)
	X

While the above layout reflects the wording of the standard, for the purposes of your workings in the examination, the following layout is recommended:

		Group	NCI
	$	$	$
Consideration transferred/Fair value of non-controlling interests		X	X
Less: net fair value of identifiable assets acquired and liabilities assumed	X		
× Group/NCI %		(X)	(X)
		X	X
			X

The NCI (non-controlling interest) column is only needed if the NCI interest is to be measured at fair value (see below). When the NCI is measured at fair value, goodwill arises that is attributable to the NCI.

3.6.3 Measuring non-controlling interest at acquisition

FAST FORWARD

> The non-controlling interest may be measured **either at fair value or at the non-controlling interest's proportionate share of the acquiree's identifiable net assets**.

The non-controlling interest now forms part of the calculation of goodwill. The question now arises as to how it should be measured.

The 'economic entity' principle (see 1.7.2) suggests that the non-controlling interest should be measured at fair value. In fact, IFRS 3 gives a **choice**:

> 'For each business combination, the acquirer shall measure any non-controlling interest in the acquiree **either at fair value or at the non-controlling interest's proportionate share of the acquiree's identifiable net assets**.' *(IFRS 3)*

Note that this choice is available on a transaction by transaction basis.

IFRS 3 suggests that for a quoted company the closest approximation to fair value will be the market price of the shares held by the non-controlling shareholders just before the acquisition by the parent.

Non-controlling interest at fair value will be different from non-controlling interest at proportionate share of the acquiree's net assets. The difference is goodwill attributable to the non-controlling interest, which may be, but often is not, proportionate to goodwill attributable to the parent.

Exam focus point

The examiner may refer to valuation at (full) fair value as the 'full goodwill' method.

3.6.4 Goodwill calculation: Simple examples

Now we will look at goodwill calculations on the two bases: the IFRS 3 proportion of net assets method and the IFRS 3 fair value method.

(a) **IFRS 3 proportion of net assets method**

On 31 December 20X8, Penn acquired 4 million of the 5 million $1 ordinary shares of Sylvania, paying $10m in cash. On that date, the fair value of Sylvania's net assets was $7.5m.

It is the group's policy to value the non-controlling interest at its proportionate share of the fair value of the subsidiary's identifiable net assets.

Calculate goodwill on the acquisition.

Answer

	$'000	$'000
Consideration transferred	10,000	
Non-controlling interest: 20% × $7.5m		1,500
Fair value of net assets acquired: 80%/20% × $7.5m	(6,000)	(1,500)
Goodwill	4,000	–

BPP note. You will see that the NCI column is not needed because the figures cancel each other out.

(b) **IFRS 3 fair value method**

On 31 December 20X8, Penn acquired 4 million of the 5 million $1 ordinary shares of Sylvania, paying $10m in cash. On that date, the fair value of Sylvania's net assets was $7.5m.

It is the group's policy to value the non-controlling interest at fair value. The market price of the shares held by the non-controlling shareholders just before the acquisition was $2.00

Calculate goodwill on the acquisition.

Answer

	$'000	$'000
Consideration transferred/FV NCI	10,000	2,000
Fair value of net assets acquired: 80%/20% × $7.5m	(6,000)	(1,500)
Goodwill	4,000	500

Goodwill attributable to non-controlling interest is $500,000

Total goodwill on the acquisition (parent + NCI) is $4m + $0.5m = $4.5m.

BPP note. The goodwill attributable to the non-controlling interest is not in proportion to that attributable to the parent. If it were in proportion, the total goodwill would be $4m × 100%/80% = $5m, and so the goodwill attributable to the NCI would be $1m.

3.6.5 Why is the goodwill attributable to the NCI not always proportionate?

In Example (b) above, the goodwill attributable to the non-controlling interest is not in proportion to that attributable to the parent. Generally, this is because owners of the parent have paid a higher price in order to obtain control. You can calculate the share price the owners of the parent must have paid – it is $10m/4m, that is $2.50 per share. The premium to acquire control may reflect the value of synergies between the parent and subsidiary.

3.6.6 Subsequent measurement of the non-controlling interest

Subsequent to acquisition the non-controlling interest will increase (or decrease) by the NCI share of any post acquisition movement in the subsidiary's reserves. IFRS 10 *Consolidated Financial Statements* requires that this is the case even if it results in the non-controlling interests having a deficit balance due to the allocation of losses.

Your calculation of non-controlling interest at the year end will look like this:

	$'000	$'000
Share capital	X	
Retained earnings	X	
Provision for unrealised profit	X	
NCI share of identifiable net assets (a × NCI %)		X
NCI share of goodwill (FV method only)		X
Non-controlling interest		X

Note that the NCI share of goodwill is added on only where the parent has opted to measure the NCI at the acquisition date at fair value.

An alternative calculation involves increasing the acquisition date fair value of the non-controlling interest by the NCI share of post-acquisition profits:

	$'000
FV of the NCI at acquisition	X
NCI share of post-acquisition profits	X
Non-controlling interest	X

Because the NCI share of goodwill is included in both the top half of the statement of financial position (within total goodwill), and in the bottom half (within the NCI), the statement of financial position will balance.

3.6.7 Goodwill impairment under the full goodwill method

Where the full goodwill method is used, IAS 36 *Impairment of Assets* requires a subsidiary's goodwill impairment loss to be allocated between the parent and the non-controlling interest on the same basis as the subsidiary's profits and losses are allocated. Thus if there is an impairment loss of $1 million in respect of a subsidiary in which the parent holds a 75% stake, $750,000 would be allocated to the parent (and debited to group retained earnings) and $250,000 would be allocated to the NCI.

It could be argued that this requirement represents an anomaly; looking back to the calculation in Section 1.7.5 (b) above, of the recognised goodwill of $4.5 million only $500,000 (ie 11%) relates to the NCI, but it will suffer 25% of any goodwill impairment.

In other words, **the impairment of the goodwill is allocated proportionately, even if the goodwill on the non-controlling interest is not itself proportionate.**

> **Exam focus point**
>
> You are required to know **both** methods of measuring the NCI for Paper 13. Questions will normally ask specifically for one or other method.
>
> There are a number of ways of presenting the information to test the fair value method:
>
> (i) As above, the subsidiary's share price just before the acquisition could be given and then used to value the non-controlling interest. It would then be a matter of multiplying the share price by the number of shares held by the non-controlling interests. (**Note.** the parent is likely to have paid more than the subsidiary's pre acquisition share price in order to gain control.)
>
> (ii) The question could simply state that the directors valued the non-controlling interest at the date of acquisition at $2 million.
>
> (iii) An alternative approach would be to give (in the question) the value of the goodwill attributable to the non-controlling interest. In this case the NCI's goodwill would be added to the parent's goodwill and to the carrying amount of the non-controlling interest itself.

4 IFRS 10 *Consolidated Financial Statements*

FAST FORWARD

IFRS 10 *Consolidated Financial Statements* provides accounting guidance on the consolidation procedures to be applied when preparing the combined financial statements of a parent and its subsidiaries.

Consolidated financial statements are prepared for a parent and its subsidiaries. We have already seen that an entity is a subsidiary when it is **controlled** by another entity.

Where a parent controls one or more subsidiaries, IFRS 10 requires, with limited exemptions, that consolidated financial statements are prepared to include **all subsidiaries, both foreign and domestic** other than:

- Those held for sale in accordance with IFRS 5
- Those held under such long-term restrictions that control cannot be operated.

The rules on exclusion of subsidiaries from consolidation are necessarily strict, because this is a common method used by entities to manipulate their results. If a subsidiary which carries a large amount of debt can be excluded, then the gearing of the group as a whole will be improved. In other words, this is a way of taking debt **off the statement of financial position**.

It has been argued that subsidiaries should be excluded from consolidation on the grounds of **dissimilar activities**, ie the activities of the subsidiary are so different to the activities of the other companies within the group that to include its results in the consolidation would be misleading. IFRS 10 rejects this argument: exclusion on these grounds is not justified because better (relevant) information can be provided about such subsidiaries by consolidating their results and then giving additional information about the different business activities of the subsidiary, eg under IFRS 8 *Operating Segments*.

4.1 Exemption from preparing group financial statements

A parent **need not present** consolidated financial statements if and only if:

(a) It is a **wholly-owned subsidiary** or it is a **partially owned subsidiary** of another entity and its other owners, including those not otherwise entitled to vote, have been informed about, and do not object to, the parent not presenting consolidated financial statements;

(b) Its securities are **not publicly traded**;

(c) It is **not in the process of issuing securities** in public securities markets; **and**

(d) The **ultimate or intermediate parent** publishes financial statements that are available for public use and comply with IFRSs, in which subsidiaries are consolidated or are measured at fair value through profit or loss in accordance with this IFRS.

A parent that does not present consolidated financial statements must comply with the IAS 27 (2011) rules on separate financial statements (discussed later in the chapter).

4.1.1 Investment Entities

IFRS 10 was amended in 2012 and again in 2014 to deal with the issue of Investment Entities. An investment entity is defined as an entity that:

(a) Obtains funds from one or more investors for the purpose of providing those investors with investment management services;

(b) Commits to its investors that its business purpose is to invest funds solely for returns from capital appreciation, investment income, or both; and

(c) Measures and evaluates the performance of substantially all of its investments on a fair value basis.

Prior to the 2012 amendment to IFRS 10, it was the case that an investment entity may have several investments meeting the definition of a subsidiary and which should therefore be consolidated, despite the fact that no true commercial group existed.

The 2012 amendment to IFRS 10 excludes investment entities from applying IFRS 3 and preparing consolidated accounts and instead requires that such investments are financial assets measured at fair value through profit or loss in accordance with IFRS 9 (see Chapter 14). The 2014 amendment to IFRS 10 clarified the application of the investment entity exception.

4.2 Consolidation procedures

The consolidation procedures required by IFRS 10 are the same as those required by its predecessor IAS 27 (2008).

4.2.1 Preparation of consolidated financial statements

In order to prepare consolidated financial statements, the following procedures are applied:

1. Assets, liabilities, income and expenses are combined on a line by line basis.
2. The carrying amount of the parent's investment in each subsidiary and the parent's proportion of equity in each subsidiary are eliminated.
3. Non-controlling interests representing the equity of subsidiaries which does not belong to the parent are recognised.

4.2.2 Intragroup transactions

As the consolidated financial statements are prepared for a group as a single economic entity, intra-group balances and transactions should be eliminated as part of the consolidation process.

4.2.3 Different reporting dates

In most cases, all group companies will prepare financial statements to the same reporting date. One or more subsidiaries may, however, prepare financial statements to a different reporting date from the parent and the bulk of other subsidiaries in the group.

In such cases the subsidiary may prepare additional statements to the reporting date of the rest of the group, for consolidation purposes. If this is not possible, the subsidiary's financial statements may still be used for the consolidation, **provided that** the gap between the reporting dates is **three months or less**.

Where a subsidiary's financial statements are drawn up to a different accounting date, **adjustments should be made** for the effects of significant transactions or other events that occur between that date and the parent's reporting date.

4.2.4 Uniform accounting policies

Consolidated financial statements should be prepared using **the same accounting policies** for like transactions and other events in similar circumstances.

Adjustments must be made where members of a group use different accounting policies, so that their financial statements are suitable for consolidation.

4.2.5 Date of inclusion/exclusion

The results of subsidiary undertakings are included in the consolidated financial statements from:

(a) The date of 'acquisition', ie the **date control passes to the parent**; to
(b) The date of 'disposal', ie the **date control passes from the parent**

Once an investment is no longer a subsidiary, it should be treated as an associate under IAS 28 (2003) (if applicable) or as a financial asset investment under IFRS 9.

4.3 Revision: Summary of techniques

The summary given below is very brief but it encompasses all the major, but basic, rules of consolidation for, firstly, the consolidated statement of financial position.

> **Knowledge brought forward from earlier studies**
>
> *Summary of technique: Consolidated statement of financial position*
>
> - **Net assets**: 100% P plus 100% S.
> - **Share capital**: P only.
> - **Reserves**: 100% P plus group share of post-acquisition retained reserves of S less consolidation adjustments.
> - **Non-controlling interest**: NCI share of S's consolidated net assets (**proportion of net assets method**).
>   NCI share of S's consolidated net assets plus NCI share of goodwill (**fair value method**).
>
> The method of consolidation is as follows:
>
> - Determine the **group structure**. Draw chart showing the percentages holdings and dates of acquisition.
> - Consider **adjustments** for:
>   - Dividends
>   - Provisions for unrealised profits (PUP)
>   - Revaluations to fair value
>   - Intragroup inventory and cash in transit
> - Combine **net assets**, cancelling any **intra-group balances**.
>   - Current accounts
>   - Debentures
> - **Share capital** of P only
>
> - Calculate the **non-controlling interest** in net assets
>
> | | |
> |---|---:|
> | NCI % of share capital | X |
> | NCI % of reserves | X |
> | NCI % of revaluations to fair value | X |
> | NCI goodwill (if NCI measured at FV at acquisition) | X |
> | NCI % of unrealised profit | (X) |
> | | X |
>
> Or
>
> | | |
> |---|---:|
> | NCI at acquisition date (either a proportion of net assets or FV) | X |
> | NCI % of post-acquisition movement in reserves | X/(X) |
> | | X |
>
> - Calculate the **goodwill (positive or negative)**
>
> | | |
> |---|---:|
> | Consideration transferred | X |
> | NCI (proportion of net assets or FV) | X |
> | Assets acquired | |
> | Share capital | (X) |
> | Pre-acquisition reserves | (X) |
> | Revaluation to fair value | (X) |
> | Goodwill | X |

- If cost is **greater than** the share of net assets acquired, then the difference is **goodwill**, which should be capitalised and retained in the statement of financial position, subject to annual impairment reviews (see Chapter 13).
- If cost is **less than** the share of net assets acquired, then the difference is a **gain on bargain purchase** (sometimes termed **negative** goodwill). The treatment of this is also discussed in Chapter 13.
- **Calculate retained earnings reserve**

	P	S	A
Per question	X	X	X
Adjustments	X(X)	X(X)	X(X)
Fair value adjustment (% × adj)		X/X)	X/(X)
Accumulated profits at acquisition	—	(X)	(X)
	X	X	X
Share of post acquisition profits of subsidiary (% × X)		X	
	X		

The technique for the preparation of a **consolidated statement of profit or loss and other comprehensive income** is given below

---

Summary of technique: Consolidated statement of profit or loss and other comprehensive income

Adjustments required for consolidation of a subsidiary are as follows.

- Eliminate **intra-group sales and purchases**.
- Eliminate any **unrealised profits** on intra-group purchases still in inventory at the year end.
- Eliminate any **intra-group** interest receivable/payable dividends receivable.
- Analyse profit for the year between owners of the parent and NCI.

For the inclusion of a subsidiary carry out the following:

- **Combine all P and S results** from turnover to profit after tax (where the acquisition is mid-year, use a time-apportioned basis).

- **Calculate NCI:**
    - Where there are no preference shares: NCI = % × profit after tax
    - Where there are preference shares an additional working is required

Unrealised profits/losses

Only where **S sells to P**, allocate the unrealised profit between NCI and P: *Debit* Group reserves, *Debit* non-controlling interest, *Credit* Inventory.

Now try the following questions to refresh your memory on the topics listed above.

Question

Revision of basic groups

Boo Co has owned 80% of Goose Co's equity since its incorporation. On 31 December 20X8 it despatched goods which cost $80,000 to Goose, at an invoiced cost of $100,000. Goose received the goods on 2 January 20X9 and recorded the transaction then. The two companies' draft financial statements as at 31 December 20X8 are shown below.

STATEMENTS OF PROFIT OR LOSS AND OTHER COMPREHENSIVE INCOME

	Boo $'000	Goose $'000
Revenue	5,000	1,000
Cost of sales	2,900	600
Gross profit	2,100	400
Other expenses	1,700	320
Profit before tax	400	80
Income tax	130	25
Profit for the year	270	55

STATEMENTS OF CHANGES IN EQUITY (SUMMARY)

	$'000	$'000
Opening balance	2,260	285
Total comprehensive income (profit) for the year	270	55
Dividends paid	(130)	–
Closing balance	2,400	340

STATEMENTS OF FINANCIAL POSITION

	Boo $'000	Boo $'000	Goose $'000	Goose $'000
Assets				
Non-current assets				
Property, plant and equipment		1,920		200
Investment in Goose		80		–
		2,000		200
Current assets				
Inventory	500		120	
Trade receivables	650		40	
Bank and cash	390		35	
		1,540		195
		3,540		395
Equity and liabilities				
Equity				
Share capital		2,000		100
Retained earnings		400		240
		2,400		340
Current liabilities				
Trade payables	1,010		30	
Tax	130		25	
		1,140		55
		3,540		395

Required

Prepare draft consolidated financial statements.

Answer

BOO GROUP
CONSOLIDATED STATEMENT OF PROFIT OR LOSS AND OTHER COMPREHENSIVE INCOME FOR THE YEAR ENDED 31 DECEMBER 20X8

	$'000
Revenue (5,000 + 1,000 – 100)	5,900
Cost of sales (2,900 + 600 – 80)	3,420
Gross profit	2,480
Other expenses (1,700 + 320)	2,020
Profit before tax	460
Income tax (130 + 25)	155
Profit for the year	305
Profit attributable to:	
Owners of the parent	294
Non-controlling interest (20% × 55)	11
	305

CONSOLIDATED STATEMENT OF CHANGES IN EQUITY (SUMMARY)
FOR THE YEAR ENDED 31 DECEMBER 20X8

	Group $'000	NCI $'000
Opening balance (balancing figure)	2,408	57
Group profit for the year (as above)	294	11
Dividends paid	(130)	–
Closing balance (per statement of financial position)	2,572	68

CONSOLIDATED STATEMENT OF FINANCIAL POSITION AS AT 31 DECEMBER 20X8

	$'000	$'000
Assets		
Non-current assets (1,920 + 200)		2,120
Current assets		
Inventory (500 + 120 + 80)	700	
Trade receivables (650 – 100 + 40)	590	
Bank and cash (390 + 35)	425	
		1,715
		3,835
Equity and liabilities		
Equity		
Share capital (Boo only)		2,000
Retained earnings (W)		572
Shareholders' funds		2,572
Non-controlling interest (20% × 340)		68
		2,640
Current liabilities		
Trade payables (1,010 + 30)	1,040	
Income tax (130 + 25)	155	
		1,195
		3,835

Working: Group retained earnings

	Boo $'000	Goose $'000
Per question	400	200
Closing inventory in transit (at cost)	80	
Intercompany sale	(100)	
Share of Goose ($240 × 80%)	192	
Group net owned profits	572	

This working is, of course, only necessary when you are not required to prepare the consolidated income statement. Here, it serves as a proof of the consolidated income statement as well as of the reserves figure in the statement of financial position.

Question — NCI at proportion of net assets

The draft statements of financial position of Oak and its subsidiary Chestnut at 30 September 20X8 are as follows:

	Oak $	Oak $	Chestnut $	Chestnut $
Non-current assets				
Land and buildings		225,000		270,000
Plant		202,500		157,500
		427,500		427,500
Investment				
Shares in Chestnut at cost		562,500		
Current assets				
Inventory	255,000		180,000	
Receivables	375,000		90,000	
Bank	112,500		22,500	
		742,500		292,500
		1,732,500		720,000
Equity				
Called up share capital – issued and fully paid				
$1 ordinary shares		1,125,000		450,000
Retained earnings		450,000		202,500
		1,575,000		652,500
Current liabilities		157,500		67,500
		1,732,500		720,000

The following information is also available:

(a) Oak purchased 360,000 shares in Chestnut some years ago when that company had a credit balance of $105,000 in retained earnings. The goodwill had been impaired and was fully written off in profit or loss by 30 September 20X7.

(b) For the purpose of the takeover, the land of Chestnut was revalued at $120,000 in excess of its book value. This was not reflected in the financial statements of Chestnut. Land is not depreciated.

(c) At 30 September 20X8 Chestnut owed Oak $15,000 for goods purchased.

(d) The inventory of Chestnut includes goods purchased from Oak at a price which includes a profit to Oak of $10,500.

(e) It is the group's policy to value the non-controlling interest at its proportionate share of the fair value of the subsidiary's identifiable net assets.

PART B BUSINESS COMBINATIONS AND GROUP FINANCIAL STATEMENTS

Required

Prepare the consolidated statement of financial position for Oak as at 30 September 20X8.

BPP hint. You don't need a separate column for non-controlling interest in the goodwill working.

Answer

OAK
CONSOLIDATED STATEMENT OF FINANCIAL POSITION AS AT 30 SEPTEMBER 20X8

	$	$
Non-current assets		
Land and buildings (W5)		615,000
Plant (202,500 + 157,500)		360,000
		975,000
Current assets		
Inventory (W6)	424,500	
Receivables (W7)	450,000	
Bank (112,500 + 22,500)	135,000	
		1,009,500
		1,984,500
Equity		
Ordinary $1 shares		1,125,000
Retained earnings (W3)		495,000
		1,620,000
Non-controlling interest (W4)		154,500
Total equity		
Current liabilities one year (W8)		210,000
		1,984,500

Workings

1. Group structure: $\dfrac{360,000}{450,000} = 80\%$

2. Goodwill

	$	$
Consideration transferred		562,500
Net assets acquired		
Share capital	450,000	
Reserves	105,000	
Revaluation surplus	120,000	
	675,000	
Group share: 80%		540,000
Goodwill – fully impaired (see W3)		22,500

3. Retained earnings

	Oak $	Chestnut $
Oak	450,000	202,500
Goodwill written off as impaired (W2)	(22,500)	
Unrealised profit	(10,500)	
Retained earnings at acquisition		(105,000)
	417,000	97,500
Chestnut × 80%	78,000	
	495,000	

4 Non-controlling interests

	$
Share capital	450,000
Retained earnings	202,500
Revaluation surplus	120,000
	772,500
20% × $772,500 =	$154,500

5 Land and buildings

	$	$
Oak		225,000
Chestnut:		
Carrying amount	270,000	
Revaluation surplus	120,000	
		390,000
		615,000

6 Inventory

	$
Oak	255,000
Chestnut	180,000
Less unrealised profit	(10,500)
	424,500

7 Receivables

	$
Oak	375,000
Chestnut	90,000
Less intragroup	(15,000)
	450,000

8 Current liabilities

	$
Oak	157,500
Chestnut	67,500
Less intragroup	(15,000)
	210,000

PART B BUSINESS COMBINATIONS AND GROUP FINANCIAL STATEMENTS

Question — Non-controlling interest at fair value

You are provided with the following statements of financial position for Shark and Minnow.

STATEMENTS OF FINANCIAL POSITION AS AT 31 OCTOBER 20X0

	Shark $'000	Shark $'000	Minnow $'000	Minnow $'000
Non-current assets, at book value				
Plant		325		70
Fixtures		200		50
		525		120
Investment				
Shares in Minnow at cost		200		
Current assets				
Inventory at cost	220		70	
Receivables	145		105	
Bank	100		0	
		465		175
		1,190		295
Equity				
$1 Ordinary shares		700		170
Retained earnings		215		50
		915		220
Current liabilities				
Payables		275		55
Bank overdraft		0		20
		275		75
		1,190		295

The following information is also available:

(a) Shark purchased 70% of the issued ordinary share capital of Minnow four years ago, when the retained earnings of Minnow were $20,000. There has been no impairment of goodwill.

(b) For the purposes of the acquisition, plant in Minnow with a book value of $50,000 was revalued to its fair value of $60,000. The revaluation was not recorded in the financial statements of Minnow. Depreciation is charged at 20% using the straight-line method.

(c) Shark sells goods to Minnow at a mark-up of 25%. At 31 October 20X0, the inventories of Minnow included $45,000 of goods purchased from Shark.

(d) Minnow owes Shark $35,000 for goods purchased and Shark owes Minnow $15,000.

(e) It is the group's policy to value the non-controlling interest at fair value.

(f) The market price of the shares of the non-controlling shareholders just before the acquisition was $1.50.

Required

Prepare the consolidated statement of financial position of Shark as at 31 October 20X0.

Answer

SHARK
CONSOLIDATED STATEMENT OF FINANCIAL POSITION AS AT 31 OCTOBER 20X0

	$'000	$'000
Non-current assets		
Plant (W4)	397	
Fixtures (200 + 50)	250	
		647
Intangible asset: Goodwill (W1)		77
		724
Current assets		
Inventory (W5)	281	
Receivables (W6)	200	
Bank	100	
		581
		1,305
Capital and reserves		
Share capital		700
Retained earnings (W2)		221
		921
Non-controlling interests (W3)		84
Total equity		1,005
Current liabilities		
Payables (W7)	280	
Bank overdraft	20	
		300
		1,305

Workings

1 *Goodwill*

		Group		NCI
	$'000	$'000		$'000
Consideration transferred/FV NCI		200		76.5
(30% × 170,000 × $1.50)				
Net assets acquired				
Share capital	170			
Retained earnings	20			
Revaluation surplus (60 – 50)	10			
	200			
Group/NCI share: 70%/30%		140		60.0
Goodwill in parent		60		16.5

$76.5m

2 *Retained earnings*

	Shark $'000	Minnow $'000
Shark	215.0	50.0
PUP (W5)	(9.0)	
Excess depn on plant (W4)		(8.0)
Retained earnings at acquisition		(20.0)
	206.0	22.0
Minnow (22 × 70%)	15.4	
	221.4	

PART B BUSINESS COMBINATIONS AND GROUP FINANCIAL STATEMENTS

3 *Non-controlling interests*

	$'000	$'000
Share capital		170
Revaluation surplus	10	
Less excess depreciation (W4)	(8)	
		2
Retained earnings		50
		222
NCI in sub's identifiable net assets: 30% × $222,000		67
Goodwill attributable to NCI (W1)		17
Non-controlling interest		84

4 *Plant*

	$'000	$'000
Shark		325
Minnow		
Per question	70	
Revaluation surplus (60 – 50)	10	
Depreciation thereon (10 × 20% × 4)	(8)	
		72
		397

5 *Inventory*

	$'000	$'000
Shark		220
Minnow	70	
Less PUP (45 × $^{25}/_{125}$)	(9)	
		61
		281

6 *Receivables*

	$'000	$'000
Shark		145
Less intragroup		(35)
		110
Minnow	105	
Less intragroup	(15)	
		90
		200

7 *Payables*

	$'000	$'000
Shark		275
Less intragroup		(15)
		260
Minnow	55	
Less intragroup	(35)	
		20
		280

5 IFRS 3 – further issues

FAST FORWARD

Goodwill arising on consolidation is the excess of the fair value of the consideration transferred plus the non-controlling interest over the fair value of the identifiable assets and liabilities acquired.

We have already considered the basic requirements of IFRS 3, and considered the calculation of goodwill:

	$
Consideration transferred	X
Amount of any non-controlling interests	X
	X
Less net acquisition-date fair value of identifiable assets acquired and liabilities assumed	(X)
	X

Goodwill is specifically calculated as the difference between the consideration transferred plus the non-controlling interest and the **fair value** of the **identifiable** net assets of the acquiree.

Consideration must therefore be given to the fair value of the identifiable net assets of the acquiree, and in particular:

1. The meaning of identifiable and the recognition principles applied to the assets and liabilities of the acquiree, and
2. The measurement principle and establishing the fair value of the identifiable assets and liabilities of the acquiree.

5.1 Recognition principles

An asset or liability is identifiable if it is either:

- Separable ie capable of being separated from the entity and sold or transferred either individually or with a related contract or
- Arises from contractual or other legal rights, regardless of whether those rights are transferable from the entity.

Identifiable assets and liabilities are recognised as net assets of the acquiree within the goodwill calculation where:

- They meet the definition of assets and liabilities in the *Conceptual Framework;* and
- Are part of the business combination transaction rather than the result of separate transactions.

There are limited exceptions to the recognition principles and these are considered later in this section.

5.1.1 Recognition of intangible assets

It is important to note that as a result of the recognition principles, an acquirer must recognise acquired identifiable intangible assets (such as internally generated brand names, patents or customer relationships), even if the acquiree did not recognise the assets in its own financial statements).

5.1.2 Restructuring costs and future losses

An acquirer should not recognise liabilities for future losses or other costs expected to be incurred as a result of the business combination.

IFRS 3 explains that a plan to restructure a subsidiary following an acquisition is not a present obligation of the acquiree at the acquisition date. Neither does it meet the definition of a contingent liability. Therefore an acquirer **should not recognise a liability for** such **a restructuring plan** as part of allocating the cost of the combination unless the subsidiary was already committed to the plan before the acquisition.

This **prevents creative accounting**. An acquirer cannot set up a provision for restructuring or future losses of a subsidiary and then release this to profit or loss in subsequent periods in order to reduce losses or smooth profits.

5.2 Measurement principles

IFRS 3 requires that the identifiable assets and liabilities of an acquiree are measured at their acquisition date fair value. Fair value is defined by IFRS 13 *Fair Value Measurement*.

Key term

> **Fair value**. The price that would be received to sell an asset or paid to transfer a liability in an orderly transaction between market participants at the measurement date.

The IFRS 13 guidance with regard to establishing fair value is applicable to business combinations. This is covered in Chapter 11.

Again, there are some exceptions listed within IFRS 3 to the measurement principles.

5.3 Exceptions to the recognition and measurement principles

IFRS 3 provides limited exceptions to the recognition and measurement principles discussed above.

5.3.1 Contingent liabilities

Contingent liabilities of the acquirer are **recognised** if their **fair value can be measured reliably**. A **contingent liability** must be recognised even if the outflow is not probable, provided there is a present obligation.

This is a departure from the normal rules in IAS 37; contingent liabilities are not normally recognised, but only disclosed.

After their initial recognition, the acquirer should measure contingent liabilities that are recognised separately at the higher of:

(a) The amount that would be recognised in accordance with IAS 37
(b) The amount initially recognised

5.3.2 Income taxes

A deferred tax asset or liability arising from the assets acquired and liabilities assumed in a business combination is recognised and measured in accordance with IAS 12 *Income Taxes*.

5.3.3 Employee benefits

A liability (or asset) related to the acquiree's employee benefit arrangements is recognised in accordance with IAS 19 *Employee Benefits*.

5.3.4 Share-based payment transactions

A liability or an equity instrument related to the share-based payment transactions of the acquiree is measured in accordance with the method in IFRS 2 *Share-based Payment*.

5.3.5 Assets held for sale

An acquired non-current asset or disposal group that is classified as held for sale at the acquisition date is measured in accordance with IFRS 5 *Non-current Assets Held for Sale and Discontinued Operations*.

5.3.6 Indemnification assets

The measurement of an indemnification asset should be consistent with the measurement of the indemnified item, for example an employee benefit or a contingent liability.

5.3.7 Reacquired rights

Reacquired rights are valued on the basis of the remaining contractual term of the related contract regardless of whether market participants would consider potential contractual renewals in determining its fair value.

5.4 Consolidation adjustments

In order to comply with IFRS 3, we must ensure that the subsidiary's identifiable net assets are all included in the goodwill calculation at their **fair value**. They will also be recognised in the consolidated statement of financial position at this amount.

In the case of items which are recognised by the acquiree in its own financial statements but not held at fair value, there are two possible ways of achieving this.

(a) The **subsidiary company** might **incorporate any necessary revaluations** in its own books of account. In this case, we can proceed directly to the consolidation, taking asset values and reserves figures straight from the subsidiary company's statement of financial position.

(b) The **revaluations** may be made as a **consolidation adjustment without being incorporated** in the subsidiary company's books. In this case, we must make the necessary adjustments to the subsidiary's statement of financial position as a working. Only then can we proceed to the consolidation.

Note. Remember that when depreciating assets are revalued, there may be a corresponding alteration in the amount of depreciation charged and accumulated.

Where an asset is not recognised by the acquiree, however is identifiable and meets the recognition principles of IFRS 3, the second approach must be used ie a consolidation adjustment is required.

5.5 Example: Fair value adjustments

P Co acquired 75% of the ordinary shares of S Co on 1 September 20X5. At that date the fair value of S Co's non-current assets was $23,000 greater than their carrying amount, and the balance of retained earnings was $21,000. The statements of financial position of both companies at 31 August 20X6 are given below. S Co has not incorporated any revaluation in its books of account.

P CO
STATEMENT OF FINANCIAL POSITION AS AT 31 AUGUST 20X6

	$	$
Assets		
Non-current assets		
Property, plant and equipment	63,000	
Investment in S Co at cost	51,000	
		114,000
Current assets		82,000
Total assets		196,000
Equity and liabilities		
Equity		
Ordinary shares of $1 each	80,000	
Retained earnings	96,000	
		176,000
Current liabilities		20,000
Total equity and liabilities		196,000

PART B BUSINESS COMBINATIONS AND GROUP FINANCIAL STATEMENTS

S CO
STATEMENT OF FINANCIAL POSITION AS AT 31 AUGUST 20X6

	$	$
Assets		
Property, plant and equipment		28,000
Current assets		43,000
Total assets		71,000
Equity and liabilities		
Equity		
Ordinary shares of $1 each	20,000	
Retained earnings	41,000	
		61,000
Current liabilities		10,000
Total equity and liabilities		71,000

If S Co had revalued its non-current assets at 1 September 20X5, an addition of $3,000 would have been made to the depreciation charged to profit or loss for 20X5/X6. It is the group's policy to value the non-controlling interest at acquisition at its proportionate share of the fair value of the subsidiary's net assets.

Required

Prepare P Co's consolidated statement of financial position as at 31 August 20X6.

Solution

S Co has not incorporated the revaluation in its draft statement of financial position. Before beginning the consolidation workings we must therefore adjust the company's balance of profits at the date of acquisition and at the year end.

S Co adjusted balance of retained earnings

	$	$
Balance per financial statements at 1 September 20X5		21,000
Consolidation adjustment: revaluation surplus		23,000
∴ Pre-acquisition profits for consolidation purposes		44,000
Profit for year ended 31 August 20X6		
Per draft financial statements $(41,000 – 21,000)	20,000	
Consolidation adjustment: increase in depreciation		
Charge	(3,000)	
		17,000
Adjusted balance of retained earnings at 31 August 20X6		61,000

In the consolidated statement of financial position, S Co's non-current assets will appear at their revalued amount: $(28,000 + 23,000 – 3,000) = $48,000. The consolidation workings can now be drawn up.

1   Goodwill

	$	$
Consideration transferred		51,000
Non-controlling interest (64,000 × 25%)		16,000
		67,000
Share of net assets acquired as represented by		
Ordinary share capital	20,000	
Retained earnings		
$(21,000 + 23,000)	44,000	
		(64,000)
Goodwill		3,000

2 Retained earnings

	P Co $	S Co $
Per question	96,000	41,000
Pre-acquisition profits		(21,000)
Depreciation adjustment		(3,000)
Post-acquisition S Co		17,000
Group share in S Co ($17,000 × 75%)	12,750	
Group retained earnings	108,750	

3 Non-controlling interest

	$
Share capital (25% × $20,000)	5,000
Retained earnings (25% × $61,000)	15,250
	20,250

P CO CONSOLIDATED STATEMENT OF FINANCIAL POSITION AS AT 31 AUGUST 20X6

	$	$
Assets		
Property, plant and equipment $(63,000 + 48,000)	111,000	
Goodwill	3,000	
		114,000
Current assets $(82,000 + 43,000)		125,000
		239,000
Equity and liabilities		
Equity		
Ordinary shares of $1 each	80,000	
Retained earnings	108,750	
		188,750
Non-controlling interest		20,250
		209,000
Current liabilities $(20,000 + 10,000)		30,000
		239,000

Question — Fair value

An asset is recorded in S Co's books at its historical cost of $4,000. On 1 January 20X5 P Co bought 80% of S Co's equity and attributed a fair value of $3,000 to the asset. At that date it had been depreciated for two years out of an expected life of four years on the straight line basis. There was no expected residual value. On 30 June 20X5 the asset was sold for $2,600. What is the profit or loss on disposal of this asset to be recorded in S Co's financial statements and in P Co's consolidated financial statements for the year ended 31 December 20X5?

Answer

S Co: Carrying amount at disposal (at historical cost) = $4,000 × (4 − 2½)/4 = $1,500
∴ Profit on disposal = $1,100 (depreciation charge for the year = $500)

P Co: Carrying amount at disposal (at fair value) = $3,000 × (2 − ½)/2 = $2,250
∴ Profit on disposal for consolidation = $350 (depreciation for the year = $750)

The non-controlling interest would be credited with 20% of both items as part of the one line entry in the income statement.

PART B BUSINESS COMBINATIONS AND GROUP FINANCIAL STATEMENTS

Question
More fair values

Tyzo Co prepares financial statements to 31 December. On 1 September 20X7 Tyzo Co acquired 6 million $1 shares in Kono Co at $2.00 per share. At that date Kono Co produced the following interim financial statements.

	$m		$m
Property, plant and equipment (note 1)	16.0	Trade payables	3.2
Inventories (note 2)	4.0	Taxation	0.6
Receivables	2.9	Bank overdraft	3.9
Cash in hand	1.2	Non-current loans	4.0
		Share capital ($1 shares)	8.0
		Reserves	4.4
	24.1		24.1

Notes

1. The property, plant and equipment of Kono Co had a fair value of $16.8 million at 1 September 20X7.

2. The inventories of Kono Co which were shown in the interim financial statements are raw materials at cost. They would have cost $4.2 million to replace at 1 September 20X7.

3. On 1 September 20X7 Tyzo Co took a decision to rationalise the group so as to integrate Kono Co. The costs of the rationalisation were estimated to total $3.0 million and the process was due to start on 1 March 20X8. No provision for these costs has been made in the financial statements given above.

4. Kono Co has disclosed a contingent liability relating to litigation of $200,000 in its interim financial statements.

5. Tyzo Group values the non-controlling interest using the full goodwill method. The market value of the shares not purchased by Tyzo Co on 1 September 20X7 was $1.75.

Required

Compute the goodwill on consolidation of Kono Co that will be included in the consolidated financial statements of the Tyzo Co group for the year ended 31 December 20X7, explaining your treatment of the items mentioned above. You should refer to the provisions of relevant accounting standards.

Answer

Goodwill on consolidation of Kono Co

		Group $m	NCI $m
Consideration ($2.00 × 6m)		12.0	
Non-controlling interest (2m × $1.75)			3.5
Group share of fair value of net assets acquired			
Share capital	8.0		
Pre-acquisition reserves	4.4		
Fair value adjustments			
Property, plant and equipment (16.8 – 16.0)	0.8		
Inventories (4.2 – 4.0)	0.2		
Contingent liability	(0.2)		
	(13.2)		
Group share/NCI share		(9.9)	(3.3)
Goodwill		2.1	0.2
Total Goodwill			2.3

Notes on treatment

(a) Share capital and pre-acquisition profits represent the carrying amount (book value) of the net assets of Kono Co at the date of acquisition. Adjustments are then required to this carrying amount in order to give the fair value of the net assets at the date of acquisition. For short-term monetary items, fair value is their carrying amount on acquisition.

(b) The fair value of the property, plant and equipment is $0.8m in excess of book value.

(c) The fair value of the raw materials is their replacement cost. In this case that amount is $4.2m.

(d) The rationalisation costs cannot be reported in pre-acquisition results under IFRS 3 as they are not a liability of Kono Co at the acquisition date.

(e) The contingent liability should be included as part of the acquisition net assets of Kono even though it is recognised in Kono's individual financial statements. However, the amount at which it is disclosed is not necessarily the fair value at which a third party would assume the liability. If the probability of an outflow of resources is low, then the fair value will be lower than $200,000.

5.6 Goodwill arising on acquisition

Goodwill should be carried in the statement of financial position at **cost less any accumulated impairment losses**. The treatment of goodwill is covered in detail in Chapter 13.

5.7 Adjustments after the initial accounting is complete

Sometimes the fair values of the acquiree's identifiable assets and liabilities and/or of the consideration transferred can only be determined **provisionally** by the **end of the period in which the combination takes place**. In this situation, the acquirer **should account for the combination using those provisional values**. The acquirer should **recognise any adjustments** to those provisional values as a result of completing the initial accounting:

(a) **Within the measurement period** (a maximum of 12 months from the acquisition date), and
(b) **From** the acquisition date (ie retrospectively)

This means that:

(a) The **carrying amount** of an item that is recognised or adjusted as a result of completing the initial accounting shall be calculated **as if its fair value** at the acquisition date **had been recognised from that date.**

(b) **Goodwill should be adjusted** from the acquisition date by an amount equal to the adjustment to the fair value of the item being recognised or adjusted.

Any further adjustments after the initial accounting is complete should be **recognised only to correct an error** in accordance with IAS 8 *Accounting Policies, Changes in Accounting Estimates and Errors*. Any subsequent changes in estimates are dealt with in accordance with IAS 8 (ie the effect is recognised in the current and future periods). IAS 8 requires an entity to account for an error correction retrospectively, and to present financial statements as if the error had never occurred by restating the comparative information for the prior period(s) in which the error occurred.

5.8 Reverse acquisitions

IFRS 3 also addresses a certain type of acquisition, known as a **reverse acquisition or takeover**. This is where Company A acquires ownership of Company B through a share exchange. (For example, a private entity may arrange to have itself 'acquired' by a smaller public entity as a means of obtaining a stock exchange listing.) The number of shares issued by Company A as consideration to the shareholders of Company B is so great that control of the combined entity after the transaction is with the shareholders of Company B.

PART B BUSINESS COMBINATIONS AND GROUP FINANCIAL STATEMENTS

In legal terms Company A may be regarded as the parent or continuing entity, but IFRS 3 states that, as it is the Company B shareholders who control the combined entity, **Company B should be treated as the acquirer**. Company B should apply the acquisition (or purchase) method to the assets and liabilities of Company A.

> **Exam focus point**
>
> Look out for a reverse takeover in the exam – it may look like a normal acquisition. You must analyse the takeover deal given in a question carefully to determine the correct treatment.

5.9 Example

Burke Co is a private company that wishes to obtain a stock exchange listing. It has therefore been agreed that Allister Co, a listed company will acquire Burke by means of a share for share exchange. The terms of the deal are that Allister will issue 2.5 of its own shares in exchange for each one in Burke.

At the acquisition date, the statements of financial position of the two companies are as follows:

	Allister $'000	Burke $'000
Non-current assets	1,300	3,000
Current assets	500	700
	1,800	3,700
Ordinary shares	300	600
Retained earnings	800	1,400
	1,100	2,000
Non-current liabilities	400	1,100
Current liabilities	300	600
	1,800	3,700

The following information is relevant:

1. Allister's share capital is made up of 100,000 shares; Burke's is made up of 60,000 shares
2. All of the shareholders in Burke agree to the deal.
3. The fair value of each share in Burke on the acquisition date is $40; the market price of each share in Allister is $12. The fair value of the shares in Burke is agreed to be a reliable estimate.
4. The fair value of the non-current assets of Allister is $200,000 higher than book value.

Prepare the consolidated statement of financial position at the acquisition date.

Solution

As a result of this transaction, Allister will issue 150,000 new shares to the shareholders of Burke. As a result shares will be held in Allister as follows:

- 100,000 shares owned by the original shareholders in Allister (40%)
- 150,000 shares owned by the previous shareholders in Burke (60%)

The shareholders of Burke will therefore achieve control of the new combined entity, thus indicating that this is a reverse acquisition.

Although Allister is the legal acquirer and Burke is the legal acquiree, from an accounting point of view, this position is reversed and Burke is treated as the acquirer and Allister as the acquiree. The consolidated accounts are therefore prepared on the basis that Burke is the parent entity.

This creates the issue of how to measure goodwill when the parent entity (Burke) has not paid any form of consideration. IFRS 3 requires that the cost of the combination is presumed to be equal to the market value of the shares which Burke would have to issue in order for the original shareholders of Allister to own 40% of the shares in Burke (ie the same proportion that the original shareholders of Allister own in the combined entity).

There are 60,000 shares in Burke, therefore a further 40,000 would theoretically be issued in order that the original shareholders of Allister owned 40% of the combined entity were Burke the legal parent company. (40%/60% × 60,000 shares).

The cost of the combination is therefore 40,000 shares × $40 fair value of Burke shares on the date of the acquisition ie $1.6 million. Goodwill is calculated as the consideration transferred less the fair value of Allister's net assets. There is no non-controlling interest because 100% of Burke's shares were acquired.

This theoretical share issue must also be taken into account when reporting share capital.

Goodwill working

	$'000
Cost of combination	1,600
Net assets of acquiree (Allister)	
Share capital	(300)
Retained earnings	(800)
FV adjustment	(200)
Goodwill	300

Consolidated statement of financial position at the acquisition date

	$'000
Non-current assets (1,300 + 3,000 + 200)	4,500
Goodwill	300
Current assets (500 + 700)	1,200
	6,000
Share capital (600 actual + 1,600 theoretical)	2,200
Retained earnings (Burke only as no post acquisition period)	1,400
	3,600
Non-current liabilities (400 + 1,100)	1,500
Current liabilities (300 + 600)	900
	6,000

6 Associates

> **FAST FORWARD**
>
> IAS 28 deals with identifying and accounting for associates.

IAS 28 *Investments in Associates and Joint Ventures* provides accounting guidance on identifying and accounting for an associate.

In Section 2 we established that an associate is an entity over which the investor has significant influence. We also saw that significant influence is defined as 'the power to participate in the financial and operating policy decisions of the investee but is not control or joint control of those policies'.

This section of the chapter therefore concentrates on accounting for associates.

6.1 The equity method

IAS 28 requires all investments in associates to be accounted for using the equity method, **unless** the investment is classified as 'held for sale' in accordance with IFRS 5 in which case it should be accounted for under IFRS 5 (see Chapter 18).

6.1.1 Exemptions from applying the equity method

An investor is exempt from applying the equity method if:

(a) It is a parent exempt from preparing consolidated financial statements under IFRS 10; or

(b) All of the following apply:

  (i) The investor is a **wholly-owned subsidiary** or it is a **partially owned subsidiary** of another entity and its other owners, including those not otherwise entitled to vote, have been informed about, and do not object to, the investor not applying the equity method;

  (ii) Its securities are **not publicly traded**;

  (iii) It is **not in the process of issuing securities** in public securities markets; and

  (iv) The **ultimate or intermediate parent** publishes financial statements available for public use that comply with IFRSs, in which subsidiaries are consolidated or are measured at fair value through profit or loss in accordance with IFRS 10.

The use of the equity method should be **discontinued** from the date that the investor **ceases to have significant influence.**

From that date, the investor shall account for the investment in accordance with IFRS 9 *Financial Instruments*. The fair value of the investment at the date that it ceases to be an associate shall be regarded as its fair value on initial measurement as a financial asset under IFRS 9.

6.2 Consolidated financial statements

> **FAST FORWARD**
>
> The **equity method** should be applied in the consolidated financial statements:
>
> - **Statement of financial position**: investment in associate measured at cost plus (or minus) the group's share of the associate's post-acquisition retained profits (or losses)
>
> - **Statement of profit or loss and other comprehensive income**: group share of associate's profit after tax.

Many of the procedures required to apply the equity method are the same as are required for full consolidation. In particular, **intra-group unrealised profits** must be excluded.

Even if the investor pays more than asset value for its investment in its associate, there is no separate presentation of any goodwill. It is subsumed within the cost figure.

6.2.1 Consolidated statement of profit or loss and other comprehensive income

The basic principle is that the investing company (X Co) should take account of its **share of the earnings** of the associate, Y Co, whether or not Y Co distributes the earnings as dividends. X Co achieves this by adding to consolidated profit the group's share of Y Co's profit after tax (and where relevant, adding to consolidated other comprehensive income the group's share of other comprehensive income).

Notice the difference between this treatment and the **consolidation** of a subsidiary company's results. If Y Co were a subsidiary X Co would take credit for the whole of its sales revenue, cost of sales etc and would then make adjustments to allocate any profit or loss (and other comprehensive income) attributable to the non-controlling interest.

Under equity accounting, the associate's sales revenue, cost of sales and so on are **not amalgamated** with those of the group. Instead the group share of the associate's profit after tax for the year is presented as a separate line item in arriving at consolidated profit before tax. Where relevant the group share of the associate's other comprehensive income is presented as a separate line item in arriving at consolidated total comprehensive income.

6.2.2 Consolidated statement of financial position

A figure for **investment in associates** is shown which, at the time of the acquisition, must be stated at cost. This amount will increase (decrease) each year by the amount of the group's share of the associate's profit (loss) and, where relevant, other comprehensive income for the year.

6.3 Example: Associate

P Co, a company with subsidiaries, acquires 25,000 of the 100,000 $1 ordinary shares in A Co for $60,000 on 1 January 20X8. In the year to 31 December 20X8, A Co earns profits after tax of $24,000, from which it declares a dividend of $6,000.

How will A Co's results be accounted for in the individual and consolidated financial statements of P Co for the year ended 31 December 20X8?

Solution

In the **individual financial statements** of P Co, the investment will be recorded on 1 January 20X8 at cost. Unless there is an impairment in the value of the investment (see below), this amount will remain in the individual statement of financial position of P Co permanently. The only entry in P Co's individual statement of profit or loss and other comprehensive income will be to record the dividends received. For the year ended 31 December 20X8, P Co will:

DEBIT	Cash	$1,500	
CREDIT	Profit or loss: income from shares in associated companies		$1,500

In the **consolidated financial statements** of P Co equity accounting principles will be used to account for the investment in A Co. Consolidated profit after tax will include the group's share of A Co's profit after tax (25% × $24,000 = $6,000). To the extent that this has been distributed as dividend, it is already included in P Co's individual financial statements and will automatically be brought into the consolidated results. That part of the group's profit share which has not been distributed as dividend ($6,000 – $1,500 = $4,500) will be brought into consolidation by the following adjustment.

DEBIT	Investment in associates	$4,500	
CREDIT	Profit or loss: income from shares in associates		$4,500

The asset 'Investment in associates' is then stated at $64,500, being cost plus the group share of post-acquisition retained profits.

6.4 Consolidated statement of profit or loss and other comprehensive income

The treatment of associates' profits in the following proforma should be studied carefully.

6.4.1 Pro-forma consolidated statement of profit or loss and other comprehensive income

The following is a **suggested layout** (using the figures given in the illustration above) for an income statement for a company having subsidiaries as well as associates.

	$'000
Revenue	1,400
Cost of sales	770
Gross profit	630
Distribution costs and administrative expenses	290
	340
Interest and similar income receivable	30
	370
Finance costs	(20)
	350

PART B   BUSINESS COMBINATIONS AND GROUP FINANCIAL STATEMENTS

	$'000
Share of profit (after tax) of associate	17
Profit before taxation	367
Income tax expense	
Parent company and subsidiaries	145
Profit for the year	222
Profit attributable to:	
Owners of the parent	200
Non-controlling interest	22
	222

6.4.2 Statement of profit or loss and other comprehensive income: Investor with no subsidiaries

The treatment required by the standard is given above. The following layout is suggested.

	$
Revenue	X
Cost of sales	(X)
Gross profit	X
Distribution costs/administrative expenses	(X)
	X
Finance costs	X
Share of profit after tax of associate	X
Profit before taxation	(X)
	X
Taxation	X
Profit for the year	X

6.5 Consolidated statement of financial position

As explained earlier, the consolidated statement of financial position will contain an **asset 'Investment in associates'**. The amount at which this asset is stated will be its original cost plus the group's share of any **profits earned since acquisition** which have not been distributed as dividends.

6.6 Example: Consolidated statement of financial position

On 1 January 20X6 the net identifiable assets of A Co amount to $220,000, financed by 100,000 $1 ordinary shares and retained earnings of $120,000. P Co, a company with subsidiaries, acquires 30,000 of the shares in A Co for $75,000. During the year ended 31 December 20X6 A Co's profit after tax is $30,000, from which dividends of $12,000 are paid.

Show how P Co's investment in A Co would appear in its consolidated statement of financial position at 31 December 20X6.

Solution

CONSOLIDATED STATEMENT OF FINANCIAL POSITION
AS AT 31 DECEMBER 20X6 (extract)

	$
Non-current assets	
Investment in associate	
Cost	75,000
Group share of post-acquisition retained earnings	
(30% × $18,000)	5,400
	80,400

Question Associate 1

Set out below are the draft financial statements of Parent Co and its subsidiaries and of Associate Co. Parent Co acquired 40% of the equity capital of Associate Co three years ago when the latter's retained earnings stood at $40,000.

SUMMARISED STATEMENT OF FINANCIAL POSITION

	Parent Co & subsidiaries $'000	Associate Co $'000
Property, plant and equipment	220	170
Investment in Associate at cost	60	–
Loan to Associate Co	20	–
Current assets	100	50
Loan from Parent Co	–	(20)
	400	200
Share capital ($1 shares)	250	100
Retained earnings	150	100
	400	200

SUMMARISED STATEMENTS OF PROFIT OR LOSS AND OTHER COMPREHENSIVE INCOME

	Parent Co & subsidiaries $'000	Associate Co $'000
Profit before tax	95	80
Tax	35	30
Profit for the period	60	50

You are required to prepare the summarised consolidated financial statements of Parent Co.

Answer

PARENT CO CONSOLIDATED STATEMENT OF PROFIT OR LOSS AND OTHER COMPREHENSIVE INCOME	$'000
Profit from operations	95
Share of profits of associate (50 × 40%)	20
Profit before tax	115
Income tax expense	35
Profit attributable to the owners of Parent Co	80

PARENT CO CONSOLIDATED STATEMENT OF FINANCIAL POSITION	$'000
Assets	
Property, plant and equipment	220
Interest in associate (see note)	104
Current assets	100
Total assets	424
Equity and liabilities	
Share capital	250
Retained earnings (W)	174
Total equity and liabilities	424

Note	$'000
Interest in associate
Cost	60
Share of post-acquisition retained earnings 40% × (100 – 40)	24
84
Loan to associate	20
104

Workings: retained earnings

	Parent & subsidiaries $'000	Associate $'000
Per question	150	100
Pre-acquisition		40
Post-acquisition		60
Group share in associate ($60 × 40%)	24	
Group retained earnings	174	

Question: Associate 2

Alfred Co bought 25,000 ordinary shares on 31 December 20X8 in Grimbald Co at a cost of $38,000. Grimbald Co has 100,000 ordinary shares in issue.

During the year to 31 December 20X9 Grimbald Co made a profit before tax of $82,000 and the taxation charge on the year's profits was $32,000. A dividend of $20,000 was paid on 31 December out of these profits.

Calculate the amount in respect of the associate which should be presented in the 20X8 and 20X9 consolidated financial statements of the Alfred group.

Answer

At 31 December 20X8 (the date the investment was made), the investment in the associate should be presented in the consolidated statement of financial position at its cost of $38,000.

The amounts in the 20X9 consolidated financial statements are as follows.

CONSOLIDATED STATEMENT OF PROFIT OR LOSS AND OTHER COMPREHENSIVE INCOME

	$
Group share of associate's profit after tax (25% × (82,000 – 32,000))	12,500

CONSOLIDATED STATEMENT OF FINANCIAL POSITION

	$
Interest in associate	45,500
The asset 'interest in associate' comprises:	
Cost	38,000
Share of post-acquisition retained earnings (12,500 – (25% × 20,000 dividend paid)	7,500
	45,500

The following points are also relevant and are similar to a parent-subsidiary consolidation situation:

(a) Use financial statements drawn up to the **same reporting date.**

(b) If this is impracticable, adjust the financial statements for **significant transactions/ events** in the intervening period. The difference between the reporting date of the associate and that of the investor must be no more than three months.

(c) Use **uniform accounting policies** for like transactions and events in similar circumstances, adjusting the associate's statements to reflect group policies if necessary.

(d) If an associate has **cumulative preferred shares** held by outside interests, calculate the share of the investor's profits/losses after adjusting for the preferred dividends (whether or not declared).

6.7 'Upstream' and 'downstream' transactions

'Upstream' transactions are, for example, sales of assets from an associate to the investor. 'Downstream' transactions are, for example, sales of assets from the investor to an associate.

Profits and losses resulting from 'upstream' and 'downstream' transactions between an investor (including its consolidated subsidiaries) and an associate are eliminated to the extent of the investor's interest in the associate. This is very similar to the procedure for eliminating intra-group transactions between a parent and a subsidiary. The important thing to remember is that **only the group's share is eliminated**.

The double entry is as follows, where A% is the parent's holding in the associate, and PUP is the provision for unrealised profit.

DEBIT	Retained earnings of parent	PUP × A%
CREDIT	Group inventories	PUP × A%

For upstream transactions (associate sells to parent/subsidiary) where the parent holds the inventories.

OR

DEBIT	Retained earnings of parent/subsidiary	PUP × A%
CREDIT	Investment in associate	PUP × A%

For downstream transactions, (parent/subsidiary sells to associate) where the associate holds the inventory.

6.8 Example: Downstream transaction

A Co, a parent with subsidiaries, holds 25% of the equity shares in B Co. During the year, A Co makes sales of $1,000,000 to B Co at cost plus a 25% mark-up. At the year-end, B Co has all these goods still in inventories.

Solution

A Co has made an unrealised profit of $200,000 (1,000,000 × 25/125) on its sales to the associate. The group's share of this is 25%, ie $50,000. This must be eliminated.

The double entry is:

DEBIT	A Co: Retained earnings	$50,000	
CREDIT	Investment in associate (B Co)		$50,000

Because the sale was made to the associate, the group's share of the unsold inventories forms part of the investment in associate at the year end. If the sale had been from the associate B to A, ie an upstream transaction, the double entry would have been.

DEBIT	A Co: Retained earnings	$50,000	
CREDIT	A Co: Inventories		$50,000

If preparing the consolidated statement of profit or loss and other comprehensive income, you would deduct the $50,000 from the group share of the associate's profit.

6.9 Associate's losses

When the equity method is being used and the investor's share of losses of the associate equals or exceeds its interest in the associate, the investor should **discontinue** including its share of further losses. The investment is reported at nil value. The interest in the associate is normally the carrying amount of the investment in the associate, but it also includes any other non-current interests, for example, preference shares or long term receivables or loans.

After the investor's interest is reduced to nil, **additional losses** should only be recognised where the investor has incurred obligations or made payments on behalf of the associate (for example, if it has guaranteed amounts owed to third parties by the associate).

6.10 Impairment losses

IFRS 9 *Financial Instruments* sets out a list of indications that a financial asset (including an investment in an associate) may have become impaired. Any impairment loss is recognised in accordance with IAS 36 *Impairment of Assets* for each associate individually, reducing the carrying amount of any associate affected. Any reversal of that impairment loss is recognised in accordance with IAS 36 to the extent that the recoverable amount of the investment subsequently increases.

6.11 Section summary

		$
Statement of profit or loss and OCI	Profit before tax: Parent and subsidiary + associate's profit after tax	
	Tax: Parent and subsidiary only	
Statement of financial position	Interests in associated companies should be stated at:	
	Cost	X
	Share of post-acquisition retained earnings	X
		X

Also disclose group's share of post-acquisition reserves of associated companies and movements therein.

7 Joint arrangements

> IFRS 11 *Joint Arrangements* provides guidance on identifying, classifying and accounting for joint arrangements. A joint arrangement is classified as either a joint operation or a joint venture.

Two or more persons may decide to enter into a business arrangement together without wishing to form a long-term partnership. Usually the parties agree to place limitations on their activities, for example, a joint arrangement to manufacture and sell 'total eclipse of the sun' souvenirs could be limited by time, while a joint arrangement to buy and sell a bankrupt's inventory (a fairly common occurrence in practice) comes to an end when all the inventory has been sold.

Joint arrangements are often found when each party can **contribute in different ways** to the venture. For example, one party may provide finance, another purchases or manufactures goods, while a third offers marketing skills.

IFRS 11 *Joint Arrangements* was issued in June 2011 and replaced IAS 31 *Interests in Joint Ventures*. The new standard considers the different forms of joint arrangement how each form should be accounted for.

7.1 Definition of a joint arrangement

A joint arrangement is an arrangement of which two or more parties have **joint control**.

7.1.1 Joint control

Joint control is defined as 'the contractually agreed sharing of control of an arrangement which exists only when decisions about the relevant activities require the unanimous consent of the parties sharing control.'

Therefore:

- Where there is no contractual arrangement to establish joint control, then there is no joint control;
- Where unanimous consent is not required to make decisions then there is no joint control.

IFRS 11 makes additional points about joint arrangements and joint control:

- No single party controls the arrangement on its own.
- A party with joint control of an arrangement can prevent any of the other parties from controlling the arrangement.
- An arrangement can be a joint arrangement even if not all parties have joint control; some parties to a joint arrangement may participate but not have joint control.
- Judgement should be applied when assessing whether a party has joint control of an arrangement.

Example: Joint control

Three parties establish an arrangement. Adam has 50% of the voting rights in the arrangement, Brent has 30% and Cranberry has 20%. The contractual arrangement between the parties specifies that at least 75% of votes are required to make decisions about relevant activities of the arrangement.

In this case, Adam can block a decision, however does not control the arrangement alone as it needs the agreement of Brent. Therefore, Adam and Brent have joint control of the arrangement as decisions about relevant activities cannot be made without them agreeing. Cranberry is a participating party to the arrangement, however does not have joint control.

7.1.2 Contractual arrangement

IFRS 11 states that the contractual arrangement required to establish joint control may be evidenced in a number of ways including:

- A written contract between the controlling parties
- Minutes of discussions between controlling parties
- Incorporation of the arrangement in the articles or by-laws of the joint arrangement

The contractual arrangement will deal with issues such as:

(a) The purpose, activity and duration of the joint venture

(b) The appointment of the board of directors and voting rights of the controlling parties

(c) Capital contributions by the controlling parties

(d) The sharing by the controlling parties of the output, income, expenses or results of the joint venture

One party may be identified in the contractual arrangement as the operator or manager of the joint venture. This does not indicate that that party controls the joint arrangement, simply that they are acting within the financial and operating policies agreed by the controlling parties in accordance with the contractual arrangement.

If it is evident that the operator does have control of the activity then the arrangement is a subsidiary of the operator rather than a joint operation or venture.

7.2 Types of joint arrangement

IFRS 11 classes joint arrangements as either **joint operations** or **joint ventures**. The classification of a joint arrangement as a joint operation or a joint venture depends upon the rights and obligations of the parties to the arrangement.

- A **joint operation** is a joint arrangement whereby the parties that have joint control of the arrangement have **rights to the assets, and obligations for the liabilities**, relating to the arrangement.

- A **joint venture** is a joint arrangement whereby the parties that have joint control of the arrangement have **rights to the net assets** of the arrangement.

A joint arrangement that is not structured through a separate entity is always a joint operation; a joint arrangement that is structured through a separate entity may be either a joint operation or a joint venture.

Detailed guidance is provided in the appendices to IFRS 11 in order to help assess whether an arrangement is a joint operation or joint venture. The guidance requires that consideration is given to, for example, the wording contained within contractual arrangements.

7.3 Accounting for joint arrangements

7.3.1 Joint operations

IFRS 11 requires that a joint operator recognises line-by-line the following in relation to its interest in a joint operation:

(a) Its assets, including its share of any jointly held assets;
(b) Its liabilities, including its share of any jointly incurred liabilities;
(c) Its revenue from the sale of its share of the output arising from the joint operation;
(d) Its share of the revenue from the sale of the output by the joint operation; and
(e) Its expenses, including its share of any expenses incurred jointly.

This treatment is applicable in both the separate and consolidated financial statements of the joint operator.

7.3.2 Joint ventures

In its consolidated financial statements, IFRS 11 requires that a joint venturer recognises its interest in a joint venture as an investment and accounts for that investment using the equity method in accordance with IAS 28 *Investments in Associates and Joint Ventures* unless the entity is exempted from applying the equity method (see Section 6.1.1 which is also applicable to joint ventures).

In its separate financial statements, a joint venturer should account for its interest in a joint venture in accordance with IAS 27 *Separate Financial Statements* (see Section 9).

7.4 Applying IAS 28 to joint ventures

The consolidated statement of financial position is prepared by:

- Including the interest in the joint venture at cost plus share of post-acquisition total comprehensive income

- Including the group share of the post-acquisition total comprehensive income in group reserves

The consolidated statement of profit or loss and other comprehensive income will include:

- The group share of the joint venture's profit or loss
- The group share of the joint venture's other comprehensive income.

The use of the equity method should be **discontinued** from the date on which the joint venturer ceases to have joint control over, or have significant influence on, a joint venture.

7.4.1 Transactions between a joint venture and a joint venture

Upstream transactions

A joint venturer may **sell or contribute assets** to a joint venture so making a profit or loss. Any such gain or loss should, however, only be recognised to the extent that it reflects the substance of the transaction.

Therefore:

- Only the **gain** attributable to the interest of the other joint venturers should be recognised in the financial statements.
- The full amount of any **loss** should be recognised when the transaction shows evidence that the net realisable value of current assets is less than cost, or that there is an impairment loss.

Downstream transactions

When a joint venturer purchases assets from a joint venture, the joint venturer should not recognise its share of the profit made by the joint venture on the transaction in question until it resells the assets to an independent third party, ie until the profit is realised.

Losses should be treated in the same way, **except** losses should be recognised immediately if they represent a reduction in the net realisable value of current assets, or a permanent decline in the carrying amount of non-current assets.

Question — Inventories

Kirstan Co contributes inventories to a 50:50 joint venture it has undertaken with Pirstan Co. The recorded historical cost of the inventories is $2m.

What gain or loss should Kirstan Co recognise in its financial statements when the fair value (net realisable value) of the inventories is estimated at the date of transfer and recorded by the joint venture as:

(a) $2.2m?
(b) $1.8m?

Answer

(a) Kirstan Co has made a profit of $0.2m, but only 50% of this can be considered as realised, ie that part attributable to the other venturer. Kirstan Co should therefore recognise a gain of $0.1m.

(b) A loss of $0.2m has been made on the inventories, the entire amount of which should be recognised by Kirstan Co. It is known that the loss will be made, even though the inventories have not yet been sold, and so prudence requires that the full loss should be recognised.

7.4.2 Acquisition of an interest in a joint operation

Initially IFRS 11 did not provide any guidance on how to account for an interest in a joint operation that is also a business as defined by IFRS 3 *Business Combinations*.

As a result of this lack of guidance, diversity arose in practice. For example, when a joint operator purchases an interest for a price that is greater than the total of the fair values of the identifiable net assets of the operation (a premium), this may be recognised as a separate asset (ie goodwill) or is allocated to the identifiable assets on the basis of their relative fair values. Acquisition costs may be either capitalised or recognised as an expense.

An amendment to IFRS 11 in May 2014 clarified that a joint operator which acquires an interest in a joint operation which meets the definition of a business will be required to apply the relevant principles for accounting for a business combination in IFRS 3 and other standards, and to disclose the relevant information required by those standards.

8 Disclosure of interests in other entities

IFRS 12 requires disclosures in respect of the significant judgements and assumptions made when determining type of investment, interests in subsidiaries, interests in associates and interests in joint ventures.

IFRS 12 *Disclosure of Interests in Other Entities* was issued in 2011 collating the consolidated financial statement disclosure requirements in respect of subsidiaries, associates and joint arrangements into one standard.

The standard does not apply to the separate financial statements of the investor, which are instead covered by IAS 27 *Separate Financial Statements*.

The following sections list the disclosures required by IFRS 12.

8.1 Significant judgements and assumptions

An entity should disclose information about significant judgements and assumptions that it has made in determining:

1. That it has control of another entity.
2. That it has joint control over an arrangement.
3. That it has significant influence over another entity.
4. That a joint arrangement structured through a separate entity is either a joint operation or a joint venture.
5. That it is an investment entity.

8.2 Interests in subsidiaries

Information must be disclosed which enables users of the consolidated financial statements

(a) To understand the composition of the group and the interest that non-controlling interests have in the group's activities and cash flows

(b) To evaluate:

   (i) The nature and extent of significant restrictions on an entity's ability to access or use assets and settle liabilities of the group

   (ii) The nature of and changes in the risks associated with an entity's interests in consolidated structured entities

   (iii) The consequences of changes in an entity's ownership interest in a subsidiary that do not result in a loss of control (see Chapter 8)

   (iv) The consequences of losing control in a subsidiary during the reporting period (see Chapter 8)

8.3 Interests in joint arrangements and associates

An entity shall disclose information that enables users of the financial statements to evaluate:

(a) The nature, extent and financial effects of its interests in joint arrangements and associates, including the nature and effects of its contractual relationship with the other investors with joint control of, or significant influence over, joint arrangements and associates

(b) The nature of, and changes in, the risks associated with its interests in joint ventures and associates.

9 Separate financial statements of investor

FAST FORWARD

IAS 27 is applied when accounting for subsidiaries, associates and joint ventures in the separate financial statements of the investor. It requires that these investments are accounted for either at cost or in accordance with IFRS 9.

As part of the 'package' of consolidation standards issued in 2011, the IASB revised and renamed IAS 27 as *Separate Financial Statements.*

The revised standard is applied when accounting for investments in subsidiaries, associates and joint ventures when an entity elects, or is required to present separate financial statements.

Note that an investment entity which is required to account for all subsidiaries in accordance with IFRS 9 presents separate financial statements as its only financial statements.

9.1 Accounting treatment in separate statement of financial position

When separate financial statements are prepared by an investor, investments in subsidiaries, joint ventures and associates are accounted for either:

(a) At cost;
(b) In accordance with IFRS 9; or
(c) Using the equity method as described in IAS 28.

The same accounting must be applied to each category of investments.

Where investments are accounted for at cost, should they become classified as held for sale, they are accounted for in accordance with IFRS 5 *Non-current Assets Held for Sale and Discontinued Operations.*

An amendment to IAS 27 was issued in August 2014 which allows parent companies to use the equity method to value subsidiaries, joint ventures and associates in their own (separate) financial statements. The use of the equity method in this way was formerly permissible, but in 2003 the option was removed and all investments had to be accounted in accordance with financial asset rules (ie at cost or fair value).

9.2 Accounting treatment in separate statement of profit or loss and other comprehensive income

The investor should recognise a dividend from a subsidiary, associate or joint venture in profit or loss when its right to receive a dividend is established.

9.3 Disclosure requirements

IAS 27 requires the following disclosures in separate financial statements:

1. When an investor elects not to prepare consolidated financial statements and instead prepares separate financial statements, it must disclose:

    (i) The fact that the financial statements are separate financial statements and details of the exemption from consolidation
    (ii) A detailed list of investments in subsidiaries, associates and joint ventures

2. When consolidated financial statements are also prepared:

    (i) Details of the related consolidated financial statements
    (ii) The fact that the statements are separate financial statements and the reason why they are prepared if not required by law
    (iii) A detailed list of investments in subsidiaries, associates and joint ventures
    (iv) A description of the method used to account for the investments

3. When an investment entity prepares separate financial statements as its only financial statements, that fact is disclosed and IFRS 12 disclosures are also required.

10 Current developments

Although the IASB has recently completed an overhaul of its consolidations standards, it continues to make improvements through narrow scope amendments to the revised and new standards.

Chapter roundup

- The following statements are relevant:
  - IAS 27 *Separate Financial Statements*
  - IAS 28 *Investments in Associates and Joint Ventures*
  - IFRS 3 *Business Combinations*
  - IFRS 10 *Consolidated Financial Statements*
  - IFRS 11 *Joint Arrangements*
  - IFRS 12 *Disclosure of Interests in Other Entities*

- Investments are classified as subsidiaries, associates, joint arrangements or financial asset investments. The accounting treatment applied differs depending on the type of investment.

- The non-controlling interest may be measured **either at fair value or at the non-controlling interest's proportionate share of the acquiree's identifiable net assets**.

- **IFRS 10 *Consolidated Financial Statements*** provides accounting guidance on the consolidation procedures to be applied when preparing the combined financial statements of a parent and its subsidiaries.

- **Goodwill arising on consolidation** is the excess of the fair value of the consideration transferred plus the non-controlling interest over the fair value of the identifiable assets and liabilities acquired.

- **IAS 28** deals with identifying and accounting for associates.

- The **equity method** should be applied in the consolidated financial statements:
  - **Statement of financial position**: investment in associate measured at cost plus (or minus) the group's share of the associate's post-acquisition retained profits (or losses)
  - **Statement of profit or loss and other comprehensive income**: group share of associate's profit after tax.

- IFRS 11 *Joint Arrangements* provides guidance on identifying, classifying and accounting for joint arrangements. A joint arrangement is classified as either a joint operation or a joint venture.

- IFRS 12 requires disclosures in respect of the significant judgements and assumptions made when determining type of investment, interests in subsidiaries, interests in associates and interests in joint ventures.

- IAS 27 is applied when accounting for subsidiaries, associates and joint ventures in the separate financial statements of the investor. It requires that these investments are accounted for either at cost or in accordance with IFRS 9.

Quick quiz

1. What are the three elements of control within the definition of control as defined within IFRS 10 *Consolidated Financial Statements*?

2. If a company holds 20% or more of the voting shares of another company, it is presumed to have significant influence. True or false?

3. What is significant influence?

4. What is a non-controlling interest?

5. How is the non-controlling interest on acquisition to be valued?

6. How should an investment in a subsidiary be accounted for in the separate financial statements of the parent?

7. Describe the requirement of IFRS 3 in relation to the remeasurement of a subsidiary company's assets.

8. When land and buildings are acquired in a business combination, how should they normally be measured?

9. Which party to a business combination is the acquirer?

10. An associate is a _____ in which an investor has _____, but which is not a subsidiary or a joint venture of the investor. *Complete the blanks.*

11. What is the effect of the equity method on the statement of profit or loss and other comprehensive income and the statement of financial position?

12. Joint control exists where shared control is established in a _____. It exists only where decisions about the relevant activities require the _____ of the parties sharing control.

13. What forms of evidence of a contractual agreement might exist?

14. How should a joint venturer account for its share of a joint venture?

Answers to quick quiz

1. An investor controls an investee if the investor has:
   (i) Power over the investee
   (ii) Exposure, or rights, to variable returns from its involvement with the investee
   (iii) The ability to use its power over the investee to affect the amount of the investor's returns.

2. True.

3. The power to participate in, but not to control, the financial and operating decisions of the investee.

4. The part of the profit or loss and the net assets attributable to interests not owned by the parent.

5. Either at fair value or at the non-controlling interest's proportionate share of the acquiree's identifiable net assets.

6. (a) At cost or
   (b) Under IFRS 9 or
   (c) Using the equity method as described in IAS 28.

7. Fair value is not affected by the acquirer's intentions. Therefore only intentions after acquisition are reflected in the statement of comprehensive income after acquisition.

8. At fair value, by reference to their market value.

9. The acquirer is the entity that obtains control of the other combining entities or businesses.

10. An associates is an **entity** in which an investor has **significant influence**, but which is not a subsidiary or a joint venture of the investor.

11. (a) *Statement of profit or loss and other comprehensive income.* Investing entity includes its share of the earnings of the associate, by adding its share of profit after tax.

    (b) *Statement of financial position.* Investment in associates is included in assets at cost adjusted by the relevant share of post-acquisition retained profits/losses.

12. Joint control exists where shared control is established in a contractual agreement. It exists only where decisions about the relevant activities require the unanimous consent of the parties sharing control.

13. - Written contract between the parties
    - Minutes of discussions between the venturers
    - incorporation of the arrangement in the articles or by-laws of the joint arrangement

14. Equity accounting should be applied in accordance with IAS 28 (2011).

PART B BUSINESS COMBINATIONS AND GROUP FINANCIAL STATEMENTS

End of chapter question

Akkeal (AIA May 2004 – amended)

The following are the income statements for four limited liability companies for the financial year ended 31 March 20X4.

STATEMENTS OF PROFIT OR LOSS AND OTHER COMPREHENSIVE INCOME FOR THE YEAR ENDED 31 MARCH 20X4

	Akkeal $'000	Belloan $'000	Curtyn $'000	Dojin $'000
Revenue	16,400	8,870	13,800	11,300
Cost of sales	(5,600)	(4,200)	(5,900)	(8,100)
Gross profit	10,800	4,670	7,900	3,200
Operating expenses	(5,780)	(3,370)	(4,700)	(1,540)
Profit from operations	5,020	1,300	3,200	1,660
Dividends receivable	1,247	600	0	0
Investment income	233	97	140	0
Finance cost	(333)	(240)	(350)	0
Profit before taxation	6,167	1,757	2,990	1,660
Tax	(1,800)	(500)	(700)	(400)
Profit for the period	4,367	1,257	2,290	1,260

The following additional information is available:

- Belloan is a subsidiary of Akkeal. Akkeal owns 60% of the ordinary shares in Belloan.

- Curtyn is an associate of Akkeal. Akkeal owns 30% of the ordinary shares in Curtyn.

- Dojin is a joint venture between Akkeal and three other companies which each own 25% of the ordinary shares in Dojin and have established joint control via written agreement.

- During the financial year ended 31 March 20X4 Belloan made sales to Akkeal. The invoice value of these sales to Akkeal was $1,500,000. This represented cost to Belloan plus a mark-up of 20%. 10% of these goods remained unsold at 31 March 2004.

- All goodwill acquired in business combinations had been fully written off by 1 April 20X3.

- In each company each ordinary share carries one vote and there are no voting rights other than those attaching to the ordinary shares.

- Akkeal is a publicly listed company and its issued ordinary share capital throughout the year was 20 million shares.

- Dividends paid by the four companies during the year ended 31 March 20X4 were:

    Akkeal: Ordinary dividends paid $2,000,000
    Belloan: Ordinary dividends paid $700,000
    Curtyn: Ordinary dividends $1,500,000
    Dojin: Ordinary dividends $880,000

Required

Prepare the consolidated statement of profit or loss and other comprehensive income of Akkeal in accordance with IFRS 10 *Consolidated Financial Statements*, IAS 28 (2011) *Investments in Associates and Joint Ventures*. You should

- Include a figure for earnings per share calculated and disclosed in accordance with IAS 33 *Earnings per Share*.

(25 marks)

Complex groups

Topic list	Syllabus reference
1 Multi-entity structures	13.2
2 Consolidating sub-subsidiaries	13.2
3 Direct holdings in sub-subsidiaries	13.2
4 Associates held by subsidiaries	13.2

Introduction

This chapter introduces the first of several more complicated consolidation topics. The best way to tackle these questions is to be logical and to carry out the consolidation on a **step by step** basis.

In questions of this nature, it is very helpful to sketch a **diagram of the group structure**, as we have done. This clarifies the situation and it should point you in the right direction: always sketch the group structure as your first working and double check it against the information in the question.

PART B BUSINESS COMBINATIONS AND GROUP FINANCIAL STATEMENTS

1 Multi-entity structures

FAST FORWARD

When a holding company has **several subsidiaries**, the consolidated statement of financial position shows a single figure for non-controlling interests and for goodwill arising on consolidation. In cases where there are several subsidiary companies, the technique is to open up a single non-controlling interest working and a columnar goodwill working.

1.1 Introduction

In this section we shall consider how the principles of the preparation of the statement of financial position may be applied to more complex structures of companies within a group.

(a)   Several subsidiary companies

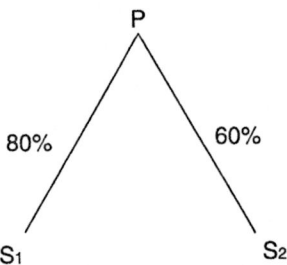

You have already seen this type of structure in your previous studies.

(b)   Sub-subsidiaries

P holds a controlling interest in S which in turn holds a controlling interest in SS. SS is therefore a subsidiary of a subsidiary of P, in other words, a **sub-subsidiary** of P.

(c)   **Direct holdings in sub-subsidiaries: 'D' shaped groups**

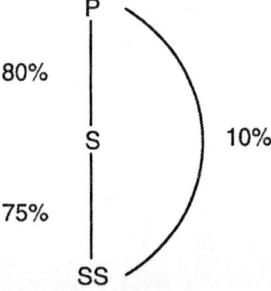

In this example, SS is a sub-subsidiary of P with additional shares held directly by P.

In practice, groups are usually larger, and therefore more complex, but the procedures for consolidation of large groups will not differ from those we shall now describe for smaller ones.

1.2 A parent company which has several subsidiaries

Where a company P has several subsidiaries S_1, S_2, S_3 and so on, the technique for consolidation is exactly as previously described. **Cancellation** is from the holding company, which has assets of investments in subsidiaries S_1, S_2, S_3, to each of the several subsidiaries.

The consolidated statement of financial position will show:

(a) A single figure for **non-controlling interest**; and
(b) A single figure for **goodwill** arising.

A single working should be used for each of the constituents of the consolidated statement of financial position: one working for goodwill, one for non-controlling interest, one for retained earnings (reserves), and so on.

1.3 Sub-subsidiaries

A slightly different problem arises when there are sub-subsidiaries in the group, which is how should we **identify the non-controlling interest** in the retained earnings of the group? Suppose P owns 80% of the equity of S, and that S in turn owns 60% of the equity of SS.

It would appear that in this situation:

(a) P owns 80% of 60% = 48% of SS
(b) The non-controlling interest in S owns 20% of 60% = 12% of SS
(c) The non-controlling interest in SS itself owns the remaining 40% of the SS equity

SS is nevertheless a **sub-subsidiary** of P, because it is a subsidiary of S which in turn is a subsidiary of P. The chain of control thus makes SS a sub-subsidiary of P which owns only 48% of its equity.

The total non-controlling interest in SS may be checked by considering a **dividend** of $100 paid by SS where S then distributes its share of this dividend in full to its own shareholders.

		$
S will receive	$60	
P will receive	80% × $60 =	48
Leaving for the total non-controlling interest in SS		52
		100

Effective interest

Top owns 60% of the equity of Middle Co, which owns 75% of the equity of Bottom Co. Calculate Top Co's effective holding in Bottom Co.

Answer

Top owns 60% of 75% of Bottom Co = 45%.

PART B BUSINESS COMBINATIONS AND GROUP FINANCIAL STATEMENTS

1.4 Date of effective control

The date the sub-subsidiary comes under the **control of the holding company** is either:

(a) The date P acquired S if S already holds shares in SS; or
(b) If S acquires shares in SS later, then that later date.

The dates of acquisition and the order in which the group is built up will make a difference to how we calculate goodwill and non-controlling interest.

1.5 Pro-forma goodwill calculation

Before we progress to the complex group calculations, here is a reminder of how IFRS 3 *Business Combinations* requires goodwill to be measured.

	$
Consideration transferred	X
Amount of any non-controlling interests	X
Fair value of acquirer's previously held equity interest	X
Less net acquisition-date fair value of identifiable assets acquired and liabilities assumed	X
	X

While the above layout reflects the wording of the standard, for the purposes of your workings in the examination, the following layout is recommended.

		Group	NCI
	$	$	$
Consideration transferred/Fair value of non-controlling interests		X	X
Less: Net fair value of identifiable assets acquired and liabilities assumed	X		
× Group/NCI %		(X)	(X)
		X	X
		X	

The NCI (non-controlling interest) column is only needed if the NCI interest is to be measured at fair value. As we saw in Chapter 6, when the NCI is measured at fair value, goodwill arises that is attributable to the NCI.

2 Consolidating sub-subsidiaries

FAST FORWARD

> When dealing with **sub-subsidiaries,** you will need to calculate effective interest owned by the group and by the non-controlling interest.
>
> The **date of acquisition** is important when dealing with sub-subsidiaries.
>
> Remember that it is the post-acquisition reserves from a **group perspective** which are relevant.

Exam focus point

> Don't panic when a question seems very complicated – sketch the group structure and analyse the information in the question methodically.

The basic consolidation method is as follows:

(a) **Net assets**: show what the group controls.
(b) **Equity (capital and reserves)**: show who owns the net assets included elsewhere in the statement of financial position. Reserves (retained earnings), therefore, are based on **effective holdings**.

2.1 Example: Subsidiary acquired first

The draft statements of financial position of P Co, S Co and SS Co on 30 June 20X7 were as follows:

	P Co $	S Co $	SS Co $
Assets			
Non-current assets			
Property, plant and equipment	105,000	125,000	180,000
Investments, at cost			
80,000 shares in S Co	120,000	–	–
60,000 shares in SS Co	–	110,000	–
Current assets	80,000	70,000	60,000
	305,000	305,000	240,000
Equity and liabilities			
Equity			
Ordinary shares of $1 each	80,000	100,000	100,000
Retained earnings	195,000	170,000	115,000
	275,000	270,000	215,000
Payables	30,000	35,000	25,000
	305,000	305,000	240,000

P Co acquired its shares in S Co on 1 July 20X4 when the reserves of S Co stood at $40,000; and

S Co acquired its shares in SS Co on 1 July 20X5 when the reserves of SS Co stood at $50,000.

It is the group's policy to measure the non-controlling interest at acquisition at its proportionate share of the fair value of the subsidiary's net assets.

Required

Prepare the draft consolidated statement of financial position of P Group at 30 June 20X7.

Note. Assume no impairment of goodwill.

Solution

This is **two acquisitions** from the point of view of the P group. In 20X4, the group buys 80% of S. Then in 20X5 S (which is now part of the P group) buys 60% of SS.

P buys 80% of S, then S (80% of S from the group's point of view) buys 60% of SS.

Having calculated the non-controlling interest and the P group interest (see working 1 below), the workings can be constructed. You should, however, note the following.

(a) Group structure working (see working 1).

(b) **Goodwill working**: compare the costs of investments with the effective group interests acquired (80% of S Co and 48% of SS Co).

(c) **Non-controlling interest working**: bring in the total non-controlling interests in S Co's share capital and retained earnings (20%), and the total non-controlling interests in SS Co's share capital and retained earnings (52%).

(d) **Retained earnings working**: bring in the share of S Co's and SS Co's post-acquisition retained earnings in the normal way.

PART B BUSINESS COMBINATIONS AND GROUP FINANCIAL STATEMENTS

1 Group structure

Effective interests in SS:
P Group (80% × 60%) = 48%
NCI = 52%

2 Goodwill

	P in S		S in SS	
	$	$	$	$
Consideration transferred		120,000	(80% × 110,000)	88,000
Fair value of identifiable NA acquired:				
Share capital	100,000		100,000	
Retained earnings	40,000		50,000	
	140,000		150,000	
Group share	80%		48%	
		(112,000)		(72,000)
		8,000		16,000
				24,000

3 Non-controlling interests

	S	SS
	$	$
Net assets per Q	270,000	215,000
Less investment in SS	(110,000)	–
	160,000	215,000
	× 20%	× 52%
	32,000	111,800
	$ 143,800	

Note. The cost of the investment in SS Co must be split between the non-controlling interest and the parent company. Only the latter is shown in the goodwill workings to ensure that we have only P Co's share of the goodwill arising in the S Co subgroup appearing in the consolidated statement of financial position. This is done by taking the group share of the subsidiary's 'cost' in the goodwill working and by deducting the cost from the net assets allocated to the non-controlling interests.

4 Retained earnings

	P Co	S Co	SS Co
	$	$	$
Per question	195,000	170,000	115,000
Pre-acquisition		(40,000)	(50,000)
Post-acquisition		130,000	65,000
Group share:			
In S Co ($130,000 × 80%)	104,000		
In SS Co ($65,000 × 48%)	31,200		
Group retained earnings	330,200		

P CO
CONSOLIDATED STATEMENT OF FINANCIAL POSITION AT 30 JUNE 20X7

	$
Assets	
Non-current assets	
Property, plant and equipment ($105,000 + $125,000 + $180,000)	410,000
Goodwill (W2)	24,000
Current assets ($80,000 + $70,000 + $60,000)	210,000
	644,000
Equity	
Ordinary shares of $1 each fully paid	80,000
Retained earnings (W4)	330,200
	410,200
Non-controlling interest (W3)	143,800
	554,000
Payables ($30,000 + $35,000 + $25,000)	90,000
	644,000

2.2 Example: Subsidiary acquired first: Non-controlling interest at fair value

Now let us consider the impact on the calculations if the full goodwill method is applied.

The draft statements of financial position of P Co, S Co and SS Co on 30 June 20X7 were as follows.

	P Co $	S Co $	SS Co $
Assets			
Non-current assets			
Property, plant and equipment	105,000	125,000	180,000
Investments, at cost			
80,000 shares in S Co	120,000	–	–
60,000 shares in SS Co	–	110,000	–
Current assets	80,000	70,000	60,000
	305,000	305,000	240,000
Equity and liabilities			
Equity			
Ordinary shares of $1 each	80,000	100,000	100,000
Retained earnings	195,000	170,000	115,000
	275,000	270,000	215,000
Payables	30,000	35,000	25,000
	305,000	305,000	240,000

P Co acquired its shares in S Co on 1 July 20X4 when the reserves of S Co stood at $40,000; and S Co acquired its shares in SS Co on 1 July 20X5 when the reserves of SS Co stood at $50,000.

It is the group's policy to measure the non-controlling interest at fair value at the date of acquisition. The fair value of the non-controlling interest in S on 1 July 20X4 was $29,000. The fair value of the 52% non-controlling interest in SS on 1 July 20X5 was $80,000.

Required

Prepare the draft consolidated statement of financial position of P Group at 30 June 20X7.

Note. Assume no impairment of goodwill.

Solution

The main difference from the example in 2.1 above is that extra columns are needed in the goodwill calculation for the goodwill attributable to the non-controlling interest. As explained in Chapter 6, the goodwill attributable to the non-controlling interest is also added to the NCI figure at the year end.

P CO
CONSOLIDATED STATEMENT OF FINANCIAL POSITION AT 30 JUNE 20X7

	$
Assets	
Non-current assets	
Property, plant and equipment (as before)	410,000
Goodwill (W2)	27,000
Current assets (as before)	210,000
	647,000
Equity	
Ordinary shares of $1 each fully paid	80,000
Retained earnings (W4)	330,200
3	410,200
Non-controlling interest (W3)	146,800
	557,000
Payables (as before)	90,000
	647,000

1   *Group structure*

Effective interests in SS:
P Group (80% × 60%) = 48%
NCI = 52%

2   *Goodwill*

	P in S				S in SS	
	Group		NCI		Group	NCI
	$	$	$	$	$	$
Consideration transferred/ FV NCI		120,000		29,000 (80% × 110,000)	88,000	80,000
Fair value of identifiable net assets acquired						
Share capital	100,000				100,000	
Retained earnings	40,000				50,000	
	140,000				150,000	
Group/NCI Share	(80%)		(20%)	(48%)		(52%)
		(112,000)	(28,000)		(72,000)	(78,000)
		8,000	1,000		16,000	2,000

$27,000

3 Non-controlling interests

The non-controlling interest working in this example has one extra step: adding on the non-controlling interest in goodwill as calculated in working 2. The cost of investment in SS is again deducted as the NCI is being calculated on the net assets that have been consolidated (see note above).

	S $	SS $
Net assets per Q	270,000	215,000
Less investment in SS	(110,000)	-
	160,000	215,000
	× 20%	× 52%
	32,000	111,800
Non-controlling interests in goodwill (W2)	1,000	2,000
	33,000	113,800

146,800

4 Retained earnings

	P Co $	S Co $	SS Co $
Per question	195,000	170,000	115,000
Pre-acquisition		(40,000)	(50,000)
Post-acquisition		130,000	65,000
Group share:			
In S Co ($130,000 × 80%)	104,000		
In SS Co ($65,000 × 48%)	31,200		
Group retained earnings	330,200		

2.3 Date of acquisition

Care must be taken when consolidating sub-subsidiaries, because (usually) either:

(a) The parent company acquired the subsidiary **before** the subsidiary bought the sub-subsidiary (as in the examples above); **or**

(b) The parent holding company acquired the subsidiary **after** the subsidiary bought the sub-subsidiary.

The rule to remember here, when considering pre- and post-acquisition profits, is that we are only interested in the consolidated results of the **parent company**. We will use the example above to demonstrate the required approach.

2.4 Example: Sub-subsidiary acquired first

Using the figures in Section 2.1, assume that:

(a) S Co purchased its holding in SS Co on 1 July 20X4
(b) P Co purchased its holding in S Co on 1 July 20X5

The retained earnings figures on the respective dates of acquisition are the same, but on the date P Co purchased its holding in S Co, the retained earnings of SS Co were $60,000.

In this version, there is only **one** acquisition from the perspective of P group: ie on 1 July 20X5 it acquires S and SS as a 'job lot'. Putting it another way, it acquires a **pre-existing group**.

So we do **one** calculation of goodwill looking at what P paid – ie the $120,000, versus what it acquired – ie 80% of the **consolidated** net assets of S and 48% of the **consolidated** net assets of SS.

Solution

The point here is that SS Co only became part of the P group on 1 July 20X5, **not** on 1 July 20X4. This means that only the retained earnings of SS Co arising **after** 1 July 20X5 can be included in the post-acquisition reserves of P Co group. Goodwill arising on the acquisition will be calculated by comparing the cost of the investment to the consolidated separable net assets of S (as represented by share capital and consolidated retained earnings, net of all goodwill).

P CO
CONSOLIDATED STATEMENT OF FINANCIAL POSITION AS AT 30 JUNE 20X7

	$
Non-current assets	
Property, plant and equipment (as before)	410,000
Goodwill (W2)	19,200
	429,200
Current assets (as before)	210,000
	639,200
Equity and liabilities	
Ordinary shares $1 each, fully paid	80,000
Retained earnings (W4)	325,400
	405,400
Non-controlling interest (W3)	143,800
	549,200
Payables (as before)	90,000
	639,200

Workings

1 *Group structure*

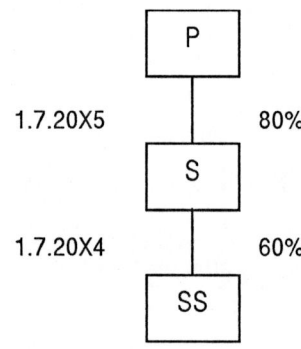

P owns an effective interest of 48% in SS. NCI in SS is 52%.

2 *Goodwill*

The working should be set out as:

		$	$
Consideration transferred			120,000
Less:			
Fair value of identifiable assets and liabilities acquired			
S	Share capital	100,000	
	Pre-acquisition retained earnings	40,000	
	Less investment in SS	(110,000)	
		30,000	
	80%		(24,000)

Note. Cost of investment in sub-sub is always deducted because we are looking at the net assets that would actually appear in the consolidated SOFP

7: COMPLEX GROUPS

			$	$
SS	Share capital		100,000	
	Pre-acquisition retained earnings		60,000	
			160,000	
		48%		(76,800)
				19,200

3 Non-controlling interests

The cost of investment in SS is again deducted as the NCI is being calculated on the net assets that have been consolidated (see note above).

	S $	SS $
Net assets per Q	270,000	215,000
Less investment in SS	(110,000)	–
	160,000	215,000
	× 20%	× 52%
	32,000	111,800

$ 143,800

4 Retained earnings

	$
P Co (as before)	195,000
S Co (as before)	104,000
SS Co (115 – 60) × 48%	26,400
	325,400

2.5 Example: Sub-subsidiary acquired first: Non-controlling interest at fair value

Now we shall reconsider the example in Section 2.4 above, but this time assume that the group measures the non-controlling interest at a fair value of $95,000 on the date of acquisition.

The revised goodwill and non-controlling interest workings are as follows:

Goodwill

The working should be set out as:

		$	Group $	NCI $
Consideration transferred/FV of the NCI			120,000	95,000
Less:				
Fair value of identifiable assets and liabilities acquired				
S	Share capital	100,000		
	Pre-acquisition retained earnings	40,000		
	Less investment in SS	(110,000)		
		30,000		
	80%/20%		(24,000)	(6,000)
SS	Share capital	100,000		
	Pre-acquisition retained earnings	60,000		
		160,000		
	48%/52%		(76,800)	(83,200)
			9,200	5,800
Total goodwill				25,000

PART B BUSINESS COMBINATIONS AND GROUP FINANCIAL STATEMENTS

Non-controlling interests

	S $	SS $
Net assets per Q	270,000	215,000
Less investment in SS	(110,000)	–
	160,000	215,000
	× 20%	× 52%
	32,000	111,800

	$
	143,800
Goodwill	5,800
NCI	149,600

Remember – the rest of the balances in the consolidated statement of financial position are the same, regardless of which method is used to measure the non-controlling interest.

Question — Sub-subsidiary

The statements of financial position of Antelope Co, Yak Co and Zebra Co at 31 March 20X4 are summarised as follows.

	Antelope Co $	Antelope Co $	Yak Co $	Yak Co $	Zebra Co $	Zebra Co $
Assets						
Non-current assets						
Freehold property		100,000		100,000		–
Plant and machinery		210,000		80,000		3,000
		310,000		180,000		3,000
Investments in subsidiaries						
Shares, at cost	110,000		6,200		–	
Loan account	–		3,800		–	
Current accounts	10,000		12,200		–	
		120,000		22,200		3,000
Current assets						
Inventories	170,000		20,500		15,000	
Receivables	140,000		50,000		1,000	
Cash at bank	60,000		16,500		4,000	
		370,000		87,000		20,000
		800,000		289,200		23,000
Equity and liabilities						
Equity						
$1 Ordinary share capital	200,000		100,000		10,000	
Retained earnings	379,600		129,200		(1,000)	
		579,600		229,200		9,000
Current liabilities						
Trade payables	160,400		40,200		800	
Due to Antelope Co	–		12,800		600	
Due to Yak Co	–				12,600	
Taxation	60,000		7,000		–	
		220,400		60,000		14,000
		800,000		289,200		23,000

Antelope Co acquired 75% of the shares of Yak Co in 20X1 when the credit balance on the retained earnings of that company was $40,000. No dividends have been paid since that date. Yak Co acquired

80% of the shares in Zebra Co in 20X3 when there was a debit balance on the retained earnings of that company of $3,000. Subsequently $500 was received by Zebra Co and credited to its retained earnings, representing the recovery of a bad debt written off before the acquisition of Zebra's shares by Yak Co.

During the year to 31 March 20X4 Yak Co purchased inventory from Antelope Co for $20,000 which included a profit mark-up of $4,000 for Antelope Co. At 31 March 20X4 one half of this amount was still held in the inventories of Yak Co. Group accounting policies are to make a full allowance for unrealised intra-group profits.

It is the group's policy to measure the non-controlling interest at its proportionate share of the fair value of the subsidiary's net assets.

Prepare the draft consolidated statement of financial position of Antelope Co at 31 March 20X4. (Assume no impairment of goodwill.)

State how your answer would differ if the non-controlling interest were measured at fair value given the following information:

- The fair value of a share in Y immediately prior to its acquisition by A was $1.50
- The fair value of a share in Z immediately prior to its acquisition by Y was 75c

Answer

Effective interests in Z:
A Group (75% × 80%) = 60%
NCI = 40%

Workings

1 Goodwill

	A in Y		Y in Z	
	$	$	$	$
Consideration transferred		110,000	(75% × 6,200)	4,650
Fair value of identifiable NA acquired:				
Share capital	100,000		10,000	
Retained earnings: ($3,000) + $500	40,000		(2,500)	
	140,000		7,500	
Group share	75%		60%	
		(105,000)		(4,500)
		5,000		150

$5,150

PART B BUSINESS COMBINATIONS AND GROUP FINANCIAL STATEMENTS

2 *Non-controlling interests*

	Yak $	Zebra $
Net assets per Q	229,200	9,000
Less investment in Zebra	(6,200)	–
	223,000	9,000
	× 25%	× 40%
	55,750	3,600

59,350

3 *Retained earnings*

	Antelope $	Yak $	Zebra $
Per question	379,600	129,200	(1,000)
Adjustment bad debt recovery			(500)
Pre-acquisition profit/losses		(40,000)	3,000
Post-acquisition profits		89,200	1,500
Group share			
In Yak ($89,200 × 75%)	66,900		
In Zebra ($1,500 × 60%)	900		
Unrealised profit in inventories Sitting in parent ($4,000) × ½)	(2,000)		
Group retained earnings	445,400		

ANTELOPE CO
CONSOLIDATED STATEMENT OF FINANCIAL POSITION AS AT 31 MARCH 20X4

	$	$
Assets		
Non-current assets		
Freehold property ($100,000 + $100,000)		200,000
Plant and machinery ($210,000 + $80,000 + $3,000)		293,000
		493,000
Goodwill (W1)		5,150
		498,150
Current assets		
Inventories (($170,000 + $20,500 + $15,000 – 2,000)	203,500	
Receivables ($140,000 + $50,000 + $1,000)	191,000	
Cash at bank ($60,000 + $16,500 + $4,000)	80,500	
		475,000
		973,150
Equity and liabilities		
Equity		
Ordinary share capital		200,000
Retained earnings (W3)		445,400
Shareholders' funds		645,400
Non-controlling interests (W2)		59,350
		704,750
Current liabilities		
Trade payables ($160,400 + $40,200 + $800)	201,400	
Taxation ($60,000 + $7,000)	67,000	
		268,400
		973,150

If Antelope adopted a policy of measuring the non-controlling interest at fair value, workings 1 and 2 would change as follows:

1   Goodwill

	A in Y		Y in Z		
	$	$	$	$	$
Consideration transferred	110,000		(75% × 6,200)	4,650	
Fair value of NCI					
25,000 shares × $1.50		37,500			
4,000 shares × 75c					3,000
Fair value of identifiable NA acquired:					
Share capital	100,000		10,000		
Retained earnings: ($3,000) + $500	40,000		(2,500)		
	140,000		7,500		
Group share 75%/25%	(105,000)	(35,000)	60%/40% (4,500)		(3,000)
	5,000	2,500		150	–

7,650 (total brace over Y in Z columns)

2   Non-controlling interests

	Yak	Zebra
	$	$
Net assets per Q	229,200	9,000
Less investment in Zebra	(6,200)	–
	223,000	9,000
	× 25%	× 40%
	55,750	3,600
NCI goodwill	2,500	–
	58,250	3,600

61,850

Therefore reported goodwill would be $7,650 and the non-controlling interest would be $61,850. All other amounts in the consolidated statement of financial position would remain the same.

2.6 Section summary

You should follow this **step by step approach** in all questions using the single-stage method. This applies to Section 3 below as well.

Step 1   Sketch the **group structure** and check it to the question.

Step 2   **Add details** to the sketch of dates of acquisition, holdings acquired (percentage and nominal values) and cost.

Step 3   **Goodwill working**: compare costs of investment with the **effective** group interests acquired.

Step 4   **Non-controlling interest working**: total NCI in subsidiary plus total NCI in sub-subsidiary.

Step 5   **Reserves working**: include the group share of subsidiary and sub-subsidiary post-acquisition retained earnings (effective holdings again).

Step 6   Prepare the **consolidated statement of financial position** (and statement of profit or loss and other comprehensive income if required).

PART B BUSINESS COMBINATIONS AND GROUP FINANCIAL STATEMENTS

3 Direct holdings in sub-subsidiaries

Consider the following structure, sometimes called a **'D-shaped' group**.

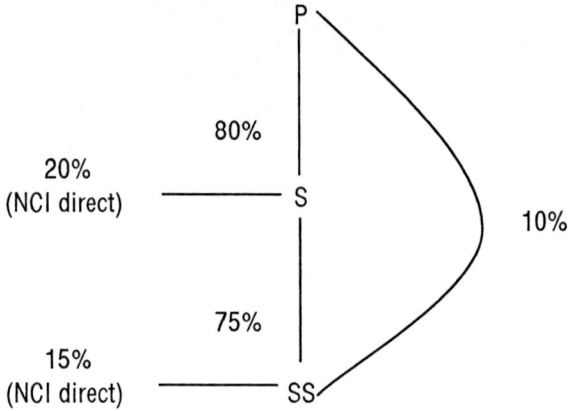

In the structure above, there is:

(a)	A **direct** non-controlling share in S of		20%
(b)	A **direct** non-controlling share in SS of	15%	
(c)	An **indirect** non-controlling share in SS of 20% × 75% =	15%	
			30%

The effective interest in SS is:

Group 80% × 75% indirect	=	60%
Direct		10%
		70%
∴ NCI		30%
		100%

Having ascertained the structure and non-controlling interests, proceed as for a typical sub-subsidiary situation.

  Question   'D' shaped group

The draft statements of financial position of Hulk Co, Molehill Co and Pimple Co as at 31 May 20X5 are as follows.

	Hulk Co		Molehill Co		Pimple Co	
	$	$	$	$	$	$
Assets						
Non-current assets						
Property, plant and equipment		90,000		60,000		60,000
Investments in subsidiaries(cost)						
Shares in Molehill Co	90,000		–		–	
Shares in Pimple Co	25,000		42,000		–	
		115,000		42,000		–
		205,000		102,000		60,000
Current assets		40,000		50,000		40,000
		245,000		152,000		100,000

7: COMPLEX GROUPS

	Hulk Co		Molehill Co		Pimple Co	
	$	$	$	$	$	$
Equity and liabilities						
Equity						
Ordinary shares $1	100,000		50,000		50,000	
Retained earnings	45,000		32,000		25,000	
Other reserves	50,000		20,000		–	
		195,000		102,000		75,000
Non-current liabilities						
12% loan		–		10,000		–
		195,000		112,000		75,000
Current liabilities						
Payables		50,000		40,000		25,000
		245,000		152,000		100,000

(a) Hulk Co acquired 60% of the shares in Molehill on 1 January 20X3 when the balance on that company's retained earnings was $8,000 (credit) and there were no other reserves.

(b) On 1 January 20X4 Hulk acquired 20% of the shares of Pimple Co and Molehill acquired 60% of the shares of Pimple Co when that company's retained earnings stood at $15,000.

(c) There has been no payment of dividends by either Molehill or Pimple since they became subsidiaries.

(d) There was no impairment of goodwill.

(e) It is the group's policy to measure the non-controlling interest at acquisition at fair value. The fair value of the non-controlling interest in Molehill at acquisition was $45,000; the fair value of a share in Pimple immediately prior to the acquisition date was $1.75.

Required

Prepare the consolidated statement of financial position of Hulk Co as at 31 May 20X5.

Answer

The direct non-controlling interest in Molehill Co is	40%
The direct non-controlling interest in Pimple Co is	20%
The indirect non-controlling interest in Pimple Co is (40% of 60%)	24%
The total non-controlling interest in Pimple Co is	44%

The group share of Molehill Co is 60% and of Pimple Co is (100 – 44)% = 56%

PART B BUSINESS COMBINATIONS AND GROUP FINANCIAL STATEMENTS

Workings

1 Goodwill

    Hulk in Molehill

		Group $	NCI $
Consideration transferred/fair value of NCI		90,000	45,000
Fair value of net assets acquired			
share capital	50,000		
Retained earnings	8,000		
	58,000 × 60% /40%	(34,800)	(23,200)
		55,200	21,800

Molehill/Hulk in Pimple

		Group $	NCI $
Consideration transferred by Molehill (60% × 42,000)		25,200	
Consideration transferred by Hulk		25,000	
Fair value of NCI (44% × 50,000 × $1.75)			38,500
		50,200	
Fair value of net assets acquired			
Share capital	50,000		
Retained earnings	15,000		
	65,000	(36,400)	(28,600)
	× 56% / 44%		
		13,800	9,900

Total goodwill: 55,200 + 21,800 + 13,800 + 9,900 = 100,700

2 Non-controlling interests

	Molehill $	Pimple $
Net assets per question	102,000	75,000
Investment in Pimple	(42,000)	–
	60,000	75,000
	× 40%	× 44%
	24,000	33,000
Goodwill	21,800	9,900
	45,800	42,900

$88,700

3 Retained earnings

	Hulk $	Molehill $	Pimple $
Per question	45,000	32,000	25,000
Pre-acquisition profits		(8,000)	(15,000)
Post-acquisition retained earnings		24,000	10,000
Group share:			
In Molehill ($24,000 × 60%)	14,400		
In Pimple ($10,000 × 56%)	5,600		
Group retained earnings	65,000		

4   Other reserves

	$
Hulk Co	50,000
Molehill Co: all post-acquisition ($20,000 × 60%)	12,000
	62,000

HULK CO
CONSOLIDATED STATEMENT OF FINANCIAL POSITION AS AT 31 MAY 20X8

	$	$
Assets		
Non-current assets		
Property, plant and equipment ($90,000 + $60,000 + $60,000)	210,000	
Goodwill (W1)	100,700	
		310,700
Current assets ($40,000 + $50,000 + $40,000)		130,000
		440,700
Equity and liabilities		
Equity		
Ordinary shares $1	100,000	
Retained earnings (W3)	65,000	
Other reserves (W4)	62,000	
Shareholders' funds	227,000	
Non-controlling interests (W2)	88,700	
		315,700
Non-current liabilities		
12% loan		10,000
		325,700
Current liabilities		
Payables ($50,000 + $40,000 + $25,000)		115,000
		440,700

4 Associates held by subsidiaries

Now let us consider a vertical group where the subsidiary holds an associate rather than a sub-subsidiary:

Here, P controls S which has a significant influence in A and therefore A is an associate of P by virtue of the fact that P has indirect significant influence over it. P's effective holding in A is 15% (60% × 25%)

There is also a 40% non-controlling interest in the subsidiary and that non-controlling interest has a 10% (40% × 25%) interest in the associate. Therefore the non-controlling interest shown in the consolidated financial statements of the group should include the **non-controlling interest of the subsidiary's interest** in the results and net assets of the associated company.

This means that the group financial statements must include the 'gross' share of net assets, pre-tax profits and tax, in accounting for the **non-controlling interest separately**. The relevant amounts for inclusion in the consolidated financial statements based on the above illustration would be as follows.

CONSOLIDATED STATEMENT OF PROFIT OR LOSS AND OTHER COMPREHENSIVE INCOME

Operating profit (P 100% + S 100%)

Share of profit after tax of associate (A 25%)

Tax (P 100% + S 100%)

Non-controlling interest (S 40% + A 10%)

Retained profits (P 100% + S 60% + A 15%)

CONSOLIDATED STATEMENT OF FINANCIAL POSITION

Investment in associated company (figures based on 25% holding)

Non-controlling interest ((40% × shareholders' funds of S) + (10 × post-acquisition retained earnings of A))

Unrealised reserves (15% × post-acquisition reserves of A)

Group retained earnings ((100% × P) + (60% × post-acquisition of S))

4.1 Example

Parker Co has held an 80% investment in Swiffen Co for a number of years, acquired when the retained earnings of Swiffen were $50,000. Swiffen recently acquired a 40% holding in Aspin Co when the reserves of that company were $40,000. The summarised statements of financial position of the three companies at 31 December 20X9 were as follows:

	Parker $'000	Swiffen $'000	Aspin $'000
Non-current assets	320	220	105
Investment in S/A	80	22	
Current assets	15	40	18
	415	282	123
Share capital	50	30	15
Retained earnings	240	170	95
	290	200	110
Liabilities	125	82	13
	415	282	123

Other relevant information is as follows:

- Parker Co measures the non-controlling interest as a proportion of the fair value of net assets acquired.
- At the date of acquisition, Swiffen's statement of financial position included land with a market value $10,000 in excess of its book value.
- During the year Parker has sold goods to Swiffen. Current account balances at the year end agree at $2,000. At the year end Swiffen is holding inventory purchased from Parker at a cost of $2,000. The original cost of this inventory to Parker was $1,000.
- There has been no impairment of the goodwill in Swiffen or investment in Aspin.

Prepare the consolidated statement of financial position of the Swiffen group at 31 December 20X9.

Solution

CONSOLIDATED STATEMENT OF FINANCIAL POSITION OF THE SWIFFEN GROUP AT 31 DECEMBER 20X9

	$'000
Non-current assets (320 + 220 + 10)	550
Investment in associate (W2)	44
Goodwill (W3)	8
Current assets (15 + 40 – 2 – 1 (PUP))	52
	654
Share capital	50
Retained earnings (W5)	352.6
Non-controlling interest (W6)	46.4
Liabilities (125 + 82 – 2)	205
	654

Workings

1   *Group structure*

2   *Investment in Associate*

	$'000
Cost	22
Group share of post acquisition profits (95 – 40) × 40%	22
	44

3   *Goodwill*

	$'000
Consideration transferred	80
NCI (90 × 20%)	18
Net assets acquired	98
Share capital	(30)
Reserves	(50)
FV adjustment	(10)
Goodwill	8

4   Retained earnings

	P $	S $	A $
At 31.12.X9	240	170	95
At acquisition		(50)	(40)
		120	55
PUP	(1)		
S × 80%	96.0		
A × 32%	17.6		
	352.6		

5   Non-controlling interest

	$'000
S: 20% × (200 + 10)	42.0
A: 8% × (95 – 40)	4.4
	46.4

Chapter roundup

- When a holding company has **several subsidiaries**, the consolidated statement of financial position shows a single figure for non-controlling interests and for goodwill arising on consolidation. In cases where there are several subsidiary companies, the technique is to open up a single non-controlling interest working and a columnar goodwill working.
- When dealing with **sub-subsidiaries,** you will need to calculate effective interest owned by the group and by the non-controlling interest.
- The **date of acquisition** is important when dealing with sub-subsidiaries.
- Remember that it is the post-acquisition reserves from a **group perspective** which are relevant

Quick quiz

1. B Co owns 60% of the equity of C Co which owns 75% of the equity of D Co. What is the total non-controlling interest percentage ownership in D Co?

2. What is the basic consolidation method for sub-subsidiaries?

3. P Co owns 25% of R Co's equity and 75% of Q Co's equity. Q Co owns 40% of R Co's equity. What is the total non-controlling interest percentage ownership in R Co?

Answers to quick quiz

1.
   ```
   B
   │ 60%
   C
   │ 75%
   D
   ```
   Non-controlling interest = 25% + (40% of 75%) = 55%

2.
   - Net assets: show what the group controls
   - Equity (capital and reserves): show who owns the net assets

3.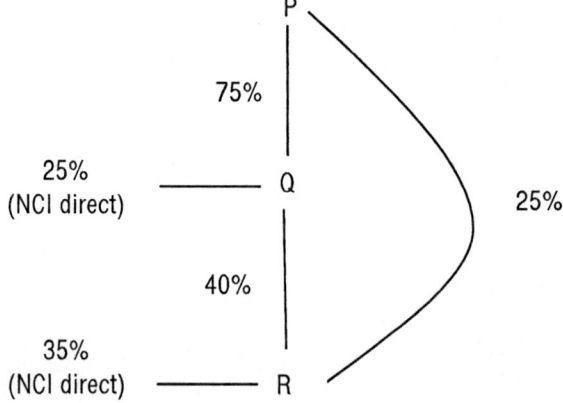

   Total non-controlling interest in R is 35% + (25% × 40%) = 45%

End of chapter question

Insolo (AIA November 2007)

The following are the summarised statements of financial position of Insolo, Vanior and Transbuy, three limited liability companies, as at 31 October 20X7, the end of the companies' most recent financial year:

STATEMENTS OF FINANCIAL POSITION AS AT 31 OCTOBER 20X7

ASSETS	Insolo	Vanior	Transbuy
Non-current assets	$	$	$
Property, plant and equipment	4,568,900	3,556,000	4,280,700
Investments, at cost	3,869,500	2,801,600	34,200
	8,438,400	6,357,600	4,314,900
Current assets			
Inventories, at cost	440,000	186,500	230,800
Trade receivables	539,080	306,750	401,200
Other receivables	87,090	34,000	16,500
Cash and cash equivalents	236,700	186,300	207,530
	1,302,870	713,550	856,030
Total assets	9,741,270	7,071,150	5,170,930
LIABILITIES AND EQUITY			
Non-current liabilities	500,000	420,000	320,800
Current liabilities			
Trade payables	539,080	345,620	412,090
Other payables	66,900	18,700	14,500
Taxation	164,200	88,600	65,400
	770,180	452,920	491,990
Equity			
Share capital			
Ordinary shares of $1	2,000,000	2,250,000	1,800,000
Preference shares of $1	400,000	200,000	300,000
Retained earnings	6,071,090	3,748,230	2,258,140
	9,741,270	7,071,150	5,170,930

The following additional information is available:

(i) Insolo purchased 1,350,000 ordinary shares in Vanior paying $2.85 per share on 1 November 2004 when Vanior's reserves were $1,262,500. For the purposes of the acquisition some land owned by Vanior was agreed to have a fair value $400,000 higher than its carrying value. The land is not depreciated and the acquisition valuation was not recorded in the financial statements of Vanior. All other assets and liabilities were recorded in the statement of financial position of Vanior at their fair values.

(ii) Vanior purchased 1,260,000 ordinary shares paying $2.15 per share and 60,000 preference shares paying $1.25 per share in Transbuy on 1 November 2005 when Transbuy's reserves were $662,857. All assets and liabilities of Transbuy were recorded in its statement of financial position at their fair values as at 1 November 20X5. During the year ended 31 October 20X6 the goodwill arising on the acquisition of Transbuy was impaired by $220,000.

(iii) Included in the inventory of Vanior as at 31 October 20X7 were items valued at $100,000. These items had been purchased from Insolo and the original cost of the items to Insolo was $68,200. Vanior had invoices totalling $41,200 payable to Insolo as at 31 October 20X7.

PART B BUSINESS COMBINATIONS AND GROUP FINANCIAL STATEMENTS

(iv) Included in the inventory of Transbuy as at 31 October 20X7 were items valued at $80,000. These items had been purchased from Vanior which purchased them from a non-related company for $55,700. Transbuy had invoices totalling $53,200 payable to Vanior as at 31 October 20X7.

(v) It is the group's policy to measure the non-controlling interest at acquisition at its proportionate share of the fair value of the subsidiary's net assets.

Required

(a) Calculate the goodwill paid by each holding company on the acquisition of its subsidiary.

(6 marks)

(b) Prepare the consolidated statement of financial position of Insolo as at 31 October 20X7 showing all supportive workings clearly. **(19 marks)**

(Total 25 marks)

Changes in group structures

Topic list	Syllabus reference
1 Disposals	13.2 + 13.3
2 Business combinations achieved in stages	13.2 + 13.3
3 Bonus issues and capital reductions	13.2 + 13.3
4 Changes in direct ownership	13.2 + 13.3
5 Demergers	13.2 + 13.3

Introduction

Complex consolidation issues are likely to come up in the exam. Your approach should be the same as for more simple consolidation questions: **methodical and logical**. If you understand the basic principles of consolidation, you should be able to tackle these complicated questions.

1 Disposals

> **Disposals** can drop a subsidiary holding to associate status, non-current asset investment status or to zero, or a the parent might still retain a subsidiary with a reduced holding. You should be able to deal with all these situations. Remember particularly how to deal with **goodwill**.

1.1 Types of disposal

1.1.1 Disposals where control is lost

There are three main kinds of disposals in which control is lost:

(a) Full disposal: all the holding is sold (say, 80% to nil)
(b) Subsidiary to associate (say, 80% to 30%)
(c) Subsidiary to financial asset investment (say, 80% to 10%)

1.1.2 Disposals where control is retained

There is only one kind of disposal where control is retained: **subsidiary to subsidiary**, for example an 80% holding to a 60% holding.

Disposals where control is lost are treated differently from disposals where control is retained. There is a reason for this.

1.2 General principle: 'crossing an accounting boundary'

Under IFRS 3 *Business Combinations* disposal occurs only when one entity loses control over another, which is generally when its holding is decreased to less than 50%. The Deloitte guide: *Business Combinations and Changes in Ownership Interests* calls this **'crossing an accounting boundary'**.

On disposal of a controlling interest, any retained interest (an associate or financial asset investment) is measured at fair value on the date that control is lost. This fair value is used in the calculation of the gain or loss on disposal, and also becomes the carrying amount for subsequent accounting for the retained interest.

If the **50%** boundary is **not crossed**, as when the interest in a subsidiary is reduced, the event is treated as a **transaction between owners**.

> Whenever you cross the 50% boundary, calculate a gain or loss on disposal, revalue any retained investment to fair value, and report a gain or loss in profit or loss for the year. If you do not cross the 50% boundary, no gain or loss is reported; instead there is an adjustment to the parent's equity.

The following diagram, from the *Deloitte* guide, may help you visualise the boundary.

Transactions that trigger remeasurement of a retained interest

8: CHANGES IN GROUP STRUCTURES

As you will see from the diagram, the situation in Section 1.1.2, where an interest in a subsidiary is reduced from say 80% to 60%, does not involve crossing that all-important 50% threshold.

1.3 Effective date of disposal

The effective date of disposal is **when control passes**: the date for accounting for an entity ceasing to be a subsidiary is the date on which its former parent relinquishes its control over that entity. The consolidated statement of profit or loss and other comprehensive income should include the results of a subsidiary up to the date of its disposal. IFRS 5 on disclosure of discontinued operations (see Chapter 18) will have an impact here.

1.4 Control lost: calculation of group gain on disposal

A proforma calculation is shown below. This needs to be adapted for the circumstances in the question, in particular whether it is a full or partial disposal.

		$
Fair value of consideration received		X
Fair value of any interest retained		X
Less:	net assets × share (%) held at date control lost	(X)
	goodwill less any NCI in goodwill at date control lost	(X)
Add/less:	gains/(losses) previously recognised in OCI	X/(X)
Group profit/(loss)		X/(X)

Following IAS 1 *Presentation of Financial Statements*, this gain may need to be disclosed separately if it is material.

1.4.1 Analogy: trading in a large car for a smaller one

It may seem counter-intuitive that the investment retained is now part of the 'proceeds' for the purposes of calculating the gain. One way of looking at it is to imagine that you are selling a larger car and putting part of the proceeds towards a smaller one. If the larger car you are selling cost you less than the smaller car and cash combined, you have made a profit. Likewise, the company making the disposal sold a larger stake to gain, at fair value, a smaller stake and some cash on top, which is the 'consideration received'.

This analogy is not exact, but may help.

1.5 Control lost: Calculation of gain in parent's separate financial statements

This calculation is more straightforward: the proceeds are compared with the carrying value of the investment sold. The investment will be held at cost or in accordance with IFRS 9 *Financial Instruments*.

	$
Fair value of consideration received	X
Less carrying value of investment disposed	(X)
Add/(less) fair value changes previously recognised in OCI (if designated as FV through OCI)	X/(X)
Profit/(loss) on disposal	X/(X)

The profit on disposal is generally taxable, and the **tax charge based on the parent's gain** rather than the group's.

1.6 Disposals where control is lost: Accounting treatment

For a **full disposal**, apply the following treatment:

(a) **Statement of profit or loss and other comprehensive income**

  (i) Consolidate results and non-controlling interest to the date of disposal.
  (ii) Show the group profit or loss on disposal.

(b) **Statement of financial position**

There will be no non-controlling interest and no consolidation as there is no subsidiary at the date the statement of financial position is being prepared.

For **partial disposals**, use the following treatments:

(a) **Subsidiary to associate**

(i) **Statement of profit or loss and other comprehensive income**

(1) Treat the investment as a subsidiary up to the date of disposal, ie consolidate for the correct number of months and show the non-controlling interest in that amount.

(2) Show the profit or loss on disposal.

(3) Treat as an associate thereafter.

(ii) **Statement of financial position**

(1) The investment remaining is at its fair value at the date of disposal (to calculate the gain).

(2) Equity account (as an associate) thereafter, using the fair value as the new 'cost'. (Post-'acquisition' retained earnings are added to this cost in future years to arrive at the carrying value of the investment in the associate in the statement of financial position.)

(b) **Subsidiary to financial asset investment**

(i) **Statement of profit or loss and other comprehensive income**

(1) Treat the investment as a subsidiary up to the date of disposal, ie consolidate.
(2) Show profit or loss on disposal.
(3) Show dividend income only thereafter.

(ii) **Statement of financial position**

(1) The investment remaining is at its fair value at the date of disposal (to calculate the gain).

(2) Thereafter, treat as a financial asset under IFRS 9.

1.7 Disposals where control is retained

Control is retained where the disposal is from **subsidiary to subsidiary.** The accounting treatment is treatment is as follows.

1.7.1 Statement of profit or loss and other comprehensive income

(a) The subsidiary is **consolidated in full** for the whole period.

(b) The **non-controlling interest in the statement of profit or loss and other comprehensive income** will be based on the percentages before and after disposal, ie time apportion.

(c) There is no profit or loss on disposal.

1.7.2 Statement of financial position

(a) The non-controlling interest in the statement of financial position is based on the year end percentage.

(b) The change (increase) in non-controlling interests is shown as an adjustment to the parent's equity.

(c) Goodwill on acquisition is unchanged in the consolidated statement of financial position.

1.7.3 Adjustment to the parent's equity

This reflects the fact that the non-controlling share has increased (as the parent's share has reduced). A subsidiary to subsidiary disposal is, in effect, **a transaction between owners**. Specifically, it is a reallocation of ownership between parent and non-controlling equity holders. **The goodwill is unchanged**, because it is a historical figure, unaffected by the reallocation. The adjustment to the parent's equity is calculated as follows.

	$
Fair value of consideration received	X
Increase in NCI in net assets at disposal	(X)
Increase in NCI in goodwill at disposal *	(X)
Adjustment to parent's equity	X

*__Note.__ This line is only required where non-controlling interests are measured at fair value at the date of acquisition (ie where there is an increase in the non-controlling interest share of goodwill already recognised).

If you are wondering why the decrease in shareholding is treated as a transaction between owners, look back to Chapter 6. IFRS 3 views **the group as an economic entity**, and views **all providers of equity**, including non-controlling interests, as **owners of the group**. Non-controlling shareholders are not outsiders, they are owners of the group just like the parent.

You can practise the adjustment to parent's equity in the example and question below.

1.7.4 Gain in the parent's separate financial statements

This is calculated as for disposals where control is lost: see Section 1.5 above.

1.8 Example: Partial disposals

Chalk Co bought 100% of the voting share capital of Cheese Co on its incorporation on 1 January 20X2 for $160,000. Cheese Co earned and retained $240,000 from that date until 31 December 20X7. At that date the statements of financial position of the companies and the group were as follows.

	Chalk Co $'000	Cheese Co $'000	Consolidated $'000
Investment in Cheese	160	–	–
Other net assets	1,000	500	1,500
	1,160	500	1,500
Share capital	400	160	400
Retained earnings	560	240	800
Current liabilities	200	100	300
	1,160	500	1,500

It is the group's policy to value the non-controlling interest at its proportionate share of the fair value of the subsidiary's identifiable net assets.

On 1 January 20X8 Chalk Co sold 40% of its shareholding in Cheese Co for $280,000 in cash. The profit on disposal (ignoring tax) in the financial statements of the parent company is calculated as follows.

	Chalk $'000
Fair value of consideration received	280
Carrying value of investment (40% × 160)	64
Profit on sale	216

We now move on to calculate the adjustment to equity for the group financial statements.

Because only 40% of the 100% subsidiary has been sold, leaving a 60% subsidiary, **control is retained**. This means that there is **no group profit on disposal in profit or loss for the year**. Instead, there is an **adjustment to the parent's equity**, which affects group retained earnings.

PART B BUSINESS COMBINATIONS AND GROUP FINANCIAL STATEMENTS

> **Point to note**
>
> Remember that, when control is retained, the disposal is just a transaction between owners. The non-controlling shareholders are owners of the group, just like the parent.

The adjustment to parent's equity is calculated as follows.

	$'000
Fair value of consideration received	280
Increase in non-controlling interest in net assets at the date of disposal (40% × (160 + 240))	160
Adjustment to parent's equity	120

This increases group retained earnings and does not go through group profit or loss for the year. (Note that there is no goodwill in this example, or non-controlling interest in goodwill, as the subsidiary was acquired on incorporation.)

Solution 1

The statements of financial position immediately after the sale will appear as follows:

	Chalk Co $'000	Cheese Co $'000	Consolidated $'000
Investment in Cheese (160 – 64)	96		
Other net assets (Chalk 1,000 + 280)	1,280	500	1,780
	1,376	500	1,780
Share capital	400	160	400
Retained earnings*	776	240	920
Non-controlling interest	–	–	160
Equity	1,176		1,480
Current liabilities	200	100	300
	1,376	500	1,780

*Chalk's retained earnings are $560,000 + $216,000 profit on disposal. Group retained earnings are increased by the adjustment above: $800,000 + $120,000 = $920,000.

Solution 2

Using the above example, assume that Chalk Co sold 60% of its holding in Cheese Co for $440,000 in cash. The fair value of the 40% holding retained was $200,000. The gain or loss on disposal in the books of the parent company would be calculated as follows:

	Parent company $'000
Fair value of consideration received	440
Carrying value of investment (60 × 160)	96
Profit on sale	344

This time control is lost, so there will be a gain in group profit or loss, calculated as follows:

	$'000
Fair value of consideration received	440
Fair value of investment retained	200
Less Chalk's share of consolidated carrying value at date control lost (100% × (160 + 240)	(400)
Group profit on sale	240

Note that there was no goodwill arising on the acquisition of Cheese, otherwise this too would be deducted in the calculation.

The statements of financial position would now appear as follows:

	Chalk Co $'000	Cheese Co $'000	Consolidated $'000
Investment in Cheese (Note 1)	64		200
Other net assets (Chalk 1,000 + 440)	1,440	500	1,440
	1,504	500	1,640
Share capital	400	160	400
Retained earnings (Note 2)	904	240	1,040
Current liabilities	200	100	200
	1,504	500	1,640

Notes

1 The investment in Cheese is measured at prorata cost (40% × 160) in Chalk's SOFP but at fair value in the group SOFP. In fact it is equity accounted at fair value at date control lost plus share of post-'acquisition' retained earnings. But there are no retained earnings yet because control has only just been lost.

2 Chalk's retained earnings are $560,000 (per question) plus parent's profit on the sale of $344,000, ie $904,000. Group retained earnings are $800,000 (per question) plus group profit on the sale of $240,000, ie $1,040,000.

The following comprehensive question should help you get to grips with disposal problems. Try to complete the whole question without looking at the solution, and then check your answer very carefully. **Give yourself at least two hours.** This is a very difficult question.

Exam focus point

Questions may involve part-disposals leaving investments with both subsidiary and associate status.

Question Disposal

Smith Co bought 80% of the share capital of Jones Co for $324,000 on 1 October 20X5. At that date Jones Co's retained earnings balance stood at $180,000. The statements of financial position at 30 September 20X8 and the summarised statements of profit or loss and other comprehensive income to that date are given below.

	Smith Co $'000	Jones Co $'000
Non-current assets	360	270
Investment in Jones Co	324	–
Current assets	370	370
	1,054	640
Equity		
$1 ordinary shares	540	180
Retained earnings	414	360
Current liabilities	100	100
	1,054	640
Profit before tax	153	126
Tax	(45)	(36)
Profit for the year	108	90

No entries have been made in the financial statements for any of the following transactions.

Assume that profits accrue evenly throughout the year.

It is the group's policy to value the non-controlling interest at its proportionate share of the fair value of the subsidiary's identifiable net assets.

Ignore taxation.

PART B BUSINESS COMBINATIONS AND GROUP FINANCIAL STATEMENTS

Required

Prepare the consolidated statement of financial position and statement of profit or loss and other comprehensive income at 30 September 20X8 in each of the following circumstances. (Assume no impairment of goodwill.)

(a) Smith Co sells its entire holding in Jones Co for $650,000 on 30 September 20X8.

(b) Smith Co sells one quarter of its holding in Jones Co for $160,000 on 30 June 20X8.

(c) Smith Co sells one half of its holding in Jones Co for $340,000 on 30 June 20X8, and the remaining holding (fair value $250,000) is to be dealt with as an associate.

(d) Smith Co sells one half of its holding in Jones Co for $340,000 on 30 June 20X8, and the remaining holding (fair value $250,000) is to be dealt with as a financial asset.

Answer

(a) *Complete disposal at year end (80% to 0%)*

CONSOLIDATED STATEMENT OF FINANCIAL POSITION
AS AT 30 SEPTEMBER 20X8

	$'000
Non-current assets	360
Current assets (370 + 650)	1,020
	1,380
Equity	
$1 ordinary shares	540
Retained earnings (W2)	740
Current liabilities	100
	1,380

CONSOLIDATED STATEMENT OF PROFIT OR LOSS AND OTHER COMPREHENSIVE INCOME
FOR THE YEAR ENDED 30 SEPTEMBER 20X8

	$'000
Profit before tax (153 + 126)	279
Profit on disposal (W1)	182
Tax (45 + 36)	(81)
	380
Profit attributable to:	
Owners of the parent	362
Non-controlling interest (20% × 90)	18
	380

Workings

1   *Profit on disposal of Jones Co*

	$'000	$'000
Fair value of consideration received		650
Less share of consolidated carrying value when control lost:		
net assets (540 × 80%)	432	
Goodwill (see Note)	36	
		(468)
		182

Note: goodwill

	$'000
Consideration transferred	324
Acquired: 80% × (180 + 180)	(288)
	36

2   *Retained earnings carried forward*

	$'000
Smith per question	414
Jones: 80% × (360 − 180)	144
Profit on disposal (W1)	182
	740

Or:

	$'000
Brought forward Smith (414 − 108 profit for year)	306
Jones: 80% × (360 − (180 + 90 profit for year))	72
Profit for year attributable to owners (per statement of profit or loss and other comprehensive income)	362
	740

(b) *Partial disposal: subsidiary to subsidiary (80% to 60%)*

CONSOLIDATED STATEMENT OF FINANCIAL POSITION AS AT 30 SEPTEMBER 20X8

	$'000
Non-current assets (360 + 270)	630
Goodwill (part (a))	36
Current assets (370 + 160 + 370)	900
	1,566
Equity	
$1 ordinary shares	540
Retained earnings (W2)	610
	1,150
Non-controlling interest (40% × 540)	216
Current liabilities (100 + 100)	200
	1,566

CONSOLIDATED STATEMENT OF PROFIT OR LOSS AND OTHER COMPREHENSIVE INCOME FOR THE YEAR ENDED 30 SEPTEMBER 20X8

	$'000	$'000
Profit before tax (153 + 126)		279
Tax (45 + 36)		(81)
Profit for the period		198
Profit attributable to:		
Owners of the parent		175.5
Non-controlling interest		
20% × 90 × 9/12	13.5	
40% × 90 × 3/12	9.0	
		22.5
		198.0

Workings

1   *Adjustment to parent's equity on disposal of 20% of Jones*

	$'000	$'000
Fair value of consideration received		160.0
Less increase in NCI in net assets at disposal		
20% × (540 − (3/12 × 90))		(103.5)
		56.5

PART B BUSINESS COMBINATIONS AND GROUP FINANCIAL STATEMENTS

2   Group retained earnings

	Smith $'000	Jones 60% $'000	Jones 20% sold $'000
Per question/at date of disposal (360 – (90 × 3/12))	414.0	360	337.5
Adjustment to parent's equity on disposal (W1)	56.5		
Retained earnings at acquisition		(180)	(180.0)
		180	157.5
Jones: share of post acq'n. earnings (180 × 60%)	108.0		
Smith: share of post acq'n. earnings (157.5 × 20%)	31.5		
	610.0		

Or:

	$'000
Brought forward As before (306 + 72)	378.0
Adjustment on disposal (W1)	56.5
Profit for year attributable to owners (per statement of profit or loss and other comprehensive income)	175.5
	610.0

(c) (i) *Partial disposal: subsidiary to associate (80% to 40%)*

CONSOLIDATED STATEMENT OF FINANCIAL POSITION AS AT 30 SEPTEMBER 20X8

	$'000
Non-current assets	360
Investment in associate (W3)	259
Current assets (370 + 340)	710
	1,329
Equity	
$1 ordinary shares	540
Retained earnings (W2)	689
Current liabilities	100
	1,329

CONSOLIDATED STATEMENT OF PROFIT OR LOSS AND OTHER COMPREHENSIVE INCOME FOR THE YEAR ENDED 30 SEPTEMBER 20X8

	$'000
Profit before tax (153 + 9/12 × 126)	247.5
Profit on disposal (W1)	140.0
Share of profit of associate (90 × 3/12 × 40%)	9.0
Tax 45 + (9/12 × 36)	(72.0)
Profit for the period	324.5
Profit attributable to:	
Owners of the parent	311.0
Non-controlling interest (20% × 90 × 9/12)	13.5
	324.5

Workings

1   *Profit on disposal in Smith Co*

	$'000	$'000
Fair value of consideration received		340
Fair value of 40% investment retained		250
Less share of consolidated carrying value when control lost		
80% × ((540 – (90 × 3/12))	414	
Goodwill (part (a))	36	
		(450)
		140

2   *Group retained earnings*

	Smith $'000	Jones 40% $'000	Jones 40% sold $'000
Per question/at date of disposal (360 – (90 × 3/12))	414	360	337.5
Group profit on disposal (W1)	140		
Retained earnings at acquisition		(180)	(180.0)
		180	157.5
Jones: share of post acq'n. earnings (180 × 40%)	72		
Jones: share of post acq'n. earnings (157.5 × 40%)	63		
	689		

Or:

	$'000
Brought forward As before (306 + 72)	378
Profit for year attributable to owners (per statement of profit or loss and other comprehensive income)	311
	689

3   *Investment in associate*

	$'000
Fair value at date control lost (new 'cost')	250
Share of post 'acq'n' retained reserves (90 × 3/12 × 40%)	9
	259

(d)   *Partial disposal: subsidiary to financial asset (80% to 40%)*

CONSOLIDATED STATEMENT OF FINANCIAL POSITION
AS AT 30 SEPTEMBER 20X8

	$'000
Non-current assets	360
Investment (fair value at date of disposal)	250
Current assets (370 + 340)	710
	1,320
Equity	
$1 ordinary shares	540
Retained earnings (W)	680
Current liabilities	100
	1,320

CONSOLIDATED STATEMENT OF PROFIT OR LOSS AND OTHER COMPREHENSIVE INCOME
FOR THE YEAR ENDED 30 SEPTEMBER 20X8

	$'000
Profit before tax (153 + (9/12 × 126))	247.5
Profit on disposal (See (c) above)	140.0
Tax (45 + (9/12 × 36))	(72.0)
Profit for the period	315.5
Profit attributable to:	
Owners of the parent	302.0
Non-controlling interest	13.5
	315.5

Working: retained earnings

	Smith $'000	Jones $'000
Per question/at date of disposal (360 – (90 × 3/12))	414	337.5
Group profit on disposal (W1)	140	
Retained earnings at acquisition		(180.0)
		157.5
Smith: share of post acq'n. earnings (157.5 × 80%)	126	
	680	

Or:

	$'000
Brought forward As before (306 + 72)	378
Profit for year attributable to owners (per statement of profit or loss)	302
	680

1.9 Section summary

Disposals occur frequently in Paper 13 consolidation questions.

- The effective date of disposal is when **control is lost**.
- Treatment of **goodwill** is according to IFRS 3.
- Disposals may be **full** or **partial**, to subsidiary, associate or investment status.
    - **If control is lost,** the interest retained is **fair valued** and becomes part of the calculation of the gain on disposal.
    - **If control is retained**, the change in non-controlling interests is shown as **an adjustment to parent's equity**.
- **Gain or loss** on disposal is calculated for the parent company and the group.

2 Business combinations achieved in stages

Transactions of the type described in this chapter can be very complicated and certainly look rather daunting. Remember and apply the **basic techniques** and you should find such questions easier than you expected.

Business combinations achieved in stages (step acquisitions) can lead to a company becoming a non-current asset investment, an associate and then a subsidiary over time. Make sure you can deal with each of these situations.

A parent company may acquire a controlling interest in the shares of a subsidiary as a result of **several successive share purchases**, rather than by purchasing the shares all on the same day. Business combinations achieved in stages may also be known as 'step acquisitions' or 'piecemeal acquisitions'.

Point to note | Business combinations achieved in stages are in many ways a mirror image of disposals. The same principles underly both.

2.1 Types of business combination achieved in stages

There are three possible types of business combinations achieved in stages:

(a) A previously held **interest**, say 10%, with **no significant influence** (accounted for under IFRS 9) is **increased to a controlling interest** of 51% or more.

(b) A **previously held equity interest**, say 35%, accounted for as an **associate** under IAS 28 (2011) *Investments in Associates and Joint Ventures*, is increased to a controlling interest of 51% or more.

(c) A **controlling interest** in a subsidiary is **increased**, say from 60% to 80%.

The first two transactions are treated in the same way, but the third is not. There is a reason for this.

2.2 General principle: 'crossing an accounting boundary'

Under IFRS 3 a business combination occurs only when one entity **obtains control over another**, which is generally when 51% or more has been acquired. The Deloitte guide: *Business Combinations and Changes in Ownership Interests* calls this '**crossing an accounting boundary**'.

When this happens, the original investment – whether an investment under IFRS 9 with no significant influence, or an associate – is **remeasured at fair value at the acquisition date**. This **previously held interest** at fair value, together with any consideration transferred, is the **'cost' of the combination** used in calculating the goodwill.

If the 50% **boundary is not crossed**, as when the interest in a subsidiary is increased, the event is treated as a **transaction between owners**.

> Whenever you cross the 50% boundary, the original investment is revalued to fair value, and a gain or loss is reported in profit or loss for the year. If you do not cross the 50% boundary, no gain or loss is reported; instead there is an adjustment to the parent's equity.

The following diagram, from the *Deloitte* guide may help you visualise the boundary.

Transactions that trigger remeasurement of an existing interest

As you will see from the diagram, the third situation (c) in Section 2.1, where an interest in a subsidiary is increased from, say, 60% to 80%, does not involve crossing that all-important 50% threshold. Likewise, purchases of stakes of up to 50% do not involve crossing the boundary, and therefore do not trigger a calculation of goodwill.

Exam focus point

> In an exam, if you get a question with a business combination achieved in stages, ignore all purchases made before control is achieved, that is purchases bringing the total holding to less than 50%.

2.3 Investment or associate becomes a subsidiary: calculation of goodwill

The previously held investment is remeasured to fair value, with any gain being reported in profit and loss, and the goodwill calculated as follows.

	Group	NCI
Consideration transferred/Fair value of NCI	X	X
Fair value of acquirer's previously held equity interest	X	
Less: Net fair value of identifiable assets acquired and liabilities assumed × Group/NCI %	(X)	(X)
	X	X

Note. You only need the NCI column if NCI at acquisition is measured at fair value.

2.3.1 Analogy: Trading in a small car for a larger one

It may seem counter-intuitive that the previous investment is now part of the 'cost' for the purposes of calculating the goodwill. One way of looking at it is to imagine that you are part-exchanging a small car for a larger one. The value of the car you trade in is put towards the cost of the new vehicle, together with your cash (the 'consideration transferred'). Likewise, the company making the acquisition has part-exchanged its smaller investment – at fair value – for a larger one, and must naturally pay on top of that to obtain the larger investment.

This analogy is not exact, but may help.

Try the following question to get the hang of the calculation of goodwill and profit on de-recognition of the investment.

Question — Piecemeal acquisition 1

Good, whose year end is 30 June 20X9 has a subsidiary, Will, which it acquired in stages. The details of the acquisition are as follows:

Date of acquisition	Holding acquired %	Retained earnings at acquisition $m	Purchase consideration $m
1 July 20X7	20	270	120
1 July 20X8	60	450	480

The share capital of Will has remained unchanged since its incorporation at $300m. The fair values of the net assets of Will were the same as their carrying amounts at the date of the acquisition. Good did not have significant influence over Will at any time before gaining control of Will. The group policy is to measure non-controlling interest at its proportionate share of the fair value of the subsidiary's identifiable net assets. The fair value at 1 July 20X8 of Good's original 20% holding in Will is $160m.

Required

(a) Calculate the goodwill on the acquisition of Will that will appear in the consolidated statement of financial position at 30 June 20X9.

(b) Calculate the profit on the remeasurement of the previously held investment in Will to be reported in group profit or loss for the year ended 30 June 20X9.

Answer

(a) *Goodwill (at date control obtained)*

	$m	$m
Consideration transferred		480
Fair value of previously held equity interest		160
Fair value of identifiable assets acquired and liabilities assumed		
Share capital	300	
Retained earnings	450	
	750	
× 80%		(600)
		40

(b) *Profit on remeasurement of previously held equity interest*

	$m
Fair value at date control obtained	160
Cost	(120)
	40

In this short example, the figures for goodwill and profit on derecognition are the same. In the more complicated examples, such as the one in Section 2.5 below, they may different because the investment (a financial asset) may be revalued before or after control was obtained.

2.4 Increase in previously held controlling interest: adjustment to parent's equity

An example of this would be where an investment goes from a 60% subsidiary to an 80% subsidiary. The 50% threshold has not been crossed, so there is no re-measurement to fair value and no gain or loss to profit or loss for the year. The increase is treated as a **transaction between owners**. As with disposals, ownership has been **reallocated** between parent and non-controlling shareholders.

Accordingly the parent's equity is adjusted. The required adjustment is calculated by comparing the consideration paid with the decrease in non-controlling interest. (As the parent's share has increased, the NCI share has decreased.) The **calculation is as follows**:

	$
Fair value of consideration paid	(X)
Decrease in NCI in net assets at date of transaction	X
Decrease in NCI in goodwill at date of transaction *	X
Adjustment to parent's equity	(X)

*Note. This line is only required where non-controlling interests are measured at fair value at the date of acquisition (ie where there is an decrease in the non-controlling interest share of goodwill already recognised).

Remember that IFRS 3 views **the group as an economic entity,** and **views all providers of equity,** including non-controlling interests, as **owners of the group**.

You can practise this adjustment in the example below.

2.5 Comprehensive example: Step acquisition of a subsidiary

Peace acquired 25% of Miel on 1.1.20X1 for $2,020,000 (equivalent to the fair value of $10.10 per share acquired on that date) when Miel's reserves were standing at $5,800,000. The fair value of Miel's identifiable assets and liabilities at that date was $7,200,000. Both Peace and Miel are stock market listed entities.

PART B BUSINESS COMBINATIONS AND GROUP FINANCIAL STATEMENTS

A further 35% stake in Miel was acquired on 30 September 20X2 for $4,025,000 (equivalent to the fair value of $14.375 per share acquired on that date) giving Peace control over Miel. The fair value of Miel's identifiable assets and liabilities at that date was $9,400,000, and Miel's reserves stood at $7,800,000.

Summarised statements of financial position of the two companies at 31 December 20X2 show:

	Peace $'000	Miel $'000
Non-current assets		
Property, plant and equipment	38,650	7,600
Investment in Miel	7,020	–
	45,670	7,600
Current assets	12,700	2,200
	58,370	9,800
Equity		
Share capital ($1)	10,200	800
Reserves	40,720	7,900
	50,920	8,700
Liabilities	7,450	1,100
	58,370	9,800

The difference between the fair value of the identifiable assets and liabilities of Miel and their book value relates to the value of a plot of land. The land had not been sold by 31 December 20X2.

For consistency with the measurement of other shares, Peace applies IFRS 9 and holds all investments in subsidiaries and associates as financial assets at fair value through OCI in its separate financial statements as permitted by IAS 27 (2011).

At 31 December 20X2, the fair value of Peace's 60% holding in Miel was $7,020,000 (equivalent to $14.625 per share).

The investment in Miel figure at 31.12.20X2 is therefore made up of:

	$'000
Purchase of 25% stake at cost	2,020
Fair value adjustments on 25% stake to 30.9.X2 [($14.375 – $10.10) × 200,000 shares]	855
	2,875
Purchase of 35% stake at cost	4,025
	6,900
Fair value adjustments on 60% stake to 31.12.X2 [($14.625 – $14.375) × 480,000 shares]	120
Fair value of 60% stake at 31.12.X2	7,020

Group policy is to measure non-controlling interests at the date of acquisition at their proportionate share of the net fair value of the identifiable assets acquired and liabilities assumed.

No impairment losses on recognised goodwill have been necessary to date.

Required

(a) Prepare the consolidated statement of financial position of Peace Group as at 31 December 20X2 in the following circumstances:

  (i) The 25% interest in Miel allowed Peace significant influence over the financial and operating policy decisions of Miel.

  (ii) The other 75% of shares were held by a single shareholder and Peace was allowed no influence in the running of Miel until acquiring control.

(b) Show the consolidated current assets, non-controlling interests and reserves figures if Peace acquired an **additional** 10% interest in Miel on 1 January 20X3 for $1,200,000 in cash.

8: CHANGES IN GROUP STRUCTURES

Solution

Parts (a)(i) and (a)(ii) to the example would generate the same overall answer.

(a) PEACE GROUP
CONSOLIDATED STATEMENT OF FINANCIAL POSITION AS AT 31 DECEMBER 20X2

	$'000
Non-current assets	
Property, plant and equipment (38,650 + 7,600 + (W2) 800)	47,050
Goodwill (W3)	1,260
	48,310
Current assets (12,700 + 2,200)	14,900
	63,210
Equity attributable to owners of the parent	
Share capital	10,200
Reserves (W5)/(W6)	40,660
	50,860
Non-controlling interests (W4)	3,800
	54,660
Liabilities (7,450 + 1,100)	8,550
	63,210

Workings

1 *Group structure*

```
         Peace
           |
           |   1.1.X1     30.9.X2
           |   25%    +   35%   =  60%
           |                   ∴ Non-controlling interests = 40%
          Miel
```

2 *Fair value adjustments*

Measured at date control achieved (only)

	At acquisition 30.9.X2 $'000	Movement $'000	At year end 31.12.X2 $'000
Land (9,400 – (800 + 7,800))	800	–	800

3 *Goodwill*

	$'000	$'000
Consideration transferred		4,025
FV of P's previously held equity interest		2,875
Fair value of identifiable assets acq'd & liabilities assumed:		
Share capital	800	
Reserves	7,800	
Fair value adjustments (W2)	800	
	9,400	
× 60%		(5,640)
		1,260

PART B BUSINESS COMBINATIONS AND GROUP FINANCIAL STATEMENTS

4 *Non-controlling interests*

	$'000	$'000
Net assets at year end per question	8,700	
Fair value adjustment (W2)	800	
	9,500	
× 40%		3,800

5 *Consolidated reserves (if previously held as an associate) (a)(i)*

	$'000 Peace	$'000 Miel 35%	$'000 Miel 25%
Per question	40,720	7,900	7,900
Profit on derecognition of investment *	355		
Fair value movement (W2)			(0)
Reserves at acquisition		(7,800)	(5,800)
		100	2,100
Share of post acquisition reserves			
Miel 35% (100 × 35%)	35		
Miel 25% (2,100 × 25%)	525		
Less: Fair value gain recognised in Peace's separate FS (855 + 120)	(975)		
	40,660		

* *Profit on derecognition of 25% associate*

	$'000
Fair value at date control obtained	2,875
P's share of carrying value (2,020 + ((7,800 – 5,800) × 25%))	(2,520)
	355

6 *Consolidated reserves (if previously held as a financial asset) (a)(ii)*

	$'000 Peace	$'000 Miel
Per question	40,720	7,900
Profit on derecognition of investment*	855	
Fair value movement (W2)		(0)
Reserves at acquisition		(7,800)
		100
Miel - Share of post-acquisition reserves (100 × 60%)	60	
Less: Fair value gain recognised in Peace's separate FS (855 + 120)	(975)	
	40,660	

* *Profit on derecognition of 25% investment*

	$'000
Fair value at date control obtained	2,875
Cost	(2,020)
	855

The profit would be the same whether the financial asset had been revalued or not, as any revaluation above original cost previously recognised in other comprehensive income is transferred to profit or loss.

(b) Current assets (14,900 – 1,200)   13,700

Non-controlling interests

	$'000	$'000
Net assets at year end per question	8,700	
Fair value adjustment (W2)	800	
	9,500	
× (40% – 10%)		2,850

Consolidated reserves

	$'000
Per part (a)	40,660
Adjustment to parent's equity on acq'n of 10% (W)	(250)
	40,410

Note. No other figures in the statement of financial position are affected.

Working: Adjustment to parent's equity on acquisition of additional 10% of Miel

	$'000
Fair value of consideration paid	(1,200)
Decrease in NCI in net assets at acq'n (9,500 × 10%)	950
	(250)

2.6 Comprehensive example: Step acquisition of a subsidiary with non-controlling interest at fair value

The facts are the same as in Section 2.5 above, except that group policy is to measure non-controlling interests at the date of acquisition at fair value.

Solution

Parts (a)(i) and (a)(ii) to the example would generate the same overall answer.

(a) PEACE GROUP
CONSOLIDATED STATEMENT OF FINANCIAL POSITION AS AT 31 DECEMBER 20X2

	$'000
Non-current assets	
Property, plant and equipment (38,650 + 7,600 + (W2) 800)	47,050
Goodwill (W3)	2,100
	49,150
Current assets (12,700 + 2,200)	14,900
	64,050
Equity attributable to owners of the parent	
Share capital	10,200
Reserves (W5)/(W6)	40,660
	50,860
Non-controlling interests (W4)	4,640
	55,500
Liabilities (7,450 + 1,100)	8,550
	64,050

PART B BUSINESS COMBINATIONS AND GROUP FINANCIAL STATEMENTS

Workings

1 *Group structure*

```
Peace
 │
 │ 1.1.X1    30.9.X2
 │  25%   +   35%   =  60%
 │                     ∴ Non-controlling interests = 40%
Miel
```

2 *Fair value adjustments*

Measured at date control achieved (only)

	At acquisition 30.9.X2 $'000	Movement $'000	At year end 31.12.X2 $'000
Land (9,400 – (800 + 7,800))	800	–	800

3 *Goodwill*

	Group $'000	$'000	NCI $'000
Consideration transferred		4,025	
FV NCI (800 × $14.375 × 40%)			4,600
FV P's previously held equity interest		2,875	
Fair value of identifiable assets acq'd & liabilities assumed:			
Share capital	800		
Reserves	7,800		
Fair value adjustments (W2)	800		
	9,400		
× 60%/40%		(5,640)	(3,760)
		1,260	840
		2,100	

4 *Non-controlling interests*

	$'000	$'000
Net assets at year end per question	8,700	
Fair value adjustment (W2)	800	
	9,500	
× 40%		3,800
NCI in goodwill (W3)		840
		4,640

5 *Consolidated reserves (if previously held as an associate) (a)(i)*

	$'000 Peace	$'000 Miel 35%	$'000 Miel 25%
Per question	40,720	7,900	7,900
Profit on derecognition of investment	355		
Fair value movement (W2)			(0)
Reserves at acquisition		(7,800)	(5,800)
		100	2,100
Share of post acquisition reserves			
Miel 35% (100 × 35%)	35		
Miel 25% (2,100 × 25%)	525		
Less: Fair value gain recognised in Peace's separate FS (855 + 120)	(975)		
	40,660		

8: CHANGES IN GROUP STRUCTURES

* *Profit on derecognition of 25% associate*

	$'000
Fair value at date control obtained	2,875
P's share of carrying amount (2,020 + (7,800 – 5,800) × 25%)	(2,520)
	355

6 *Consolidated reserves (if previously held as a financial asset) (a)(ii)*

	$'000 Peace	$'000 Miel
Per question	40,720	7,900
Profit on derecognition of investment*	855	
Fair value movement (W2)		(0)
Reserves at acquisition		(7,800)
		100
Miel – Share of post acquisition reserves (100 × 60%)	60	
Less: Fair value gain recognised in Peace's separate FS (855 + 120)	(975)	
	40,660	

* *Profit on derecognition of 25% investment*

	$'000
Fair value at date control obtained	2,875
Cost	(2,020)
	855

The profit would be the same whether the financial asset had been revalued or not, as any revaluation above original cost previously recognised in other comprehensive income is transferred to profit or loss.

2.7 Section summary

Where control is **achieved in stages:**

- **Remeasure** any previously held equity interest to **fair value at the date control is achieved.**
- Report any **gain in profit or loss.**
- Where a **controlling interest is increased**, treat as a transaction between owners and **adjust parent's equity.**

3 Bonus issues and capital reductions

Exam focus point

You may be asked to deal with a capital reorganisation, such as a bonus issue or a capital reduction. These are both straightforward.

3.1 Bonus issues

A bonus issue is simply a **capitalisation of retained earnings** and therefore there is no alteration in the percentage holding of any party. When calculating goodwill, it is easiest to ignore the effect of the bonus issue and simply use the retained earnings and share capital as at acquisition.

3.2 Capital reductions

A capital reduction will involve a **reduction in the par (nominal) value of shares in issue.** In acquisition accounting, we are using calculations which show the net assets acquired (as represented by pre-acquisition retained earnings and share capital), so any change in the nominal value of the shares at a later date is irrelevant and should be ignored.

PART B   BUSINESS COMBINATIONS AND GROUP FINANCIAL STATEMENTS

4 Changes in direct ownership

FAST FORWARD

Changes in direct ownership (ie internal group reorganisations) can take many forms. Apart from divisionalisation, all other internal reorganisations will not affect the consolidated financial statements, but they will affect the financial statements of individual companies within the group.

Groups will reorganise on occasions for a variety of reasons:

(a) A group may want to float a business to reduce the gearing of the group. The holding company will initially transfer the business into a separate company.

(b) Companies may be transferred to another business during a divisionalisation process.

(c) The group may 'reverse' into another company to obtain a stock exchange quotation.

(d) Internal reorganisations may create efficiencies of group structure for tax purposes.

Such reorganisations involve a restructuring of the relationships within a group. Companies may be transferred to another business during a divisionalisation process. There is generally no effect on the consolidated financial statements, **provided that** no non-controlling interests are affected, because such reorganisations are only internal. The impact on the individual companies within the group, however, can be substantial. A variety of different transactions are described here, **only involving 100% subsidiaries**.

4.1 New top holding company

A new top holding company might be needed as a vehicle for flotation or to improve the co-ordination of a diverse business. The new company, H, will issue its own shares to the holders of the shares in S.

4.2 Subsidiary moved up

This transaction is shown in the diagram below. It might be carried out to allow S_1 to be **sold** while S_2 is retained, or to **split diverse businesses**.

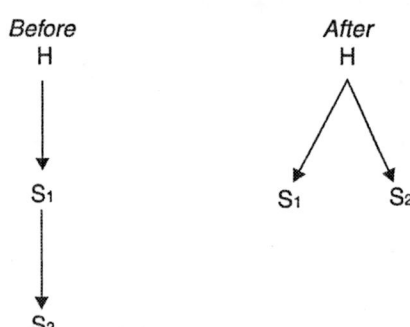

S_1 could transfer its investment in S_2 to H as a dividend *in specie* or by H paying cash. A share for share exchange is not possible because an allotment by H to S_1 is void. A **dividend *in specie*** is simply a dividend paid other than in cash.

S_1 must have sufficient **distributable profits** for a dividend *in specie*. If the investment in S_2 has been revalued then that can be treated as a realised profit for the purposes of determining the legality of the distribution.

For example, suppose the statement of financial position of S_1 is as follows:

	$m
Investment in S_2 (cost $100m)	900
Other net assets	100
	1,000
Share capital	100
Revaluation reserve	800
Retained earnings	100
	1,000

It appears that S_1 cannot make a distribution of more than $100m. If, however, S_1 makes a distribution in kind of its investment in S_2, then the **revaluation reserve** can be treated as realised.

It is not clear how H should account for the transaction. The carrying value to S_2 might be used, but there may be **no legal rule**. H will need to write down its investment in S_1 at the same time. A transfer for cash is probably easiest, but there are still legal pitfalls as to what is distributable, depending on how the transfer is recorded.

There will be **no effect** on the group financial statements as the group has stayed the same: it has made no acquisitions or disposals.

4.3 Subsidiary moved along

This is a transaction which is treated in a very similar manner to that described above.

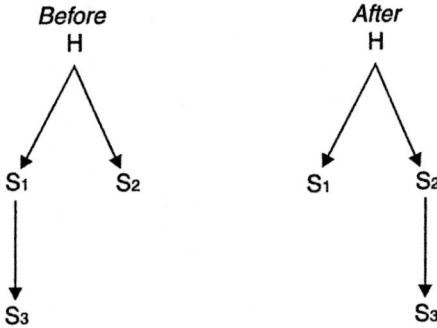

The problem of an effective distribution does not arise here because the holding company did not buy the subsidiary. There may be problems with **financial assistance** if S_2 pays less than the fair value to purchase S_3 as a prelude to S_1 leaving the group.

4.4 Subsidiary moved down

This situation could arise if H is in one country and S_1 and S_2 are in another. A **tax group** can be formed out of such a restructuring.

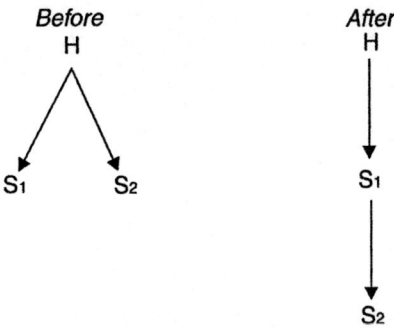

If S_1 paid cash for S_2, the transaction would be straightforward (as described above). It is unclear whether H should recognise a gain or loss on the sale if S_2 is sold for more or less than carrying value. S_1 would only be deemed to have made a distribution (avoiding any advance tax payable) only if the **price was excessive**.

4.5 Divisionalisation

This type of transaction involves the **transfer of businesses** from subsidiaries into just one company. The businesses will all be similar and this is a means of rationalising and streamlining. The savings in administration costs can be quite substantial. The remaining shell company will leave the cash it was paid on an intragroup balance as it is no longer trading. The accounting treatment is generally straightforward.

5 Demergers

> **FAST FORWARD**
>
> **Demergers** are not unusual in practice and are not difficult to account for. Concentrate on the substance of the transactions undertaken and follow the instructions in the question.

A demerger will usually involve **splitting up an existing group** into two or more separate groups. This is usually done to separate different types of trade, particularly when it is intended to sell one of the resulting parts.

There are a number of ways to carry out such a transaction.

(a) P transfers shares in S_1 to its **shareholders** as a dividend *in specie*.

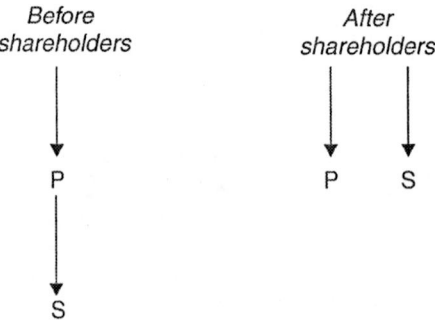

(b) P transfers a trade to **another company** S, often formed for the purpose, and in exchange S issues shares to P's shareholders.

(c) P transfers shares in S_1 to **another company** S_2, who in return issues shares to the shareholders in P.

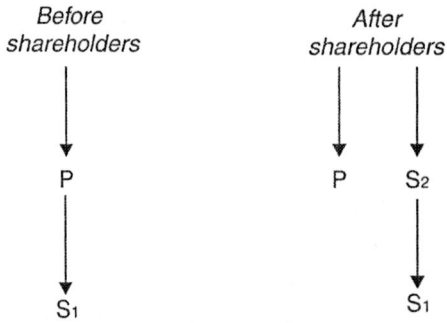

Most importantly, you should note that the transaction will **always** involve a **distribution by P to its shareholders**, even though this point may seem obscure at times.

5.1 Example: Demerger

Guinevere Co, a subsidiary of Arthur Co, is to be demerged from the group. A new company, Lancelot Co, is to be created and it will issue its shares to the shareholders of Arthur in return for the investment in Guinevere. The statements of financial position on the day before the demerger were as follows.

	Arthur plc $'000	Guinevere Co $'000	Arthur Group $'000
Investment in Guinevere	3,000		
Other net assets	7,200	4,800	12,000
	10,200	4,800	12,000
Share capital	6,000	3,000	6,000
Retained earnings	4,200	1,800	6,000
	10,200	4,800	12,000

In exchange for Arthur's holding in Guinevere, Lancelot Co issues 3 million $1 shares to Arthur Co's shareholders.

Solution

In effect this is a distribution by Arthur to its shareholders. The net assets of the company are reduced by $3m and the net assets of the group are reduced by $4.8m, the value of Guinevere. It is usual to show such treatment as movements on retained earnings.

	Company $'000	Group $'000
Retained earnings		
Balance before demerger	4,200	6,000
Demerger of Guinevere	(3,000)	(4,800)
Balance after demerger	1,200	1,200

PART B   BUSINESS COMBINATIONS AND GROUP FINANCIAL STATEMENTS

Chapter roundup

- **Disposals** can drop a subsidiary holding to associate status, financial asset investment status or to zero, or a the parent might still retain a subsidiary with a reduced holding. You should be able to deal with all these situations. Remember particularly how to deal with **goodwill**.

- Transactions of the type described in this chapter can be very complicated and certainly look rather daunting. Remember and apply the **basic techniques** and you should find such questions easier than you expected.

- **Business combinations achieved in stages (step acquisitions)** can lead to a company becoming a financial asset investment, an associate and then a subsidiary over time. Make sure you can deal with each of these situations.

- **Changes in direct ownership** (ie internal group reorganisations) can take many forms. Apart from divisionalisation, all other internal reorganisations will not affect the consolidated financial statements, but they will affect the financial statements of individual companies within the group.

- **Demergers** are not unusual in practice and are not difficult to account for. Concentrate on the substance of the transactions undertaken and follow the instructions in the question.

Quick quiz

1   Control is always lost when there is a disposal of shares in a subsidiary. True or false?

2   Why is the fair value of the interest retained used in the calculation of a gain on disposal where control is lost?

3   When is the effective date of disposal of shares in a subsidiary?

4   Subside owns 60% of Diary at 31 December 20X8. On 1 July 20X9, it buys a further 20% of Diary. How should this transaction be treated in the group financial statements at 31 December 20X9.

5   Ditch had a 75% subsidiary, Dodge, at 30 June 20X8. On 1 January 20X9, it sold two-thirds of this investment, leaving it with a 25% holding, over which it retained significant influence. How will the remaining investment in Dodge appear in the group financial statements for the year ended 30 June 20X9?

6   Why might a group undertake an internal reconstruction?

Answers to quick quiz

1. False. Control may be retained if the investee is still a subsidiary after the disposal, even though the parent owns less and the non-controlling interest owns more.

2. It is viewed as part of the consideration received.

3. When control passes

4. As a transaction between owners, with an adjustment to the parent's equity to reflect the difference between the consideration paid and the decrease in non-controlling interest.

5. At its fair value at the date of disposal plus a 25% share of the profits accrued between the date of disposal and the year end, less any impairment at the year end.

6.
   - To reduce group's gearing
   - Divisionalisation
   - For Stock Exchange quotation purposes
   - For tax purposes

End of chapter question

Mozart, Constanza and Salzburg (AIA May 2006)

The following are the summarised statements of profit or loss of Mozart, Constanza and Salzburg (three limited liability companies) for the year ended 31 December 20X5.

	Mozart $	Constanza $	Salzburg $
Revenue	9,850,000	7,684,000	5,464,500
Cost of sales	(6,402,500)	(4,610,400)	(4,371,600)
Gross profit	3,447,500	3,073,600	1,092,900
Operating expenses	(1,419,900)	(565,200)	(362,170)
Profit from operations	2,027,600	2,508,400	730,730
Proceeds from sale of shares in Salzburg	1,050,000		
Income from shares in group companies	360,000	–	–
Profit before tax	3,437,600	2,508,400	730,730
Income tax	(608,280)	(752,520)	(219,219)
Profit for the year	2,829,320	1,755,880	511,511

PART B BUSINESS COMBINATIONS AND GROUP FINANCIAL STATEMENTS

The summarised statements of financial position of the three companies as at 31 December 20X5 were:

	Mozart $	Constanza $	Salzburg $
Assets			
Non-current assets			
Property, plant and equipment	5,548,450	3,370,400	2,374,200
Investments, at cost	3,660,000	–	–
	9,208,450	3,370,400	2,374,200
Current assets	1,133,000	724,000	430,000
Total assets	10,341,450	4,094,400	2,804,200
Liabilities			
Current liabilities	767,950	434,400	318,200
Equity			
Ordinary shares of $1	5,000,000	2,000,000	1,500,000
Reserves	4,573,500	1,660,000	986,000
	9,573,500	3,660,000	2,486,000
	10,341,450	4,094,400	2,804,200

Mozart purchased 60% of the equity of Constanza for $1.40 a share in 20X2 when Constanza's reserves were $455,000. Mozart also purchased 60% of the equity of Salzburg for $2.20 a share in 20X3 when Salzburg's reserves were $785,000.

On 30 June 20X5 Mozart sold 525,000 of its shares in Salzburg for $2.00 a share. After the sale there were four shareholders in Salzburg – all limited liability companies. The shareholders put in place a contractual agreement to run Salzburg as a joint venture as from 1 July 20X5. The fair value of the group's interest in the joint venture was equal to its proportionate share of Salzburg's net assets at that date. At the date of disposal, the goodwill relating to the acquisition of Salzburg had been written down to zero.

During the year ended 31 December 20X5 Constanza paid dividends totalling $600,000. Salzburg did not pay any dividends.

The statement of profit or loss of Mozart does not include the profit or loss on the sale of the shares in Salzburg because the company accountant is not sure how this should be calculated or reported. Nor does he know how to report the tax effects of the sale of the shares. The rate of income tax is 30%. The accountant has reported the sales proceeds as income for the year.

It is the group's policy to value the non-controlling interest at its proportionate share of the fair value of the subsidiary's identifiable net assets.

Required

(a) Advise, with appropriate calculations, how the profit or loss on the disposal of the shares in Salzburg would be reported in:

   (i) Mozart's individual statement of profit or loss and other comprehensive income; and

   (ii) Mozart's consolidated statement of profit or loss and other comprehensive income for the year ended 31 December 20X5. **(6 marks)**

(b) Prepare the consolidated statement of financial position of Mozart as at 31 December 20X5. Show full supportive workings. **(19 marks)**

(Total 25 marks)

Foreign currency translation

Topic list	Syllabus reference
1 Foreign currency translation	13.2
2 IAS 21: Individual company	13.2
3 IAS 21: Consolidated financial statements	13.2
4 Hyperinflation	13.1

Introduction

Many of the largest companies in any country, while based there, have subsidiaries and other interests all over the world: they are truly **global companies** and so foreign currency consolidations take place frequently in practice.

1 Foreign currency translation

> Questions on foreign currency translation have always been popular with examiners. In general you are required to prepare **consolidated financial statements** for a group which includes a foreign subsidiary.

If a company trades overseas, it will buy or sell assets in foreign currencies. For example, an Indian company might buy materials from Canada, and pay for them in US dollars, and then sell its finished goods in Germany, receiving payment in Euros, or perhaps in some other currency. If the company owes money in a foreign currency at the end of the accounting year, or holds assets which were bought in a foreign currency, those liabilities or assets must be translated into the local currency (in this text $), in order to be shown in the books of account.

A company might have a subsidiary abroad (ie a foreign entity that it owns), and the subsidiary will trade in its own local currency. The subsidiary will keep books of account and prepare its annual financial statements in its own currency. However, at the year end, the holding company must consolidate the results of the overseas subsidiary into its group financial statements, a process which requires the assets and liabilities and the profits of the subsidiary to be translated from the foreign currency into $.

If foreign currency exchange rates remained constant, there would be no accounting problem. As you will be aware, however, foreign exchange rates are continually changing, and it is not inconceivable for example, that the rate of exchange between the Polish zloty and sterling might be Z6.2 to £1 at the start of the accounting year, and Z5.6 to £1 at the end of the year (in this example, a 10% increase in the relative strength of the zloty).

There are two distinct types of foreign currency transaction, conversion and translation.

1.1 Conversion gains and losses

Conversion is the process of exchanging amounts of one foreign currency for another. For example, suppose a local company buys a large consignment of goods from a supplier in Germany. The order is placed on 1 May and the agreed price is €124,250. At the time of delivery the rate of foreign exchange was €3.50 to $1. The local company would record the amount owed in its books as follows:

DEBIT	Inventory account (124,250 ÷ 3.5)	$35,500	
CREDIT	Payables account		$35,500

When the local company comes to pay the supplier, it needs to obtain some foreign currency. By this time, however, if the rate of exchange has altered to €3.55 to $1, the cost of raising €124,250 would be (÷ 3.55) $35,000. The company would need to spend only $35,000 to settle a debt for inventories 'costing' $35,500. Since it would be administratively difficult to alter the value of the inventories in the company's books of account, it is more appropriate to record a profit on conversion of $500.

DEBIT	Payables account	$35,500	
CREDIT	Cash		$35,000
CREDIT	Profit on conversion		$500

Profits (or losses) on conversion would be included in profit or loss for the year in which conversion (whether payment or receipt) takes place.

Suppose that another home company sells goods to a Chinese company, and it is agreed that payment should be made in Chinese Yuan at a price of Y116,000. We will further assume that the exchange rate at the time of sale is Y10.75 to $1, but when the debt is eventually paid, the rate has altered to Y10.8 to $1. The company would record the sale as follows:

DEBIT	Receivables account (116,000 ÷ 10.75)	$10,800	
CREDIT	Sales account		$10,800

When the Y116,000 are paid, the local company will convert them into $, to obtain (÷ 10.8) $10,750. In this example, there has been a loss on conversion of $50 which will be written off to profit of loss for the year:

DEBIT	Cash	$10,750
DEBIT	Loss on conversion	$50
CREDIT	Payables account	$10,800

There are **no accounting difficulties** concerned with foreign currency conversion gains or losses, and the procedures described above are uncontroversial.

1.2 Translation

Foreign currency translation, as distinct from conversion, does not involve the act of exchanging one currency for another. **Translation is required at the end of an accounting period when a company still holds assets or liabilities in its statement of financial position which were obtained or incurred in a foreign currency.**

These assets or liabilities might consist of any of the following:

(a) An individual home company holding individual **assets** or **liabilities** originating in a foreign currency 'deal'.

(b) An individual home company with a separate **branch** of the business operating abroad which keeps its own books of account in the local currency.

(c) A home company which wishes to consolidate the **results of a foreign subsidiary**.

There has been great **uncertainty** about the method which should be used to translate the following:

- Value of assets and liabilities from a foreign currency into $ for the year end statement of financial position

- Profits of an independent foreign branch or subsidiary into $ for the annual statement of profit or loss and other comprehensive income

Suppose, for example, that a Belgian subsidiary purchases a piece of property for €2,100,000 on 31 December 20X7. The rate of exchange at this time was €70 to $1. During 20X8, the subsidiary charged depreciation on the building of €16,800, so that at 31 December 20X8, the subsidiary recorded the asset as follows:

	€
Property at cost	2,100,000
Less accumulated depreciation	16,800
Carrying amount	2,083,200

At this date, the rate of exchange has changed to €60 to $1.

The local holding company must translate the asset's value into $, but there is a **choice of exchange rates**.

(a) Should the rate of exchange for translation be the rate which existed at the date of purchase, which would give a carrying amount of 2,083,200 ÷ 70 = $29,760?

(b) Should the rate of exchange for translation be the rate existing at the end of 20X8 (the closing rate of €60 to $1)? This would give a carrying amount of $34,720.

Similarly, should depreciation be charged to group profit or loss at the rate of €70 to $1 (the historical rate), €60 to $1 (the closing rate), or at an average rate for the year (say, €64 to $1)?

1.3 Consolidated financial statements

If a parent has a subsidiary whose financial statements are presented in a foreign currency, those financial statements must be translated into the local currency before they can be included in the consolidated financial statements.

- Should the subsidiary's financial statements be translated as if the subsidiary is an extension of the parent?

- Or should they be translated as if the subsidiary is a separate business?

Where the affairs of a foreign operation are very closely interlinked with those of the investing company, it should be included in the consolidated financial statements as if the transactions had been entered into by the investing company in its own currency. Non-monetary assets and depreciation are translated at **historic rate** and sales, purchase and expenses at **average rate**. **Exchange differences** arising on retranslation are reported as part of **profit or loss** on ordinary activities.

Where a foreign operation is effectively a separate business, the **closing rate** is used for most items in the financial statements. **Exchange differences** are taken **directly** to **equity** (and reported in other comprehensive income).

We will look at the consolidation of foreign subsidiaries in much more detail in Section 3 of this chapter.

2 IAS 21: Individual company

The questions discussed above are addressed by IAS 21 *The Effects of Changes in Foreign Exchange Rates*. We will examine those matters which affect single company financial statements here.

2.1 Definitions

These are some of the definitions given by IAS 21.

Key terms

> **Foreign currency.** A currency other than the functional currency of the entity.
>
> **Functional currency.** The currency of the primary economic environment in which the entity operates.
>
> **Presentation currency.** The currency in which the financial statements are presented.
>
> **Exchange rate.** The ratio of exchange for two currencies.
>
> **Exchange difference.** The difference resulting from translating a given number of units of one currency into another currency at different exchange rates.
>
> **Closing rate.** The spot exchange rate at the year end date.
>
> **Spot exchange rate.** The exchange rate for immediate delivery.
>
> **Monetary items.** Units of currency held and assets and liabilities to be received or paid in a fixed or determinable number of units of currency.
>
> (IAS 21)

Each entity – whether an individual company, a parent of a group, or an operation within a group (such as a subsidiary, associate or branch) – should determine its **functional currency** and **measure its results and financial position in that currency**.

For most individual companies the functional currency will be the currency of the country in which they are located and in which they carry out most of their transactions. Determining the functional currency is much more likely to be an issue where an entity operates as part of a group. IAS 21 contains detailed guidance on how to determine an entity's functional currency and we will look at this in Section 3.

An entity can present its financial statements in any currency (or currencies) it chooses. IAS 21 deals with the situation in which financial statements are presented in a currency other than the functional currency.

Again, this is unlikely to be an issue for most individual companies. Their presentation currency will normally be the same as their functional currency (the currency of the country in which they operate). A company's presentation currency may be different from its functional currency if it operates within a group and we will look at this in Section 3.

2.2 Foreign currency transactions: initial recognition

IAS 21 states that a foreign currency transaction should be recorded, on initial recognition in the functional currency, by applying the exchange rate between the reporting currency and the foreign currency **at the date of the transaction** to the foreign currency amount.

An **average rate** for a period may be used if exchange rates do not fluctuate significantly.

2.3 Reporting at subsequent year ends

The following rules apply at each subsequent year end:

(a) Report foreign currency **monetary items** using the **closing rate**.

(b) Report **non-monetary items** (eg non-current assets, inventories) which are carried at **historical cost** in a foreign currency using the **exchange rate at the date of the transaction** (historical rate).

(c) Report **non-monetary items** which are carried at **fair value** in a foreign currency using the exchange rates that existed **when the values were determined**.

2.4 Recognition of exchange differences

Exchange differences occur when there is a **change in the exchange rate** between the transaction date and the date of settlement of monetary items arising from a foreign currency transaction.

Exchange differences arising on the settlement of monetary items (receivables, payables, loans, cash in a foreign currency) or on translating an entity's monetary items at rates different from those at which they were translated initially, or reported in previous financial statements, should be **recognised in profit or loss** in the period in which they arise.

There are two situations to consider:

(a) The transaction is **settled in the same period** as that in which it occurred: all the exchange difference is recognised in that period.

(b) The transaction is **settled in a subsequent accounting period**: the exchange difference recognised in each intervening period up to the period of settlement is determined by the change in exchange rates during that period.

In other words, where a monetary item has not been settled at the end of a period, it should be **restated using the closing exchange rate** and any gain or loss recognised in profit or loss.

Question — Entries

White Cliffs Co, whose year end is 31 December, buys some goods from Rinka SA of France on 30 September. The invoice value is €40,000 and is due for settlement in equal instalments on 30 November and 31 January.

The exchange rate moved as follows:

	€ = $1
30 September	1.60
30 November	1.80
31 December	1.90
31 January	1.85

Required

State the accounting entries in the books of White Cliffs Co.

Answer

The purchase will be recorded in the books of White Cliffs Co using the rate of exchange ruling on 30 September.

DEBIT	Purchases	$25,000	
CREDIT	Trade payables		$25,000

Being the $ cost of goods purchased for €40,000 (€40,000 ÷ €1.60/$1)

On 30 November, White Cliffs must pay €20,000. This will cost €20,000 ÷ €1.80/$1 = $11,111 and the company has therefore made an exchange gain of $12,500 − $11,111 = $1,389.

DEBIT	Trade payables	$12,500	
CREDIT	Profit or loss: exchange gains		$1,389
CREDIT	Cash		$11,111

On 31 December, the year end, the outstanding liability will be recalculated using the rate applicable to that date: €20,000 ÷ €1.90/$1 = $10,526. A further exchange gain of $1,974 has been made and will be recorded as follows:

DEBIT	Trade payables	$1,974	
CREDIT	Profit or loss: exchange gains		$1,974

The total exchange gain of $3,363 will be included in the operating profit for the year ending 31 December.

On 31 January, White Cliffs must pay the second instalment of €20,000. This will cost them $10,811 (€20,000 ÷ €1.85/$1).

DEBIT	Trade payables	$10,526	
	Profit or loss: exchange losses	$285	
CREDIT	Cash		$10,811

When a gain or loss on a non-monetary item is recognised in other comprehensive income, any **related exchange differences** should also be **recognised in other comprehensive income**. This might happen, for example, where property is revalued.

3 IAS 21: Consolidated financial statements

3.1 Definitions

The following definitions are relevant here.

Key terms

> **Foreign operation.** A subsidiary, associate, joint venture or branch of a reporting entity, the activities of which are based or conducted in a country or currency other than those of the reporting entity.
>
> **Net investment in a foreign operation.** The amount of the reporting entity's interest in the net assets of that operation. (IAS 21)

3.2 Determining functional currency

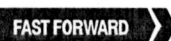

> You may have to make the decision yourself as to whether the subsidiary has the same functional currency as the parent or a different functional currency from the parent. This determines whether the subsidiary is treated as an **extension of the parent** or as a **net investment**.

A holding or parent company with foreign operations must **translate the financial statements** of those operations into its own reporting currency before they can be consolidated into the group financial statements. In theory there are two methods: **the method used depends** upon **whether** the foreign operation has the **same functional currency as the parent**.

IAS 21 states that an entity should consider the following factors in determining its functional currency:

(a) The currency that mainly **influences sales prices** for goods and services (often the currency in which prices are denominated and settled)

(b) The currency of the **country whose competitive forces and regulations** mainly determine the sales prices of its goods and services

(c) The currency that mainly **influences labour, material and other costs** of providing goods or services (often the currency in which prices are denominated and settled)

Sometimes the functional currency of an entity is not immediately obvious. Management must then exercise judgement and may also need to consider:

(a) The currency in which **funds from financing activities** (raising loans and issuing equity) are generated

(b) The currency in which **receipts from operating activities** are usually retained

Where a parent has a foreign operation a number of factors are considered:

(a) Whether the activities of the foreign operation are carried out as an **extension of the parent**, rather than being carried out with a **significant degree of autonomy**

(b) Whether **transactions with the parent** are a high or a low proportion of the foreign operation's activities

(c) Whether **cash flows** from the activities of the foreign operation **directly affect the cash flows of the parent** and are readily available for remittance to it

(d) Whether the activities of the foreign operation are **financed from its own cash flows** or by **borrowing from the parent**

To sum up: in order to determine the functional currency of a foreign operation it is necessary to consider the **relationship** between the foreign operation and its parent:

- If the foreign operation carries out its business as though it were an **extension of the parent's operations**, it almost certainly has the **same functional currency** as the parent.

- If the foreign operation is **semi-autonomous** it almost certainly has **a different functional currency** from the parent.

The translation method used has to reflect the economic reality of the relationship between the reporting entity (the parent) and the foreign operation.

3.2.1 Same functional currency as the reporting entity

In this situation, the foreign operation normally carries on its business as though it were an **extension of the reporting entity's operations**. For example, it may only sell goods imported from, and remit the proceeds directly to, the reporting entity.

Any **movement in the exchange rate** between the reporting currency and the foreign operation's currency will have an **immediate impact** on the reporting entity's cash flows from the foreign operations. In other words, changes in the exchange rate affect the **individual monetary items** held by the foreign operation, **not** the reporting entity's net investment in that operation.

3.2.2 Different functional currency from the reporting entity

Exam focus point

Many exam questions consist of a foreign operation consolidation.

In this situation, although the reporting entity may be able to exercise control, the foreign operation normally operates in a **semi-autonomous** way. It accumulates cash and other monetary items, generates income and incurs expenses, and may also arrange borrowings, all **in its own local currency**.

A change in the exchange rate will produce **little or no direct effect on the present and future cash flows** from operations of either the foreign operation or the reporting entity. Rather, the change in exchange rate affects the reporting entity's **net investment** in the foreign operation, not the individual monetary and non-monetary items held by the foreign operation.

> **Exam focus point**
>
> Where the foreign operation's functional currency is different from the parent's, the financial statements need to be translated before consolidation.

3.3 Accounting treatment: Same functional currency as the reporting entity

Where a foreign operation has the same functional currency as its parent, it will almost certainly keep its accounting records in its functional currency, even if this is not the same as the local currency. This means that the financial statements of the foreign operation **do not need to be translated**.

In theory, the foreign operation could keep its accounting records and prepare individual financial statements in the local currency. In this situation, the foreign operation's transactions should be translated **as if they had been those of the parent**. The same procedures used for individual company financial statements should be applied (see Section 2 above).

We can summarise the treatment here:

(a) **Statement of profit or loss and other comprehensive income:** translate using actual rates.
An average for a period may be used, but not where there is significant fluctuation and the average is therefore unreliable.

(b) **Non-monetary items**: translate using an historical rate at the date of purchase (or revaluation to fair value, or reduction to realisable/recoverable amount). This includes inventories and non-current assets (and their depreciation).

(c) **Monetary items**: translate at the closing rate.

(d) **Exchange differences**: report as part of profit or loss for the year.

IAS 21 does not directly cover this situation or this method of translation as it assumes that where a foreign operation has the same functional currency as the parent the foreign operation always prepares financial statements in the functional currency.

3.4 Accounting treatment: Different functional currency from the reporting entity

The financial statements of the foreign operation must be translated to the functional currency of the parent. Different procedures must be followed here, because the functional currency of the parent is the **presentation currency** of the foreign operation.

(a) The **assets and liabilities** shown in the foreign operation's statement of financial position are translated at the **closing rate** at the year end, regardless of the date on which those items originated. The balancing figure in the translated statement of financial position represents the reporting entity's net investment in the foreign operation.

(b) Amounts in the **statement of profit or loss and other comprehensive income** should be translated at the rate ruling at the date of the transaction (an **average rate** will usually be used for practical purposes).

(c) **Exchange differences** arising from the re-translation at the end of each year of the parent's net investment should be **reported in other comprehensive income and taken to equity**, not included in profit or loss for the year, until the disposal of the net investment.

3.5 Example: Different functional currency from the reporting entity

A dollar-based company, Stone Co, set up a foreign subsidiary on 30 June 20X7. Stone subscribed €24,000 for share capital when the exchange rate was €2 = $1. The subsidiary, Brick Inc, borrowed €72,000 and bought a non-monetary asset for €96,000. Stone Co prepared its financial statements on 31 December 20X7 and by that time the exchange rate had moved to €3 = $1. As a result of highly unusual circumstances, Brick Inc sold its asset early in 20X8 for €96,000. It repaid its loan and was liquidated. Stone's capital of €24,000 was repaid in February 20X8 when the exchange rate was €3 = $1.

Required

Account for the above transactions as if the entity has a different functional currency from the parent.

Solution

From the above it can be seen that Stone Co will record its initial investment at $12,000 (€24,000 ÷ €2/$1) which is the starting cost of its shares. The statement of financial position of Brick Inc at 31 December 20X7 is summarised below.

	€'000
Non-monetary asset	96
Share capital	24
Loan	72
	96

This may be translated as follows.

	$'000
Non-monetary asset (€3 = $1)	32
Share capital and reserves (retained earnings) (balancing figure)	8
Loan (€3 = $1)	24
	32
Exchange gain/(loss) for 20X7	(4)

The exchange loss is the differences between the value of the original investment ($12,000) and the total of share capital and reserves (retained earnings) as disclosed by the above statements of financial position.

On liquidation, Stone Co will receive $8,000 (€24,000 converted at €3 = $1). No gain or loss will arise in 20X8.

3.6 Some practical points

The following points apply:

(a) For consolidation purposes calculations are simpler if a subsidiary's share capital is translated at the **historical rate** (the rate when the investing company acquired its interest) and reserves are found as a balancing figure.

(b) **Dividends declared** by a subsidiary should always be translated at the actual rate on the dates of payment. This is because the investing company will record the items at these rates in its own books.

> **FAST FORWARD**
>
> You must be able to calculate **exchange differences**.
>
> **Practising** examination questions is the best way of learning this topic.

3.7 Summary of method

A summary of the translation method is given below, which shows the main steps to follow in the consolidation process.

PART B BUSINESS COMBINATIONS AND GROUP FINANCIAL STATEMENTS

Exam focus point

You should learn this summary.

Step	Translation
Step 1 Translate the **closing statement of financial position** (net assets/shareholders' funds) and use this for preparing the consolidated statement of financial position in the normal way.	Use the **closing rate** at the year end for all items (see note).
Step 2 Translate the **statement of profit or loss and other comprehensive income**. (In all cases, dividends should be translated at the rate ruling when the dividend was paid.)	Use the **average rate** for the year for all items (but see comment on dividends). The figures obtained can then be used in preparing the consolidated statement of profit or loss and other comprehensive income.
Step 3 Translate the **shareholders' funds** (net assets) at the beginning of the year.	Use the **closing rate** at the beginning of the year (the opening rate for the current year).
Step 4 Calculate the **total exchange difference** for the year as follows. \$ Closing net assets at closing rate (Step 1) X Less opening net Assets at opening rate (Step 3) X X Less retained profit per translated statement of profit or loss and other comprehensive income (Step 2) X Exchange differences X Group share (%) X It may be necessary to adjust for any profits or losses taken direct to reserves during the year.	This stage will be **unnecessary** unless you are asked to state the total exchange differences or are asked to prepare a statement of the movement on reserves, where the exchange difference will be shown. For **exam purposes** you can translate the closing shareholders' funds as follows. (a) Share capital + pre-acquisition reserves at historical rate. (b) Post-acquisition reserves as a balancing figure.

Note. As mentioned above, the share capital may be translated at the historical rate. The reserves will then be the balancing figure. The advantage of this method is that it simplifies the 'cancellation' of the share capital on consolidation.

Question Consolidated financial statements

The abridged statements of financial position and statements of profit or loss and other comprehensive income of Darius Co and its foreign subsidiary, Xerxes Inc, appear below.

DRAFT STATEMENT OF FINANCIAL POSITION AS AT 31 DECEMBER 20X9

	Darius Co $	Darius Co $	Xerxes Inc €	Xerxes Inc €
Assets				
Non-current assets				
Plant at cost	600		500	
Less depreciation	(250)		(200)	
		350		300
Investment in Xerxes				
100 €1 shares		25		–
		375		300
Current assets				
Inventories	225		200	
Receivables	150		100	
		375		300
		750		600
Equity and liabilities				
Equity				
Ordinary $1/€1 shares	300		100	
Retained earnings	300		280	
		600		380
Non-current loans		50		110
Current liabilities		100		110
		750		600

STATEMENTS OF PROFIT OR LOSS AND OTHER COMPREHENSIVE INCOME
FOR THE YEAR ENDED 31 DECEMBER 20X9

	Darius Co $	Xerxes Inc €
Profit before tax	200	160
Tax	100	80
Profit after tax, retained	100	80

The following further information is given.

(a) Darius Co has had its interest in Xerxes Inc since the incorporation of the company.

(b) Depreciation is 8% per annum on cost.

(c) There have been no loan repayments or movements in the cost of non-current assets during the year. The opening inventory of Xerxes Inc was €120. Assume that inventory turnover times are very short.

(d) Exchange rates: €4 to $1 when Xerxes Inc was incorporated
€2.5 to $1 when Xerxes Inc acquired its non-current assets
€2 to $1 on 31 December 20X8
€1.6 to $1 average rate of exchange year ending 31 December 20X9
€1 to $1 on 31 December 20X9.

Required

Prepare the summarised consolidated financial statements of Darius Co.

PART B BUSINESS COMBINATIONS AND GROUP FINANCIAL STATEMENTS

Answer

Step 1 The statement of financial position of Xerxes Inc at 31 December 20X9, other than share capital and retained earnings, should be translated at € 1 = $1.

SUMMARISED STATEMENT OF FINANCIAL POSITION AT 31 DECEMBER 20X9

	$	$
Non-current assets (NBV)		300
Current assets		
Inventories	200	
Receivables	100	
		300
		600
Non-current liabilities		110
Current liabilities		110

∴ Shareholders' funds = 600 – 110 – 110 = $380

Since Darius Co acquired the whole of the issued share capital on incorporation, the post-acquisition retained earnings including exchange differences will be the value of shareholders' funds arrived at above, less the original cost to Darius Co of $25. Post-acquisition retained earnings = $380 – $25 = $355.

SUMMARISED CONSOLIDATED STATEMENT OF FINANCIAL POSITION AS AT 31 DECEMBER 20X9

		$	$
Assets			
Non-current assets (net carrying amount)	$(350 + 300)		650
Current assets			
Inventories	$(225 + 200)	425	
Receivables	$(150 + 100)	250	
			675
			1,325
Equity and liabilities			
Equity			
Ordinary $1 shares (Darius only)			300
Retained earnings	$(300 + 355)		655
			955
Non-current liabilities: loans	$(50 + 110)		160
Current liabilities	$(100 + 110)		210
			1,325

Note. It is quite unnecessary to know the amount of the exchange differences when preparing the consolidated statement of financial position.

Step 2 The statement of profit or loss and other comprehensive income should be translated at average rate (€1.6 = $1).

SUMMARISED STATEMENT OF PROFIT OR LOSS AND OTHER COMPREHENSIVE INCOME OF XERXES INC FOR THE YEAR ENDED 31 DECEMBER 20X9

	$
Profit before tax	100
Tax	50
Profit after tax, retained	50

SUMMARISED CONSOLIDATED STATEMENT OF PROFIT OR LOSS AND OTHER COMPREHENSIVE INCOME FOR THE YEAR ENDED 31 DECEMBER 20X9

		$
Profit before tax	$(200 + 100)	300
Tax	$(100 + 50)	150
Profit after tax, retained	$(100 + 50)	150

Step 3 The equity interest at the beginning of the year can be found as follows.

	€
Equity value at 31 December 20X9	380
Retained profit for year	80
Equity value at 31 December 20X8	300

Translated at € 2 = $1, this gives $150

Step 4 The exchange difference can now be calculated.

	$
Equity interest at 31 December 20X9 (stage 1)	380
Equity interest at 1 January 20X9 (stage 3)	150
	230
Less retained profit (stage 2)	50
Exchange gain	180

CONSOLIDATED STATEMENT OF MOVEMENTS ON RESERVES
FOR THE YEAR ENDED 31 DECEMBER 20X9

	$
Consolidated reserves at 31 December 20X8	325
Exchange gains arising on consolidation	180
Retained profit for the year	150
Consolidated reserves at 31 December 20X9	655

Notes

1. The post-acquisition reserves of Xerxes Inc at the beginning of the year must have been $150 – $25 = $125 and the reserves of Darius Co must have been $300 – $100 = $200. The consolidated reserves must therefore have been $325.

2. The exchange gains arising on consolidation are reported as a separate line item in 'other comprehensive income'.

3.8 Analysis of exchange differences

The exchange differences in the above exercise could be reconciled by splitting them into their component parts.

Exam focus point
Such a split is not required by IAS 21, but it may help your understanding of the subject.

The exchange difference consists of those exchange gains/losses arising from:

- Translating **income/expense items** at the exchange rates at the date of transactions, whereas **assets/liabilities** are translated at the closing rate.

- Translating the **opening net investment** (opening net assets) in the foreign entity at a closing rate different from the closing rate at which it was previously reported.

This can be demonstrated using the above question.

Using the opening statement of financial position and translating at €2 = $1 and €1 = $1 gives the following.

	€2 = $1 $	€1 = $1 $	Difference $
Non-current assets at net carrying amount (€300 + (depreciation of 8% of €500) = €340)	170	340	170
Inventories (€120)	60	120	60
Net current monetary liabilities (balancing figure)	(25)	(50)	(25)
Total = €410 (see below)	205	410	205
Shareholders' funds (€380 – €80 = €300)	150	300	150
Loans (€110)	55	110	55
Total = €410	205	410	205

PART B BUSINESS COMBINATIONS AND GROUP FINANCIAL STATEMENTS

Translating the statement of profit or loss and other comprehensive income using €1.60 = $1 and €1 = $1 gives the following results.

	€1.60 = $1 $	€1 = $1 $	Difference $
Profit before tax, depreciation and increase in inventory values	75	120	45
Increase in inventory values	50	80	30
	125	200	75
Depreciation	(25)	(40)	(15)
	100	160	60
Tax	(50)	(80)	(30)
Profit after tax, retained	50	80	30

The overall position is then:

	$	$
Gain on non-current assets ($170 – $15)		155
Loss on loan		(55)
Gain on inventories ($60 + $30)	90	
Loss on net monetary current assets/ Liabilities (all other differences) ($45 – $30 – $25)	(10)	
		80
Net exchange gain: as above		180

3.9 Non-controlling interest

In problems involving non-controlling interest the following points should be noted.

(a) The figure for **non-controlling interest in the statement of financial position** will be the appropriate proportion of the translated share capital and reserves of the subsidiary. In addition, it may be necessary to show any dividend payable to the NCI as a liability. Dividends payable should be translated at the closing rate for this purpose.

(b) The **non-controlling interest in the statement of profit or loss and other comprehensive income** will be the appropriate proportion of dollar profits available for distribution. If the functional currency of the subsidiary is the same as that of the parent, this profit will be arrived at **after** charging or crediting the exchange differences.

3.10 Example: Non-controlling interest

The summarised financial statements of Camrumite Inc are shown below.

STATEMENT OF FINANCIAL POSITION AS AT 31 DECEMBER 20X3

	€
Non-current assets	10,000
Net monetary assets	5,000
	15,000
Equity (share capital and reserves)	15,000

STATEMENT OF CHANGES IN EQUITY FOR THE YEAR ENDED 31 DECEMBER 20X3

	€
Profit after tax	3,080
Dividends payable	1,680
Retained profit	1,400

60% of the issued capital of Camrumite Inc is owned by Bates Co, a company based in another country.

There have been no movements in non-current assets during the year. The depreciation charge for the year was €560.

The exchange rate has moved as follows:

Date on which non-current assets were acquired	€8 = $1
1 January 20X3	€5 = $1
Average for the year ended 31.12.X3	€7 = $1
31 December 20X3	€8 = $1

You are required to calculate the figures for non-controlling interest to be included in the consolidated financial statements of Bates Co.

Show the movements on the non-controlling interest account during the year.

Solution

Translating the shareholders' funds using the closing rate as at 31 December 20X3 gives €15,000 ÷ 8 = $1,875. The non-controlling interest in the statement of financial position will be 40% × $1,875 = $750.

The dividend payable translated at the closing rate is €1,680 ÷ 8 = $210. The amount payable to the non-controlling shareholders is 40% × $210 = $84.

The profit after tax translated at the average rate is €3,080 ÷ 7 = $440. The non-controlling interest in the statement of profit or loss and other comprehensive income is therefore 40% × $440 = $176.

At the beginning of the year the share capital and reserves must have been €15,000 – €1,400 = €13,600. Translating this at the rate ruling on 1 January 20X3 gives €13,600 ÷ 5 = $2,720. The non-controlling interest at 1 January 20X3 was 40% × $2,720 = $1,088.

	$	$
Shareholders' funds as at 1 January 20X3		2,720
Add: profit for year	440	
less dividends	210	
		230
		2,950
Less shareholders' funds at 31 December 20X3		1,875
Exchange loss		1,075
Non-controlling interest therein $1,075 × 40%		430

The non-controlling interest can be summarised as follows:

	$
Balance at 1 January 20X3	1,088
Non-controlling interest in profit for the year	176
Non-controlling interest in exchange losses	(430)
	834
Balance at 31 December 20X3	750
Dividend payable to non-controlling shareholders	84
	834

3.11 Further matters relating to foreign operations

3.11.1 Goodwill and fair value adjustments

Goodwill and fair value adjustments arising on the acquisition of a foreign operation should be treated as assets and liabilities of the acquired entity. This means that they should be expressed in the functional currency of the foreign operation and translated at the **closing rate**.

Here is a layout for calculating goodwill and the exchange gain or loss. The parent holds 90% of the shares. NCI is valued as the proportionate share of the fair value of the subsidiary's identifiable net assets.

Goodwill

	F'000	F'000	Rate	$'000
Consideration transferred (12,000 × 6)		72,000		
Non-controlling interest		6,600		
66,000 × 10%		78,600		
Less:				
Less share capital	40,000			
Pre acquisition retained earnings	26,000			
		(66,000)		
At 1.4.X1		12,600	6**	2,100
Foreign exchange gain		–	Balance	420
At 31.3.X7		12,600	5***	2,520

** Historic rate
*** Closing rate

3.11.2 Consolidation procedures

Follow normal consolidation procedures, except that where an exchange difference arises on **long or short-term intra-group monetary items**, these cannot be offset against other intra-group balances. This is because these are commitments to convert one currency into another, thus exposing the reporting entity to a gain or loss through currency fluctuations.

If the foreign operation's **reporting date** is different from that of the parent, it is acceptable to use the financial statements made up to that date for consolidation, as long as adjustments are made for any significant changes in rates in the interim.

3.11.3 Hyperinflationary economies

We will look at IAS 29 *Financial Reporting in Hyperinflationary Economies* in Section 4. The financial statements of a foreign operation operating in a hyperinflationary economy must be adjusted under IAS 29 before they are translated into the parent's reporting currency and then consolidated. When the economy **ceases to be hyperinflationary**, and the foreign operation ceases to apply IAS 29, the amounts restated to the price level at the date the entity ceased to restate its financial statements should be used as the historical costs for translation purposes.

3.11.4 Disposal of foreign entity

When a parent disposes of a foreign entity, the cumulative amount of deemed exchange differences relating to that foreign entity should be **reclassified from equity to profit or loss** (ie recognised as **income** or **expense**) in the same period in which the gain or loss on disposal is recognised. Effectively, this means that these exchange differences are recognised once by taking them to reserves and then are recognised for a second time ('recycled') by transferring them to profit or loss (the statement of profit or loss and other comprehensive income) on disposal of the foreign operation.

3.11.5 In the parent's financial statements

In the parent company's own financial statements, exchange differences arising on a **monetary item** that is effectively part of the parent's net investment in the foreign entity should be recognised **in profit or loss** in the separate financial statements of the reporting entity or the individual financial statements of the foreign operation, as appropriate.

3.12 Change in functional currency

The functional currency of an entity can be changed only if there is a change to the underlying transactions, events and conditions that are relevant to the entity. For example, an entity's functional currency may change if there is a change in the currency that mainly influences the sales price of goods and services.

Where there is a change in an entity's functional currency, the entity translates all items into the new functional currency **prospectively** (ie from the date of the change) using the exchange rate at the date of the change.

3.13 Tax effects of exchange differences

IAS 12 *Income Taxes* should be applied when there are tax effects arising from gains or losses on foreign currency transactions and exchange differences arising on the translation of the financial statements of foreign operations.

3.14 Foreign associates

Foreign associates will be companies with substantial autonomy from the group and so their **functional currency will be different** from that of the parent.

3.15 Section summary

- Where the functional currency of a foreign operation is **different** from that of the parent/reporting entity, they need to be translated before consolidation
    - Operation is semi-autonomous
    - Translate assets and liabilities at **closing rate**
    - Translate statement of profit or loss and other comprehensive income at **average rate**
    - Exchange differences through **reserves/equity**

4 Hyperinflation

FAST FORWARD

IAS 29 *Financial Reporting in Hyperinflationary Economies* requires financial statements of entities operating within a hyperinflationary economy to be restated in terms of measuring units current at the year end.

In a hyperinflationary economy, **money loses its purchasing power very quickly**. Comparisons of transactions at different points in time, even within the same accounting period, are misleading. It is therefore considered inappropriate for entities to prepare financial statements without making adjustments for the **fall in the purchasing power of money over time**.

IAS 29 *Financial Reporting in Hyperinflationary Economies* applies to the **primary financial statements** of entities (including consolidated financial statements and statements of cash flows) whose functional currency is the currency of a hyperinflationary economy. In this section, we will identify the hyperinflationary currency as $H.

The standard does not define a **hyperinflationary economy** in exact terms, although it indicates the characteristics of such an economy, for example, where the cumulative inflation rate over three years approaches or exceeds 100%.

Question — Hyperinflation

What other factors might indicate a hyperinflationary economy?

Answer

These are examples, but the list is not exhaustive.

(a) The population prefers to retain its wealth in non-monetary assets or in a relatively stable foreign currency. Amounts of local currency held are immediately invested to maintain purchasing power.

(b) The population regards monetary amounts not in terms of the local currency but in terms of a relatively stable foreign currency. Prices may be quoted in that currency.

(c) Sales/purchases on credit take place at prices that compensate for the expected loss of purchasing power during the credit period, even if that period is short.

(d) Interest rates, wages and prices are linked to a price index.

The reported value of **non-monetary assets**, in terms of current measuring units, increases over time. For example, if a non-current asset is purchased for $H1,000 when the price index is 100, and the price index subsequently rises to 200, the value of the asset in terms of current measuring units (ignoring accumulated depreciation) will rise to $H2,000.

In contrast, the value of **monetary assets and liabilities**, such as a debt for 300 units, is unaffected by changes in the prices index, because it is an actual money amount payable or receivable. If a customer owes $H300 when the price index is 100, and the debt is still unpaid when the price index has risen to 150, the customer still owes just $H300. The purchasing power of monetary assets, however, will decline over time as the general level of prices goes up.

4.1 Requirement to restate financial statements in terms of measuring units current at the year end

In most countries, financial statements are produced on the basis of either:

(a) **Historical cost**, except to the extent that some assets (eg property and investments) may be revalued, or

(b) **Current cost**, which reflects the changes in the values of specific assets held by the entity.

In a hyperinflationary economy, neither of these methods of financial reporting are meaningful unless adjustments are made for the fall in the purchasing power of money. IAS 29 therefore requires that the **primary financial statements** of entities in a hyperinflationary economy should be produced by restating the figures prepared on either a historical cost basis or a current cost basis in terms of **measuring units current at the year end**.

Key term

> **Measuring unit current at the year end date.** This is a unit of local currency with a purchasing power as at the date of the statement of financial position, measured by reference to a general prices index.

Financial statements that are not restated (ie that are prepared on a historical cost basis or current cost basis without adjustments) may be presented as **additional statements** by the entity, but this is discouraged. The primary financial statements are those that have been restated.

After the assets, liabilities, equity and statement of profit or loss and other comprehensive income of the entity have been restated, there will be a **net gain or loss on monetary assets and liabilities (the 'net monetary position')** and this should be recognised separately in profit or loss for the period.

4.2 Making the adjustments

IAS 29 recognises that the resulting financial statements, after restating all items in terms of measuring units current at the year end, will **lack precise accuracy**. However, it is more important that certain procedures and judgements should be applied consistently from year to year. The implementation guidelines to the standard suggest what these procedures should be.

4.3 Statement of financial position: Historical cost

Where the entity produces its financial statements on a historical cost basis, the following procedures should be applied:

(a) Items that are not already expressed in terms of measuring units current at the year end should be restated, using a **general prices index**, so that they are valued in measuring units current at the year end.

(b) **Monetary assets and liabilities** are not restated, because they are already expressed in terms of measuring units current at the year end.

(c) Assets that are **already stated at market value or net realisable value** need not be restated, because they too are already valued in measuring units current at the year end.

(d) Any assets or liabilities **linked by agreement to changes in the general level of prices**, such as indexed-linked loans or bonds, should be adjusted in accordance with the terms of the agreement to establish the amount outstanding as at the year end.

(e) All **other non-monetary assets**, eg tangible non-current assets, intangible non-current assets (including accumulated depreciation/amortisation) investments and inventories, should be restated in terms of measuring units as at the year end, by applying a general prices index.

The **method of restating** these assets should normally be to multiply the original cost of the assets by a factor: (prices index at year end /prices index at date of acquisition of the asset). For example, if an item of machinery was purchased for $H2,000 units when the prices index was 400 and the prices index at the year end is 1,000, the restated value of the non-current asset (before accumulated depreciation) would be:

$$\$H2,000 \times (1,000/400) = \$H5,000$$

If, in the above example, the non-current asset has been held for half its useful life and has no residual value, the **accumulated depreciation** would be restated as $H2,500. (The depreciation charge for the year should be the amount of depreciation based on historical cost, multiplied by the same factor as above: 1,000/400.)

If an asset has been **revalued** since it was originally purchased (eg a property), it should be restated in measuring units at the year end date by applying a factor: (prices index at year end/prices index at revaluation date) to the revalued amount of the asset.

If the restated amount of a non-monetary asset **exceeds its recoverable amount** (ie its net realisable value or fair value), its value should be reduced accordingly.

The **owners' equity** (all components) as at the start of the accounting period should be restated using a general prices index from the beginning of the period.

4.4 Statement of profit or loss and other comprehensive income: historical cost

In the statement of profit or loss and other comprehensive income, all amounts of income and expense should be **restated in terms of measuring units current at the year end**. All amounts therefore need to be restated by a factor that allows for the change in the prices index since the item of income or expense was first recorded.

4.5 Gain or loss on net monetary position

In a period of inflation, an entity that holds monetary assets (cash, receivables) will suffer a fall in the purchasing power of these assets. By the same token, in a period of inflation, the value of monetary liabilities, such as a bank overdraft or bank loan, declines in terms of current purchasing power.

(a) If an entity has an **excess of monetary assets over monetary liabilities**, it will suffer a loss over time on its net monetary position, in a period of inflation, in terms of measuring units as at 'today's date'.

(b) If an entity has an **excess of monetary liabilities over monetary assets**, it will make a gain on its net monetary position, in a period of inflation.

4.6 Example: Hyperinflationary financial statements

An entity maintains an unchanged position over time. At 1 January, when the general prices index was 100, its statement of financial position was as follows:

	$H
Assets	
Non-monetary assets	2,000
Monetary assets	2,000
	4,000
Liabilities and equity	
Monetary liabilities	1,000
Equity	3,000
	4,000

Suppose that the general prices index rises to 150 at 31 December.

Required

Show the adjustments required in the statement of financial position.

Solution

Restating this statement of financial position in terms of measuring units when the prices index is 50% higher gives the following.

	$H
Assets	
Non-monetary assets ($\times$ 150/100)	3,000
Monetary assets	2,000
	5,000
Liabilities and equity	
Monetary liabilities	1,000
Equity ($\times$ 150/100)	4,500
	5,500

The entity has suffered a loss on its net monetary position of $H500, in terms of measuring units at the current date $H(5,500 – 5,000). This is because it has held net monetary assets of $H1,000 during the period.

In the financial statements of an entity reporting in the currency of a hyperinflationary economy, the gain or loss on the net monetary position:

(a) May be derived as the **difference between total assets and total equity and liabilities**, after restating the non-monetary assets, owners' equity, statement of profit or loss and other comprehensive income items and index-linked items; **or**

(b) May be estimated by **applying the change in the general prices index** for the period to the weighted average of the net monetary position of the entity in the period.

The gain or loss on the net monetary position should be **included in net income** and disclosed separately. (Any adjustment that was made to index-linked items can be set off against this net monetary gain or loss.)

4.7 Current cost financial statements: Restating the financial statements

A similar procedure is required to restate the financial statements of an entity that prepares its financial statements using a current cost basis.

(a) Items stated in the statement of financial position at current cost do not need to be restated. Other items should be restated in the same way as for adjusting financial statements prepared on a historical cost basis.

(b) In the **statement of profit or loss and other comprehensive income**, cost of sales and depreciation are generally reported at current costs at the time of consumption and sales and other expenses at money amounts at the time they occurred. These items will need to be restated in terms of measuring units as at the year end by making a prices index adjustment.

(c) There will be a **gain or loss on the net monetary position**, which will be established in the same way as for financial statements based on historical cost.

4.8 Economies ceasing to be hyperinflationary economies

When an economy ceases to be a hyperinflation economy, entities reporting in the currency of the economy are no longer required to produce financial statements in compliance with IAS 29.

Suppose for example that in 20X4 an entity reports in compliance with IAS 29, but in 20X5 it reverts to historical cost accounting because the economy is no longer a hyperinflationary economy. As a starting point for reverting to historical cost reporting, the entity should use the amounts expressed in terms of measuring units as at the end of 20X4 as the basis for its carrying amounts in 20X5 and subsequent years.

4.9 Disclosures

IAS 29 calls for the following disclosures:

- The fact that the **financial statements have been restated** for the changes in general purchasing power.
- Whether the financial statements as shown are based on **historical cost or current cost**.
- The **identity of the prices index** used to make the restatements, its level at the year end the movement in the index during the current and the previous reporting periods.

In financial statements prepared under IAS 29, corresponding figures for the previous year should be **restated using the general prices index**.

4.10 Hyperinflation and changes in foreign exchange rates

IAS 21 *The Effects of Changes in Foreign Exchange Rates* was covered earlier in this chapter. A parent may have a foreign operation whose functional currency is the currency of a hyperinflationary economy. When the parent prepares consolidated financial statements it should:

(a) **Restate the financial statements** of the foreign operation in accordance with IAS 29; **before**

(b) **Translating all amounts** from the foreign operation's functional currency to the presentation currency **at the closing rate**.

The following example is a simple illustration of the problems that can arise where a foreign subsidiary operates in a hyperinflationary economy.

4.11 Example: 'Disappearing assets'

A company has a subsidiary in a country which suffers from hyperinflation. On 31 December 20X2 the subsidiary acquired freehold land for $H1,000,000. At that date the exchange rate was $H4 = $1 and the relevant price index was 100.

At 31 December 20X3 the exchange rate was $H10 = $1 and the price index was 300.

Required

Show the value at which the freehold land is included in the consolidated financial statements of the parent at 31 December 20X3 if the subsidiary's financial statements:

(a) Are not restated to reflect current price levels;

(b) Are restated to reflect current price levels.

Solution

(a) *Without restatement*

Assuming that the subsidiary has a different functional currency ($H) from that of its parent ($) the statement of financial position is translated at the closing rate.

At 31 December 20X3 the land is included at $100,000 ($H1,000,000 @ 10).

At 31 December 20X2 (the date of purchase) its was stated at $250,000 ($H1,000,000 @ 4). Therefore there has been an exchange loss of $150,000 (which may significantly reduce equity) and the land appears to have fallen to only 40% of its original value.

(b) *With restatement*

At 31 December 20X3 the land is included at $300,000 ($H1,000,000 × 300/100 @ 10).

The value of the land is now adjusted so that it reflects the effect of inflation over the year and the 'disappearing assets' problem is overcome.

Where the financial statements of an entity whose functional currency is that of a hyperinflationary economy are translated into a different presentation currency, **comparative amounts** should be those that were presented as current year amounts in the relevant prior year financial statements (ie **not adjusted** for subsequent changes in the price level or subsequent changes in exchange rates).

4.12 Section summary

- IAS 29 does not define **hyperinflationary economies**, but they have various characteristics.
- Financial statements should be **restated based on a measuring unit current** at the year end
    - **Monetary assets/liabilities** do not need to be restated
    - **Non-monetary assets/liabilities** must be restated by applying a general prices index
    - **Items of income/expense** must be restated
    - **Gain/loss on net monetary items** must be reported in profit or loss for the year

9: FOREIGN CURRENCY TRANSLATION

Chapter roundup

- Questions on foreign currency translation have always been popular with examiners. In general you are required to prepare **consolidated financial statements** for a group which includes a foreign subsidiary.

- You may have to make the decision yourself as to whether the subsidiary has the same functional currency as the parent or a different functional currency from the parent. This determines whether the subsidiary is treated as an **extension of the parent** or as a **net investment**.

- You must be able to calculate **exchange differences**.
  Practising examination questions is the best way of learning this topic.

- **IAS 29** *Financial Reporting in Hyperinflationary Economies* requires financial statements of entities operating within a hyperinflationary economy to be restated in terms of measuring units current at the year end.

Quick quiz

1. What is the difference between conversion and translation?

2. Define 'monetary' items according to IAS 21.

3. How should foreign currency transactions be recognised initially in an individual entity's financial statements?

4. What factors must management take into account when determining the functional currency of a foreign operation?

5. How should goodwill and fair value adjustments be treated on consolidation of a foreign operation?

6. When can an entity's functional currency be changed?

Answers to quick quiz

1   (a) Conversion is the process of exchanging one currency for another.
    (b) Translation is the restatement of the value of one currency in another currency.

2   Money held and assets and liabilities to be received or paid in fixed or determinable amounts of money.

3   Use the exchange rate at the date of the transaction. An average rate for a period can be used if the exchange rates did not fluctuate significantly.

4   See Section 3.2

5   Treat as assets/liabilities of the foreign operation and translate at the closing rate.

6   Only if there is a change to the underlying transactions relevant to the entity.

End of chapter question

Eufonion (AIA November 2008)

(a) According to IAS 21 *The Effects of Changes in Foreign Exchange Rates*, how should a company decide what its functional currency is? **(5 marks)**

(b) Until recently Eufonion, a UK limited liability company, reported using the euro (€) as its functional currency. However, on 1 November 20X7 the company decided that its functional currency should now be the dollar ($).

The summarised statement of financial position of Eufonion as at 31 October 20X8 in € million was as follows:

	€m
ASSETS	
Non-current assets	420
Current assets	
Inventories	26
Trade and other receivables	42
Cash and cash equivalents	8
	76
Total assets	496
EQUITY AND LIABILITIES	
Equity	
Share capital	200
Retained earnings	107
	307
Non-current liabilities	85
Current liabilities	
Trade and other payables	63
Current taxation	41
	104
Total liabilities	189
Total equity and liabilities	496

Non-current liabilities includes a loan of $70 million which was raised in dollars ($) and translated at the closing rate of $1 = €0.72425.

Trade receivables includes an amount of $20 million invoiced in dollars ($) to an American customer which has been translated at the closing rate of $1 = €0.72425.

9: FOREIGN CURRENCY TRANSLATION

All items of property, plant and equipment were purchased in euros (€) except for plant which was purchased in British pounds (£) in 2007 and which cost £150 million. This was translated at the exchange rate of £1 = €1.46015 as at the date of purchase. The carrying value of the equipment was £90 million as at 31 October 20X8.

Required

Translate the statement of financial position of Eufonion as at 31 October 20X8 into dollars ($m), the company's new functional currency. **(5 marks)**

(c) The directors of Eufonion (as in (b) above) are now considering using the British pound (£) as the company's presentation currency for the financial statements for the year ended 31 October 20X9.

Required

Advise the directors how they should translate the company's statement of profit or loss and other comprehensive income for the year ended 31 October 20X9 and its statement of financial position as at 31 October 20X9 into the new presentation currency. **(6 marks)**

(d) Discuss whether or not a reporting entity should be allowed to present its financial statements in a currency which is different to its functional currency.

(4 marks)

(Total 20 marks)

PART B BUSINESS COMBINATIONS AND GROUP FINANCIAL STATEMENTS

Group statements of cash flows

Topic list	Syllabus reference
1 Cash flows and funds flows	13.2
2 IAS 7 *Statement of Cash Flows:* Single company	13.2
3 Consolidated statements of cash flows	13.2
4 Foreign currency translation and the statement of cash flows	13.2
5 Examiner's guide to approaching an exam question	13.2

Introduction

A statement of cash flows is an additional primary statement of **great value** to users of financial statements for the extra information it provides.

You should be familiar with the basic principles, techniques and definitions relating to statements of cash flows from your earlier studies. This chapter develops the principles and preparation techniques to include **consolidated financial statements**.

1 Cash flows and funds flows

FAST FORWARD

Statements of cash flows are a useful addition to the financial statements of companies because it is recognised that accounting profit is not the only indicator of a company's performance.

Statements of cash flows concentrate on the sources and uses of cash and are a useful indicator of a company's **liquidity and solvency**.

1.1 Funds flows

'Funds statements' have been used in the past and are still used in some countries. They are generally deficient in that they often do not specify the 'focus' of the statement, ie the **definition of funds** to be adopted by the reporting entity. Some companies will report movements in net liquid funds, some in working capital, some in net borrowings and some in total external financing. This means that a whole range of different funds flow statements might be given in financial statements.

In spite of this problem, some standards on funds flow require that the 'all financial resources' approach should be adopted in presentation. This means that the definition of funds adopted by the company is effectively ignored as **all movements in financial resources** have to be shown, whether they affect the 'funds' or not. For example, if a company adopted a working capital definition of funds, it would still have to show a conversion of shares into debt in the statement, even though this has no impact on working capital 'funds'.

The overall effect of such an approach is a **lack of uniformity and definition**, the result of which is often a simple mathematical exercise comparing opening and closing statement of financial position. It is also perceived as relatively meaningless to most users.

1.2 Cash flows: Advantages

Cash flows are much easier to understand as a concept. The main advantages of using cash flow accounting (including both historical and forecast cash flows) are as follows:

(a) **Survival** of a company depends on its ability to generate cash. Cash flow accounting directs attention towards this critical issue.

(b) Cash flow is more **comprehensive** than 'profit' which is dependent on accounting conventions and concepts.

(c) Creditors (long- and short-term) are more interested in an entity's **ability to repay** them than in its profitability. Whereas 'profits' might indicate that cash is likely to be available, cash flow accounting is more direct with its message.

(d) Cash flow reporting provides a better means of **comparing** the results of different companies than traditional profit reporting.

(e) Cash flow reporting satisfies the **needs of all users** better.

  (i) For **management**. It provides the sort of information on which decisions should be taken (in management accounting, 'relevant costs' to a decision are future cash flows). Traditional profit accounting does not help with decision-making.

  (ii) For **shareholders and auditors**. Cash flow accounting can provide a satisfactory basis for stewardship accounting.

  (iii) For **creditors and employees**. Their information needs will be better served by cash flow accounting.

(f) **Cash flow forecasts** are easier to prepare, as well as more useful, than profit forecasts.

(g) Statements of cash flows can be **audited more easily** than financial statements based on the accruals concept.

(h) The accruals concept is confusing, and cash flows are more **easily understood**.

(i) Cash flow accounting can be both **retrospective**, and also include a **forecast** for the future. This is of great information value to all users of accounting information.

(j) Forecasts can subsequently be monitored by the use of **variance statements** which compare actual cash flows against the forecast.

Looking at the same question from a different angle, readers of financial statements can be **misled** by the profit figure.

(a) Shareholders might believe that if a company makes a profit after tax of, say $100,000 then this is the amount which it could afford to pay as a **dividend**. Unless the company has sufficient cash available to stay in business and also to pay a dividend, the shareholders' expectations would be wrong.

(b) Employees might believe that if a company makes profits, it can afford to pay **higher wages** next year. This opinion may not be correct: the ability to pay wages depends on the availability of cash.

(c) Creditors might consider that a profitable company is a **going concern**.

   (i) If a company builds up large amounts of **unsold inventories** of goods, their cost would not be chargeable against profits, but cash would have been used up in making them, thus weakening the company's liquid resources.

   (ii) A company might capitalise large **development costs**, having spent considerable amounts of money on R & D, but only charge small amounts against current profits. As a result, the company might show reasonable profits, but get into severe difficulties with its liquidity position.

(d) Management might suppose that if their company makes a historical cost profit, and reinvests some of those profits, then the company must be **expanding**. This is not the case: in a period of inflation, a company might have a historical cost profit but a current cost accounting loss, which means that the operating capability of the firm will be declining.

(e) **Survival** of a business entity depends not so much on profits as on its ability to pay its debts when they fall due. Such payments might include expense items such as material purchases, wages, interest and taxation etc but also capital payments for new non-current assets and the repayment of loan capital when this falls due (eg on the redemption of debentures).

2 IAS 7 *Statement of Cash Flows:* Single company

FAST FORWARD

> You need to be aware of the **format** of the statement as laid out in **IAS 7**. Setting out the format is an essential first stage in preparing the statement, so this format must be learnt.

The aim of IAS 7 is to provide information to users of financial statements about the cash flows of an entity's **ability to generate cash and cash equivalents**, as well as indicating the cash needs of the entity. The statement of cash flows provides **historical** information about cash and cash equivalents, classifying cash flows between operating, investing and financing activities.

2.1 Scope

A statement of cash flows should be presented as an **integral part** of an entity's financial statements. All types of entity can provide useful information about cash flows as the need for cash is universal, whatever the nature of their revenue-producing activities. Therefore **all entities are required by the standard to produce a statement of cash flows**.

2.2 Benefits of cash flow information

The use of statements of cash flows is very much **in conjunction** with the rest of the financial statements. Users can gain further appreciation of the change in net assets, of the entity's financial position (liquidity and solvency) and the entity's ability to adapt to changing circumstances by affecting the amount and timing of cash flows. Statements of cash flows **enhance comparability** as they are not affected by differing accounting policies used for the same type of transactions or events.

Cash flow information of a historical nature can be used as an indicator of the amount, timing and certainty of future cash flows. Past forecast cash flow information can be **checked for accuracy** as actual figures emerge. The relationship between profit and cash flows can be analysed as can changes in prices over time.

2.3 Definitions

The standard gives the following definitions, the most important of which are **cash** and **cash equivalents**.

Key terms

> **Cash** comprises cash on hand and demand deposits.
>
> **Cash equivalents** are short-term, highly liquid investments that are readily convertible to known amounts of cash and which are subject to an insignificant risk of changes in value.
>
> **Cash flows** are inflows and outflows of cash and cash equivalents.
>
> **Operating activities** are the principal revenue-producing activities of the entity and other activities that are not investing or financing activities.
>
> **Investing activities** are the acquisition and disposal of non-current assets and other investments not included in cash equivalents.
>
> **Financing activities** are activities that result in changes in the size and composition of the equity capital and borrowings of the entity.
> (IAS 7)

2.4 Cash and cash equivalents

The standard expands on the definition of cash equivalents: they are not held for investment or other long-term purposes, but rather to meet short-term cash commitments. To fulfil the above definition, an investment's **maturity date should normally be three months from its acquisition date**. It would usually be the case then that equity investments (ie shares in other companies) are **not** cash equivalents. An exception would be where preferred shares were acquired with a very close maturity date.

Loans and other borrowings from banks are classified as investing activities. In some countries, however, **bank overdrafts** are repayable on demand and are treated as part of an entity's total cash management system. In these circumstances an overdrawn balance will be included in cash and cash equivalents. Such banking arrangements are characterised by a balance which fluctuates between overdrawn and credit.

Movements between different types of cash and cash equivalent are not included in cash flows. The investment of surplus cash in cash equivalents is part of cash management, not part of operating, investing or financing activities.

2.5 Presentation of a statement of cash flows

IAS 7 requires statements of cash flows to report cash flows during the period classified by **operating, investing and financing activities**.

The manner of presentation of cash flows from operating, investing and financing activities **depends on the nature of the entity**. By classifying cash flows between different activities in this way users can see the impact on cash and cash equivalents of each one, and their relationships with each other. We can look at each in more detail.

2.5.1 Operating activities

This is perhaps the key part of the statement of cash flows because it shows whether, and to what extent, companies can **generate cash from their operations**. It is these operating cash flows which must, in the end, pay for all cash outflows relating to other activities, ie paying loan interest, dividends and so on.

Most of the components of cash flows from operating activities will be those items which **determine the profit or loss of the entity**, ie they relate to the main revenue-producing activities of the entity. The standard gives the following as examples of cash flows from operating activities:

- Cash receipts from the sale of goods and the rendering of services
- Cash receipts from royalties, fees, commissions and other revenue
- Cash payments to suppliers for goods and services
- Cash payments to and on behalf of employees
- Cash payments/refunds of income taxes unless they can be specifically identified with financing or investing activities
- Cash receipts and payments from contracts held for dealing or trading purposes

Certain items may be included in the profit or loss for the period which do *not* relate to operational cash flows. For example the profit or loss on the sale of a piece of plant will be included in profit or loss, but the cash flows will be classed as from **investing activities**.

2.5.2 Investing activities

The cash flows classified under this heading show the extent of new investment in **assets which will generate future profit and cash flows**. The standard gives the following examples of cash flows arising from investing activities.

- Cash payments to acquire property, plant and equipment, intangibles and other non-current assets, including those relating to capitalised development costs and self-constructed property, plant and equipment
- Cash receipts from sales of property, plant and equipment, intangibles and other non-current assets
- Cash payments to acquire shares or debentures of other entities
- Cash receipts from sales of shares or debentures of other entities
- Cash advances and loans made to other parties
- Cash receipts from the repayment of advances and loans made to other parties
- Cash payments for or receipts from futures/forward/option/swap contracts except where the contracts are held for dealing purposes, or the payments/receipts are classified as financing activities

2.5.3 Financing activities

This section of the statement of cash flows shows the share of cash which the entity's capital providers have claimed during the period. This is an indicator of **likely future interest and dividend payments**. The standard gives the following examples of cash flows which might arise under these headings.

- Cash proceeds from issuing shares
- Cash payments to owners to acquire or redeem the entity's shares
- Cash proceeds from issuing debentures, loans, notes, bonds, mortgages and other short or non-current borrowings
- Cash repayments of amounts borrowed
- Cash payments by a lessee for the reduction of the outstanding liability relating to a lease

2.6 Reporting cash flows from operating activities

The standard offers a choice of method for this part of the statement of cash flows.

(a) **Direct method**: disclose major classes of gross cash receipts and gross cash payments

(b) **Indirect method**: profit or loss is adjusted for the effects of transactions of a non-cash nature, any deferrals or accruals of past or future operating cash receipts or payments, and items of income or expense associated with investing or financing cash flows

The **direct method is the preferred method** because it discloses information not available elsewhere in the financial statements, which could be of use in estimating future cash flows. The example in Section 2.11 shows both methods.

2.6.1 Using the direct method

There are different ways in which the **information about gross cash receipts and payments** can be obtained. The most obvious way is simply to extract the information from the accounting records. This may be a laborious task, however, and the indirect method below may be easier.

2.6.2 Using the indirect method

This method is undoubtedly **easier** from the point of view of the preparer of the statement of cash flows. The profit or loss for the period is adjusted for the following.

(a) Changes during the period in inventories, operating receivables and payables
(b) Non-cash items, eg depreciation, provisions, profits/losses on the sales of assets
(c) Other items, the cash flows from which should be classified under investing or financing activities.

A **proforma** of such a calculation is as follows and this method may be more common in the exam.

	$
Profit before taxation (statement of profit or loss and OCI)	X
Add depreciation	X
Loss (profit) on sale of non-current assets	X
(Increase)/decrease in inventories	(X)/X
(Increase)/decrease in receivables	(X)/X
Increase/(decrease) in payables	X/(X)
Cash generated from operations	X
Interest (paid)/received	(X)
Income taxes paid	(X)
Net cash flows from operating activities	X

It is important to understand why **certain items are added and others subtracted**. Note the following points.

(a) Depreciation is not a cash expense, but is deducted in arriving at the profit figure in the statement of profit or loss and other comprehensive income. It makes sense, therefore, to eliminate it by adding it back.

(b) By the same logic, a loss on a disposal of a non-current asset (arising through underprovision of depreciation) needs to be added back and a profit deducted.

(c) An increase in inventories means less cash – you have spent cash on buying inventory.

(d) An increase in receivables means the company's debtors have not paid as much, and therefore there is less cash.

(e) If we pay off payables, causing the figure to decrease, again we have less cash.

2.6.3 Indirect versus direct

The direct method **is encouraged** where the necessary information is not too costly to obtain, but IAS 7 does not require it. In practice, therefore, the direct method is rarely used. It could be argued that companies ought to monitor their cash flows carefully enough on an ongoing basis to be able to use the direct method at minimal extra cost.

2.7 Interest and dividends

Cash flows from interest and dividends received and paid should each be **disclosed separately**. Each should be classified in a consistent manner from period to period as either operating, investing or financing activities.

Dividends paid by the entity can be classified in **one of two ways**:

(a) As a **financing cash flow**, showing the cost of obtaining financial resources.

(b) As a component of **cash flows from operating activities** so that users can assess the entity's ability to pay dividends out of operating cash flows.

2.8 Taxes on income

Cash flows arising from taxes on income should be **separately disclosed** and should be classified as cash flows from operating activities **unless** they can be specifically identified with financing and investing activities.

Taxation cash flows are often **difficult to match** to the originating underlying transaction, so most of the time all tax cash flows are classified as arising from operating activities.

2.9 Components of cash and cash equivalents

The components of cash and cash equivalents should be disclosed and a **reconciliation** should be presented, showing the amounts in the statement of cash flows reconciled with the equivalent items reported in the statement of financial position.

It is also necessary to disclose the **accounting policy** used in deciding the items included in cash and cash equivalents, in accordance with IAS 1 *Presentation of Financial Statements*, but also because of the wide range of cash management practices worldwide.

2.10 Other disclosures

All entities should disclose, together with a **commentary by management**, any other information likely to be of importance. Disclosure is required of restrictions on the use of or access to any part of cash equivalents. Disclosure is encouraged of:

(a) The amount of undrawn borrowing facilities which are available.

(b) Cash flows which increased operating capacity compared to cash flows which merely maintained operating capacity.

2.11 Example: Statement of cash flows

In the next section we will look at the procedures for preparing a statement of cash flows. First, look at this **example**, adapted from the example given in the standard.

2.11.1 Direct method

STATEMENT OF CASH FLOWS (DIRECT METHOD)
YEAR ENDED 20X7

	$m	$m
Cash flows from operating activities		
Cash receipts from customers	30,150	
Cash paid to suppliers and employees	(27,600)	
Cash generated from operations	2,550	
Interest paid	(270)	
Income taxes paid	(900)	
Net cash from operating activities		1,380

PART B BUSINESS COMBINATIONS AND GROUP FINANCIAL STATEMENTS

	$m	$m
Cash flows from investing activities		
Purchase of property, plant and equipment	(900)	
Proceeds from sale of equipment	20	
Interest received	200	
Dividends received	200	
Net cash used in investing activities		(480)
Cash flows from financing activities		
Proceeds from issue of share capital	250	
Proceeds from non-current borrowings	250	
Payment of lease liabilities	(90)	
Dividends paid*	(1,200)	
Net cash used in financing activities		(790)
Net increase in cash and cash equivalents		110
Cash and cash equivalents at beginning of period (Note)		120
Cash and cash equivalents at end of period (Note)		230

* This could also be shown as an operating cash flow

2.11.2 Indirect method

STATEMENT OF CASH FLOWS (INDIRECT METHOD)
YEAR ENDED 20X7

	$m	$m
Cash flows from operating activities		
Profit before taxation	3,390	
Adjustments for:		
Depreciation	450	
Investment income	(500)	
Interest expense	400	
	3,740	
Increase in trade and other receivables	(500)	
Decrease in inventories	1,050	
Decrease in trade payables	(1,740)	
Cash generated from operations	2,550	
Interest paid	(270)	
Income taxes paid	(900)	
Net cash from operating activities		1,380
Cash flows from investing activities		
Purchase of property, plant and equipment	(900)	
Proceeds from sale of equipment	20	
Interest received	200	
Dividends received	200	
Net cash used in investing activities		(480)
Cash flows from financing activities		
Proceeds from issue of share capital	250	
Proceeds from non-current borrowings	250	
Payment of lease liabilities	(90)	
Dividends paid*	(1,200)	
Net cash used in financing activities		(790)
Net increase in cash and cash equivalents		110
Cash and cash equivalents at beginning of period (Note)		120
Cash and cash equivalents at end of period (Note)		230

10: GROUP STATEMENTS OF CASH FLOWS

	20X7 $m	20X6 $m
Cash on hand and balances with banks	40	25
Short-term investments	190	95
Cash and cash equivalents	230	120

*Note. This could also be shown as an operating cash flow

2.12 Current developments

The IASB issued an Exposure Draft in December 2014, *Disclosure Initiative Proposed Amendments to IAS 7*, which resulted in amendments to IAS 7 being issued in 2016. The amendments seeks to improve information provided to users of financial statements about an entity's financing activities, excluding equity items; and disclosures that help those users to understand the liquidity of an entity.

To meet the first objective, an entity should disclose a reconciliation of the amounts in the opening and closing statements of financial position for each item for which cash flows have been, or would be, classified as financing activities in the statement of cash flows, excluding equity items. The result of requiring this reconciliation is that investors will be provided with improved disclosures about an entity's debt and movements in debt during the reporting period.

To meet the second objective, the IASB has extended the disclosures required by IAS 7 about an entity's liquidity and proposes disclosures about the restrictions that affect the decisions of an entity to use cash and cash equivalent balances, including tax liabilities that would arise on the repatriation of foreign cash and cash equivalent balances.

2.13 Section summary

FAST FORWARD

> Remember the **step-by-step preparation procedure** and use it for all the questions you practise.

Remember the steps involved in preparation of a statement of cash flows.

Step 1 Set out the proforma leaving plenty of space.

Step 2 Complete the reconciliation of profit before tax to net cash flow from operating activities, as far as possible.

Step 3 Calculate the following where appropriate.

- Tax paid
- Dividends paid
- Purchase and sale of non-current assets
- Issues of shares
- Repayment of loans

Step 4 Work out the profit if not already given using: opening and closing balances, tax charge and dividends.

Step 5 Slot the figures into the statement and any notes required.

PART B BUSINESS COMBINATIONS AND GROUP FINANCIAL STATEMENTS

Question — Single company

Kane Co's statement of profit or loss and other comprehensive income for the year ended 31 December 20X8 and statements of financial position at 31 December 20X7 and 31 December 20X8 were as follows.

KANE CO

STATEMENT OF PROFIT AND LOSS AND OTHER COMPREHENSIVE INCOME FOR THE YEAR ENDED 31 DECEMBER 20X8

	$'000	$'000
Sales		720
Raw materials consumed	70	
Staff costs	94	
Depreciation	118	
Loss on disposal of non-current asset	18	
		300
		420
Interest payable		28
Profit before tax		392
Income tax expense		124
Profit for the year		268

KANE CO
STATEMENT OF FINANCIAL POSITION AS AT 31 DECEMBER

	20X8		20X7	
	$'000	$'000	$'000	$'000
Assets				
Non-current assets				
Cost	1,596		1,560	
Depreciation	318		224	
		1,278		1,336
Current assets				
Inventory	24		20	
Trade receivables	76		58	
Bank	48		56	
		148		134
Total assets		1,426		1,470
Equity and liabilities				
Equity				
Share capital	360		340	
Share premium	36		24	
Retained earnings	686		490	
		1,082		854
Non-current liabilities				
Non-current loans		200		500
Current liabilities				
Trade payables	42		30	
Taxation	102		86	
		144		116
		1,426		1,470

During the year, the company paid $90,000 for a new piece of machinery.

Required

Prepare a statement of cash flows for Kane Co for the year ended 31 December 20X8 in accordance with the requirements of IAS 7, using the indirect method.

Answer

KANE CO
STATEMENT OF CASH FLOWS FOR THE YEAR ENDED 31 DECEMBER 20X8

	$'000	$'000
Net cash flow from operating activities		
Operating profit	420	
Depreciation charges (W)	118	
Loss on sale of tangible non-current assets	18	
Increase in inventories (24 – 20)	(4)	
Increase in receivables (76 – 58)	(18)	
Increase in payables (42 – 30)	12	
Cash generated from operations	546	
Interest paid	(28)	
Dividends paid (268 + 490 – 686)	(72)	
Tax paid (86 + 124 – 102)	(108)	
Net cash flow from operating activities		338
Cash flows from investing activities		
Payments to acquire tangible non-current assets	(90)	
Receipts from sales of tangible non-current assets (W)	12	
Net cash outflow from investing activities		(78)
Cash flows from financing activities		
Issues of share capital (360 + 36 – 340 – 24)	32	
Non-current loans repaid (500 – 200)	(300)	
Net cash flows from financing		(268)
Decrease in cash and cash equivalents		(8)
Cash and cash equivalents at 1.1.X8		56
Cash and cash equivalents at 31.12.X8		48

Working: non-current asset disposals

COST

	$'000		$'000
At 1.1.X8	1,560	At 31.12.X8	1,596
Purchases	90	Disposals (balance)	54
	1,650		1,650

ACCUMULATED DEPRECIATION

	$'000		$'000
At 31.1.X8	318	At 1.1.X8	224
Depreciation on disposals (balance)	24	Charge for year	118
	342		342
Carrying amount of disposals			30
Net loss reported			(18)
Proceeds of disposals			12

3 Consolidated statements of cash flows

Consolidated cash flows should not present a great problem if you understand how to deal with acquisitions and disposals of subsidiaries, non-controlling interest and dividends.

Consolidated statements of cash flows follow the same principles as for single company statements, with some additional complications.

Cash flows that are **internal to the group** should be eliminated in the preparation of a consolidated statement of cash flows. Where a subsidiary **joins or leaves** a group during a financial year the cash flows of the group should include the cash flows of the subsidiary concerned for the same period as that for which the group's statement of profit or loss and other comprehensive income includes the results of the subsidiary.

3.1 Acquisitions and disposals of subsidiaries and other business units

An entity should present separately the aggregate cash flows arising from acquisitions and from disposals of subsidiaries or other business units and classify them as **investing activities**.

Disclosure is required of the following, in aggregate, in respect of both acquisitions and disposals of subsidiaries or other business units during the period.

- Total purchase/disposal consideration
- Portion of purchase/disposal consideration discharged by means of cash/cash equivalents
- Amount of cash/cash equivalents in the subsidiary or business unit disposed of
- Amount of assets and liabilities other than cash/cash equivalents in the subsidiary or business unit acquired or disposed of, summarised by major category

The amounts shown in the statements of cash flows for purchase or disposal of subsidiaries or business units will be the amounts paid or received **net** of cash/cash equivalents acquired or disposed of.

3.2 Consolidation adjustments and non-controlling interest

The group statement of cash flows should only deal with flows of cash and cash equivalents external to the group, so all intra-group cash flows should be eliminated. **Dividends paid to non-controlling interest** should be included under the heading 'cash flow from financing' and disclosed separately.

3.3 Example: Non-controlling interest

The following are extracts of the consolidated results for Jarvis Co for the year ended 31 December 20X8.

CONSOLIDATED STATEMENT OF PROFIT OR LOSS AND OTHER COMPREHENSIVE INCOME (EXTRACT)

	$'000
Group profit before tax	90
Income tax expense	(30)
Profit for the year	60
Profit attributable to:	
Owners of the parent	45
Non-controlling interest	15
	60

CONSOLIDATED STATEMENT OF FINANCIAL POSITION (EXTRACT)

	20X1	20X2
	$'000	$'000
Non-controlling interest	300	306

Calculate the dividends paid to the non-controlling interest during the year.

Solution

The non-controlling interest share of profit after tax represents retained profit plus dividends paid.

NON-CONTROLLING INTEREST

	$'000		$'000
Dividend paid	9	Balance b/fwd	300
Balance c/fwd	306	Profit for period (I/S)	15
	315		315

3.4 Associates and joint ventures

In respect of associates and joint ventures accounted for using the equity method, only the actual cash flows from sales or purchases between the group and the associate/joint venture, and investments in and dividends from the entity should be included in the consolidated statement of cash flows. Dividends should be included in **operating cash flows**, where they are shown within operating profit in the statement of profit or loss and other comprehensive income.

3.5 Example: Associate

The following are extracts of the consolidated results of Pripon Co for the year ended 31 December 20X8.

CONSOLIDATED STATEMENT OF PROFIT OR LOSS AND OTHER COMPREHENSIVE INCOME (EXTRACT)

	$'000
Group profit before tax	150
Share of associate's profit after tax	30
	180
Tax	75
Profit after tax	105

CONSOLIDATED STATEMENT OF FINANCIAL POSITION (EXTRACTS)

	20X1 $'000	20X2 $'000
Investment in associate	264	276

Calculate the dividend received from the associate.

Solution

ASSOCIATE

	$'000		$'000
Balance b/fwd	264	Dividend from associate	18
Profit after tax	30	Balance c/fwd	276
	294		294

3.6 Lease transactions

When rentals under a lease are paid the **capital and interest elements are split out** and included under the 'financing' heading and interest paid respectively.

3.7 Section summary

The preparation of consolidated statements of cash flows will, in many respects, be the same as those for single companies, with the following **additional complications**:

- Acquisitions and disposals of subsidiary
- Cancellation of intra-group transactions
- Non-controlling interest
- Associates and joint ventures

PART B BUSINESS COMBINATIONS AND GROUP FINANCIAL STATEMENTS

 Question — Consolidated cash flow

Topiary Co is a 40 year old company producing garden statues carved from marble. Twenty-two years ago it acquired a 100% interest in a marble importing company, Hardstuff Co. In 20W9 it acquired a 40% interest in a competitor, Landscapes Co and on 1 January 20X7 it acquired a 75% interest in Garden Furniture Designs. The draft consolidated financial statements for the Topiary Group are as follows:

DRAFT CONSOLIDATED STATEMENT OF PROFIT OR LOSS AND OTHER COMPREHENSIVE INCOME
FOR THE YEAR ENDED 31 DECEMBER 20X7

	$'000	$'000
Operating profit		4,455
Share of profits after tax of associates		1,050
Income from non-current investments		600
Interest payable		(450)
Profit before taxation		5,655
Tax on profit		
Income tax	1,173	
Deferred taxation	312	
Tax attributable to investment income	135	
		(1,620)
Profit for the year		4,035
Attributable to:		
Owners of the parent		3,735
Non-controlling interest		300
		4,035

DRAFT CONSOLIDATED STATEMENT OF FINANCIAL POSITION
AS AT 31 DECEMBER

	20X6		20X7	
	$'000	$'000	$'000	$'000
Assets				
Non-current assets				
Property, plant and equipment				
Buildings at carrying amount		6,600		6,225
Machinery: cost	4,200		9,000	
aggregate depreciation	(3,300)		(3,600)	
carrying amount		900		5,400
		7,500		11,625
Goodwill				300
Investments in associates		3,000		3,300
Other investments		1,230		1,230
		11,730		16,455
Current assets				
Inventories	3,000		5,925	
Receivables	3,825		5,550	
Cash	5,460		13,545	
		12,285		25,020
		24,015		41,475

	20X6		20X7	
	$'000	$'000	$'000	$'000
Equity and liabilities				
Equity				
Share capital: 25c shares	6,000		11,820	
Share premium account	6,285		8,649	
Retained earnings	7,500		10,335	
	19,785		30,804	
Non-controlling interest	–		345	
Total equity		19,785		31,149
Non-current liabilities				
Obligations under leases	510		2,130	
Loans	1,500		4,380	
Deferred tax	39		90	
		2,049		6,600
Current liabilities				
Trade payables	840		1,500	
Obligations under leases	600		720	
Income tax	651		1,386	
Accrued interest and finance charges	90		120	
		2,181		3,726
		24,015		41,475

Notes

1. There had been no acquisitions or disposals of buildings during the year.

   Machinery costing $1.5m was sold for $1.5m resulting in a profit of $300,000. New machinery was acquired in 20X7 including additions of $2.55m acquired under leases.

2. Information relating to the acquisition of Garden Furniture Designs

	$'000
Machinery	495
Inventories	96
Trade receivables	84
Cash	336
Trade payables	(204)
Income tax	(51)
	756
Non-controlling interest	(189)
	567
Goodwill	300
	867
2,640,000 shares issued as part consideration	825
Balance of consideration paid in cash	42
	867

3. Loans were issued at a discount in 20X7 and the carrying amount of the loans at 31 December 20X7 included $120,000 representing the finance cost attributable to the discount and allocated in respect of the current reporting period.

Required

Prepare a consolidated statement of cash flows for the Topiary Group for the year ended 31 December 20X7 as required by IAS 7, using the indirect method. There is no need to provide notes to the statement of cash flows.

PART B BUSINESS COMBINATIONS AND GROUP FINANCIAL STATEMENTS

Answer

TOPIARY CO
CONSOLIDATED STATEMENT OF CASH FLOWS
FOR THE YEAR ENDED 31 DECEMBER 20X7

	$'000	$'000
Cash flows from operating activities		
Profit before tax	6,090	
Adjustments for:		
Depreciation (W1)	975	
Profit on sale of plant	(300)	
Share of associate's profits	(1,485)	
Investment income	(600)	
Interest payable	450	
Operating profit before working capital changes	5,130	
Increase in trade and other receivables (5,500 – 3,825 – 84)	(1,641)	
Increase in inventories (5,925 – 3,000 – 96)	(2,829)	
Increase in trade payables (1,500 – 840 – 204)	456	
Cash generated from operations	1,116	
Interest paid (W2)	(300)	
Income taxes paid (W3)	(750)	
Net cash from operating activities		66
Cash flows from investing activities		
Purchase of subsidiary (W4)	294	
Purchase of property, plant and equipment (W5)	(3,255)	
Proceeds from sale of plant	1,500	
Dividends from investment (600 – 135)	465	
Dividends from associate (W6)	750	
Net cash used in investing activities		(246)
Cash flows from financing activities		
Issue of ordinary share capital (W8)	7,359	
Issue of loan notes (W9)	2,760	
Capital payments under leases (W10)	(810)	
Dividends paid to owners (3,735 + 7,500 – 10,335)	(900)	
Dividends paid to non-controlling interest (W7)	(144)	
Net cash flows from financing activities		8,265
Net increase in cash and cash equivalents		8,085
Cash and cash equivalents at 1.1.X7		5,460
Cash and cash equivalents at 31.12.X7		13,545

Workings

1   Depreciation charges

	$'000	$'000
Freehold buildings (6,600 – 6,225)		375
Plant		
Closing balance	3,600	
Opening balance	3,300	
	300	
Depreciation on disposal	300	
		600
		975

2 Interest

	$'000
Accrued interest b/f	90
Expense	450
Discount	(120)
Less accrued interest c/f	(120)
	300

3 Taxation

	$'000	$'000
Opening balance		
Income tax	651	
Deferred tax	39	
		690
Statement of profit or loss and OCI (1,173 + 312)		1,485
Closing balances		
Income tax	1,386	
Deferred tax	90	
		(1,476)
		699
On acquisition		51
Cash outflow		750

4 Purchase of subsidiary

	$'000
Cash received on acquisition	336
Less cash consideration	(42)
Cash inflow	294

5 Purchase of tangible non-current assets: machinery

	$'000	$'000
Cost at 31 December 20X7		9,000
Cost at 1 January 20X7		4,200
		4,800
Disposal		1,500
		6,300
On acquisition	495	
Leased	2,550	
		(3,045)
Cash outflow		3,255

6 Dividends from associate

	$'000
Opening balance	3,000
Share of profit after tax	1,050
	4,050
Closing balance	3,300
	750

7 Non-controlling interest

	$'000
Opening balance	
Profit for year	300
On acquisition	189
	489
Closing balance	(345)
Cash outflow	144

PART B BUSINESS COMBINATIONS AND GROUP FINANCIAL STATEMENTS

8 Issue of ordinary share capital

	$'000	$'000
Closing balance		
Shares	11,820	
Premium	8,649	
		20,469
Non-cash consideration		
Shares	660	
Premium	165	
		(825)
Opening balance		
Shares	6,000	
Premium	6,285	
		(12,285)
Cash inflow		7,359

9 Issue of loan notes

	$'000
Closing balance	4,380
Opening balance	1,500
	2,880
Finance cost	120
Cash inflow	2,760

10 Capital payments under leases

	$'000	$'000
Opening balances		
Current		600
Non-current		510
		1,110
New lease commitment		2,550
Closing balances		
Current	720	
Non-current	2,130	
		(2,850)
Cash outflow		810

4 Foreign currency translation and the statement of cash flows

> **FAST FORWARD**
>
> A **foreign exchange difference** in a group statement of cash flows must be analysed into its constituent parts.

> **Exam focus point**
>
> Questions on this topic are possible. They normally feature cash flows from an individual transaction but you may be asked to deal with a foreign subsidiary.

4.1 Individual companies

Receipts and payments should be translated into the reporting currency at the **rate ruling** at the date on which the receipt or payment is made.

Exchange differences **do not give rise to cash flows** and therefore they would not be reflected in the statement of cash flows.

4.2 Group companies

The main problems relating to foreign exchange differences are when dealing with the cash flows of an overseas subsidiary. IAS 7 requires that all cash flows relating to an overseas subsidiary be translated at the exchange rates between the functional currency and the foreign currency at the date of the cash flows. Where the average rate is used to translate the subsidiary's statement of profit and loss and other comprehensive income then the subsidiary's cash flows will also be translated using this rate.

If the **average rate** is used, then merely using the statement of financial position to derive the figures would not be appropriate as the resulting statement of cash flows would not comply with IAS 7, some items being translated at the closing rate. The practical answer to this problem is to use the following method (which would be time consuming in practice).

Step 1 Produce a statement of cash flows for each subsidiary.

Step 2 Translate each into dollars using the average rate.

Step 3 Consolidate them into the group statement of cash flows (after eliminating intra-group items).

The other main point to note is that the exchange differences on translation must be **analysed into their constituent parts**, namely long-term assets, receivables, cash, payables and non-controlling interests. In the example shown below, the split is given.

4.3 Example: Foreign currency translation

The draft statements of financial position and statements of profit or loss and other comprehensive income of Guinevere Co are as follows.

CONSOLIDATED STATEMENTS OF FINANCIAL POSITION

AS AT 31 DECEMBER

	20X8		20X7	
	$'000	$'000	$'000	$'000
Assets				
Non-current assets				
Property, plant and equipment	32,907		22,926	
Financial assets	6,300		6,300	
		39,207		29,226
Current assets				
Inventories	21,735		18,300	
Receivables	19,230		21,633	
Cash and cash equivalents	2,859		495	
		43,824		40,428
		83,031		69,654
Equity and liabilities				
Equity				
Share capital	15,000		15,000	
Share premium	9,000		9,000	
Reserves	34,476		21,909	
	58,476		45,909	
Non-controlling interests	7,557		5,991	
		66,033		51,900
Non-current liabilities				
Loans		3,006		4,230

PART B BUSINESS COMBINATIONS AND GROUP FINANCIAL STATEMENTS

	20X8		20X7	
	$'000	$'000	$'000	$'000
Current liabilities				
Trade payables	5,760		5,070	
Income taxes	8,232		8,454	
		13,992		13,524
		83,031		69,654

There were no non-current asset disposals during the year. The depreciation charge for the year was $5,931,000. There were no non-current asset payables at either year end.

Receivables as at 31 December 20X8 include called up share capital not paid of $3,705,000 (20X7: $8,238,000).

CONSOLIDATED STATEMENT OF PROFIT OR LOSS AND OTHER COMPREHENSIVE INCOME
FOR THE YEAR ENDED 31 DECEMBER 20X8

	$'000
Group operating profit	20,865
Income from financial assets	144
Interest payable	(522)
Group profit before tax	20,487
Income tax expense	(8,490)
Group profit after tax	11,997
Attributable to:	
Owners of the parent	11,319
Non-controlling interest	678
	11,997

Note: reserves

	$'000
Reserves as at 1 January 20X8	21,909
Profit for the year	11,319
Dividends	(1,674)
Exchange gain on translation (Note 1)	4,068
Exchange loss on loan	(1,146)
Reserves as at 31 December 20X8	34,476

Note 1: Exchange gain
The exchange gain on translation is made up as follows.

	$'000
Non-current assets	3,684
Inventories	1,179
Receivables	633
Cash	117
Payables	(189)
Non-controlling interest	(1,356)
	4,068

Required

Prepare the group statement of cash flows for Guinevere Co for the year ended 31 December 20X8, in accordance with IAS 7.

Solution

STATEMENT OF CASH FLOWS FOR THE YEAR ENDED 31 DECEMBER 20X8

	$'000	$'000
Cash flows from operating activities		
Net profit before tax	20,487	
Adjustments for:		
Depreciation	5,931	
Investment income	(144)	
Interest expense	522	
Operating profit before working capital changes	26,796	
Increase in trade and other receivables		
(19,230 – 3,705 – 21,633 + 8,238 – 633)	(1,497)	
Increase in inventories (21,735 – 18,300 – 1,179)	(2,256)	
Increase in trade payables (5,760 – 5,070 – 189)	501	
Cash generated from operations	23,544	
Interest paid	(522)	
Income taxes paid (8,454 + 8,490 – 8,232)	(8,712)	
Net cash from operating activities		14,310
Cash flows from investing activities		
Dividends received	144	
Dividends paid to non-controlling interest		
(5,991 + 678 + 1,356 – 7,557)	(468)	
Payments to acquire long-term assets		
(5,931 + 32,907 – 22,926 – 3,684)	(12,228)	
Net cash used in investing activities		(12,552)
Cash flows from financing activities		
Proceeds of share issue (8,238 – 3,705)	4,533	
Repayment of loans (3,006 – 4,230 – 1,146)	(2,370)	
Dividends paid	(1,674)	
Net cash from financing activities		489
Increase in cash and cash equivalents		2,247
Cash and cash equivalents at 1.1.X8		495
Effect of exchange rate changes		117
Cash and cash equivalents at 31.12.X8		2,859

5 Examiner's guide to approaching an exam question

The Paper 13 examiner has produced the following guidance with regard to approaching a statement of cash flows exam question.

The first point to note is that the IAS 7 **principles** are the same whether you are preparing a statement of cash flows for a group or for an individual company. These are as follows:

- *Cash and cash equivalents.* IAS 7 requires the presentation of information about the historical changes in cash and cash equivalents.

- Cash flows **must** be analysed between:

    - *Operating activities.* Operating cash flows may be presented using the direct method (which is preferred by the IASB) or the indirect method (which is preferred by entities in practice and by examiners in examinations).

    - *Investing activities*

    - *Financing activities*

It is important to learn the definitions of all the above headings. You may be asked to use your judgement to decide where an item should be presented or whether an item is a 'cash or cash equivalent' or should be included elsewhere on the statement. With respect to this, cash flows concerning interest and

PART B BUSINESS COMBINATIONS AND GROUP FINANCIAL STATEMENTS

dividends received and paid may be classified as operating, investing or financing, provided the classification is consistent from one period to the next. Cash flows arising from income taxes are **normally** to be classified as operating **unless** they can be specifically identified as referring to investing or financing activities.

Steps in the preparation of a group statement of cash flows:

1   Draft out a pro forma group statement of cash flows with the headings required by IAS 7.

    This means that your statement would look something like this:

    XYZ Group
    Consolidated statement of cash flows
    for the year ended...........

	$m
Cash flows from operating activities	
	–
	=
Cash generated from operations	X
Interest paid	
Income taxes paid	
Net cash used in/generated by operating activities	X
Cash flows from investing activities	
Net cash used in/generated by investing activities	X
Cash flows from financing activities	
Net cash used in/generated by financing activities	X
Net increase/decrease in cash and cash equivalents	X
Cash and cash equivalents at the beginning of the year	X
Effects of exchange rates changes on the balance of cash held in foreign currencies	X
Cash and cash equivalents at the end of the year	X

    Leave plenty of space between the headings so that you can fill in the missing information as you go through the question. If the question asks you to use the indirect method there will usually be much more space required between 'cash flows from operating activities' and 'cash generated from operations' than if it asks you to use the direct method. This is because when using the direct method there is no need to present all the accrual adjustments such as depreciation, gain on disposal of plant and equipment, impairment losses, net foreign exchange gains/losses etc.

2   Begin with the 'cash flows from operating activities' section and complete the statement as far as you can. If you are using the indirect method (as is likely at Paper 13 level), this must begin with 'profit for the year'. This is normally taken directly from the statement of profit or loss and other comprehensive income. However the examiner may require you to make adjustments to this figure before you include it in the group statement of cash flows if, for example, there have been errors in its calculation (as in the May 2010 exam). Next, read through the question and include on the statement of cash flows any adjustments necessary to the 'profit for the year' figure for accrual items which have been included in its calculation but which have not resulted in cash flows.

    Note above comment concerning the importance of learning the definitions and the possible inclusion of interest, dividends and income taxes in operating, investing or financing cash flows. If the question has given you information concerning company policy in this respect, then include those cash flows as directed. That is, include any interest, dividends or tax cash flows in operating activities if so directed by the question.

3	Read through the question and calculate cash flows with respect to investing activities; for example, proceeds from disposal of property, payments for intangible assets etc. Insert the figures onto the group statement of cash flows.
4	Read through the question and calculate cash flows with respect to financing activities; for example, payments to buy back shares, proceeds from borrowings, repayment of borrowings etc. Insert the figures onto the group statement of cash flows.
5	Make sure you have correctly dealt with the group implications of a cash flow statement. This will normally involve:
	(a) Include dividends received from associates and net cash flows from acquiring and disposing of subsidiaries and associates in investing activities.
	(b) Include proceeds from disposal of partial interest in subsidiaries in financing activities.
6	Complete the group statement of cash flows by inserting figures for cash equivalents.

Remember that the Paper 13 exam questions are more advanced than the Paper 11 questions and will be more complex. Note therefore that, as mentioned in point 2 above, when you get to step 2 and before beginning to enter figures onto the group statement of cash flows, check to see whether the question requires you to make any amendments to any of the figures as a result, for example, of a finance director misunderstanding an IFRS's requirements.

Chapter roundup

- **Statements of cash flows** are a useful addition to the financial statements of companies because it is recognised that accounting profit is not the only indicator of a company's performance.

- Statements of cash flows concentrate on the sources and uses of cash and are a useful indicator of a company's **liquidity and solvency**.

- You need to be aware of the **format** of the statement as laid out in **IAS 7**. Setting out the format is an essential first stage in preparing the statement, so this format must be learnt.

- Remember the **step-by-step preparation procedure** and use it for all the questions you practise.

- **Consolidated cash flows** should not present a great problem if you understand how to deal with acquisitions and disposals of subsidiaries, non-controlling interest and dividends.

- **A foreign exchange difference** in a group statement of cash flows must be analysed into its constituent parts.

Quick quiz

1. What is the objective of IAS 7?
2. What are the benefits of cash flow information according to IAS 7?
3. What are the standard headings required by IAS 7 to be included in a statement of cash flows?
4. What is the 'indirect method' of preparing a statement of cash flows?
5. How should an acquisition or disposal of a subsidiary be shown in the statement of cash flows?

Answers to quick quiz

1. To provide users of financial statements with information about the entity's ability to generate cash and cash equivalents, and the entity's cash needs.

2. See Section 2.2

3. Operating, investing and financing activities.

4. The profit or loss for the period is adjusted for non-cash items; changes in inventories, receivables and payables from operations; and other items resulting from investing or financing activities.

5. Cash flows from acquisitions and disposal, net of cash acquired/disposed of, are disclosed separately under investing activities.

End of chapter question

Porter

The following consolidated financial statements relate to Porter, a public limited company:

PORTER GROUP: STATEMENT OF FINANCIAL POSITION AS AT 31 MAY 20X6

	20X6 $m	20X5 $m
Non-current assets		
Property, plant and equipment	958	812
Goodwill	15	10
Investment in associate	48	39
	1,021	861
Current assets		
Inventories	154	168
Trade receivables	132	112
Financial assets measured at fair value	16	0
Cash and cash equivalents	158	48
	460	328
	1,481	1,189
Equity attributable to owners of the parent		
Share capital ($1 ordinary shares)	332	300
Share premium account	212	172
Retained earnings	188	165
Revaluation surplus	101	54
	833	691
Non-controlling interests	84	28
	917	719
Non-current liabilities		
Non-current borrowings	380	320
Deferred tax liability	38	26
	418	346
Current liabilities		
Trade and other payables	110	98
Interest payable	8	4
Current tax payable	28	22
	146	124
	1,481	1,189

PART B BUSINESS COMBINATIONS AND GROUP FINANCIAL STATEMENTS

PORTER GROUP: STATEMENT OF PROFIT OR LOSS AND OTHER COMPREHENSIVE INCOME
FOR THE YEAR ENDED 31 MAY 20X6

	$m
Revenue	956
Cost of sales	(634)
Gross profit	322
Other income	6
Distribution costs	(97)
Administrative expenses	(115)
Finance costs	(16)
Share of profit of associate	12
Profit before tax	112
Income tax expense	(34)
PROFIT FOR THE YEAR	78
Other comprehensive income:	
Gains on property revaluation	58
Share of other comprehensive income of associate	8
Income tax relating to components of other comprehensive income	(17)
Other comprehensive income for the year, net of tax	49
TOTAL COMPREHENSIVE INCOME FOR THE YEAR	127
Profit attributable to:	
Owners of the parent	68
Non-controlling interests	10
	78
Total comprehensive income attributable to:	
Owners of the parent	115
Non-controlling interests	12
	127

The following information relates to the consolidated financial statements of Porter:

(a) During the period, Porter acquired 60% of a subsidiary. The purchase was effected by issuing shares of Porter on a 1 for 2 basis, at their market value on that date of $2.25 per share, plus $26m in cash.

A statement of financial position of the subsidiary, prepared at the acquisition date for consolidation purposes, showed the following position:

	$m
Property, plant and equipment	92
Inventories	20
Trade receivables	16
Cash and cash equivalents	8
	136
Share capital ($1 shares)	80
Reserves	40
	120
Trade payables	12
Income taxes payable	4
	136

An impairment test conducted at the year end, resulted in a write-down of goodwill relating to another wholly owned subsidiary. This was charged to cost of sales.

Group policy is to value non-controlling interests at the date of acquisition at the proportionate share of the fair value of the acquiree's identifiable assets acquired and liabilities assumed.

10: GROUP STATEMENTS OF CASH FLOWS

(b) Depreciation charged to the consolidated profit or loss amounted to $44m. There were no disposals of property, plant and equipment during the year.

(c) Other income represents gains on financial assets measured at fair value. The financial assets represent investments in quoted shares were purchased shortly before the year end with surplus cash, and are expected to be sold after the year end. No dividends have yet been received.

(d) Included in 'trade and other payables' is the $ equivalent of an invoice for 102m shillings for some equipment purchased from a foreign supplier. The asset was invoiced on 5 March 20X6, but had not been paid for at the year end, 31 May 20X6.

Exchange gains or losses on the transaction have been included in administrative expenses. Relevant exchange rates were as follows:

	Shillings to $1
5 March 20X6	6.8
31 May 20X6	6.0

(e) Movement on retained earnings was as follows:

	$m
At 31 May 20X5	165
Total comprehensive income	68
Dividends paid	(45)
At 31 May 20X6	188

Required

Prepare a consolidated statement of cash flows for Porter for the year ended 31 May 20X6 in accordance with IAS 7 *Statement of Cash Flows*, using the indirect method.

Notes to the statement of cash flows are not required.

(Total 25 marks)

Accounting and reporting techniques

Interim reporting, first-time adoption and fair values

Topic list	Syllabus reference
1 IAS 34 *Interim Financial Reporting*	13.4
2 IFRS 1 *First-time Adoption of International Financial Reporting Standards*	13.4
3 IFRS 13 *Fair Value Measurement*	13.4

Introduction

This chapter deals with three accounting standards:

- IAS 34 *Interim Financial Reporting*, which provides guidance on the content of interim financial reports for those companies which produce them;
- IFRS 1 *First-time Adoption of IFRS*, which explains the procedures which companies adopting IFRS for the first time should follow, and
- IFRS 13 *Fair Value Measurement*, which provides guidance on establishing the fair value of items, when other IFRS require measurement at fair value.

PART C ACCOUNTING AND REPORTING TECHNIQUES

1 IAS 34 *Interim Financial Reporting*

FAST FORWARD

> IAS 34 complements stock exchange rules on interim financial reporting in many countries, but it may provide a blueprint for developing markets.

IAS 34 recommends that **entities should produce interim financial reports** and, for entities that do publish such reports, it lays down principles and guidelines for their production.

The following definitions are used in IAS 34.

Key terms

- **Interim period** is a financial reporting period shorter than a full financial year.
- **Interim financial report** means a financial report containing either a complete set of financial statements (as described in IAS 1) or a set of condensed financial statements (as described in this standard) for an interim period. (IAS 34)

1.1 Scope

The standard does not make the preparation of interim financial reports **mandatory**, taking the view that this is a matter for governments, securities regulators, stock exchanges or professional accountancy bodies within each country to decide. The IASB does, however, strongly recommend to governments etc. that interim financial reporting should be a requirement for companies whose equity or debt securities are **publicly traded**.

(a) An interim financial report should be produced by such companies for **at least the first six months of their financial year** (ie a half year financial report).

(b) The report should be **available no later than 60 days** after the end of the interim period.

Thus, a company with a year ending 31 December would be required as a minimum to prepare an interim report for the half year to 30 June, and this report should be available before the end of August.

1.2 Minimum components

The proposed standard specifies the **minimum component elements** of an interim financial report:

- Condensed statement of financial position
- Condensed statement of profit or loss and other comprehensive income
- Condensed statement of changes in equity
- Condensed statement of cash flows
- Selected note disclosures

The rationale for requiring only condensed statements and selected note disclosures is that entities need not duplicate information in their interim report that is contained in their report for the previous financial year. Interim statements should **focus more on new events, activities and circumstances**.

1.3 Form and content

Where **full financial statements** are given as interim financial statements, they should comply with IAS 1 *Presentation of Financial Statements*, otherwise IAS 34 specifies minimum contents.

The **condensed statement of financial position** should include, as a minimum, each of the headings and sub-totals as were in the statement of financial position at the end of the previous financial year, thus providing a summary of the economic resources of the entity and its financial structure.

The **condensed statement of profit or loss and other comprehensive income** (whether presented as a single statement or as two separate statements) should include, as a minimum, each of the headings and sub-totals shown for the previous financial year, together with the earnings per share and diluted earnings per share.

The **condensed statement of cash flows** should show, as a minimum, the three major sub-totals of cash flow as required by IAS 7 *Statement of Cash Flows*, namely: cash flows from operating activities, cash flows from investing activities and cash flows from financing activities.

The **condensed statement of changes in equity** should include, as a minimum, each of the headings and sub-totals as were contained in the statement of changes in equity for the previous financial year of the entity.

1.3.1 Significant events and transactions and selected explanatory notes

IAS 34 states that the interim financial report should include an explanation of events and transactions that are significant in providing an understanding of the changes in financial position and performance of the entity since the end of the last annual reporting period.

In addition to disclosing significant events and transactions, the notes to the interim report should include the following (unless the information is contained elsewhere in the report).

- A statement that the **same accounting policies and methods of computation** have been used for the interim statements as were used for the most recent annual financial statements. If not, the nature of the differences and their effect should be described. (The accounting policies for preparing the interim report should only differ from those used for the previous annual financial statements in a situation where there has been a change in accounting policy since the end of the previous financial year, and the new policy will be applied for the annual financial statements of the current financial period.)

- Explanatory comments on the **seasonality or 'cyclicality'** of operations in the interim period. For example, if a company earns most of its annual profits in the first half of the year, because sales are much higher in the first six months, the interim report for the first half of the year should explain this fact.

- The **nature and amount** of items during the interim period affecting assets, liabilities, capital, net income or cash flows, that are unusual, due to their nature, incidence or size.

- The **issue or repurchase** of equity or debt securities.

- Nature and amount of any **changes in estimates** of amounts reported in an earlier interim report during the financial year, or in prior financial years if these affect the current interim period.

- **Dividends paid** on ordinary shares and the dividends paid on other shares.

- **Segmental results** for the operating segments of the entity (see IFRS 8).

- Any **significant events since the end of the interim period**.

- Effect of the acquisition or disposal of subsidiaries during the interim period.

- Any significant change in a **contingent liability or a contingent asset** since the end of the reporting period.

The entity should also disclose the fact that the interim report has been produced **in compliance with** IAS 34 on interim financial reporting.

Question — Disclosures

Give some examples of the type of events or transactions which require disclosure if significant.

Answer

The following are examples from IAS 34. The list is not exhaustive.

(a) The write-down of inventories or reversal of a write-down

(b) Recognition of an impairment loss or its reversal

(c) The reversal of provisions for restructuring costs

(d) Acquisitions and disposals of property, plant and equipment

(e) Commitments for the purchase of property, plant and equipment

(f) Litigation settlements

(g) Correction of prior period errors

(h) Changes in the business or economic circumstances that affect the fair value of financial instruments

(i) Any loan default or breach of loan agreement not remedied by the end of the reporting period

(j) Related party transactions

(k) Changes in the classification of financial assets due to a change in the purpose or use of those assets

(l) Changes in contingent liabilities and assets.

1.4 Periods covered

The standard requires that interim financial reports should provide financial information for the following periods or as at the following dates:

- **Statement of financial position data** as at the end of the current interim period, and comparative data as at the end of the most recent financial year.

- **Statement of profit or loss and other comprehensive income data** for the current interim period and cumulative data for the current year to date, together with comparative data for the corresponding interim period and cumulative figures for the previous financial year.

- **Statement of cash flow data** should be cumulative for the current year to date, with comparative cumulative data for the corresponding interim period in the previous financial year.

- **Data for the statement of changes in equity** should be for both the current interim period and for the year to date, together with comparative data for the corresponding interim period, and cumulative figures, for the previous financial year.

1.5 Materiality

Materiality should be assessed in relation to the interim period financial data. It should be recognised that interim measurements **rely to a greater extent on estimates** than annual financial data.

1.6 Recognition and measurement principles

A large part of IAS 34 deals with recognition and measurement principles, and guidelines as to their practical application. The **guiding principle** is that an entity should use the **same recognition and measurement principles in its interim statements as it does in its annual financial statements.**

This means, for example, that a cost that would not be regarded as an asset in the year-end statement of financial position should not be regarded as an asset in the statement of financial position for an interim period. Similarly, an accrual for an item of income or expense for a transaction that has not yet occurred (or a deferral of an item of income or expense for a transaction that has already occurred) is inappropriate for interim reporting, just as it is for year-end reporting.

Applying this principle of recognition and measurement may result, in a subsequent interim period or at the year-end, in a **remeasurement** of amounts that were reported in a financial statement for a previous interim period. **The nature and amount of any significant remeasurements should be disclosed.**

1.6.1 Revenues received occasionally, seasonally or cyclically

Revenue that is received as an occasional item, or within a seasonal or cyclical pattern, should not be anticipated or deferred in interim financial statements, if it would be inappropriate to anticipate or defer the revenue for the annual financial statements. In other words, the principles of revenue recognition should be applied consistently to the interim reports and year-end reports.

1.6.2 Costs incurred unevenly during the financial year

These should only be anticipated or deferred (ie treated as accruals or prepayments) if it would be appropriate to anticipate or defer the expense in the annual financial statements. For example, it would be appropriate to anticipate a cost for property rental where the rental is paid in arrears, but it would be inappropriate to anticipate part of the cost of a major advertising campaign later in the year, for which no expenses have yet been incurred.

The standard goes on, in an appendix, to deal with **specific applications** of the recognition and measurement principle. Some of these examples are explained below, by way of explanation and illustration.

1.6.3 Payroll taxes or insurance contributions paid by employers

In some countries these are assessed on an annual basis, but paid at an uneven rate during the course of the year, with a large proportion of the taxes being paid in the early part of the year, and a much smaller proportion paid later on in the year. In this situation, it would be appropriate to use an estimated average annual tax rate for the year in an interim statement, not the actual tax paid. This treatment is appropriate because it reflects the fact that the taxes are assessed on an annual basis, even though the payment pattern is uneven.

1.6.4 Cost of a planned major periodic maintenance or overhaul

The cost of such an event later in the year must not be anticipated in an interim financial statement **unless** there is a legal or constructive obligation to carry out this work. The fact that a maintenance or overhaul is planned and is carried out annually is not of itself sufficient to justify anticipating the cost in an interim financial report.

1.6.5 Other planned but irregularly-occurring costs

Similarly, these costs such as charitable donations or employee training costs, should not be accrued in an interim report. These costs, even if they occur regularly and are planned, are nevertheless discretionary.

1.6.6 Year-end bonus

A year end bonus should not be provided for in an interim financial statement *unless* there is a constructive obligation to pay a year end bonus (eg a contractual obligation, or a regular past practice) and the size of the bonus can be reliably measured.

1.6.7 Holiday pay

The same principle applies here. If holiday pay is an enforceable obligation on the employer, then any unpaid accumulated holiday pay may be accrued in the interim financial report.

1.6.8 Non-monetary intangible assets

The entity might incur expenses during an interim period on items that might or will generate non-monetary intangible assets. IAS 38 *Intangible Assets* requires that costs to generate non-monetary intangible assets (eg development expenses) should be recognised as an expense when incurred **unless** the costs form part of an identifiable intangible asset. Costs that were initially recognised as an expense cannot subsequently be treated instead as part of the cost of an intangible asset. IAS 34 states that interim financial statements should adopt the same approach. This means that it would be inappropriate in an interim financial statement to 'defer' a cost in the expectation that it will eventually be part of a non-monetary intangible asset that has not yet been recognised: such costs should be treated as an expense in the interim statement.

1.6.9 Depreciation

Depreciation should only be charged in an interim statement on non-current assets that have been acquired, not on non-current assets that will be acquired later in the financial year.

1.6.10 Foreign currency translation gains and losses

These should be calculated by the same principles as at the financial year end, in accordance with IAS 21 *The Effects of Changes in Foreign Exchange Rates*.

1.6.11 Tax on income

An entity will include an expense for income tax (tax on profits) in its interim statements. The **tax rate** to use should be the estimated average annual tax rate for the year. For example, suppose that in a particular jurisdiction, the rate of tax on company profits is 30% on the first $200,000 of profit and 40% on profits above $200,000. Now suppose that a company makes a profit of $200,000 in its first half year, and expects to make $200,000 in the second half year. The rate of tax to be applied in the interim financial report should be 35%, not 30%, ie the expected average rate of tax for the year as a whole. This approach is appropriate because income tax on company profits is charged on an annual basis, and an effective annual rate should therefore be applied to each interim period.

As another illustration, suppose a company earns pre-tax income in the first quarter of the year of $30,000, but expects to make a loss of $10,000 in each of the next three quarters, so that net income before tax for the year is zero. Suppose also that the rate of tax is 30%. In this case, it would be inappropriate to anticipate the losses, and the tax charge should be $9,000 for the first quarter of the year (30% of $30,000) and a negative tax charge of $3,000 for each of the next three quarters, if actual losses are the same as anticipated.

Where the tax year for a company does not coincide with its financial year, a separate estimated weighted average tax rate should be applied for each tax year, to the interim periods that fall within that tax year.

Some countries give entities tax credits against the tax payable, based on amounts of capital expenditure or research and development, etc. Under most tax regimes, these credits are calculated and granted on an annual basis; therefore it is appropriate to include anticipated tax credits within the calculation of the estimated average tax rate for the year, and apply this rate to calculate the tax on income for interim periods. However, if a tax benefit relates to a specific one-time event, it should be recognised within the tax expense for the interim period in which the event occurs.

1.6.12 Inventory valuations

Within interim reports, inventories should be valued in the same way as for year-end financial statements. It is recognised, however, that it will be necessary to rely more heavily on estimates for interim reporting than for year-end reporting.

In addition, it will normally be the case that the net realisable value of inventories should be estimated from selling prices and related costs to complete and dispose at interim dates.

1.7 Use of estimates

Although accounting information must be reliable and free from material error, it may be necessary to sacrifice some accuracy and reliability for the sake of timeliness and cost-benefits. This is particularly the case with interim financial reporting, where there will be much less time to produce reports than at the financial year end. The standard therefore recognises that estimates will have to be used to a greater extent in interim reporting, to assess values or even some costs, than in year-end reporting.

An appendix to IAS 34 gives some examples of the use of estimates.

(a) **Inventories.** An entity might not need to carry out a full inventory count at the end of each interim period. Instead, it may be sufficient to estimate inventory values using sales margins.

(b) **Provisions**. An entity might employ outside experts or consultants to advise on the appropriate amount of a provision as at the year end. It will probably be inappropriate to employ an expert to make a similar assessment at each interim date. Similarly, an entity might employ a professional valuer to revalue fixed assets at the year end, whereas at the interim date(s) the entity will not rely on such experts.

(c) **Income taxes**. The rate of income tax (tax on profits) will be calculated at the year end by applying the tax rate in each country/jurisdiction to the profits earned there. At the interim stage, it may be sufficient to estimate the rate of income tax by applying the same 'blended' estimated weighted average tax rate to the income earned in all countries/jurisdictions.

The principle of **materiality** applies to interim financial reporting, as it does to year-end reporting. As already noted the assessment of materiality in interim financial reports will rely more heavily on estimates than in year-end reports. Materiality should be assessed in relation to the interim financial statements themselves, and should be independent of 'annual materiality' considerations.

1.8 Section summary

- IAS 34 in concept makes **straightforward proposals** for the production of interim financial reports by entities.
- It is essential to apply **principles of recognition and measurement** that will prevent entities from 'massaging' the interim figures.
- The **detail** in the guidelines is therefore very important, and the application of the recognition and measurement principles to particular valuations and measurements needs to be understood.

2 IFRS 1 *First-time Adoption Of International Financial Reporting Standards*

FAST FORWARD

> IFRS 1 sets out the precise way in which an entity should implement a change from local accounting standards to IFRS.

IFRS 1 sets out the precise way in which companies should implement a **change from local accounting standards (their previous GAAP) to IFRS**.

The standard is intended to ensure that an entity's **first IFRS financial statements** contain **high quality information** that is transparent for users and comparable over all periods presented; provides a suitable starting point for accounting under IFRS; and can be generated at a cost that does not exceed the benefits to users.

Key terms

Date of transition to IFRS. The beginning of the earliest period for which an entity presents full comparative information under IFRS in its first IFRS financial statements.

Deemed cost. An amount used as a surrogate for cost or depreciated cost at a given date.

Fair value. The price that would be received to sell an asset or paid to transfer a liability in an orderly transaction between market participants at the measurement date.

First IFRS financial statements. The first annual financial statements in which an entity adopts International Financial Reporting Standards (IFRS), by an explicit and unreserved statement of compliance with IFRS.

Opening IFRS statement of financial position. An entity's statement of financial position (published or unpublished) at the date of transition to IFRS.

Previous GAAP. The basis of accounting that a first time adopter used immediately before adopting IFRS.

> **Reporting date.** The end of the latest period covered by financial statements or by an interim financial report.
> (IFRS 1)

IFRS 1 **only applies** where an entity prepares IFRS financial statements **for the first time**. Changes in accounting policies made by an entity that already applies IFRS should be dealt with by applying either IAS 8 *Accounting Policies, Changes in Accounting Estimates and Errors* or specific transitional requirements in other standards.

2.1 Making the transition to IFRS

An entity should:

(a) Select accounting policies that comply with IFRS **at the reporting date** for the entity's first IFRS financial statements.

(b) Prepare an **opening IFRS statement of financial position** at the **date of transition to IFRS.** This is the starting point for subsequent accounting under IFRS. The date of transition to IFRS is the beginning of the earliest comparative period presented in an entity's first IFRS financial statements.

(c) **Disclose the effect** of the change in the financial statements.

2.2 Example: Reporting date and opening IFRS statement of financial position

An listed company has a 31 December year end and will be required to comply with IFRS from 1 January 20X5.

Required

What is the date of transition to IFRS?

Solution

The company's first IFRS financial statements will be for the **year ended 31 December 20X5**.

IFRS 1 requires that at least one year's comparative figures are presented in the first IFRS financial statements. The comparative figures will be for the year ended 31 December 20X4.

Therefore the date of transition to IFRS is **1 January 20X4** and the company prepares an opening IFRS statement of financial position at this date.

2.3 Preparing the opening IFRS statement of financial position

IFRS 1 states that in its opening IFRS statement of financial position an entity shall:

(a) **Recognise all assets and liabilities** whose recognition is required by IFRS

(b) Not recognise items as assets or liabilities if IFRS do not permit such recognition

(c) **Reclassify items** that it recognised under previous GAAP as one type of asset, liability or component of equity, but are a different type of asset liability or component of equity under IFRS

(d) **Apply IFRS in measuring** all recognised assets and liabilities

This involves restating the statement of financial position prepared at the same date under the entity's previous GAAP so that it complies with IFRS in force **at the first reporting date**. In our example above, the company prepares its opening IFRS statement of financial position at **1 January 20X4**, following accounting policies that comply with IFRS in force at **31 December 20X5**.

The accounting policies that an entity uses in its opening IFRS statement of financial position may differ from those it used for the same date using its previous GAAP. The resulting adjustments are recognised directly **in retained earnings** (in equity) **at the date of transition**. (This is because the adjustments arise from events and transactions before the date of transition to IFRS.)

An entity's **estimates** under IFRS at the date of transition must be **consistent** with those made at the same date under previous GAAP, (after adjustments to reflect any difference in accounting policies), unless there is **objective evidence** that those estimates were **in error**.

2.4 Exemptions from other IFRS

These enabled an entity not to apply certain requirements of specific accounting standards retrospectively in drawing up its opening IFRS statement of financial position. Their purpose was to ensure that the cost of producing IFRS financial statements did not exceed the benefits to users.

These exemptions have now been deleted from IFRS 1 as part of the 2014–2016 IFRS Improvements cycle. It is considered that they have now served their purpose and are no longer needed.

2.4.1 Business combinations

IFRS 3 *Business Combinations* need not be applied retrospectively to business combinations that occurred before the date of the opening IFRS statement of financial position. This has the following consequences:

(a) Combinations keep the **same classification** (eg acquisition, uniting of interests) as in the previous GAAP financial statements.

(b) **All acquired assets and liabilities are recognised** other than:

- Some financial assets and financial liabilities derecognised under the previous GAAP (derivatives and special purpose entities must be recognised);
- Assets (including goodwill) and liabilities that were not recognised under previous GAAP and would not qualify for recognition under IFRS.

Any resulting change is recognised by **adjusting retained earnings** (ie equity) unless the change results from the recognition of an intangible asset that was previously subsumed within goodwill.

(c) **Items which do not qualify for recognition** as an asset or liability under IFRS must be excluded from the opening IFRS statement of financial position. For example, intangible assets that do not qualify for separate recognition under IAS 38 must be reclassified as part of goodwill.

(d) The carrying amount of **goodwill** in the opening IFRS statement of financial position is the same as its carrying amount **under previous GAAP**. However, goodwill must be tested for impairment at the transition date.

2.4.2 Property, plant and equipment

An entity may measure an item of property, plant and equipment at its **fair value at the transition** date and then use the fair value as its **deemed** cost at that date.

An entity may use a **previous GAAP revaluation**, or a valuation for the purpose of a privatisation or initial public offering, as the deemed cost at the transition date, so long as the revaluation was **broadly comparable** to fair value or depreciated replacement cost at the date of the valuation.

These exemptions are also available for:

(a) Investment properties measured under the cost model in IAS 40 *Investment Property*
(b) Intangible assets that meet the recognition criteria and the criteria for revaluation in IAS 38

2.4.3 Cumulative translation differences

IAS 21 requires some exchange differences is to be classified as a separate component of equity, for example, differences arising when a the financial statements of a foreign operation are translated. The cumulative translation differences must be included in the gain or loss on disposal of the foreign operation. Under the exemption, the **cumulative translation differences for all foreign operations are deemed to be zero at the transition date**. The gain or loss on a subsequent disposal of a foreign operation will exclude translation differences that arose before the transition date. Later translation differences will be included.

2.4.4 Compound financial instruments

IAS 32 *Financial Instruments: Presentation* requires compound financial instruments to be split at inception into separate liability and equity components. If the liability component is no longer outstanding at the date of the translation to IFRS, the split is not required.

2.4.5 Designation of previously recognised financial instruments

When financial assets are first recognised, they may be designated as financial assets measured at fair value in accordance with IFRS 9 *Financial Instruments*. Financial liabilities may be designated as fair value through profit or loss in accordance with IFRS 9.

Note. An entity may make such a designation at the date of transition to IFRS.

2.4.6 Share-based payment transactions

An entity is encouraged, but not required, to apply IFRS 2 *Share-based Payment* to:

(a) Equity instruments that were granted and vested before the date of transition to IFRS or 1 January 2005 (whichever is the later)

(b) Liabilities arising from share-based payment transactions that were settled before the date of transition to IFRS

Question
IFRS 1

Russell Co will adopt International Financial Reporting Standards (IFRS) for the first time in its financial statements for the year ended 31 December 20X4.

In its previous financial statements for 31 December 20X2 and 20X3, which were prepared under local GAAP, the company made a number of routine accounting estimates, including accrued expenses. It also recognised a general provision for liabilities, calculated at a fixed percentage of its retained profits for the year. This is required under its local GAAP.

Subsequently, some of the accruals were found to be overestimates and some were found to be underestimates.

Required

Discuss how the matters above should be dealt with in the IFRS financial statements of Russell Co for the year ended 31 December 20X4.

Answer

Provided that the routine accounting estimates have been made in a manner consistent with IFRS no adjustments are made in the first IFRS financial statements. The only exception to this is if the company has subsequently discovered that these estimates were in error. Although there were some overestimates and some underestimates, this is probably not the case here.

The general provision is a different matter. This provision would definitely not have met the criteria for recognition under IAS 37 *Provisions, Contingent Liabilities and Contingent Assets* and therefore it will not be recognised in the opening IFRS statement of financial position (1 January 20X3) or at subsequent year ends.

2.5 Presentation and disclosure

An entity's first IFRS financial statements must include **at least**:

(a) Three statements of financial position;
(b) Two statements of profit or loss and other comprehensive income;
(c) Two separate statements of profit or loss (if presented);
(d) Two statements of cash flows; and
(e) Two statements of changes in equity and related notes.

An entity must also **explain the effect** of the transition from previous GAAP to IFRS on its financial position, financial performance and cash flows by providing **reconciliations**:

(a) Of **equity** reported under previous GAAP to equity under IFRS at the **date of transition** and at the **end of the last period presented in accordance with previous GAAP**.

(b) Of **total comprehensive income** reported under previous GAAP to total comprehensive income reported under IFRS for the latest period in the entity's most recent financial statements.

The reconciliations must give sufficient detail to enable users to understand the material adjustments to the statement of financial position and statement of profit or loss and other comprehensive income.

If an entity presented a statement of cash flows under its previous GAAP, it should also explain the material **adjustments to the statement of cash flows**.

If an entity recognised or reversed any **impairment losses** for the first time in preparing its opening IFRS statement of financial position, it must provide the disclosures that IAS 36 *Impairment of Assets* would have required if the entity had recognised those impairment losses or reversals in the period beginning with the date of transition to IFRS.

If an entity corrects **errors made under previous GAAP**, the reconciliations must distinguish the correction of errors from changes in accounting policies.

Where **fair value has been used as deemed cost** for a non-current asset in the opening IFRS statement of financial position, the financial statements must disclose the aggregate of fair values and the aggregate adjustments to the carrying amounts reported under previous GAAP for each line in the opening IFRS statement of financial position.

2.5.1 Change in accounting policy

IAS 8 does not apply to the changes in accounting policies that occur when an entity first adopts IFRS or to changes in those policies until after the first IFRS financial statements are presented.

Therefore IAS 8's disclosure requirements do not apply to the first IFRS financial statements.

If, after the issue of its first IFRS interim report but before the issue of its first IFRS financial statements, an entity changes its accounting policies or use of IFRS 1 exemptions, it must update its reconciliations between IFRS and the previous GAAP accordingly.

2.6 Interim financial reports

IFRS 1 applies to any interim financial report that an entity presents under IAS 34 *Interim Financial Reporting* for part of the period covered by the first IFRS financial statements.

Where interim financial reports are presented, an entity should provide the same reconciliations required for full financial statements and described above. Material adjustments to the statement of cash flows, if any, should also be disclosed.

2.7 Managing the change to International Standards

The implementation of the above technical aspects is likely to entail careful management in most companies. Here are some of the **change management considerations** that should be addressed:

PART C   ACCOUNTING AND REPORTING TECHNIQUES

(a) **Accurate assessment of the task involved.** Underestimation or wishful thinking may hamper the effectiveness of the conversion and may ultimately prove inefficient.

(b) **Proper planning.** This should take place at the overall project level, but a **detailed** task **analysis** could be drawn up to **control work performed**.

(c) **Human resource management.** The project must be properly structured and staffed.

(d) **Training.** Where there are **skills gaps**, remedial training should be provided.

(e) **Monitoring and accountability.** A relaxed 'it will be alright on the night' attitude could spell danger. Implementation **progress** should be **monitored** and **regular meetings** set up so that participants can **personally account for what they are doing** as well as **flag up any problems** as early as possible. **Project drift should be avoided.**

(f) **Achieving milestones.** Successful completion of key steps and tasks should be appropriately acknowledged, ie what managers call 'celebrating success', so as to **sustain motivation and performance**.

(g) **Physical resourcing.** The need for IT **equipment** and **office space** should be properly assessed.

(h) **Process review.** Care should be taken not to perceive the change as a one-off quick fix. Any charge in **future systems** and processes should be assessed and properly implemented.

(i) **Follow-up procedures.** As with general good management practice, the **follow up procedures** should be planned in to **make sure that the changes stick** and that any further changes are identified and addressed.

2.8 Section summary

You need to be able to advise an entity making the change from previous GAAP to IFRS on:

- The **general rules** (including the date of the **opening IFRS statement of financial position**)
- The **exemptions** available
- How to deal with **estimates** in previous financial statements
- **Explaining the effects** of the change on the financial statements (preparing reconciliations)
- The **practical aspects** of managing the change

3 IFRS 13 *Fair Value Measurement*

FAST FORWARD

IFRS 13 *Fair Value Measurement* establishes a single source of guidance for fair value measurement under IFRS.

Exam focus point

Fair value is very much a current issue. Not only is it the subject of a recently completed joint project between the IASB and the US FASB, but it has become even more important as a result of the economic downturn. As well as explaining and applying the requirements of IFRS 13, you could be asked to explain the advantages and disadvantages of measuring assets and liabilities at fair value.

IFRS 13 *Fair Value Measurement* was issued by the IASB in May 2011 and is applicable to most areas of accounting. The standard defines fair value, provides guidance on its determination and introduces consistent requirements for disclosures on fair value measurements. The standard does not include requirements on when fair value measurement is required, but instead prescribes how fair value is to be measured if another standard requires it.

3.1 Scope

IFRS 13 will apply where another IFRS requires or allows fair value measurements or related disclosures, with the following exceptions:

- Share-based payments (Chapter 20)

- Leasing transactions (Chapter 15)
- Other standards where measurement is similar to fair value but not fair value eg net realisable value in IAS 2 *Inventories* and value in use in IAS 36 *Impairment of Assets*.

IFRS 13 also gives relief from its disclosure requirements in respect of:

- Plan assets measured at fair value in accordance with IAS 19 *Employee Benefits*.
- Assets for which the recoverable amount is fair value less costs of disposal in accordance with IAS 36.
- Retirement benefit plan investments measured at fair value under IAS 26 *Accounting and Reporting by Retirement Benefit Plans*. This standard is outside the scope of Paper 13.

3.2 Definitions

Key terms

Fair value is defined by IFRS 13 as **'the price that would be received to sell an asset or paid to transfer a liability in an orderly transaction between market participants at the measurement date.'**

Other important definitions are given below:

Key terms

Transaction costs The costs to sell an asset or transfer a liability in the principal (or most advantageous) market for the asset or liability that are directly attributable to the disposal of an asset or transfer of a liability and that:

(i) Result directly from and are essential to that transaction
(ii) Would not have been incurred had the decision to sell the asset or transfer the liability not been made.

Market participants are buyers and sellers in the principal (or most advantageous) market for the asset or liability.

Principal market is the market with the greatest volume and level of activity for the asset or liability.

Most advantageous market is the market that maximises the amount that would be received to sell the asset or minimises the amount that would be paid to transfer the liability after taking into account transport and transaction costs.

Active market is a market in which transactions for the asset or liability take place with sufficient frequency and volume to provide pricing information on an ongoing basis.

Entry price The price paid to acquire an asset or received to assume a liability in an exchange transaction.

Exit price The price that would be received to sell an asset or paid to transfer a liability.

Inputs The assumptions that market participants would use when pricing as asset or liability.

3.3 General considerations in measuring fair value

IFRS 13 stipulates the following factors that should be considered in fair value measurement:

(a) The asset or liability
(b) The market
(c) Market participants
(d) The price

3.3.1 The asset or liability

A fair value measurement relates to a particular asset or liability and should therefore take into account the specific characteristics of the asset or liability, if market participants consider these when pricing the item.

Such characteristics may include the condition and location of the item and any restrictions on sale or use at the measurement date.

IFRS 13 may be applied to an individual asset or liability or a group of related assets and liabilities eg a business.

3.3.2 Example: Characteristics of the asset or liability

A donor contributes land in a residential area to a not-for-profit neighbourhood association. The land is currently used as a playground and the donor specifies that as long as the association owns the land, it must continue to be used as a playground. There is, however, no restriction on the further sale of the land. The land is sought after by a number of residential property developers.

In this case, the donor restriction on use of the land is specific to the association, and the restriction would not be transferred to market participants. Therefore the fair value of the land is the higher of its fair value used as a playground and its fair value as a site for residential development, regardless of the restriction of use of the land by the association.

3.3.3 The market

Under IFRS 13, fair value is determined based on a transaction in the principal market. The **principal market** is the market with the greatest volume and level of activity for the asset or liability.

If there is no principal market, the **most advantageous market** is used. This is the market in which the entity could achieve the most beneficial price.

The principal market (or most advantageous market if there is no principal market) is assumed to be the market in which the entity normally transacts, unless there is evidence to the contrary.

IFRS 13 prohibits the adjustment of fair value for transaction costs, but it does require that these are considered in the determination of the most advantageous market. IFRS 13 does, however allow fair value to be adjusted for transport costs, where location is a characteristic of the asset.

3.3.4 Example: Most advantageous market

An asset is sold in two different markets as follows:

	Market A $	Market B $
Price	27	25
Transport costs	(3)	(2)
	24	23
Transaction costs	(3)	(1)
	21	22

There is no principal market for the asset. What is its fair value?

Solution

As a principal market for the asset does not exist, its fair value is measured using the price in the most advantageous market.

Transaction costs are considered in the determination of the most advantageous markets, but are not taken into consideration in determining fair value.

The most advantageous market is Market B where the net price achieved is $22.

The transaction price of the asset (before transaction costs) in this market is $23, and therefore this is fair value.

3.3.5 Market participants

IFRS 13 emphasises that a fair value measurement is based on the assumptions of market participants who are:

- Independent (not a related party)
- Knowledgeable (have a reasonable understanding of the asset or liability and the transaction)
- Able to transact in the asset or liability
- Willing to transact in the asset or liability (motivated but not forced to transact).

Market participants seek to maximise the fair value of an asset or minimise the fair value of a liability in a transaction to sell the asset or transfer the liability.

IFRS 13 does not require that specific market participants are identified, but instead that a profile of potential market participants is developed.

3.3.6 The price

Under IFRS 13, fair value is based on **exit price** (the price that would be received to sell an asset or paid to transfer a liability) rather than transaction price or entry price (the price that was paid to acquire an asset or received to assume a liability). The exit price concept is based on current expectations about the sale or transfer price from the perspective of market participants.

3.4 Specific considerations in measuring fair value

As well as the general considerations listed above, IFRS 13 stipulates specific factors that should be considered when measuring:

(a) Non-financial assets
(b) Liabilities and equity
(c) Financial instruments

3.4.1 Non-financial assets

The fair value of a non-financial asset is measured based on its **highest and best use** from a market participant's perspective, taking into account whether a particular use is:

- Physically possible (eg it may not be physically possible to use marshland for residential development)
- Legally permissible (eg it is not legally permissible to build on green belt land)
- Financially feasible (eg the costs of using a property in a particular way may not produce the investment return required by market participants).

The **highest and best use** of an asset is assumed to be an entity's current use of a non-financial asset, unless market or other factors suggest otherwise. Some entities will not use an asset at its highest and best use, for example if they are holding an asset defensively in order to restrict availability to others. In this case, measurement is still based on the highest and best use and disclosure is made of the fact that the asset is not used in that way.

3.4.2 Example: Highest and best use

An entity acquires land in a business combination. The land is currently developed for industrial use as a site for a factory. Nearby sites have recently been developed for residential use as sites for high-rise apartment buildings. On the basis of that development, the entity determined that the land could be used as a site for residential use because market participants would take into account the potential to develop the site when pricing the land.

Therefore the highest and best use of the land is the highest of:

(a) The value of the land as currently developed for industrial use

(b) The value of the land as a vacant site for residential use, taking into account the costs of demolishing the factory and other costs necessary to convert the land to a vacant site.

3.4.3 Liabilities and equity

IFRS 13 makes several points relevant in the fair value measurement of liabilities and equity:

Fair value measurement assumes a liability or an entity's own equity instrument is transferred to a market participant at the measurement date, In particular it is assumed that:

(a) A liability remains outstanding and the market participant would be required to fulfil the obligation

(b) An entity's own equity instrument would remain outstanding and the market participant would take on the rights and responsibilities associated with the instrument.

　(i) Where liabilities and equity instruments are held by other parties as assets, and a quoted price is unavailable for the transfer of such an instrument, the fair value of the liability/equity to the issuer is measured from the perspective of the market participant that holds the asset.

　(ii) Where liabilities and equity instruments are **not** held by other parties as assets, and a quoted price is unavailable for the transfer of such an instrument, the fair value of the liability/equity is measured using a valuation technique from the perspective of the market participant that owes the liability or has a claim on the equity.

　(iii) The fair value of a liability should reflect the effect of non-performance risk (the risk that an entity will not fulfil an obligation).

3.4.4 Financial instruments

In markets for securities, financial instruments and commodities, dealers generally buy at the bid price and sell at the ask price. Where this is relevant, the price within the bid-ask spread that is most representative of fair value in the circumstances is used to measure fair value.

IFRS 13 does not, however disallow the use of other pricing conventions that are used by market participants, such as mid-market pricing. Once management has established which convention it is using, this must be applied consistently.

3.5 Valuation techniques

Unless transactions are directly observable in a market (in which case the determination of fair value can be relatively straightforward), a valuation technique is used. IFRS 13 identifies 3 valuation techniques that may be used to determine fair value:

(a) The **market approach**, in which an entity uses prices and other relevant information generated by market transactions involving identical or comparable assets, liabilities or groups of assets and liabilities.

(b) The **income approach**, in which an entity converts future amounts (eg cash flows, income and expenses) to a single discounted (ie current) amount.

(c) The **cost approach** in which an entity determines a value which reflects the amount that would be required currently to replace the service capacity of an asset (often referred to as current replacement cost).

A valuation technique should be selected which maximises the use of relevant observable inputs, such as closing prices on a stock exchange, and minimises the use of unobservable inputs. Once selected the technique should be applied consistently unless alternative techniques provide a more representative measure of fair value. Any changes are regarded as changes in accounting estimate, although the IAS 8 disclosures are not required.

3.6 Fair value at initial recognition

When an asset is acquired or a liability assumed in an exchange transaction, the transaction price is the price paid to acquire the asset or received to assume the liability. This is the **entry price**. Fair value is, however, determined by reference to the **exit price**. This may be the same as the transaction price/entry price in some instances (eg when the transaction to buy an asset takes place in the market in which it would be sold). It may not be the same, if the entry price transaction:

(a) Is between related parties
(b) Takes place under duress eg if the seller is in financial difficulty
(c) Takes place in a market other than the principal (or most advantageous market)

3.7 Fair value hierarchy

A fair value measurement is ranked according to the IFRS 13 fair value hierarchy in order to increase consistency and comparability of fair value measurements. This ranking is **based on the type of inputs** rather than the valuation technique used. A fair value measurement is classified as the same level of the fair value hierarchy as the lowest level input that is significant to the measurement.

The levels are:

- **Level 1 inputs** Unadjusted quoted prices in active markets for identical assets or liabilities that the entity can access at the measurement date.

- **Level 2** Other observable inputs for the asset or liability such as quoted prices in active markets for similar assets or liabilities or quoted prices for identical assets or liabilities in markets which are not active.

- **Level 3** Unobservable inputs developed by an entity using the best information available where there is little or no market activity for the asset or liability at the measurement date.

3.8 Disclosure

Extensive disclosures are required in order to help users of the financial statements assess:

- For both recurring and non-recurring fair value measurements, valuation techniques and inputs used to measure fair values.

- For recurring fair value measurements which use significant level 3 (unobservable) inputs, the effect of the measurements on profit or loss and other comprehensive income for the period.

Recurring fair value measurements are those which require regular updating eg those in relation to investment properties; non-recurring fair value measurements are those which are required only in particular circumstances eg when an asset becomes held for sale and is measured at fair value less costs to sell.

The minimum disclosures for each class of asset and liability measured at fair value after initial recognition are as follows:

(a) The fair value measurement at the end of the reporting period (for both recurring and non-recurring fair value measurements).

(b) For non-recurring fair value measurements, the reasons for measurement.

(c) For recurring and non-recurring fair value measurements, the level in which they are categorised in the fair value hierarchy.

(d) For assets and liabilities that are measured at fair value on a recurring basis, details of any transfers between level 1 and level 2.

(e) For recurring and non-recurring level 2 and 3 fair value measurements, a description of the valuation technique and inputs used.

(f) Changes in valuation technique and reasons for the change.

(g) Quantitative information about significant unobservable inputs used in level 3 fair values unless those inputs are not developed by the reporting entity when measuring fair value.

3.9 Fair value: advantages and problems

IFRS 9 requires that some types of financial instrument are measured at fair value. Other IFRS allow the use of fair value (for example, for non-current assets). Fair value is believed to provide more relevant information than historical cost because:

(a) For some types of financial asset, historical cost can be zero, which does not reflect the underlying reality.

PART C ACCOUNTING AND REPORTING TECHNIQUES

(b) Fair values should have more predictive value.

(c) Some assets are traded on an active market or held for their investment potential (rather than being held to be used in the business).

(d) Fair value often reflects the way risks are managed (for financial instruments).

(e) For assets such as property fair value provides information on the resources actually available to an entity.

However, **fair value is not without problems**:

(a) Some of the changes in fair value will never be realised, which makes the figure reported in the statement of profit or loss and other comprehensive income misleading (particularly if changes in value are recognised in profit or loss).

(b) Fair value may not be reliable, and in a non-active market it may be irrelevant.

(c) Fair valuing investment properties and financial assets can result in volatile profits (as gains and losses impact profit or loss).

(d) Fair value is irrelevant where management does not intend to sell an asset.

In an economic downturn, fair value measurement means that many companies suffer significant losses and many assets lose their value. Financial instruments, property, intangibles (such as goodwill and development costs) and defined benefit pension plans can all be affected, as has been seen recently, particularly in the case of a number of financial institutions.

Chapter roundup

- IAS 34 complements stock exchange rules on interim financial reporting in many countries, but it may provide a blueprint for developing markets.
- IFRS 1 sets out the precise way in which an entity should implement a change from local accounting standards to IFRS.
- IFRS 13 *Fair Value Measurement* establishes a single source of guidance for fair value measurement under IFRS.

Quick quiz

1. Under IAS 34 depreciation should only be charged on non-current assets .... (complete the blanks).

2. IFRS 1 permits a previous GAAP revaluation to be used as deemed cost at the date of transition.

    True ☐
    False ☐

3. How is fair value defined in IFRS 13?

4. What valuation techniques are suggested by IFRS 13 to establish fair value?

5. What type of inputs are classified as Level 1 in the IFRS 13 fair value hierarchy?

Answers to quick quiz

1. That have been acquired.
2. True. This is a specific 'exception'.
3. Fair value is the price that would be received to sell an asset or paid to transfer a liability in an orderly transaction between market participants at the measurement date.
4. The market approach, the income approach and the cost approach.
5. Unadjusted, quoted prices in active markets for identical assets or liabilities that the entity can access at the measurement date.

End of chapter question

Tollirene (AIA May 2004)

Tollirene is a publicly quoted limited liability company operating in a country which is to adopt international accounting standards as from 1 January 20X5. Tollirene currently uses a variety of domestic accounting standards and tax rules to prepare its financial statements and is therefore subject to the requirements of IFRS 1 *First-time Adoption of International Financial Reporting Standards*.

Tollirene has six subsidiaries. Three of the subsidiaries are also holding companies – but none are listed. All the subsidiaries have a financial year end of 31 December. The companies comprising the group have prepared their financial statements for the year ended 31 December 20X3 and Tollirene is currently finalising the consolidated financial statements for the year ended 31 December 20X3.

The chief executive officer of Tollirene would like to know how the move to International Accounting Standards will affect the group and has asked for your help.

Required

Report to the chief executive officer of Tollirene explaining:

- The impact of IFRS 1 on the group of companies, and
- The impact (if any) on the preparation of the financial statements for the years ended 31 December 20X3, 20X4 and 20X5.

(25 marks)

Tangible non-current assets and inventory

Topic list	Syllabus reference
1 The definition of an asset	13.4
2 Revision of IASs 16, 20 and 23	13.4
3 IAS 36 *Impairment of Assets*	13.4
4 Impairment: cash-generating units	13.4
5 IAS 40 *Investment Property*	13.4
6 IAS 2 *Inventories*	13.4

Introduction

We look again here at the **IASB definition of an asset**, as given in the *Conceptual Framework*, and compare it with the definitions given by other standard-setters, particularly FASB in the USA and the Financial Reporting Council (FRC) in the UK.

You have covered several of the relevant standards relating to non-current assets in your earlier studies. These are straightforward and are revised briefly in Section 2, with some questions for you to try. If you have any problems, **go back to your earlier study material**.

The IASB has a standard covering the **impairment of assets**. This is a controversial topic and you must understand the relevant standard. **IAS 36** is discussed in depth in Section 3.

Investment properties are discussed in detail in Section 5.

The topic of **inventories** is revised in Section 6.

PART C ACCOUNTING AND REPORTING TECHNIQUES

1 The definition of an asset

> **FAST FORWARD**
>
> You must learn the IASB *Conceptual Framework* **definition of an asset**: a present economic resource controlled by the entity as a result of past events. An economic resource is a right that has the potential to produce economic benefits.
>
> This definition was changed when the *Conceptual Framework* was revised in 2018. It still ties in closely with the definitions produced by **other standard-setters**, particularly FASB (USA) and FRC (UK).

Asset have been defined in many different ways and for many purposes. The definition of an asset is important because it directly affects the **treatment** of such items. A good definition will prevent abuse or error in the accounting treatment: otherwise some assets might be treated as expenses, and some expenses might be treated as assets.

1.1 IASB definition

> **FAST FORWARD**
>
> The definition has three important characteristics:
> - Economic benefits
> - Control (ownership)
> - Transaction to acquire has taken place (it is a past event)

Remember the definition of an asset in the IASB's *Conceptual Framework*.

Key term

> **Asset**: A present economic resource controlled by the entity as a result of past events. An economic resource is a right that has the potential to produce economic benefits.

The definition of an asset was changed when the *Conceptual Framework* was revised in 2018. The old definition was that an asset was 'a resource controlled by the entity as a result of past events, and from which future economic benefits are expected to flow to the entity.' The key change in the definition is that to be recognised as an asset, economic benefits do not need to be likely.

1.2 Financial Reporting Council (FRC): UK

In the FRC's *Statement of Principles,* Chapter 3 *The Elements of Financial Statements* assets are defined as follows.

Key term

> **Asset** are rights or other access to future economic benefits controlled by an entity as a result of past transactions or events.

The *Statement* goes on to discuss various aspects of this definition, and it is broadly consistent with the IASB's *Conceptual Framework*. The *Statement* then goes further in discussing the complementary natures of assets and liabilities.

1.3 Financial Accounting Standards Board (FASB): USA

The definition given by the FASB in its *Statement of Concepts* is very similar.

Key term

> **Asset** are probable future economic benefits obtained or controlled by a particular entity as a result of past transactions or events.

'Probable' is given in its general meaning merely to reflect the fact that no future outcome can be predicted with total certainty. This definition is more in line with the old *Conceptual Framework* 2010 definition, which required it to be expected that economic benefits would flow to the entity.

1.4 Comparison of definitions

It is clear from what we have seen so far that a general consensus seems to exist in the standard-setting bodies as to the definition of an asset. That definition encompasses **three important characteristics**:

- Economic benefit
- Control (ownership)
- The transaction to acquire control has already taken place

1.5 Definition of a non-current asset

Non-current assets may be defined as follows:

> A **non-current asset** is one intended for use on a continuing basis in the company's activities, ie it is not intended for resale or consumption in its normal operating cycle.

Essentially, an asset is classified as non-current when it does not meet the criteria to be classified as current. IAS 1 paragraph 66 specifies the following criteria for making the distinction between current and non-current assets.

An entity shall classify an asset as current when:

(a) It expects to realise the asset, or intends to sell or consume it, in its normal operating cycle;

(b) It holds the asset primarily for the purpose of trading;

(c) It expects to realise the asset within 12 months after the reporting period; or

(d) The asset is cash or a cash equivalent (as defined in IAS 7) unless the asset is restricted from being exchanged or used to settle a liability for at least 12 months after the reporting period.

An entity shall classify all other assets as non-current.

2 Revision of IASs 16, 20 and 23

> **FAST FORWARD**
>
> You should already be familiar with many standards relating to **non-current assets** from Papers 1 and 11. If not, go back to your earlier study material.
> - IAS 16 *Property, Plant and Equipment*
> - IAS 20 *Accounting for Government Grants and Disclosure of Government Assistance*
> - IAS 23 *Borrowing Costs*

You have studied these standards for earlier papers, but they are fairly straightforward. Read the summary of knowledge brought forward and try the relevant questions. If you have any difficulty, go back to your earlier study material and re-read it.

2.1 IAS 16 *Property, Plant and Equipment*

Knowledge brought forward from earlier studies

IAS 16 *Property, Plant and Equipment*

Definitions

- **Property, plant and equipment** are tangible items with the following properties:
    - Held by an entity for use in the production or supply of goods or services, for rental to others, or for administrative purposes; and
    - Expected to be used during more than one period

- **Cost** is the amount of cash or cash equivalents paid or the fair value of the other consideration given to acquire an asset at the time of its acquisition or construction.
- **Residual value** is the estimated amount that an entity would currently obtain from disposal of the asset, after deducting the estimated costs of disposal, if the asset were already of the age and in the condition expected at the end of its useful life.
- **Fair value** is the price that would be received to sell an asset or paid to transfer a liability in an orderly transaction between market participants at the measurement date.
- **Carrying amount** is the amount at which an asset is recognised after deducting any accumulated depreciation and accumulated impairment losses.

Recognition

As with all assets, **recognition** depends on two criteria:

- It is probable that future economic benefits associated with the item will flow to the entity
- The cost of the item can be measured reliably

These recognition criteria apply to **subsequent expenditure** as well as costs incurred initially (ie, there are no longer separate criteria for recognising subsequent expenditure).

Initial measurement

Once recognised as an asset, items should **initially be measured at cost,** including:

- **Purchase price**, plus import duties less trade discount/rebate
- **Directly attributable costs** of bringing the asset to working condition for intended use
- **Initial estimate** of the **costs of dismantling and removing the item** and **restoring the site** on which it is located.

IAS 16 also provides additional guidance on **directly attributable costs** included in the cost of an item of property, plant and equipment.

(a) These costs bring the asset to the location and condition necessary for it to be capable of operating in the manner intended by management, including those costs to test whether the asset is functioning properly.

(b) These are determined after deducting the net proceeds from selling any items produced when bringing the asset to its location and condition.

The standard also states that **income and related expenses** of operations that are incidental to the construction or development of an item of property, plant and equipment should be recognised in profit or loss.

IAS 16 specifies that **exchanges of items of property, plant and equipment**, regardless of whether the assets are similar, are measured at **fair value**, unless the exchange transaction lacks commercial substance or the fair value of neither of the assets exchanged can be measured reliably. If the acquired item is not measured at fair value, its cost is measured at the carrying amount of the asset given up.

Expenditure incurred in replacing or renewing a component of an item of property, plant and equipment shall be **recognised in the carrying amount of the item**. The carrying amount of the replaced or renewed component asset shall be derecognised. A similar approach is also applied when a separate component of an item of property, plant and equipment is identified in respect of a major inspection to enable the continued use of the item.

Measurement subsequent to initial recognition.

IAS 16 allows a choice between measurement models:

- **Cost model**: carry asset at cost less accumulated depreciation and any accumulated impairment losses

- **Revaluation model**: carry asset at revalued amount, ie fair value less subsequent accumulated depreciation and any subsequent accumulated impairment losses. (IAS 16 makes clear that the revaluation model is available only if the fair value of the item can be measured reliably).

Where the revaluation model is adopted certain rules apply:

1 When an item of property, plant and equipment is revalued, the whole class of assets to which it belongs should be revalued.

2 Revaluations must be kept up to date; the frequency of valuation depends on the volatility of fair values of individual assets. Where the current fair value is significantly different from carrying value then a revaluation should be carried out.

3 All items within a class should be revalued at the same time to prevent selective revaluation and to avoid disclosing a mixture of costs and values from different dates in the financial statements. A rolling basis of revaluation is allowed if the revaluations are kept up to date and the revaluation of a class of assets is completed in a short period of time.

Fair value is measured in accordance with IFRS 13 (see Chapter 11)

A revaluation is accounted for as follows:

- An increase in value is recognised in other comprehensive income and carried in a revaluation surplus
- A decrease is an expense in profit or loss after cancelling a previous revaluation surplus
- Additional disclosure required

Depreciation

- Depreciation is based on the carrying amount in the statement of financial position. It must be determined separately for each significant part of an item.
- Where an asset has been revalued the excess of the depreciation charge over historical cost depreciation can be transferred to realised earnings in the statement of changes in equity.
- The residual value and useful life of an asset, as well as the depreciation method, must be reviewed at least at each financial year end. Changes are changes in accounting estimates and are accounted for prospectively as adjustments to future depreciation.
- Depreciation of an asset ceases when the asset is derecognised or reclassified as held for sale (IFRS 5).

    Depreciation does not cease when the asset becomes idle or is retired from active use unless the asset is fully depreciated. However, under usage methods of depreciation the depreciation charge can be zero while there is no production.

Derecognition

An asset is derecognised either on disposal or when no future economic benefits are expected from its use.

Any gain or loss arising at derecognition (such as a gain on disposal) is included in profit or loss in the accounting period in which when the asset is derecognised (unless required otherwise by IFRS).

A further point worth emphasising here is the relationship between the accounting treatment of **impairments and revaluations**.

(a) An **impairment loss** should be treated in the same way as a **revaluation decrease**, ie the decrease should be recognised as an expense. However, a revaluation decrease (or impairment loss) should be charged directly against any related revaluation surplus to the extent that the decrease does not exceed the amount held in the revaluation surplus in respect of that same asset.

(b) A **reversal of an impairment** loss should be treated in the same way as a **revaluation increase**, ie a revaluation increase should be recognised as income to the extent that it reverses a revaluation decrease or an impairment loss of the same asset previously recognised as an expense.

PART C ACCOUNTING AND REPORTING TECHNIQUES

Question — Depreciation

What are the purposes of providing for depreciation?

Answer

The financial statements of a business try to recognise that the cost of a non-current asset is gradually consumed as the asset wears out. This is done by gradually writing off the asset's cost in profit or loss over several accounting periods. This process is known as depreciation, and is an example of the accrual assumption. Depreciation should be allocated on a systematic basis to each accounting period during the useful life of the asset.

With regard to the accrual principle, it is fair that the profits should be reduced by the depreciation charge, this is not an arbitrary exercise. Depreciation is not, as is sometimes supposed, an attempt to set aside funds to purchase new non-current assets when required. Depreciation is not generally provided on freehold land because it does not 'wear out' (unless it is held for mining).

2.1.1 Example: Revaluation surplus

Binkie Co has an item of land carried in its books at $13,000. Two years ago a slump in land values led the company to reduce the carrying value from $15,000. This was recognised as an expense in profit or loss. There has been a surge in land prices in the current year, however, and the land now has a fair value measured in accordance with IFRS 13 of $20,000.

Account for the revaluation in the current year.

Solution

The double entry is:

DEBIT	Asset value (statement of financial position)	$7,000	
CREDIT	Profit or loss		$2,000
	Other comprehensive income (revaluation surplus)		$5,000

The case is similar for a **decrease in value** on revaluation. Any decrease should be recognised as an expense, except where it offsets a previous increase taken as a revaluation surplus in equity. Any decrease greater than the previous upwards increase in value must be taken as an expense in profit or loss.

2.1.2 Example: Revaluation decrease

Let us simply swap round the example given above. The original cost was $15,000, revalued upwards to $20,000 two years ago. The fair value has now fallen to $13,000.

Account for the decrease in value.

Solution

The double entry is:

DEBIT	Other comprehensive income (revaluation surplus)	$5,000	
DEBIT	Profit or loss	$2,000	
CREDIT	Asset value (statement of financial position)		$7,000

There is a further complication when a **revalued asset is being depreciated**. As we have seen, an upward revaluation means that the depreciation charge will increase. Normally, a revaluation surplus is only realised when the asset is sold, but when it is being depreciated, part of that surplus is being realised as the asset is used. The amount of the surplus realised is the difference between depreciation charged on the revalued amount and the depreciation which would have been charged on the asset's original cost. **This amount can be transferred to retained (ie realised) earnings in the statement of changes in equity, NOT through the profit or loss.**

2.1.3 Example: revaluation and depreciation

Crinckle Co bought an asset for $10,000 at the beginning of 20X6. It had a useful life of five years. On 1 January 20X8 the asset was revalued to $12,000. The expected useful life has remained unchanged (ie three years remain).

Account for the revaluation and state the treatment for depreciation from 20X8 onwards.

Solution

On 1 January 20X8 the carrying amount of the asset is $10,000 − (2 × $10,000 ÷ 5) = $6,000. For the revaluation:

DEBIT	Asset value (statement of financial position)	$6,000
CREDIT	Other comprehensive income (revaluation surplus)	$6,000

The depreciation for the next three years will be $12,000 ÷ 3 = $4,000, compared to depreciation on cost of $10,000 ÷ 5 = $2,000. So each year, the extra $2,000 can be treated as part of the surplus which has become realised:

DEBIT	Statement of changes in equity (revaluation surplus)	$2,000
CREDIT	Statement of changes in equity (retained earnings)	$2,000

This is a movement on equity only, not an item in total comprehensive income.

2.1.4 Basis of depreciation and amortisation

In 2014 the IASB issued a clarification of acceptable methods of depreciation and amortisation, which amended IAS 16 *Property, Plant and Equipment* and IAS 38 *Intangible Assets* to the effect that revenue-based methods of depreciation and amortisation will be disallowed or restricted.

The amendments are to be applied prospectively for annual periods beginning on or after 1 January 2016, with earlier application permitted.

Depreciation should reflect the consumption of the asset's future economic benefits (IAS 16, para. 60). Even though revenue could sometimes be considered to be a measurement of the output generated by the asset, revenue does not, as a matter of principle, reflect the way in which an asset is used or consumed. (For example, revenue may be affected by inflation.) Revenue-based depreciation is no longer allowed for property, plant and equipment (IAS 16) and there is a rebuttable presumption that revenue-based amortisation is inappropriate for intangible assets (IAS 38). This presumption can be overcome only when either revenue and consumption of economic benefits of an asset are 'highly correlated' or the asset is expressed as a measure of revenue (for example, the right to receive a certain amount of income). To use a revenue-based method, an entity will need to show that there is more than just an element of relationship between revenue generation and the consumption of benefits.

This change is likely to affect media companies, for example, who may move towards recognising lower amortisation expenses, and therefore higher profits, in the earlier years of the life of an asset.

2.1.5 Example

Alphaplayer Ltd will release a new game on 1 November 2015. Sales volumes and revenues for the game are projected to be as shown below. Total development costs for the game are £20m.

Year	Average price per unit	Sales volume (million units)	Revenue (£m)
2015	45.0	2.2	99
2016	30.4	5.4	164
2017 onwards	26.4	1.4	37

Required

Calculate the amortisation expense to be shown in the statement of profit or loss for the year ended 31 December 2015 assuming (a) amortisation is based on revenue and (b) amortisation is based on sales volume.

PART C   ACCOUNTING AND REPORTING TECHNIQUES

Solution

Based on revenue, amortisation in the year ended 31 December 2015 will be 33% × £20m= £6.6m. Based on sales volume, it will be 24.4% × £20m = £4.8m.

2.2 Government grants

IAS 20 is very straightforward. The question after the following summary covers the accounting problem it tackled.

> **Knowledge brought forward from earlier studies**

IAS 20 *Accounting for Government Grants And Disclosure Of Government Assistance*

Definitions

- **Government assistance**. Action by government designed to provide an economic benefit specific to an entity or range of entities qualifying under certain criteria. This does not include benefits provided only indirectly through action affecting general trading conditions.
- **Government grants**. Assistance by government in the form of transfers of resources to an entity in return for past or future compliance with certain conditions relating to the operating activities of the entity. They exclude those forms of government assistance which cannot reasonably have a value placed upon them and transactions with government which cannot be distinguished from the normal trading transactions of the entity.
- **Grants related to assets**. Government grants whose primary condition is that an entity qualifying for them should purchase, construct or otherwise acquire non-current assets. Subsidiary conditions may also be attached, restricting the type or location of the assets or the periods during which they are to be acquired or held.
- **Grants related to income**. Government grants other than those related to assets.
- **Forgivable loans**. Loans which the lender undertakes to waive repayment of under certain prescribed conditions.

Accounting treatment

- **Recognise government grants and forgivable loans** once compliance with conditions and receipt/waiver are both reasonably assured.
- Grants are recognised under the **income approach**: recognise grants as income to match them with related costs that they have been received to compensate.
- Use a **systematic basis** of matching over the relevant periods.
- Grants for **depreciable assets** should be recognised as income on the same basis as the asset is depreciated.
- Grants for **non-depreciable assets** should be recognised as income over the periods in which the cost of meeting the obligation is incurred.
- A grant may be **split into parts** and allocated on different bases where there are a series of conditions attached.
- Where **related costs have already been incurred**, the grant may be recognised as income in full immediately.
- A grant in the form of a **non-monetary asset** may be valued at fair value or a nominal value.
- **Grants related to assets** may be presented in the statement of financial position *either* as **deferred income** *or* deducted in arriving at the carrying amount of the asset.
- **Grants related to income** may be presented in the statement of profit or loss *either* as a **separate credit** *or* **deducted** from the related expense.
- Repayment of government grants should be accounted for as a **revision of an accounting estimate**.

Disclosure

- **Accounting policy** note.
- **Nature and extent** of government grants and other forms of assistance received.
- **Unfulfilled conditions** and other contingencies attached to recognised government assistance.

Question — Government grants

IAS 20 suggests that there are two approaches to recognising government grants: a capital approach (credit directly to owners' interests) and an income approach. IAS 20 requires the use of the income approach, but what are the arguments in support of each method?

Answer

IAS 20 gives the following arguments in support of each method.

Capital approach

(a) The grants are a **financing device**, so should go through the statement of financial position. In the statement of profit or loss they would simply offset the expenses which they are financing. No repayment is expected by the Government, so the grants should be credited directly to owners' interests (equity).

(b) Grants are **not earned**, they are incentives without related costs, so it would be wrong to take them to profit or loss.

Income approach

(a) The grants are **not received from owners** so should not be credited directly to owners' interests (equity).

(b) Grants are **not given or received for nothing**. They are earned by compliance with conditions and by meeting obligations. There are therefore associated costs with which the grant can be matched in the statement of profit or loss as these costs are being compensated by the grant.

(c) Grants are an extension of **fiscal policies** and so as income and other taxes are charged against income, so grants should be credited to income.

2.3 IAS 23 *Borrowing Costs*

This is another straightforward standard. In March 2007, the IASB issued a revised IAS 23 and amended the accounting treatment of borrowing costs. Read the following section carefully.

Knowledge brought forward from earlier studies

Key term

IAS 23 *Borrowing Costs*

- IAS 23 deals with the treatment of borrowing costs, often associated with the construction of **self-constructed assets**, but which can also be applied to an asset purchased that takes time to get ready for use/sale.

Definitions

- **Borrowing costs**: Interest and other costs incurred by an entity in connection with the borrowing of funds.
- **Qualifying asset**: An asset that necessarily takes a substantial period of time to get ready for its intended use or sale.

PART C ACCOUNTING AND REPORTING TECHNIQUES

Accounting treatment

- **Recognition**: Borrowing costs that are directly attributable to the acquisition, construction or production of a qualifying asset should be capitalised (where it is probable they will result in future economic benefit and the costs can be measured reliably). All other borrowing costs should be recognised as an expense in the period in which they are incurred.
- **Borrowing costs eligible for capitalisation** are those that would have been avoided otherwise. Use judgement where a range of debt instruments is held for general finance.
- **Amount of borrowing costs available for capitalisation** is actual borrowing costs incurred less any investment income from temporary investment of those borrowings.
- For borrowings obtained generally, apply the **capitalisation rate** to the expenditure on the asset (weighted average borrowing cost). It must not exceed actual borrowing costs.
- Capitalisation of borrowing costs **commences** when the entity first meets all the following conditions:
    - (a) it incurs expenditure on the asset
    - (b) it incurs borrowing costs
    - (c) it undertakes activities necessary to prepare the asset for use or sale
- **Capitalisation is suspended** if active development is interrupted for extended periods. (Necessary temporary delays or technical/administrative work will not cause suspension).
- **Capitalisation ceases** (normally) when physical construction of the asset is substantially completed, capitalisation should cease when each stage or part that is capable of being used separately is completed.

Disclosure

- **Accounting policy** note.
- Amount of **borrowing costs capitalised** during the period.
- **Capitalisation rate** used to determine borrowing costs eligible for capitalisation.

Question — Borrowing costs 1

Rechno borrowed $15m to finance the construction of two assets, both of which were expected to take a year to build. Construction started 1 January 20X8. The loan facility was drawn down on 1 January 20X8, and was utilised as follows, with the remaining funds invested temporarily.

	Asset X $m	Asset Y $m
1 January 20X8	2.5	5.0
1 July 20X8	2.5	5.0

The loan rate was 10% and Rechno can invest surplus funds at 8%.

Required

Ignoring compound interest, calculate the borrowing costs which may be capitalised for each of the assets and consequently the cost of each asset as at 31 December 20X8.

Answer

		Asset X $'000	Asset Y $'000
Borrowing costs			
To 30 June 20X8	$2.5m/$5.0m × 10% × 6/12	125	250
To 31 December 20X8	$5.0m/$10m × 10% × 6/12	250	500
		375	750
Less investment income			
To 30 June 20X8	$2.5m/$5.0m × 8% × 6/12	(100)	(200)
		275	550

	$'000	$'000
Cost of assets		
Expenditure incurred	5,000	10,000
Borrowing costs	275	550
	5,275	10,550

Question
Borrowing costs 2

Zenzi had the following loans in place at the beginning and end of 20X8.

	1 January 20X8 $m	31 December 20X8 $m
10.0% Bank loan repayable 20Y3	120	120
9.5% Bank loan repayable 20Y1	80	80
8.9% debenture repayable 20Y8	–	150

The 8.9% debenture was issued to fund the construction of a qualifying asset (a piece of mining equipment), construction of which began on 1 July 20X8.

On 1 January 20X8, Zenzi began construction of another qualifying asset, a piece of machinery for a hydro-electric plant, using existing borrowings. Expenditure drawn down for the construction was: $30m on 1 January 20X8, $20m on 1 October 20X8.

Required

Calculate the borrowing costs to be capitalised for the hydro-electric plant machine.

Answer

Capitalisation rate = weighted average rate = $(10\% \times \frac{120}{120+80}) + (9.5\% \times \frac{80}{120+80}) = 9.8\%$

Borrowing costs = ($30m × 9.8%) + ($20m × 9.8% × 3/12)
= $3.43m

3 IAS 36 *Impairment of Assets*

FAST FORWARD

IAS 36 *Impairment of Assets* covers a controversial topic and it affects both intangible and tangible non-current assets.

There is an established principle that assets should not be carried at above their recoverable amount. IAS 36 describes the procedures which should be followed in order to ensure that this is not the case. This is a very relevant standard in the light of the ongoing global economic downturn.

3.1 Scope

IAS 36 applies to all tangible, intangible and financial assets except for:

1. Inventories (IAS 2)
2. Assets arising from contracts (IFRS 15)
3. Deferred tax assets (IAS 12)
4. Assets arising from employee benefits (IAS 19)
5. Financial assets within the scope of IFRS 9
6. Investment property measured at fair value (IAS 40)
7. Non-current assets classified as held for sale in accordance with IFRS 5

Other assets are excluded from the scope of IAS 36. However, these relate to IAS 41 *Agriculture* and IFRS 4 *Insurance Contracts* and these standards do not form part of the Paper 13 syllabus.

These assets are excluded from IAS 36 because rules for recognising and measuring impairment are already included in the relevant standard.

3.2 The basic principle

Key terms

> **Impairment**: a fall in the value of an asset or cash-generating unit, so that its 'recoverable amount' is now less than its carrying amount in the statement of financial position.
>
> **Carrying amount**: is the amount at which an asset is recognised in the statement of financial position after deducting accumulated depreciation (amortisation) and any impairment losses thereon.
>
> (See IAS 16 and IAS 36)

The basic principle underlying IAS 36 is relatively straightforward. If an asset's value in the financial statements is higher than its realistic value, measured as its 'recoverable amount', the asset is judged to have suffered an impairment loss. It should therefore be reduced in value, by the amount of the **impairment loss**. The amount of the impairment loss should be **recognised as an expense in profit or loss** immediately.

The main accounting issues to consider are therefore as follows:

(a) When should an asset be tested for impairment?
(b) How should the **recoverable amount** of the asset be measured?
(c) How should an 'impairment loss' be **reported in the financial statements**?

3.3 Frequency of impairment testing

An asset must be tested for impairment when there is an indication of impairment at the reporting date. In addition IAS 36 requires certain assets to be tested for impairment annually. These are:

- Goodwill acquired in a business combination
- Intangible assets with an indefinite useful life
- Intangible assets which are not yet available for use.

3.3.1 Indications of impairment

An entity should carry out a **review of its assets at the end of each reporting period**, to assess whether there are any indications of impairment. The concept of **materiality** applies, and only material impairment needs to be identified.

IAS 36 suggests how **indications of a possible impairment** of assets might be recognised. The following must be considered as a minimum:

(a) **External sources of information**

  (i) A fall in the asset's market value that is more significant than would normally be expected from passage of time or normal use.

  (ii) A significant adverse change in the technological, market, legal or economic environment of the business in which the assets are employed has taken place or will take place in the near future.

  (iii) An increase in market interest rates or market rates of return on investments likely to materially affect the discount rate used in calculating value in use.

  (iv) The carrying amount of the entity's net assets being more than its market capitalisation.

(b) **Internal sources of information**

   (i) Evidence of obsolescence or physical damage.

   (ii) Significant adverse changes have or are expected to take place which will change the manner of use of the asset, such as the asset becoming idle, plans to discontinue or restructure the operation or plans to dispose of the asset earlier than expected, leading to changes to an asset's useful life.

   (iii) Evidence that an asset is performing worse than expected.

   (iv) Cash outflows related to the operation and maintenance of an asset are significantly higher than budgeted.

   (v) Cash inflows from an asset are significantly lower than budgeted.

3.4 Performing an impairment test: Measuring the recoverable amount of the asset

FAST FORWARD

> Impairment is determined by comparing the carrying amount of the asset with its **recoverable amount**.
>
> The recoverable amount of an asset is the higher of the asset's **fair value less costs of disposal** and its **value in use**.

Where there are indications of impairment or the asset in question requires annual testing, an impairment test must be performed. This involves comparing its carrying amount with its recoverable amount. An asset is impaired when its carrying amount exceeds its recoverable amount.

What is an asset's recoverable amount?

Key term

> The **recoverable amount of an asset** is the **higher** of:
>
> (a) The asset's fair value less costs of disposal; and
> (b) Its value in use. (IAS 36)

3.4.1 Fair value less costs of disposal

An asset's fair value less costs of disposal is fair value established in accordance with IFRS 13 *Fair Value Measurement* (see Chapter 11) less any selling costs. Selling costs include sales transaction costs, such as legal expenses, other than those that have been recognised as liabilities.

3.4.2 Value in use

The concept of 'value in use' is very important. It is defined as the present value of future cash flows expected to be derived from an asset or cash-generating unit.

Key term

> The **value in use** of an asset is measured by:
>
> – Estimating cash inflows and outflows from the use and eventual disposal of the asset
> – Discounting those cash flows to present value

There are therefore two elements to the calculation of value in use: cash flows and an appropriate discount rate.

Cash flows

The cash flows which must be taken into consideration include all future cash inflows and outflows from the continuing use and ultimate disposal of the asset. They should:

- Be based on reasonable and supportable assumptions
- Be based on the most **recent budgets or financial forecasts** up to a maximum period of five years ahead, unless a longer period can be justified
- Exclude the effects of future restructurings or improving / enhancing the asset's performance (including servicing the asset)
- Not include income tax receipts or payments or cash flows from financing activities
- Assume disposal at arm's length

Cash flows beyond the period covered by the most recent forecasts should be estimated by extrapolating projections based on the budgets using a steady or declining growth rate for subsequent years, unless an increasing rate can be justified. The growth rate should not exceed the long-term average growth rate for the products, industries or country in which the entity is based or market in which the asset is used unless a higher rate can be justified.

Foreign currency future cash flows should be forecast in the currency in which they will arise and discounted using a rate appropriate for that currency. The resulting figure should then be translated into the reporting currency at the spot rate at the date of the calculation ie year end.

Discount rate

The **discount rate** should be a pre-tax rate (or rates) that reflects the current assessment of the time value of money and the risks specific to the asset. The discount rate should not include a risk weighting if the underlying cash flows have already been adjusted for risk.

3.5 Recognition and measurement of an impairment loss

Where the carrying amount of an asset exceeds its recoverable amount, the asset must be written down to the recoverable amount. The amount written off the asset is referred to as an impairment loss.

The accounting entries will depend on whether the impaired asset is held at historic cost or a revalued amount.

The rule for assets at **historic cost** is:

Rule to learn
> The impairment loss is recognised as an expense in profit or loss.

The rule for assets held at a **revalued amount** (such as property revalued under IAS 16) is:

Rule to learn
> The impairment loss is to be treated as a revaluation decrease under the relevant IFRS. In other words:
> - To the extent that there is a revaluation surplus held in respect of the asset, the impairment loss should be charged to that revaluation surplus
> - Any excess should be recognised in profit or loss

3.5.1 Example: recognition of impairment loss 1

At 31 December 20X9, Kilnsey Co identified a possible indication of impairment relating to one of its properties. The property was purchased on 1 January 20X4 at a cost of $400,000 and depreciation on a 2% straight-line basis commenced immediately. On 1 January 20X9 the company adopted a policy of revaluing all properties and the property was revalued to $405,000. Its total useful life remained unchanged and the company made an annual reserve transfer in respect of the excess depreciation. At 31 December 20X9 the impairment test revealed a value in use of $330,000 and fair value less costs of disposal of $320,000.

How should the impairment be recognised?

Solution

	$
Cost of property on 1.1.X4	400,000
Depreciation to 1.1.X9 2% × $400,000 × 5 years	(40,000)
	360,000
Revaluation surplus	45,000
Valuation at 1.1.X9	405,000
Depreciation for y/e 31.12.X9 ($405,000/45 years)	(9,000)
Carrying amount at 31.12.X9	396,000
Impairment loss	(66,000)
Recoverable amount	330,000

The revaluation surplus at the date of the impairment is $44,000 (the $45,000 surplus on revaluation less one year's transfer of excess depreciation to retained earnings). Therefore $44,000 of the impairment loss reduces the revaluation surplus to $nil and the remaining $22,000 is charged to profit or loss.

3.5.2 Example: Recognition of an impairment loss 2

A company that extracts natural gas and oil has a drilling platform in the Caspian Sea. It is required by legislation of the country concerned to remove and dismantle the platform at the end of its useful life. Accordingly, the company has included an amount in its financial statements for removal and dismantling costs, and is depreciating this amount over the platform's expected life.

The company is carrying out an exercise to establish whether there has been an impairment of the platform.

(a) Its carrying amount in the statement of financial position is $3m.

(b) The company has received an offer of $2.8m for the platform from another oil company. The bidder would take over the responsibility (and costs) for dismantling and removing the platform at the end of its life.

(c) The present value of the estimated cash flows from the platform's continued use is $3.3m.

(d) The carrying amount in the statement of financial position for the provision for dismantling and removal is currently $0.6m.

What should be the carrying amount of the drilling platform in the statement of financial position, and what, if anything, is the impairment loss?

Solution

Fair value less costs of disposal	=	$2.8m
Value in use	=	PV of cash flows from use less the carrying amount of the provision/liability = $3.3m – $0.6m = $2.7m
Recoverable amount	=	Higher of these two amounts, ie $2.8m
Carrying amount	=	$3m
Impairment loss	=	$0.2m

The carrying amount should be reduced to $2.8m.

3.6 Depreciating an impaired asset

After an impairment loss is recorded, the new carrying amount of the impaired asset, less any residual value should be spread over its remaining useful life.

Both the residual value and useful life may need to be reassessed in the light of the impairment.

3.7 Reversal of an impairment loss

An impairment loss on an individual asset can be reversed should recoverable amount exceed carrying amount subsequent to the initial loss (with the exception of goodwill, which we shall see in the next section).

Rule to learn

> An impairment loss recognised for an asset in prior years should be reversed if, and only if, there has been a change in the estimates used to determine the asset's recoverable amount since the last impairment loss was recognised.

Indicators that an impairment loss may have reversed mirror those indicators that an impairment loss has occurred. Even where no reversal of impairment loss is recognised, these indicators may indicate that the useful life, residual value or depreciation method applied to an asset may require reassessment.

The impairment loss can be reversed to the extent that the increased carrying amount of an individual asset does not exceed the amount that the asset would have been carried at had there been no initial impairment.

3.7.1 Recognising the reversal of an impairment loss

The accounting entries for the reversal of an impairment loss depend on whether the reversal relates to an asset held at historic cost or revalued amount:

- An impairment reversal is recognised in profit or loss when it relates to an asset held at historic cost

- In relation to a revalued asset, the reversal is recognised in profit or loss to the extent that the original impairment loss was recognised in profit or loss and as a revaluation surplus thereafter.

3.7.2 Example: Reversal of an impairment loss

Continuing with the example in Section 3.5.1 above, let's now assume that the estimates used to determine recoverable amount have been revised and the recoverable amount at 31 December 20Y0 is calculated as $370,000.

At 31 December 20Y0 the carrying amount of the property is:

	$
Carrying amount at 31.12.X9 after impairment	330,000
Depreciation in year (330,000/44 years)	(7,500)
Carrying amount at 31.12.Y0	322,500

The recoverable amount of the property is assessed as $370,000, meaning a potential reversal of $47,500 ($370,000 – $322,500) of the impairment loss. The reversal cannot, however, increase the value of the asset above the value that it would have had, had the impairment loss not occurred. Therefore a check is required:

	$
Carrying amount at 31.12.X9 before impairment	396,000
Depreciation in year (as in y/e 31.12.X9) (405,000/45 years)	(9,000)
Carrying amount at 31.12.Y0 had impairment not occurred	387,000

In this case the reversal will not increase the carrying amount above $387,000 and therefore the full $47,500 reversal can be recognised as follows:

- $22,000 in profit or loss to reverse the impairment loss recognised in profit or loss, and
- $25,500 as a revaluation surplus.

12: TANGIBLE NON-CURRENT ASSETS AND INVENTORY

4 Impairment: Cash-generating units

FAST FORWARD

Where the recoverable amount of a single asset can not be estimated, the impairment test must be performed for the cash-generating unit (CGU) to which that asset belongs.

IAS 36 goes into quite a large amount of detail about the important concept of cash-generating units. As a basic rule, the recoverable amount of an asset should be calculated for the **asset individually** as we saw in the last section of the chapter. However, there will be occasions when it is not possible to estimate such a value for an individual asset, particularly in the calculation of value in use. This is because cash inflows and outflows cannot be attributed to the individual asset.

If it is not possible to calculate the recoverable amount for an individual asset, the recoverable amount of the asset's cash-generating unit should be measured instead.

Key term

A cash-generating unit is the smallest identifiable group of assets that generates cash inflows that are largely independent of the cash inflows of other assets or groups of assets.

(IAS 36)

Question — Cash generating unit 1

Can you think of some examples of how a cash-generating unit would be identified?

Answer

Here are two possibilities.

(a) A mining company owns a private railway that it uses to transport output from one of its mines. The railway now has no market value other than as scrap, and it is impossible to identify any separate cash inflows from the use of the railway itself. Consequently, if the mining company suspects an impairment in the value of the railway, it should treat the mine as a whole as a cash-generating unit, and measure the recoverable amount of the mine as a whole.

(b) A bus company has an arrangement with a town's authorities to run a bus service on four routes in the town. Separately identifiable assets are allocated to each of the bus routes, and cash inflows and outflows can be attributed to each individual route. Three routes are running at a profit and one is running at a loss. The bus company suspects that there is an impairment of assets on the loss-making route. However, the company will be unable to close the loss-making route, because it is under an obligation to operate all four routes, as part of its contract with the local authority. Consequently, the company should treat all four bus routes together as a cash-generating unit, and calculate the recoverable amount for the unit as a whole.

Question — Cash generating unit 2

Minimart belongs to a retail store chain Maximart. Minimart makes all its retail purchases through Maximart's purchasing centre. Pricing, marketing, advertising and human resources policies (except for hiring Minimart's cashiers and sales force) are decided by Maximart. Maximart also owns five other stores in the same city as Minimart (although in different neighbourhoods) and 20 other stores in other cities. All stores are managed in the same way as Minimart. Minimart and four other stores were purchased five years ago and goodwill was recognised.

What is the cash-generating unit for Minimart?

> **Answer**

In identifying Minimart's cash-generating unit, an entity considers whether, for example:

(a) Internal management reporting is organised to measure performance on a store-by-store basis.
(b) The business is run on a store-by-store profit basis or on a region/city basis.

All Maximart's stores are in different neighbourhoods and probably have different customer bases. So, although Minimart is managed at a corporate level, Minimart generates cash inflows that are largely independent from those of Maximart's other stores. Therefore, it is likely that Minimart is a cash-generating unit.

> **Question**   Cash generating unit 3

Mighty Mag Publishing Co owns 150 magazine titles of which 70 were purchased and 80 were self-created. The price paid for a purchased magazine title is recognised as an intangible asset. The costs of creating magazine titles and maintaining the existing titles are recognised as an expense when incurred. Cash inflows from direct sales and advertising are identifiable for each magazine title. Titles are managed by customer segments. The level of advertising income for a magazine title depends on the range of titles in the customer segment to which the magazine title relates. Management has a policy to abandon old titles before the end of their useful lives and replace them immediately with new titles for the same customer segment.

What is the cash-generating unit for an individual magazine title?

> **Answer**

It is likely that the recoverable amount of an individual magazine title can be assessed. Even though the level of advertising income for a title is influenced, to a certain extent, by the other titles in the customer segment, cash inflows from direct sales and advertising are identifiable for each title. In addition, although titles are managed by customer segments, decisions to abandon titles are made on an individual title basis.

Therefore, it is likely that individual magazine titles generate cash inflows that are largely independent one from another and that each magazine title is a separate cash-generating unit.

If an active market exists for the output produced by the asset or a group of assets, this asset or group of assets should be identified as a cash-generating unit, even if some or all of the output is used internally.

Cash-generating units should be identified consistently from period to period for the same type of asset unless a change is justified.

4.1 Testing a CGU for impairment

When performing an impairment test on a cash-generating unit (CGU), the carrying amount of the CGU's assets should be compared with the recoverable amount of the same assets.

In some cases identifying the assets of a cash-generating unit is not straightforward. This is particularly true when one asset is shared between a number of CGUs or goodwill can be attributed to a number of CGUs.

We shall deal with these 'corporate assets' (shared assets) and goodwill in the next sections, but first let's consider a simple example of allocating assets to CGUs.

4.1.1 Example: Cash-generating units

Fourways Co is made up of four cash-generating units. All four units are being tested for impairment.

(a) Property, plant and equipment and separate intangibles would be allocated to cash-generating units as far as possible.

(b) Current assets such as inventories, receivables and prepayments would be allocated to the relevant cash-generating units.

(c) The figure for each cash-generating unit resulting from this exercise would be compared to the relevant recoverable amount, computed on the same basis.

4.2 Corporate assets

Corporate assets are group or divisional assets such as a head office building, IT equipment or a research centre. Essentially, corporate assets are assets that do not generate cash inflows independently from other assets, and their carrying amount cannot be fully attributed to a cash-generating unit under review.

IAS 36 requires that these corporate assets are allocated to CGUs on a 'reasonable and consistent' basis before an impairment test takes place.

Where such an allocation is not possible, the entity should:

(i) Compare the carrying amount of the CGU (excluding the corporate asset) with its recoverable amount and recognise any impairment loss

(ii) Identify the smallest group of cash-generating units that includes the cash-generating unit to which the corporate asset belongs and to which a portion of the carrying amount of the asset can be allocated on a reasonable and consistent basis

(iii) Compare the carrying amount of that group of cash-generating units (including the portion of the corporate asset allocated to the group of units) with the recoverable amount of the group of units and recognise any impairment loss

4.2.1 Example: Allocation of a corporate asset to CGUs

Rombald Co has four divisions which are also cash-generating units: 1, 2, 3 and 4. The carrying amounts of these divisions are $150,000, $600,000, $300,000 and $250,000 respectively.

The divisions are managed from a head office with a carrying amount of $650,000. What is the carrying amount of each division after this corporate asset has been allocated to the divisions for the purpose of impairment testing?

Solution

	Division A	Division B	Division C	Division D	Total
Carrying amount	150,000	600,000	300,000	250,000	1,300,000
Allocation of corporate asset	150/1,300 × $650 = 75,000	600/1,300 × $650 = 300,000	300/1,300 × $650 = 150,000	250/1,300 × $650 = 125,000	
Total carrying amount of each CGU	225,000	900,000	450,000	375,000	

4.3 Goodwill

For the purpose of impairment testing, goodwill acquired in a business combination must be **allocated** to each of the **cash-generating units** that are expected to benefit from the synergies of the combination.

Where goodwill cannot be allocated on a non-arbitrary basis to individual cash-generating units, it should be allocated to groups of cash-generating units

Each unit (or group of units) to which the goodwill is so allocated should:

(a) Represent the **lowest level** within the entity at which the goodwill is monitored for internal management purposes.

(b) Not be **larger than a reporting segment** determined in accordance with IFRS 8 *Operating Segments*.

It may be impractical to complete the allocation of goodwill before the first reporting date after a business combination, particularly if the acquirer is accounting for the combination for the first time using provisional values. The initial allocation of goodwill must be completed before the end of the first reporting period beginning after the acquisition date.

4.3.1 Impairment testing and goodwill

Where goodwill has been allocated to individual CGUs, those CGUs should be tested annually for impairment by comparing their carrying amount (including the allocated goodwill) with their recoverable amount (including goodwill).

Where goodwill is attributable to a number of CGUs but cannot be allocated to those CGUs on an individual basis:

1. Each individual CGU to which goodwill is attributable and for which indications of impairment have been identified should be tested for impairment by comparing their carrying amount (excluding goodwill) with their recoverable amount (excluding goodwill); and then

2. The CGUs to which the goodwill is attributable should be tested for impairment on an aggregate basis by comparing their aggregate carrying amount (including goodwill) with their aggregate recoverable amount (including goodwill).

4.3.2 Example: Impairment testing and goodwill

Skipton Co has identified 6 CGUs within its organisation. Goodwill arising on a business combination is attributable to four of these. Explain the requirements of IAS 36 with regard to impairment testing if:

(a) The goodwill can be allocated to the four CGUs to which it is attributed
(b) The goodwill cannot be allocated to the four CGUs to which it is attributed.

Solution

(a) The two CGUs to which no goodwill is attributed are tested for impairment only if there are indications of impairment by comparing their carrying amount with their recoverable amount.

The four CGUs to which goodwill is attributed and allocated must be tested for impairment annually, since it is a requirement of IAS 36 that goodwill is tested annually. The carrying amount of each CGU (including the allocation of goodwill) must be compared with its recoverable amount (including goodwill) in turn.

(b) Again, the two CGUs to which no goodwill is attributed are tested for impairment only if there are indications of impairment by comparing their carrying amount with their recoverable amount.

The four CGUs to which goodwill is attributed are tested on an individual basis for impairment only if there are indications of impairment by comparing their carrying amount (excluding goodwill) with their recoverable amount (excluding goodwill).

The four CGUs to which goodwill is attributed are tested annually on an aggregate basis (due to the IAS 36 requirement to test goodwill for impairment annually) by comparing their aggregate carrying amount (including goodwill) with their aggregate recoverable amount (including goodwill).

4.3.3 Goodwill and non-controlling interests

In addition to the problem of allocating goodwill to CGUs, there may be a further problem where there is a non-controlling interest in the business combination which created the goodwill.

Chapter 6 explained that IFRS 3 allows two methods of measuring non-controlling interests in a subsidiary:

(a) As the non-controlling interest's proportionate share of the acquiree's identifiable net assets; or
(b) At the **fair value** of the non-controlling interest.

Where the non-controlling interest is measured at fair value, the reported goodwill is 'full' goodwill. This includes the goodwill 'belonging' to the non-controlling interest as well as the goodwill 'belonging' to the parent.

Where the non-controlling interest is measured as a proportion of net assets, the reported goodwill is the parent's goodwill only.

When performing an impairment test, we must ensure that we are comparing like with like. The recoverable amount of a CGU (or group of CGUs) includes all of its goodwill, and therefore it is important that the carrying amount of the CGU (or group of CGUs) does as well.

Therefore where the non-controlling interest is measured as a proportion of net assets and the reported goodwill is the parent goodwill only, an adjustment should be made to notionally gross up the reported goodwill to include the goodwill attributable to the non-controlling interest.

The goodwill is grossed up in proportion to ownership.

4.3.4 Example: Non-controlling interests

On 1 January 20X4 a parent acquires an 80% interest in a subsidiary for $1,600,000, when the identifiable net assets of the subsidiary are $1,500,000. The subsidiary is a cash-generating unit.

The non-controlling interest is measured as the proportionate share of the acquiree's net assets.

At 31 December 20X4, the recoverable amount of the subsidiary is $1,000,000. The carrying amount of the subsidiary's identifiable net assets is $1,350,000.

Calculate the impairment loss at 31 December 20X4.

Solution

At 31 December 20X4 the cash-generating unit consists of the subsidiary's identifiable net assets (carrying amount $1,350,000) and goodwill of $400,000 ($1,600,000 − (80% × $1,500,000)). For the purposes of the impairment test goodwill is grossed up to reflect the 20% non-controlling interest.

	Goodwill $'000	Identifiable net assets $'000	Total $'000
Carrying amount	400	1,350	1,750
Unrecognised non-controlling interest	100	–	100
	500	1,350	1,850
Recoverable amount			(1,000)
Impairment loss			850

We shall come back to this example in a moment to see how the impairment loss is allocated between the assets of the cash-generating unit.

4.4 Recognising an impairment loss in a CGU

An impairment loss should be recognised for a **cash-generating unit** if (and only if) the recoverable amount for the cash-generating unit is less than the carrying amount in the statement of financial position for all the assets in the unit.

When an impairment loss is recognised for a cash-generating unit (or group of CGUs), the loss should be allocated between the assets in the unit in the following order:

(a) First, to the **goodwill** allocated to the cash-generating unit
(b) Then to all other assets in the cash-generating unit, on a **pro rata basis**

Any loss allocated to assets held at historic cost should be recognised in profit or loss; any loss allocated to revalued assets is treated as a revaluation decrease.

In allocating an impairment loss, the carrying amount of an asset should not be reduced below the highest of:

(a) Its fair value less costs of disposal (so no loss will be allocated to current assets, because they are already measured at the lower of cost and NRV)
(b) Its value in use (if determinable)
(c) Zero

Any remaining amount of an impairment loss should be recognised as a liability if required by another IFRS.

Where goodwill is impaired in a cash-generating unit, the impairment loss must be allocated between the parent and the non-controlling interest goodwill. This is true even if the non-controlling interest goodwill is notional and the result of a grossing up exercise.

4.4.1 Example: Allocation of impairment loss to CGU

Now let's revisit the example in Section 4.3.2 above.

The impairment loss of $850,000 should be allocated between the parent and the non-controlling interest goodwill in the first instance and then to the other assets of the CGU as follows.

	Goodwill (80%) $'000	Goodwill (NCI) $'000	Identifiable net assets $'000	Total $'000
Carrying amounts	400	100	1,350	1,850
Impairment	(400)	(100)	(350)	(850)
	–	–	1,000	1,000

The NCI goodwill is a notional amount and the $100,000 impairment loss allocated against it is also notional. It is therefore not recognised in profit or loss.

The entity does, however, recognise an impairment of $750,000 ($400,000 + $350,000) in its financial statements, all of it allocated to the owners of the parent.

Now let's assume that the recoverable amount of the cash-generating unit was $1,400,000 and therefore the impairment loss was $450,000 ($1,850,000 – $1,400,000).

This loss is allocated in its entirety to the $500,000 goodwill balance. It must be split between the parent and NCI on the same basis as that which profit or loss is allocated:

	Goodwill (80%) $'000	Goodwill (NC1) $'000
Carrying amounts	400	100
Impairment (80%/20% × $450,000)	(360)	(90)
	40	10

As before, only the impairment in relation to the parent's goodwill is recognised.

4.4.2 Example: Allocation of impairment loss to CGU 2 (non-controlling interest at fair value)

On 1 January 20X4 a parent acquires an 80% interest in a subsidiary for $1,600,000, when the identifiable net assets of the subsidiary are $1,500,000. The subsidiary is a cash-generating unit.

The non-controlling interest is measured at its fair value of $350,000.

At 31 December 20X4, the recoverable amount of the subsidiary is $1,000,000. The carrying amount of the subsidiary's identifiable net assets is $1,350,000.

Calculate the impairment loss at 31 December 20X4 and allocate it to the assets of the CGU.

Solution

At 31 December 20X4 the cash-generating unit consists of the subsidiary's identifiable net assets (carrying amount $1,350,000) and goodwill of $450,000 ($1,600,000 + $350,000 − $1,500,000)). Goodwill includes the amount attributable to the 20% non-controlling interest.

	Goodwill $'000	Identifiable net assets $'000	Total $'000
Carrying amount	450	1,350	1,800
Recoverable amount			(1,000)
Impairment loss			800

The impairment loss should be allocated as follows.

	Goodwill $'000	Identifiable net assets $'000	Total $'000
Carrying amounts	450	1,350	1,800
Impairment	(450)	(350)	(800)
Recoverable amount	–	1,000	1,000

The whole of the impairment loss is recognised in profit or loss.

4.4.3 Example: Impairment loss

A company has acquired another business for $4.5m: identifiable net assets are valued at $4.0m and goodwill at $0.5m.

An asset with a carrying amount of $1.0m is destroyed in a terrorist attack. The asset was not insured and has no scrap value. The loss of the asset, without insurance, has prompted the company to estimate whether there has been an impairment of assets in the acquired business and what the amount of any such loss is. The recoverable amount of the acquired business has been estimated at $3.1m.

Solution

The destroyed asset should be derecognised and a loss on abandonment of $1.0m recognised as an expense in profit or loss.

After this, the carrying amount of the business is $3.5m ($4.0m + $0.5m − $1.0m). The recoverable amount is measured as $3.1m and therefore there is an impairment loss of $0.4m. The impairment loss will be recognised in profit or loss. The loss will all be allocated to goodwill.

The carrying amount of the assets will now be $3.0m for identifiable assets and $0.1m for goodwill.

4.5 Reversal of an impairment loss

As with an individual asset, an impairment loss in relation to a cash-generating unit can be reversed, with one exception: any loss recognised for goodwill.

The reversal is allocated pro rata to the assets (other than goodwill) of the CGU, however the increased carrying amount of each asset cannot exceed the lower of:

- Its recoverable amount; and
- The amount that the asset would have been carried at had there been no initial impairment.

The reversal is recognised in profit or loss to the extent that it relates to a non-revalued asset and treated as a revaluation increase to the extent that it relates to a revalued asset.

Rule to learn

> An impairment loss recognised for an asset (other than goodwill) in prior years should be reversed if, and only if, there has been a change in the estimates used to determine the asset's recoverable amount since the last impairment loss was recognised.

Question — Reversal of impairment loss

A cash-generating unit comprising a factory, plant and equipment etc and associated goodwill becomes impaired because the product it makes is overtaken by a technologically more advanced model produced by a competitor. The recoverable amount of the cash-generating unit falls to $60m, resulting in an impairment loss of $80m, allocated as follows.

	Carrying amounts before impairment $m	Carrying amounts after impairment $m
Goodwill	40	–
Patent (with no market value)	20	–
Tangible non-current assets	80	60
Total	140	60

After three years, the entity makes a technological breakthrough of its own, and the recoverable amount of the cash-generating unit increases to $90m. The carrying amount of the tangible non-current assets had the impairment not occurred would have been $70m.

Required

Calculate the reversal of the impairment loss.

Answer

The reversal of the impairment loss is recognised to the extent that it increases the carrying amount of the tangible non-current assets to what it would have been had the impairment not taken place, ie a reversal of the impairment loss of $10m is recognised and the tangible non-current assets written back to $70m. Reversal of the impairment is not recognised in relation to the goodwill and patent because the effect of the external event that caused the original impairment has not reversed – the original product is still overtaken by a more advanced model.

4.6 Disclosure

IAS 36 calls for substantial disclosure about impairment of assets. The information to be disclosed includes the following:

- For each class of assets, the amount of **impairment losses recognised** and the amount of any **impairment losses reversed** split between profit or loss and other comprehensive income.
- For each impairment loss recognised or reversed, a description of the circumstances, the amount, a description of the nature of the asset or CGU, the recoverable amount and whether it reflects fair value less costs or disposal or value in use.

12: TANGIBLE NON-CURRENT ASSETS AND INVENTORY

A narrow scope amendment to IAS 36 was issued in May 2013. This clarified the disclosure requirements, which had become unclear since the issue of IFRS 13. The standard now states that for each asset (including goodwill) or cash-generating unit for which an impairment loss has been recognised/reversed during the period, the following should be disclosed:

- The recoverable amount of the asset/CGU and whether it is based on (i) value in use or (ii) fair value less cost to sell.
- If based on (ii), the basis on which on which it was determined, including:
  - The level of the fair value hierarchy (see IFRS 13) within which the measurement of the asset/CGU is categorised.
  - For those categorised within Levels 2 or 3 of the fair value hierarchy:
    - A description of the valuation techniques used, and whether/why that technique has changed
    - Each key assumption used

In addition, the basis on which recoverable amount has been determined shall be disclosed for each CGU for which carrying amount of goodwill/intangible assets with indefinite useful life is significant, even if no impairment has taken place.

4.7 Section summary

The main aspects of IAS 36 to consider are:

- **Indications** of impairment of assets
- **Measuring recoverable amount**, as the higher of fair value less costs of disposal and value in use
- **Measuring value in use**
- **Cash-generating units**
- **Accounting treatment** of an impairment loss, for individual assets and cash-generating units
- **Reversal** of an impairment loss

5 IAS 40 *Investment Property*

FAST FORWARD

> IAS 40 *Investment Property* defines investment property as property **held to earn rentals or for capital appreciation** or both, rather than for:
> - Use in production or supply of goods or services
> - Sale in the ordinary course of business

An entity may own land or a building **as an investment** rather than for use in the business. It may therefore generate cash flows largely independently of other assets which the entity holds.

Consider the following definitions.

Key terms

Investment property is property (land or a building – or part of a building – or both) held (by the owner or by the lessee as a right-of-use asset) to earn rentals or for capital appreciation or both, rather than for:

(a) Use in the production or supply of goods or services or for administrative purposes, or
(b) Sale in the ordinary course of business

Owner-occupied property is property held by the owner (or by the lessee as a right-of-use asset) for use in the production or supply of goods or services or for administrative purposes.

Fair value is the price that would be received to sell an asset or paid to transfer a liability in an orderly transaction between market participants at the measurement date.

Cost is the amount of cash or cash equivalents paid or the fair value of other consideration given to acquire an asset at the time of its acquisition or construction.

Carrying amount is the amount at which an asset is recognised in the statement of financial position.

Examples of investment property include:

(a) **Land held for non-current capital appreciation** rather than for short-term sale in the ordinary course of business

(b) Land held for a currently undetermined future use

(c) A **building** owned by the reporting entity (or a right-of-use asset relating to a building held by the entity) and **leased out under an operating lease**

(d) A building that is vacant but is held to be leased out under an operating lease

(e) Property that is being constructed or developed for future use as investment property

Question — Investment property

Rich Co owns a piece of land. The directors have not yet decided whether to build a factory on it for use in its business or to keep it and sell it when its value has risen.

Would this be classified as an investment property under IAS 40?

Answer

Yes. If an entity has not yet determined whether it will use the land as an owner-occupied property or for short-term sale in the ordinary course of business, the land is considered to be held for capital appreciation and classified as investment property.

5.1 The objective of IAS 40

The objective of IAS 40 *Investment Property* is to prescribe the accounting treatment for investment property and related disclosure requirements.

The standard includes investment property held as a right-of use asset or leased out under an operating lease. However, IAS 40 does not deal with matters covered in IFRS 16 *Leases*.

IAS 40 *Investment Property* defines investment property as property held to earn rentals or for capital appreciation or both, rather than for:

- Use in the production or supply of goods and services or for administrative purposes; or
- Sale in the ordinary course of business.

You now know what **is** investment property under IAS 40. Below are examples of items that are **not investment property**.

Type of non-investment property	Applicable IAS
Property held for sale in the ordinary course of business	IAS 2 *Inventories*
Property being constructed or developed on behalf of third parties	IFRS 15 *Revenue from Contracts with Customers*
Owner-occupied property	IAS 16 *Property, Plant and Equipment*

5.2 Recognition

Investment property should be recognised as an asset when **two conditions** are met.

(a) It is **probable** that the **future economic benefits** that are associated with the investment property will **flow to the entity**.

(b) The **cost** of the investment property can be **measured reliably**.

5.3 Initial measurement

An investment property should be measured initially at its **cost,** including transaction costs.

A property interest held as a right-of use asset and classified as an investment property shall be measured initially at its cost in accordance with IFRS 16. The right of use asset is measured at the total of the initial measurement of the lease liability, plus any payments made before commencement, less any initial direct costs incurred by the lessee, plus any expected dismantling/restoration costs.

5.4 Measurement subsequent to initial recognition

FAST FORWARD

Entities can choose between:

- A **fair value model,** with fair value measured in accordance with IFRS 13 and changes in fair value being recognised in profit or loss
- A **cost model** – the treatment most commonly used under IAS 16

IAS 40 requires an entity to **choose between two models.**

- The fair value model
- The cost model

Whatever policy it chooses should be applied to **all of its investment property**.

5.4.1 Fair value model

IAS 40 is the first standard in which the IASB allowed a fair value model for non-financial assets. This is not the same as a revaluation, where increases in carrying amount above a cost-based measure are recognised as revaluation surplus. Under the fair value model **all changes in fair value are recognised in profit or loss**.

Fair value is established in accordance with IFRS 13, taking into account rental income from current leases and other assumptions that market participants would use when pricing investment property under current market conditions.

An entity that chooses the fair value model should measure all of its investment property at fair value unless fair value cannot be measured reliably. In this case, the IAS 16 cost model should be applied going forward. Where investment property is under construction and fair value cannot be reliably measured, but it is expected that the fair value will be measurable when the property is complete, the cost model is applied during construction until fair value becomes measurable or construction is complete, if earlier.

5.4.2 Cost model

The cost model is the **cost model in IAS 16**. Investment property should be measured at **depreciated cost, less any accumulated impairment losses**. An entity that chooses the cost model should **disclose the fair value of its investment property**.

5.4.3 Changing models

Once the entity has chosen the fair value or cost model, it should apply it to all its investment property. It **should not change from one model to the other unless the change results in the financial statements providing reliable and more relevant information**. IAS 40 states that it is highly unlikely that a change from the fair value model to the cost model will result in a more relevant presentation.

5.5 Transfers

Transfers to or from investment property should **only** be made **when there is a change in use**. For example, owner occupation commences so the investment property will be treated under IAS 16 as an owner-occupied property.

When there is a transfer from investment property carried at fair value to owner-occupied property or inventories, the property's cost for subsequent accounting under IAS 16 or IAS 2 should be its fair value at the date of change in use.

Conversely, an owner-occupied property may become an investment property and need to be carried at fair value. An entity should apply IAS 16 up to the date of change in use. It should treat any difference at that date between the carrying amount of the property under IAS 16 and its fair value as a revaluation under IAS 16.

5.6 Disposals

Derecognise (eliminate from the statement of financial position) an investment property on disposal or when it is permanently withdrawn from use and no future economic benefits are expected from its disposal.

Any **gain or loss** on disposal is the difference between the net disposal proceeds and the carrying amount of the asset. It should generally be **recognised as income or expense in profit or loss**.

Compensation from third parties for investment property that was impaired, lost or given up shall be recognised in profit or loss when the compensation becomes receivable.

5.7 Disclosure requirements

These relate to:

- Choice of fair value model or cost model
- Criteria for classification as investment property
- Assumptions in determining fair value
- Use of independent professional valuer (encouraged but not required)
- Rental income and expenses
- Any restrictions or obligations

5.7.1 Fair value model – additional disclosures

An entity that adopts this model must also disclose a **reconciliation** of the carrying amount of the investment property at the beginning and end of the period.

IFRS 13 *Fair Value Measurement* disclosures are also relevant where the fair value model is used.

5.7.2 Cost model – additional disclosures

These relate mainly to the depreciation method as well as a **reconciliation** of the carrying amount of the investment property at the beginning and end of the period. In addition, an entity which adopts the cost model **must disclose the fair value** of the investment property.

12: TANGIBLE NON-CURRENT ASSETS AND INVENTORY

5.8 Decision tree

The decision tree below summarises which IFRSs apply to various kinds of property.

Exam focus point

Learn this decision tree – it will help you tackle most of the problems you are likely to meet in the exam!

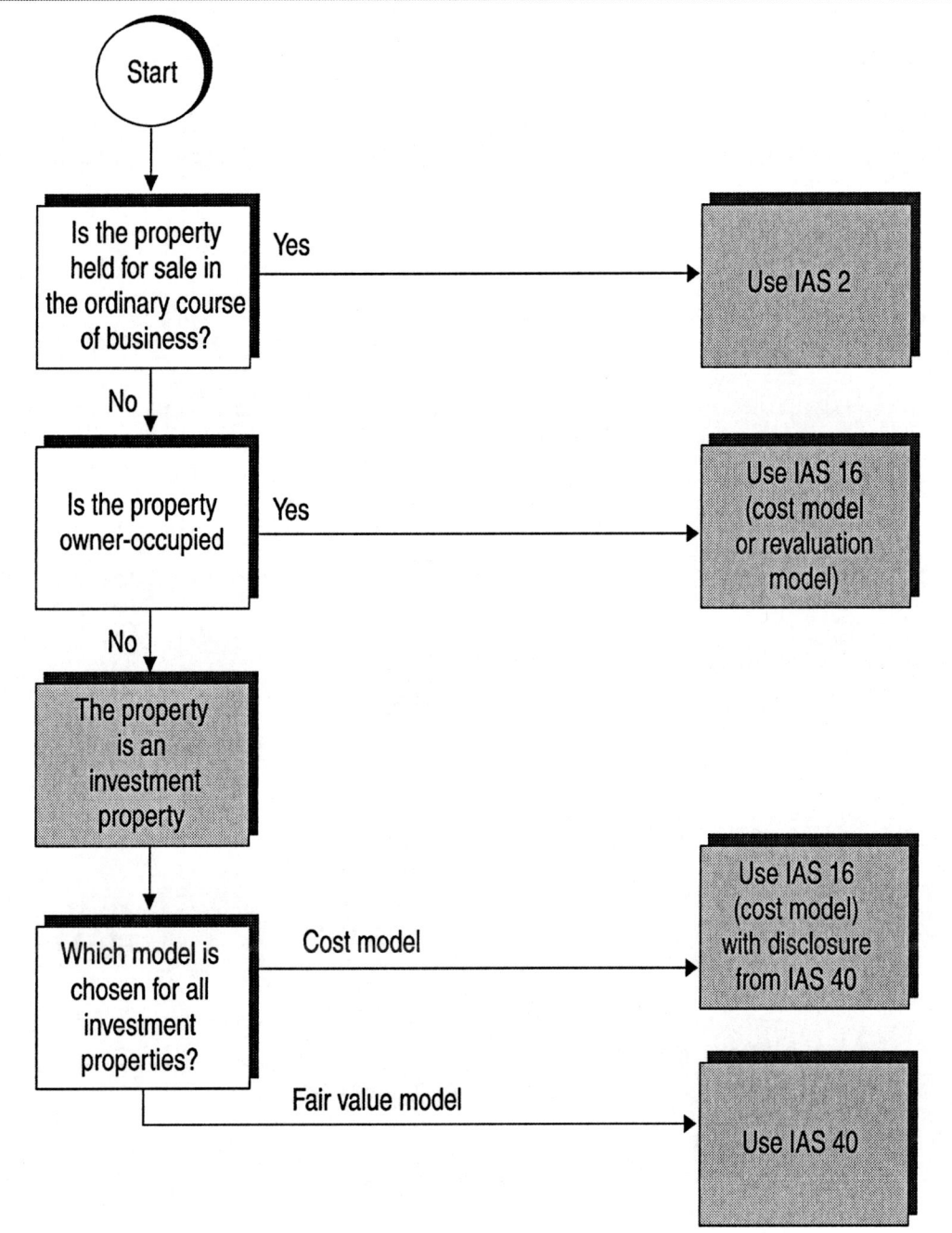

PART C   ACCOUNTING AND REPORTING TECHNIQUES

6 IAS 2 *Inventories*

You have studied inventories in your earlier studies, so this section is a quick revision of that.

FAST FORWARD IAS 2 requires that inventories are measured at the lower of cost and net realisable value

6.1 Introduction

In most businesses the value put on inventory is an important factor in the determination of profit. Inventory valuation is, however, a highly subjective exercise and consequently there is a wide variety of different methods used in practice.

6.2 IAS 2 *Inventories*

IAS 2 lays out the required accounting treatment for inventories. The major area of contention is the cost **value of inventory** to be recorded. This is recognised as an asset of the entity until the related revenues are recognised (ie the item is sold) at which point the inventory is recognised as an expense (ie cost of sales). Part or all of the cost of inventories may also be expensed if a write-down to **net realisable value** is necessary. The IAS also provides guidance on the cost formulas that are used to assign costs to inventories.

In other words, the fundamental accounting assumption of **accruals** requires costs to be matched with associated revenues. In order to achieve this, costs incurred for goods which remain unsold at the year end must be carried forward in the statement of financial position and matched against future revenues.

6.3 Scope

The following items are **excluded** from the scope of the standard.

- Work in progress under **long-term contracts** (covered by IFRS 15 *Revenue from Contracts with Customers*, see Chapter 21)
- **Financial instruments** (ie shares, bonds)
- **Biological assets**

6.4 Definitions

The following definitions are important.

Key terms

- **Inventories** are assets:
    - Held for sale in the ordinary course of business;
    - In the process of production for such sale; or
    - In the form of materials or supplies to be consumed in the production process or in the rendering of services.
- **Net realisable value** is the estimated selling price in the ordinary course of business less the estimated costs of completion and the estimated costs necessary to make the sale.   (IAS 2)
- **Fair value** is the price that would be received to sell an asset or paid to transfer a liability in an orderly transaction between market participants at the measurement date.   (IFRS 13)

Inventories can **include** any of the following:

- **Goods purchased and held for resale**, eg goods held for sale by a retailer, or land and buildings held for resale
- **Finished goods** produced

- **Work in progress** being produced
- Materials and supplies awaiting use in the production process (**raw materials**)

6.5 Measurement of inventories

The standard states that **'Inventories should be measured at the lower of cost and net realisable value.'**

> **Exam focus point**
>
> This is a very important rule and you will be expected to apply it in the exam.

6.6 Cost of inventories

The cost of inventories will consist of all costs of:

- **Purchase**
- **Costs of conversion**
- **Other costs** incurred in bringing the inventories to their **present location and condition**

6.6.1 Costs of purchase

The standard lists the following as comprising the costs of purchase of inventories.

- **Purchase price** PLUS
- **Import duties** and other taxes PLUS
- Transport, handling and any other cost **directly attributable** to the acquisition of finished goods, services and materials LESS
- **Trade discounts**, rebates and other similar amounts

6.6.2 Costs of conversion

Costs of conversion of inventories consist of two main parts:

(a) Costs **directly related** to the units of production, eg direct materials, direct labour.

(b) Fixed and variable **production overheads** that are incurred in converting materials into finished goods, allocated on a systematic basis.

You may have come across the terms 'fixed production overheads' or 'variable production overheads' elsewhere in your studies. The standard defines them as follows.

> **Key terms**
>
> - **Fixed production overheads** are those indirect costs of production that remain relatively constant regardless of the volume of production, eg the cost of factory management and administration.
> - **Variable production overheads** are those indirect costs of production that vary directly, or nearly directly, with the volume of production, eg indirect materials and labour. (IAS 2)

The standard emphasises that fixed production overheads must be allocated to items of inventory on the basis of the **normal capacity of the production facilities**. This is an important point.

(a) **Normal capacity** is the expected achievable production based on the average over several periods/seasons, under normal circumstances.

(b) The above figure should take account of the capacity lost through **planned maintenance**.

(c) If it approximates to the normal level of activity then the **actual level of production** can be used.

(d) **Low production** or **idle plant** will **not** result in a higher fixed overhead allocation to each unit.

(e) **Unallocated overheads** must be recognised as an expense in the period in which they were incurred.

(f) When production is **abnormally high**, the fixed production overhead allocated to each unit will be reduced, so avoiding inventories being stated at more than cost.

(g) The allocation of variable production overheads to each unit is based on the **actual use** of production facilities.

6.6.3 Other costs

Any other costs should only be recognised if they are incurred in bringing the inventories to their **present location and condition**.

The standard lists types of cost which **would not be included** in cost of inventories. Instead, they should be recognised as an **expense** in the period they are incurred.

(a) **Abnormal amounts** of wasted materials, labour or other production costs

(b) **Storage costs** (except costs which are necessary in the production process before a further production stage)

(c) **Administrative overheads** not incurred to bring inventories to their present location and conditions

(d) **Selling costs**

6.6.4 Techniques for the measurement of cost

Two techniques are mentioned by the standard, both of which produce results which **approximate to cost**, and so both of which may be used for convenience.

(a) **Standard costs** are set up to take account of normal production values: amount of raw materials used, labour time etc. They are reviewed and revised on a regular basis.

(b) **Retail method** is often used in the retail industry where there is a large turnover of inventory items, which nevertheless have similar profit margins. The only practical method of inventory valuation may be to take the total selling price of inventories and deduct an overall average profit margin, thus reducing the value to an approximation of cost. The percentage will take account of reduced price lines. Sometimes different percentages are applied on a department basis.

6.7 Cost formulae

Cost of inventories should be assigned by **specific identification** of their individual costs for:

(a) Items that are **not ordinarily interchangeable**
(b) Goods or services produced and segregated for **specific projects**

Specific costs should be attributed to individual items of inventory when they are segregated for a specific project, but not where inventories consist of a large number of interchangeable (ie identical or very similar) items. In the latter case the rule is as specified below.

6.7.1 Interchangeable items

Rule to learn

The cost of inventories should be assigned by using the **first-in, first-out (FIFO)** or **weighted average cost** formulas. The LIFO formula (last in, first out) is **not permitted** by IAS 2.

You should be familiar with these methods from your earlier studies. Under the weighted average cost method, a recalculation can be made after each purchase, **or alternatively only at the period end**.

6.8 Net realisable value (NRV)

As a general rule assets should not be carried at amounts greater than those expected to be realised from their sale or use. In the case of inventories this amount could fall below cost when items are **damaged or become obsolete**, or where the **costs to completion have increased** in order to make the sale.

In fact we can identify the principal situations in which **NRV is likely to be less than cost**, ie where there has been:

(a) An **increase in costs** or a **fall in selling price**
(b) A **physical deterioration** in the condition of inventory
(c) **Obsolescence** of products
(d) A decision as part of the company's marketing strategy to manufacture and sell products at a **loss**
(e) **Errors in production or purchasing**

A write down of inventories would normally take place on an item by item basis, but similar or related items may be **grouped together**. This grouping together is acceptable for, say, items in the same product line, but it is not acceptable to write down inventories based on a whole classification (eg finished goods) or a whole business.

The assessment of NRV should take place **at the same time** as estimates are made of selling price, using the most reliable information available. Fluctuations of price or cost should be taken into account if they relate directly to **events after the reporting period,** which confirm conditions existing at the end of the period.

The reasons why inventory is held must also be taken into account. Some inventory, for example, may be held to satisfy a firm contract and its NRV will therefore be the **contract price**. Any additional inventory of the same type held at the period end will, in contrast, be assessed according to general sales prices when NRV is estimated.

Net realisable value must be reassessed at the end of each period and compared again with cost. If the NRV has risen for inventories held over the end of more than one period, then the previous write down must be **reversed** to the extent that the inventory is then valued at the lower of cost and the new NRV. This may be possible when selling prices have fallen in the past and then risen again.

On occasion a write down to NRV may be of such size, incidence or nature that it must be **disclosed separately**.

6.9 Recognition as an expense

The following treatment is required **when inventories are sold**:

(a) The **carrying amount** is recognised as an expense in the period in which the related revenue is recognised.

(b) The amount of any **write-down of inventories** to NRV and all losses of inventories are recognised as an expense in the period the write-down or loss occurs.

(c) The amount of any **reversal of any write-down of inventories**, arising from an increase in NRV, is recognised as a reduction in the amount of inventories recognised as an expense in the period in which the reversal occurs.

6.10 Consistency – different cost formulas for inventories

IAS 2 allows two cost formulas (FIFO or weighted average cost) for inventories that are ordinarily interchangeable or are not produced and segregated for specific projects. The issue is whether an entity may use different cost formulas for different types of inventories.

IAS 2 provides that an entity should use **the same cost formula for all inventories having similar nature and use to the entity.** For inventories with different nature or use (for example, certain commodities used in one business segment and the same type of commodities used in another business segment), different cost formulas may be justified. A difference in geographical location of inventories (and in the respective tax rules), by itself, is not sufficient to justify the use of different cost formulas.

PART C   ACCOUNTING AND REPORTING TECHNIQUES

Chapter roundup

- You must learn the IASB *Conceptual Framework* **definition of an asset**: a present economic resource controlled by the entity as a result of past events. An economic resource is a right that has the potential to produce economic benefits.

- This definition was changed when the *Conceptual Framework* was revised in 2018. It still ties in closely with the definitions produced by **other standard-setters**, particularly FASB (USA) and FRC (UK).

- The definition has three important characteristics:
    - **Economic benefits**
    - **Control (ownership)**
    - **Transaction to acquire has taken place (it is a past event)**

- You should already be familiar with many standards relating to **non-current assets** from Papers 1 and 11. If not, go back to your earlier study material.
    - IAS 16 *Property, Plant and Equipment*
    - IAS 20 *Accounting for Government Grants and Disclosure of Government Assistance*
    - IAS 23 *Borrowing Costs*

- **IAS 36 *Impairment of Assets*** covers a controversial topic and it affects both intangible and tangible non-current assets.

- Impairment is determined by comparing the carrying amount of the asset with its **recoverable amount**.

- The recoverable amount of an asset is the higher of the asset's **fair value less costs of disposal** and **its value in use**.

- Where the recoverable amount of a single asset cannot be estimated, the impairment test must be performed for the cash-generating unit to which that asset belongs.

- IAS 40 *Investment Property* defines investment property as property **held to earn rentals or for capital appreciation** or both, rather than for:
    - Use in production or supply of goods or services
    - Sale in the ordinary course of business.

- Entities can choose between:
    - A **fair value model**, with fair value measured in accordance with IFRS 13 and changes in fair value being recognised in profit or loss
    - A **cost model** – the treatment most commonly used under IAS 16

- IAS 2 requires that inventories are measured at the lower of cost and net realisable value.

Quick quiz

1. How does the IASB *Conceptual Framework* define an asset?
2. How might a non-current asset be defined?
3. Define an impairment.
4. How is value in use calculated?
5. What is a cash-generating unit?
6. Investment property **must** be valued at fair value. True or false?

Answers to quick quiz

1. A resource controlled by the entity as a result of past events and from which future economic benefits are expected to flow to the entity.

2. One intended for use on a continuing basis in the company's activities.

3. A fall in the value of an asset, so that its recoverable amount is now less than its carrying amount.

4. The present value of estimated future cash flows generated by the asset, including its estimated net disposal value (if any).

5. The smallest identifiable group of assets for which independent cash flows can be identified and measured.

6. False, it can be valued at cost or fair value.

PART C ACCOUNTING AND REPORTING TECHNIQUES

End of chapter question

NCH (AIA May 2006)

NCH is a pharmaceutical company which has a factory in Ireland the sole activity of which is the manufacture of a popular drug. NCH has patents which ensure that it has been the sole manufacturer of this drug and the company has priced the drug accordingly and has enjoyed high levels of profit.

However, NCH's sole manufacturing rights are currently being challenged in the courts, and it now looks probable that the company will lose its protection which was due to run until the end of 20X8. This will reduce not only the number of units of this drug the company will be able to sell but also the selling price it will be able to charge.

The net assets employed in the Irish factory as at 31 March 20X6 were:

	Carrying value €	Fair Value less costs of disposal €
Net assets	131,500,000	115,144,500
Apportioned head office assets	850,000	150,000
	132,350,000	115,294,500

The scrap value of the net assets employed in the manufacturing unit is estimated to be €1,000,000 as at 31 March 20X9.

The following figures come from the company's internal budgets for the drug:

Budgets for the year ended 31 March	20X7	20X8	20X9
Sales in units			
– estimated as at end of 20X4	1,500,000	1,650,000	1,700,000
– estimated as at end of 20X5	1,500,000	500,000	500,000
Unit costs and revenues	€	€	€
– estimated as at end of 20X4	40.00	40.00	40.00
– estimated as at end of 20X5	40.00	35.00	30.00
Materials	(18.00)	(18.00)	(18.00)
Other production costs	(4.20)	(4.20)	(4.20)
Apportioned head office costs	(1.80)	(1.80)	(1.80)
Income per unit (20X4 estimates)	16.00	11.00	6.00
Income per unit (20X5 estimates)	16.00	6.00	1.00
Discount rate for equivalent level of risk	5%	5%	5%
Expected rate of inflation	3%	3%	4%
Real cost of capital	8.15%	8.15%	9.20%

Required

(a) Calculate the values necessary for the impairment review as at 31 March 20X6 for the Irish factory.

(14 marks)

(b) Advise as to whether the carrying value of the factory should be revised, the new carrying value and the amount of any impairment loss. **(3 marks)**

(c) Advise on the way in which an impairment loss should be treated in the following circumstances:

(i) The asset was previously revalued; and **(3 marks)**

(ii) The impairment loss cannot be allocated to a particular non-current asset. **(5 marks)**

(Total 25 marks)

Intangible non-current assets

Topic list	Syllabus reference
1 IAS 38 *Intangible Assets*	13.4
2 Goodwill and IFRS 3	13.4

Introduction

We begin our examination of intangible non-current assets with a discussion of IAS 38.

Goodwill and its treatment is a controversial area, as is the accounting for items similar to goodwill, such as brands. Goodwill is very important in **group financial statements**.

1 IAS 38 *Intangible Assets*

The objectives of the standard are:

(a) To establish the criteria for when an intangible asset may or should be **recognised**
(b) To specify how intangible assets should be **measured**
(c) To specify the **disclosure requirements** for intangible assets

It applies to all intangible assets with certain **exceptions**: deferred tax assets (IAS 12 *Income Taxes*), leases that fall within the scope of IFRS 16 *Leases*, financial assets, insurance contracts, assets arising from employee benefits (IAS 19 *Employee Benefits*), non-current assets held for sale and mineral rights and exploration and extraction costs for minerals etc (although intangible assets used to develop or maintain these rights are covered by the standard). Also, it does **not** apply to goodwill acquired in a business combination, which is dealt with under IFRS 3 *Business Combinations.*

1.1 Definition and recognition of an intangible asset

FAST FORWARD

Intangible assets are defined by IAS 38 as non-monetary assets without physical substance. They must be:

- **Identifiable**
- **Controlled** as a result of a past event
- Expected to provide **future economic benefits**

An intangible asset is recognised in the financial statements where:

- It is probable that future economic benefits attributable to the asset will flow to the entity; and
- The cost can be measured reliably.

The definition of an intangible asset is a key aspect of the standard, because the rules for deciding whether or not an intangible asset is **recognised** in the financial statements of an entity are based on the definition of what an intangible asset is.

Key term

An **intangible asset** is an identifiable non-monetary asset without physical substance The asset must be a resource:

(a) Controlled by the entity as a result of events in the past
(b) From which future economic benefits are expected to flow

Examples of items that might be considered as intangible assets include computer software, patents, copyrights, motion picture films, customer lists, franchises and fishing rights. An item should not be recognised as an intangible asset, however, unless it **fully meets the definition** in the standard. The guidelines go into great detail on this matter.

1.1.1 Intangible asset: Must be identifiable

An intangible asset must be identifiable (in order to distinguish it from goodwill).

(a) It must be separable, ie capable of being sold separately from the entity's other operations; or

(b) It must arise from contractual or other legal rights, even if those legal rights cannot be sold separately from the entity owning them.

1.1.2 Intangible asset: Control by the entity

Another element of the definition of an intangible asset is that it must be under the control of the entity as a result of a past event. The entity must therefore be able to enjoy the future economic benefits from the asset, and prevent the access of others to those benefits. A **legally enforceable right** is evidence of such control, but is not always a **necessary** condition.

(a) Control over **technical knowledge or know-how** only exists if it is protected by a **legal right**.

(b) The skill of employees, arising out of the benefits of **training costs**, are most unlikely to be recognisable as an intangible asset, because an entity does not control the future actions of its staff.

(c) Similarly, **market share and customer loyalty** cannot normally be intangible assets, since an entity cannot control the actions of its customers.

1.1.3 Intangible asset: Future economic benefits

The requirement to provide future economic benefits forms part of the definition of an intangible asset and is also one of the recognition criteria relevant to an intangible asset.

Rule to learn

> An intangible asset should be recognised if, and only if **both** the following are true:
>
> (a) It is probable that the **future economic benefits** that are attributable to the asset will **flow to the entity**.
>
> (b) The **cost can be measured reliably**

Economic benefits may come from the **sale** of products or services, or from a **reduction in expenditures** (cost savings).

Management has to exercise its judgement in assessing the degree of certainty attached to the flow of economic benefits to the entity. External evidence is best.

1.2 Application of definition and recognition criteria to internally generated assets

FAST FORWARD

> **Internally-generated goodwill** cannot be recognised as an asset but other internally-generated assets may be, eg R & D.

Before we go on to consider the 'reliable measurement' of the cost of an intangible asset, we shall apply the above definition and the first of the recognition criteria to some specific (and commonly examined) internally generated intangible assets.

1.2.1 Internally generated goodwill

Rule to learn

> Internally generated goodwill may **not** be recognised as an **asset**.

The standard deliberately precludes recognition of internally generated goodwill because it is not an identifiable resource that can be measured reliably at cost.

1.2.2 Research

Research activities by definition do not meet the criteria for recognition under IAS 38. This is because, at the research stage of a project, it cannot be certain that future economic benefits will probably flow to the entity from the project. There is too much uncertainty about the likely success or otherwise of the project. **Research costs should therefore be recognised as an expense in profit or loss as they are incurred**.

Examples of research costs

(a) Activities aimed at obtaining new knowledge

(b) The search for, evaluation and final selection of, applications of research findings or other knowledge

(c) The search for alternatives for materials, devices, products, processes, systems or services

(d) The formulation, design evaluation and final selection of possible alternatives for new or improved materials, devices, products, systems or services

1.2.3 Development

Development costs **should be recognised** as intangible assets provided that all the following can be demonstrated.

(a) The technical feasibility of completing the intangible asset so that it will be available for use or sale.

(b) The intention to complete the intangible asset and use or sell it.

(c) The ability to use or sell the intangible asset.

(d) How the intangible asset will generate probable future economic benefits. Among other things, the entity should demonstrate the existence of a market for the output of the intangible asset or the intangible asset itself or, if it is to be used internally, the usefulness of the intangible asset.

(e) The ability to measure the expenditure attributable to the intangible asset during its development reliably.

In contrast with research costs, development costs are incurred at a later stage in a project, and the probability of success should be more apparent. Examples of development costs include the following.

(a) The design, construction and testing of pre-production or pre-use prototypes and models

(b) The design of tools, jigs, moulds and dies involving new technology

(c) The design, construction and operation of a pilot plant that is not of a scale economically feasible for commercial production

(d) The design, construction and testing of a chosen alternative for new or improved materials, devices, products, processes, systems or services

1.2.4 Other internally generated assets

The standard **prohibits** the recognition of **internally generated brands, mastheads, publishing titles and customer lists** and similar items as intangible assets. These all fail to meet one or more (in some cases all) the definition and recognition criteria and in some cases are probably indistinguishable from internally generated goodwill.

1.3 Initial measurement

FAST FORWARD

Intangible assets should initially be measured at cost, but subsequently they can be carried at **cost or at a fair value** measured in accordance with IFRS 13 *Fair Value Measurement*.

An intangible asset is initially measured at cost. The application of this rule to purchased and internally generated assets is considered below.

1.3.1 Separately acquired assets

If an intangible asset is **acquired separately**, its cost can usually be measured reliably as its purchase price (including incidental costs of purchase such as legal fees, and any costs incurred in getting the asset ready for use).

In accordance with IAS 20 *Accounting for Government Grants and Disclosure of Government Assistance*, intangible assets acquired by way of government grant and the grant itself may be recorded initially either at cost (which may be zero) or fair value.

1.3.2 Assets acquired as part of a business combination

When an intangible asset is acquired as **part of a business combination** (ie an acquisition or takeover), the cost of the intangible asset is its fair value at the date of the acquisition.

IFRS 3 explains that the fair value of intangible assets acquired in business combinations can normally be measured with sufficient reliability to be **recognised separately** from goodwill.

IFRS 13 should be applied in establishing the fair value of assets acquired as part of a business combination (see Chapter 11).

1.3.3 Exchanges of assets

If one intangible asset is exchanged for another, the cost of the intangible asset is measured at fair value unless:

(a) The exchange transaction lacks commercial substance; or
(b) The fair value of neither the asset received nor the asset given up can be measured reliably.

Otherwise, its cost is measured at the carrying amount of the asset given up.

1.3.4 Internally generated intangible assets

The cost of an internally generated intangible asset should comprise only those costs that can be **directly attributed** or allocated on a reasonable and consistent basis to creating, producing or preparing the asset for its intended use. The principles underlying the costs which may or may not be included are similar to those for other than non-current assets and inventory.

The cost of an internally operated intangible asset is the sum of the **expenditure incurred from the date when** the intangible asset first **meets the recognition criteria**. If, as often happens, considerable costs have already been recognised as expenses before management could demonstrate that the criteria have been met, this earlier expenditure should not be retrospectively recognised at a later date as part of the cost of an intangible asset.

Question
Recognition criteria

Doug Co is developing a new production process. During 20X3, expenditure incurred was $100,000, of which $90,000 was incurred before 1 December 20X3 and $10,000 between 1 December 20X3 and 31 December 20X3. Doug Co can demonstrate that, at 1 December 20X3, the production process met the criteria for recognition as an intangible asset. The recoverable amount of the know-how embodied in the process is estimated to be $50,000.

How should the expenditure be treated?

Answer

At the end of 20X3, the production process is recognised as an intangible asset at a cost of $10,000. This is the expenditure incurred since the date when the recognition criteria were met, that is 1 December 20X3. As the estimated recoverable amount of at $50,000 is greater than cost, no impairment loss need be recognised. The $90,000 expenditure incurred before 1 December 20X3 is expensed, because the recognition criteria were not met. It will never form part of the cost of the production process recognised in the statement of financial position.

1.4 Recognition of an expense

All expenditure related to an intangible which does not meet the criteria for recognition either as an identifiable intangible asset or as goodwill arising on an acquisition should be **expensed as incurred**. The IAS gives examples of such expenditure.

- Start up costs
- Training costs
- Advertising costs
- Business relocation costs

Prepaid costs for services, for example advertising or marketing costs for campaigns that have been prepared but not launched, can still be recognised as a **prepayment**.

1.5 Measurement of intangible assets subsequent to initial recognition

The standard allows two methods of valuation for intangible assets after they have been first recognised.

Applying the **cost model**, an intangible asset should be **carried at its cost**, less any accumulated depreciation and less any accumulated impairment losses.

Under the **revaluation model** an intangible asset is carried at a revalued amount, which is its **fair value** at the date of revaluation less any subsequent accumulated amortisation and any subsequent accumulated impairment losses.

A number of rules apply where the revaluation model is applied:

(a) The fair value must be able to be measured reliably with reference to an **active market** in that type of asset.

(b) The **entire class** of intangible assets of that type must be revalued at the same time (to prevent selective revaluations).

(c) If an intangible asset in a class of revalued intangible assets cannot be revalued because there is **no active market** for this asset, the asset should be carried at its **cost less any accumulated amortisation and impairment losses**.

(d) Revaluations should be made with such **regularity** that the carrying amount does not differ from that which would be determined using fair value at the year end.

Point to note

> This treatment is **not** available for the **initial recognition** of intangible assets. This is because the cost of the asset must be reliably measured.

The guidelines state that it is **uncommon for an active market** to exist for an intangible asset; therefore the revaluation model will usually not be available. For example, although copyrights, publishing rights and film right can be sold, each has a unique sale value. In such cases, revaluation to fair value would be inappropriate. A fair value might be obtainable however for assets such as fishing rights or quotas or taxi cab licences.

1.5.1 Accounting for a revaluation

Where an intangible asset is revalued upwards to a fair value, the amount of the revaluation should be recognised in other comprehensive income and carried in equity under the heading of a **revaluation surplus**.

However, if a revaluation surplus is a **reversal of a revaluation decrease** that was previously recognised as an expense in profit or loss, the increase is recognised in profit or loss.

Where the carrying amount of an intangible asset is revalued downwards, the amount of the **downward revaluation** should be charged as an expense against income, unless the asset has previously been revalued upwards. A revaluation decrease should be first charged against any previous revaluation surplus in respect of that asset.

Question — Downward valuation

An intangible asset is measured by a company at fair value. The asset was revalued by $400 in 20X3, and there is a revaluation surplus of $400 in the statement of financial position. At the end of 20X4, the asset is valued again, and a downward valuation of $500 is required.

Required

State the accounting treatment for the downward revaluation.

> **Answer**
>
> In this example, the downward valuation of $500 is first set against the revaluation surplus of $400. The revaluation surplus will be reduced to 0 and a charge of $100 made as an expense in 20X4.

When the revaluation model is used, and an intangible asset is revalued upwards, the cumulative revaluation **surplus may be transferred to retained earnings** when the surplus is eventually realised. The surplus would be realised when the asset is disposed of. However, the surplus may also be realised over time as the **asset is used** by the entity. The amount of the surplus realised each year is the difference between the amortisation charge for the asset based on the revalued amount of the asset, and the amortisation that would be charged on the basis of the asset's historical cost. The realised surplus in such case should be transferred from revaluation surplus directly to retained earnings in the statement of changes in equity, and should not be recognised in profit or loss.

1.6 Amortisation of intangibles

An entity should **assess** the useful life of an intangible asset, which may be **finite or indefinite**. An intangible asset with a finite useful life should be amortised over its **expected useful life**, with the amortisation charge recognised in profit or loss.

1.6.1 Assessment of useful life

An intangible asset has an indefinite useful life when there is **no foreseeable limit** to the period over which the asset is expected to generate net cash inflows for the entity.

Many factors are considered in determining the useful life of an intangible asset, including: expected usage; typical product life cycles; technical, technological, commercial or other types of obsolescence; the stability of the industry; expected actions by competitors; the level of maintenance expenditure required; and legal or similar limits on the use of the asset, such as the expiry dates of related leases. Computer software and many other intangible assets normally have short lives because they are susceptible to technological obsolescence. However, uncertainty does not justify choosing a life that is unrealistically short.

The useful life of an intangible asset that arises from **contractual or other legal rights** should not exceed the period of the rights, but may be shorter depending on the period over which the entity expects to use the asset.

1.6.2 Residual value

The **residual value** of an intangible asset with a finite useful life is **assumed to be zero** unless a third party is committed to buying the intangible asset at the end of its useful life or unless there is an active market for that type of asset (so that its expected residual value can be measured) and it is probable that there will be a market for the asset at the end of its useful life.

1.6.3 Amortisation period and amortisation method

Amortisation should start when the asset is **available for use**. It should cease at the earlier of the date that the asset is classified **as held for sale** in accordance with IFRS 5 *Non-current Assets Held for Sale and Discontinued Operations* and the date that the asset is **derecognised**.

The amortisation method used should reflect the **pattern in which the asset's future economic benefits are consumed**. If such a pattern cannot be predicted reliably, the straight-line method should be used.

The amortisation period and the amortisation method used for an intangible asset with a finite useful life should be **reviewed at each financial year end**.

In 2014 the IASB issued a clarification of acceptable methods of depreciation and amortisation, which amended IAS 16 *Property, Plant and Equipment* and IAS 38 to the effect that revenue-based methods of depreciation and amortisation will be disallowed or restricted.

The amendments are to be applied prospectively for annual periods beginning on or after 1 January 2016, with earlier application permitted.

Depreciation should reflect the consumption of the asset's future economic benefits (IAS 16, para. 60). Even though revenue could sometimes be considered to be a measurement of the output generated by the asset, revenue does not, as a matter of principle, reflect the way in which an asset is used or consumed. (For example, revenue may be affected by inflation). Revenue-based depreciation is no longer allowed for property, plant and equipment (IAS 16) and there is a **rebuttable presumption that revenue-based amortisation is inappropriate for intangible assets** (IAS 38). This presumption can be overcome only when either revenue and consumption of economic benefits of an asset are 'highly correlated' or the asset is expressed as a measure of revenue (for example, the right to receive a certain amount of income). To use a revenue-based method, an entity will need to show that there is more than just an element of relationship between revenue generation and the consumption of benefits.

This change is likely to affect media companies, for example, who may move towards recognising lower amortisation expenses, and therefore higher profits, in the earlier years of the life of an asset.

1.7 Intangible assets with indefinite useful lives

FAST FORWARD

Impairment rules follow IAS 36. There are substantial disclosure requirements.

An intangible asset with an indefinite useful life **should not be amortised**. but in accordance with IAS 36 *Impairment of Assets* should be tested for impairment at least annually.

The useful life of an intangible asset that is not being amortised should be **reviewed each year** to determine whether it is still appropriate to assess its useful life as indefinite. Reassessing the useful life of an intangible asset as finite rather than indefinite is an indicator that the asset may be impaired and therefore it should be tested for impairment.

Question
Useful life

It may be difficult to establish the useful life of an intangible asset, and judgement will be needed. Consider how to determine the useful life of a **purchased** brand name and how to provide evidence that its useful life might in fact exceed 20 years.

Answer

Factors to consider would include the following:

(a) Legal protection of the brand name and the control of the entity over the (illegal) use by others of the brand name (ie control over pirating)
(b) Age of the brand name
(c) Status or position of the brand in its particular market
(d) Ability of the management of the entity to manage the brand name and to measure activities that support the brand name (eg advertising and PR activities)
(e) Stability and geographical spread of the market in which the branded products are sold
(f) Pattern of benefits that the brand name is expected to generate over time
(g) Intention of the entity to use and promote the brand name over time (as evidenced perhaps by a business plan in which there will be substantial expenditure to promote the brand name)

1.8 Disposals/retirements of intangible assets

An intangible asset should be eliminated from the statement of financial position when it is disposed of or when there is no further expected economic benefit from its future use. On disposal the gain or loss arising from the **difference between the net disposal proceeds and the carrying amount** of the asset should be taken to the statement of profit or loss and other comprehensive income as a gain or loss on disposal (ie treated as income or expense).

1.9 Disclosure requirements

The standard has fairly extensive disclosure requirements for intangible assets. The financial statements should disclose the **accounting policies** for intangible assets that have been adopted.

For **each class of intangible assets**, disclosure is required of the following:

- The **method of amortisation** used
- The **useful life** of the assets or the amortisation rate used
- The **gross carrying amount**, the **accumulated amortisation** and the **accumulated impairment losses** as at the beginning and the end of the period
- A **reconciliation of the carrying amount** as at the beginning and at the end of the period (additions, retirements/disposals, revaluations, impairment losses, impairment losses reversed, amortisation charge for the period, net exchange differences, other movements)
- The carrying amount of **internally-generated intangible assets**

The financial statements should also disclose the following:

- In the case of intangible assets that are assessed as having a indefinite useful life, the carrying amounts and the reasons supporting that assessment
- For intangible assets acquired by way of a **government grant** and initially recognised at fair value, the **fair value initially recognised**, the **carrying amount** and whether they are subsequently measured under the cost model or the revaluation model
- The carrying amount, nature and remaining amortisation period of any intangible asset that is **material to the financial statements of the entity as a whole**
- The existence (if any) and amounts of intangible assets whose **title is restricted** and of intangible assets that have been **pledged as security** for liabilities
- The amount of any **commitments for the future acquisition of intangible assets**

Where intangible assets are accounted for at revalued amounts, disclosure is required of the following:

- The **effective date of the revaluation** (by class of intangible assets)
- The **carrying amount** of revalued intangible assets
- The carrying amount that would have been shown (by class of assets) **if the cost model had been used**, and the amount of amortisation that would have been charged
- The amount of any **revaluation surplus** on intangible assets, as at the beginning and end of the period, and movements in the surplus during the year (and any restrictions on the distribution of the balance to shareholders)

The financial statements should also disclose the amount of research and development expenditure that have been charged as expenses of the period.

IFRS 13 disclosures are also relevant where intangible assets are measured at fair value in accordance with that standard (see Chapter 11).

1.10 Section summary

- An intangible asset must be identifiable, ie separable or arising from contractual or other legal rights.
- An intangible asset should be recognised if, and only if, it is probable that future economic benefits will flow to the entity and the cost of the asset can be measured reliably.
- An asset is initially recognised at cost and subsequently carried either at cost or revalued amount.
- Costs that do not meet the recognition criteria should be expensed as incurred.
- An intangible asset with a finite useful life should be amortised over its useful life. An intangible asset with an indefinite useful life should not be amortised.

Question
List

As an aid to your revision, list the examples given in IAS 38 of activities that might be included in either research or development.

Answer

IAS 38 gives these examples.

Research

- Activities aimed at obtaining new knowledge
- The search for applications of research findings or other knowledge
- The search for product or process alternatives
- The formulation and design of possible new or improved product or process alternatives

Development

- The evaluation of product or process alternatives
- The design, construction and testing of pre-production prototypes and models
- The design of tools, jigs, moulds and dies involving new technology
- The design, construction and operation of a pilot plant that is not of a scale economically feasible for commercial production

Question
Project

Forkbender Co develops and manufactures exotic cutlery and has the following projects in hand.

	Project 1 $'000	Project 2 $'000	Project 3 $'000	Project 4 $'000
Deferred development Expenditure b/f 1.1.X8	280	450	–	–
Development expenditure Incurred during the year				
Salaries, wages and so on	35	29	60	20
Overhead costs	2	5	–	3
Materials and services	3	13	11	4
Patents and licences	1	2	–	–
Market research	–	10	2	–

Project 1 was originally expected to be highly profitable but this is now in doubt, since the scientist in charge of the project is now behind schedule, with the result that competitors are gaining ground.

Project 2: commercial production started during the year. Sales were 20,000 units in 20X8 and future sales are expected to be: 20X8 30,000 units; 20X9 60,000 units; 20Y0 40,000 units; 20Y1 30,000 units. There are no sales expected after 20Y1.

Project 3: these costs relate to a new project, which meets the criteria for deferral of expenditure and which is expected to last for three years.

Project 4 is another new project, involving the development of a 'loss leader', expected to raise the level of future sales.

The company's policy is to defer development costs, where permitted by IAS 38. Expenditure carried forward is written off evenly over the expected sales life of projects, starting in the first year of sale.

Required

Show how the above projects should be treated in the accounting statements of Forkbender Co for the year ended 31 December 20X8 in accordance with best accounting practice. Justify your treatment of each project.

Answer

Project 1 expenditure, including that relating to previous years, should all be written off in 20X8, as there is now considerable doubt as to the profitability of the project.

Since commercial production has started under Project 2 the expenditure previously deferred should now be amortised. This will be done over the estimated life of the product, as stated in the question.

Project 3: the development costs should be deferred.

Since *Project 4* is not expected to be profitable; its development costs should not be deferred.

STATEMENT OF FINANCIAL POSITION AS AT 31 DECEMBER 20X8 (extract)

	$'000
NON-CURRENT ASSETS	
Intangible assets	
Development costs (Note 2)	480

NOTES TO THE FINANCIAL STATEMENTS

1 *Accounting policies*

   Research and development

   Research and development expenditure is written off as incurred, except that development costs incurred on an individual project are carried forward when their future recoverability can be foreseen with reasonable assurance. Any expenditure carried forward is amortised over the period of sales from the related project.

2 *Development costs*

	$'000	$'000
Balance brought forward 1 January 20X8		730
Development expenditure incurred during 20X8	188	
Development expenditure amortised during 20X8	438	
		(250)
Balance carried forward 31 December 20X8		480

Note. IAS 38 would not permit the inclusion of market research in deferred development costs. Market research costs might, however, be carried forward separately under the accruals principle.

Workings

	1 $'000	2 $'000	3 $'000	4 $'000	Total $'000
B/F	280	450			730
Salaries etc.	35		60	20	115
Overheads	2			3	5
Materials etc.	3		11	4	18
Patents etc.	1				1
C/F	0	(360)	(71)	–	(431)
Written off	321	*90	–	27	438

* **Note.** Calculated as 1/5 of carrying amount of the asset.

2 Goodwill and IFRS 3

FAST FORWARD

If a business has **goodwill**, it means that the value of the business is greater than the value of its identifiable net assets. The valuation of goodwill is extremely subjective and fluctuates constantly. For this reason, goodwill other than that acquired in a business combination is **not** shown as an asset in the statement of financial position.

Goodwill can be created in a number of different ways, for example **by good relationships** between a business and its customers.

(a) By building up a **reputation** (by word of mouth perhaps) for high quality products or high standards of service

(b) By **responding promptly and helpfully** to queries and complaints from customers

(c) Through the **personality of the staff** and their attitudes to customers

The value of goodwill to a business might be **extremely significant**. However, goodwill is not usually valued in the financial statements of a business at all, and we should not normally expect to find an amount for goodwill in its statement of financial position. For example, the welcoming smile of the bar staff may contribute more to a bar's profits than the fact that a new electronic cash register has recently been acquired. Even so, whereas the cash register will be recorded in the financial statements as a non-current asset, the value of staff would be ignored for accounting purposes.

On reflection, we might agree with this omission of goodwill from the financial statements of a business.

(a) The goodwill is **inherent** in the business but it has not been paid for, and it does not have an 'objective' value. We can guess at what such goodwill is worth, but such guesswork would be a matter of individual opinion, and not based on hard facts.

(b) Goodwill **changes** from day to day. One act of bad customer relations might damage goodwill and one act of good relations might improve it. Staff with a favourable personality might retire or leave to find another job, to be replaced by staff who need time to find their feet in the job, etc. Since goodwill is continually changing in value, it cannot realistically be recorded in the financial statements of the business.

2.1 Goodwill acquired in a business combination

FAST FORWARD

When someone **purchases a business**, the purchaser and vendor will fix an agreed price which may include an element in respect of goodwill. The way in which goodwill is then valued is not an accounting problem, but a matter of agreement between the two parties.

Goodwill acquired in a business combination is then carried in the statement of financial position as an intangible asset under the requirements of **IFRS 3**. It must be reviewed for impairment annually.

There is one exception to the general rule that goodwill has no objective valuation. This is **when a business is sold**. People wishing to set up in business have a choice of how to do it – they can either buy their own non-current assets and inventory and set up their business from scratch, or they can buy up an existing business from a proprietor willing to sell it. When a buyer purchases an existing business, he will have to purchase not only its non-current assets and inventory (and perhaps take over its accounts payable and receivable too) but also the goodwill attributable to the business.

> **Exam focus point**
>
> Goodwill acquired in a business combination is shown in the statement of financial position because its measurement results from a market transaction. It has no tangible substance, and so it is an **intangible non-current asset**.

2.2 How is goodwill measured?

When a business is sold, any goodwill acquired in a business combination must be recognised in the financial statements of the enlarged group. The value of the goodwill is a **matter for the purchaser and seller to agree upon** as a result of agreeing the purchase/sale price. However, two methods of valuation are worth mentioning here.

(a) The seller and buyer agree on a price **without specifically quantifying the goodwill**. Goodwill will then be the difference between the price agreed and the fair value of the identifiable net assets acquired.

(b) However, the calculation of goodwill often precedes the fixing of the purchase price and becomes a **central element of negotiation**. There are many ways of arriving at a value for goodwill and most of them are related to the profit record of the business in question.

No matter how goodwill is calculated within the total agreed purchase price, the goodwill shown by the purchaser in its financial statements will be **the difference between the consideration transferred and the fair value of the identifiable net assets acquired**. If A values his identifiable net assets at $40,000 and goodwill at $21,000, and B agrees to pay $61,000 for the business but values the identifiable net assets at only $38,000, then the goodwill in B's books will be $61,000 – $38,000 = $23,000.

2.3 IFRS 3 *Business Combinations*

IFRS 3 covers the accounting treatment of goodwill acquired in a business combination.

It is possible to define goodwill in different ways. The IFRS 3 definition of goodwill is different from the more traditional definition and emphasises benefits, rather than the method of calculation.

> **Key term**
>
> **Goodwill.** An asset representing future economic benefits arising from other assets acquired in a business combination that are not individually identified and separately recognised. (IFRS 3)
>
> **Goodwill.** Any excess of the cost of acquisition over the acquirer's interest in the fair value of the identifiable assets and liabilities acquired as at the date of the exchange transaction. (Traditional)

Goodwill acquired in a business combination is **recognised as an asset** and is initially measured at **cost**. Cost is the excess of the cost of the combination plus the non-controlling interest less the net fair value of the acquiree's identifiable assets and liabilities.

After initial recognition goodwill acquired in a business combination is measured **at cost less any accumulated impairment losses**. It is **not amortised**. Instead it is tested for impairment at least annually, in accordance with IAS 36 *Impairment of Assets*.

2.3.1 Goodwill and non-controlling interests

IFRS 3 views the **group as an economic entity**. This means that it treats **all provides of equity including non-controlling interests as shareholders in the group**, even if they re not shareholders in the parent.

Thus goodwill attributable to the non-controlling interest may be recognised. (See also Chapter 6.)

2.3.2 Bargain purchase

A gain on a bargain purchase arises when the net of the acquisition-date amounts of the identifiable assets acquired and the liabilities assumed exceeds the consideration transferred (see Chapter 6). This difference is sometimes called **negative goodwill**.

A bargain purchase might arise, for example, in a business combination that is a forced sale in which the seller is acting under compulsion. However, the recognition or measurement exceptions for particular items may also result in recognising a gain (or change the amount of a recognised gain) on a bargain purchase.

Before recognising a gain on a bargain purchase, the acquirer must reassess whether it has correctly identified all of the assets acquired and all of the liabilities assumed and must recognise any additional assets or liabilities that are identified in that review. The acquirer must then review the procedures used to measure the amounts this IFRS requires to be recognised at the acquisition date for all of the following:

(a) The identifiable assets acquired and liabilities assumed

(b) The non-controlling interest in the accquiree, if any

(c) For a business combination achieved in stages, the acquirer's previously held interest in the acquiree

(d) The consideration transferred

The purpose of this review is to ensure that the measurements appropriately reflect all the available information as at the acquisition date.

Any excess (ie, negative goodwill) remaining should be **recognised immediately in profit or loss**.

IFRS 3 requires extensive **disclosures** about goodwill acquired in business combinations. These include a **reconciliation** of the carrying amount of goodwill at the beginning and end of the period, showing separately:

(a) The gross amount and accumulated impairment losses at the beginning of the period
(b) Additional goodwill recognised during the period
(c) Impairment losses recognised during the period
(d) Net exchange differences arising during the period, and
(e) The gross amount and accumulated impairment losses at the end of the period

Question — Characteristics of goodwill

What are the main characteristics of goodwill which distinguish it from other intangible non-current assets? To what extent do you consider that these characteristics should affect the accounting treatment of goodwill? State your reasons.

Answer

Goodwill may be distinguished from other intangible non-current assets by reference to the following characteristics.

(a) It is incapable of realisation separately from the business as a whole.

(b) Its value has no reliable or predictable relationship to any costs which may have been incurred.

(c) Its value arises from various intangible factors such as skilled employees, effective advertising or a strategic location. These indirect factors cannot be valued.

(d) The value of goodwill may fluctuate widely according to internal and external circumstances over relatively short periods of time.

(e) The assessment of the value of goodwill is highly subjective.

It could be argued that, because goodwill is so different from other intangible non-current assets, it does not make sense to account for it in the same way. Thus the capitalisation and amortisation treatment would not be acceptable. Furthermore, because goodwill is so difficult to value, any valuation may be misleading, and it is best eliminated from the statement of financial position altogether. However, there are strong arguments for treating it like any other intangible non-current asset. This issue remains controversial.

Chapter roundup

- **Intangible assets** are defined by **IAS 38** as non-monetary assets without physical substance. They must be:
    - **Identifiable**
    - **Controlled** as a result of a past event
    - Expected to provide **future economic benefits**

- An intangible asset is recognised in the financial statements where:
    - It is probable that future economic benefits attributable to the asset will flow to the entity; and
    - The cost can be measured reliably.

- **Internally-generated goodwill** cannot be recognised as an asset but other internally-generated assets may be, eg R & D.

- Intangible assets should initially be measured at cost, but subsequently they can be carried at **cost or at a fair value** measured in accordance with IFRS 13 *Fair Value Measurement*.

- **Impairment** rules follow **IAS 36**. There are substantial disclosure requirements.

- If a business has **goodwill**, it means that the value of the business is greater than the value of its identifiable net assets. The valuation of goodwill is extremely subjective and fluctuates constantly. For this reason, goodwill other than that acquired in a business combination is **not** shown as an asset in the statement of financial position.

- When someone **purchases a business**, the purchaser and vendor will fix an agreed price which may include an element in respect of goodwill. The way in which goodwill is then valued is not an accounting problem, but a matter of agreement between the two parties.

- **Goodwill acquired in a business combination** is then carried in the statement of financial position as an intangible asset under the requirements of **IFRS 3**. It must be reviewed for impairment annually.

Quick quiz

1. Internally generated goodwill can be recognised. True or false?
2. How should research and development costs be treated under IAS 38?
3. When can a revaluation surplus on intangible assets be transferred to retained earnings?
4. Over what period should an intangible asset normally be amortised?
5. How should the gain or loss on the disposal of an intangible asset be calculated?
6. Why is it unusual to record goodwill as an asset in the financial statements?
7. What is goodwill acquired in a business combination?
8. What method of accounting for goodwill acquired in a business combination is required by IFRS 3?
9. Over what period should goodwill be amortised?
10. What treatment does IFRS 3 prescribe for a gain on a bargain purchase?

Answers to quick quiz

1. False
2. - Research costs are recognised as an expense in profit or loss as they are incurred
   - Development costs should be recognised as intangible assets if the criteria in Section 1.7.2 are met
3. When the surplus is eventually realised
4. Over its useful life, which may be finite or indefinite
5. The difference between the net disposal proceeds and the carrying value
6. The value of goodwill is usually inherent in the business but does not have an 'objective' value
7. The excess of the consideration transferred plus the non-controlling interest over the identifiable net assets acquired
8. Cost less accumulated impairment losses
9. Goodwill should not be amortised
10. Before recognising a gain, measurement procedures for assets and liabilities and for consideration must be reviewed. Any gain remaining is recognised in profit or loss immediately

End of chapter question

Grimsel (AIA November 2007)

(a) Explain what is meant by 'component depreciation' and its status under International Accounting Standards. **(3 marks)**

(b) Trin, a limited liability company, owns its business premises. It has just installed extensive specialised machinery and fittings in the premises. The estimated remaining useful life is ten years for the building and six years for the machinery and fittings. Trin knows that decommissioning the machinery and fittings in six years' time will cost around $910,000 at current prices.

Required

Explain and justify how Trin should account for the costs of decommissioning its machinery and fittings. **(3 marks)**

(c) Cozz, a limited liability company, has an asset, purchased on 1 November 20X2, which was reported in its statement of financial position as at 1 November 20X6 as follows:

	$
Cost	240,000
Accumulated depreciation	118,000
	122,000

The accumulated depreciation figure is made up as follows:

	$
Four years' depreciation based on the asset's estimated life of 12 years	80,000
Impairment recognised during the year ended 31 October 20X5	20,000
Impairment recognised during the year ended 31 October 20X6	18,000
	118,000

As at 31 October 20X7 there was no change to the estimate of this asset's economic life or residual value. The asset's recoverable amount was estimated to be $125,000 as at 31 October 20X7. Cozz reports this class of assets at historical cost.

PART C ACCOUNTING AND REPORTING TECHNIQUES

Required

What charge will Cozz make in its statement of profit or loss and other comprehensive income for the year ended 31 October 20X7 for this asset and how will the asset be reported in the statement of financial position as at 31 October 20X7? **(6 marks)**

(d) The following is the summarised statement of financial position of Grimsel, a limited liability company, as at 31 October 20X7:

	$'000	$'000
ASSETS		
Non-current assets		
Property, plant and equipment		7,540
Current assets		
Inventory	2,230	
Receivables	4,120	
Cash	430	
		6,780
		14,320
LIABILITIES AND EQUITY		
Current liabilities		3,775
Non-current liabilities		12,500
Equity		
Issued share capital	5,000	
Accumulated losses	6,955	
		(1,955)
		14,320

Grimsel has been a very successful company in its time. However, a series of losses due to a declining share in the market and demands from its bankers for repayment of significant bank debt included in current and non-current liabilities have left its shareholders keen to sell.

Brenner, another limited liability company, operates in the same line of business as Grimsel. Brenner has been very successful and sees an opportunity to acquire Grimsel at a bargain price.

Brenner has successfully concluded negotiations with Grimsel and has agreed a price of $2,000,000 for all the issued share capital of Grimsel.

The following additional information is available:

(i) The values of all the assets and liabilities identified in Grimsel's statement of financial position were agreed as fair values for the purposes of the purchase with the exception of the following assets:

Fair values	$'000
Property, plant and equipment	8,000
Inventory	2,000
Receivables	3,710

(ii) Grimsel has a deferred income tax asset of $2,200,000. This is not shown in Grimsel's statement of financial position because it was unlikely that Grimsel would be able to recover this amount because of its continuing losses. Brenner is trading profitably in the same type of business and will be able to realise this benefit.

(iii) Grimsel has significant patents which were internally developed. These patents are still useful and a fair value of $1,000,000 has been established in accordance with IFRS 13.

(iv) Brenner will also take over Grimsel's customer list. This is a sensitive area. While the customer list was not of much value to Grimsel, the directors of Brenner feel that it could be of significant value but wish to continue keeping it off the statement of financial position. The fair value of the customer list to Brenner has been measured at $1,500,000 in accordance with IFRS 13.

Required

Applying the rules in IFRS 3 calculate the amount of goodwill arising on the acquisition of Grimsel by Brenner. **(8 marks)**

(e) Summarise the guidance in IFRS 3 when goodwill turns out to be a negative. **(5 marks)**

(Total 25 marks)

PART C ACCOUNTING AND REPORTING TECHNIQUES

Financial instruments

Topic list	Syllabus reference
1 Financial instruments	13.4
2 Presentation of financial instruments	13.4
3 Recognition of financial instruments	13.4
4 Measurement of financial instruments	13.4
5 Hedging	13.4
6 Embedded derivatives	13.4
7 Disclosure of financial instruments	13.4

Introduction

Financial instruments sounds like a daunting subject, and indeed this is a complex and controversial area. The numbers involved in financial instruments are often huge, but don't let this put you off. In this chapter we aim to simplify the topic as much as possible and to focus on the important issues.

The debate over **measurement and recognition** of financial instruments is very closely connected to the '**off balance sheet finance debate**' (see Chapter 21). Before the issue of IAS 32 and IAS 39 many financial instruments were not recognised or disclosed in financial statements at all.

IFRS 9 *Financial Instruments* was issued in final form in July 2014, replacing IAS 39.

1 Financial instruments

> **FAST FORWARD**
>
> Financial instruments can be very complex, particularly **derivative instruments**, although **primary instruments** are more straightforward.

1.1 Background

If you read the financial press you will probably be aware of **rapid international expansion** in the use of financial instruments. These vary from straightforward, traditional instruments, eg bonds, through to various forms of so-called 'derivative instruments'.

We can perhaps summarise the reasons why a project on the accounting for financial instruments was considered necessary as follows.

(a) The **significant growth of financial instruments** over recent years has outstripped the development of guidance for their accounting.

(b) The topic is of **international concern;** other national standard-setters are involved as well as the IASB.

(c) There have been **high-profile disasters** involving derivatives which, while not caused by accounting failures, raised questions about accounting and disclosure practices.

There are three accounting standards on financial instruments:

(a) IAS 32 *Financial Instruments: Presentation*, which deals with:

   (i) The classification of financial instruments between liabilities and equity
   (ii) Presentation of certain compound instruments

(b) IFRS 7 *Financial Instruments: Disclosures*, which revised, simplified and incorporated disclosure requirements previously in IAS 32.

(c) IFRS 9 *Financial instruments*, issued in final form in July 2014, replaces IAS 39 *Financial Instruments: Recognition and Measurement*. The standard covers:

   (i) Recognition and derecognition
   (ii) The measurement of financial instruments
   (iii) Impairment
   (iv) General hedge accounting (not macro hedge accounting, which is a separate IASB project, currently at the discussion paper stage)

IAS 32 provides the basic rules on the presentation of financial instruments, and IAS 39 / IFRS 9 build upon these. IAS 32 is therefore covered in Section 2 of this chapter.

1.2 Definitions

The most important definitions are relevant to all the standards.

> **FAST FORWARD**
>
> The important definitions to learn are:
> - **Financial asset**
> - **Financial liability**
> - **Equity instrument**

Key terms

> **Financial instrument.** Any contract that gives rise to both a financial asset of one entity and a financial liability or equity instrument of another entity.
>
> **Financial asset.** Any asset that is:
>
> (a) Cash;
>
> (b) An equity instrument of another entity;
>
> (c) A contractual right to receive cash or another financial asset from another entity; or to exchange financial instruments with another entity under conditions that are potentially favourable to the entity; or
>
> (d) A contract that will or may be settled in the entity's own equity instruments and is:
>
>   (i) A non-derivative for which the entity is or may be obliged to receive a variable number of the entity's own equity instruments; or
>
>   (ii) A derivative that will or may be settled other than by the exchange of a fixed amount of cash or another financial asset for a fixed number of the entity's own equity instruments.
>
> **Financial liability.** Any liability that is:
>
> (a) A contractual obligation:
>
>   (i) To deliver cash or another financial asset to another entity; or
>
>   (ii) To exchange financial instruments with another entity under conditions that are potentially unfavourable to the entity; or
>
> (b) A contract that will or may be settled in the entity's own equity instruments and is:
>
>   (i) A non-derivative for which the entity is or may be obliged to deliver a variable number of the entity's own equity instruments; or
>
>   (ii) A derivative that will or may be settled other than by the exchange of a fixed amount of cash or another financial asset for a fixed number of the entity's own equity instruments.
>
> **Equity instrument.** Any contract that evidences a residual interest in the assets of an entity after deducting all of its liabilities.
>
> **Fair value.** The price that would be received to sell an asset or paid to transfer a liability in an orderly transaction between market participants at the measurement date.
>
> **Derivative.** A financial instrument or other contract with all three of the following characteristics:
>
> (a) Its value changes in response to the change in a specified interest rate, financial instrument price, commodity price, foreign exchange rate, index of prices or rates, credit rating or credit index, or other variable (sometimes called the 'underlying');
>
> (b) It requires no initial net investment or an initial net investment that is smaller than would be required for other types of contracts that would be expected to have a similar response to changes in market factors; and
>
> (c) It is settled at a future date.   (IAS 32, IFRS 9 and IFRS 13)

We should clarify some points arising from these definitions. Firstly, one or two terms above should themselves be defined.

(a) A '**contract**' need not be in writing, but it must comprise an agreement that has 'clear economic consequences' and which the parties to it cannot avoid, usually because the agreement is enforceable in law.

(b) An '**entity**' here could be an individual, partnership, incorporated body or government agency.

1.2.1 Financial assets and liabilities

The definitions of **financial assets and financial liabilities** may seem rather circular, referring as they do to the terms financial asset and financial instrument. The point is that there may be a chain of contractual rights and obligations, but it will lead ultimately to the receipt or payment of cash **or** the acquisition or issue of an equity instrument.

Examples of **financial assets** include:

(a) Trade receivables
(b) Options
(c) Shares (when used as an investment).

Examples of **financial liabilities** include:

(a) Trade payables
(b) Debenture loans payable
(c) Redeemable preference (non-equity) shares
(d) Forward contracts standing at a loss.

As we have already noted, financial instruments include both of the following.

(a) **Primary instruments**: eg receivables, payables and equity securities

(b) **Derivative (or secondary) instruments**: eg financial options, futures and forwards, interest rate swaps and currency swaps, **whether recognised or unrecognised**.

IAS 32 makes it clear that the following items are **not** financial instruments:

- **Physical assets**, eg inventories, property, plant and equipment, leased assets and intangible assets (patents, trademarks etc). Where a contract is expected to be satisfied by **physical** delivery (eg of wheat or gold), it is **not** a financial instrument. This is known as the 'normal purchase/sale exemption'.

- **Prepaid expenses**, deferred revenue and most warranty obligations

- Liabilities or assets that are **not contractual** in nature

- Contractual rights/obligations that **do not involve transfer of a financial asset**, eg commodity futures contracts, operating leases

Question — Why not?

Can you give the reasons why the first two items listed above do not qualify as financial instruments?

Answer

Refer to the definitions of financial assets and liabilities given above.

(a) **Physical assets**: control of these creates an opportunity to generate an inflow of cash or other assets, but it does not give rise to a present right to receive cash or other financial assets.

(b) **Prepaid expenses, etc**: the future economic benefit is the receipt of goods/services rather than the right to receive cash or other financial assets.

(c) **Deferred revenue, warranty obligations**: the probable outflow of economic benefits is the delivery of goods/services rather than cash or another financial asset.

Contingent rights and obligations meet the definition of financial assets and financial liabilities respectively, even though many do not qualify for recognition in financial statements. The definition is met because the contractual rights or obligations exist because of a past transaction or event (eg assumption of a guarantee).

1.3 Derivatives

A **derivative** is a financial instrument that **derives** its value from the price or rate of an underlying item. Common **examples** of derivatives include the following:

(a) **Forward contracts**: agreements to buy or sell an asset at a fixed price at a fixed future date

(b) **Futures contracts**: similar to forward contracts except that contracts are standardised and traded on an exchange

(c) **Options**: rights (but not obligations) for the option holder to exercise at a pre-determined price; the option writer loses out if the option is exercised

(d) **Swaps**: agreements to swap one set of cash flows for another (normally interest rate or currency swaps).

The nature of derivatives often gives rise to **particular problems**. The **value** of a derivative (and the amount at which it is eventually settled) depends on **movements** in an underlying item (such as an exchange rate). This means that settlement of a derivative can lead to a very different result from the one originally envisaged. A company which has derivatives is exposed to **uncertainty and risk** (potential for gain or loss) and this can have a very material effect on its financial performance, financial position and cash flows.

Yet because a derivative contract normally has **little or no initial cost**, under traditional accounting it **may not be recognised** in the financial statements at all. Alternatively it may be recognised at an amount which bears no relation to its current value. This is clearly **misleading** and leaves users of the financial statements unaware of the **level of risk** that the company faces. IAS 32, IAS 39 and subsequently IFRS 9 were developed in order to correct this situation.

1.4 Section summary

- Three accounting standards are relevant:

    - **IFRS 9** *Financial Instruments*, now complete with the final version published in July 2014
    - **IAS 32** *Financial Instruments: Presentation*
    - **IFRS 7** *Financial Instruments: Disclosures*

- The definitions of **financial asset, financial liability** and **equity instrument** are fundamental to the standards.

- Financial instruments include:

    - **Primary** instruments
    - **Derivative** instruments

2 Presentation of financial instruments

2.1 Objective

The objective of IAS 32 is to establish principles for presenting financial instruments as liabilities or equity and for offsetting financial assets and financial liabilities. It applies to the classification of financial instruments, from the perspective of the issuer, into financial assets, financial liabilities and equity instruments; the classification of related interest, dividends, losses and gains; and the circumstances in which financial assets and financial liabilities should be offset.

2.2 Scope

IAS 32 should be applied in the presentation and disclosure of **all types of financial instruments**, whether recognised or unrecognised.

Certain items are **excluded**.

- Interests in subsidiaries (IFRS 10)
- Interests in associates (IAS 28)
- Interests in joint ventures (IAS 28, IFRS 11)
- Pensions and other post-retirement benefits (IAS 19)

unless the interest is accounted for under IAS 39/IFRS 9

- Insurance contracts (IFRS 4)
- Financial instruments, contracts and obligations under share-based payment transactions (IFRS 2)

2.3 Liabilities and equity

> **FAST FORWARD**
>
> A financial instrument must be classified as a **financial asset**, a **financial liability** or **equity** according to its **substance**.
>
> The critical feature of a financial liability is the **contractual obligation to deliver cash** or another financial asset.

The main principle of IAS 32 here is that financial instruments should be presented according to their **substance, not merely their legal form**. In particular, entities which issue financial instruments should classify them (or their component parts) as **either financial liabilities or equity**.

The classification of a financial instrument as a liability or as equity depends on the following:

- The **substance of the contractual arrangement** on initial recognition
- The definitions of a **financial liability** and an **equity instrument**

How should a **financial liability be distinguished from an equity instrument**? The critical feature of a **liability** is an **obligation** to transfer economic benefit. Therefore, a financial instrument is a financial liability if there is a **contractual obligation** on the issuer either to deliver cash or another financial asset to the holder or to exchange another financial instrument with the holder under potentially unfavourable conditions to the issuer.

The financial liability exists **regardless of the way in which the contractual obligation will be settled**. The issuer's ability to satisfy an obligation may be restricted, eg by lack of access to foreign currency, but this is irrelevant as it does not remove the issuer's obligation or the holder's right under the instrument.

Where the above critical feature is **not** met, then the financial instrument is an **equity instrument**. IAS 32 explains that although the holder of an equity instrument may be entitled to a *pro rata* share of any distributions out of equity, the issuer does **not** have a contractual obligation to make such a distribution.

Although substance and legal form are often **consistent with each other**, this is not always the case. In particular, a financial instrument may have the legal form of equity, but in substance it is in fact a liability. Other instruments may combine features of both equity instruments and financial liabilities.

For example, many entities issue **preference shares** which must be **redeemed** by the issuer for a fixed (or determinable) amount at a fixed (or determinable) future date. Alternatively, the holder may have the right to require the issuer to redeem the shares at or after a certain date for a fixed amount. In such cases, the issuer has an **obligation**. Therefore, the instrument is a **financial liability** and should be classified as such.

The classification of the financial instrument is made when it is **first recognised** and this classification will continue until the financial instrument is removed from the entity's statement of financial position.

2.4 Contingent settlement provisions

An entity may issue a financial instrument where the way in which it is settled depends on:

(a) The occurrence or non-occurrence of uncertain future events; or
(b) The outcome of uncertain circumstances;

that are beyond the control of both the holder and the issuer of the instrument. For example, an entity might have to deliver cash instead of issuing equity shares. In this situation it is not immediately clear whether the entity has an equity instrument or a financial liability.

Such financial instruments should be classified as **financial liabilities** because the issuer does not have an unconditional right to avoid settlement by delivery of cash or another financial asset, unless the possibility of settlement is remote.

2.5 Settlement options

When a derivative financial instrument gives one party a **choice** over how it is settled (eg the issuer can choose whether to settle in cash or by issuing shares) the instrument is a **financial asset** or a **financial liability** unless **all the alternative choices** would result in it being an equity instrument.

2.6 Compound financial instruments

> **FAST FORWARD**
>
> **Compound instruments** are split into **equity** and **liability** components and presented in the statement of financial position accordingly.

Some financial instruments contain both a liability and an equity element. In such cases, IAS 32 requires the component parts of the instrument to be **classified separately**, according to the substance of the contractual arrangement and the definitions of a financial liability and an equity instrument.

One of the most common types of compound instrument is **convertible debt**. This creates a primary financial liability of the issuer and grants an option to the holder of the instrument to convert it into an equity instrument (usually ordinary shares) of the issuer. This is the economic equivalent of the issue of conventional debt plus a warrant to acquire shares in the future.

Although in theory there are several possible ways of calculating the split, the following method is recommended:

(a) Calculate the value for the liability component.
(b) Deduct this from the instrument's carrying value as a whole to leave a residual value for the equity component.

The reasoning behind this approach is that an entity's equity is its residual interest in its assets amount after deducting all of its liabilities.

The **sum of the carrying amounts** assigned to liability and equity will always be equal to the carrying amount that would be ascribed to the instrument **as a whole**.

2.7 Example: Valuation of compound instruments

Rathbone Co issues 2,000 convertible bonds at the start of 20X2. The bonds have a three-year term, and are issued at par with a face value of $1,000 per bond, giving total proceeds of $2,000,000. Interest is payable annually in arrears at a nominal annual interest rate of 6%. Each bond is convertible at any time up to maturity into 250 common shares.

When the bonds are issued, the prevailing market interest rate for similar debt without conversion options is 9%. At the issue date, the market price of one common share is $3. The dividends expected over the three-year term of the bonds amount to 14c per share at the end of each year. The risk-free annual interest rate for a three-year term is 5%.

Required

What is the value of the equity component in the bond?

Solution

The liability component is valued first, and the difference between the proceeds of the bond issue and the fair value of the liability is assigned to the equity component. The present value of the liability component is calculated using a discount rate of 9%, the market interest rate for similar bonds having no conversion rights, as shown.

	$
Present value of the principal: $2,000,000 payable at the end of three years ($2m × 0.772)*	1,544,000
Present value of the interest: $120,000 payable annually in arrears for three years ($120,000 × 2.531)*	303,725
Total liability component	1,847,720
Equity component (balancing figure)	152,280
Proceeds of the bond issue	2,000,000

* These figures can be obtained from discount and annuity tables.

The split between the liability and equity components remains the same throughout the term of the instrument, even if there are changes in the **likelihood of the option being exercised**. This is because it is not always possible to predict how a holder will behave. The issuer continues to have an obligation to make future payments until conversion, maturity of the instrument or some other relevant transaction takes place.

Question — Definite variables

On 1 January 20X1, EFG issued 10,000 5% convertible bonds at their par value of $50 each. The bonds will be redeemed on 1 January 20X6. Each bond is convertible at the option of the holder at any time during the five year period. Interest on the bond will be paid annually in arrears.

The prevailing market interest rate for similar debt without conversion options at the date of issue was 6%.

At what value should the equity element of the financial instrument be recognised in the financial statements of EFG at the date of issue?

Answer

Top tip. The method to use here is to find the present value of the principal value of the bond, $500,000 (10,000 × $50) and the interest payments of $25,000 annually (5% × $500,000) at the market rate for non-convertible bonds of 6%, using discount factor tables. The difference between this total and the principal amount of $500,000 is the equity element.

	$
Present value of principal $500,000 × 0.747	373,500
Present value of interest $25,000 × 4.212	105,300
Liability value	478,800
Principal amount	500,000
Equity element	21,200

2.8 Treasury shares

If an entity **reacquires its own equity instruments**, those instruments ('treasury shares') shall be **deducted from equity**. No gain or loss shall be recognised in profit or loss on the purchase, sale, issue or cancellation of an entity's own equity instruments. Consideration paid or received shall be recognised directly in equity.

2.9 Interest, dividends, losses and gains

As well as looking at statement of financial position presentation, IAS 32 considers how financial instruments affect the statement of profit or loss and other comprehensive income (and movements in equity). The treatment varies according to whether interest, dividends, losses or gains relate to a financial liability or an equity instrument.

(a) Interest, dividends, losses and gains relating to a financial instrument (or component part) classified as a **financial liability** should be recognised as **income or expense** in profit or loss.

(b) Distributions to holders of a financial instrument classified as an **equity instrument** should be **debited directly to equity** by the issuer.

(c) **Transaction costs** of an equity transaction (when an entity issues or acquires its own equity) shall be accounted for as a **deduction from equity** (unless they are directly attributable to the acquisition of a business, in which case they are accounted for under IFRS 3).

You should look at the requirements of IAS 1 *Presentation of Financial Statements* for further details of disclosure.

2.10 Offsetting a financial asset and a financial liability

A financial asset and financial liability should **only** be **offset**, with the net amount reported in the statement of financial position, when an entity:

(a) Has a **legally enforceable right of set off**; and

(b) Intends to settle on a **net basis**, or to realise the asset and settle the liability simultaneously, ie at the same moment.

This will reflect the expected **future cash flows** of the entity in these specific circumstances. In all other cases, financial assets and financial liabilities are presented separately.

2.11 Section summary

- Financial instruments issued to raise capital must be classified as **liabilities** or **equity**.
- The **substance** of the financial instrument is more important than its **legal form**.
- The **critical feature of a financial liability** is the contractual obligation to deliver cash or another financial instrument.
- **Compound instruments** are split into equity and liability parts and presented accordingly.
- **Interest, dividends, losses and gains** are treated according to whether they relate to an equity instrument or a financial liability.

Question
Classification

During the financial year ended 28 February 20X5, MN issued the two financial instruments described below. For **each** of the instruments, identify whether it should be classified as a financial liability or equity, **explaining in not more than 40 words each** the reason for your choice. In each case you should refer to the relevant International Accounting Standard or International Financial Reporting Standard.

(i) Redeemable preferred shares with a coupon rate 8%; the shares are redeemable on 28 February 20X9 at premium of 10%.

(ii) A grant of share options to senior executives; the options may be exercised from 28 February 20X8.

Answer

(i) **Financial liability**. The preference shares require regular distributions to the holders but more importantly have the debt characteristic of being redeemable. Therefore according to IAS 32 *Financial Instruments: Presentation* they must be classified as debt.

(ii) **Equity.** According to IFRS 2 *Share-based Payment* the grant of share options must be recorded as equity in the statement of financial position. It is an alternative to cash as a method of payment for the provision of services by the directors.

Note. IAS 32 requires that if the holder of a financial instrument can require the issuer to redeem it for cash or another financial asset ('puttable instrument') it should be classified as a liability. Some ordinary shares and partnership interests allow the holder to 'put' the instrument (that is to require the issuer to redeem it in cash). Such shares might more usually be considered as equity, but application of IAS 32 results in their being classified as liabilities.

However, IAS 32 allows entities to classify such instruments as equity, so long as they meet certain conditions, ie because they represent a residual interest in the net assets of the entity. It further requires that instruments imposing an obligation on an entity to deliver to another party a pro rata share of the net assets only on liquidation should be classified as equity.

3 Recognition of financial instruments

> **FAST FORWARD**
>
> IFRS 9 states that **all financial assets and liabilities** should be **recognised in the statement of financial position, including derivatives.**

IFRS 9 *Financial Instruments* establishes principles for recognising and measuring financial assets and liabilities.

3.1 Scope

IFRS 9 applies to **all entities** and to **all types of financial instruments except** those specifically excluded, as listed below.

(a) Investments in **subsidiaries, associates, and joint ventures** that are accounted for under IFRS 10, IAS 27 or IAS 28.

(b) **Leases** covered in IFRS 16

(c) **Employee benefit plans** covered in IAS 19

(d) Equity instruments **issued by the entity** eg ordinary shares issued, or options and warrants

(e) **Insurance contracts** covered in IFRS 4

(f) Any **forward contracts between an acquirer and a selling shareholder** to buy or sell an acquiree **that will result in a business combination at a future acquisition date** covered under IFRS 3.

(g) **Loan commitments** that cannot be settled net in cash or another financial instrument

(h) Financial instruments, contracts and obligations under **share-based payment transactions**, covered in IFRS 2

(i) Rights to payments to reimburse the entity for expenditure it is required to make to settle a liability recognised as a provision under IAS 37

(j) Rights and obligations within the scope of IFRS 15.

3.2 Initial recognition

IFRS 9 requires that financial instruments are recognised in the statement of financial position when the entity becomes a party to the **contractual provisions of the instrument.**

Point to note

An important consequence of this is that all derivatives should be included in the statement of financial position.

Notice that this is **different** from the recognition criteria in the *Conceptual Framework* and in most other standards. Items are normally recognised when there is a probable inflow or outflow of resources and the item has a cost or value that can be measured reliably.

3.2.1 Example: Initial recognition

An entity has entered into two separate contracts.

(a) A firm commitment (an order) to buy a specific quantity of iron.

(b) A forward contract to buy a specific quantity of iron at a specified price on a specified date, provided delivery of the iron is not taken.

Contract (a) is a **normal trading contract**. The entity does not recognise a liability for the iron until the goods have actually been delivered. (Note that this contract is not a financial instrument because it involves a physical asset, rather than a financial asset.)

Contract (b) is a **financial instrument**. Under IFRS 9, the entity recognises a financial liability (an obligation to deliver cash) on the **commitment date**, rather than waiting for the closing date on which the exchange takes place.

Note that planned future transactions, no matter how likely, are not assets and liabilities of an entity – the entity has not yet become a party to the contract.

3.2.2 Classification of financial assets

IFRS 9 requires that on recognition financial assets are classified as measured at either:

- **Amortised cost;**
- **Fair value through other comprehensive income;** or
- **Fair value through profit or loss**

This classification is made on the basis of both:

(a) The **entity's business model** for managing the financial assets; and
(b) The **contractual cash flow** characteristics of the financial asset.

A financial asset is classified as measured at **amortised cost** where:

(a) The objective of the business model within which the asset is held is to hold assets in order to collect contractual cash flows; **and**

(b) The contractual terms of the financial asset give rise on specified dates to cash flows that are solely payments of principal and interest on the principal amount outstanding.

All other financial assets are measured at fair value.

A financial asset must be classified and measured at **fair value through other comprehensive income** (unless designated at inception as at fair value through profit or loss) if it meets both of the following criteria:

(a) The financial asset is held within a business model whose objective is achieved by **both** collecting contractual cash flows and selling financial assets; and

(b) The contractual terms of the financial asset give rise on specified dates to cash flows that are solely payments of principal and interest.

All other debt instruments must be measured at fair value through profit or loss.

An application of these rules means that:

- **Equity investments** may not be classified as measured at amortised cost and must be measured at measured at **fair value through profit and loss**. This is because contractual cash flows on specified dates are not a characteristic of equity instruments. However, if an equity investment is **not held for**

trading, an entity can make an irrevocable election at initial recognition to measure it at **fair value through other comprehensive income** with only dividend income recognised in profit or loss.

- **Derivatives** are measured at fair value.
- **Debt instruments** may be classified as measured at either amortised cost or fair value depending on whether they meet the criteria above. For example, a debt instrument that is held for trading would be measured at fair value through profit or loss. The objective of holding the asset is to realise a short-term gain (a change in fair value), not to receive payments of interest and principal (the contractual cash flows).

Even where the criteria are met at initial recognition, a debt instrument may be classified (irrevocably) as measured at fair value through profit or loss if doing so eliminates or significantly reduces a **measurement or recognition inconsistency** (sometimes referred to as an 'accounting mismatch') that would otherwise arise from measuring assets or liabilities or recognising the gains and losses on them on different bases.

The IFRS 9 requirement to classify financial assets on recognition as one of three types is a significant simplification of the previous IAS 39 rules. These required financial assets to be classified as one of four types, being:

- Fair value through profit or loss
- Held to maturity
- Available for sale, and
- Loans and receivables

3.2.3 Classification of financial liabilities

On initial **recognition**, IFRS 9 requires that financial liabilities are **classified as measured at** either:

- Fair value through profit or loss; or
- Amortised cost

Where the liability is measured at amortised cost, transaction costs are deducted from the initial measurement.

A financial liability is classified as fair value through profit or loss if:

(a) It is held for trading; or

(b) Upon initial recognition it is irrevocably designated as fair value through profit or loss. This is permitted when it results in more relevant information because:

    (i) It eliminates or significantly reduces a measurement or recognition inconsistency ('accounting mismatch'); or

    (ii) It is a group of financial liabilities or financial assets and liabilities and its performance is evaluated on a fair value basis, in accordance with a documented risk management or investment strategy.

Derivatives are always measured at fair value through profit or loss.

3.2.4 Re-classification of financial instruments

On initial recognition, financial assets must be classified in accordance with IFRS 9. In some cases they may be subsequently reclassified.

IFRS 9 requires that when an entity changes its business model for managing financial assets, it should reclassify all affected financial assets. This reclassification applies only to debt instruments, as equity instruments must be classified as measured at fair value.

IFRS 9 prohibits the reclassification of financial liabilities.

The Application guidance to IFRS 9 includes examples of circumstances when a reclassification is required or is not permitted.

3.3 Derecognition

Derecognition is the removal of a previously recognised financial instrument from an entity's statement of financial position. IFRS 9 provides the rules relating to the derecognition of both financial assets and financial liabilities.

3.3.1 Derecognition of financial assets

An entity should derecognise a **financial asset** when:

(a) The **contractual rights** to the cash flows from the financial asset **expire**; or

(b) The entity **transfers substantially all the risks and rewards of ownership** of the financial asset to another party.

Question — Risks and rewards

Can you think of an example of a situation in which:

(a) An entity has transferred substantially all the risks and rewards of ownership?
(b) An entity has retained substantially all the risks and rewards of ownership?

Answer

IFRS 9 includes the following examples:

(a) (i) An unconditional sale of a financial asset
    (ii) A sale of a financial asset together with an option to repurchase the financial asset at its fair value at the time of repurchase

(b) (i) A sale and repurchase transaction where the repurchase price is a fixed price or at the sale price plus a lender's return
    (ii) A sale of a financial asset together with a total return swap that transfers the market risk exposure back to the entity

Exam focus point: The principle here is that of **substance over form**.

3.3.2 Derecognition of financial liabilities

An entity should derecognise a **financial liability** when it is **extinguished** – ie, when the obligation specified in the contract is discharged or cancelled or expires.

Where an existing borrower and lender exchange one financial liability for another with substantially different terms, this is accounted for as an extinguishment of the original financial liability and recognition of a new financial liability.

Equally a substantial modification of the terms of an existing financial liability (or part of it) is accounted for as an extinguishment of the original financial liability and recognition of a new financial liability.

A modification is substantial where the discounted present value of cash flows under the new terms, discounted using the original effective interest rate, is at least 10% different from the discounted present value of the cash flows of the original financial liability.

3.3.3 Partial derecognition

It is possible for only **part** of a financial asset or liability to be derecognised. This is allowed if the part comprises:

(a) Only specifically identified cash flows; or
(b) Only a fully proportionate (*pro rata*) share of the total cash flows.

For example, if an entity holds a bond it has the right to two separate sets of cash inflows: those relating to the principal and those relating to the interest. It could sell the right to receive the interest to another party while retaining the right to receive the principal.

3.3.4 Gain or loss on derecognition

On derecognition, the amount to be included in profit or loss for the period is calculated as follows:

Formula to learn

	$	$
Carrying amount of asset/liability (or the portion of asset/liability) transferred	X	
Less: Proceeds received/paid	X	
Any cumulative gain or loss reported as other comprehensive income	X	
		(X)
Difference to profit or loss		X

Where only part of a financial asset is derecognised, the carrying amount of the asset should be allocated between the part retained and the part transferred based on their relative fair values on the date of transfer. A gain or loss should be recognised based on the proceeds for the portion transferred.

3.4 Section summary

- **All financial assets** and **liabilities** should be **recognised in the statement of financial position**, including derivatives.
- **Financial assets** should be classified as measured at either amortised cost, fair value though other comprehensive income or fair value through profit or loss when first recognised.
- **Financial liabilities** should be classified as either fair value through profit or loss or measured at amortised cost when first recognised.
- In limited circumstances reclassifications of financial assets can be made.
- Financial assets should be derecognised when the rights to the cash flows from the asset expire or where substantially all the risks and rewards of ownership are transferred to another party.
- Financial liabilities should be derecognised when they are extinguished.

4 Measurement of financial instruments

Financial instruments should initially be measured at **fair value** (which is usually, but not always equal to cost). Subsequently they are measured in accordance with IFRS 9 classification.

Throughout this section, there are several references to the measurement of financial instruments at **fair value**. Financial instruments fall within the scope of IFRS 13 *Fair Value Measurement* and therefore fair value is established by reference to the requirements of this standard. Detailed guidance can be found in Chapter 11.

4.1 Initial measurement

Financial instruments are initially measured at their **fair value**. This is usually, but not always, equal to the transaction price (ie consideration given or received).

An **exception** is where part of the consideration given is for something other than the financial asset. In this case, for example, a financial asset is initially measured at fair value as evidenced by a quoted price in an active market for an identical asset (ie an IFRS 13 level 1 input) or based on a valuation technique that uses only data from observable markets. The difference between the fair value at initial recognition and the transaction price is recognised as a gain or loss.

In the case of financial instruments classified as measured at **amortised cost, transaction costs** that are **directly attributable** to the acquisition or issue of the financial instrument increase this amount for a financial asset and decrease this amount for a financial liability.

4.2 Subsequent measurement of financial assets

Under IFRS 9, financial assets are measured subsequent to recognition at:

- **Amortised cost** with interest recognised in profit or loss;
- **Fair value** with changes in value recognised in **other comprehensive income** for debt instruments meeting the criteria;
- **Fair value** with changes in value recognised in other comprehensive income for equity instruments where the election has been made; or
- **Fair value** with changes in value normally recognised in **profit or loss**.

> **Exam focus point**
>
> Remember, derivatives **must** be remeasured to fair value. This is because it would be misleading to measure them at cost.

4.2.1 Financial assets measured at fair value

Where a financial asset is classified as measured at fair value, fair value is established at each period end using the methods prescribed by IFRS 13 *Fair Value Measurement*.

4.2.2 Example: Equity investment not held for trading

On 6 May 20X8 Embsay Co acquires an equity investment with the intention of holding it in the long-term and elects to recognise changes in fair value in other comprehensive income. The investment cost $500,000, which was its fair value at the acquisition date. At Embsay Co's year end of 31 December 20X8, the fair value of the investment is $545,000. How is the asset initially and subsequently measured?

Solution

- The asset is initially recognised at the fair value of the consideration, being $500,000
- At the period end its fair value is remeasured to $545,000
- This results in the recognition of $45,000 in other comprehensive income.

4.2.3 Financial assets measured at amortised cost

> **Key terms**
>
> **Amortised cost** of a financial asset or financial liability is the amount at which the financial asset or liability is measured at initial recognition minus principal repayments, plus or minus the cumulative amortisation using the effective interest method of any difference between that initial amount and the maturity amount, and for financial assets, adjusted for any loss allowance.
>
> The **effective interest method** is the method that is used in the calculation of the amortised cost of a financial asset or a financial liability and in the allocation and recognition of the interest revenue or interest expense in profit or loss over the relevant period.
>
> The **effective interest rate** is the rate that exactly discounts estimated future cash payments or receipts through the expected life of the financial asset or financial liability to the gross carrying amount of a financial asset or to the amortised cost of a financial liability.
>
> (IFRS 9)

4.2.4 Example: Financial asset at amortised cost

On 1 January 20X1 Abacus Co purchases a debt instrument for its fair value of $1,000. The debt instrument is due to mature on 31 December 20X5 and will be redeemed at par. The instrument has a principal amount of $1,250 and the instrument carries fixed interest at 4.72% that is paid annually. The effective interest rate is 10%.

How should Abacus Co account for the debt instrument over its five year term?

Solution

Abacus Co will receive interest of $59 ($1,250 × 4.72%) each year and $1,250 when the instrument matures.

Abacus must allocate the discount of $250 and the interest receivable over the five year term at a constant rate on the carrying amount of the debt. To do this, it must apply the effective interest rate of 10%.

The following table shows the allocation over the years.

Year	Amortised cost at beginning of year $	Statement of profit or loss: Interest income for year (@10%) $	Interest received during year (cash inflow) $	Amortised cost at end of year $
20X1	1,000	100	(59)	1,041
20X2	1,041	104	(59)	1,086
20X3	1,086	109	(59)	1,136
20X4	1,136	113	(59)	1,190
20X5	1,190	119	(1,250 + 59)	–

Each year the carrying amount of the financial asset is increased by the interest income for the year and reduced by the interest actually received during the year.

4.3 Subsequent measurement of financial liabilities

After initial recognition, all financial liabilities should be measured at **amortised cost**, with the exception of financial liabilities at fair value through profit or loss (including most derivatives). These should be measured at **fair value**, but where the fair value **is not capable of reliable measurement**, they should be measured at **cost**.

4.3.1 Financial liabilities measured at amortised cost

The definitions seen above in relation to financial assets at amortised cost remain relevant here. Again, their application is best seen through examples.

Question — Financial liabilities measured at amortised cost 1

Galaxy Co issues a bond for $503,778 on 1 January 20X2. No interest is payable on the bond, but it will be redeemed on 31 December 20X4 for $600,000. The bond has **not** been designated as at fair value through profit or loss.

Required

Calculate the charge to the statement of profit or loss of Galaxy Co for the year ended 31 December 20X2 and the balance outstanding at 31 December 20X2.

Answer

The bond is a 'deep discount' bond and is a financial liability of Galaxy Co. It is measured at amortised cost. Although there is no interest as such, the difference between the initial cost of the bond and the price at which it will be redeemed is a finance cost. This must be allocated over the term of the bond at a constant rate on the carrying amount.

To calculate amortised cost we need to calculate the effective interest rate of the bond:

$\dfrac{600{,}000}{503{,}778} = 1.191$ over three years

To calculate an annual rate, we take the cube root, $(1.191)^{1/3} = 1.06$, so the annual interest rate is 6%.

The charge to profit or loss for the year ended 31 December 20X2 is $30,226 ($503,778 × 6%).

The balance outstanding at 31 December 20X2 is $534,004 ($503,778 + $30,226).

Question — Financial liabilities measured at amortised cost 2

On 1 January 20X3 Deferred issued $600,000 loan notes. Issue costs were $200. The loan notes do not carry interest, but are redeemable at a premium of $152,389 on 31 December 20X4. The effective finance cost of the debentures is 12%.

What is the finance cost in respect of the loan notes for the year ended 31 December 20X4?

- A $72,000
- B $76,194
- C $80,613
- D $80,640

Answer

C   The premium on redemption of the preferred shares represents a finance cost. The effective rate of interest must be applied so that the debt is measured at amortised cost (IFRS 9).

At the time of issue, the loan notes are recognised at their net proceeds of $599,800 ($600,000 − $200).

The finance cost for the year ended 31 December 20X4 is $80,613, calculated as follows:

	B/f $	Interest @ 12% $	C/f $
20X3	599,800	71,976	671,776
20X4	671,776	80,613	752,389

Question: Financial liabilities measured at amortised cost 3

On 1 January 20X5, an entity issued a debt instrument with a coupon rate of 3.5% at a par value of $6,000,000. The directly attributable costs of issue were $120,000. The debt instrument is repayable on 31 December 20Y1 at a premium of $1,100,000.

What is the total amount of the finance cost associated with the debt instrument?

- A $1,470,000
- B $1,590,000
- C $2,570,000
- D $2,690,000

Answer

D

Issue costs	120,000
Interest $6,000,000 × 3.5% × 7 years	1,470,000
Premium on redemption	1,100,000
Total finance cost	2,690,000

4.3.2 Financial liabilities measured at fair value through profit or loss

Financial liabilities which are held for trading and classified as fair value through profit or loss are remeasured to fair value each year in accordance with IFRS 13 *Fair Value Measurement* with any gain or loss recognised in profit or loss.

Question: Financial liabilities: subsequent measurement

After initial recognition, all financial liabilities should be measured at amortised cost.

True ☐
False ☐

Answer

False. Financial liabilities classified as at fair value through profit or loss should be measured at fair value, unless this is not reliable, in which case they should be measured at amortised cost.

4.4 Impairment and uncollectability of financial assets

The impairment model in IFRS 9 is based on the premise of providing for expected losses (rather than only recognising losses after an event has occurred). The amount of expected credit losses is updated at each reporting date to reflect changes in credit risk since initial recognition.

4.4.1 Example

Artabank issues a 10 year loan for $10 million on 1 January 20X1. Artabank considers the risk associated with comparable instruments (ie ones with similar credit risk) using information at its disposal including general financial and economic data. Based on its analysis, Artabank estimates that the loan at initial recognition has a probability of default of 0.5% over the next 12 months.

At the reporting date (before payment on the loan is due), there has been no change in the probability of default over 12 months and there has been no change in credit risk. If the customer defaults, Artabank has estimated that in the event of a default, it will be able to recover 60% of the loan amount.

Requirement

Calculate the loss allowance based on the expected losses over a 12 month period.

Solution

The loss allowance is 0.5% × 40% × $10,000,000 = $20,000.

4.5 Exceptions to treatment of liabilities

The exceptions to the above treatment of financial liabilities are:

(a) It is part of a hedging arrangement (see Section 5)

(b) It is a financial liability designated as at fair value through profit or loss and the entity is required to present the effects of changes in the liability's **credit risk** in other comprehensive income (see 4.4.1 below).

4.5.1 Credit risk

IFRS 9 requires that financial liabilities which are **designated as measured at fair value through profit or loss are treated differently**. In this case the gain or loss in a period must be classified into:

- Gain or loss **resulting from credit risk**; and
- **Other** gain or loss.

This provision of IFRS 9 was in response to an anomaly regarding changes in the credit risk of a financial liability.

Changes in a financial liability's credit risk affect the fair value of that financial liability. This means that when an entity's creditworthiness deteriorates, the fair value of its issued debt will decrease (and *vice versa*). For financial liabilities measured using the fair value option, this causes **a gain (or loss) to be recognised in profit or loss for the year**. For example:

STATEMENT OF PROFIT OR LOSS AND OTHER COMPREHENSIVE INCOME (EXTRACT)
PROFIT OR LOSS FOR THE YEAR

	$'000
Liabilities at fair value (except derivatives and liabilities held for trading)	
Change in fair value	100
Profit (loss) for the year	100

Many users of financial statements found this result to be **counter-intuitive** and confusing. Accordingly, IFRS 9 requires the gain or loss as a result of credit risk to be recognised in other comprehensive income, unless it creates or enlarges an **accounting mismatch**, in which case it is recognised in profit or loss. The other gain or loss (not the result of credit risk) is recognised in profit or loss.

On derecognition any gains or losses recognised in other comprehensive income are **not** transferred to **profit or loss**, although the cumulative gain or loss may be transferred within equity.

4.5.2 Example

On 1 July 20X3 Bravo plc issued 8% 10 year redeemable bonds at their par value of $10,000,000. LIBOR is used as a benchmark rate by Bravo and the coupon rate for these bonds was based on LIBOR plus 7%. LIBOR was 1% at 1 July 2013 and was 0.75% at 30 June 20X4. At 30 June 2014, the market value of the bonds was $10,254,000, implying an interest rate of 7.6%.

Required

Calculate and explain the amounts to be shown in the financial statements of Bravo plc for the year ended 30 June 20X4 in respect of the bonds issued.

Solution

(1) Compute the liability's internal rate of return at the start of the period using the observed market price of the liability and the liability's contractual cash flows at the start of the period. Deduct from this rate of return the observed (benchmark) interest rate at the start of the period, to arrive at an instrument-specific component of the internal rate of return.

(2) Calculate the present value of the cash flows associated with the liability using the liability's contractual cash flows at the end of the period and a discount rate equal to the sum of (i) the observed (benchmark) interest rate at the end of the period and (ii) the instrument-specific component of the internal rate of return.

(3) The difference between the observed market price of the liability at the end of the period and the amount determined above is the change in fair value that is not attributable to changes in the observed (benchmark) interest rate. This is the amount to be presented in other comprehensive income.

At 1 July 20X3 the interest rate offered by the bonds is 8%. This consists of LIBOR – 1% – plus an instrument-specific component of 7%. The market value at 30 June 20X4 implies an interest rate of 7.6% (this can be calculated as the internal rate of return of the cash flows). This reflects a decrease of 0.25 percentage points in LIBOR and an increase in credit risk (assuming no other changes), as explained below.

Interest rate at 1 July 20X3	8.00%
Decrease in LIBOR	–0.25%
Implied change in credit risk (balancing figure)	–0.15%
Interest rate at 30 June 20X4	7.60%

	$'000	$'000
Market value at 30 June 20X4	10,254	
PV of future cashflows at instrument specific rate (W1)	10,160	
Increase in liability to be presented in OCI		94
Market value at 1 July 20X3	10,000	
Increase in liability to be presented in profit or loss		160
Total increase		254

(W1) The discount rate to be used is equal to the sum of (i) the observed (benchmark) interest rate at the end of the period ie 0.75% and (ii) the instrument-specific component of the internal rate of return. This gives a discount rate of 0.75% plus 7.00% = 7.75%. The present value of contractual cashflows is as follows:

Time	Cash $'000	DR 7.75%	PV $'000
1 – 9	800	6.312	5,050
9	10,000	0.511	5,110
			10,160

4.6 Section summary

- Financial instruments are initially measured at fair value. Where financial instruments are classified as measured at amortised cost, transaction costs increase this amount for financial assets and decrease this amount for financial liabilities.

- Financial assets are subsequently measured at:
  - Fair value with changes in value recognised in other comprehensive income
  - Fair value with changes in value recognised in profit or loss, or
  - Amortised cost with interest recognised in profit or loss

- Financial liabilities are subsequently measured at fair value or amortised cost with gains and losses recognised in profit or loss

5 Hedging

FAST FORWARD

Hedge accounting is allowed in certain strictly defined circumstances.

5.1 Introduction

IFRS 9 **requires hedge accounting** where there is a **designated hedging relationship** between a hedging instrument and a hedged item. It is **prohibited otherwise**.

Key terms

Hedging, for accounting purposes, means designating one or more hedging instruments so that their change in fair value is an offset, in whole or in part, to the change in fair value or cash flows of a hedged item.

A **hedged item** is an asset, liability, firm commitment, or forecasted future transaction that:

(a) Exposes the entity to risk of changes in fair value or changes in future cash flows, and that
(b) Is designated as being hedged.

A **hedging instrument** is a designated derivative or (in limited circumstances) another financial asset or liability whose fair value or cash flows are expected to offset changes in the fair value or cash flows of a designated hedged item. (A non-derivative financial asset or liability may be designated as a hedging instrument for hedge accounting purposes only if it hedges the risk of changes in foreign currency exchange rates.)

Hedge effectiveness is the degree to which changes in the fair value or cash flows of the hedged item attributable to a hedged risk are offset by changes in the fair value or cash flows of the hedging instrument.

(IFRS 9)

In simple terms, entities hedge to reduce their exposure to risk and uncertainty, such as changes in prices, interest rates or foreign exchange rates. Hedge accounting recognises hedging relationships by allowing (for example) losses on a hedged item to be offset against gains on a hedging instrument.

Generally only assets, liabilities etc that involve external parties can be designated as hedged items. The foreign currency risk of an intragroup monetary item (eg payable/receivable between two subsidiaries) may qualify as a hedged item in the group financial statements if it results in an exposure to foreign exchange rate gains or losses that are not fully eliminated on consolidation. This can happen (per IAS 21) when the transaction is between entities with different functional currencies.

In addition, the foreign currency risk of a highly probable group transaction may qualify as a hedged item if it is in a currency other than the functional currency of the entity and the foreign currency risk will affect profit or loss.

5.2 IFRS 9's new model for hedge accounting

The hedge accounting rules in IFRS 9's predecessor, IAS 39 *Financial Instruments: Recognition and Measurement*, were criticised as being complex and not reflecting the entity's risk management activities, nor the extent to which they are successful. The IASB addressed these issues in IFRS 9 and the revised rules appear in the July 2014 version of the standard.

5.2.1 Why change the hedge accounting requirements?

(a) **The IAS 39 provisions were not based on consistent principles.** The provisions were rules-based, which led to inconsistency and arbitrariness.

(b) **The IAS 39 rules did not provide sufficient information on risk management.** Increasingly users of financial statements have said that they wish to understand the risks that an entity faces, and the entity's strategy in managing those risks. Many believed that the IAS 39 requirements did not provide such an understanding.

(c) **The IAS 39 rules on hedging did not reflect risk management practice.** For example:

  (i) **There were instances where hedge accounting cannot be applied to groups of items, whereas for risk management purposes, items are often hedged on a group basis.** One example of this is equities making up an index such as the FTSE 100. These have an apparent economic link, but under the IAS 39 rules they could not be grouped together for hedging purposes, because they did not have similar risk characteristics.

  (ii) IAS 39 did not allow components of non-financial items to be hedged but entities usually hedge components of such items. For instance, an entity may wish to hedge the oil price component of the jet fuel price exposure by entering into a forward contract for crude oil. Under the IAS 39 rules, the entity could only hedge the price of jet fuel itself or the foreign currency risk.

  (iii) IAS 39 did not allow net positions to be hedged. However, companies often hedge net positions. For example, they may hedge a net foreign exchange position of $60m that is made up of an asset of $200m and a liability of $140m.

(d) IAS 39's rules **were confusing and complex**.

(e) IAS 39's rules provided **insufficient disclosures** in the financial statements about an entity's risk management activities.

(f) IAS 39 permitted hedge accounting only if a hedge is highly effective, both prospectively and retrospectively. IAS 39 regarded a hedge as highly effective if the offset is within the range of 80 to 125%. This was a purely quantitative test and has been felt to be narrow and arbitrary.

5.2.2 Principles-based model

IFRS 9 contains a new, **principles based model** for hedge accounting that aims to **align accounting with risk management activities**. This will combine the following.

(a) A **management view**, that aims to use information produced internally for risk management purposes,

(b) An **accounting view** that seeks to address the risk management issue of the timing of recognition of gains and losses.

(c) An **objective-based assessment** for hedge effectiveness, replacing the somewhat arbitrary 80%–125% 'bright line' test of IAS 39.

5.3 Conditions for hedge accounting

Before a hedging relationship qualifies for hedge accounting, **all** of the following **conditions** must be met.

(a) The hedging relationship **consists only of eligible hedging instruments and eligible hedged items**.

(b) There must **be formal documentation** (including identification of the hedged item, the hedging instrument, the nature of the risk that is to be hedged and how the entity will assess the hedging instrument's effectiveness in offsetting the exposure to changes in the hedged item's fair value or cash flows attributable to the hedged risk).

(c) The hedging relationship meets all of the following hedge effectiveness criteria

  (i) There is an **economic relationship** between the hedged item and the hedging instrument, ie the hedging instrument and the hedged item have values that generally move in the opposite direction because of the same risk, which is the hedged risk;

(ii) The **effect of credit risk does not dominate the value** changes that result from that economic relationship, ie the gain or loss from credit risk does not frustrate the effect of changes in the underlyings on the value of the hedging instrument or the hedged item, even if those changes were significant; and

(iii) The **hedge ratio of the hedging relationship** (quantity of hedging instrument vs quantity of hedged item) is the same as that resulting from the quantity of the hedged item that the entity **actually hedges** and the quantity of the hedging instrument that the entity **actually uses** to hedge that quantity of hedged item.

5.4 Example: Hedging

A company owns inventories of 20,000 gallons of oil which cost $400,000 on 1 December 20X3.

In order to hedge the fluctuation in the market value of the oil the company signs a futures contract to deliver 20,000 gallons of oil on 31 March 20X4 at the futures price of $22 per gallon.

The market price of oil on 31 December 20X3 is $23 per gallon and the futures price for delivery on 31 March 20X4 is $24 per gallon.

Required

Explain the impact of the transactions on the financial statements of the company:

(a) Without hedge accounting
(b) With hedge accounting

Solution

The futures contract was intended to protect the company from a fall in oil prices (which would have reduced the profit when the oil was eventually sold). However, oil prices have actually risen, so that the company has made a loss on the contract.

Without hedge accounting:

The futures contract is a derivative and therefore must be re-measured to fair value under IFRS 9. The loss on the futures contract is recognised in profit or loss:

DEBIT	Profit or loss (20,000 × 24 – 22)	$40,000	
CREDIT	Financial liability		$40,000

With hedge accounting:

The loss on the futures contract is recognised in the profit or loss as before.

The inventories are revalued to fair value:

	$
Fair value at 31 December 20X3 (20,000 × 23)	460,000
Cost	(400,000)
Gain	60,000

The gain is also recognised in profit or loss:

DEBIT	Inventory	$60,000	
CREDIT	Profit or loss		$60,000

The net effect on the profit or loss is a gain of $20,000 compared with a loss of $40,000 without hedging.

The **standard** identifies three types of **hedging relationship**.

PART C ACCOUNTING AND REPORTING TECHNIQUES

Key terms

> **Fair value hedge**: a hedge of the exposure to changes in fair value of a recognised asset or liability or an unrecognised firm commitment, or a component of any such item, that is attributable to a particular risk and could affect profit or loss.
>
> **Cash flow hedge**: a hedge of the exposure to variability in cash flows that
>
> (a) Is attributable to a particular risk associated with all, or a component of, a recognised asset or liability (such as all or some future interest payments on variable-rate debt) or a highly probable forecast transaction; and
>
> (b) Could affect profit or loss.
>
> **Hedge of a net investment in a foreign operation**: IAS 21 defines a net investment in a foreign operation as the amount of the reporting entity's interest in the net assets of that operation. (IFRS 9)

The hedge in the example above is a **fair value hedge** (it hedges exposure to changes in the fair value of a recognised asset: the oil).

This is a highly controversial topic and therefore, likely to be examined, probably in Section B.

5.5 Accounting treatment

5.5.1 Fair value hedges

Hedging instrument

The **gain or loss** resulting from **re-measuring** the hedging instrument at fair value is **recognised in profit or loss**. However, **if** the hedging instrument hedges **an equity instrument** for which an entity has **elected** to present **changes in fair value in other comprehensive income**, then the **gain or loss** on the hedging instrument must be recognised in **other comprehensive income**.

Hedged item

The gain or loss on the hedged item attributable to the **hedged risk** should **adjust the carrying amount** of the hedged item and be **recognised in profit or loss**. If the hedged item is a **financial asset through other comprehensive income** (mandatory), the **gain or loss** on the hedged item is also **recognised through profit or loss**.

However, if the hedged item is an **investment in an equity instrument held at fair value through other comprehensive income**, the **gains and losses on both** the hedged investment and the hedging instrument will be **recognised in other comprehensive income**.

This ensures that hedges of investments of equity instruments held at fair value through other comprehensive income can be accounted for as hedges.

5.5.2 Example: fair value hedge

On 1 July 20X6 Joules acquired 10,000 ounces of a material which it held in its inventory. This cost $200 per ounce, so a total of $2 million. Joules was concerned that the price of this inventory would fall, so on 1 July 20X6 he sold 10,000 ounces in the futures market for $210 per ounce for delivery on 30 June 20X7. On 1 July 20X6 the conditions for hedge accounting were all met.

At 31 December 20X6, the end of Joules' reporting period, the fair value of the inventory was $220 per ounce while the futures price for 30 June 20X7 delivery was $227 per ounce. On 30 June 20X7 the trader sold the inventory and closed out the futures position at the then spot price of $230 per ounce.

The IFRS 9 hedging criteria have been met.

Required

Set out the accounting entries in respect of the above transactions.

Solution

At 31 December 20X6 the increase in the fair value of the inventory was $200,000 (10,000 × ($220 – $200)) and the increase in the forward contract liability was $170,000 (10,000 × ($227 – $210)). The IFRS 9 hedge accounting criteria have been met, so hedge accounting was permitted.

31 December 20X6	Debit $	Credit $
Profit or loss	170,000	
Financial liability		170,000
(To record the loss on the forward contract)		
Inventories	200,000	
Profit or loss		200,000
(To record the increase in the fair value of the inventories)		

At 30 June 20X7 the increase in the fair value of the inventory was another $100,000 (10,000 × ($230 – $220)) and the increase in the forward contract liability was another $30,000 (10,000 × ($230 – $227)).

30 June 20X7	Debit $	Credit $
Profit or loss	30,000	
Financial liability		30,000
(To record the loss on the forward contract)		
Inventories	100,000	
Profit or loss		100,000
(To record the increase in the fair value of the inventories)		
Profit or loss	2,300,000	
Inventories		2,300,000
(To record the inventories now sold)		
Cash	2,300,000	
Profit or loss – revenue		2,300,000
(To record the revenue from the sale of inventories)		
Financial liability	200,000	
Cash		200,000
(To record the settlement of the net balance due on closing the financial liability)		

Note that because the fair value of the material rose, Joules made a profit of only £100,000 on the sale of inventories. Without the forward contract, the profit would have been £300,000 (2,300,000 – 2,000,000). In the light of the rising fair value the trader might in practice have closed out the futures position earlier, rather than waiting until the settlement date.

5.5.3 Cash flow hedges

These hedge the risk of change in value of future cash flows from a recognised asset or liability (or highly probable forecast transaction) that could affect profit or loss, eg hedging a variable rate interest income stream. The hedging instrument is accounted for as follows:

(a) The portion of the gain or loss on the hedging instrument that is effective (ie up to the value of the loss or gain on cash flow hedged) is recognised in other comprehensive income ('items that may be reclassified subsequently to profit or loss') and the cash flow hedge reserve.

(b) Any excess is recognised immediately in profit or loss.

The amount that has been accumulated in the cash flow hedge reserve is then accounted for as follows:

(a) If a hedged forecast transaction subsequently results in the recognition of a non-financial asset or non-financial liability, the amount shall be removed from the cash flow reserve and be included directly in the initial cost or carrying amount of the asset or liability;

(b) For all other cash flow hedges, the amount shall be reclassified from other comprehensive income to profit or loss in the same period(s) that the hedged expected future cash flows affect profit or loss.

5.5.4 Example: Cash flow hedge

Bets Co signs a contract on 1 November 20X1 to purchase an asset on 1 November 20X2 for €60,000,000. Bets reports in US$ and hedges this transaction by entering into a forward contract to buy €60,000,000 on 1 November 20X2 at US$1: €1.5.

Spot and forward exchange rates at the following dates are:

	Spot	Forward (for delivery on 1.11.X2)
1.11.X1	US$1: €1.45	US$1: €1.5
31.12.X1	US$1: €1.20	US$1: €1.24
1.11.X2	US$1: €1.0	US$1: €1.0 (actual)

The IFRS 9 hedging criteria have been met.

Required

Show the double entries relating to these transactions at 1 November 20X1, 31 December 20X1 and 1 November 20X2.

Solution

Entries at 1 November 20X1

The value of the forward contract at inception is zero so no entries recorded (other than any transaction costs), but risk disclosures will be made.

The contractual commitment to buy the asset would be disclosed if material (IAS 16).

Entries at 31 December 20X1

Gain on forward contract:

	$
Value of contract at 31.12.X1 (€60,000,000/1.24)	48,387,096
Value of contract at 1.11.X1 (€60,000,000/1.5)	40,000,000
Gain on contract	8,387,096

Compare to movement in value of asset (unrecognised):

Increase in $ cost of asset

(€60,000,000/1.20 – €60,000,000/1.45) $8,620,690

As this is higher, the hedge is deemed fully effective at this point:

DEBIT Financial asset (Forward a/c) $8,387,096
CREDIT Equity $8,387,096

Entries at 1 November 20X2

Additional gain on forward contract

	$
Value of contract at 1.11.X2 (€60,000,000/1.0)	60,000,000
Value of contract at 31.12.X1 (€60,000,000/1.24)	48,387,096
Gain on contract	11,612,904

Compare to movement in value of asset (unrecognised):

Increase in $ cost of asset

(€60,000,000/1.0 – €60,000,000/1.2) $10,000,000

Therefore, the hedge is not fully effective during this period, but it still meets the IFRS 9 hedging criteria (and hence hedge accounting can be used):

DEBIT Financial asset (Forward a/c)	$11,612,904	
CREDIT Equity		$10,000,000
CREDIT Profit or loss		$1,612,904

Purchase of asset at market price

DEBIT Asset (€60,000,000/1.0)	$60,000,000	
CREDIT Cash		$60,000,000

Settlement of forward contract

DEBIT Cash	$20,000,000	
CREDIT Financial asset (Forward a/c)		$20,000,000

Realisation of gain on hedging instrument

The cumulative gain of $18,387,096 recognised in equity is removed from equity (the cash flow hedge reserve) and included directly in the initial cost of the asset.

5.5.5 Rebalancing hedging relationships

Rebalancing denotes adjustments to the designated quantities of the hedged item or the hedging instrument of an already existing hedging relationship for the purpose of maintaining a hedge ratio that complies with the hedge.

IFRS 9 requires rebalancing to be undertaken if the risk management objective remains the same, but the hedge effectiveness requirements are no longer met. Where the risk management objective for a hedging relationship has changed, rebalancing does not apply and the hedging relationship must be discontinued.

5.5.6 Discontinuing

An entity cannot voluntarily discontinue hedge accounting as it could under the old IAS 39. Under IFRS 9, an entity is **not allowed to discontinue hedge accounting where the hedging relationship still meets the risk management objective and continues to meet all other qualifying criteria.**

Hedge accounting should be discontinued only when the hedging relationship ceases to meet the qualifying criteria. This includes instances when the hedging instrument expires or is sold, terminated or exercised. Discontinuing hedge accounting can either affect a hedging relationship in its entirety, or only a part of it. If only part of the hedging relationship is affected, hedge accounting continues for the remainder of the hedging relationship.

5.5.7 Premium paid for options

Under IFRS 9, **the part of an option that reflects time value premium should be treated as a cost of hedging**, which will be presented in other comprehensive income. This is intended to decrease inappropriate volatility in profit or loss and it should be more consistent with risk management practices.

Under IAS 39 the time value premium was treated as if it was a derivative held for trading purposes. This created volatility in profit or loss for the year. It did not reflect the way risk managers saw it: when hedging, risk managers viewed the time value premium paid as a cost of hedging rather than a speculative trading position.

5.5.8 Forward element of forward contracts and foreign currency basis spreads

When an entity separates the forward element and the spot element of a forward contract and designates as the hedging instrument only the change in the value of the spot element, or when an entity excludes the foreign currency basis spread from a hedge the entity may recognise the change in value of the excluded portion in other comprehensive income. The change in value of the excluded portion will later be removed or reclassified from equity as a single amount or on an amortised cost basis (depending on the nature of the hedged item) and ultimately **recognised in profit or loss.**

5.5.9 Hedges of a group of items

IFRS 9 **permits** the designation of a group of assets as a hedged item provided that the following **three conditions** are met.

(a) It consist of items that are eligible individually for hedging

(b) The items in the group are managed together on a group basis for the purposes of risk management.

5.5.10 Accounting for hedges of credit risk using credit derivatives

IFRS 9 **permits certain credit exposures to be designated at fair value through profit or loss** if a credit derivative that is measured at fair value through profit or loss is used to manage the credit risk of all, or a part of, the exposure on a fair value basis.

A credit exposure may be a financial instrument within or outside the scope of IFRS 9, for example, loan commitments, that is managed for credit risk. The designation would be permitted if both of the following apply.

(a) The name of the credit exposure matches the reference entity of the credit derivative.

(b) The seniority of the financial instrument matches that of the instruments that can be delivered in accordance with the credit derivative.

If the qualifying criteria are no longer met and the instrument is not otherwise required to be measured at fair value through profit or loss, the entity must discontinue measuring the financial instrument that gave rise to the credit risk at fair value through profit or loss.

5.5.11 Disclosures

IFRS 7 *Financial Instruments: Disclosures* is revised by IFRS 9.

Disclosures relating to hedging must be presented in a **single note** (or alternatively a **separate section**) of the financial statements. In that way, all the effects of hedging are seen together in detail in this note.

5.6 Section summary

- **Hedge accounting** means designating one or more instruments so that their change in fair value is **offset** by the change in fair value or cash flows of another item.

- **Hedge accounting** is permitted in certain circumstances, provided **the qualifying criteria are met.**

- There are three types of hedge: **fair value** hedge; **cash flow** hedge; hedge of a **net investment in a foreign operation**. Only the first two are examinable.

- The accounting treatment of a hedge **depends on its type**.

6 Embedded derivatives

> **FAST FORWARD**
>
> An **embedded derivative** is a derivative instrument that is combined with a non-derivate **host contract** to form a single hybrid instrument.

Certain contracts that are not themselves derivatives (and may not be financial instruments) include derivative contracts that are 'embedded' within them. These non-derivatives are called **host contracts**.

> **Key term**
>
> An **embedded derivative** is a derivative instrument that is combined with a non-derivative host contract to form a single hybrid instrument.

6.1 Examples of host contracts

Possible examples include:

(a) A lease
(b) A debt or equity instrument
(c) An insurance contract
(d) A sale or purchase contract
(e) A long term contract

6.2 Examples of embedded derivatives

Possible examples include:

(a) A bond which is redeemable in five years' time with part of the redemption price being based on the increase in the FTSE 100 Index.

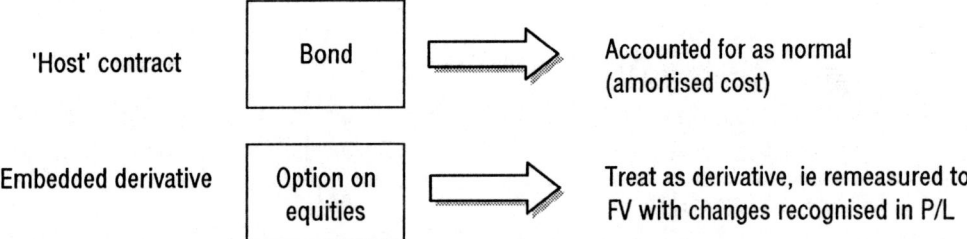

(b) A construction contract priced in a foreign currency. The construction contract is a non-derivative contract, but the changes in foreign exchange rate is the embedded derivative.

6.3 Accounting treatment of embedded derivatives

6.3.1 Financial asset host contract

Where the host contract is a financial asset within the scope of the standard, the classification and **measurement rules of the standard are applied to the entire hybrid contract**.

This is a simplification of the IAS 39 rules, and different from the treatment of financial liability host contracts (see below).

6.3.2 Other host contracts

Where the host contract is not a financial asset within the scope of IFRS 9, the standard requires that an embedded derivative be **separated from its host contract** and accounted for as a derivative when the following conditions are met:

(a) The economic characteristics and risks of the embedded derivative are not closely related to the economic characteristics and risks of the host contract.

(b) A separate instrument with the same terms as the embedded derivative would meet the definition of a derivative.

(c) The hybrid (combined) instrument is not measured at fair value with changes in fair value recognised in the profit or loss (a derivative embedded in a financial liability need not be separated out if the entity holds the combined instrument at fair value through profit or loss).

7 Disclosure of financial instruments

> **IFRS 7** specifies the **disclosures** required for financial instruments. The standard requires qualitative and quantitative disclosures about exposure to risks arising from financial instruments and specifies minimum disclosures about credit risk, liquidity risk and market risk. IFRS 13 disclosure requirements are also relevant where financial instruments are measured at fair value.

The IASB maintains that users of financial instruments need information about an entity's exposures to risks and how those risks are managed, as this information can **influence a user's assessment of the financial position and financial performance of an entity** or of the amount, timing and uncertainty of its **future cash flows**.

There have been new techniques and approaches to measuring risk management, which highlighted the need for guidance.

7.1 General requirements

The extent of disclosure required depends on the extent of the entity's use of financial instruments and on its exposure to risk. IFRS 7 **adds to the requirements previously in IAS 32** by requiring:

- Enhanced statement of financial position and statement of profit or loss and other comprehensive income disclosures

- Disclosures about an allowance account when one is used to reduce the carrying amount of impaired financial instruments.

The standard requires **qualitative and quantitative disclosures about exposure to risks** arising from financial instruments, and specifies minimum disclosures about **credit risk**, **liquidity risk** and **market risk**.

7.2 Objective

The objective of the IFRS is to require entities to provide disclosures in their financial statements that enable users to evaluate:

(a) The significance of financial instruments for the entity's financial position and performance

(b) The nature and extent of risks arising from financial instruments to which the entity is exposed during the period and at the reporting date, and how the entity manages those risks.

The principles in IFRS 7 complement the principles for recognising, measuring and presenting financial assets and financial liabilities in IAS 32 *Financial Instruments: Presentation*, IAS 39 *Financial Instruments: Recognition and Measurement* and IFRS 9 *Financial Instruments*.

7.3 Classes of financial instruments and levels of disclosure

The entity must group financial instruments into classes **appropriate to the nature of the information disclosed**. An entity must decide in the light of its circumstances how much detail it provides. Sufficient information must be provided to permit reconciliation to the line items presented in the statement of financial position.

7.3.1 Statement of financial position

The following must be disclosed:

(a) **Carrying amount** of financial assets and liabilities by IFRS 9 category

(b) **Reason for any reclassification** of a financial asset between fair value and amortised cost (and *vice versa*)

(c) Information to enable users of financial statements to evaluate the effect of netting arrangements on financial position (ie rights of set off). In order to achieve this, disclosure must be made of the gross amounts of recognised financial assets and liabilities, the amounts that are set off and the net amounts presented in the statement of financial position.

(d) The **carrying amount** of financial assets the entity has **pledged as collateral** for liabilities or contingent liabilities and the associated terms and conditions.

(e) When financial assets are impaired by credit losses and the entity records the impairment in a separate account (eg an **allowance account** used to record individual impairments or a similar account used to record a collective impairment of assets) rather than directly reducing the carrying amount of the asset, it must disclose a **reconciliation** of changes in that account during the period for each class of financial assets.

(f) The **existence of multiple embedded derivatives**, where compound instruments contain these.

(g) Defaults and breaches.

(h) **Details** of the assets and exposure to risk where the entity has made a **transfer** such that part or all of the financial assets do not qualify for derecognition.

7.3.2 Statement of profit or loss and other comprehensive income

The entity must disclose the following **items of income, expense, gains or losses**, either on the face of the financial statements or in the notes:

(a) Net gains/losses by IFRS 9 category (broken down as appropriate: eg interest, fair value changes, dividend income)

(b) Interest income/expense

(c) Impairment losses by class of financial asset.

7.3.3 Other disclosures

(1) Entities must disclose in the summary of **significant accounting policies** the measurement basis used in preparing the financial statements and the other accounting policies that are relevant to an understanding of the financial statements, as per IAS 1.

(2) Disclosures must be made relating to hedge accounting so as to provide information about:

  (a) An entity's risk management strategy and how it is applied to manage risk;

  (b) How the entity's hedging activities may affect the amount, timing and uncertainty of its future cash flows; and

  (c) The effect that hedge accounting has had on the entity's statement of financial position, statement of comprehensive income and statement of changes in equity.

Disclosures relating to hedging must be presented in a **single note** or **separate section** of the financial statements.

(3) Disclosures must be made relating to **fair value by class** in a way that allows comparison with carrying amount for those financial instruments **measured at amortised cost**. (Financial assets and liabilities may only be offset to the extent that their carrying amounts are offset in the statement of financial position).

Disclosures of fair value are not required when the carrying amount is a reasonable approximation of fair value (eg receivables).

The disclosure requirements of IFRS 13 *Fair Value Measurement* are also relevant where financial instruments are held at fair value (see Chapter 11).

7.3.4 Example: Fair value disclosures required by IFRS 7

Background

On 1 January 20X1 an entity purchases for $15 million financial assets that are not traded in an active market. The entity has only one class of such financial assets.

The transaction price of $15 million is the fair value at initial recognition.

After initial recognition, the entity will apply a valuation technique to establish the financial assets' fair value. This valuation technique includes variables other than data from observable markets.

At initial recognition, the same valuation technique would have resulted in an amount of $14 million, which differs from fair value by $1 million.

The entity has cumulative existing differences of $5 million at 1 January 20X1.

Application of requirements

The entity's 20X2 disclosure would include the following:

Accounting policies

The entity uses the following valuation technique to determine the fair value of financial instruments that are not traded in an active market: [description of technique, not included in this example]. Differences may arise between the fair value at initial recognition (which, in accordance with IFRS 9, is generally the transaction price) and the amount determined at initial recognition using the valuation technique. Any such differences are [description of the entity's accounting policy].

In the notes to the financial statements

As discussed in note X, the entity uses [name of valuation technique] to measure the fair value of the following financial instruments that are not traded in an active market. However, in accordance with IFRS 9, the fair value of an instrument at inception is generally the transaction price. If the transaction price differs from the amount determined at inception using the valuation technique, that difference is [description of the entity's accounting policy].

The differences yet to be recognised in profit or loss are as follows:

	31 Dec 20X2 $m	31 Dec 20X1 $m
Balance at beginning of year	5.3	5.0
New transactions	–	1.0
Amounts recognised in profit or loss during the year	(0.7)	(0.8)
Other increases	–	0.2
Other decreases	(0.1)	(0.1)
Balance at end of year	4.5	5.3

Disclosures of fair value are **not required** if carrying value is a reasonable approximation to fair value, or if fair value cannot be measured reliably.

7.4 Nature and extent of risks arising from financial instruments

In undertaking transactions in financial instruments, an entity may assume or transfer to another party one or more of **different types of financial risk** as defined below. The disclosures required by the standard show the extent to which an entity is exposed to these different types of risk, relating to both recognised and unrecognised financial instruments.

Type of risk	Description
Credit risk	The risk that one party to a financial instrument will cause a financial loss for the other party by failing to discharge an obligation.
Currency risk	The risk that the fair value or future cash flows of a financial instrument will fluctuate because of changes in foreign exchange rates.

Type of risk	Description
Interest rate risk	The risk that the fair value or future cash flows of a financial instrument will fluctuate because of changes in market interest rates.
Liquidity risk	The risk that an entity will encounter difficulty in meeting obligations associated with financial liabilities.
Market risk	The risk that the fair value or future cash flows of a financial instrument will fluctuate because of changes in market prices. Market risk comprises three types of risk: currency risk, interest rate risk and other price risk.
Other price risk	The risk that the fair value or future cash flows of a financial instrument will fluctuate because of changes in market prices (other than those arising from interest rate risk or currency risk), whether those changes are caused by factors specific to the individual financial instrument or its issuer, or factors affecting all similar financial instruments traded in the market.

7.4.1 Qualitative disclosures

For each type of risk arising from financial instruments, an entity must disclose:

(a) The **exposures to risk** and how they arise

(b) Its objectives, policies and processes for managing the risk and the methods used to measure the risk

(c) Any **changes** in (a) or (b) from the previous period.

7.4.2 Quantitative disclosures

For each financial instrument risk, **summary quantitative data** about risk exposure at the end of the reporting period must be disclosed. This should be based on the information provided internally to key management personnel. More information should be provided if this is unrepresentative of risk exposure during the reporting period.

Information about **credit risk** must be disclosed by class of financial instrument:

(a) Maximum exposure at the reporting date, ie without deduction of collateral

(b) A description of collateral held as security and of other credit enhancements and their financial effect

(c) Information about the credit quality of financial assets that are neither **past due** nor impaired

(d) An age analysis for financial assets that are either past due or impaired

(e) Collateral taken possession of and other credit enhancements obtained, including the nature and carrying amount of the assets and policy for disposing of or using assets not readily convertible into cash.

For **liquidity risk** entities must disclose:

(a) A maturity analysis of financial liabilities
(b) A description of the way risk is managed

Disclosures required in connection with **market risk** are:

(a) Sensitivity analysis, showing the effects on profit or loss and equity of changes in each market risk and the method and assumptions used.

(b) If the sensitivity analysis reflects interdependencies between risk variables, such as interest rates and exchange rates, an explanation of the method used, its objective and its **limitations** must also be disclosed.

7.5 Capital disclosures

Certain disclosures about managing **capital** are required. An entity's capital does not relate solely to financial instruments, but has more general relevance. Accordingly, those disclosures are included in IAS 1, rather than in IFRS 7.

Chapter roundup

- Financial instruments can be very complex, particularly **derivative instruments**, although **primary instruments** are more straightforward.
- The important definitions to learn are:
  - **Financial asset**
  - **Financial liability**
  - **Equity instrument**
- A financial instrument must be classified as a **financial asset**, a **financial liability** or **equity** according to its **substance**.
- The critical feature of a financial liability is the **contractual obligation to deliver cash** or another financial asset.
- **Compound instruments** are split into **equity** and **liability** components and presented in the statement of financial position accordingly.
- IFRS 9 states that **all financial assets and liabilities** should be **recognised in the statement of financial position, including derivatives**.
- Financial instruments are initially measured at **fair value** (which is usually, but not always equal to cost). Subsequently they are measured in accordance with their IFRS 9 classification.
- **Hedge accounting** is allowed in certain strictly defined circumstances.
- An **embedded derivative** is a derivative instrument that is combined with a non-derivate **host contract** to form a single hybrid instrument.
- **IFRS 7** specifies the **disclosures** required for financial instruments. The standard requires qualitative and quantitative disclosures about exposure to risks arising from financial instruments and specifies minimum disclosures about credit risk, liquidity risk and market risk. IFRS 13 disclosure requirements are also relevant where financial instruments are measured at fair value.

Quick quiz

1. Which issues are dealt with by IAS 32?
2. Define the following:
   (a) Financial asset
   (b) Financial liability
   (c) Equity instrument
3. What items are **not** financial instruments according to IAS 32?
4. What is the critical feature used to identify a financial liability?
5. How should compound instruments be presented in the statement of financial position?
6. Define interest rate risk and credit risk.
7. When should a financial asset be derecognised?
8. How are financial instruments initially measured?
9. What is hedging?
10. Name the three types of hedging relationship identified by IFRS 9.

PART C ACCOUNTING AND REPORTING TECHNIQUES

Answers to quick quiz

1. Classification; presentation; offsetting
2. See Key Terms, Section 1.2
3. Physical assets; prepaid expenses; non-contractual assets or liabilities; contractual rights not involving transfer of financial assets
4. The contractual obligation to deliver cash or another financial asset to the holder
5. By calculating the present value of the liability component and then deducting this from the instrument as a whole to leave a residual value for the equity component
6. See table, under Section 6.4
7. Financial assets should be derecognised when the rights to the cash flows from the asset expire or where substantially all the risks and rewards of ownership are transferred to another party
8. At the fair value of the consideration given or received ie cost
9. See Key Terms, Section 5.1
10. Fair value hedge; cash flow hedge; hedge of a net investment in a foreign operation

End of chapter question

Financial instruments (AIA May 2004)

This question should be answered applying the provisions of IAS 32 *Financial Instruments: Presentation* and IFRS 9 *Financial Instruments*.

(a) Alpha, a non-listed company, has issued 2,400,000 ordinary shares with a face value of $1. The company incurred costs of $49,880 in connection with the issue. These have been analysed as follows.

	$
Feasibility study	6,480
Publicity and printing costs	11,500
Management time spent negotiating the issue	8,500
Legal fees and costs	23,400

Required

Advise the directors of Alpha how these issue costs should be treated in the financial statements.

(4 marks)

(b) Gamma issues $10,000,000 bonds at par at the start of Year 1. The bonds bear interest at 9% per annum and are redeemable in 15 years at par. Gamma has the option to redeem the bonds after four years at a premium of 25%.

Required

Advise how the above should be treated in Gamma's Statements of profit or loss and other comprehensive income for Years 1 to 4 if Gamma decides to redeem the bonds at the end of Year 4.

(4 marks)

(c) Theta issues $800,000 debt at the start of Year 1. The debt is repayable after five years at a premium of $250,000. The debt bears interest at 5.5% per year for the first year. The interest is to be paid annually just after the end of the financial year. The rate of interest will increase by 0.5% each year after the first so that by Year 5 it will be 7.5%. The rate of interest implicit in the cash flows associated with this debt issue is 11.37351% per year.

Required

Advise how:

(i) The interest; and
(ii) The debt

Should be reported in the financial statements for the first two years.

(7 marks)

(Total 15 marks)

PART C ACCOUNTING AND REPORTING TECHNIQUES

Leasing contracts

Topic list	Syllabus reference
1 Introduction to leases	13.4
2 Lessee accounting	13.4
3 Lessor accounting	13.4
4 Sale and leaseback transactions	13.4
5 Disclosure	13.4

Introduction

Leasing transactions are extremely common in business and you will often come across them in both your business and personal capacity. You should be familiar with the more straightforward aspects of this topic from your earlier studies, but we will go through these aspects in full as leasing can be very complicated. The first section of this chapter goes over some of that basic groundwork, before the chapter moves on to more complicated aspects.

1 Introduction to leases

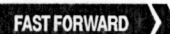

IFRS 16 *Leases* covers accounting for lease transactions by both lessees and lessors.

1.1 Identifying a lease

A **lease** is a contract that conveys to the customer ('lessee') the right to use an asset for a period of time in exchange for consideration. A contract contains a lease if the customer has the right to control the use of an identified asset for a period of time. The customer controls an asset if both of the following conditions are met:

- The customer has right to obtain substantially all of the economic benefits from use of the identified asset.

- The customer has the right to direct the use of the identified asset. (IFRS 16)

A customer can **obtain substantially all of the economic benefits from use** of the asset either directly by using or holding the asset or indirectly by sub-leasing the asset. Economic benefits include the primary output of the asset (for example, goods produced by a machine) and any other economic benefits from using the asset (such as rental income from a tenant).

A customer has the right to **direct the use** of an identified asset throughout the period of use if one of the following applies:

(a) The customer has the right to direct how and for what purpose the asset is used; or

(b) Decisions about how and for what purpose the asset is used are predetermined (for example because of the way that the asset was designed and constructed) and the customer has the right to determine how to operate the asset (operating the asset itself or directing others to operate the asset) without the supplier having the right to change those operating instructions; or

(c) Decisions about how and for what purpose the asset is used are predetermined and the customer designed the asset.

Legal ownership of the asset does not indicate which party controls the asset.

The following flowchart from IFRS can be used to determine whether a **contract** contains a **lease**.

(IFRS 16)

1.2 Development of IFRS 16 *Leases*

IFRS 16 *Leases* has been developed over a number of years in response to concerns about shortcomings in the previous standard IAS 17 *Leases*.

IAS 17 focused on transactions in which leasing an asset was economically similar to purchasing the asset being leased (the 'underlying asset'). When a lease was determined to be economically similar to purchasing the underlying asset, the lease was classified as a **finance lease** and the associated asset and liability were recognised and included reported on a company's statement of financial position. Otherwise the lease was classified as an **operating lease** and did not result in recognition of assets or liabilities: such leases were referred to as 'off balance sheet leases'. Off balance sheet leases were accounted for similarly to service contracts, with the company reporting a rental expense in the income statement (typically the same amount in each period of the lease – a so called straight-line lease expense).

Listed companies using IFRS or US GAAP disclosed almost US$3 trillion of off balance sheet lease commitments in 2014. The absence of information about leases, in particular non-recognition of assets and liabilities meant that investors and analysts did not have a complete picture of the financial position of a company, and were unable to properly compare companies that borrow to buy assets with those that lease assets. Many users of financial statements – investors, lenders and analysts – routinely adjusted the amounts shown in the statement of financial position to reflect the obligations associated with operating leases.

1.2.1 Accounting treatment by lessees

IFRS 16 eliminates the classification of leases as either operating leases or finance leases for a lessee. All contracts containing leases result in the recognition of an asset - in respect of the resource being used - and a liability – in respect of the obligation to make payments to the supplier over the life of the contract

The most significant effect of the new requirements in IFRS 16 will be an increase in lease assets and financial liabilities. Accordingly, for companies with material 'off balance sheet leases', there will be a change to the assets and liabilities included in the statement of financial position and this will result in changes to key financial ratios such as leverage.

IFRS 16 also changes the nature of expenses related to 'off balance sheet leases'. Applying IAS 17 companies would record an operating expense in respect of the payments made to use the resource, typically on a straight-line basis over the life of the contract. Applying IFRS 16 will result in a depreciation expense in respect of the leased asset and (included within operating expenses) and an interest expense on lease liabilities (included within finance expenses). Although the depreciation charge may be calculated on a straight-line basis the interest expense reduces over the life of the lease as lease payments are made (thus reducing the outstanding liability over time). This results in a gradual year on year reduction total expense as an individual lease matures. However, as many companies hold a portfolio of leases that start and end in different reporting periods this difference is unlikely to be significant.

(IFRS *Project Summary*)

1.2.2 Accounting treatment by lessors

Feedback received by the IASB during the consultation process for IFRS 16 indicated that user groups generally did not wish to see substantial changes to the way in which lessors accounted for leases. Most users of financial statements did not make adjustments on lessors' financial statements for the effects of leases, indicating that they had the information that they needed. Based on the feedback received the IASB concluded that the lessor accounting requirements in IAS 17 were well understood and did not require fundamental change.

Under IFRS 16 lessors continue to distinguish between finance leases and operating leases.

To address concerns about the lack of information about a lessor's risk exposure, IFRS 16 requires lessors to make additional disclosures, including information about assets subject to operating leases and residual value risk.

1.3 Key definitions – lessor accounting

> **FAST FORWARD**
>
> Make sure you learn these **important definitions from IAS 17 which are still applicable to lessor accounting**:
>
> - Finance lease
> - Operating lease
> - Minimum lease payments
> - Interest rate implicit in the lease
> - Guaranteed and unguaranteed residual value
> - Gross and net investment in the lease

Key terms

Finance lease. A lease that transfers substantially all the risks and rewards incidental to ownership of an asset. Title may or may not eventually be transferred.

Operating lease. A lease other than a finance lease.

Minimum lease payments. The payments over the lease term that the lessee is or can be required to make, excluding contingent rent, costs for services and taxes to be paid by and be reimbursable to the lessor, together with:

(a) For a lessee, any amounts guaranteed by the lessee or by a party related to the lessee

(b) For a lessor, any residual value guaranteed to the lessor by one of the following.

  (i) The lessee
  (ii) A party related to the lessee
  (iii) An independent third party financially capable of meeting this guarantee

However, if the lessee has the option to purchase the asset at a price which is expected to be sufficiently lower than fair value at the date the option becomes exercisable for it to be reasonably certain, at the inception of the lease, that the option will be exercised, the minimum lease payments comprise the minimum payments payable over the lease term to the expected date of exercise of this purchase option and the payment required to exercise it

Interest rate implicit in the lease.

The discount rate that, at the inception of the lease, causes the aggregate present value of

(a) The minimum lease payments; and
(b) The unguaranteed residual value

to be equal to the sum of

(a) The fair value of the leased asset; and
(b) Any initial direct costs.

Initial direct costs are **incremental costs** that are directly attributable to **negotiating** and **arranging** a lease, except for such costs incurred by manufacturer or dealer lessors. Examples of initial direct costs include amounts such as **commissions, legal fees** and relevant internal costs.

Lease term. The non-cancellable period for which the lessee has contracted to lease the asset together with any further terms for which the lessee has the option to continue to lease the asset, with or without further payment, when at the inception of the lease it is reasonably certain that the lessee will exercise the option.

A **non-cancellable lease** is a lease that is cancellable only in one of the following situations.

(a) Upon the occurrence of some remote contingency
(b) With the permission of the lessor
(c) If the lessee enters into a new lease for the same or an equivalent asset with the same lessor
(d) Upon payment by the lessee of an additional amount such that, at inception, continuation of the lease is reasonably certain

The **inception of the lease** is the earlier of the date of the lease agreement and the date of commitment by the parties to the principal provisions of the lease. As at this date:

(a) A lease is classified as either an operating lease or a finance lease; and
(b) In the case of a finance lease, the amounts to be recognised at the commencement of the lease term are determined.

Economic life is either:

(a) The period over which an asset is expected to be economically usable by one or more users; or
(b) The number of production or similar units expected to be obtained from the asset by one or more users.

PART C ACCOUNTING AND REPORTING TECHNIQUES

Key terms (cont'd)

Useful life is the estimated remaining period, from the beginning of the lease term, without limitation by the lease term, over which the economic benefits embodied in the asset are expected to be consumed by the entity.

Fair value is the amount for which an asset could be exchanged, or a liability settled, between knowledgeable, willing parties in an arm's length transaction.

Guaranteed residual value is:

(a) For a lessee, that part of the residual value which is guaranteed by the lessee or by a party related to the lessee (the amount of the guarantee being the maximum amount that could, in any event, become payable).

(b) For a lessor, that part of the residual value which is guaranteed by the lessee or by a third party unrelated to the lessor who is financially capable of discharging the obligations under the guarantee.

Unguaranteed residual value is that portion of the residual value of the leased asset, the realisation of which by the lessor is not assured or is guaranteed solely by a party related to the lessor.

Gross investment in the lease is the aggregate of:

(a) The minimum lease payments receivable by the lessor under a finance lease; and
(b) Any unguaranteed residual value accruing to the lessor.

Net investment in the lease is the gross investment in the lease discounted at the interest rate implicit in the lease.

Unearned finance income is the difference between:

(a) The gross investment in the lease; and
(b) The net investment in the lease.

The **lessee's incremental borrowing rate of interest** is the rate of interest the lessee would have to pay on a similar lease or, if that is not determinable, the rate that, at the inception of the lease, the lessee would incur to borrow over a similar term, and with a similar security, the funds necessary to purchase the asset.

Variable lease payments are payments made by a lessee to a lessor that vary because of changes in facts or circumstances occurring after the commencement date, other than the passage of time (eg percentage of sales, amount of usage, price indices, market rates of interest). (IFRS 16/IAS 17)

Some of these definitions are only of relevance once we look at lessor accounting in Section 3.

Question   Identifying a lease

Which of the following transactions, taken from the IFRS 16 Illustrative Examples, would result in recognising a lease?

Scenario 1

A utility company (the customer) enters into a contract with a power company (the supplier) to purchase all of the electricity produced by a new solar farm for 20 years. The solar farm is explicitly specified in the contract and the supplier can not substitute electricity from a different source. The customer specified the location and design of farm; the supplier is responsible for building the solar farm to specifications, and then operating and maintaining it. The supplier will retain ownership of the farm. There are no decisions to be made about whether, when or how much electricity will be produced because the design of the asset has predetermined those decisions. The supplier will receive tax credits relating to the construction and ownership of the solar farm, while the customer will receive renewable energy credits that accrue from the use of the farm to generate power.

Scenario 2

A utility company (the customer) enters into a contract with a power company (the supplier) to purchase all of the electricity produced by a single specified power plant for three years. The power plant is explicitly specified in the contract and the supplier can not substitute electricity from a different source. The contract sets out the quantity and timing of power that the power plant will produce throughout the period of use, which cannot be changed in the absence of extraordinary circumstances (for example, emergency situations). The supplier designed the power plant when it was constructed some years before entering into the contract with customer (the customer had no involvement in that design). The power plant is owned by the supplier and is operated by the supplier on a day to day basis in accordance with industry-approved operating practices.

Answer

Scenario 1

The contract contains a lease.

There is an identified asset because the solar farm is explicitly specified in the contract, and the supplier does not have the right to substitute the specified solar farm.

The customer has the right to control the use of the solar farm throughout the 20-year period of use because:

(i) **The customer has the right to obtain substantially all of the economic benefits** from use of the solar farm over the 20-year period of use. The customer has exclusive use of the solar farm; it takes all of the electricity produced by the farm over the 20-year period of use as well as the renewable energy credits that are a by-product from use of the solar farm. Although the supplier will receive economic benefits from the solar farm in the form of tax credits, those economic benefits relate to the ownership of the solar farm rather than the use of the solar farm and, thus, are not considered in this assessment.

(ii) **The customer has the right to direct the use of the solar farm.** Neither the customer, nor the supplier, decides how and for what purpose the solar farm is used during the period of use because those decisions are predetermined by the design of the asset (ie the design of the solar farm has, in effect, programmed into the asset any relevant decision-making rights about how and for what purpose the solar farm is used throughout the period of use). The customer does not operate the solar farm; the supplier makes the decisions about the operation of the solar farm. However, the customer's design of the solar farm has given it the right to direct the use of the farm. Because the design of the solar farm has predetermined how and for what purpose the asset will be used throughout the period of use, the customer's control over that design is substantively no different from the customer controlling those decisions.

Scenario 2

The contract does not contain a lease.

There is an identified asset because the power plant is explicitly specified in the contract, and the supplier does not have the right to substitute the specified plant.

The customer has the right to obtain substantially all of the economic benefits from use of the power plant over the three years of the contract. The customer will take all of the electricity produced by the plant during those three years.

However, **the customer does not have the right to direct the use of the power plant.** How and for what purpose the plant is used (ie whether, when and how much power the plant will produce) is predetermined in the contract. The customer has no right to change how and for what purpose the plant is used during the period of use. The customer has no other decision-making rights about the use of the power plant during the period of use (for example, it does not operate the power plant) and did not design the plant. The supplier is the only party that can make decisions about the plant during the period of use by making the decisions about how the plant is operated and maintained. The customer has the same rights regarding the use of the plant as if it were one of many customers obtaining power from the plant.

(IFRS *16 Illustrative example 9*)

2 Lessee accounting

FAST FORWARD — If a contract contains a lease the customer recognises an asset and a liability in the statement of financial position.

2.1 Identification of a lease

A contract contains a lease if the customer has the right to control the use of an identified asset for a period of time. The customer controls an asset if both of the following conditions are met.

- The customer has right to obtain substantially all of the economic benefits from use of the identified asset.
- The customer has the right to direct the use of the identified asset.

2.2 Accounting treatment

Where a contract contains a lease the customer recognises

- A **right-of-use asset** in respect of the resource that is controlled by the customer; and
- A **liability** in respect of the obligation to make future payments

(IFRS 16)

Key terms

Lease. A contract, or part of a contract, that conveys the right to use an asset, **the underlying asset**, for a period of time in exchange for consideration.

Underlying asset. An asset that is the subject of a lease, for which the right to use that asset has been provided by a **lessor** to a **lessee**.

Right-of-use asset. An asset that represents a lessee's right to use an **underlying asset** for the **lease term**.

- **Lease payments.** Payments made by a **lessee** to a **lessor** relating to the right to use an **underlying asset** during the **lease term**, comprising:
  - (a) Fixed payments, less any **lease incentives**
  - (b) **Variable lease payments** that depend on an index or rate
  - (c) The exercise price of a purchase option if the lessee is reasonably certain to exercise that option
  - (d) Payment of lease termination penalties if applicable

- **Interest rate implicit in the lease**.

  The discount rate that, at the inception of the lease, causes the aggregate present value of:
  - (a) The lease payments; and
  - (b) The **unguaranteed residual value**

  to be equal to the sum of:
  - (a) The fair value of the **underlying asset**; and
  - (b) Any initial direct costs.

- **Lessee's incremental borrowing rate.** The rate of interest that a **lessee** would have to pay to borrow over a similar term, and with a similar security, the funds necessary to obtain an asset of similar value to the **right of use asset** in a similar economic environment.

- **Unguaranteed residual value.** That portion of the residual value of the underlying asset, the realisation of which by the lessor is not assured.

> - **Variable lease payments**. The portion of payments made by a **lessee** to a **lessor** for the right to use an **underlying asset** during the **lease term** that varies because of changes in facts or circumstances occurring after the commencement date, other than the passage of time.
> - **Lease term**. The non-cancellable period for which the lessee has contracted to lease the asset together with any further terms for which the lessee has the option to continue to lease the asset, with or without further payment, when at the inception of the lease it is reasonably certain that the lessee will exercise the option and any periods covered by an option to terminate the lease if the lessee is reasonably certain not to exercise that option (IFRS 16: para.18)
> - **Short-term lease**. A lease that at the commencement date has a term of 12 months or less and does not contain a purchase option.
> - **Lease incentives**. Payments made by the **lessor** to the **lessee**, or the reimbursement or assumption by the lessor of costs of the lessee. (IFRS 16: Appendix A)

The **asset** is **initially measured** at the amount of the lease liability plus any initial direct costs incurred by the lessee. Such costs are often incurred in connection with securing or negotiating a lease. Only those costs which are directly attributable to activities performed by the lessee to obtain a finance lease should be added to the amount recognised as an asset.

In **subsequent periods** the **asset** is measured using a cost model ie at cost less accumulated depreciation and impairment losses. The asset is measured at fair value if (i) the asset is an investment property and the lessee measures its investment property at fair value under IAS 40 or (ii) the asset relates to a class of PPE to which the lessee applies IAS 16's revaluation model.

The **liability** is **initially measured** at the present value of the lease payments payable over the lease term, discounted at the **rate implicit in the lease**. (If that rate cannot be readily determined the lessee uses their **incremental borrowing rate**.)

In **subsequent periods** the liability is remeasured to reflect the unwinding of the discount and any payments made to reduce the outstanding finance.

Remeasurement of the liability also reflects any reassessments or modifications (for example, changes in the lease term, changes in future variable payments).

The statement of profit or loss and other comprehensive income will include:

- the **depreciation charge** associated with the leased asset (as well as any impairment losses and, possibly, revaluation gains and losses); and
- The **finance expense** associated with the financing element of the lease contract.

2.3 Allocating the finance charge

When the lessee makes a rental payment it will comprise two elements:

(a) An **interest charge** on the finance provided by the lessor. This proportion of each payment is interest payable in the statement of profit or loss of the lessee.

(b) A repayment of part of the **capital cost** of the asset. In the lessee's books this proportion of each rental payment must be debited to the lessor's account to reduce the outstanding liability.

The accounting problem is to decide what proportion of each instalment paid by the lessee represents interest, and what proportion represents a repayment of the capital advanced by the lessor. This is done by the actuarial method, using the interest rate implicit in the lease.

2.4 Example: Apportionment of rental payments

(This is based on IFRS 16 Illustrative example 13)

A lessee enters into a five-year lease of a building which has a remaining useful life of 10 years. Lease payments are $50,000 per annum, payable at the beginning of each year.

The lessee incurs initial direct costs of $20,000 and receives lease incentives of $5,000. There is no transfer of the asset at the end of the lease and no purchase option.

The interest rate implicit in the lease is not immediately determinable but the lessee's incremental borrowing rate is 5%.

At the commencement date the lessee pays the initial $50,000, incurs the direct costs and receives the lease incentives.

The lease liability is measured at the present value of the remaining four payments:

	$
$50,000/1.05$	47,619
$50,000/1.05^2$	45,351
$50,000/1.05^3$	43,192
$50,000/1.05^4$	41,135
	177,297

Assets and liabilities will initially be recognised as follows:

		Debit $	Credit $
Right-of-use asset:			
Initial payment	50,000		
Discounted liability	177,297		
Initial direct costs	20,000		
Incentives received	(5,000)		
		242,297	
Lease liability			177,297
Cash	(50,000 + 20,000 – 5,000)		65,000
		242,297	242,297

At the end of Year 1 the liability will be measured as:

	$
Opening balance	177,297
Interest 5%	8,865
	186,162
Current liability	50,000
Non-current liability	136,162
	186,162

The right of use asset will be depreciated over five years, being the shorter of the lease term and the useful life of the underlying asset.

Now we will see how this would work out if the lease payments were made **in arrears**.

At the commencement date the lessee would incur the direct costs and receive the lease incentives.

The lease would be measured at the present value of **five** payments:

	$
$50,000/1.05$	47,619
$50,000/1.05^2$	45,351
$50,000/1.05^3$	43,192
$50,000/1.05^4$	41,135
$50,000/1.05^5$	39,176
	216,473

Assets and liabilities would be recognised as follows:

	Debit $	Credit $
Right-of-use asset:		
Discounted liability	216,473	
Direct costs	20,000	
Lease incentives	(5,000)	
	231,473	
Lease liability		216,473
Cash (20,000 – 5,000)		15,000
	231,473	231,473

At the end of Year 1 the liability will be measured as:

	$
Opening balance	216,473
Interest 5%	10,824
Lease payment Year 1	(50,000)
Year-end balance	177,297

In order to ascertain the split between non-current and current liabilities, we work out the balance at the end of Year 2:

	$
Opening balance	177,297
Interest 5%	8,865
Lease payment Year 2	(50,000)
Year-end balance	136,162

The statement of financial position will show:

	$
Non-current liability	136,162
Current liability (177,297 – 136,162)	41,135
	177,297

Note that when payments are made in arrears the next instalment due will contain interest, so this is effectively deducted to arrive at the capital repayment.

2.5 Exemptions

For practical purposes IFRS 16 allows the following exemptions from the requirements to recognise lease assets and liabilities:

- Short-term leases (12 months or less)
- Leases for which the underlying asset is of low value

During the preparation of IFRS 16 and in response to feedback from consultation the IASB concluded that the benefits of requiring a lessee to apply all of the requirements in IFRS 16 to short-term leases and to a large number of low value leases do not outweigh the associated costs.

The assessment of whether an underlying asset is of low value is performed on an absolute basis. Leases of low-value assets qualify for the exemption regardless of whether those leases are material to the lessee. The assessment is not affected by the size, nature or circumstances of the lessee. Accordingly, different lessees are expected to reach the same conclusions about whether a particular underlying asset is of low value.

An underlying asset can be of low value only if:

(a) The lessee can benefit from use of the underlying asset on its own or together with other resources that are readily available to the lessee; and

(b) The underlying asset is not highly dependent on, or highly interrelated with, other assets for which the underlying asset is of low value

Examples of low value items given in the standard are tablet and personal computers, small items of office furniture and telephones.

2.6 Disclosure requirements

The objective of the disclosure requirements in IFRS 16 is for lessees to disclose information gives a basis for users to assess the effect that leases have on the financial position, financial performance and cash flows of the lessee.

The following should be disclosed:

(a) Depreciation charge for right-of-use assets by class of underlying asset;

(b) Interest expense on lease liabilities;

(c) The expense relating to short-term leases

(d) The expense relating to leases of low-value assets

(e) The expense relating to variable lease payments not included in the measurement of lease liabilities;

(f) Income from subleasing right-of-use assets;

(g) Total cash outflow for leases;

(h) Additions to right-of-use assets;

(i) Gains or losses arising from sale and leaseback transactions; and

(j) The carrying amount of right-of-use assets at the end of the reporting period by class of underlying asset

3 Lessor accounting

FAST FORWARD | Under IFRS 16 lessors continue to distinguish between finance leases and operating leases.

3.1 Finance lease or operating lease?

The following diagram can be used to determine whether a lease is a **finance lease** or an **operating lease**.

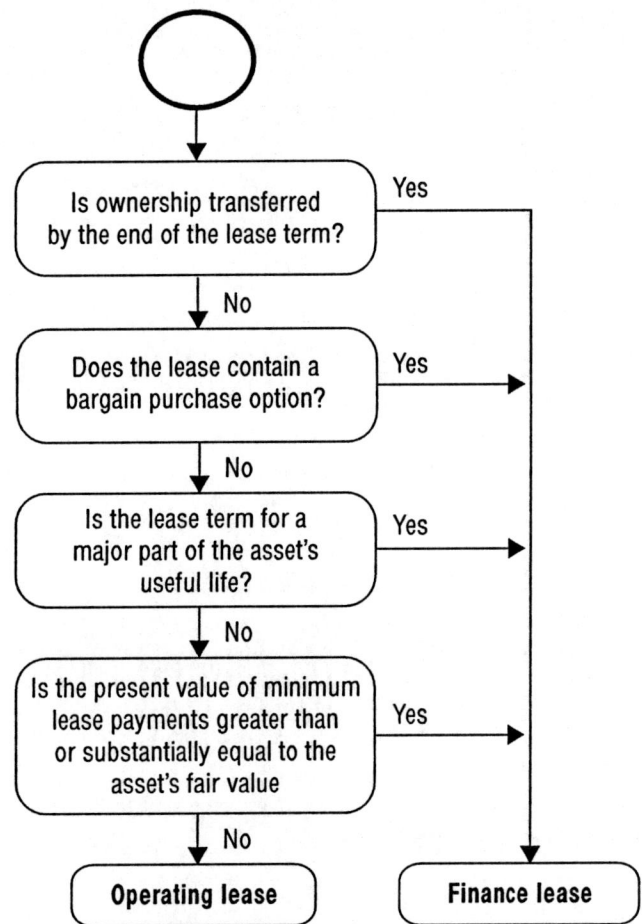

Several of the **definitions** given in Section 1 of this chapter are relevant to lessor accounting in particular and you should go back and look at them.

- Unguaranteed residual value
- Gross investment in the lease
- Unearned finance income
- Net investment in the lease

3.2 Example: Gross investment

Willco Co has just purchased a lorry from Drogon Trucks Co for $50,000. The lorry has been leased to Newton Freight Co on a two-year lease requiring annual payments in arrears of $13,500. Drogon Trucks have agreed to buy the truck back at open market value at the end of the lease.

Newton Freight Co have guaranteed that the value of the lorry after two years will be not less than $30,000. A realistic estimate of its value at that time is $33,000, ie the unguaranteed residual value is $3,000.

What is the gross investment in the lease at the start of the lease?

Solution

At the start of the lease the 'minimum lease payments' will be the rentals due of $27,000 plus the guaranteed residual of $30,000 giving $57,000. The gross investment in the lease will be the minimum lease payments of $57,000 plus the unguaranteed residual of $3,000 ($33,000 – $30,000) giving $60,000.

3.3 Example: Net investment

It will be apparent from the definition of net investment above that when any residual amount receivable by the lessor is insignificant (as is usually the case in normal full payout leases), the net investment in the lease will be equal to the cash selling price of the leased asset.

Consider again the example given in Section 2.2, this time from the point of view of the lessor.

PART C ACCOUNTING AND REPORTING TECHNIQUES

Solution

	Years ending 31 December			
	20X0	20X1	20X2	20X3
	$	$	$	$
Net investment in the lease	7,710			
Less deposit	(2,000)			
Balance outstanding	5,710	4,566	3,251	1,739
Finance income at 15%	856	685	488	261
Instalment received	(2,000)	(2,000)	(2,000)	(2,000)
Balance outstanding at period end	4,566	3,251	1,739	–

The lessor's statement of financial position and notes will include the following amounts for each year.

	As at 31 December		
	20X3	20X4	20X5
	$	$	$
Finance lease receivables	4,566	3,251	1,739
Of which: due in one year (2,000 – 685) and (2,000 – 488)	1,315	1,512	1,739
due in more than one year	3,251	1,739	–

Note that under the assumptions of this question the total net investments shown above are the same as the obligations shown in the lessee's statement of financial position. This would not have been the case had the lessee based its disclosure on a present value found using its cost of borrowing rather than the implied rate in the lease.

3.4 Operating leases

An **asset** held for use in operating leases by a lessor should be recorded as a non-current asset and depreciated over its useful life. The basis for depreciation should be consistent with the lessor's policy on similar non-lease assets and follow the guidance in IAS 16.

Income from an operating lease, excluding charges for services such as insurance and maintenance, should be recognised on **a straight-line basis** over the period of the lease (even if the receipts are not on such a basis), unless another systematic and rational basis is more representative of the time pattern in which the benefit from the leased asset is receivable.

Initial direct costs incurred by lessors in negotiating and arranging an operating lease should be **added to the carrying amount** of the leased asset and recognised as an expense over the lease term on the same basis as lease income, ie capitalised and amortised over the lease term.

Lessors should refer to IAS 36 in order to determine whether a leased asset has become impaired.

A lessor who is a **manufacturer or dealer** should not recognise any selling profit on entering into an operating lease because it is not the equivalent of a sale.

3.5 Example: Operating lease

Martin Co has supplied an asset to a customer for a period of 12 months commencing 1 July 20X1 and has correctly classified the contract as an operating lease. The customer receives the first three months rent free and pays $12,000 per month starting in the fourth month.

What income should Martin Co recognise in its statement f profit or loss for the year ended 31 December 20X1?

Solution

The income will be recognised on a straight line basis over the life of the contract. Total income is $12,000 × 9 = $108,000. Income for the six months ended 31 December 20X1 should therefore be $108,000 × 6/12 = $54,000.

4 Sale and leaseback transactions

FAST FORWARD

In a sale and leaseback transaction, an asset is sold by a vendor and then the same asset is **leased back** to the same vendor. The lease payment and sale price are normally interdependent because they are negotiated as part of the same package.

4.1 Sale or not?

To determine whether the transfer of an asset is accounted for as a sale an entity applies the requirements of IFRS 15 *Revenue from Contracts with Customers* for determining when a performance obligation is satisfied.

4.1.1 Transfer is a sale

If the transfer satisfies the IFRS 15 requirement to be accounted for as a sale:

- The seller/lessee measures the right-of-use asset arising from the leaseback at the proportion of the previous carrying amount of the asset that relates to the **right-of use retained** by the seller/lessee.
- The seller/lessee only recognises the amount of any gain or loss on the sale that relates to the **rights transferred** to the buyer (IFRS 16: para. 100).

If the fair value of the consideration for the sale does not equal the fair value of the asset, or if the lease payments are not at market rates, the following adjustments should be made:

- Any below-market terms should be accounted for as a prepayment of lease payments (the shortfall in consideration received from the lessor is treated as a lease payment made by the lessee).
- Any above-market terms are accounted for as additional financing provided by the buyer/lessor (the additional amount paid by the lessor is treated as additional liability, **not** as gain on the sale) (IFRS 16: para. 101).

4.1.2 Transfer is not a sale

If the transfer does not satisfy the IFRS 15 requirements to be accounted for as a sale, the seller continues to recognise the transferred asset and the transfer proceeds are treated as a financial liability, accounted for in accordance with IFRS 9. The transaction is more in the nature of a secured loan.

4.2 Example: sale and leaseback

[Adapted from IFRS 16 Illustrated example 24]

The seller/lessee sells a building to the buyer/lessor for $800,000 cash. The carrying amount of the building prior to the sale was $600,000. The seller/lessee arranges to lease the building back for five years at $120,000 per annum, payable in arrears. The remaining useful life is 15 years.

The transaction satisfies the performance obligations in IFRS 15, so will be accounted for as a sale and leaseback.

At the date of sale the fair value of the building was $750,000, so the excess $50,000 paid by the buyer is recognised as additional financing provided by the buyer/lessor.

The interest rate implicit in the lease is 4.5% and the present value of the annual payments is:

	$
$120,000/1.045$	114,833
$120,000/1.045^2$	109,888
$120,000/1.045^3$	105,155
$120,000/1.045^4$	100,627
$120,000/1.045^5$	96,294
	526,797

Of this, $476,797 relates to the lease and $50,000 relates to the additional financing.

At the commencement date, the seller/lessee measures the right-of-use asset arising from the leaseback of the building at the proportion of the previous carrying amount of the building that relates to the right-of-use retained. This is calculated as carrying amount × discounted lease payments/fair value.

In our example: $600,000 × 476,797/750,000 = $381,437

The seller/lessee only recognises the amount of gain that relates to the rights transferred. The gain on sale of the building is $150,000 (750,000 – 600,000), of which:

(a) 150,000 × 476,797/750,000 = $95,360 – relates to the rights retained
(b) The balance – 150,000 – 95,360 = $54,640 – relates to the rights transferred to the buyer

At the commencement date the lessee accounts for the transaction as follows:

	Debit $	Credit $
Cash	800,000	
Right-of-use asset	381,437	
Building		600,000
Financial liability		526,797
Gain on rights transferred		54,640
	1,181,437	1,181,437

The right-of-use asset will be depreciated over five years, the gain will be recognised in profit or loss and the financial liability will be increased each year by the interest charge and reduced by the lease payments.

5 Disclosures

There are separate disclosure requirements for lessees and lessors under IFRS 16.

5.1 Lessees

A lessee is requires to disclose:

- Depreciation charge for right-of-use assets by class of underlying asset
- Interest expense on lease liabilities
- Expenses relating to short-term leases and leases of low-value assets
- Expense relating to variable lease payments
- Income from subleasing right-of-use assets
- Total cash outflow for leases
- Additions to right-of-use assets
- Gains or losses arising from sale and leaseback transactions
- Carrying amount of right-of-use assets at the end of the period.

5.2 Lessors

A lessor is required to disclose:

For finance leases:

- Selling profit or loss;
- Finance income on net investment in the lease; and
- Income relating to variable lease payments not included in the net investment in the lease

Also:

- Information in respect of significant changes in the carrying amount of the net investment in finance leases
- Maturity analysis of lease payments receivable

For operating leases:

Lease income, separately disclosing income relating to variable lease payments that do not depend on an index or rate.

IAS 16 requirements in relation to assets subject to an operating lease

Lessors should also disclose information in respect of the nature of leasing activities and how associated risk is managed.

> **Exam focus point**
>
> The **disclosure requirements** for both lessees and lessors should force disclosure of sale and leaseback transactions. IAS 1 *Presentation of Financial Statements* should be considered.

PART C ACCOUNTING AND REPORTING TECHNIQUES

Chapter roundup

- IFRS 16 covers accounting for lease transactions by both lessees and lessors.
- Make sure you learn these **important definitions from IAS 17 which are still applicable to lessor accounting**:
    - Finance lease
    - Operating lease
    - Minimum lease payments
    - Interest rate implicit in the lease
    - Guaranteed and unguaranteed residual value
    - Gross and net investment in the lease
- If a contract contains a lease the customer recognises an asset and a liability in the statement of financial position.
- **Under IFRS 16 lessors continue to distinguish between finance leases and operating leases.**
- **In** a sale and leaseback transaction, an asset is sold by a vendor and then the same asset is **leased back** to the same vendor. The lease payment and sale price are normally interdependent because they are negotiated as part of the same package.
- There are separate disclosure requirements for lessees and lessors under IFRS 16.
- **Lessee accounting**:

    Record an asset and a liability in the statement of financial position. Apportion the finance charge to give a constant periodic rate of return.

- **Lessor accounting**:
    - The definition of a **finance lease** is very important: it is a lease that transfers all the risks and rewards of ownership of the asset, regardless of whether legal title passes.
    - **Finance leases**: record the amount due from the lessor in the statement of financial position at the net investment in the lease, recognise finance income to give a constant periodic rate of return.
    - **Operating leases**: record as non-current asset and depreciate over useful life, record income on a straight-line basis over the lease term.

Quick quiz

1. List the disclosure requirements for lessees under leases.
2. What are the conditions for determining that a customer controls an identified asset?
3. Distinguish between a finance lease and an operating lease.

Answers to quick quiz

1. (a) Depreciation charge for right-of-use assets by class of underlying asset;
   (b) Interest expense on lease liabilities;
   (c) The expense relating to short-term leases
   (d) The expense relating to leases of low-value assets
   (e) The expense relating to variable lease payments not included in the measurement of lease liabilities;
   (f) Income from subleasing right-of-use assets;
   (g) Total cash outflow for leases;
   (h) Additions to right-of-use assets;
   (i) Gains or losses arising from sale and leaseback transactions; and
   (j) The carrying amount of right-of-use assets at the end of the reporting period by class of underlying asset

2. The customer controls an asset if both of the following conditions are met.
   - The customer has right to obtain substantially all of the economic benefits from use of the identified asset.
   - The customer has the right to direct the use of the identified asset.

3. (a) A finance lease transfers substantially all the risks and rewards incident to ownership of an asset. Title may or may not be transferred eventually
   (b) An operating lease is a lease other than a finance lease

End of chapter question

Trench Quarries (AIA May 2010 amended)

(Trench Quarries is a public liability company and an independent quarry operator. The company provides ready-mixed concrete to major building contractors. At 31 March 2010 the company has a lease of a machine in operation at one of its quarries and wishes to know how this contract should be accounted for in the company's financial statements.

On 1 October 2009 the company entered into a five year agreement to lease a machine used to crush rock. Trench Quarries and the lessor became committed to the main provisions of the lease at that date. The machine was delivered on 1 October 2009, at which date its estimated useful life was six years. The following information concerns the lease agreement:

Initial direct costs paid by Trench Quarries	$0.2 million
Present value of lease payments	$8.1 million
Lease payments payable in advance	$0.8 million per month

The machine was due to commence commercial production on 1 October 2009 but, due to difficulties in training Trench Quarry operators, did not do so until 1 January 2010. As a result the lessor allowed the lease payments to begin on 1 January 2010.

Required

(a) Advise the appropriate accounting treatment of the above lease agreement to comply with IFRS 16 *Leases*. **(10 marks)**

(b) Explain the reasons for the introduction of IFRS 16 *Leases* and analyse the likely effect on companies that had accounted for some leases as operating leases under IAS 17. **(10 marks)**

(Total 20 marks)

Employee benefits

Topic list	Syllabus reference
1 IAS 19 *Employee Benefits*	13.4
2 Short-term employee benefits	13.4
3 Post-employment benefits	13.4
4 Defined contribution plans	13.4
5 Defined benefit plans: Recognition and measurement	13.4
6 Defined benefit plans: Other matters	13.4
7 Other long-term benefits	13.4
8 Termination benefits	13.4

Introduction

An increasing number of companies and other entities now provide a **pension and other employee benefits** as part of their employees' remuneration package. In view of this trend, it is important that there is standard best practice for the way in which employee benefit costs are **recognised, measured, presented and disclosed** in the sponsoring entities' financial statements.

1 IAS 19 *Employee Benefits*

IAS 19 *Employee Benefits* is a long and complex standard covering both short-term and long-term (post-employment) benefits. The complications arise when dealing with **post-employment benefits**.

IAS 19 covers **all employee benefit costs**, except share-based payment, not only retirement benefit (pension) costs. Before we look at IAS 19, we should consider the nature of employee benefit costs and why there is an accounting problem which must be addressed by a standard.

1.1 The conceptual nature of employee benefit costs

When a company or other entity employs a new worker, that worker will be offered a **package of pay and benefits**. Some of these will be short-term and the employee will receive the benefit at about the same time as he or she earns it, for example basic pay, overtime etc. Other employee benefits are **deferred**, however, the main example being retirement benefits (ie a pension).

The cost of these deferred employee benefits to the employer can be viewed in various ways. They could be described as **deferred salary** to the employee. Alternatively, they are a **deduction** from the employee's true gross salary, used as a tax-efficient means of saving. In some countries, tax efficiency arises on retirement benefit contributions because they are not taxed on the employee, but they are allowed as a deduction from taxable profits of the employer.

1.2 Accounting for employee benefit costs

Accounting for **short-term employee benefit costs** tends to be quite straightforward, because they are simply recognised as an expense in the employer's financial statements of the current period.

Accounting for the cost of **deferred employee benefits** is much more difficult. This is because of the large amounts involved, as well as the long time scale, complicated estimates and uncertainties. In the past, entities accounted for these benefits simply by charging profit or loss on the basis of actual payments made. This led to substantial variations in reported profits of these entities and disclosure of information on these costs was usually sparse.

1.3 IAS 19 *Employee Benefits*

IAS 19 was amended in 2011, with significant changes made to the measurement, recognition and disclosure of employee benefits.

The standard prescribes the following:

(a) When the cost of employee benefits should be **recognised as a liability or an expense**
(b) The **amount** of the liability or expense that should be recognised

As a basic rule, the standard states the following:

(a) A **liability** should be recognised when an employee has provided a service in exchange for benefits to be received by the employee at some time in the future.

(b) An **expense** should be recognised when the entity enjoys the economic benefits from a service provided by an employee regardless of when the employee received or will receive the benefits from providing the service.

The basic problem is therefore fairly straightforward. An entity will often enjoy the **economic benefits** from the services provided by its employees in advance of the employees receiving all the employment benefits from the work they have done, for example they will not receive pension benefits until after they retire.

1.4 Categories of employee benefits

The standard recognises four categories of employee benefits, and proposes a different accounting treatment for each. These four categories are as follows:

1 **Short-term benefits** including:

- Wages and salaries
- Social security contributions
- Paid annual leave
- Paid sick leave
- Paid maternity/paternity leave
- Profit shares and bonuses paid within 12 months of the year end
- Paid jury service
- Paid military service
- Non-monetary benefits, eg medical care, cars, free goods

2 **Post-employment benefits**, eg pensions and post-employment medical care

3 **Other long-term benefits**, eg profit shares, bonuses or deferred compensation payable later than 12 months after the year end, sabbatical leave, long-service benefits

4 **Termination benefits**, eg early retirement payments and redundancy payments

Benefits may be paid to the employees themselves, to their dependants (spouses, children, etc) or to third parties.

Benefits under share-option schemes and the like are accounted for under IFRS 2 *Share-based Payment* (see Chapter 20).

1.5 Definitions

IAS 19 uses a great many important definitions. They are grouped together here, but you should refer back to them as necessary as you work through the rest of this chapter.

Key terms

Definitions of employee benefits

Employee benefits are all forms of consideration given by an entity in exchange for service rendered by employees or for the termination of employment.

Short-term employee benefits are employee benefits (other than termination benefits) that are expected to be settled wholly before 12 months after the end of the annual reporting period in which the employees render the related service.

Post-employment benefits are employee benefits (other than termination benefits and short-term employee benefits) which are payable after the completion of employment.

Other long-term employee benefits are all employee benefits other than short-term employee benefits, post-employment benefits and termination benefits.

Termination benefits are employee benefits provided in exchange for the termination of an employee's employment as a result of either:

(a) An entity's decision to terminate an employee's employment before the normal retirement date; or

(b) An employee's decision to accept an offer of benefits in exchange for the termination of employment.

Definitions relating to classification of plans

Post-employment benefit plans are formal or informal arrangements under which an entity provides post-employment benefits for one or more employees.

Defined contribution plans are post-employment benefit plans under which an entity pays fixed contributions into a separate entity (a fund) and will have no legal or constructive obligation to pay further contributions if the fund does not hold sufficient assets to pay all employee benefits relating to employee service in the current and prior periods.

Defined benefit plans are post-employment benefit plans other than defined contribution plans.

Multi-employer plans are defined contribution plans (other than state plans) or defined benefit plans (other than state plans) that:

(a) Pool the assets contributed by various entities that are not under common control, and

(b) Use those assets to provide benefits to employees of more than one entity, on the basis that contribution and benefit levels are determined without regard to the identity of the entity that employs the employees concerned.

Definitions relating to the net defined benefit liability (asset)

The **net defined benefit liability (asset)** is the deficit or surplus, adjusted for any effect of limiting a net defined benefit asset to the asset ceiling.

The **deficit or surplus** is:

(a) The present value of the defined benefit obligation; less
(b) The fair value of plan assets (if any).

The **asset ceiling** is the present value of any economic benefits available in the form of refunds from the plan or reductions in future contributions to the plan.

The **present value of a defined benefit** obligation is the present value, without deducting any plan assets, of expected future payments required to settle the obligation resulting from employee service in the current and prior periods.

Plan assets comprise:

(a) Assets held by a long-term employee benefit fund; and
(b) Qualifying insurance policies

Asset held by a long-term employee benefit fund are assets (other than non-transferable financial instruments issued by the reporting entity) that:

(a) Are held by an entity (a fund) that is legally separate from the reporting entity and exists solely to pay or fund employee benefits; and

(b) Are available to be used only to pay or fund employee benefits, are not available to the reporting entity's own creditors (even in bankruptcy), and cannot be returned to the reporting entity, unless either:

   (i) The remaining assets of the fund are sufficient to meet all the related employee benefit obligations of the plan or the reporting entity; or

   (ii) The assets are returned to the reporting entity to reimburse it for employee benefits already paid

A **qualifying insurance policy** is an insurance policy issued by an insurer that is not a related party (as defined in IAS 24) of the reporting entity, if the proceeds of the policy:

(a) Can be used only to pay or fund employee benefits under a defined benefit plan; and

(b) Are not available to the reporting entity's own creditors (even in bankruptcy) and cannot be paid to the reporting entity, unless either:

   (i) The proceeds represent surplus assets that are not needed for the policy to meet all the related employee benefit obligations; or

   (ii) The proceeds are returned to the reporting entity to reimburse it for employee benefits already paid.

> **Fair value** is the price that would be received to sell an asset or paid to transfer a liability in an orderly transaction between market participants at the measurement date.
>
> *Definitions relating to defined benefit cost*
>
> **Service cost** comprises:
>
> (a) **Current service cost**, which is the increase in the present value of the defined benefit obligation resulting from employee service in the current period;
>
> (b) **Past service cost**, which is the change in the present value of the defined benefit obligation for employee service in prior periods, resulting from a plan amendment (the introduction or withdrawal of, or changes to, a defined benefit plan) or a curtailment (a significant reduction by the entity in the number of employees covered by a plan); and
>
> (c) And gain or loss on settlement.
>
> **Net interest on the net defined benefit liability (asset)** is the change during the period in the net defined benefit liability (asset) that arises from the passage of time.
>
> **Remeasurements of the net defined benefit liability (asset)** comprise:
>
> (a) Actuarial gains and losses;
>
> (b) The return on plan assets, excluding amounts included in net interest on the net defined benefit liability (asset); and
>
> (c) Any change in the effect of the asset ceiling, excluding amounts included in net interest on the net defined benefit liability (asset).
>
> **Actuarial gains and losses** are changes in the present value of the defined benefit obligation resulting from:
>
> (a) Experience adjustments (the effects of differences between the previous actuarial assumptions and what has actually occurred); and
>
> (b) The effects of changes in actuarial assumptions.
>
> The **return on plan assets** is interest, dividends and other income derived from the plan assets, together with realised and unrealised gains or losses on the plan assets, less:
>
> (a) Any costs of managing plan assets; and
>
> (b) Any tax payable by the plan itself, other than tax included in the actuarial assumptions used to measure the present value of the defined benefit obligation.
>
> A **settlement** is a transaction that eliminates all further legal or constructive obligations for part or all of the benefits provided under a defined benefit plan, other than a payment of benefits to, or on behalf of, employees that is set out in the terms of the plan and included in the actuarial assumptions.
>
> (IAS 19 [amended 2011])

1.6 Section summary

There are **two key issues** or problems to consider.

- It may be necessary to rely on **actuarial assumptions** about what the future amount of benefits payable will be.
- If benefits are payable later than 12 months after the end of the accounting period, the future benefits payable should be **discounted** to a present value.

2 Short-term employee benefits

Accounting for short-term employee benefits is fairly straightforward, because there are **no actuarial assumptions** to be made, and there is **no requirement to discount** future benefits (because they are all, by definition, payable no later than 12 months after the end of the accounting period).

2.1 Recognition and measurement

The rules for short-term benefits are essentially an application of **basic accounting principles and practice**.

(a) **Unpaid short-term employee benefits** as at the end of an accounting period should be recognised as a liability (an accrued expense). Any short-term benefits **paid in advance** should be recognised as a prepayment (to the extent that it will lead to, eg a reduction in future payments or a cash refund).

(b) The **cost of short-term employee benefits** should be recognised as an **expense** in the period when the economic benefit is given, as employment costs (except insofar as employment costs may be included within the cost of an asset, eg property, plant and equipment).

2.2 Short-term absences

There may be **short-term accumulating paid absences**. These are absences for which an employee is paid, and if the employee's entitlement has not been used up at the end of the period, they are carried forward to the next period. An example is paid holiday leave, where any unused holidays in one year are carried forward to the next year. The cost of the benefits of such absences should be **charged as an expense** as the employees render service that increases their entitlement to future paid absences.

There may be **short-term non-accumulating paid absences**. These are absences for which an employee is paid when they occur, but an **entitlement to the absences does not accumulate**. The employee can be absent, and be paid, but only if and when the circumstances arise. Examples are maternity/paternity pay, (in most cases) sick pay, and paid absence for jury service. The cost of these should be recognised when the absences occur.

2.3 Example: Unused holiday leave

A company gives its employees an annual entitlement to paid holiday leave. If there is any unused leave at the end of the year, employees are entitled to carry forward the unused leave for up to 12 months. At the end of 20X9, the company's employees carried forward in total 50 days of unused holiday leave. Employees are paid $100 per day.

Required

State the required accounting for the unused holiday carried forward.

Solution

The cost of $5,000 short-term accumulating compensated absences should be recognised as a liability and an expense in the year when the entitlement arises, ie in 20X9.

Question — Sick leave

Plyman Co has 100 employees. Each is entitled to five working days of paid sick leave for each year, and unused sick leave can be carried forward for one year. Sick leave is taken on a LIFO basis (ie firstly out of the current year's entitlement and then out of any balance brought forward).

As at 31 December 20X8, the average unused entitlement is two days per employee. Plyman Co expects (based on past experience which is expected to continue) that 92 employees will take five days or less sick leave in 20X9, the remaining eight employees will take an average of 6½ days each.

Required

State the required accounting for sick leave.

Answer

Plyman Co expects to pay an additional 12 days of sick pay as a result of the unused entitlement that has accumulated at 31 December 20X8, ie 1½ days × 8 employees. Plyman Co should recognise a liability equal to 12 days of sick pay.

2.4 Profit sharing or bonus plans

Profit shares or bonuses payable within 12 months after the end of the accounting period should be recognised as an expected cost when the entity has a **present obligation to pay it**, ie when the employer has no real option but to pay it. This will usually be when the employer recognises the profit or other performance achievement to which the profit share or bonus relates.

2.5 Example: Profit sharing plan

Mooro Co runs a profit sharing plan under which it pays 3% of its profit for the year to its employees if none have left during the year. Mooro Co estimates that this will be reduced by staff turnover to 2.5% in 20X9.

Required

Which costs should be recognised by Mooro Co for the profit share?

Solution

Mooro Co should recognise a liability and an expense of 2.5% of profit.

2.6 Disclosure

There are **no specific disclosure requirements for short-term employee benefits** in the standard.

3 Post-employment benefits

> **FAST FORWARD**
>
> There are **two types of post-employment benefit plan:**
> - Defined contribution plans
> - Defined benefit plans
>
> **Defined contribution plans** are simple to account for because it is the contributions payable which are promised and the eventual benefits depend on them.
>
> **Defined benefit plans** are much more difficult to account for because it is the eventual benefits which are promised and the total contributions depend on them.

Many employers provide post-employment benefits for their employees after they have stopped working. **Pension schemes** are the most obvious example, but an employer might provide post-employment death benefits to the dependants of former employees, or post-employment medical care.

Post-employment benefit schemes are often referred to as '**plans**'. The 'plan' receives regular contributions from the employer (and sometimes from current employees as well) and the money is invested in assets, such as stocks and shares and other investments. The post-employment benefits are paid out of the income from the plan assets (dividends, interest) or from money from the sale of some plan assets.

There are two types or categories of post-employment benefit plan, as given in the definitions in Section 1.5 above.

(a) **Defined contribution plans**. With such plans, the employer (and possibly current employees too) pay regular contributions into the plan of a given or 'defined' amount each year. The contributions are invested, and the size of the post-employment benefits paid to former employees depends on how well or how badly the plan's investments perform. If the investments perform well, the plan will be able to afford higher benefits than if the investments performed less well.

(b) **Defined benefit plans**. With these plans, the size of the post-employment benefits is determined in advance, ie the benefits are 'defined'. The employer (and possibly current employees too) pay contributions into the plan, and the contributions are invested. The size of the contributions is set at an amount that is expected to earn enough investment returns to meet the obligation to pay the post-employment benefits. If, however, it becomes apparent that the assets in the fund are insufficient, the employer will be required to make additional contributions into the plan to make up the expected shortfall. On the other hand, if the fund's assets appear to be larger than they need to be, and in excess of what is required to pay the post-employment benefits, the employer may be allowed to take a 'contribution holiday' (ie stop paying in contributions for a while).

It is important to make a clear distinction between the following.

(a) **Funding** a defined benefit plan, ie paying contributions into the plan
(b) **Accounting for** the cost of funding a defined benefit plan

Before we examine accounting for both these types of scheme, we need to mention a couple of other issues addressed by the standard.

3.1 Multi-employer plans

These were defined above. IAS 19 requires an entity to **classify** such a plan as a defined contribution plan or a defined benefit plan, depending on its terms (including any constructive obligation beyond those terms).

For a multi-employer plan that is a **defined benefit plan**, the entity should account for its proportionate share of the defined benefit obligation, plan assets and cost associated with the plan in the same way as for any other defined benefit plan and make full disclosure.

When there is **insufficient information** to use defined benefit accounting, then the multi-employer plan should be accounted for as a defined contribution plan and additional disclosures made (that the plan is in fact a defined benefit plan and information about any known surplus or deficit).

3.2 State plans

These plans are **established by legislation** to cover some or all entities and are operated by government or its agent. These plans cannot be controlled or influenced by the entity. State plans should be treated in the same way as multi-employer plans by the entity.

3.3 Insured benefits

Insurance premiums paid by an employer to fund an employee post-employment benefit plan should be accounted for as **defined contributions** to the plan, **unless** the employer has a legal or constructive obligation to pay the employee benefits directly when they fall due **or** to make further payments in the event that the insurance company does not pay all the post-employment benefits (relating to service given in prior years and the current period) for which insurance has been paid.

3.4 Examples: Insured benefits

For example, Employer A pays insurance premiums to fund post-employment medical care for former employees. It has no obligation beyond paying the annual insurance premiums. The premium paid each year should be accounted for as a defined contribution.

Employer B similarly pays insurance premiums for the same purpose, but retains the liability to pay for the medical benefits itself. In the case of Employer B, the rights under the insurance policy should be recognised as an asset, and it should account for the obligation to employees as a liability as if there were no insurance policy.

3.5 Section summary

- There are two categories of **post-retirement benefits**:
    - Defined contribution schemes
    - Defined benefit schemes
- **Defined contribution schemes** provide benefits commensurate with the fund available to produce them.
- **Defined benefit schemes** provide promised benefits and so contributions are based on estimates of how the fund will perform.
- **Defined contribution scheme costs** are easy to account for and this is covered in the next section.
- The main part of the rest of this chapter deals with the more difficult question of how **defined benefit scheme costs** are accounted for.

4 Defined contribution plans

Accounting for payments into defined contribution plans is straightforward.

(a) The **obligation** is determined by the amount payable into the plan in each period.

(b) There are no actuarial assumptions to make.

(c) If the obligation is settled in the current period (or at least no later than 12 months after the end of the current period) there is **no requirement for discounting**.

IAS 19 requires the following.

(a) **Contributions** to a defined contribution plan should be recognised as an **expense** in the period they are payable (except to the extent that labour costs may be included within the cost of assets).

(b) Any liability for **unpaid contributions** that are due as at the end of the period should be recognised as a **liability** (accrued expense).

(c) Any **excess contributions** paid should be recognised as an asset (prepaid expense), but only to the extent that the prepayment will lead to, eg a reduction in future payments or a cash refund.

In the (unusual) situation where contributions to a defined contribution plan do not fall due entirely within 12 months after the end of the period in which the employees performed the related service, then these should be **discounted**. The discount rate to be used is discussed below.

Disclosure requirements

(a) A **description** of the plan
(b) The amount recognised as an **expense** in the period

5 Defined benefit plans: Recognition and measurement

Accounting for defined benefit plans is much more complex. The complexity of accounting for defined benefit plans stems largely from the following factors.

(a) The future benefits (arising from employee service in the current or prior years) **cannot be estimated exactly**, but whatever they are, the employer will have to pay them, and the liability should therefore be recognised now. To estimate these future obligations, it is necessary to use **actuarial assumptions**.

(b) The obligations payable in future years should be valued, by discounting, on a **present value** basis. This is because the obligations may be settled in many years' time.

(c) If actuarial assumptions change, the amount of required contributions to the fund will change, and there may be **remeasurements**. A contribution into a fund in any period is not necessarily the total for that period, due to remeasurements.

Most of the definitions given in the standard (shown in Section 1) are to do with defined benefit plans.

5.1 Outline of the method

> **FAST FORWARD** There is a **four-step method** for accounting for the expenses and liability of a defined benefit pension plan.

An outline of the method used for an employer to account for the expenses and obligation of a defined benefit plan is given below. The stages will be explained in more detail later.

Step 1 — Determining the deficit or surplus. This involves:

Section 5.3

(i) Using an actuarial technique, the projected unit credit method, to make a reliable estimate of the ultimate cost to the entity of the benefit that employees have earned in return for their service in the current and prior periods. This requires an entity to consider **actuarial assumptions** ie estimates about variables such as employee turnover and future increases in salary that will affect the future benefit. (see **Section 5.3.1**)

(ii) Discounting the benefit in order to determine the present value of the defined benefit obligation and the current service cost. (see **Section 5.3.3**)

(iii) Deducting the fair value of the plan assets from the present value of the defined benefit obligation. (see **Section 5.3.4**)

Step 2 — Determining the amount of the net defined benefit liability (asset) as the amount of the deficit or surplus determined in (a), adjusted for any effect of limiting a net defined benefit asset to the asset ceiling.

Section 5.4

Step 3 — Determining amounts to be recognised in profit or loss:

Section 5.5

(i) Current service cost (calculated using the projected unit credit method – see **Section 5.3**)

(ii) Any past service cost and gain or loss on settlement

(iii) Net interest on the defined benefit liability (asset)

Step 4 — Determining the remeasurements of the net defined benefit liability (asset) to be recognised in other comprehensive income, comprising:

Section 5.5

(i) Actuarial gains and losses

(ii) Return on plan assets excluding amounts included in net interest on the defined benefit liability (asset)

(iii) Any change in the effect of the asset ceiling, excluding amounts included in net interest on the net defined benefit liability (asset).

5.2 Constructive obligation

IAS 19 makes it very clear that it is not only its legal obligation under the formal terms of a defined benefit plan that an entity must account for, but also for any **constructive obligation** that it may have. A constructive obligation, which will arise from the entity's informal practices, exist when the entity has no realistic alternative but to pay employee benefits, for example if any change in the informal practices would cause unacceptable damage to employee relationships.

16: EMPLOYEE BENEFITS

5.3 Determining the deficit or surplus

5.3.1 The Projected Unit Credit Method

FAST FORWARD

> Future benefits are attributed to services performed by employees using the **Projected Unit Credit Method**.

With this method, it is assumed that each period of service by an employee gives rise to an **additional unit of future benefits**. The present value of that unit of future benefits can be calculated, and attributed to the period in which the service is given as the current service cost. The units, each measured separately, build up to the overall obligation. The accumulated present value of (discounted) future benefits will incur interest over time, and an interest expense should be recognised.

The method relies on a number of actuarial assumptions – some of which are non-financial such as employee turnover and mortality rates, and some of which are financial, such as expected future salaries. These are discussed in the next section.

In practice, the mathematics will be complex. Here is a simplified example, using figures rounded to whole numbers.

5.3.2 Example: Projected Unit Credit Method

An employer pays a lump sum to employees when they retire. The lump sum is equal to 1% of their salary in the final year of service, for every year of service they have given.

(a) An employee is expected to work for 5 years (actuarial assumption)
(b) His salary is expected to rise by 7% pa (actuarial assumption)
(c) His salary in 20X1 is $10,000
(d) The discount rate applied is 10% pa

Required

Calculate the amounts chargeable to each of years 20X1 to 20X5 and the closing obligation each year, assuming no change in actuarial assumptions.

Solution

Since his salary in 20X1 is $10,000, his salary in 20X5 is expected to be $13,107 (£10,000 × 1.07^4). His lump sum entitlement is therefore expected to be 1% of $13,107 ie $131 for each year's service, giving $655 in total.

Using the Projected Unit Credit Method, and assuming that the actuarial assumptions do not change over the years 20X1 to 20X5, and that the employee does leave at the end of 20X5, the calculations are as follows:

Future benefit attributable to:	20X1 $	20X2 $	20X3 $	20X4 $	20X5 $
Prior years	0	131	262	393	524
Current year (1% of final salary)	131	131	131	131	131
Prior and current years total	131	262	393	524	655

The future benefit builds up to $655 over the five years, at the end of which the employee is expected to leave and the benefit is payable.

These figures, however, have not been discounted. The benefit attributable to the current year should be discounted, in this example at 10%, from the end of 20X5.

	20X1 $	20X2 $	20X3 $	20X4 $	20X5 $
Opening obligation (note 1)	–	89	196	324	476
Interest (note 2)	–	9	20	33	48
Current service cost (note 3)	89	98	108	119	131
Closing obligation (note 4)	89	196	324	476	655

Notes

1 The opening obligation is the closing obligation of the previous period, brought forward.
2 Interest is 10% of this opening obligation (rounded to the nearest $).
3 The current service cost is the future obligation attributed to the current period (in this example $131 in each year), discounted back by 10% for 4, 3, 2 and 1 years respectively.
4 The closing obligation is the total of the opening obligation brought forward, the interest charged on that amount and the current year service cost.
5 The calculations in the example above assume that actuarial forecasts are exactly correct. If these were to prove incorrect (which is likely in practice), there could be an adjustment to make, resulting in an actuarial gain or an actuarial loss.

5.3.3 Actuarial assumptions

Actuarial assumptions made should be unbiased and based on market expectations.

Actuarial assumptions are needed **to estimate the size of the future (post-employment) benefits** that will be payable under a defined benefit plan. The main categories of actuarial assumptions are as follows.

(a) **Demographic assumptions** are about mortality rates before and after retirement, the rate of employee turnover, early retirement, claim rates under medical plans for former employees, and so on.

(b) **Financial assumptions** are the expected return on plan assets, future salary levels (allowing for seniority and promotion as well as inflation) and the future rate of increase in medical costs (not just inflationary cost rises, but also cost rises specific to medical treatments and to medical treatments required given the expectations of longer average life expectancy).

The standard requires actuarial assumptions to be neither too cautious nor too imprudent: they should be **'unbiased'**. They should also be based on **'market expectations'** at the year end, over the period during which the obligations will be settled.

5.3.4 Discount rate

The example above shows how the post-employment benefit obligation estimated based on actuarial assumptions is discounted in order to determine the present value of the defined benefit obligation and current service cost in each year.

The **discount rate** adopted should be determined by reference to **market yields** (at the year end) on high quality fixed-rate corporate bonds. In the absence of a 'deep' market in such bonds, the yields on comparable government bonds should be used as reference instead. The maturity of the corporate bonds that are used to determine a discount rate should have a term to maturity that is consistent with the expected maturity of the post-employment benefit obligations, although a single weighted average discount rate is sufficient.

5.3.5 Fair value of plan assets

The fair value of plan assets are deducted from the present value of the defined benefit obligation or give the net deficit or surplus.

Plan assets are:

(a) Assets such as stocks and shares, held by a fund that is legally separate from the reporting entity, which exists solely to pay employee benefits.

(b) Insurance policies, issued by an insurer that is not a related party, the proceeds of which can only be used to pay employee benefits.

Investments which may be used for purposes other than to pay employee benefits are not plan assets.

The standard requires that the plan assets are measured at fair value, defined in accordance with IFRS 13 *Fair Value Measurement* as 'the price that would be received to sell an asset or paid to transfer a liability in an orderly transaction between market participants at the measurement date.'

IAS 19 includes the following **specific requirements:**

(a) The plan assets should exclude any contributions due from the employer but not yet paid.

(b) Plan assets are reduced by any liabilities of the fund that do not relate to employee benefits, such as trade and other payables.

5.4 The net defined benefit (asset) in the statement of financial position

In the statement of financial position, the amount recognised as a **defined benefit liability** (which may be a negative amount, ie an asset) should be the following:

(a) The **present value of the defined obligation** at the year end, **minus**

(b) The **fair value of the assets of the plan** as at the year end (if there are any) out of which the future obligations to current and past employees will be directly settled.

Where there is a net defined benefit asset, the amount of this may be limited by the 'asset ceiling'. We shall discuss this in more detail later in the chapter.

5.5 Amounts to be recognised in the statement of profit or loss and other comprehensive income

Step three of the four step plan is determining amounts to be recognised in the statement of profit or loss and other comprehensive income.

All of the gains and losses that affect the plan obligation and plan asset must be recognised. The **components of defined benefit cost must be recognised as follows** in the statement of profit or loss and other comprehensive income:

Component	*Recognised in*
(a) **Service cost**	Profit or loss
(b) **Net interest on the net defined benefit liability**	Profit or loss
(c) **Remeasurements of the net defined benefit liability (asset)**	Other comprehensive income (not reclassified to profit or loss)

5.5.1 Service costs

These include:

(a) **Current service cost,** this is the increase in the present value of the defined benefit obligation resulting from employee services during the period. The measurement and recognition of this cost was introduced in Section 5.3.2.

(b) **Past service cost,** which is the change in the obligation relating to service in **prior periods.** This results from amendments or curtailments to the pension plan; and

(c) Any **gain or loss on settlement.**

The detail relating to points (b) and (c) above will be covered in a later section. First we shall continue with the basic elements of accounting for defined benefit pension costs.

5.5.2 Net interest on the net defined benefit liability

IAS 19 requires that annual interest should be calculated on the **net defined benefit liability (asset)**. It therefore incorporates two elements:

(i) An interest charge arising on the unwinding of the discount on the defined benefit obligation as time passes; and

(ii) Interest income recognised on the plan assets.

The calculation is of net interest is:

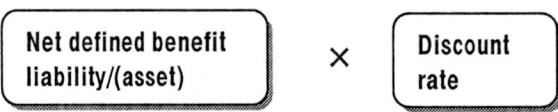

The **net defined benefit liability/(asset)** should be determined as at the **start** of the accounting period, taking account of changes during the period as a result of contributions paid into the scheme and benefits paid out.

Many exam questions include the assumption that all payments into and out of the scheme take place at the end of the year, so that the interest calculations can be based on the opening balances.

The **discount rate** is that determined by reference to **market yields** (at the year end) on high quality fixed-rate corporate bonds, as discussed in Section 5.3.4.

5.5.3 Remeasurements of the net defined benefit liability (asset)

Remeasurements of the net defined benefit liability/(asset) comprise:

(a) Actuarial gains and losses;

(b) The return on plan assets, (excluding amounts included in net interest on the net defined benefit liability/(asset); and

(c) Any change in the effect of the asset ceiling, (excluding amounts included in net interest on the net defined benefit liability/(asset).

The gains and losses relating to points (a) and (b) above will arise in every defined benefit scheme so we will look at these in this section. The asset ceiling is a complication that is not relevant in every case, so it is dealt with separately, later in the chapter.

Actuarial gains and losses

At the end of each accounting period, a new valuation, using updated assumptions, should be carried out on the obligation. Actuarial gains or losses arise because of the following.

- **Actual events** (eg employee turnover, salary increases) differ from the actuarial assumptions that were made to estimate the defined benefit obligations
- The effect of **changes to assumptions** concerning benefit payment options
- **Estimates are revised** (eg different assumptions are made about future employee turnover, salary rises, mortality rates, and so on)
- The effect of changes to the **discount rate.**

Actuarial gains and losses are recognised in other comprehensive income. They are **not reclassified to profit or loss.**

Return on plan assets

A new valuation of the plan assets is carried out at each period end, using current fair values. Any difference between the new value, and what has been recognised up to that date (normally the opening balance, interest, and any cash payments into or out of the plan) is treated as a 'remeasurement' and recognised in other comprehensive income.

5.5.4 Example

At 1 January 20X2 the fair value of the assets of a defined benefit plan were valued at $1,100,000 and the present value of the defined benefit obligation was $1,250,000. On 31 December 20X2, the plan received contributions from the employer of $490,000 and paid out benefits of $190,000.

The current service cost for the year was $360,000 and a discount rate of 6% is to be applied to the net liability/(asset).

After these transactions, the fair value of the plan's assets at 31 December 20X2 was $1.5m. The present value of the defined benefit obligation was $1,553,600.

Required

Calculate the actuarial gains or losses and the return on plan assets and illustrate how this pension plan will be treated in the statement of profit or loss and other comprehensive income and statement of financial position for the year ended 31 December 20X2.

Solution

It is always useful to set up a working reconciling the assets and obligation:

	Assets $	Obligation $
Fair value/present value at 1/1/X2	1,100,000	1,250,000
Interest (1,100,000 × 6%)/(1,250,000 × 6%)	66,000	75,000
Current service cost		360,000
Contributions received	490,000	
Benefits paid	(190,000)	(190,000)
Return on plan assets (balancing figure)	34,000	–
Actuarial loss (balancing figure)	–	58,600
	1,500,000	1,553,600

The following accounting treatment is required.

(a) In the **statement of profit or loss and other comprehensive income**, the following amounts will be recognised:

In profit or loss	$
Current service cost	360,000
Net interest on net defined benefit liability (75,000 – 66,000)	9,000
In other comprehensive income	
Remeasurement losses on defined benefit liability	(24,600)

(b) In the **statement of financial position**, the net defined benefit liability of $53,600 (1,553,600 – 1,500,000) will be recognised.

5.6 Section summary

The recognition and measurement of defined benefit plan costs are complex issues.

- Learn and understand the definitions of the various elements of a defined benefit pension plan
- Learn the **outline method** of accounting (see Section 5.1)
- Learn the recognition method for the:
    - Statement of financial position
    - Statement of profit or loss and other comprehensive income

6 Defined benefit plans: Other matters

6.1 Past service cost and gains and losses on settlement

> **FAST FORWARD**
>
> You should know how to deal with **past service cost**.

In Section 5.5.1 we identified that the total service cost may comprise not only the current service costs but also past service cost and gains and losses on settlement. This section explain these issues and their accounting treatment.

6.1.1 Past service cost

Past service cost is the change in the present value of the defined benefit obligation resulting from a plan **amendment** or **curtailment**.

A plan **amendment** arises when an entity either introduces a defined benefits plan or **changes the benefits payable** under an existing plan. As a result, the entity has taken on additional obligations that it has not previously provided for. For example, an employer might decide to introduce a medical benefits scheme for former employees. This will create a new defined benefit obligation, that has not yet been provided for.

A **curtailment occurs when an entity significantly reduces the number of employees covered by a plan.** This could result from an isolated event, such as closing a plant, discontinuing an operation or the termination or suspension of a plan.

Past service costs can be either **positive** (if the changes increase the obligation) or **negative** (if the change reduces the obligation).

6.1.2 Gains and losses on settlement

A **settlement** occurs either when an employer enters into a transaction to eliminate part or all of its post-employment benefit obligations (other than a payment of benefits to or on behalf of employees under the terms of the plan and included in the actuarial assumptions).

A curtailment and settlement might **happen together**, for example when an employer brings a defined benefit plan to an end by settling the obligation with a one-off lump sum payment and then scrapping the plan.

The gain or losses on a settlement is the difference between:

(a) The **present value of the defined benefit obligation** being settled, as valued on the date of the settlement; and

(b) The **settlement price**, including any plan assts transferred and any payments made by the entity directly in connection with the settlement.

6.1.3 Accounting for past service cost and gains and losses on settlement

An entity should **remeasure the obligation** (and the related plan assets, if any) using current actuarial assumptions, before determining past service cost or a gain or loss on settlement.

The rules for recognition for these items are:

Past service costs are recognised at the earlier of the following dates:

(a) When the plan amendment or curtailment occurs, and

(b) When the entity recognises related restructuring costs (in accordance with IAS 37 *Provisions, Contingent Liabilities and Contingent Assets,* see Chapter 19) or termination benefits

6.2 Asset ceiling test

When we looked at the recognition of the net defined benefit liability/(asset) in the statement of financial position at the beginning of Section 5 the term 'asset ceiling' was mentioned. This term relates to a threshold established by IAS 19 to ensure that any defined benefit asset (ie a pension surplus) is carried at no more than its recoverable amount. In simple terms, this means that any net asset is restricted to the amount of cash savings that will be available to the entity in future.

6.3 Net defined benefit assets

A net defined benefit asset may arise if the plan has been overfunded or if actuarial gains have arisen. This meets the definition of an asset (as stated in the *Conceptual Framework*) because **all** of the following apply:

(a) The entity **controls a resource** (the ability to use the surplus to generate future benefits).

(b) That control is the **result of past events** (contributions paid by the entity and service rendered by the employee).

(c) **Future benefits** are available to the entity in the form of a reduction in future contributions or a cash refund, either directly or indirectly to another plan in deficit.

The **asset ceiling** is the present value of those future benefits. The discount rate used is the same as that used to calculate the net interest on the net defined benefit liability/(asset). The net defined benefit asset would be reduced to the asset ceiling threshold. Any related write down would be treated as a **remeasurement** and recognised in **other comprehensive income.**

If the asset ceiling adjustment was needed in a subsequent year, the changes in its value would be treated as follows:

(a) **Interest** (as it is a discounted amount) recognised in profit or loss as part of the net interest amount

(b) **Other changes** recognised in profit or loss

6.4 Employee contributions

In some entities, employees also make contributions to the retirement plan. These contributions reduce the cost to the entity of providing the benefits, and so are deducted from service cost.

In November 2013, a narrow scope amendment was issued to IAS 19 to clarify in which periods these contributions should be deducted:

- If the amounts of the contributions are independent of the numbers of years of service, the entity is permitted (but may choose not to) recognise them as reduction of service cost in the period in which the service is rendered, instead of attributing them to periods of service.

- If the amounts are dependent on the number of years of service, then those amounts must be attributed to periods of service using the same attribution method used to allocate service cost to periods of service.

6.5 Suggested approach and question

The suggested approach to defined benefit schemes is to deal with the change in the obligation and asset in the following order.

Step	Item	Recognition	
1	**Record opening figures:** • Asset • Obligation		
2	**Interest cost on obligation** • Based on discount rate and PV obligation at start of period. • Should also reflect any changes in obligation during period.	DEBIT CREDIT	Interest cost (SPLOCI) (X% × b/d obligation) PV defined benefit obligation (SOFP)
3	**Interest on plan assets** • Based on discount rate and asset value at start of period. • Technically, this interest is also time apportioned on contributions less benefits paid in the period.	DEBIT CREDIT	Plan assets (SOFP) Interest cost (SPLOCI) (X% × b/d assets)
4	**Current service cost** • Increase in the present value of the obligation resulting from employee service in the current period.	DEBIT CREDIT	Current service cost (SPLOCI) PV defined benefit obligation (SOFP)
5	**Contributions** • As advised by actuary.	DEBIT CREDIT	Plan assets (SOFP) Company cash
6	**Benefits** • Actual pension payments made.	DEBIT CREDIT	PV defined benefit obligation (SOFP) Plan assets (SOFP)
7	**Past service cost** • Increase/decrease in PV obligation as a result of introduction or improvement of benefits.	**Positive (increase in obligation):** DEBIT CREDIT **Negative (decrease in obligation):** DEBIT CREDIT	 Past service cost (SPLOCI) PV defined benefit obligation (SOFP) PV defined benefit obligation (SOFP) Past service cost (SPLOCI)
8	**Gains and losses on settlement** • Difference between the value of the obligation being settled and the settlement price	**Gain** DEBIT CREDIT **Loss** DEBIT CREDIT	 PV defined benefit obligation (SOFP) Service cost (SPLOCI) Service cost (SPLOCI) PV defined benefit obligation (SOFP)
9	**Remeasurements: actuarial gains and losses** • Arising from annual valuations of obligation. • On obligation, differences between actuarial assumptions and actual experience during the period, or changes in actuarial assumptions.	**Gain** DEBIT CREDIT **Loss** DEBIT CREDIT	 PV defined benefit obligation (SOFP) Other comprehensive income (SPLOCI) Other comprehensive income (SPLOCI) PV defined benefit obligation (SOFP)

16: EMPLOYEE BENEFITS

Step	Item	Recognition
10	**Remeasurements: return on assets** • Arising from annual valuations of plan assets	**Gain** DEBIT FV plan assets (SOFP) CREDIT Other comprehensive income (SPLOCI) **Loss** DEBIT Other comprehensive income (SPLOCI) CREDIT FV plan assets (SOFP)
11	**Disclose in accordance with the standard**	See comprehensive question.

Exam focus point

It would be useful for you to do one last question on accounting for post-employment defined benefit schemes.

Question — Comprehensive

For the sake of simplicity and clarity, all transactions are assumed to occur at the year end.

The following data applies to the post employment defined benefit compensation scheme of BCD Co.
Discount rate: 10% (each year)
Present value of obligation at start of 20X2: $1m
Market value of plan assets at start of 20X2: $1m

The following figures are relevant:

	20X2	20X3	20X4
	$'000	$'000	$'000
Current service cost	140	150	150
Benefits paid out	120	140	150
Contributions paid by entity	110	120	120
Present value of obligation at year end	1,200	1,650	1,700
Fair value of plan assets at year end	1,250	1,450	1,610

Additional information:

(1) At the end of 20X3, a division of the company was sold. As a result of this, a large number of the employees of that division opted to transfer their accumulated pension entitlement to their new employer's plan. Assets with a fair value of $48,000 were transferred to the other company's plan and the actuary has calculated that the reduction in BCD's defined benefit liability is $50,000. The year end valuations in the table above were carried out **before** this transfer was recorded.

(2) At the end of 20X4, a decision was taken to make a one-off additional payment to former employees currently receiving pensions from the plan. This was announced to the former employees before the year end. This payment was not allowed for in the original terms of the scheme. The actuarial valuation of the obligation in the table above **includes** the additional liability of $40,000 relating to this additional payment.

Required

Show how the reporting entity should account for this defined benefit plan in each of years 20X2, 20X3 and 20X4.

Answer

The actuarial gain or loss is established as a balancing figure in the calculations, as follows:

Present value of obligation

	20X2 $'000	20X3 $'000	20X4 $'000
PV of obligation at start of year	1,000	1,200	1,600
Interest cost (10%)	100	120	160
Current service cost	140	150	150
Past service cost			40
Benefits paid	(120)	(140)	(150)
Settlements		(50)	
Actuarial (gain)/loss on obligation: balancing figure	80	320	(100)
PV of obligation at end of year	1,200	1,600*	1,700

*(1,650 – 50)

Market value of plan assets

	20X2 $'000	20X3 $'000	20X4 $'000
Market value of plan assets at start of year	1,000	1,250	1,402
Interest on plan assets (10%)	100	125	140
Contributions	110	120	120
Benefits paid	(120)	(140)	(150)
Settlements	–	(48)	–
Return on plan assets: balancing figure	160	95	98
Market value of plan assets at year end	1,250	1,402*	1,610

*(1,450 – 48)

In the statement of financial position, the liability that is recognised is calculated as follows:

	20X2 $'000	20X3 $'000	20X4 $'000
Present value of obligation	1,200	1,600	1,700
Market value of plan assets	1,250	1,402	1,610
Liability/(asset) in statement of financial position	(50)	198	90

The following will be recognised in profit or loss for the year:

	20X2 $'000	20X3 $'000	20X4 $'000
Current service cost	140	150	150
Past service cost	–	–	40
Net interest on defined benefit liability (asset)	–	(5)	20
Gain on settlement of defined benefit liability		2	
Expense recognised in profit or loss	140	147	210

The following remeasurements will be recognised in other comprehensive income for the year:

	20X2 $'000	20X3 $'000	20X4 $'000
Actuarial (gain)/loss on obligation	80	320	(100)
Return on plan assets	(160)	(95)	(98)

7 Other long-term benefits

FAST FORWARD

Other long-term employment benefits are accounted for in the same way as defined benefit pension plans with the exception of remeasurements, which are recognised in profit or loss rather than other comprehensive income.

In Section 5.5.1 we identified that the total service cost may comprise not only the current service.

There may be other long-term employment benefits, in addition to post-employment benefits. These include **bonuses** and **profit shares** payable 12 months or more after the end of the reporting period, and **long-term sabbatical leave**.

The measurement of other long-term employee benefits is not usually subject to the same degree of uncertainty as the measurement of post-employment benefits. Therefore a simplified method of accounting is adopted in which remeasurements are not recognised in other comprehensive income.

(a) The surplus or deficit in an other long-term employee benefit plan is measured as for a defined benefit pension plan; and

(b) The net total of the following is recognised in profit or loss except to the extent that another IFRS permits their inclusion in the cost of an asset:

   (i) Service cost
   (ii) Net interest on the net defined benefit liability (asset)
   (iii) Remeasurements of the net defined benefit liability (asset)

There are no specific disclosure requirements with respect to these benefits.

8 Termination benefits

FAST FORWARD

Termination benefits are recognised as a liability and expense when an entity can no longer withdraw the offer of the termination benefit or recognises any related restructuring costs.

Termination benefits are benefits to employees arising as a consequence of **termination of their employment**; they arise from either:

(i) An entity's decision to terminate employment; or

(ii) An employee's decision to accept an entity's offer of benefits in exchange for termination of employment eg the payment of a lump sum to an employee who volunteers for early retirement.

8.1 Recognition of termination benefits

The standard requires that these costs should be recognised in full as a liability and an expense at the earlier of:

- The date on which the entity can no longer withdraw the offer of benefits; or
- When the entity recognises costs for a restructuring that is within the scope of IAS 37 and involves the payment of termination benefits.

8.2 Measurement of termination benefits

Termination benefits should be measured in accordance with the nature of the employee benefit:

- If the termination benefits are expected to be settled wholly before 12 months after the end of the accounting period in which the termination benefit is recognised, the requirements for short-term employment benefits are applied;
- If the termination benefits are not expected to be settled wholly before 12 months after the end of the annual reporting period, the requirements for other long-term employee benefits are applied.

PART C ACCOUNTING AND REPORTING TECHNIQUES

Chapter roundup

- **IAS 19 *Employee Benefits*** is a long and complex standard covering both short-term and long-term (post-employment) benefits. The complications arise when dealing with **post-employment benefits**.
- There are **two types of post-employment benefit plan**:
    - Defined contribution plans
    - Defined benefit plans
- **Defined contribution plans** are simple to account for because it is the contributions payable which are promised and the eventual benefits depend on them.
- **Defined benefit plans** are much more difficult to account for because it is the eventual benefits which are promised and the total contributions depend on them.
- There is a **four-step method** for accounting for the expenses and liability of a defined benefit pension plan.
- Future benefits are attributed to services performed by employees using the **Projected Unit Credit Method**.
- **Actuarial assumptions** made should be unbiased and based on market expectations.
- You should know how to deal with **past service cost**.
- **Other long-term employment benefits** are accounted for in the same way as defined benefit pension plans with the exception of remeasurements, which are recognised in profit or loss rather than other comprehensive income.
- **Termination benefits** are recognised as a liability and expense when an entity can no longer withdraw the offer of the termination benefit or recognises any related restructuring costs.

Quick quiz

1. What are the four categories of employee benefits given by IAS 19?
2. What is the difference between defined contribution and defined benefit plans?
3. What is a 'constructive obligation' compared to a legal obligation?
4. Which gains and losses on a defined benefit liability (asset) should be recognised in profit or loss?
5. Which gains and losses on a defined benefit liability (asset) should be recognised in other comprehensive income?
6. How should termination benefits be recognised?

    A   Provided for as part of the costs of employment when incurred
    B   Part of a special provision for future liabilities
    C   Recognised in full as a liability and expense when a future obligation is recognised
    D   Amortised over the period of employment

Answers to quick quiz

1. - Short-term
   - Post-employment
   - Other long-term
   - Termination

2. See Section 3

3. A constructive obligation exists when the entity has no realistic alternative than to pay employee benefits.

4. Current service cost + past service cost + gains or losses on settlement + net interest on the defined benefit liability (asset).

5. Actuarial gains and losses + return on plan assets other that that included in net interest + change in the effect of the asset ceiling other than that included in net interest.

6. C   Recognised in full as a liability and an expense in the accounting period when the entity recognises a demonstrable obligation to pay the benefits in the future

End of chapter question

Employee benefits (AIA May 2008 – adapted)

The following information relates to the defined benefit employee compensation scheme of an entity:

Present value of obligation at start of 20X8 ($'000)	20,000
Market value of plan assets at start of 20X8 ($'000)	20,000
Discount rate per year	8%

	20X8	20X9
	$'000	$'000
Current service cost	1,250	1,430
Benefits paid out	987	1,100
Contributions paid by entity	1,000	1,100
Present value of obligation at end of the year	23,000	25,500
Market value of plan assets at end of the year	21,500	22,300

Assume that all transactions occur at the end of the year.

Required

(i) Calculate the present value of the defined benefit plan obligation as at the start and end of 20X8 and 20X9 showing clearly any actuarial gain or loss on the plan obligation for each year. **(4 marks)**

(ii) Calculate the market value of the defined benefit plan assets as at the start and end of 20X8 and 20X9 showing clearly any remeasurement on the plan assets for each year. **(4 marks)**

(iii) Show the total charge in respect of this plan in the statement of profit or loss and other comprehensive income for 20X8 and the statement of profit or loss and other comprehensive income for 20X9.

(4 marks)

(Total 12 marks)

PART C ACCOUNTING AND REPORTING TECHNIQUES

Taxation

Topic list	Syllabus reference
1 Current tax revised	13.4
2 Deferred tax	13.4
3 Taxable temporary differences	13.4
4 Deductible temporary differences	13.4
5 Measurement and recognition of deferred tax	13.4
6 Presentation and disclosure of taxation	13.4
7 Deferred taxation and business combinations	13.4

Introduction

In almost all countries entities are taxed on the basis of their trading income. In some countries this may be called corporation or corporate tax, but we will follow the terminology of IAS 12 *Income Taxes* and call it **income tax**.

There are two main systems for taxing corporate income: the **classical system** and the **imputation system**: go back to your earlier study material if necessary. For this chapter we will assume a classical system. Of course, each country will be different in its tax legislation and its method of accounting for taxation may reflect this.

There are two aspects of income tax which must be accounted for: **current tax** and **deferred tax**. Current tax is revised briefly in Section 1. The rest of this chapter is concerned with deferred tax, which students invariably find difficult.

Section 7 introduces a new aspect of deferred tax, relating to **business combinations**. This represents one of the most complex areas of deferred tax.

Note. Throughout this chapter we will assume a current corporate income tax rate of 30% and a current personal income tax rate of 20%, unless otherwise stated.

PART C ACCOUNTING AND REPORTING TECHNIQUES

1 Current tax revised

FAST FORWARD

Taxation consists of **two components**.

- Current tax
- Deferred tax

Current tax is the amount payable to the tax authorities in relation to the trading activities during the period. It is generally straightforward and is covered in Section 1.

Deferred tax is an accounting measure, used to match the tax effects of transactions with their accounting impact. It is quite complex, and is covered from Section 2.

These are some of the definitions given in IAS 12 *Income Taxes*. We will look at the rest later.

Key terms

Accounting profit. Profit or loss for a period before deducting tax expense.

Taxable profit (tax loss). The profit (loss) for a period, determined in accordance with the rules established by the taxation authorities, upon which income taxes are payable (recoverable).

Tax expense (tax income). The aggregate amount included in the determination of profit or loss for the period in respect of current tax and deferred tax.

Current tax. The amount of income taxes payable (recoverable) in respect of the taxable profit (tax loss) for a period. (IAS 12)

Remember the difference between current and deferred tax.

(a) **Current tax** is the amount **actually payable** to the tax authorities in relation to the trading activities of the entity during the period.

(b) **Deferred tax** is an **accounting measure**, used to match the tax effects of transactions with their accounting impact and thereby produce less distorted results.

1.1 Recognition of current tax liabilities and assets

IAS 12 requires any **unpaid tax** in respect of the current or prior periods to be recognised as a **liability**.

Conversely, any **excess tax** paid in respect of current or prior periods over what is due should be recognised as an asset.

Question — Current tax

In 20X8 Darton Co had taxable profits of $120,000 and the rate of tax is 30%. In the previous year (20X7) income tax on 20X7 profits had been estimated as $30,000.

Required

Calculate tax payable and the charge for 20X8 if the tax due on 20X7 profits was subsequently agreed with the tax authorities as:

(a) $35,000
(b) $25,000

Any under- or overpayments are not settled until the following year's tax payment is due.

Answer

(a)

	$
Tax due on 20X8 profits ($120,000 × 30%)	36,000
Underpayment for 20X7	5,000
Tax charge and liability	41,000

(b)

	$
Tax due on 20X8 profits (as above)	36,000
Overpayment for 20X7	(5,000)
Tax charge and liability	31,000

Taking this a stage further, IAS 12 also requires recognition as an asset of the benefit relating to any tax loss that can be **carried back** to recover current tax of a previous period. This is acceptable because it is probable that the benefit will flow to the entity **and** it can be reliably measured.

1.2 Example: Tax losses carried back

In 20X7 Eramu Co paid $50,000 in tax on its 20X7 profits. In 20X8 the company made tax losses of $24,000. The local tax authority rules allow losses to be carried back to offset against current tax of prior years. The rate of tax is 30%

Required

Show the double entry in 20X8.

Solution

Tax relief due on losses = 30% × $24,000 = $7,200.

The double entry will be:

DEBIT	Tax recoverable (statement of financial position)	$7,200	
CREDIT	Tax relief (statement of profit or loss and other comprehensive income)		$7,200

The tax receivable will be shown as an asset until the repayment is received from the tax authorities.

1.3 Measurement

Measurement of current tax liabilities (assets) for the current and prior periods is very simple. They are measured at the **amount expected to be paid to (recovered from) the tax authorities**. The tax rates (and tax laws) used should be those enacted (or substantively enacted) by the end of the reporting period.

1.4 Recognition of current tax

Normally, current tax is recognised as income or expense and included in the profit or loss for the period, except in two cases.

(a) Tax arising from a **business combination** which is an acquisition is treated differently (see Part B of this text and Section 7 of this chapter).

(b) Tax arising from a transaction or event which is recognised **directly in other comprehensive income or in equity** (in the same or a different period).

The rule in (b) is logical. If a transaction or event is charged or credited directly to other comprehensive income/equity, rather than to profit or loss, then the related tax should be also. An example of such a situation is where, under IAS 8 *Accounting Policies, Changes in Accounting Estimates and Errors*, an adjustment is made to the **opening balance of retained earnings** due to either a change in accounting policy that is applied retrospectively, or to the correction of a fundamental error.

1.5 Presentation

In the statement of financial position, **tax assets and liabilities** should be shown separately from other assets and liabilities.

Current tax assets and liabilities can be **offset**, but this should happen only when certain conditions apply.

(a) The entity has a **legally enforceable right** to set off the recognised amounts.

(b) The entity intends to settle the amounts on a **net basis**, or to realise the asset and settle the liability at the same time.

The **tax expense (income)** related to the profit or loss from ordinary activities should be shown in the statement of profit or loss and other comprehensive income.

The **disclosure requirements** of IAS 12 are extensive and we will look at these later in the chapter.

2 Deferred tax

Deferred tax assets and liabilities arise from taxable and deductible temporary differences.

2.1 What is deferred tax?

When a company recognises an asset or liability, it expects to **recover or settle the carrying amount** of that asset or liability. In other words, it expects to sell or use up assets, and to pay off liabilities. What happens if that recovery or settlement is likely to make future tax payments larger (or smaller) than they would otherwise have been if the recovery or settlement had no tax consequences? In these circumstances, IAS 12 requires companies to recognise a **deferred tax liability** (or **deferred tax asset**).

2.2 Definitions

Here are the definitions relating to deferred tax given in IAS 12.

Key terms

Deferred tax liabilities are the amounts of income taxes payable in future periods in respect of taxable temporary differences.

Deferred tax assets are the amounts of income taxes recoverable in future periods in respect of:

- Deductible temporary differences
- The carryforward of unused tax losses
- The carryforward of unused tax credits

Temporary differences are differences between the carrying amount of an asset or liability in the statement of financial position and its tax base. Temporary differences may be either:

(a) **Taxable temporary differences**, which are temporary differences that will result in taxable amounts in determining taxable profit (tax loss) of future periods when the carrying amount of the asset or liability is recovered or settled

(b) **Deductible temporary differences**, which are temporary differences that will result in amounts that are deductible in determining taxable profit (tax loss) of future periods when the carrying amount of the asset or liability is recovered or settled.

The **tax base** of an asset or liability is the amount attributed to that asset or liability for tax purposes.

(IAS 12)

2.3 Tax base

We can expand on the definition given above by stating that the **tax base of an asset** is the amount that will be deductible for tax purposes against any taxable economic benefits that will flow to the entity when it recovers the carrying value of the asset. Where those economic benefits are not taxable, the tax base of the asset is the same as its carrying amount.

Question — Tax base 1

State the tax base of each of the following assets.

(a) A machine cost $10,000. For tax purposes, depreciation of $3,000 has already been deducted in the current and prior periods and the remaining cost will be deductible in future periods, either as depreciation or through a deduction on disposal. Revenue generated by using the machine is taxable, any gain on disposal of the machine will be taxable and any loss on disposal will be deductible for tax purposes.

(b) Interest receivable has a carrying amount of $1,000. The related interest revenue will be taxed on a cash basis.

(c) Trade receivables have a carrying amount of $10,000. The related revenue has already been included in taxable profit (tax loss).

(d) A loan receivable has a carrying amount of $1m. The repayment of the loan will have no tax consequences.

(e) Dividends receivable from a subsidiary have a carrying amount of $5,000. The dividends are not taxable.

Answer

(a) The tax base of the machine is $7,000.
(b) The tax base of the interest receivable is nil.
(c) The tax base of the trade receivables is $10,000.
(d) The tax base of the loan is $1m.
(e) The tax base of the dividend is $5,000.

In the case of (e), in substance the entire carrying amount of the asset is deductible against the economic benefits. There is no taxable temporary difference. An alternative analysis is that the accrued dividends receivable have a tax base of nil and a tax rate of nil is applied to the resulting taxable temporary difference ($5,000). Under both analyses, there is no deferred tax liability.

In the case of a **liability**, the tax base will be its carrying amount, less any amount that will be deducted for tax purposes in relation to the liability in future periods. For revenue received in advance, the tax base of the resulting liability is its carrying amount, less any amount of the revenue that will **not** be taxable in future periods.

Question — Tax base 2

State the tax base of each of the following liabilities.

(a) Current liabilities include accrued expenses with a carrying amount of $1,000. The related expense will be deducted for tax purposes on a cash basis.

(b) Current liabilities include interest revenue received in advance, with a carrying amount of $10,000. The related interest revenue was taxed on a cash basis.

(c) Current liabilities include accrued expenses with a carrying amount of $2,000. The related expense has already been deducted for tax purposes.

(d) Current liabilities include accrued fines and penalties with a carrying amount of $100. Fines and penalties are not deductible for tax purposes.

(e) A loan payable has a carrying amount of $1m. The repayment of the loan will have no tax consequences.

Answer

(a) The tax base of the accrued expenses is nil.
(b) The tax base of the interest received in advance is nil.
(c) The tax base of the accrued expenses is $2,000.
(d) The tax base of the accrued fines and penalties is $100.
(e) The tax base of the loan is $1m.

IAS 12 gives the following examples of circumstances in which the carrying amount of an asset or liability will be **equal to its tax base**.

- **Pre-paid expenses** which have already been deducted in determining an entity's current tax liability for the current or earlier periods.
- A **loan payable** which is measured at the amount originally received and this amount is the same as the amount repayable on final maturity of the loan.
- **Accrued expenses** which will never be deductible for tax purposes.
- **Accrued income** which will never be taxable.

2.4 Temporary differences

You may have found the definition of temporary differences somewhat confusing. Remember that accounting profits form the basis for computing **taxable profits**, on which the tax liability for the year is calculated. However, accounting profits and taxable profits are different. There are two reasons for the differences.

(a) **Permanent differences**. These occur when certain items of revenue or expense are excluded from the computation of taxable profits (for example, entertainment expenses may not be allowable for tax purposes).

(b) **Temporary differences**. These occur when items of revenue or expense are included in both accounting profits and taxable profits, but not for the same accounting period. For example, an expense which is allowable as a deduction in arriving at taxable profits for 20X7 might not be included in the financial statements until 20X8 or later. In the long run, the total taxable profits and total accounting profits will be the same (except for permanent differences) so that timing differences originate in one period and are capable of reversal in one or more subsequent periods. Deferred tax is the tax attributable to **temporary differences**.

The distinction made in the definition between **taxable temporary differences** and **deductible temporary differences** can be made clearer by looking at the explanations and examples given in the standard and its appendices.

2.4.1 Section summary

- Deferred tax is an **accounting measure**. It does **not** represent tax payable to the tax authorities.
- The **tax base** of an asset or liability is the value of that asset or liability for tax purposes.
- You should understand the difference between **permanent and temporary differences**.
- Deferred tax is the tax attributable to **temporary differences**.

3 Taxable temporary differences

Rule to learn

> The rule to remember here is that:
>
> 'All taxable temporary differences give rise to a deferred tax liability.'

The following are examples of circumstances that give rise to taxable temporary differences.

3.1 Transactions that affect the statement of profit or loss and other comprehensive income

- **Interest revenue** received in arrears and included in accounting profit on the basis of time apportionment. It is included in taxable profit, however, on a cash basis.
- **Sale of goods revenue** included in accounting profit when the goods are delivered, but only included in taxable profit when cash is received.
- **Depreciation** of an asset accelerated for tax purposes. When new assets are purchased, allowances may be available against taxable profits which exceed the amount of depreciation chargeable on the assets in the financial statements for the year of purchase.
- **Development costs** which have been capitalised will be amortised in profit or loss, but they were deducted in full from taxable profit in the period in which they were incurred.
- **Prepaid expenses** already been deducted on a cash basis in determining the taxable profit of the current or previous periods.

3.2 Transactions that affect the statement of financial position

- **Depreciation of an asset** is not deductible for tax purposes. No deduction will be available for tax purposes when the asset is sold/scrapped.
- A borrower records a **loan** at proceeds received (amount due at maturity) less transaction costs. The carrying amount of the loan is subsequently increased by amortisation of the transaction costs against accounting profit. The transaction costs were, however, deducted for tax purposes in the period when the loan was first recognised.
- A **loan** payable is measured on initial recognition at net proceeds (net of transaction costs). The transaction costs are amortised to accounting profit over the life of the loan. Those transaction costs are not deductible in determining the taxable profit of future, current or prior periods.
- The liability component of a **compound financial instrument** (eg a convertible bond) is measured at a discount to the amount repayable on maturity, after assigning a portion of the cash proceeds to the equity component (see IAS 32 *Financial Instruments: Presentation*). The discount is not deductible in determining taxable profit.

3.3 Fair value adjustments and revaluations

- **Current investments** or financial instruments are carried at fair value. This exceeds cost, but no equivalent adjustment is made for tax purposes.
- Property, plant and equipment is **revalued** by an entity (under IAS 16 *Property, Plant and Equipment*), but no equivalent adjustment is made for tax purposes. This also applies to non-current investments.

The standard also looks at the deferred tax implications of business combinations and consolidations. We will look at these in Section 7.

Remember the rule we gave you above, that all taxable temporary differences give rise to a deferred tax liability? There are **two circumstances** given in the standards where this does **not** apply.

(a) The deferred tax liability arises from the initial recognition of **goodwill**.

(b) The deferred tax liability arises from the **initial recognition** of an asset or liability in a transaction which:

   (i) Is **not** a business combination (see Section 7); **and**
   (ii) At the time of the transaction affects neither accounting profit nor taxable profit.

Try to **understand the reasoning** behind the recognition of deferred tax liabilities on taxable temporary differences.

(a) When an **asset is recognised**, it is expected that its carrying amount will be recovered in the form of economic benefits that flow to the entity in future periods.

(b) If the carrying amount of the asset is **greater than** its tax base, then taxable economic benefits will also be greater than the amount that will be allowed as a deduction for tax purposes.

(c) The difference is therefore a **taxable temporary difference** and the obligation to pay the resulting income taxes in future periods is a **deferred tax liability**.

(d) As the entity recovers the carrying amount of the asset, the taxable temporary difference will **reverse** and the entity will have taxable profit.

(e) It is then probable that economic benefits will flow from the entity in the form of **tax payments**, and so the recognition of all deferred tax liabilities (except those excluded above) is required by IAS 12.

3.3.1 Example: Taxable temporary differences

A company purchased an asset costing $1,500. At the end of 20X8 the carrying amount is $1,000. The cumulative depreciation for tax purposes is $900 and the current tax rate is 25%.

Required

Calculate the deferred tax liability for the asset.

Solution

First, what is the tax base of the asset? It is $1,500 – $900 = $600.

In order to recover the carrying value of $1,000, the entity must earn taxable income of $1,000, but it will only be able to deduct $600 as a taxable expense. The entity must therefore pay income tax of $400 × 25% = $100 when the carrying value of the asset is recovered.

The entity must therefore recognise a deferred tax liability at the end of 20X8 of $400 × 25% = $100, recognising the difference between the carrying amount of $1,000 and the tax base of $600 as a taxable temporary difference.

3.4 Timing differences

Some temporary differences are often called **timing differences**, when income or expense is included in accounting profit in one period, but is included in taxable profit in a different period. The main types of taxable temporary differences which are timing differences and which result in deferred tax liabilities are included in the examples given above.

- **Interest received** which is accounted for on an accruals basis, but which for tax purposes is included on a cash basis.
- Accelerated depreciation for tax purposes.
- Capitalised and amortised **development costs**.

We will look briefly at other circumstances where temporary differences arise. Those relating to business combinations and group financial statements will be examined in Section 7.

3.5 Revalued assets

Under IAS 16 assets may be revalued. If this affects the taxable profit for the current period, the tax base of the asset changes and **no temporary difference** arises.

If, however (as in some countries), the revaluation does **not** affect current taxable profits, the tax base of the asset is not adjusted. Consequently, the taxable flow of economic benefits to the entity as the carrying value of the asset is recovered will differ from the amount that will be deductible for tax purposes. The difference between the carrying amount of a revalued asset and its tax base is a temporary difference and gives rise to a **deferred tax liability or asset**.

3.6 Initial recognition of an asset or liability

A temporary difference can arise on initial recognition of an asset or liability, eg if part or all of the cost of an asset will not be deductible for tax purposes. The **nature of the transaction** which led to the initial recognition of the asset is important in determining the method of accounting for such temporary differences.

If the transaction affects **either** accounting profit or taxable profit, an entity will **recognise any deferred tax liability or asset**. The resulting deferred tax expense or income will be recognised in the statement of profit or loss and other comprehensive income.

Where a transaction affects **neither accounting profit nor taxable profit** it would be normal for an entity to recognise a deferred tax liability or asset and adjust the carrying amount of the asset or liability by the same amount. However, IAS 12 does **not** permit this recognition of a deferred tax asset or liability as it would make the financial statements less transparent. This will be the case both on initial recognition and subsequently, nor should any subsequent changes in the unrecognised deferred tax liability or asset as the asset is depreciated be made.

3.7 Example: Initial recognition

As an example of the last paragraph, suppose Petros Co intends to use an asset which cost $10,000 in 20X7 through its useful life of five years. Its residual value will then be nil. The tax rate is 40%. Any capital gain on disposal would not be taxable (and any capital loss not deductible). Depreciation of the asset is not deductible for tax purposes.

Required

State the deferred tax consequences in each of years 20X7 and 20X8.

Solution

At the end of 20X7, as it recovers the carrying amount of the asset, Petros Co will earn taxable income of $10,000 and pay tax of $4,000. The resulting deferred tax liability of $4,000 would not be recognised because it results from the initial recognition of the asset.

At the end of 20X8, the carrying amount of the asset is now $8,000. In earning taxable income of $8,000, the entity will pay tax of $3,200. Again, the resulting deferred tax liability of $3,200 is not recognised, because it results from the initial recognition of the asset.

The following question on accelerated depreciation should clarify some of the issues and introduce you to the calculations which may be necessary in the exam.

Question — Deferred tax

Jonquil Co buys equipment for $50,000 and depreciates it on a straight-line basis over its expected useful life of five years. For tax purposes, the equipment is depreciated at 25% per annum on a straight-line basis. Tax losses may be carried back against taxable profit of the previous five years. In year 20X0, the entity's taxable profit was $25,000. The tax rate is 40%.

PART C ACCOUNTING AND REPORTING TECHNIQUES

Required

Assuming nil profits/losses after depreciation in years 20X1 to 20X5 show the current and deferred tax impact in years 20X1 to 20X5 of the acquisition of the equipment.

Answer

Jonquil Co will recover the carrying amount of the equipment by using it to manufacture goods for resale. Therefore, the entity's current tax computation is as follows:

	\multicolumn{5}{c}{Year}
	20X1 $	20X2 $	20X3 $	20X4 $	20X5 $
Taxable income*	10,000	10,000	10,000	10,000	10,000
Depreciation for tax purposes	12,500	12,500	12,500	12,500	0
Taxable profit (tax loss)	(2,500)	(2,500)	(2,500)	(2,500)	10,000
Current tax expense (income) at 40%	(1,000)	(1,000)	(1,000)	(1,000)	4,000

*ie nil profit plus ($50,000 ÷ 5) depreciation add-back.

The entity recognises a current tax asset at the end of years 20X1 to 20X4 because it recovers the benefit of the tax loss against the taxable profit of year 20X0.

The temporary differences associated with the equipment and the resulting deferred tax asset and liability and deferred tax expense and income are as follows:

	\multicolumn{5}{c}{Year}
	20X1 $	20X2 $	20X3 $	20X4 $	20X5 $
Carrying amount	40,000	30,000	20,000	10,000	0
Tax base	37,500	25,000	12,500	0	0
Taxable temporary difference	2,500	5,000	7,500	10,000	0
Opening deferred tax liability	0	1,000	2,000	3,000	4,000
Deferred tax expense (income): bal fig	1,000	1,000	1,000	1,000	(4,000)
Closing deferred tax liability @ 40%	1,000	2,000	3,000	4,000	0

The entity recognises the deferred tax liability in years 20X1 to 20X4 because the reversal of the taxable temporary difference will create taxable income in subsequent years. The entity's statement of profit or loss and other comprehensive income is as follows:

	\multicolumn{5}{c}{Year}
	20X1 $	20X2 $	20X3 $	20X4 $	20X5 $
Income	10,000	10,000	10,000	10,000	10,000
Depreciation	10,000	10,000	10,000	10,000	10,000
Profit before tax	0	0	0	0	0
Current tax expense (income)	(1,000)	(1,000)	(1,000)	(1,000)	4,000
Deferred tax expense (income)	1,000	1,000	1,000	1,000	(4,000)
Total tax expense (income)	0	0	0	0	0
Profit for the period	0	0	0	0	0

3.8 Section summary

- With one or two exceptions, all taxable temporary differences give rise to a **deferred tax liability**.
- Many taxable temporary differences are **timing differences**.
- Timing differences arise when income or an expense is included in accounting profit in one period, but in taxable profit in a **different period**.

4 Deductible temporary differences

Refer again to the definition given in Section 2 above.

Rule to learn

> The rule to remember here is that:
>
> 'All deductible temporary differences give rise to a deferred tax asset.'

There is a proviso, however. The deferred tax asset must also satisfy the **recognition criteria** given in IAS 12. This is that a deferred tax asset should be recognised for all deductible temporary differences to the extent that it is **probable that taxable profit will be available** against which it can be utilised. Before we look at this issue in more detail, let us consider the examples of deductible temporary differences given in the standard.

4.1 Transactions that affect the statement of profit or loss and other comprehensive income

- **Retirement benefit costs** (pension costs) are deducted from accounting profit as service is provided by the employee. They are not deducted in determining taxable profit until the entity pays either retirement benefits or contributions to a fund. (This may also apply to similar expenses.)

- **Accumulated depreciation** of an asset in the financial statements is greater than the accumulated depreciation allowed for tax purposes up to the end of the reporting period.

- The **cost of inventories** sold before the end of the reporting period is deducted from accounting profit when goods/services are delivered, but is deducted from taxable profit when the cash is received. (**Note.** There is also a taxable temporary difference associated with the related trade receivable, as noted in Section 3 above.)

- The **NRV** of inventory, or the **recoverable amount** of an item of property, plant and equipment falls and the carrying value is therefore **reduced**, but that reduction is ignored for tax purposes until the asset is sold.

- **Research costs** (or organisation/other start-up costs) are recognised as an expense for accounting purposes but are not deductible against taxable profits until a later period.

- Income is **deferred** in the statement of financial position, but has already been included in taxable profit in current/prior periods.

- A **government grant** is included in the statement of financial position as deferred income, but it will not be taxable in future periods. (**Note.** A deferred tax asset may *not* be recognised here according to the standard.)

4.2 Fair value adjustments and revaluations

Current investments or **financial instruments** may be carried at fair value which is less than cost, but no equivalent adjustment is made for tax purposes.

Other situations discussed by the standard relate to **business combinations** and consolidation (see Section 7).

4.3 Recognition of deductible temporary differences

We looked earlier at the important recognition criteria above. As with temporary taxable differences, there are also circumstances where the overall rule for recognition of deferred tax asset is **not** allowed. This applies where the deferred tax asset arises from **initial recognition** of an asset or liability in a transaction which is not a business combination, **and** at the time of the transaction, affects neither accounting nor taxable profit/tax loss.

Let us lay out the reasoning behind the recognition of deferred tax assets arising from deductible temporary differences.

(a) When a **liability is recognised**, it is assumed that its carrying amount will be settled in the form of outflows of economic benefits from the entity in future periods.

(b) When these resources flow from the entity, part or all may be deductible in determining taxable profits of a **period later** than that in which the liability is recognised.

(c) A **temporary tax difference** then exists between the carrying amount of the liability and its tax base.

(d) A **deferred tax asset** therefore arises, representing the income taxes that will be recoverable in future periods when that part of the liability is allowed as a deduction from taxable profit.

(e) Similarly, when the carrying amount of an asset is **less than its tax base**, the difference gives rise to a deferred tax asset in respect of the income taxes that will be recoverable in future periods.

4.3.1 Example: Deductible temporary differences

Pargatha Co recognises a liability of $10,000 for accrued product warranty costs on 31 December 20X7. These product warranty costs will not be deductible for tax purposes until the entity pays claims. The tax rate is 25%.

Required

State the deferred tax implications of this situation.

Solution

What is the tax base of the liability? It is nil (carrying amount of $10,000 less the amount that will be deductible for tax purposes in respect of the liability in future periods).

When the liability is settled for its carrying amount, the entity's future taxable profit will be reduced by $10,000 and so its future tax payments by $10,000 × 25% = $2,500.

The difference of $10,000 between the carrying amount ($10,000) and the tax base (nil) is a deductible temporary difference. The entity should therefore recognise a deferred tax asset of $10,000 × 25% = $2,500 **provided that** it is probable that the entity will earn sufficient taxable profits in future periods to benefit from a reduction in tax payments.

4.4 Taxable profits in future periods

When can we be sure that sufficient taxable profit will be available against which a deductible temporary difference can be utilised? IAS 12 states that this will be assumed when sufficient **taxable temporary differences** exist which relate to the same taxation authority and the same taxable entity. These should be expected to reverse as follows:

(a) In the same period as the expected reversal of the deductible temporary difference.

(b) In periods into which a tax loss arising from the deferred tax asset can be carried back or forward.

Only in these circumstances is the deferred tax asset **recognised**, in the period in which the deductible temporary differences arise.

What happens when there are **insufficient taxable temporary differences** (relating to the same taxation authority and the same taxable entity)? It may still be possible to recognise the deferred tax asset, but only to the following extent.

(a) **Taxable profits** are sufficient in the same period as the reversal of the deductible temporary difference (or in the periods into which a tax loss arising from the deferred tax asset can be carried forward or backward), ignoring taxable amounts arising from deductible temporary differences arising in future periods.

(b) **Tax planning opportunities** exist that will allow the entity to create taxable profit in the appropriate periods.

With reference to (b), **tax planning opportunities** are actions that an entity would take in order to create or increase taxable income in a particular period before the expiry of a tax loss or tax credit carryforward. For example, in some countries it may be possible to increase or create taxable profit by electing to have interest income taxed on either a received or receivable basis, or deferring the claim for certain deductions from taxable profit.

In any case, where tax planning opportunities **advance taxable profit** from a later period to an earlier period, the utilisation of a tax loss or a tax credit carryforward will still depend on the existence of future taxable profit from sources other than future originating temporary differences.

If an entity has a **history of recent losses**, then this is evidence that future taxable profit may not be available (see below).

4.5 Initial recognition of an asset or liability

Consider Section 3.6 on **initial recognition of an asset or liability**. The example given by the standard is of a non-taxable government grant related to an asset, deducted in arriving at the carrying amount of the asset. For tax purposes, however, it is **not** deducted from the asset's depreciable amount (ie its tax base). The carrying amount of the asset is less than its tax base and this gives rise to a deductible temporary difference. Section 3.6 applies to this type of transaction.

4.6 Unused tax losses and unused tax credits

An entity may have unused tax losses or credits (ie which it can offset against taxable profits) at the end of a period. Should a deferred tax asset be recognised in relation to such amounts? IAS 12 states that a deferred tax asset may be recognised in such circumstances **to the extent that it is probable future taxable profit will be available against which the unused tax losses/credits can be utilised.**

The **criteria for recognition** of deferred tax assets here is the same as for recognising deferred tax assets arising from deductible differences. The existence of **unused tax losses** is strong evidence, however, that future taxable profit may not be available. So where an entity has a history of recent tax losses, a deferred tax asset arising from unused tax losses or credits should be recognised only to the extent that the entity has sufficient taxable temporary differences or there is other convincing evidence that sufficient taxable profit will be available against which the unused losses/credits can be utilised by the entity.

In these circumstances, the following criteria should be considered when assessing the probability that taxable profit will be available against which unused tax losses/credits can be utilised.

- Existence of **sufficient taxable temporary differences** (same tax authority/taxable entity) against which unused tax losses/credits can be utilised before they expire
- Probability that the entity will have **taxable profits** before the unused tax losses/credits expire
- Whether the unused tax losses result from **identifiable causes**, unlikely to recur
- Availability of **tax planning opportunities** (see above)

To the extent that it is **not probable** that taxable profit will be available, the deferred tax asset is **not** recognised.

4.7 Reassessment of unrecognised deferred tax assets

For **all** unrecognised deferred tax assets, at each year end an entity should **reassess the availability of future taxable profits** and whether part or all of any unrecognised deferred tax assets should now be recognised. This may be due to an improvement in trading conditions which is expected to continue.

4.8 Section summary

- Deductible temporary differences give rise to a **deferred tax asset**.
- Deferred tax assets can only be recognised when **sufficient future taxable profits** exist against which they can be utilised.

5 Measurement and recognition of deferred tax

5.1 Basis of provision of deferred tax

IAS 12 adopts the full provision method of providing for deferred tax. The **full provision method** has the **advantage** that it recognises that each timing difference at the year end has an effect on future tax payments. If a company claims an accelerated tax allowance on an item of plant, future tax assessments will be bigger than they would have been otherwise. Future transactions may well affect those assessments still further, but that is not relevant in assessing the position at the year end. The **disadvantage** of full provision is that, under certain types of tax system, it gives rise to large liabilities that may fall due only far in the future.

5.2 Example: Full provision

Suppose that Girdo Co begins trading on 1 January 20X7. In its first year it makes profits of $5m, the depreciation charge is $1m and the tax allowances on those assets is $1.5m. The rate of corporation tax is 30%.

Solution

The tax liability is $1.35m again, but the debit to profit or loss is increased by the deferred tax liability of 30% × $0.5m = $150,000. The total charge to profit or loss is therefore $1.5m which is an effective tax rate of 30% on accounting profits (ie 30% × $5.0m). Again, no judgement is involved in using this method.

5.3 Deferral/liability methods: changes in tax rates

Where the corporate rate of income tax **fluctuates from one year to another**, a problem arises in respect of the amount of deferred tax to be credited (debited) to profit or loss in later years. The amount could be calculated using either of two methods.

(a) The **deferral method** assumes that the deferred tax account is an item of 'deferred tax relief' which is credited to profits in the years in which the timing differences are reversed. Therefore the tax effects of timing differences are calculated using tax rates current when the differences **arise**.

(b) The **liability method** assumes that the tax effects of timing differences should be regarded as amounts of tax ultimately due by or to the company. Therefore deferred tax provisions are calculated at the rate at which it is estimated that tax will be paid (or recovered) when the timing differences **reverse**.

The deferral method involves **extensive record keeping** because the timing differences on each individual capital asset must be held. In contrast, under the liability method, the total originating or reversing timing difference for the year is converted into a deferred tax amount at the current rate of tax (and if any change in the rate of tax has occurred in the year, only a single adjustment to the opening balance on the deferred tax account is required).

IAS 12 requires deferred tax assets and liabilities to be measured at the tax rates expected to apply in the period **when the asset is realised or liability settled**, based on tax rates and laws enacted (or substantively enacted) at the end of the reporting period. In other words, IAS 12 requires the **liability method** to be used.

5.4 Different rates of tax

In addition, in some countries different tax rates apply to different levels of taxable income. In such cases, deferred tax assets and liabilities should be measured using the **average rates** that are expected to apply to the taxable profit (loss) of the periods in which the temporary differences are expected to reverse.

5.5 Manner of recovery or settlement

In some countries, the way in which an entity **recovers or settles** the carrying amount of an asset or liability may affect the following.

(a) The tax rate applying when the entity recovers/settles the carrying amount of the asset/liability
(b) The tax base of the asset/liability

In such cases, the entity must consider the expected manner of recovery or settlement. Deferred tax liabilities and assets must be measured accordingly, using an **appropriate tax rate and tax base**.

5.6 Example: Manner of recovery/settlement

Richcard Co has an asset with a carrying amount of $10,000 and a tax base of $6,000. If the asset were sold, a tax rate of 20% would apply. A tax rate of 30% would apply to other income.

Required

State the deferred tax consequences if the entity:

(a) Sells the asset without further use.
(b) Expects to retain the asset and recover its carrying amount through use.

Solution

(a) A deferred tax liability is recognised of $(10,000 – 6,000) × 20% = $800.
(b) A deferred tax liability is recognised of $(10,000 – 6,000) × 30% = $1,200.

Question — Recovery 1

Emida Co has an asset which cost $100,000. At the end of 20X9 the carrying amount was $80,000 and the asset was revalued to $150,000. No equivalent adjustment was made for tax purposes. Cumulative depreciation for tax purposes is $30,000 and the tax rate is 30%. If the asset is sold for more than cost, the cumulative tax depreciation of $30,000 will be included in taxable income but sale proceeds in excess of cost will not be taxable.

Required

State the deferred tax consequences of the above. (**Hint.** Assume first that the entity expects to recover the carrying amount through use, and secondly that it will not and therefore will sell the asset instead.)

Answer

The tax base of the asset is $70,000 ($150,000 – $80,000).

If the entity expects to recover the revalued carrying amount by using the asset, it must generate taxable income of $150,000, but will only be able to deduct depreciation of $70,000. On this basis there is a deferred tax liability of $24,000 ($80,000 × 30%).

If the entity expects to recover the carrying amount by selling the asset immediately for proceeds of $150,000, the deferred tax liability will be computed as follows.

	Taxable temporary difference $	Tax rate	Deferred tax liability $
Cumulative tax depreciation	30,000	30%	9,000
Proceeds in excess of cost	50,000	Nil	–
Total	80,000		9,000

Note. The additional deferred tax that arises on the revaluation is charged to other comprehensive income: see below.

Question — Recovery 2

The facts are as in Recovery 1 above, except that if the asset is sold for more than cost, the cumulative tax depreciation will be included in taxable income (taxed at 30%) and the sale proceeds will be taxed at 40% after deducting an inflation-adjusted cost of $110,000.

Required

State the deferred tax consequences of the above (use the same hint as in Recovery 1).

Answer

If the entity expects to recover the carrying amount by using the asset, the situation is as in Recovery 1 above in the same circumstances.

If the entity expects to recover the carrying amount by selling the asset immediately for proceeds of $150,000, the entity will be able to deduct the indexed costs of $110,000. The profit of $40,000 will be taxed at 40%. In addition, the cumulative tax depreciation of $30,000 will be included in taxable income and taxed at 30%. On this basis, the tax base is $80,000 ($110,000 – $30,000), there is a taxable temporary difference of $70,000 and there is a deferred tax liability of $25,000 ($40,000 × 40% plus $30,000 × 30%).

Exam focus point

If the tax base is not immediately apparent in Recovery 2 above, it may be helpful to consider the fundamental principle of IAS 12: that an entity should recognise a deferred tax liability (asset) whenever recovery or settlement of the carrying amount of an asset or liability would make future tax payments larger (smaller) than they would be if such recovery or settlement would have no consequences.

5.7 Investment properties – manner of recovery

In 2010, IAS 12 was amended to include a rebuttable presumption that deferred tax on investment properties carried at fair value under IAS 40 *Investment Property* should be measured based on recovery through sale.

The presumption is rebutted where the investment property is depreciable and is held with the intention of consuming substantially all of the economic benefits of the property through use rather than sale, in other words where the entity expects the asset's income-generating ability to wear out whilst the asset is still owned by the entity.

5.8 Revalued non-depreciable assets – manner of recovery

Where a non-depreciable asset (freehold land) is carried at revaluation under IAS 16, no part of the carrying amount of such an asset is considered to be recovered through use. Therefore, the deferred tax liability or asset that arises from revaluation must be measured based on the tax consequences that would follow from the sale of the asset rather than through use.

In some jurisdictions, this will result in the use of a capital gains tax rate rather than the rate applicable to corporate earnings.

5.9 Discounting

IAS 12 states that deferred tax assets and liabilities **should not be discounted** because the complexities and difficulties involved. Discounting would require detailed scheduling of the timing of the reversal of each temporary difference, but this is often impracticable. If discounting were permitted but not required, this would affect comparability, so it is barred completely. However, carrying amounts determine temporary differences even when such carrying amounts are discounted (eg retirement benefit obligations: see Chapter 16).

5.10 Carrying amount of deferred tax assets

The carrying amount of deferred tax assets should be **reviewed at the end of the reporting period** and reduced where appropriate (insufficient future taxable profits). Such a reduction may be reversed in future years.

5.11 Recognition

As with current tax, deferred tax should normally be recognised as income or an expense and included in the profit or loss for the period. The exceptions are where the tax arises from the events below.

(a) A transaction or event which is recognised (in the same or a different period) **in other comprehensive income or directly in equity**.

(b) A business combination that is an **acquisition**.

The figures shown for deferred tax in profit or loss will consist of **two components**.

(a) Deferred tax relating to **timing differences**.

(b) Adjustments relating to **changes in the carrying amount of deferred tax assets/liabilities** (where there is no change in timing differences), eg changes in tax rates/laws, reassessment of the recoverability of deferred tax assets, or a change in the expected recovery of an asset.

Items in (b) will be recognised in profit or loss, **unless** they relate to items previously recognised in other comprehensive income or charged/credited to equity.

Deferred tax (and current tax) should be recognised in other comprehensive income or charged/credited directly to equity if the tax relates to items also recognised in other comprehensive income or charged/credited directly to equity (in the same or a different period).

The following show examples of from IAS.

(a) **Revaluations** of property, plant and equipment recognised in other comprehensive income (IAS 16)

(b) The effect of a **change in accounting policy** (applied retrospectively) or correction of an **error** charged/credited directly to equity (IAS 8)

Where it is not possible to determine the amount of current/deferred tax that relates to items recognised in other comprehensive income or credited/charged to equity, such tax amounts should be based on a reasonable **prorata allocation** of the entity's current/deferred tax.

5.12 Section summary

- There are two methods of calculating deferred tax when **tax rates change**.
    - **Deferral method** (use tax rates current when differences **arise**)
    - **Liability method** (use tax rate expected when differences **reverse**: per IAS 12)
- Where different rates of tax apply to different rates of income, the **manner of recovery/settlement** of assets/liabilities is important.
- Deferred tax should normally be recognised as income or an expense and **included in profit or loss** for the period.
- Deferred tax should be recognised in other comprehensive income or **charged/credited directly to equity** if the tax relates to items also recognised in other comprehensive income or charged/credited directly to equity.

6 Presentation and disclosure of taxation

FAST FORWARD

IAS 12 *Income Taxes* covers both current and deferred tax. It has substantial presentation and disclosure requirements.

IAS 12 contains rules for comprehensive presentation and disclosure of taxation items, which are summarised here.

6.1 Presentation of tax assets and liabilities

These should be **presented separately** from other assets and liabilities in the statement of financial position. Deferred tax assets and liabilities should be distinguished from current tax assets and liabilities.

In addition, deferred tax assets/liabilities should **not** be classified as current assets/liabilities, where an entity makes such as distinction.

There are only limited circumstances where **current tax** assets and liabilities may be **offset**. This should only occur if the entity:

(a) Has a legally enforceable right to set off the recognised amounts; **and**
(b) Intends either to settle on a net basis, or to realise the asset and settle the liability simultaneously.

Similar criteria apply to the **offset of deferred tax assets and liabilities**.

6.2 Presentation of tax expense

The tax expense or income related to the profit or loss from ordinary activities should be presented in the statement of profit or loss and other comprehensive income.

6.3 Disclosure

As you would expect, the major components of tax expense or income should be disclosed separately. These will generally include the following.

- **Current tax expense** (income)
- Any adjustments recognised in the period for **current tax of prior periods** (ie for over/under statement in prior years)
- Amount of **deferred tax expense (income)** relating to the origination and reversal of **temporary differences**
- Amount of **deferred tax expense (income)** relating to changes in **tax rates** or the imposition of **new taxes**
- Amount of the benefit arising from a previously unrecognised tax loss, tax credit or temporary difference of a prior period that is used to **reduce current tax expense**
- Amount of the benefit from a previously unrecognised tax loss, tax credit or temporary difference of a prior period that is used to **reduce deferred tax expense**
- Deferred tax expense arising from the **write-down**, or reversal of a previous write-down, of a deferred tax asset

There are substantial additional disclosures required by the standard. All these items should be shown separately.

- Aggregate current and deferred tax relating to items that are charged or credited to **equity**
- The amount of income tax relating to each component of other comprehensive income
- An explanation of the relationship between **tax expense (income)** and **accounting profit** in either or both of the following forms
    - A numerical reconciliation between tax expense (income) and the product of accounting profit multiplied by the applicable tax rate(s), disclosing also the basis on which the applicable tax rate(s) is (are) computed
    - A numerical reconciliation between the average effective tax rate and the applicable tax rate, disclosing also the basis on which the applicable tax rate is computed

- An explanation of **changes in the applicable tax rate(s)** compared to the previous accounting period
- The amount (and expiry date, if any) of **deductible temporary differences, unused tax losses, and unused tax credits** for which no deferred tax is recognised in the statement of financial position
- In respect of each type of **temporary difference**, and in respect of each type of **unused tax loss** and **unused tax credit**:
  - The amount of the deferred tax assets and liabilities recognised in the statement of financial position for each period presented
  - The amount of the deferred tax income or expense recognised in profit or loss, if this is not apparent from the changes in the amounts recognised in the statement of financial position
- In respect of **discontinued operations**, the tax expense relating to:
  - The gain or loss on discontinuance; **and**
  - The profit or loss from the ordinary activities of the discontinued operation for the period, together with the corresponding amounts for each prior period presented
- **Temporary differences** arising from investments in subsidiaries, branches, associates or joint arrangements, where no deferred tax liabilities have been recognised (see Section 7.4)

In addition, an entity should disclose the amount of a deferred tax asset and the nature of the evidence supporting its recognition, when:

(a) The utilisation of the deferred tax asset is dependent on future taxable profits in excess of the profits arising from the reversal of existing taxable temporary differences; and

(b) The entity has suffered a loss in either the current or preceding period in the tax jurisdiction to which the deferred tax asset relates.

7 Deferred taxation and business combinations

FAST FORWARD

You must appreciate the deferred tax aspects of **business combinations** as this aspect of deferred tax may appear in the exam.

Much of the above will be familiar to you from your earlier studies. You may be asked about the **group aspects of deferred taxation**. Everything that IAS 12 states in relation to deferred tax and business combinations is brought together in this section.

7.1 Tax bases

Remember the definition of the tax base of an asset or liability given in Section 2.3 above? In relation to business combinations and consolidations, IAS 12 gives (in an appendix) examples of circumstances that give rise to taxable temporary differences and to deductible temporary differences.

7.1.1 Circumstances that give rise to taxable temporary differences

- The carrying amount of an asset is increased to **fair value** in a business combination that is an acquisition and no equivalent adjustment is made for tax purposes
- **Unrealised losses resulting from intragroup transactions** are eliminated by inclusion in the carrying amount of inventory or property, plant and equipment
- **Retained earnings** of subsidiaries, branches, associates and joint arrangements are included in consolidated retained earnings, but income taxes will be payable if the profits are distributed to the reporting parent
- Investments in foreign subsidiaries, branches or associates or interests in foreign joint arrangements are affected by **changes in foreign exchange rates**

- An entity financial statements in its own currency for the cost of the non-monetary assets of a foreign operation that is **integral to the reporting entity's operations** but the taxable profit or tax loss of the foreign operation is determined in the foreign currency

Question — Deferred tax and business combinations 1

What are the consequences of the above situations?

Note. You may want to read through to the end of this section before you attempt this question.

Answer

(a) *Fair value adjustment*

On initial recognition, the resulting deferred tax liability increases goodwill or decreases the bargain purchase gain.

(b) *Unrealised losses*

The tax bases of the assets are unaltered.

(c) *Consolidated earnings*

IAS 12 does not allow recognition of the resulting deferred tax liability if the parent, investor or venturer is able to control the timing of the reversal of the temporary difference and it is probable that the temporary difference will not reverse in the foreseeable future.

(d) *Changes in exchange rates: investments*

There may be either a taxable temporary difference or a deductible temporary difference in this situation. IAS 12 does not allow recognition of the resulting deferred tax liability if the parent, investor or venturer is able to control the timing of the reversal of the temporary difference and it is probable that the temporary difference will not reverse in the foreseeable future.

(e) *Changes in exchange rates: use of own currency*

Again, there may be either a taxable temporary difference or a deductible temporary difference. Where there is a taxable temporary difference, the resulting deferred tax liability is recognised, because it relates to the foreign operation's own assets and liabilities, rather than to the reporting **entity**'s investment in that foreign operation. The deferred tax is charged to profit or loss.

7.1.2 Circumstances that give rise to deductible temporary differences

(a) A **liability is recognised at its fair value** in a business combination that is an acquisition, but none of the related expense is deducted in determining taxable profit until a later period.

(b) **Unrealised profits resulting from intragroup transactions** are eliminated from the carrying amount of assets, such as inventory or property, plant or equipment, but no equivalent adjustment is made for tax purposes.

(c) Investments in foreign subsidiaries, branches or associates or interests in foreign joint arrangements are affected by **changes in foreign exchange rates**.

(d) A foreign operation financial statements for its non-monetary assets in its own (functional) currency. If its taxable profit or loss is determined in a different currency (under the presentation currency method) changes in the exchange rate result in temporary differences. The resulting deferred tax is charged or credited to profit or loss.

Question — Deferred tax and business combinations 2

What are the consequences of the above situations?

Note. Again, you should read to the end of this section before you answer this question.

Answer

(a) *Fair value of liabilities*

The resulting deferred tax asset decreases goodwill or increases the bargain purchase gain.

(b) *Unrealised profits*

The tax bases of the liabilities are unaltered.

(c) *Changes in exchange rates: investments*

As noted in the prior question, there may be a taxable temporary difference or a deductible temporary difference. IAS 12 requires recognition of the resulting deferred tax asset to the extent, and only to the extent, that it is probable that:

(i) The temporary difference will reverse in the foreseeable future; and
(ii) Taxable profit will be available against which the temporary difference can be utilised.

(d) *Changes in exchange rates: use of own currency*

As noted in the prior question, there may be either a taxable temporary difference or a deductible temporary difference. Where there is a deductible temporary difference, the resulting deferred tax asset is recognised to the extent that it is probable that sufficient taxable profit will be available, because the deferred tax asset relates to the foreign operation's own assets and liabilities, rather than to the reporting **entity**'s investment in that foreign operation. The deferred tax is charged to profit or loss.

7.2 Taxable temporary differences

In a business combination, the cost of the acquisition must be allocated to the fair values of the identifiable assets and liabilities acquired as at the date of the transaction. Temporary differences will arise when the tax bases of the identifiable assets and liabilities acquired are not affected by the business combination or are affected differently. For example, the carrying amount of an asset is increased to fair value but the tax base of the asset remains at cost to the previous owner; a taxable temporary difference arises which results in a deferred tax liability and this will also affect goodwill.

7.3 Deductible temporary differences

In a business combination that is an acquisition, as in Section 7.2 above, when a **liability** is recognised on acquisition but the related costs are not deducted in determining taxable profits until a later period, a deductible temporary difference arises resulting in a deferred tax asset. A deferred tax asset will also arise when the fair value of an identifiable asset acquired is less than its tax base. In both these cases goodwill is affected (see below).

7.4 Investments in subsidiaries, branches and associates and interests in joint arrangements

When such investments are held, **temporary differences** may arise because the carrying amount of the investment (ie the parent's share of the net assets including goodwill) becomes different from the tax base (often the cost) of the investment. Why do these differences arise? These are some examples.

- There are **undistributable profits** held by subsidiaries, branches, associates and joint arrangements
- There are **changes in foreign exchange rates** when a parent and its subsidiary are based in different countries
- There is a **reduction in the carrying amount** of an investment in an associate to its recoverable amount

The **temporary difference in the consolidated financial statements** may be different from the temporary difference associated with that investment in the parent's separate financial statements when the parent carries the investment in its separate financial statements at cost or revalued amount.

IAS 12 requires entities to **recognise a deferred tax liability** for all taxable temporary differences associated with investments in subsidiaries, branches and associates, and interests in joint arrangements, **except** to the extent that both of these conditions are satisfied:

(a) The parent/investor/venturer is able to **control the timing of the reversal** of the temporary difference; **and**

(b) It is probable that the temporary difference **will not reverse** in the foreseeable future.

As well as the fact of parent control over reversal of temporary differences, it would often be **impracticable** to determine the amount of income taxes payable when the temporary differences reverses. So when the parent has determined that those profits will not be distributed in the foreseeable future, the parent does not recognise a deferred tax liability. The same applies to investments in branches.

Where a foreign operation's taxable profit or tax loss (and therefore the tax base of its non-monetary assets and liabilities) is determined in a **foreign currency**, changes in the exchange rate give rise to temporary differences. These relate to the foreign entity's own assets and liabilities, rather than to the reporting entity's investment in that foreign operation, and so the reporting entity should recognise the resulting deferred tax liability or asset. The resulting deferred tax is charged or credited to profit or loss.

An investor in an **associate** does not control that entity and so cannot determine its dividend policy. Without an agreement requiring that the profits of the associate should not be distributed in the foreseeable future, therefore, an investor should recognise a deferred tax liability arising from taxable temporary differences associated with its investment in the associate. Where an investor cannot determine the exact amount of tax, but only a minimum amount, then the deferred tax liability should be that amount.

In a **joint arrangement**, the agreement between the parties usually deals with profit sharing. When a venturer can control the sharing of profits and it is probable that the profits will not be distributed in the foreseeable future, a deferred liability is not recognised.

IAS 12 then states that a **deferred tax asset** should be recognised for all deductible temporary differences arising from investments in subsidiaries, branches and associates, and interests in joint arrangements, to the extent that (and **only** to the extent that) both these are probable:

(a) That the temporary difference will **reverse** in the foreseeable future; **and**
(b) That **taxable profit** will be available against which the temporary difference can be utilised.

The **prudence principles** discussed above for the recognition of deferred tax assets should be considered.

7.5 Recognition of deferred tax arising from business combinations

As noted above, temporary differences may arise in a business combination. IFRS 3 *Business Combinations* requires an entity to recognise any resulting deferred tax assets (to the extent that they meet the relevant recognition criteria) or deferred tax liabilities as identifiable assets and liabilities at the date of acquisition. These deferred tax assets and liabilities, consequently, will **affect goodwill or negative goodwill**. An entity will not, however, recognise deferred tax liabilities arising from the initial recognition of goodwill.

An acquirer may consider that, as a result of a business combination, it is probable that it will **recover its own deferred tax asset** that was not recognised prior to the business combination, eg by utilising unused tax losses against the future taxable profit of the acquiree. The acquirer should recognise a deferred tax asset but does not take it into account in calculating goodwill.

If deferred tax assets of an acquiree were not originally recognised as identifiable assets at the acquisition date but are **recognised subsequently**, the accounting is as follows:

(a) **If the assets are recognised during the measurement period** (see Chapter 6), **adjust (reduce) the carrying amount of goodwill** to the amount that would have been recognised if the deferred tax assets had been recognised at acquisition and **recognise the reduction in the carrying amount** of goodwill as an expense in profit or loss (this expense will cancel out the deferred tax income, leaving a nil effect on profit or loss).

(b) **Otherwise, recognise the effect in profit or loss**

The acquirer cannot, however, create a bargain purchase gain by the type (a) adjustments.

Question — Recognition

In 20X2 Jacko acquired a subsidiary, Jilly, which had deductible temporary differences of $3m. The tax rate at the date of acquisition was 30%. The resulting deferred tax asset of $0.9m was not recognised as an identifiable asset in determining the goodwill of $5m resulting from the business combination. Two years after the acquisition, Jacko decided that future taxable profit would probably be sufficient for the entity to recover the benefit of all the deductible temporary differences.

Required

(a) Consider the accounting treatment of the subsequent recognition of the deferred tax asset in 20X4.
(b) What would happen if the tax rate had risen to 40% by 20X4 or decreased to 20%?

Answer

(a) The deferred tax asset is recognised two years after the acquisition, so outside the measurement period. Jacko should recognise a deferred tax asset of $0.9m ($3m × 30%) and deferred tax income of $0.9m in profit or loss.

(b) If the tax rate rises to 40%, Jacko should recognise a deferred tax asset of $1.2m ($3m × 40%) and deferred tax income of $0.12m in profit or loss.

If the tax rate falls to 20%, Jacko should recognise a deferred tax asset of $0.6m ($3m × 20%) and deferred tax income of $0.6m in profit or loss.

7.6 Example: Deferred tax adjustments (1)

Red is a private limited company and has two 100% owned subsidiaries, Blue and Green, both themselves private limited companies. Red acquired Green on 1 January 20X2 for $5 million when the fair value of its net assets was $4 million, and the tax base of the net assets was $3.5 million. The acquisition of Green and Blue was part of a business strategy whereby Red would build up the 'value' of the group over a three year period and then list its existing share capital on the stock exchange.

(a) The following details relate to the acquisition of Green, which manufactures electronic goods.

   (i) Part of the purchase price has been allocated to intangible assets because it relates to the acquisition of a database of key customers from Green. The recognition and measurement criteria for an intangible asset under IFRS 3 *Business Combinations*/IAS 38 *Intangible Assets* do not appear to have been met but the directors feel that the intangible asset of $0.5 million will be allowed for tax purposes and have computed the tax provision accordingly. However, the tax authorities could possibly challenge this opinion.

   (ii) Green has sold goods worth $3 million to Red since acquisition and made a profit of $1 million on the transaction. The inventory of these goods recorded in Red's statement of financial position at the year end of 31 May 20X2 was $1.8 million.

   (iii) The balance on the retained earnings of Green at acquisition was $2 million. The directors of Red have decided that, during the three years to the date that they intend to list the shares of the company, they will realise earnings through future dividend payments from the subsidiary amounting to $500,000 per year. Tax is payable on any remittance or dividends and no dividends have been declared for the current year.

(b) Blue was acquired on 1 June 20X1 and is a company which undertakes various projects ranging from debt factoring to investing in property and commodities. The following details relate to Blue for the year ending 31 May 20X2.

(i) Blue has a portfolio of readily marketable government securities which are held as current assets. These investments are stated at market value in the statement of financial position with any gain or loss taken to profit or loss. These gains and losses are taxed when the investments are sold. Currently the accumulated unrealised gains are $4 million.

(ii) Blue has calculated that it requires a specific allowance of $2 million against loans in its portfolio. Tax relief is available when the specific loan is written off.

(iii) When Red acquired Blue it had unused tax losses brought forward. At 1 June 20X1, it appeared that Blue would have sufficient taxable profit to realise the deferred tax asset created by these losses but subsequent events have proved that the future taxable profit will not be sufficient to realise all of the unused tax loss.

The current tax rate for Red is 30% and for public companies is 35%.

Required

Write a note suitable for presentation to the partner of an accounting firm setting out the deferred tax implications of the above information for the Red Group of companies.

Solution

Acquisition of the subsidiaries – general

Fair value adjustments have been made in both cases and these will **affect** the **deferred tax charge for the year**. This is because the deferred tax position is viewed **from the perspective of the group as a whole**. For example, it may be possible to recognise deferred tax assets which previously could not be recognised by individual companies, because there are now sufficient tax profits available within the group to utilise unused tax losses. Therefore a **provision** should be made for **temporary differences between fair values of the identifiable net assets acquired and their carrying values** ($4 million less $3.5 million in respect of Green). **No provision should be made for the temporary difference** of $1 million arising on goodwill recognised as a result of the combination with Green.

Future listing

Red plans to seek a listing in three years' time. Therefore, it will become a **public company** and will be subject to a **higher rate of tax**. IAS 12 states that deferred tax should be measured at the **average tax rates expected to apply in the periods in which the timing differences are expected to reverse**, based on current enacted tax rates and laws. This means that Red may be paying tax at the higher rate when some of its timing differences reverse and this should be taken into account in the calculation.

Acquisition of Green

(a) The directors have calculated the tax provision on the assumption that the intangible asset of $0.5 million will be allowed for tax purposes. However, this is not certain and the directors **may eventually have to pay the additional tax**. If the directors cannot be persuaded to adjust their calculations, a **liability for the additional tax should be recognised**.

(b) The intra-group transaction has resulted in an **unrealised profit** of $0.6 million in the group financial statements and this will be **eliminated on consolidation**. The tax charge in the group statement of profit or loss and other comprehensive income includes the tax on this profit, for which **the group will not become liable to tax until the following period. From the perspective of the group, there is a temporary difference**. Because the temporary difference arises in the financial statements of Red, **deferred tax should be provided** on this difference (an asset) using the rate of tax payable by Red.

(c) **Deferred tax should be recognised on the unremitted earnings of subsidiaries** unless the parent is able to **control the timing of dividend payments** or it is **unlikely that dividends will be paid for the foreseeable future**. Red controls the dividend policy of Green and this means that there would normally be no need to make a provision in respect of unremitted profits.

However, the profits of Green **will be distributed** to Red over the next few years and **tax will be payable** on the dividends received. Therefore a **deferred tax liability should be shown**.

Acquisition of Blue

(a) A **temporary difference arises** where non-monetary assets are **revalued upwards** and the **tax treatment of the surplus is different from the accounting treatment**. In this case, the revaluation surplus has been **recognised in profit or loss** for the current period, rather than in other comprehensive income/equity but no corresponding adjustment has been made to the tax base of the investments because the gains will be taxed in future periods. Therefore the company **should recognise a deferred tax liability on the temporary difference of $4 million**.

(b) A temporary difference arises when the provision for the loss on the loan portfolio is first recognised. The general allowance is expected to increase and therefore it is unlikely that the temporary difference will reverse in the near future. However, a **deferred tax liability should still be recognised**. The temporary difference gives rise to a **deferred tax asset**. IAS 12 states that **deferred tax assets should not be recognised unless it is probable that taxable profits will be available** against which the taxable profits can be utilised. **This is affected by the situation in point (c) below**.

(c) In theory, unused tax losses give rise to a deferred tax asset. However, IAS 12 states that **deferred tax assets should only be recognised to the extent that they are regarded as recoverable**. They should be regarded as recoverable to the extent that on the basis of all the evidence available it is **probable that there will be suitable taxable profits against which the losses can be recovered**. The future taxable profit of Blue **will not be sufficient to realise all the unused tax loss. Therefore the deferred tax asset is reduced to the amount that is expected to be recovered**.

This reduction in the deferred tax asset implies that it was **overstated at 1 June 20X1**, when it was acquired by the group. As these are the first post-acquisition financial statements, **goodwill should also be adjusted**.

7.7 Example: Deferred tax adjustments 2

You are the accountant of Pay it. Your assistant is preparing the consolidated financial statements of the year ended 31 March 20X2. However, he is unsure how to account for the deferred tax effects of certain transactions as he has not studied IAS 12. These transactions are given below.

Transaction 1
During the year, Pay it sold goods to a subsidiary for $10 million, making a profit of 20% on selling price. 25% of these goods were still in the inventories of the subsidiary at 31 March 20X2. The subsidiary and Pay it are in the same tax jurisdiction and pay tax on profits at 30%.

Transaction 2
An overseas subsidiary made a loss adjusted for tax purposes of $8 million ($ equivalent). The only relief available for this tax loss is to carry it forward for offset against future taxable profits of the overseas subsidiary. Taxable profits of the oversees subsidiary suffer tax at a rate of 25%.

Required

Compute the effect of both the above transactions on the deferred tax amounts in the consolidated statement of financial position of Pay it at 31 March 20X2. You should provide a full explanation for your calculations and indicate any assumptions you make in formulating your answer.

Solution

Transaction 1

This intra-group sale will give rise to a **provision for unrealised profit** on the unsold inventory of $10,000,000 × 20% × 25% = $500,000. This provision must be made in the consolidated financial statements. However, this profit has already been taxed in the financial statements of Payit. In other words there is a **timing difference**.

In the following year when the inventory is sold outside the group, the provision will be released, but the profit will not be taxed. The timing difference therefore gives rise to a **deferred tax asset**. The asset is 30% × $500,000 = $150,000.

Deferred tax assets are recognised to the extent that they are **recoverable**. This will be the case if **it is more likely than not** that **suitable tax profits** will exist from which the reversal of the timing difference giving rise to the asset can be deducted. The asset is carried forward on this assumption.

Transaction 2

An unrelieved tax loss gives rise to a **timing difference** because the loss is recognised in the financial statements but not yet allowed for tax purposes. When the overseas subsidiary generates sufficient taxable profits, the loss will be offset against these in arriving at taxable profits.

The amount of the deferred tax asset to be carried forward is 25% × $8m = $2m.
As with Transaction 1, deferred tax assets are recognised to the extent that they are **recoverable**. This will be the case if **it is more likely than not** that **suitable tax profits** will exist from which the reversal of the timing difference giving rise to the asset can be deducted.

7.8 Presentation and disclosure

7.8.1 Offset

In consolidated financial statements, a **current** tax asset of one entity in a group is offset against a current tax liability of another entity in the group if, and only if, the entities concerned have a **legally enforceable** right to make/receive a single net payment **and** the entities intend to make/receive such a net payment or recover the asset and settle the liability simultaneously.

7.8.2 Tax expense: exchange differences

IAS 21 requires certain exchange differences to be recognised as income/expense without specifying where such differences should be presented in the statement of profit or loss and other comprehensive income. IAS 12 merely states that, where exchange differences on **deferred foreign tax liabilities or assets** are recognised in the statement of profit or loss and other comprehensive income, such differences may be classified as deferred tax expense/income if this presentation is considered most useful.

7.8.3 Disclosure

IAS 12 requires the aggregate amount of temporary differences associated with investments in subsidiaries, branches and associates and interests in joint arrangements, for which deferred tax liabilities **have not been recognised** to be disclosed separately.

7.9 Amendment: Recognition of deferred tax assets for unrealised losses

7.9.1 The issue

This amendment was issued in January 2016 in order to clarify when a deferred tax asset should be recognised for unrealised losses. For example, an entity holds a debt instrument that is falling in value, without a corresponding tax deduction, but the entity knows that it will receive the full nominal amount on the due date, and there will be no tax consequences of that repayment. The question arises of whether to recognise a deferred tax asset on this unrealised loss.

7.9.2 2016 change

The IASB clarified **that unrealised losses on debt instruments measured at fair value and measured at cost for tax purposes give rise to a deductible temporary difference** regardless of whether the debt instrument's holder expects to recover the carrying amount of the debt instrument by sale or by use.

This may seem to contradict the key requirement that an entity recognises deferred tax assets only if it is probable that it will have future taxable profits. However, the amendment also addresses the issue of what constitutes future taxable profits, and clarifies that:

(a) Unrealised losses on debt instruments measured at fair value and measured at cost for tax purposes give rise to a deductible temporary difference regardless of whether the debt instrument's holder expects to recover the carrying amount of the debt instrument by sale or by use.

(b) The carrying amount of an asset does not limit the estimation of probable future taxable profits.

(c) Estimates for future taxable profits exclude tax deductions resulting from the reversal of deductible temporary differences.

(d) An entity assesses a deferred tax asset in combination with other deferred tax assets. Where tax law restricts the utilisation of tax losses, an entity would assess a deferred tax asset in combination with other deferred tax assets of the same type.

7.9.3 Example: Deferred tax asset and unrealised loss

(Adapted from IAS 12, Illustrative Example 7)

Humbert has a debt instrument with a nominal value of $2,000,000. The fair value of the financial instrument at the company's year end of 30 June 20X4 is $1,800,000. Humbert has determined that there is a deductible temporary difference of $200,000. Humbert intends to hold the instrument until maturity on 30 June 20X5, and expects that the $2,000,000 will be paid in full. This means that the deductible temporary difference will reverse in full.

Humbert has, in addition, $60,000 of taxable temporary differences that will also reverse in full in 20X5. The company expects the bottom line of its tax return to show a tax loss of $40,000.

Assume a tax rate of 20%.

Required

Discuss, with calculations, whether Humbert can recognise a deferred tax asset under IAS 12 *Income Taxes*.

Solution

The first stage is to use the reversal of the taxable temporary difference to arrive at the amount to be tested for recognition.

Under the current requirements of IAS 12 Humbert will consider whether it has a tax liability from a taxable temporary difference that will support the recognition of the tax asset:

	$'000
Deductible temporary difference	200
Reversing taxable temporary difference	(60)
Remaining amount (recognition to be determined)	140

At least $60,000 may be recognised as a deferred tax asset.

The next stage is to calculate the future taxable profit. Following the amendment, this is done using a formula, the aim of which is to derive the amount of tax profit or loss before the reversal of any temporary difference:

	$'000
Expected tax loss (per bottom line of tax return)	(40)
Less reversing taxable temporary difference	(60)
Add reversing deductible temporary difference	200
Taxable profit for recognition test	100

Finally, the results of the above two steps should be added, and the tax calculated:

Humbert would recognise a deferred tax asset of ($60,000 + $100,000) × 20% = $32,000. This deferred tax asset would be recognised even though the company has an expected loss on its tax return.

7.10 Section summary

In relation to deferred tax and business combinations you should be familiar with:

- Circumstances that give rise to **taxable temporary differences**
- Circumstances that give rise to **deductible temporary differences**
- Their **treatment** once an acquisition takes place
- Reasons **why deferred tax arises** when investments are held
- **Recognition** of deferred tax on business combinations

Chapter roundup

- Taxation consists of **two components.**
  - Current tax
  - Deferred tax
- **Current tax** is the amount payable to the tax authorities in relation to the trading activities during the period. It is generally straightforward and is covered in Section 1.
- **Deferred tax** is an accounting measure, used to match the tax effects of transactions with their accounting impact. It is quite complex, and is covered in Section 2.
- **Deferred tax assets and liabilities** arise from taxable and deductible temporary differences.
- IAS 12 *Income Taxes* covers both current and deferred tax. It has substantial presentation and disclosure requirements.
- You must appreciate the deferred tax aspects of **business combinations** as this aspect of deferred tax may appear in the exam.

Quick quiz

1. What is the difference between 'current tax' and 'deferred tax'?
2. How should current tax be measured?

   A   The total liability, including deferred tax
   B   The amount expected to be paid to (or recovered from) the tax authorities
   C   The amount calculated on profit at current tax rates
   D   The amount calculated on profit at future tax rates

3. A taxable temporary difference does not give rise to a deferred tax liability. True or false?
4. What basis of provision for deferred tax is required by IAS 12?
5. What two methods can be used for calculating deferred tax when the tax rate changes?
6. Current tax assets and liabilities cannot be offset. True or false?
7. How do temporary differences arise when investments are held in subsidiaries, associates etc?

PART C ACCOUNTING AND REPORTING TECHNIQUES

Answers to quick quiz

1   (a) Current tax is the amount payable (recoverable) in respect of the taxable profit (tax loss) for a period.

    (b) Deferred tax is used to match the tax effects of transactions with their accounting impact.

2   B   The amount expected to be paid to (or recovered from) the tax authorities.

3   False, except when the liability arises in a business combination or affects neither accounting nor tax profit or loss

4   Full provision

5   • Deferral method
    • Liability method (required by IAS 12)

6   False. They can be offset only if the entity has a legally enforceable right to offset **and** it intends to actually carry out the offset.

7   When the carrying amounts of the investment become different to the tax base of the investment

End of chapter question

DT

DT, a public limited company, has decided to adopt the provisions of IFRS for the first time in its financial statements for the year ending 30 November 20X1. The amounts of deferred tax provided and unprovided as set out in the notes of the group financial statements for the year ending 30 November 20X0 were as follows.

	Provided $m	Unprovided $m
Tax depreciation in excess of accounting depreciation	38	12
Other temporary differences	11	14
Liabilities for health care benefits	(12)	
Losses available for offset against future taxable profits	(34)	(56)
Income tax on capital gains arising on the disposal of property which had been deferred	–	165
Tax that would arise if properties were disposed of at their revalued amounts	–	140
	3	275

The following notes are relevant to the calculation of the deferred tax liability as at 30 November 20X1.

(a) DT acquired a 100% holding in a foreign company on 30 November 20X1. The subsidiary does not plan to pay any dividends for the financial year to 30 November 20X1 or in the foreseeable future. The carrying amount in DT's consolidated financial statements of its investment in the subsidiary at 30 November 20X1 is made up as follows.

	$m
Carrying value of net assets acquired excluding deferred tax	76
Goodwill (before deferred tax and impairment losses)	14
Carrying amount/cost of investment	90

The tax base of the net assets of the subsidiary at acquisition was $60 million. No deduction is available in the subsidiary's tax jurisdiction for the cost of the goodwill.

Immediately after acquisition on 30 November 20X1, DT had supplied the subsidiary with inventories amounting to $30 million at a profit of 20% on selling price. The inventories had not been sold by the year end and the tax rate applied to the subsidiary's profit is 25%. There was no significant difference between the fair values and carrying values on the acquisition of the subsidiary.

(b) The carrying amount of the property, plant and equipment (excluding that of the subsidiary) is $2,600 million and their tax base is $1,920 million. The tax arising on the revaluation of properties of $140 million, if disposed of at their revalued amounts, is the same at 30 November 20X1 as at the beginning of the year. The revaluation of the properties is included in the carrying amount above.

Other taxable temporary differences (excluding the subsidiary) amount to $90 million as at 30 November 20X1.

(c) The liability for health care benefits in the statement of financial position had risen to $100 million as at 30 November 20X1 and the tax base is zero. Health care benefits are deductible for tax purposes when payments are made to retirees. No payments were made during the year to 30 November 20X1.

(d) Under the tax law of the country, tax losses can be carried forward for three years only. The taxable profits for the years ending 30 November were anticipated to be as follows:

20X1	20X2	20X3
$m	$m	$m
110	100	130

The auditors are unsure about the availability of taxable profits in 20X3 as the amount is based upon the projected acquisition of a profitable company. It is anticipated that there will be no future reversals of existing taxable temporary differences until after 30 November 20X3.

(e) Income tax of $165 million on the property disposed of becomes payable on 30 November 20X4 under the deferral relief provisions of the tax laws of the country. There had been no sales or revaluations of property during the year to 30 November 20X1.

(f) Income tax is assumed to be 30% for the foreseeable future in DT's jurisdiction and the company wishes to discount any deferred tax liabilities at a rate of 4% if allowed by IAS 12.

(g) There are no other temporary differences other than those set out above. The directors of DT have calculated the opening balance of deferred tax using IAS 12 to be $280 million and not the total of the provided and unprovided amounts of $278 million at the beginning of the year.

Required

Calculate the liability for deferred tax required by the DT Group at 30 November 20X1 and the deferred tax expense in profit or loss for the year ending 30 November 20X1 using IAS 12, commenting on the effect that the application of IAS 12 will have on the financial statements of the DT Group.

PART C ACCOUNTING AND REPORTING TECHNIQUES

Reporting financial performance

Topic list	Syllabus reference
1 Reporting financial performance: IAS 1 and IAS 8	13.4
2 IFRS 5 *Non-Current Assets Held for Sale and Discontinued Operations*	13.4
3 IFRS 8 *Operating Segments*	13.4
4 IAS 33 *Earnings per Share*	13.4
5 Management commentary	13.1

Introduction

This chapter covers a great many standards, but you are very familiar with some of them.

IFRS 5 *Non-Current Assets Held for Sale and Discontinued Operations* requires the segregation of information which relates to **discontinued operations** from that relating to continuing operations. It also requires the separate presentation of non-current assets held for sale.

IFRS 8 *Operating Segments* requires extensive disclosure about an entity's operating segments.

Earnings per share is important: it is used internationally as a comparative performance figure.

1 Reporting financial performance: IAS 1 and IAS 8

Go back to your earlier studies to revise **IAS 1** and **IAS 8**.

In Chapter 2 we looked at the format and content of financial statements, current assets and liabilities. In this chapter, we cover some of the other aspects of IAS 1 *Presentation of Financial Statements* and also revise IAS 8 *Accounting Policies, Changes in Accounting Estimates and Errors*.

1.1 Objectives and scope

The objective of IAS 1 is:

> 'to prescribe the basis for presentation of general purpose financial statements, in order to ensure comparability both with the entity's own financial statements of previous periods and with the financial statements of other entities.'

IAS 1 applies to all **general purpose financial statements** prepared in accordance with IFRS, ie those intended to meet the needs of users who are not in a position to demand reports tailored to their specific needs.

1.2 Purpose of financial statements

The **objective of financial statements** is to provide information about the financial position, performance and cash flows of an entity that is useful to a wide range of users in making economic decisions. They also show the result of **management stewardship** of the resources of the entity.

In order to fulfil this objective, financial statements must provide information about the following aspects of an entity's results:

- Assets
- Liabilities
- Equity
- Income and expenses (including gains and losses)
- Contributions by, and distributions to owners in their capacity as owners
- Cash flows

Along with other information in the notes and related documents, this information will assist users in predicting the entity's **future cash flows**.

1.3 Responsibility for financial statements

Responsibility for the preparation and presentation of an entity's financial statements rests with the **board of directors** (or equivalent).

1.4 Components of financial statements

As you will already know, a complete set of financial statements comprises the following components.

- Statement of financial position
- Statement of profit or loss and other comprehensive income
- Statement of changes in equity
- Statement of cash flows
- Accounting policies and other explanatory notes
- Comparative information in respect of the preceding period.

In addition, IAS 1 recognises that many entities wish to present, outside the financial statements, a **financial review** by management (which is **not** part of the financial statements), explaining the main features of the entity's performance and position, and the principal uncertainties it faces. The report may include a review of the following.

(a) **Factors/influences determining performance**: changes in the environment in which the entity operates, the entity's response to those changes and their effect, and the entity's policy for investment to maintain and enhance performance, including its dividend policy

(b) Entity's sources of funding, the policy on gearing and its risk management policies

(c) **Strengths and resources** of the entity whose value is not reflected in the statement of financial position under IFRS

Exam focus point

> IFRS are only concerned with the financial statements, so IAS 1 has no mandatory rules concerning such a review.

However, the IASB has issued an IFRS Practice Statement on Management Commentary. This is discussed later in this chapter.

1.5 Fair presentation and compliance with IFRS

Most importantly, financial statements should **present fairly** the financial position, financial performance and cash flows of an entity. **Compliance with IFRS** is presumed to result in financial statements that achieve a fair presentation.

The following points made by IAS 1 expand on this principle.

(a) **Compliance with IFRS** should be disclosed

(b) **All relevant IFRS** must be followed if compliance with IFRS is disclosed

(c) Use of an **inappropriate accounting treatment** cannot be rectified either by disclosure of accounting policies or notes/explanatory material

There may be (very rare) circumstances when management decides that compliance with a requirement of an IFRS would be so misleading that it would conflict with the *Conceptual Framework's* objective of financial statements. **Departure from the IFRS** is therefore required to achieve a fair presentation. The following should be disclosed in such an event.

(a) Management confirmation that the financial statements fairly present the entity's financial position, performance and cash flows

(b) Statement that all IFRS have been complied with **except** departure from one IFRS to achieve a fair presentation

(c) Details of the nature of the departure, why the IFRS treatment would be misleading, and the treatment adopted

(d) Financial impact of the departure

1.5.1 Extreme case disclosures

In very rare circumstances, management may conclude that compliance with a requirement in a standard or interpretation may be so **misleading** that it would **conflict with the objective** of financial statements set out in the *Conceptual Framework*, but the relevant regulatory framework prohibits departure from the requirements. In such cases the entity needs to reduce the perceived misleading aspects of compliance by **disclosing**:

(a) The title of the standard, the nature of the requirement and the reason why management has reached its conclusion.

(b) For each period, the adjustment to each item in the financial statements that would be necessary to achieve fair presentation.

IAS 1 states what is required for a fair presentation.

(a) Selection and application of **accounting policies**

(b) **Presentation of information** in a manner which provides relevant, reliable, comparable and understandable information

(c) **Additional disclosures** where required

The IAS then goes on to consider certain important assumptions which underpin the preparation and presentation of financial statements, which we might call **fundamental assumptions**.

1.6 Going concern

Key term

> The entity is normally viewed as a **going concern**, that is, as continuing in operation for the foreseeable future. Financial statements are prepared on a going concern basis unless management intends to, or has no realistic alternative but to, liquidate the entity or to cease trading.

This assumption is based on the notion that, when preparing a normal set of financial statements, it is always expected that the business will **continue to operate** for the foreseeable future (at least the next 12 months should be considered). In particular, the entity will not go into liquidation or scale down its operations in a material way.

The main significance of the going concern assumption is that the assets of the business **should not be valued at their 'break-up' value**, which is the amount that they would sell for if they were sold off piecemeal and the business were thus broken up.

If the going concern assumption is not followed, that fact must be disclosed, together with:

- The **basis** on which the financial statements have been prepared
- The **reasons** why the entity is not considered to be a going concern

1.6.1 Assessing going concern

In assessing whether the going concern assumption is appropriate, management takes into account all available information about the future. The degree of consideration depends on the facts in each case.

When an entity has a history of profitable operations and ready access to financial resources, the entity may reach a conclusion that the going concern basis of accounting is appropriate without detailed analysis.

In other cases, management may need to consider a wide range of factors relating to current and expected profitability (ie consider profit forecasts), debt repayment schedules and potential sources of replacement financing (including considering cash flow forecasts) before it can satisfy itself that the going concern basis is appropriate.

1.7 Accrual accounting

Key term

> **Accrual accounting.** Items are recognised as assets liabilities, equity, income and expenses when they satisfy the definition and recognition criteria for those elements in the *Conceptual Framework*.
>
> (IAS 1)

Entities should prepare their financial statements on the basis that transactions are recorded in them, not as the cash is paid or received, but as the revenues or expenses are **earned or incurred** in the accounting period to which they relate.

1.8 Consistency of presentation

To maintain consistency, the presentation and classification of items in the financial statements should **stay the same from one period to the next. There are two exceptions.**

(a) There is a significant change in the **nature of the operations** or a review of the financial statements presentation indicates a **more appropriate presentation**.

(b) A change in presentation is **required by an IFRS**.

1.9 Materiality and aggregation

All material items should be presented separately in the financial statements.

Amounts which are **immaterial** should be aggregated with amounts of a similar nature or function and need not be presented separately.

Key term

> **Material.** Omissions or misstatement of items are material if they could, individually or collectively, influence the economic decisions of users taken on the basis of the financial statements. Materiality depends on the size and nature of the omission or misstatement judged in the surrounding circumstances. The size or nature of the item, or a combination of both, could be the determining factor. (IAS 1)

An error which is too trivial to affect anyone's understanding of the financial statements is referred to as **immaterial**. In preparing financial statements it is important to assess what is material and what is not, so that time and money are not wasted in the pursuit of excessive detail.

Determining whether or not an item is material is a very **subjective exercise**. There is no absolute measure of materiality. It is common to apply a convenient rule of thumb (for example, to define material items as those with a value greater than 5% of the profit/(loss) disclosed by the financial statements). But some items disclosed in financial statements are regarded as particularly sensitive and even a very small misstatement of such an item would be regarded as a material error. An example in the financial statements of a limited liability company might be the amount of remuneration paid to directors of the company.

The assessment of an item as material or immaterial may **affect its treatment in the financial statements**. For example, the statement of profit or loss and other comprehensive income of a business will show the expenses incurred by the business grouped under suitable captions (heating and lighting expenses, rent and property taxes etc); but in the case of very small expenses it may be appropriate to lump them together under a caption such as 'sundry expenses', because a more detailed breakdown would be inappropriate for such immaterial amounts.

In assessing whether or not an item is material, it is not only the amount of the item which needs to be considered. The **context** is also important.

(a) If a statement of financial position shows non-current assets of $2 million and inventories of $30,000 an error of $20,000 in the depreciation calculations might not be regarded as material, whereas an error of $20,000 in the inventory valuation probably would be. In other words, the total of which the erroneous item forms part must be considered.

(b) If a business has a bank loan of $50,000 and a $55,000 balance on bank deposit account, it might well be regarded as a material misstatement if these two amounts were displayed in the statement of financial position as 'cash at bank $5,000'. In other words, incorrect presentation may amount to material misstatement even if there is no monetary error.

Users are assumed to have a reasonable knowledge of business and economic activities and accounting and a willingness to study the information with reasonable diligence.

ED2015/8: Application of Materiality to Financial Statements

A Draft Practice Statement on materiality was issued as part of the IASB's Disclosure Initiative in October 2015. The Statement was developed in response to concerns with the level of uncertainty over the application of the concept of materiality, which can result in excessive disclosure of immaterial information while important information can be obscured or even missed out of the financial statements. It provides non-mandatory guidance to assist with the application of the concept of materiality to financial statements prepared in accordance with IFRS. The statement is divided into the following three key areas (ED/2015/8: Para. IN4):

(a) **Characteristics of materiality**, including:

   (i) The pervasiveness of the concept in IFRS

   (ii) The importance of management's use of judgement

(iii) Who the primary users of the financial statements are and what decisions they make based on those financial statements

(iv) The need for a quantitative and qualitative assessment when applying the concept and

(v) The need to assess whether information is material, both individually and collectively

(b) How to apply the concept of materiality when making decisions about **presenting and disclosing information** in the financial statements, in particular:

(i) The objective of the financial statements and how it relates to materiality decisions

(ii) How to deal with immaterial information

(iii) When to aggregate and disaggregate information

(iv) Making judgements about materiality in the context of the financial statements, the notes to the financial statements, the complete set of financial statements (ie considering the financial statements as a whole) and interim reports

(c) How to assess **whether omissions and misstatements of information are material** to the financial statements. Guidance is given on:

(i) Assessing whether misstatements are material
(ii) Current period misstatements versus prior period misstatements
(iii) Dealing with misstatements that are made intentionally to mislead

It also includes a short section on applying materiality when applying recognition and measurement requirements and includes illustrative examples throughout.

1.10 Offsetting

IAS 1 does not allow **assets and liabilities to be offset** against each other unless such a treatment is required or permitted by another IFRS.

Income and expenses can be offset only when:

(a) An IAS requires/permits it; **or**

(b) Gains, losses and related expenses arising from the same/similar transactions are not material (aggregate).

1.11 Comparative information

1.11.1 Minimum comparative information

Except where IFRSs permit or require otherwise, an entity should present comparative information in respect of the preceding period for all amounts reported in the current period's financial statements. Comparative information for narrative and descriptive information should be presented if it is relevant to understanding the current period's financial statements.

As a minimum, two statements of financial position, two statements of profit or loss and other comprehensive income, two statements of profit or loss (if presented), two statements of cash flows and two statements of changes in equity and related notes should be presented in a set of financial statements.

1.11.2 Additional comparative information

Additional comparative information may be presented as long as it is prepared in accordance with IFRS. For example, a third statement of profit or loss and other comprehensive income may be presented for an additional comparative period. Where a third statement is presented (regardless of whether it is a statement of profit or loss and other comprehensive income, a statement of financial position or any other statement):

(1) The relevant notes to that statement should be presented for the third period

(2) The other main financial statements are not required (ie a full third set of financial statements is not necessary).

1.12 Disclosure of accounting policies

There should be a specific section for accounting policies in the notes to the financial statements and the following should be disclosed there.

(a) **Measurement bases** used in preparing the financial statements
(b) Each **specific accounting policy** necessary for a proper understanding of the financial statements

To be clear and understandable it is essential that financial statements should disclose the accounting policies used in their preparation. This is because **policies may vary**, not only from entity to entity, but also from country to country. As an aid to users, all the major accounting policies used should be disclosed in the same place.

There is a wide range of policies available in many accounting areas. Examples where such differing policies exist are as follows, although the list is not exhaustive.

- **General**
    - Consolidation policy
    - Conversion/translation of foreign currencies, including the treatment of exchange gains/losses
    - Overall valuation policy (eg historical cost, general purchasing power, replacement value)
    - Events subsequent to the end of the reporting period
    - Leases, hire purchase or instalment transactions and related interest
    - Taxes
    - Franchises

- **Assets**
    - Receivables
    - Inventories and related cost of goods sold
    - Depreciable assets and depreciation
    - Growing crops
    - Land held for development and related development costs
    - Investments: subsidiary and associate companies and other investments
    - Research and development
    - Patents and trademarks
    - Goodwill

- **Liabilities and provisions**
    - Warranties
    - Commitments and contingencies
    - Pension costs and retirement plans
    - Severance and redundancy payments

- **Profits and losses**
    - Methods of revenue recognition
    - Maintenance, repairs and improvements
    - Gains and losses on disposals of property
    - Reserve accounting, statutory or otherwise, including direct charges and credits to surplus accounts

1.13 Reclassification adjustments and related tax effects

Entities must present other comprehensive income split according to whether it may subsequently be reclassified to profit or loss or will not subsequently be classified to profit and loss. Where items of other comprehensive income are presented inclusive of tax and tax is disclosed separately, this must also be split according to whether it may be reclassified.

In addition to this requirement, entities must **disclose reclassification adjustments which have arisen in a period** relating to each item of other comprehensive income. These are amounts reclassified in the current period from other comprehensive income to profit and loss.

Entities should disclose **income tax relating to reclassification adjustments** for each component of other comprehensive income. This information will be useful, because often different tax rates are applied to these items than are applied to profit or loss.

1.14 Presentation of dividends

Dividends must be presented in the statement of changes in equity or in the notes. They cannot be presented in the statement of profit or loss and other comprehensive income

This reflects the fact that a dividend distribution is an owner change in equity, which must be presented separately from non-owner changes in equity.

1.15 Revision of IAS 8

You have studied this standard already but it is long and important. If you do not understand any of this or if you have problems with the revision question, go back and revise your earlier study material.

Knowledge brought forward from earlier studies

Key terms

> **IAS 8** *Accounting Policies, Changes in Accounting Estimates and Errors*
>
> *Definitions*
>
> - **Accounting policies** are the specific principles, bases, conventions, rules and practices adopted by an entity in preparing and presenting financial statements.
>
> - A **change in accounting estimate** is an adjustment of the carrying amount of an asset or a liability or the amount of the periodic consumption of an asset, that results from the assessment of the present status of, and expected future benefits and obligations associated with, assets and liabilities. Changes in accounting estimates result from new information or new developments and, accordingly, are not corrections of errors.
>
> - **Material**: as defined in IAS 1 (see above)
>
> - **Prior period errors** are omissions from, and misstatements in, the entity's financial statements for one or more prior periods arising from a failure to use, or misuse of, reliable information that:
>
>   (a) Was available when financial statements for those periods were authorised for issue; and
>
>   (b) Could reasonably be expected to have been obtained and taken into account in the preparation and presentation of those financial statements.
>
>   Such errors include the effects of mathematical mistakes, mistakes in applying accounting policies, oversights or misinterpretations of facts, and fraud.
>
> - **Retrospective application** is applying a new accounting policy to transactions, other events and conditions as if that policy had always been applied.
>
> - **Retrospective restatement** is correcting the recognition, measurement and disclosure of amounts of elements of financial statements as if a prior period error had never occurred.

- **Prospective application** of a change in accounting policy and of recognising the effect of a change in an accounting estimate, respectively, are:

    (a) Applying the new accounting policy to transactions, other events and conditions occurring after the date as at which the policy is changes; and

    (b) Recognising the effect of the change in the accounting estimate in the current and future periods affected by the change.

- **Impracticable**. Applying a requirement is impracticable when the entity cannot apply it after making every reasonable effort to do so. It is impracticable to apply a change in an accounting policy retrospectively or to make a retrospective restatement to correct an error if one of the following apply.

    (a) The effects or the retrospective application or retrospective restatement are not determinable.

    (b) The retrospective application or retrospective restatement requires assumptions about what management's intent would have been in that period.

    (c) The retrospective application or retrospective restatement requires significant estimates of amounts and it is impossible to distinguish objectively information about those estimates that: provides evidence of circumstances that existed on the date(s) at which those amounts are to be recognised, measured or disclosed; and would have been available when the financial statements for that prior period were authorised for issue from other information.

Accounting policies

- Accounting policies are determined by **applying the relevant IFRS**.

- Where there is no applicable IFRS or IFRIC management should use its **judgement** in developing and applying an accounting policy that results in information that is **relevant** and **reliable**. Management should refer to:

    (a) The requirements in IFRS and IFRICs dealing with **similar** and **related issues**.

    (b) The definitions, recognition criteria and measurement concepts for assets, liabilities and expenses in the *Conceptual Framework*.

    Management may also consider the most recent pronouncements of other standard-setting bodies that use a similar *Conceptual Framework* to develop standards, other accounting literature and accepted industry practices if these do not conflict with the sources above.

- An entity shall select and apply its accounting policies for a period **consistently** for similar transactions, other events and conditions, unless an IFRS specifically requires or permits categorisation of items for which different policies may be appropriate. If an IFRS requires or permits categorisation of items, an appropriate accounting policy shall be selected and applied consistently to each category.

Changes in Accounting Policies

- These are **rare**: only required by statute/standard-setting body/results in reliable and more relevant information.

- **Adoption of new IFRS**: follow transitional provisions of IFRS. If no transitional provisions: **retrospective** application.

- **Other changes in policy**: **retrospective** application. Adjust opening balance of each affected component of equity, ie as if new policy has always been applied.

- **Prospective** application is **no longer allowed** unless it is **impracticable** to determine the cumulative effect of the change. (See definition of impracticable above.)

- An entity should **disclose** information relevant to assessing the **impact of new IFRS** on the financial statements where these have been **issued but have not yet come into force**.

PART C ACCOUNTING AND REPORTING TECHNIQUES

Changes in Accounting Estimates

- Estimates arise because of **uncertainties inherent within them**; judgement is required but this does not undermine reliability.
- Effect of a change in accounting estimate should be included in profit or loss in:
    - Period of change, if change affects only current period; or
    - Period of change and future periods, if change affects both.

Errors

(See definition of prior period error above.)

- **Prior period errors**: correct **retrospectively**.
- This involves:
    (a) Either restating the comparative amounts for the prior period(s) in which the error occurred; or
    (b) When the error occurred before the earliest prior period presented, restating the opening balances of assets, liabilities and equity for that period

    so that the financial statements are presented as if the error had never occurred.

- Only where it is **impracticable** to determine the cumulative effect of an error on prior periods can an entity correct an error **prospectively**.

The following question will allow you to revise IAS 8.

Question — Prior period error

During 20X7 Lubi Co discovered that certain items had been included in inventory at 31 December 20X6, valued at $4.2m, which had in fact been sold before the year end. The following figures for 20X6 (as reported) and 20X7 (draft) are available.

	20X6	20X7 (draft)
	$'000	$'000
Sales	47,400	67,200
Cost of goods sold	(34,570)	(55,800)
Profit before taxation	12,830	11,400
Income taxes	(3,880)	(3,400)
Profit	8,950	8,000

Retained earnings at 1 January 20X6 were $13m. The cost of goods sold for 20X7 includes the $4.2m error in opening inventory. The income tax rate was 30% for 20X6 and 20X7.

Required

Prepare the statement of profit or loss and other comprehensive income for 20X7, with the 20X6 comparative, and retained earnings.

Answer

STATEMENT OF PROFIT OR LOSS AND OTHER COMPREHENSIVE INCOME

	20X6	20X7
	$'000	$'000
Sales	47,400	67,200
Cost of goods sold (W1)	(38,770)	(51,600)
Profit before tax	8,630	15,600
Income tax (W2)	(2,620)	(4,660)
Profit	6,010	10,940

	20X6 $'000	20X7 $'000
RETAINED EARNINGS		
Opening retained earnings		
As previously reported	13,000	21,950
Correction of prior period error (4,200 – 1,260 tax)	–	(2,940)
As restated	13,000	19,010
Profit for year	6,010	10,940
Closing retained earnings	19,010	29,950

Workings

1 Cost of goods sold

	20X6 $'000	20X7 $'000
As stated in question	34,570	55,800
inventory adjustment	4,200	(4,200)
	38,770	51,600

2 Income tax

	20X6 $'000	20X7 $'000
As stated in question	3,880	3,400
Inventory adjustment (4,200 × 30%)	1,260	1,260
	2,620	4,660

2 IFRS 5 *Non-current Assets Held for Sale and Discontinued Operations*

FAST FORWARD

IFRS 5 requires non-current assets 'held-for-sale' to be presented separately in the statement of financial position.

2.1 Background

IFRS 5 was the result of a short-term convergence project with the US Financial Accounting Standards Board (FASB).

IFRS 5 requires non-current assets and groups of assets that are 'held-for-sale' to be **presented separately** in the statement of financial position and the results of discontinued operations to be presented separately in the statement of profit or loss and other comprehensive income. This is required so that users of financial statements will be better able to make **projections** about the financial position, profits and cash flows of the entity.

Key term

Disposal group: a group of assets to be disposed of, by sale or otherwise, together as a group in a single transaction, and liabilities directly associated with those assets that will be transferred in the transaction. (In practice, a disposal group could be a subsidiary, a cash-generating unit or a single operation within an entity.) (IFRS 5)

IFRS 5 does not apply to certain assets covered by other accounting standards:

(a) Deferred tax assets (IAS 12 *Income Taxes*)

(b) Assets arising from employee benefits (IAS 19 *Employee Benefits*)

(c) Financial assets (IFRS 9 *Financial Instruments*)

(d) Investment properties accounted for in accordance with the fair value model (IAS 40 *Investment Property*)

(e) Agricultural and biological assets that are measured at fair value less costs to sell (IAS 41 *Agriculture*)*

(f) Insurance contracts (IFRS 4 *Insurance Contracts*)*

*IAS 41 and IFRS 4 are not examinable in Paper 13.

2.2 Classification of assets held-for-sale

A non-current asset (or disposal group) should be classified as **held for sale** if its carrying amount will be recovered **principally through a sale transaction** rather than **through continuing use**. A number of detailed criteria must be met:

(a) The asset must be **available for immediate sale** in its present condition.
(b) Its sale must be **highly probable** (ie significantly more likely than not).

For the sale to be highly probable, the following must apply.

(a) Management must be **committed** to a plan to sell the asset.

(b) There must be an active programme to **locate a buyer**.

(c) The asset must be marketed for sale at a **price that is reasonable** in relation to its current fair value.

(d) The sale should be expected to take place **within one year** from the date of classification.

(e) It is unlikely that significant changes to the plan will be made or that the plan will be withdrawn.

A non-current asset (or disposal group) should still be classified as held-for-sale, even if the sale has not actually taken place within one year. However, the delay must have been **caused by events or circumstances beyond the entity's control** and there must be sufficient evidence that the entity is still committed to sell the asset or disposal group. Otherwise the entity must cease to classify the asset as held-for-sale.

If an entity acquires a disposal group (eg a subsidiary) exclusively with a view to its subsequent disposal, it should classify the asset as held-for-sale only if the sale is expected to take place within one year and it is highly probable that all the other criteria will be met within a short time (normally three months).

If an entity is committed to a sale plan involving loss of control of a subsidiary, it should classify all the assets and liabilities of the subsidiary as held-for-sale when the criteria above are met, even if the entity will retain a non-controlling interest in its former subsidiary after the sale.

A non-current asset that is to be **abandoned** should not be classified as held-for-sale. This is because its carrying amount will be recovered principally through continuing use. However, a disposal group to be abandoned may meet the definition of a discontinued operation (and therefore separate disclosure may be required) when it ceases to be used (see below).

IFRS 5 was amended in September 2014 to clarify that a change in the planned method of disposal does not constitute a change in classification which requires revaluation or additional disclosure.

Question — Held for sale?

On 1 December 20X3, a company became committed to a plan to sell a manufacturing facility and has already found a potential buyer. The company does not intend to discontinue the operations currently carried out in the facility. At 31 December 20X3 there is a backlog of uncompleted customer orders. The subsidiary will not be able to transfer the facility to the buyer until after it ceases to operate the facility and has eliminated the backlog of uncompleted customer orders. This is not expected to occur until spring 20X4.

Required

Should the manufacturing facility be classified as 'held for sale' at 31 December 20X3?

Answer

The facility will not be transferred until the backlog of orders is completed; this demonstrates that the facility is not available for immediate sale in its present condition. The facility cannot be classified as 'held for sale' at 31 December 20X3. It must be treated in the same way as other items of property, plant and equipment: it should continue to be depreciated and should not be separately disclosed.

2.3 Measurement of assets held-for-sale

Key terms

Fair value: The price that would be received to sell an asset or paid to transfer a liability in an orderly transaction between market participants at the measurement date.

Costs to sell: The incremental costs directly attributable to the disposal of an asset (or disposal group), excluding finance costs and income tax expense.

Recoverable amount: The higher of an asset's fair value less costs to sell and its value in use.

Value in use: The present value of estimated future cash flows expected to arise from the continuing use of an asset and from its disposal at the end of its useful life.

A non-current asset (or disposal group) that is held for sale should be measured at the **lower of** its **carrying amount** and **fair value less costs to sell**. Fair value less costs to sell is equivalent to net realisable value. Fair value is measured in accordance with IFRS 13 *Fair Value Measurement* (see Chapter 11).

An impairment loss should be recognised where fair value less costs to sell is lower than carrying amount. Note that this is an exception to the normal rule. IAS 36 *Impairment of Assets* requires an entity to recognise an impairment loss only where an asset's recoverable amount is lower than its carrying amount. Recoverable amount is defined as the higher of net realisable value and value in use. IAS 36 does not apply to non-current assets held for sale.

IFRS 5 states that **immediately before** the asset (or disposal group) is first classified as 'held for sale' it must be **measured in accordance with applicable IFRS**. This means that if, for example, an asset is measured using the revaluation model in IAS 16 *Property, Plant and Equipment*, it must be revalued at the date on which it becomes 'held for sale'. Depreciation must be charged up to the date of classification.

Non-current assets held for sale **should not be depreciated**, even if they are still being used by the entity.

A non-current asset (or disposal group) that is **no longer classified as held for sale** (for example, because the sale has not taken place within one year) is measured at the **lower of**:

(a) Its **carrying amount** before it was classified as held for sale, adjusted for any depreciation that would have been charged had the asset not been held for sale

(b) Its **recoverable amount** at the date of the decision not to sell

2.4 Presenting discontinued operations

FAST FORWARD

The results of discontinued operations should be presented separately in the statement of profit or loss and other comprehensive income.

Key terms

Discontinued operation: a component of an entity that has either been disposed of, or is classified as held for sale, and:

(a) Represents a separate major line of business or geographical area of operations;

(b) Is part of a single co-ordinated plan to dispose of a separate major line of business or geographical area of operations; or

> (c) Is a subsidiary acquired exclusively with a view to resale.
>
> **Component of an entity:** operations and cash flows that can be clearly distinguished, operationally and for financial reporting purposes, from the rest of the entity.

An entity should **present and disclose information** that enables users of the financial statements to evaluate the financial effects of **discontinued operations** and disposals of non-current assets or disposal groups.

An entity should disclose a **single amount in the statement of profit or loss and other comprehensive income** comprising the total of:

(a) The **post-tax profit or loss** of discontinued operations; and

(b) The post-tax gain or loss recognised on the **measurement to fair value less costs to sell** or on the disposal of the assets or disposal group(s) constituting the discontinued operation.

An entity should also disclose an **analysis** of the single amount into:

(a) The revenue, expenses and pre-tax profit or loss of discontinued operations

(b) The related income tax expense

(c) The gain or loss recognised on the measurement to fair value less costs to sell or on the disposal of the assets or the discontinued operation

(d) The related income tax expense

This analysis may be presented either in the statement of profit or loss and other comprehensive income or in the notes. If it is presented in the statement of profit or loss and other comprehensive income, it should be presented in a section identified as relating to discontinued operations, ie separately from continuing operations. This analysis is not required where the discontinued operation is a newly acquired subsidiary that has been classified as held-for-sale.

An entity should disclose the **net cash flows** attributable to the operating, investing and financing activities of discontinued operations. These disclosures may be presented either in the statement of cash flows or in the notes.

The prior period amounts relating to the operations discontinued in the current period should be restated in the comparative figures in the statement of profit or loss and other comprehensive income and the statement of cash flows, but **not** in the statement of financial position.

Gains and losses on the remeasurement of a disposal group that is not a discontinued operation but is held for sale should be included in profit or loss from continuing operations.

2.5 Illustration

The following illustration is taken from the implementation guidance to IFRS 5. Profit for the period from discontinued operations would be analysed in the notes.

XYZ GROUP
STATEMENT OF PROFIT OR LOSS AND OTHER COMPREHENSIVE INCOME FOR THE YEAR ENDED 31 DECEMBER 20X2

	20X2	20X1
	$'000	*$'000*
Continuing operations		
Revenue	X	X
Cost of sales	(X)	(X)
Gross profit	X	X
Other income	X	X
Distribution costs	(X)	(X)
Administrative expenses	(X)	(X)
Other expenses	(X)	(X)
Finance costs	(X)	(X)

Share of profit of associates	X	X
Profit before tax	X	X
Income tax expense	(X)	(X)
Profit for the period from continuing operations	X	X
Discontinued operations		
Profit for the period from discontinued operations	X	X
Profit for the period	X	X
Attributable to:		
Owners of the parent	X	X
Non-controlling interest	X	X
	X	X

An alternative to this presentation would be to analyse the profit from discontinued operations in a separate column in the statement of profit or loss and other comprehensive income.

Question — Treatment of closure

On 20 October 20X3 the directors of a parent company made a public announcement of plans to close a steel works. The closure means that the group will no longer carry out this type of operation, which until recently has represented about 10% of its total turnover. The works will be gradually shut down over a period of several months, with complete closure expected in July 20X4. At 31 December output had been significantly reduced and some redundancies had already taken place. The cash flows, revenues and expenses relating to the steel works can be clearly distinguished from those of the group's other operations.

Required

How should the closure be treated in the financial statements for the year ended 31 December 20X3?

Answer

Because the steel works is being closed, rather than sold, it cannot be classified as 'held-for-sale'. In addition, the steel works is not a discontinued operation. Although at 31 December 20X3 the group was firmly committed to the closure, this has not yet taken place and therefore the steel works must be included in continuing operations. Information about the planned closure could be disclosed in the notes to the financial statements and the steel works' results should be presented as from discontinued operations (with adjustments to the comparative figures) when it ceases to be used.

2.6 Presentation of a non-current asset or disposal group classified as held-for-sale

Non-current assets and disposal groups classified as held-for-sale should be **presented separately** from other assets in the statement of financial position. The liabilities of a disposal group should be presented separately from other liabilities in the statement of financial position.

(a) Assets and liabilities held for sale **should not be offset**.

(b) The **major classes** of assets and liabilities held for sale should be **separately disclosed** either in the statement of financial position or in the notes.

(c) IFRS 5 requires non-current assets or disposal groups held for sale to be shown as a separate component of current assets/current liabilities.

For example (taken from standard)

ASSETS

Non-current assets
AAA   X

Current assets
BBB   X
CCC   X
                                                                                        ―
                                                                                        X

Non-current assets classified as held for sale   X
                                                                                        ―
                                                                                        X

Total assets   X
                                                                                        ═

EQUITY AND LIABILITIES

Equity
DDD   X

Non-current liabilities
EEE   X

Current liabilities
FFF   X
GGG   X
                                                                                        ―
Liabilities directly associated with non-current assets classified   X
as held for sale
                                                                                        X
Total equity and liabilities   X
                                                                                        ═

2.7 Additional disclosures

In the period in which a non-current asset (or disposal group) has been either classified as held-for-sale or sold the following should be disclosed.

(a) A **description** of the non-current asset (or disposal group)

(b) A description of the **facts and circumstances** of the disposal

(c) Any **gain or loss** recognised when the item was classified as held-for-sale

(d) If applicable, the **segment** in which the non-current asset (or disposal group) is presented in accordance with IFRS 8 *Operating Segments*

Where an asset previously classified as held for sale is **no longer held-for-sale**, the entity should disclose a description of the facts and circumstances leading to the decision and its effect on results. Its results should be included within those from continuing operations.

IFRS 13 *Fair Value Measurement* disclosures are also relevant to assets held-for-sale.

2.8 Current developments

The IASB and FASB have begun a project to amplify the definition of a discontinued operation in IFRS 5. An exposure draft issued in 2008 proposed:

- A revised definition of discontinued operations, expected to result in fewer items being recognised as discontinued operations than under the current IFRS 5; and

- Additional disclosure about components of an entity that have been disposed of or are classified as held for sale, even if these do not meet the definition of a discontinued operation.

The project is currently on hold.

3 IFRS 8 *Operating Segments*

3.1 Introduction

Large entities produce a wide range of products and services, often in several different countries. Further information on how the overall results of entities are made up from each of these product or geographical areas will help the users of the financial statements. This is the reason for **segment reporting**.

- The entity's **past performance** will be better understood
- The entity's **risks and returns** may be better assessed
- More **informed judgements** may be made about the entity as a whole

Risks and returns of a **diversified, multi-national company** can only be assessed by looking at the individual risks and rewards attached to groups of products or services or in different groups of products or services or in different geographical areas. These are subject to differing rates of profitability, opportunities for growth, future prospects and risks.

Segment reporting is covered by IFRS 8 *Operating Segments*.

3.2 Objective

An entity must disclose information to enable users of its financial statements to evaluate the nature and financial effects of the business activities in which it engages and the economic environments in which it operates.

3.3 Scope

Only entities whose **equity or debt securities are publicly traded** (ie on a stock exchange) need disclose segment information. In group financial statements, only **consolidated** segmental information needs to be shown. (The statement also applies to entities filing or in the process of filing financial statements for the purpose of issuing instruments in a public market.)

3.4 Definition of operating segment

> **FAST FORWARD**
>
> Reportable segments are **operating segments** or aggregations of operating segments that meet specified criteria.

You need to learn this definition, as it is crucial to the standard.

Key term

> **Operating segment**: This is a component of an entity:
>
> (a) That engages in business activities from which it may earn revenues and incur expenses (including revenues and expenses relating to transactions with other components of the same entity);
>
> (b) Whose operating results are regularly reviewed by the entity's chief operating decision maker to make decisions about resources to be allocated to the segment and assess its performance; and
>
> (c) For which discrete financial information is available.
>
> (IFRS 8)

The term 'chief operating decision maker' identifies a function, not necessarily a manager with a specific title. That function is to allocate resources and to assess the performance of the entity's operating segments.

3.5 Aggregation

Two or more operating segments may be **aggregated** if the segments have **similar economic characteristics**, and the segments are similar in **each** of the following respects:

- The **nature of the products or services**
- The **nature of the production process**

- The type or class of customer for their products or services
- The methods used to distribute their products or provide their services, and
- If applicable, the **nature of the regulatory environment**

3.6 Determining reportable segments

> **FAST FORWARD**
> IFRS 8 adopts a **management approach** to identifying reportable segments.

An entity must report separate information about **each operating segment** that:

(a) Has been identified as meeting the **definition of an operating segment**; and

(b) Where the segment total is **10% or more of total**:

   (i) **Revenue** (internal and external);

   (ii) **Reported profit or loss of all segments not reporting a loss** (or all segments in loss if greater); or

   (iii) **Assets**.

In each case the 10% test is made against the total amount for all operating segments.

At least **75% of total external revenue** must be reported by operating segments. Where this is not the case, additional segments must be identified (even if they do not meet the 10% thresholds).

Two or more operating segments **below** the thresholds may be aggregated to produce a reportable segment if the segments have similar economic characteristics, and the segments are similar in a **majority** of the aggregation criteria above.

Operating segments that do not meet **any of the quantitative thresholds** should be reported separately if management believes that information about the segment would be useful to users of the financial statements.

3.6.1 Decision tree to assist in identifying reportable segments

The following decision tree will assist in identifying reportable segments.

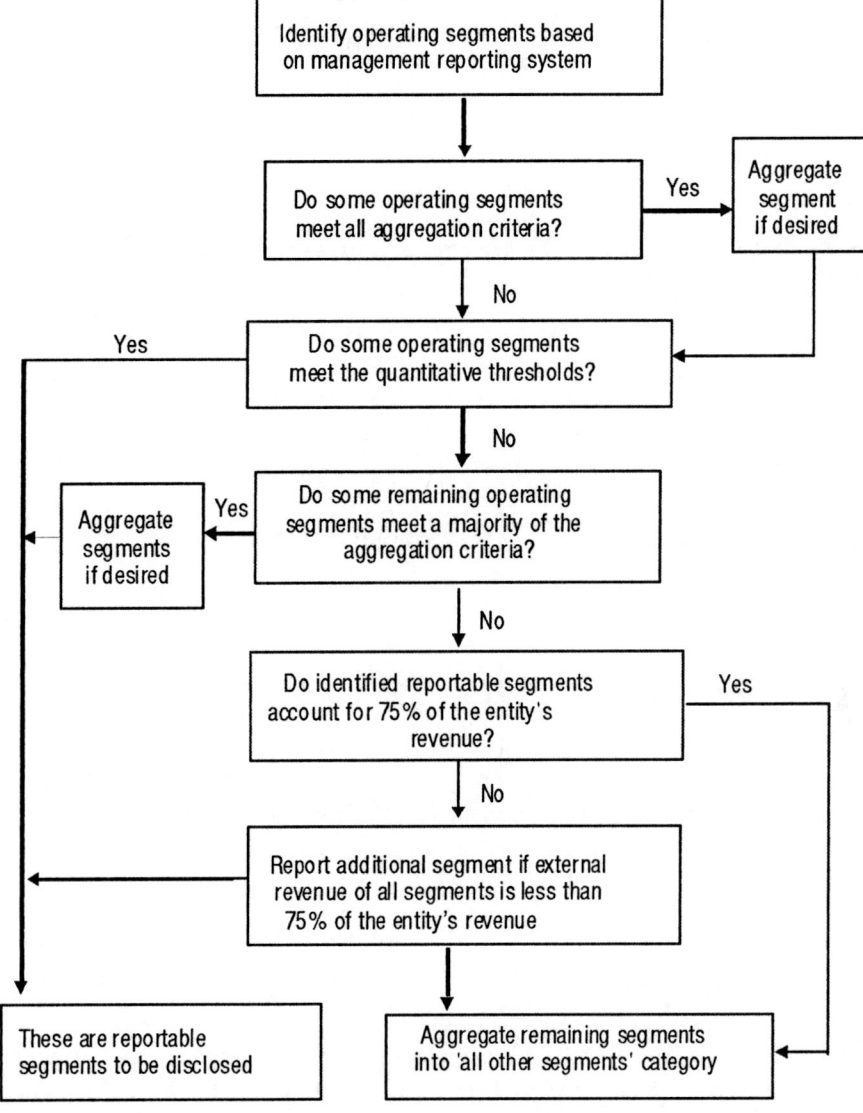

3.7 Disclosures

FAST FORWARD

- IFRS 8 disclosures are of:
    - Operating segment profit or loss
    - Segment assets
    - Segment liabilities
    - Certain income and expense items

  Disclosure under the last two headings is only required if these amounts are regularly reported to the chief operating decision maker.

- Disclosures are also required about the revenues derived from products or services and about the countries in which revenues are earned or assets held, even if that information is not reported to management for decision making.

Disclosures required by the IFRS are extensive, and best learned by looking at the example and proforma, which follow the list.

(a) Factors used to identify the entity's reportable segments

(b) **Types of products and services** from which each reportable segment derives its revenues

(c) Reportable segment revenues, profit or loss, assets, liabilities and other material items:

The amounts disclosed should be measured as they are reported to the chief operating decision maker, which is not necessarily the measurements required by IFRS.

A **reconciliation** is required of the total of each of the above items to the entity's total figures reported in its financial statements and measured under IFRS.

Reporting of a measure of **profit or loss** for each segment is compulsory. Other items are disclosed if included in the figures reviewed by or regularly provided to the chief operating decision maker.

(d) **External revenue** by each product and service (if reported basis is not products and services)

(e) Geographical information:

Notes

(1) Non-current assets excludes financial instruments, deferred tax assets, post-employment benefit assets, and rights under insurance contracts.

(2) External revenue is allocated based on the customer's location.

(f) Information about **reliance on major customers** (ie those who represent more than 10% of external revenue)

Note that amounts disclosed under (d), (e) and (f) above must be measured under IFRS.

3.7.1 Disclosure example from IFRS 8

The following example is adapted from the IFRS 8 *Implementation Guidance*, which emphasises that this is for illustrative purposes only and that the information must be presented in the most understandable manner in the specific circumstances.

The hypothetical company does not allocate tax expense (tax income) or non-recurring gains and losses to reportable segments. In addition, not all reportable segments have material non-cash items other than depreciation and amortisation in profit or loss. The amounts in this illustration, denominated as dollars, are assumed to be the amounts in reports used by the chief operating decision-maker.

	Car parts $	Motor vessel $	Software $	Electronics $	Finance $	All other $	Totals $
Revenues from external customers	3,000	5,000	9,500	12,000	5,000	1,000[a]	35,500
Intersegment revenues	–	–	3,000	1,500	–	–	4,500
Interest revenue	450	800	1,000	1,500	–	–	3,750
Interest expense	350	600	700	1,100	–	–	2,750
Net interest revenue [b]	–	–	–	–	1,000	–	1,000
Depreciation and amortisation	200	100	50	1,500	1,100	–	2,950
Reportable segment profit	200	70	900	2,300	500	100	4,070
Other material non-cash items:							
Impairment of assets	–	200	–	–	–	–	200
Reportable segment assets	2,000	5,000	3,000	12,000	57,000	2,000	81,000
Expenditure for reportable segment non-current assets	300	700	500	800	600	–	2,900
Reportable segment liabilities	1,050	3,000	1,800	8,000	30,000	–	43,850

(a) Revenues from segments below the quantitative thresholds are attributable to four operating segments of the company. Those segments include a small property business, an electronics equipment rental business, a software consulting practice and a warehouse leasing operation. None of those segments has ever met any of the quantitative thresholds for determining reportable segments.

(b) The finance segment derives a majority of its revenue from interest. Management primarily relies on net interest revenue, not the gross revenue and expense amounts, in managing that segment. Therefore, as permitted by IFRS 8, only the net amount is disclosed.

3.7.2 Suggested proforma

Information about profit or loss, assets and liabilities

	Segment A	Segment B	Segment C	All other segments	Inter segment	Entity total
Revenue – external customers	X	X	X	X	–	X
Revenue – inter segment	X	X	X	X	X	–
	X	X	X	X	(X)	X
Interest revenue	X	X	X	X	(X)	X
Interest expense	(X)	(X)	(X)	(X)	X	(X)
Depreciation and amortisation	(X)	(X)	(X)	(X)	–	(X)
Other material non-cash items	X/(X)	X/(X)	X/(X)	X/(X)	X/(X)	X/(X)
Material income/expense (IAS 1)	X/(X)	X/(X)	X/(X)	X/(X)	X/(X)	X/(X)

	Segment A	Segment B	Segment C	All other segments	Inter segment	Entity total
Share of profit of associate/JVs	X	X	X	X	–	X
Segment profit before tax	X	X	X	X	(X)	X
Income tax expense	(X)	(X)	(X)	(X)	–	(X)
Unallocated items						X/(X)
Profit for the period						X
Segment assets	X	X	X	X	(X)	X
Investments in associate/JVs	X	X	X	X	–	X
Unallocated assets						X
Entity's assets						X
Expenditures for reportable assets	X	X	X	X	(X)	X
Segment liabilities	X	X	X	X	(X)	X
Unallocated liabilities						X
Entity's liabilities						X

Information about geographical areas

	Country of domicile	Foreign countries	Total
Revenue – external customers	X	X	X
Non-current assets	X	X	X

3.8 Different ways of defining segments

IFRS 8 adopts a managerial approach. The published segment information is based on the way that the company or group is actually managed and an entity's reportable segments (called operating segments) are the ones used in its internal management reports.

It is possible to take a different approach. Under the previous standard, IAS 14, a reportable segment was 'a distinguishable component of an entity that is subject to risks and returns that are different from those of other segments'. The directors could use judgement in deciding which parts of an entity should be treated as separate reportable segments, but they were expected to take into account factors such as returns on investment, rates of growth and the potential for future development experienced by different parts of the business. This approach was called the 'risks and returns' approach.

IFRS 8 has been a controversial standard. Some users claim that the managerial approach to defining segments is too flexible and allows management to hide information, particularly the extent of their overseas operations. Some critics of IFRS 8 would like entities to be required to report all segment information by country.

3.9 Proposed changes to IFRS 8

ED/2017/2 proposes some changes and clarifications to IFRS 8 (and associated changes to IAS 34). These include:

- To clarify and emphasise the criteria for aggregating two or more operating segments may be aggregated.

- To explain more clearly the term 'chief operating decision maker' and require companies to disclose the title and role of the person or group that performs that function.

- To require companies to disclose and difference between segments as identified and segments as identified elsewhere in the annual report.

- To require companies that change their segments to provide, in the interim financial statements, additional restated segment information for prior interim periods.

3.10 Section summary

IFRS 8 is a **disclosure standard**.

- **Segment reporting** is necessary for a better understanding and assessment of:
    - Past performance
    - Risks and returns
    - Informed judgements
- IFRS 8 adopts the **managerial approach** to identifying segments
- The standard gives guidance on how segments should be **identified** and **what information should be disclosed** for each

It also sets out **requirements for related disclosures** about products and services, geographical areas and major customers.

4 IAS 33 *Earnings per Share*

FAST FORWARD

Earnings per share is a measure of the amount of profits earned by a company for each ordinary share. Earnings are profits after tax and preferred dividends.

The objective of IAS 33 is to improve the **comparison** of the performance of different entities in the same period and of the same entity in different accounting periods.

4.1 Definitions

The following definitions are given in IAS 33.

Key terms

> **Ordinary share**: an equity instrument that is subordinate to all other classes of equity instruments.
>
> **Potential ordinary share**: a financial instrument or other contract that may entitle its holder to ordinary shares.
>
> **Options, warrants and their equivalents**: financial instruments that give the holder the right to purchase ordinary shares.
>
> **Contingently issuable ordinary shares** are ordinary shares issuable for little or no cash or other consideration upon the satisfaction of certain conditions in a contingent share agreement.
>
> **Contingent share agreement**: an agreement to issue shares that is dependent on the satisfaction of specified conditions.
>
> **Dilution** is a reduction in earnings per share or an increase in loss per share resulting from the assumption that convertible instruments are converted, that options or warrants are exercised, or that ordinary shares are issued upon the satisfaction of certain conditions.
>
> **Antidilution** is an increase in earnings per share or a reduction in loss per share resulting from the assumption that convertible instruments are converted, that options or warrants are exercised, or that ordinary shares are issued upon the satisfaction of certain conditions. (IAS 33)

4.1.1 Ordinary shares

There may be more than one class of ordinary shares, but ordinary shares of the same class will have the same rights to receive dividends. Ordinary shares participate in the profit for the period **only after other types of shares**, eg preference shares classified as equity.

4.1.2 Potential ordinary shares

IAS 33 identifies the following examples of financial instrument and other contracts generating potential ordinary shares.

(a) **Debts** (financial liabilities) **or equity instruments**, including preference shares, that are convertible into ordinary shares

(b) **Share warrants and options**

(c) Shares that would be issued upon the satisfaction of **certain conditions** resulting from contractual arrangements, such as the purchase of a business or other assets

4.2 Scope

IAS 33 has the following **scope restrictions**.

(a) Only companies with (potential) ordinary shares which are **publicly traded** need to present EPS (including companies in the process of being listed).

(b) EPS need only be presented on the basis of **consolidated results** where the parent's results are shown as well.

(c) Where companies **choose** to present EPS, even when they have no (potential) ordinary shares which are publicly traded, they must do so according to IAS 33.

4.3 Basic EPS

FAST FORWARD

> You should know how to calculate **basic EPS** and how to deal with related complications (issue of shares for cash, bonus issue, share splits/reverse share splits, rights issues).
>
> **Basic EPS** is calculated by dividing the profit or loss for the period attributable to ordinary equity holders by the weighted average number of ordinary shares outstanding during the period.

Basic EPS should be calculated for **profit or loss attributable to ordinary equity holders** of the parent entity and **profit or loss from continuing operations** attributable to those equity holders (if this is presented).

Basic EPS should be calculated by dividing the **profit** or loss for the period attributable to ordinary equity holders by the **weighted average number of ordinary shares** outstanding during the period.

$$\frac{\text{Profit/(loss attributable to ordinary shareholders}}{\text{Weighted average number of ordinary shares outstanding during the period}}$$

4.3.1 Earnings

Earnings includes **all items of income and expense** (including tax and non-controlling interests) **less** profit attributable to **holders of preference shares** classified as equity, including preference dividends.

The dividends on **preference shares** classified as equity to be deducted from profit consist of the following:

(a) Dividends on non-cumulative preference shares declared in respect of the period.

(b) Dividends on cumulative preference shares required for the period, **whether or not** they have been declared (**excluding** those paid/declared during the period in respect of previous periods).

If an entity purchases its own preference shares classified as equity for more than their carrying amount, the excess should be treated as a return to the preference shareholders and deducted from profit or loss attributable to ordinary equity holders.

4.3.2 Per share

The number of ordinary shares used should be the weighted average number of ordinary shares during the period. This figure (for all periods presented) should be **adjusted for events**, other than the conversion of potential ordinary shares, that have changed the number of shares outstanding without a corresponding change in resources.

The **time-weighting factor** is the number of days the shares were outstanding compared with the total number of days in the period. A reasonable approximation is usually adequate.

Shares are usually included in the weighted average number of shares from the **date consideration is receivable** which is usually the date of issue. In other cases consider the specific terms attached to their issue (consider the substance of any contract). The treatment for the issue of ordinary shares in different circumstances is as follows.

Consideration	Start date for inclusion
In exchange for cash	When cash is receivable
On the voluntary reinvestment of dividends on ordinary or preferred shares	The dividend payment date
As a result of the conversion of a debt instrument to ordinary shares	Date interest ceases accruing
In place of interest or principal on other financial instruments	Date interest ceases accruing
In exchange for the settlement of a liability of the entity	The settlement date
As consideration for the acquisition of an asset other than cash	The date on which the acquisition is recognised
For the rendering of services to the entity	As services are rendered

Ordinary shares issued as **purchase consideration** in an acquisition should be included as of the date of acquisition because the acquired entity's results will also be included from that date.

Ordinary shares that will be issued on the **conversion** of a mandatorily convertible instrument are included in the calculation from the **date the contract is entered into**.

If ordinary shares are **partly paid**, they are treated as a fraction of an ordinary share to the extent they are entitled to dividends relative to fully paid ordinary shares.

Contingently issuable shares (including those subject to recall) are included in the computation when all necessary conditions for issue have been satisfied.

4.4 Effect on basic EPS of changes in capital structure

4.4.1 New issues/buy backs

When there has been an issue of new shares or a buy-back of shares, the corresponding figures for EPS for the previous year will be comparable with the current year because, as the weighted average of shares has risen or fallen, there has been a **corresponding increase or decrease in resources**. Money has been received when shares were issued, and money has been paid out to repurchase shares. It is assumed that the sale or purchase has been made at full market price.

There are other events, however, which change the number of shares outstanding, **without a corresponding change in resources**. In these circumstances (four of which are considered by IAS 33) it is necessary to make adjustments so that the current and prior period EPS figures are comparable.

4.4.2 Capitalisation/bonus issue and share split/reverse share split

These two types of event can be considered together as they have a similar effect. In both cases, the number of ordinary shares held by equity holders changes, but for **no consideration is received or paid**. So there is no change in resources held by the entity.

PART C ACCOUNTING AND REPORTING TECHNIQUES

This problem is solved by **adjusting the number of ordinary shares outstanding before the event** for the proportionate change in the number of shares outstanding as if the event had occurred at the beginning of the earliest period reported.

4.4.3 Rights issue

A rights issue of shares is an issue of new shares to existing equity holders **at a price below the current market value**. The offer of new shares is made on the basis of x new shares for every y shares currently held, eg a 1 for 3 rights issue is an offer of 1 new share at the offer price for every 3 shares currently held. Because the rights price is below the market price, there is a 'free', ie bonus, element in the issue.

To arrive at figures for EPS when a rights issue is made, we first calculate the **theoretical ex-rights price**. This is a weighted average value per share.

The procedures for calculating the EPS for the current year and a corresponding figure for the previous year are as follows.

(a) The **EPS for the corresponding previous period** should be multiplied by the following fraction. (**Note.** The market price on the last day of quotation is taken as the fair value immediately prior to exercise of the rights, as required by the standard.)

$$\frac{\text{Theoretical ex-rights price}}{\text{Market price on last day of quotation (with rights)}}$$

(b) To obtain the **EPS for the current year** you should:

(i) Multiply the number of shares before the rights issue by the fraction of the year before the date of issue and by the following fraction.

$$\frac{\text{Market price on last day of quotation with rights}}{\text{Theoretical ex-rights price}}$$

(ii) Multiply the number of shares after the rights issue by the fraction of the year after the date of issue and add to the figure arrived at in (i).

The total earnings should then be divided by the total number of shares so calculated.

Question — Basic EPS

Macarone Co has produced the following profit figures.

	$m
20X6	1.1
20X7	1.5
20X8	1.8

On 1 January 20X7 the number of shares outstanding was 500,000. During 20X7 the company announced a rights issue with the following details.

Rights: 1 new share for each 5 outstanding (100,000 new shares in total)

Exercise price: $5.00

Last date to exercise rights: 1 March 20X7

The market (fair) value of one share in Marcoli immediately prior to exercise on 1 March 20X7 = $11.00.

Required

Calculate the EPS for 20X6, 20X7 and 20X8.

Answer

Computation of theoretical ex-rights price

This computation uses the total fair value and number of shares.

$$\frac{\text{Fair value of all outstanding shares} + \text{total received from exercise of rights}}{\text{No shares outstanding prior to exercise} + \text{no shares issued in exercise}}$$

$$= \frac{(\$11.00 \times 500,000) + (\$5.00 \times 100,000)}{500,000 + 100,000} = \$10.00$$

Another method of calculation is:

20X6	Shares	Price $	$
Initial holding	5	11.00	55.00
Rights issue	1	5.00	5.00
	6		60.00

so $10.00 per share.

Computation of EPS

		20X6 $	20X7 $	20X8 $
20X6	EPS as originally reported $\dfrac{\$1,100,000}{500,000}$	2.20		
20X6	EPS restated for rights issue = $\dfrac{\$1,100,000}{500,000} \times \dfrac{10}{11}$	2.00		
20X7	EPS including effects of rights issue $\dfrac{\$1,500,000}{(500,000 \times 2/12 \times 11/10) + (600,000 \times 10/12)}$		2.54	
20X8	EPS = $\dfrac{\$1,800,000}{600,000}$			3.00

4.5 Diluted EPS

> **FAST FORWARD**
>
> **Diluted EPS** is calculated by adjusting the profit attributable to ordinary equity holders and the weighted average number of shares outstanding for the effects of all dilutive potential ordinary shares.

At the end of an accounting period, a company may have in issue some **securities** which do not (at present) have any 'claim' to a share of equity earnings, but **may give rise to such a claim in the future**, for example.

(a) A **separate class of equity shares** which at present is not entitled to any dividend, but will be entitled after some future date.

(b) **Convertible loan stock** or **convertible preferred shares** which give their holders the right at some future date to exchange their securities for ordinary shares of the company, at a pre-determined conversion rate.

(c) **Options or warrants.**

In such circumstances, the future number of shares ranking for dividend might increase, which in turn results in a fall in the EPS. In other words, a **future increase** in the **number of equity shares will cause a dilution or 'watering down' of equity**, and it is possible to calculate a **diluted earnings per share** (ie the

EPS that would have been obtained during the financial period if the dilution had already taken place). This will indicate to investors the possible effects of a future dilution.

4.5.1 Earnings

The earnings calculated for basic EPS should be adjusted by the **post-tax** (including deferred tax) effect of the following.

(a) Any **dividends** on dilutive potential ordinary shares that were deducted to arrive at earnings for basic EPS.

(b) **Interest recognised** in the period for the dilutive potential ordinary shares.

(c) Any **other changes in income or expenses** (fees and discount, premium accounted for as yield adjustments) that would result from the conversion of the dilutive potential ordinary shares.

The conversion of some potential ordinary shares may lead to changes in **other income or expenses**. For example, the reduction of interest expense related to potential ordinary shares and the resulting increase in profit for the period may lead to an increase in the expense relating to a non-discretionary employee profit-sharing plan. When calculating diluted EPS, the profit or loss for the period is adjusted for any such consequential changes in income or expense.

4.5.2 Per share

The number of ordinary shares is the weighted average number of ordinary shares calculated for basic EPS plus the weighted average number of ordinary shares that would be issued on the conversion of all the **dilutive potential ordinary shares** into ordinary shares.

It should be assumed that dilutive ordinary shares were converted into ordinary shares at the **beginning of the period** or, if later, at the actual date of issue. There are two other points.

(a) The computation assumes the most **advantageous conversion rate** or exercise rate from the standpoint of the holder of the potential ordinary shares.

(b) A **subsidiary, joint venture or associate** may issue potential ordinary shares that are convertible into either ordinary shares of the subsidiary, joint venture or associate, or ordinary shares of the reporting entity. If these potential ordinary shares have a dilutive effect on the consolidated basic EPS of the reporting entity, they are included in the calculation of diluted EPS.

4.6 Example: Diluted EPS

In 20X7 Farrah Co had a basic EPS of 105c based on earnings of $105,000 and 100,000 ordinary $1 shares. It also had in issue $40,000 15% Convertible Loan Stock which is convertible in two years' time at the rate of 4 ordinary shares for every $5 of stock. The rate of tax is 30%.

Required

Calculate the diluted EPS.

Solution

Diluted EPS is calculated as follows.

Step 1 **Number of shares**: the additional equity on conversion of the loan stock will be 40,000 × 4/5 = 32,000 shares

Step 2 **Earnings**: Farrah Co will save interest payments of $6,000 ($40,000 × 15%) but this increase in profits will be taxed. Hence the earnings figure may be recalculated:

	$
Gross profit $((105,000 ÷ (1 − 30%)) + 6,000)	156,000
Tax (30%)	46,800
Profit after taxation	109,200

Step 3 Calculation: Diluted EPS = $\dfrac{\$109,200}{132,000}$ = 82.7c

Step 4 Dilution: the dilution in earnings would be 105c − 82.7c = 22.3c per share.

Question — EPS 1

Ardent Co has 5,000,000 ordinary shares of 25 cents each in issue. During 20X4 the company also had in issue $2,000,000 of 10% convertible loan stock, convertible in one year's time at the rate of 3 shares per $5 of stock.

The total earnings in 20X4 were $1,750,000.

The rate of tax is 35%.

Required

Calculate the EPS and diluted EPS.

Answer

(a) EPS = $\dfrac{\$1,750,000}{5\ \text{million}}$ = 35 cents

(b) On dilution, the (maximum) number of shares in issue would be:

	Shares
Current	5,000,000
On conversion of 10% stock (2 million × 3/5)	1,200,000
	6,200,000

	$	$
Current earnings		1,750,000
Add interest saved on 10% stock		120,000
Revised earnings		1,880,000

Fully diluted EPS = $\dfrac{\$1,880,000}{6.2\ \text{million}}$ = 30.3 cents

4.6.1 Treatment of options

FAST FORWARD

You must be able to deal with **options** and all other **dilutive potential ordinary shares**.

It should be assumed that options are exercised and that the assumed proceeds would have been received from the issue of shares at the average market price of the ordinary shares during the period.

Options and other share purchase arrangements are dilutive when they would result in the issue of ordinary shares for **less than the average market price of ordinary shares during the period**. The amount of the dilution is the average market price of ordinary shares during the period less the issue price. In order to calculate diluted EPS, each transaction of this type is treated as consisting of two parts.

(a) A contract to issue a certain number of ordinary shares at their **average market price** during the period. These shares are fairly priced and are assumed to be neither dilutive nor antidilutive. They are ignored in the computation of diluted earnings per share.

(b) A contract to issue the remaining ordinary shares for **no consideration**. Such ordinary shares generate no proceeds and have no effect on the profit attributable to ordinary shares outstanding. Therefore such shares are dilutive and they are added to the number of ordinary shares outstanding in the computation of diluted EPS.

To the extent that **partly paid shares** are not entitled to participate in dividends during the period, they are considered the equivalent of **warrants** or **options**.

Employee share options with fixed or determinable terms (ie **not performance based**) and outstanding shares are treated as **options** in the calculation of diluted earnings per share. **Performance based** employee share options are treated as **contingently issuable shares** because their issue is contingent upon satisfying specified conditions in addition to the passage of time.

Question

EPS 2

Brand Co has the following results for the year ended 31 December 20X7.

Profit for year	$1,200,000
Weighted average number of ordinary shares outstanding during year	500,000 shares
Average market value of one ordinary share during year	$20.00
Weighted average number of shares under option during year	100,000 shares
Exercise price for shares under option during year	$15.00

Required

Calculate both basic and diluted earnings per share.

Answer

	Per share	Earnings $	Shares
Profit for year		1,200,000	
Weighted average shares outstanding during 20X7			500,000
Basic earnings per share	2.40		
Number of shares under option			100,000
Number of shares that would have been issued at market value: (100,000 × $15.00/$20.00)			(75,000)*
Diluted earnings per share	2.29	1,200,000	525,000

*The earnings have not been increased as the total number of shares has been increased only by the number of shares (25,000) deemed for the purpose of the computation to have been issued for no consideration.

4.6.2 Interim financial reports

Where an entity issues interim financial reports, EPS is based on the earnings and weighted average number of shares for the 'year-to-date'.

IAS 33 states that dilutive potential ordinary shares must be determined **independently for each period presented**. The number of dilutive potential ordinary shares included in the year-to-date period is not a weighted average of the dilutive potential ordinary shares included in each interim computation.

4.6.3 Contingently issuable shares

Contingently issueable (potential) ordinary shares are treated **as for basic EPS**. If the conditions have not been met, the number of contingently issueable shares included in the computation is based on the number of shares **that would be issueable** if the end of the reporting period was the end of the contingency period. Restatement is not allowed if the conditions are not met when the contingency period expires.

4.6.4 Contracts that may be settled in ordinary shares or cash

Where an entity has issued a contract that may be settled either in ordinary shares or in cash at the **issuer's option**, the entity shall **presume** that the contract will be settled **in ordinary shares**, and the resulting potential ordinary shares should be included in diluted earnings per share if the effect is dilutive.

For contracts that may be settled in ordinary shares or cash at the **holder's option**, the **more dilutive** of cash settlement and share settlement should be used in the calculation.

4.7 Dilutive potential ordinary shares

According to IAS 33, potential ordinary shares should be treated as dilutive when, and only when, their conversion to ordinary shares would **decrease profit per share** from continuing ordinary operations. How is this determined?

The **profit from continuing ordinary activities** is 'the control number', used to establish whether potential ordinary shares are dilutive or antidilutive. The profit from continuing ordinary activities is the profit from ordinary activities **after deducting** dividends on preference shares classified as equity and after excluding items relating to discontinued operations. It also excludes the effects of changes in accounting policies and of corrections of prior period errors.

Potential ordinary shares are **antidilutive** when their conversion to ordinary shares would increase earnings per share from continuing ordinary operations or decrease loss per share from continuing ordinary operations. The effects of antidilutive potential ordinary shares are ignored in calculating diluted EPS.

In considering whether potential ordinary shares are dilutive or antidilutive, each issue or series of potential ordinary shares is **considered separately, not** in aggregate. The sequence in which potential ordinary shares are considered may affect whether or not they are dilutive. Therefore, in order to maximise the dilution of basic EPS, each issue or series of potential ordinary shares is considered in sequence from the most dilutive to the least dilutive. This may sound very confusing, but the following example may help.

4.8 Example: Dilutive potential ordinary shares

Carter plc has the following results for the year ended 31 December 20X7.

Earnings: profit attributable to ordinary equity holders	$10,000,000
Ordinary shares outstanding	2,000,000
Average market value of one ordinary share during the year	$75.00
Tax rate	40%

Potential ordinary shares are as follows.

(a) Options: 100,000 with exercise price of $60

(b) Convertible preference shares: 800,000 shares entitled to a cumulative dividend of $8 per share (each preference share is convertible to two ordinary shares)

(c) 5% Convertible bond: nominal amount $100,000,000, each 1,000 bond is convertible to 20 ordinary shares and there is no amortisation of premium or discount affecting the determination of interest expense

Required

Calculate the diluted EPS.

Solution

Step 1 Calculate the increase in earnings attributable to ordinary equity holders on conversion of the potential ordinary shares.

	Increase in earnings $	Increase in number of ordinary shares	Earnings per Incremental shares $
Options			
Increase in earnings	Nil		
Incremental shares issued for no Consideration 100,000 × $(75 − 60)/$75		20,000	Nil
Convertible preference shares			
Increase in profit $8 × 800,000	6,400,000		
Incremental shares 2 × 800,000		1,600,000	4.00
5% Convertible bonds			
Increase in profit ((100,000,000 × 0.05) × (1 − 40%))	3,000,000		
Incremental shares 100,000 × 20		2,000,000	1.50

Step 2 Now calculate the diluted EPS in order of most dilutive to least dilutive.

	Profit attributable $	Ordinary shares	Per share $	
As reported	10,000,000	2,000,000	5.00	
Options		20,000		
	10,000,000	2,020,000	4.95	Dilutive
5% Convertible bonds	3,000,000	2,000,000		
	13,000,000	4,020,000	3.23	Dilutive
Convertible preference shares	6,400,000	1,600,000		
	19,400,000	5,620,000	3.45	Antidilutive

Note. Since diluted EPS is increased when taking the convertible preference shares into account (from $3.23 to $3.45), the convertible preference shares are antidilutive and are ignored in the calculation of diluted EPS. Therefore, diluted EPS is $3.23.

Potential ordinary shares are **weighted** for the period they were outstanding. Any that were cancelled or allowed to lapse during the reporting period are included in the computation of diluted EPS only for the portion of the period during which they were outstanding. Potential ordinary shares that have been converted into ordinary shares **during the reporting period** are included in the calculation of diluted EPS from the beginning of the period to the date of conversion. From the date of conversion, the resulting ordinary shares are included in basic (and therefore in diluted) EPS.

4.9 Retrospective adjustment

If the number of ordinary or potential ordinary shares outstanding **increases** as a result of a capitalisation, bonus issue or share split, or decreases as a result of a reverse share split, the calculation of basic and diluted EPS for all periods presented should be **adjusted retrospectively**.

If these changes occur **after the year end** but before issue of the financial statements, the calculations per share for the financial statements and those of any prior period should be based on the **new number of shares** (and this should be disclosed).

In addition, basic and diluted EPS of all periods presented should be adjusted for the effects of **errors**, and adjustments resulting from **changes** in **accounting policies**, accounted for retrospectively (as required by IAS 8).

An entity **does not restate diluted EPS** of any prior period for changes in the assumptions used or for the conversion of potential ordinary shares into ordinary shares outstanding.

4.10 Presentation

A entity should present in the statement of profit or loss and other comprehensive income (or the statement of profit or loss where this is presented separately), basic and diluted EPS for:

(a) Profit or loss from continuing operations; and

(b) Profit or loss for the period for each class of ordinary share that has a different right to share in the profit for the period.

The basic and diluted EPS should be presented with **equal prominence** for all periods presented.

Basic and diluted EPS for any **discontinuing operations** must also be presented.

Disclosure must still be made where the EPS figures (basic and/or diluted) are **negative** (ie a loss per share).

4.11 Disclosure

An entity should disclose the following.

(a) The amounts used as the **numerators** in calculating basic and diluted EPS, and a **reconciliation** of those amounts to the profit or loss for the period.

(b) The weighted average number of ordinary shares used as the **denominator** in calculating basic and diluted EPS, and a **reconciliation** of these denominators to each other.

(c) Instruments that could potentially dilute basic EPS but which were **not included** in the calculation because they were **antidilutive** for the period presented.

An entity should also disclose a description of ordinary share transactions or potential ordinary share transactions, other than capitalisation issues and share splits, which occur **after the year end** when they are of such importance that non-disclosure would affect the ability of the users of the financial statements to make proper evaluations and decisions (see IAS 10 *Events After the Reporting Period*). Examples of such transactions include the following:

(a) Issue of shares for cash

(b) Issue of shares when the proceeds are used to repay debt or preferred shares outstanding at the year end

(c) Redemption of ordinary shares outstanding

(d) Conversion or exercise of potential ordinary shares, outstanding at the year end, into ordinary shares

(e) Issue of warrants, options or convertible securities

(f) Achievement of conditions that would result in the issue of contingently issueable shares

EPS amounts are not adjusted for such transactions occurring after the end of the reporting period because such transactions **do not affect the amount of capital used** to produce the profit or loss for the period.

4.12 Alternative EPS figures

An entity may present **alternative EPS figures if it wishes**. However, IAS 33 lays out certain rules where this takes place.

(a) The weighted average number of shares as calculated under IAS 33 **must** be used.

(b) A **reconciliation** must be given between the component of profit used in the alternative EPS (if it is not a line item in the statement of profit or loss and other comprehensive income) and the line item for profit reported in the statement of profit or loss and other comprehensive income.

(c) The entity must indicate the basis on which the **numerator** is determined.

(d) Basic and diluted EPS must be shown with **equal prominence**.

(e) The alternative EPS figure must be shown in the notes (not in the statement of profit or loss and other comprehensive income).

4.13 Significance of earnings per share

Earnings per share (EPS) is one of the most frequently quoted statistics in financial analysis. Because of the widespread use of the price earnings **(P/E) ratio** as a yardstick for investment decisions, it became increasingly important.

It seems that reported and forecast EPS can, through the P/E ratio, have a **significant effect on a company's share price**. Thus, a share price might fall if it looks as if EPS is going to be low. This is not very rational, as EPS can depend on many, often subjective, assumptions used in preparing a historical statement, namely the statement of profit or loss and other comprehensive income. It does not necessarily bear any relation to the value of a company, and of its shares. Nevertheless, the market is sensitive to EPS.

EPS has also served as a means of assessing the **stewardship and management** role performed by company directors and managers. Remuneration packages might be linked to EPS growth, thereby increasing the pressure on management to improve EPS. The danger of this, however, is that management effort may go into distorting results to produce a favourable EPS.

4.14 Exposure draft: Simplifying earnings per share

The objective of the EPS project is to simplify and converge the calculation of EPS between IAS 33 *Earnings per Share* and its US equivalent, SFAS No. 128 *Earnings per Share*. To this end, the IASB issued, in August 2008, an Exposure Draft: *Simplifying Earnings per Share.* This focuses on:

- Simplifying the earnings per share (EPS) calculation
- Establishing a common denominator for the EPS calculation
- Reducing differences between IAS 33 and U.S. Statement of Financial Accounting Standard (SFAS) No. 28 Earnings per Share.

Other changes include the following:

(a) The ED proposes a **principle to determine which instruments would be included in the basic EPS calculation.** Under the proposed principle the weighted average number of ordinary shares would include only those instruments that give their holder the right to share in the profit or loss for the current period.

(b) For the **diluted EPS calculation**, the ED proposes that **no adjustment be made to reflect the assumed exercise or conversion of instruments measured at fair value through profit or loss**.

At the time of writing, this project has been deferred until other projects in the IASB's work plan are completed. The Board will decide whether to restart the project as part of its three-yearly agenda consultation.

4.15 Section summary

EPS is an important measure for investors.

- **Basic EPS** is straightforward, although it may require adjustments for **changes in capital structure**
- **Diluted EPS** is more complex (and more likely in an exam question). You must be able to deal with:
    - Options
    - Dilutive potential ordinary shares
    - Retrospective adjustment

5 Management commentary

FAST FORWARD

The non-mandatory IFRS Practice Statement *Management Commentary* provides guidance for those entities which publish management commentary.

In the UK, companies have historically been encouraged to produce an Operating and Financial Review (OFR), explaining the main factors underlying a company's financial position and performance, and analysing the main trends affecting this. The UK Accounting Standards Board (ASB) issued a Reporting Statement on the OFR in January 2006. The Companies Act 2006 requires all UK companies other than those classified as small to provide a Business Review (now called a Strategic Report) within their annual report. This must provide a fair review of the business and an assessment of the risks and uncertainties facing the business.

The IASB believes that the **quality of financial reports** can be improved through management commentary and consequently it issued an IFRS Practice Statement *Management Commentary* in December 2010.

This document provides a broad, non-binding framework for the presentation of narrative reporting to accompany financial statements prepared in accordance with IFRS. It is applicable from its issue date, 8 December 2010.

5.1 Definition of management commentary

The following definition is given in the Practice Statement:

Key term

Management commentary. A narrative report that provides a context within which to interpret the financial position, financial performance and cash flows of an entity. It also provides management with an opportunity to explain its objectives and its strategies for achieving those objectives.

5.2 Scope of the Practice Statement

The Practice Statement applies only to management commentary that relates to financial statements prepared in accordance with IFRS. It does not apply to any other information presented in the financial statements.

The Practice Statement does not prescribe:

- Which entities should publish management commentary
- How frequently entities should publish management commentary
- The level of assurance to which management commentary should be subjected

5.3 Identification of management commentary

The Practice Statement requires that:

- The financial statements to which management commentary relates are either be presented with the commentary or indentified within the commentary.
- Management commentary should be distinguished from other information.
- Management should explain the extent to which the Practice Statement has been followed.

5.4 Framework for management commentary

The Practice Statement provides a framework for the presentation of management commentary, which considers its purpose and the principles which underlie it.

5.4.1 Purpose

Management commentary should provide a context for the financial statements, explaining management's views about what has happened, why it has happened and what the implications are for the future. The views should be balanced to include both positive and negative circumstances.

The commentary should look at the past, the present and the future by analysing historic trends and factors likely to affect future performance, position and progress.

5.4.2 Principles

The following principles underlie a management commentary:

- Commentary should provide a **management's view** of an entity's performance, position and progress (and therefore it should derive from information that is important to management in managing the business).

- It should **supplement and complement information presented in the financial statements**, by providing explanations and background conditions in respect of amounts in the financial statements. It may also include other information that is not presented in the financial statements but which is important to management.

- It should include **forward looking information**. Such information does not predict the future, but instead sets out management's objectives for the entity and its strategies for achieving those objectives. Management should also explain how and why the performance of the entity is short of, meets or exceeds forward-looking disclosures made in the prior period management commentary.

- It should **include information which possesses the qualitative characteristics** described in the *Conceptual Framework*. The information presented should be material to the entity.

- It should provide information to help users to **assess the performance** of the entity **and actions of the management** relative to stated strategies and plans for progress.

5.5 Presentation

The Practice Statement accepts that the form of management commentary will vary from entity to entity, however requires that in all cases it is clear and straightforward.

It should focus on the most important information and specifically should:

- Be consistent with the related financial statements
- Reflect any segment information contained within the financial statements
- Not duplicate disclosures made in the notes to the accounts without providing additional analysis
- Avoid generic disclosures which do not relate specifically to the entity in question

5.6 Elements of management commentary

The Practice Statement requires that management commentary includes information that is essential to an understanding of:

(a) **The nature of the business**

- A description of the business
- The industry in which the entity operates
- Main markets and the entity's competitive position within those
- Significant features of the legal, regulatory and macro-economic environments that influence the entity
- The entity's main products, services, business processes and distribution methods
- The entity's structure and how it creates value

(b) **Management's objectives and strategies for meeting those objectives**

Eg information about how management intends to address market trends and the threats and opportunities those market trends represent provides users of the financial reports with insight that may shape their expectations about the entity's future performance.

Management should also discuss significant changes in management objectives and strategies since the previous period.

(c) **The entity's most significant resources, risks and relationships**

To include a clear description of the most important resources, risks and relationships that management believes can affect the entity's value and how those resources, risks and relationships are managed.

Resources are both financial and non-financial whilst risks may be strategic, commercial, operational or financial.

(d) **The results of operations and prospects**

To include a clear description of the entity's financial and non-financial performance, the extent to which that performance may be indicative of future performance and management's assessment of the entity's prospects.

(e) **The critical performance measures and indicators that management uses to evaluate the entity's performance against stated objectives.**

Management should disclose performance measures and indicators (both financial and non-financial) that are used by management to assess progress against its stated objectives. Management should explain why the results from performance measures have changed over the period or how the indicators have changed.

PART C ACCOUNTING AND REPORTING TECHNIQUES

Chapter roundup

- Go back to your earlier studies to revise **IAS 1** and **IAS 8**.
- **IFRS 5** requires non-current assets 'held for sale' to be presented separately in the statement of financial position.
- The results of discontinued operations should be presented separately in the statement of profit or loss and other comprehensive income.
- Reportable segments are **operating segments** or aggregations of operating segments that meet specified criteria.
- IFRS 8 adopts a **management approach** to identifying reportable segments.
- IFRS 8 disclosures are of:
    - Operating segment profit or loss
    - Segment assets
    - Segment liabilities
    - Certain income and expense items

    Disclosure under the last two headings is only required if these amounts are regularly reported to the chief operating decision maker.
- Disclosures are also required about the revenues derived from products or services and about the countries in which revenues are earned or assets held, even if that information is not reported to management for decision making.
- **Earnings per share** is a measure of the amount of profits earned by a company for each ordinary share. Earnings are profits after tax and preferred dividends.
- You should know how to calculate **basic EPS** and how to deal with related complications (issue of shares for cash, bonus issue, share splits/reverse share splits, rights issues).
- **Basic EPS** is calculated by dividing the profit or loss for the period attributable to ordinary equity holders by the weighted average number of ordinary shares outstanding during the period.
- **Diluted EPS** is calculated by adjusting the profit attributable to ordinary equity holders and the weighted average number of shares outstanding for the effects of all dilutive potential ordinary shares.
- You must be able to deal with **options** and all other **dilutive potential ordinary shares**.
- The non-mandatory IFRS Practice Statement *Management Commentary* provides guidance for those entities which publish management commentary.

Quick quiz

1. What is the full title of IAS 8? (*Fill in the blanks.*)

    Accounting……………., changes in accounting…………………… and ………………

2. For a non-current asset to be held for sale, a buyer must already have been found. True or false?

3. A non-current asset held for sale should be measured at the lower of …………..… and
   ……………………………………….(*Fill in the blanks.*)

4. All entities must disclose segment information. True or false?

5. Which numerator is used to rank dilutive shares?

6. Why is the numerator adjusted for convertible bonds when calculating diluted EPS?

Answers to quick quiz

1. Accounting **policies**, changes in accounting **estimates** and **errors**
2. False. There must be an **active programme** to locate a buyer.
3. The lower of **its carrying amount** and **fair value less costs to sell**.
4. False. Only entities whose equity or debt securities are publicly traded need disclose segment information.
5. Profit from continuing operations only
6. Because the issue of shares will affect earnings by the interest saving.

End of chapter question

Bartolo (AIA November 2004)

(a) Bartolo, a limited liability company, had an issued share capital as at 31 October 20X4 consisting of 20,000,000 ordinary shares of 50 cents each and 800,000 6.8% convertible preference shares of $1 each. The company also had in issue $5,500,000 of 12% convertible bonds.

Profit from continuing operations after tax for the year ended 31 October 20X4 was $880,000. The average market price of Bartolo plc's ordinary shares was $0.99 per share during the year ended 31 October 20X4.

Each convertible bond is convertible into 2.5 ordinary shares. Each convertible preference share is convertible into 1.25 ordinary shares. In addition, Bartolo plc's directors have options to purchase 460,000 ordinary shares at $0.85 per share in 20X6.

Income tax is 30%.

Required

Calculate Bartolo plc's diluted earnings per share for the year ended 31 October 20X4 in accordance with IAS 33 *Earnings per Share*. **(12 marks)**

(b) The issued share capital of Contessa, a limited liability company, as at 1 November 20X3 consisted of 25,000,000 ordinary shares of 60 cents each, fully paid. On 1 February 20X4 Contessa made a 1 for 10 rights issue at $1.15 per ordinary share.

Contessa's statement of profit or loss and other comprehensive income for the year ended 31 October 20X4 reports a profit on ordinary activities of $3,100,000. The statement of profit or loss and other comprehensive income for the year ended 31 October 20X3 reported a profit on ordinary activities after taxation of $2,200,000 and an earnings per share figure of 8.80 cents.

The market value of Contessa plc's ordinary shares immediately before the rights issue on 1 February 20X4 was $1.40 per share.

Required

Calculate earnings per share in accordance with IAS 33 *Earnings per Share* for the years ended 31 October 20X4 and 31 October 20X3 for disclosure in the published financial statements for the year ended 31 October 20X4. **(9 marks)**

(c) The draft statement of profit or loss and other comprehensive income of Figaro, a limited liability company, for the financial year ended 31 October 20X4 shows a profit before tax of $2,276,850, an income tax expense of $1,350,000 and a transfer from deferred taxation of $227,600. At 1 November 20X3 Figaro had in issue 4,000,000 equity shares of £1 each. On 1 July 20X4 Figaro split its share capital into 5,000,000 shares of 80 cents each. Figaro's reported earnings per share figure for the year ended 31 October 20X3 was 22.2 cents.

PART C ACCOUNTING AND REPORTING TECHNIQUES

Required

Calculate the two earnings per share figures which will be reported in the statement of profit or loss and other comprehensive income for the year ended 31 October 20X4. **(4 marks)**

(Total 25 marks)

Provisions, contingencies and events after the reporting period

Topic list	Syllabus reference
1 IAS 10 *Events After the Reporting Period*	13.4
2 IAS 37 *Provisions, Contingent Liabilities and Contingent Assets*	13.4

Introduction

You should be very familiar with IAS 10 from your earlier studies.

Provisions and IAS 37 are a topical area. An ED was issued proposing revisions, however this project is currently on hold.

1 IAS 10 *Events After the Reporting Period*

> **FAST FORWARD**
>
> IAS 10 should be familiar from your earlier studies, but it still could come up in part of a question.

You have already studied IAS 10 *Events After the Reporting Period* extensively.

Knowledge brought forward from earlier studies

IAS 10 *Events After the Reporting Period*

Definition

Events occurring after the reporting period are those events, both favourable and unfavourable, that occur between the end of the reporting period and the date on which the financial statements are authorised for issue. Two types of events can be identified:

- Those that provide further evidence of conditions that existed at the end of the reporting period, and
- Those that are indicative of conditions that arose after the reporting period.

Accounting treatment

- **Adjust** assets and liabilities where events after the year end provide further evidence of conditions existing at the year end.
- **Do not adjust**, but instead disclose, important events after the year end that do not affect condition of assets/liabilities at the year end.
- **Dividends** for period proposed/declared after the year end but before financial statements are approved should not be recognised as a liability at the year end (no obligation exists at that time) but should be disclosed as required by IAS 1 *Presentation of Financial Statements*.

Disclosure

- Nature of event
- Estimate of financial effect (or statement that estimate cannot be made)

Window dressing is the arranging of transactions, the substance of which is primarily to alter the appearance of the statement of financial performance: it is **not** falsification of financial statements. IAS 10 does allow window dressing but **disclosure** should be made of such transactions.

2 IAS 37 *Provisions, Contingent Liabilities and Contingent Assets*

> **FAST FORWARD**
>
> Under IAS 37, a **provision** should be recognised:
>
> - When an entity has a **present obligation**, legal or constructive
> - It is probable that a **transfer of economic benefits** will be required to settle it
> - A reliable estimate can be made of its amount

As we have seen with regard to events after the reporting period, financial statements must include **all the information necessary for an understanding of the company's financial position**. Provisions, contingent liabilities and contingent assets are 'uncertainties' that must be accounted for consistently if are to achieve this understanding.

2.1 Objective

IAS 37 *Provisions, Contingent Liabilities and Contingent Assets* aims to ensure that appropriate **recognition criteria** and **measurement bases** are applied to provisions, contingent liabilities and

19: PROVISIONS, CONTINGENCIES AND EVENTS AFTER THE REPORTING PERIOD

contingent assets and that **sufficient information** is disclosed in the **notes** to the financial statements to enable users to understand their nature, timing and amount.

2.2 Provisions

You will be familiar with provisions for depreciation and doubtful debts from your earlier studies. The sorts of provisions addressed by IAS 37 are, however, rather different.

Before IAS 37, there was no accounting standard dealing with provisions. Companies wanting to show their results in the most favourable light used to make large 'one off' provisions in years where a high level of underlying profits was generated. These provisions, often known as 'big bath' provisions, were then available to shield expenditure in future years when perhaps the underlying profits were not as good.

In other words, provisions were used for profit smoothing. Profit smoothing is misleading.

> **Important**
>
> The key aim of IAS 37 is to ensure that provisions are made only where there are valid grounds for them.

IAS 37 views a provision as a liability.

> **Key terms**
>
> A **provision** is a **liability** of uncertain timing or amount.
>
> A **liability** is an obligation of an entity to transfer economic benefits as a result of past transactions or events. (IAS 37)

The IAS distinguishes provisions from other liabilities such as trade payables and accruals. This is on the basis that for a provision there is **uncertainty** about the timing or amount of the future expenditure. While uncertainty is clearly present in the case of certain accruals, the uncertainty is generally much less than for provisions.

2.3 Recognition

IAS 37 states that a provision should be **recognised** as a liability in the financial statements when:

- An entity has a **present obligation** (legal or constructive) as a result of a past event
- It is probable that a **transfer of economic benefits** will be required to settle the obligation
- A **reliable estimate** can be made of the obligation

2.4 Meaning of obligation

It is fairly clear what a legal obligation is. However, you may not know what a **constructive obligation** is.

> **Key term**
>
> IAS 37 defines a **constructive obligation** as:
>
> 'An obligation that derives from an entity's actions where:
>
> - By an established pattern of past practice, published policies or a sufficiently specific current statement the entity has indicated to other parties that it will accept certain responsibilities, and
> - As a result, the entity has created a valid expectation on the part of those other parties that it will discharge those responsibilities.'

Question: Recognise a provision

In which of the following circumstances might a provision be recognised?

(a) On 13 December 20X9 the board of an entity decided to close down a division. The accounting date of the company is 31 December. Before 31 December 20X9 the decision was not communicated to any of those affected and no other steps were taken to implement the decision.

(b) The board agreed a detailed closure plan on 20 December 20X9 and details were given to customers and employees.

(c) A company is obliged to incur clean up costs for environmental damage that has already been caused.

(d) A company intends to carry out future expenditure to operate in a particular way in the future.

Answer

(a) No provision would be recognised; the decision has not been communicated so there is no obligation.

(b) A provision would be made in the 20X9 financial statements; the decision has been communicated so there is a constructive obligation.

(c) A provision for such costs is appropriate.

(d) No present obligation exists and under IAS 37 no provision would be appropriate. This is because the entity could avoid the future expenditure by its future actions, maybe by changing its method of operation.

2.4.1 Probable transfer of economic benefits

For the purpose of the IAS, a transfer of economic benefits is regarded as **'probable'** if the event is **more likely than not** to occur. This appears to indicate a probability of more than 50%. However, the standard makes it clear that where there is a number of similar obligations the probability should be based on considering the population as a whole, rather than one single item.

2.5 Example: Transfer of economic benefits

If a company has entered into a warranty obligation, then the probability of transfer of economic benefits may well be extremely small in respect of one specific item. However, when considering the population as a whole the probability of some transfer of economic benefits is quite likely to be much higher. If there is a **greater than 50% probability** of some transfer of economic benefits then a **provision** should be made for the **expected amount**.

2.5.1 Measurement of provisions

Important

> The amount recognised as a provision should be the best estimate of the expenditure required to settle the present obligation at the end of the reporting period.

The estimates will be determined by the **judgement** of the entity's management supplemented by the experience of similar transactions.

Allowance is made for **uncertainty**. Where the provision being measured involves a large population of items, the obligation is estimated by weighting all possible outcomes by their probabilities, ie **expected value**.

Question — Warranty

Parker Co sells goods with a warranty under which customers are covered for the cost of repairs of any manufacturing defect that becomes apparent within the first six months of purchase. The company's past experience and future expectations indicate the following pattern of likely repairs.

% of goods sold	Defects	Cost of repairs $m
75	None	–
20	Minor	1.0
5	Major	4.0

What is the expected cost of repairs?

The cost is found using 'expected values' (75% × $nil) + (20% × $1.0m) + (5% × $4.0m) = $400,000.

Where the effect of the **time value of money** is material, the amount of a provision should be the **present value** of the expenditure required to settle the obligation. An appropriate **discount** rate should be used.

The discount rate should be a **pre-tax rate** that reflects current market assessments of the time value of money and the risks specific to the liability. **The discount rate(s) should not reflect risks for which future cash flow estimates have been adjusted.**

2.5.2 Future events

Future events which are reasonably expected to occur (eg new legislation, changes in technology) may affect the amount required to settle the entity's obligation and should be taken into account, but only if there is objective evidence that the future events will occur.

2.5.3 Expected disposal of assets

Gains from the expected disposal of assets should not be taken into account in measuring a provision.

2.5.4 Reimbursements

Some or all of the expenditure needed to settle a provision may be expected to be recovered from a third party. If so, the **reimbursement should be recognised only when it is virtually certain that reimbursement will be received if the entity settles the obligation.**

- The reimbursement should be treated as a separate asset, and the amount recognised should not be greater than the provision itself.
- The provision and the amount recognised for reimbursement may be netted off in profit or loss.

2.5.5 Changes in provisions

Provisions should be reviewed at each year-end and adjusted to reflect the current best estimate. If it is no longer probable that a transfer of economic benefits will be required to settle the obligation, the provision should be reversed.

2.5.6 Use of provisions

A provision should be used only for expenditures for which the provision was originally recognised. Setting expenditures against a provision that was originally recognised for another purpose would conceal the impact of two different events.

2.5.7 Future operating losses

Provisions should not be recognised for future operating losses. They do not meet the definition of a liability and the general recognition criteria set out in the standard.

2.5.8 Onerous contacts

If an entity has a contract that is onerous, the present obligation under the contract **should be recognised and measured** as a provision. An example might be vacant leasehold property.

> **Key term**
>
> An **onerous contract** is a contract in which the unavoidable costs of meeting the obligations under the contract exceed the economic benefits expected to be received under it.

2.6 Examples of possible provisions

It is easier to see what IAS 37 is driving at if you look at examples of those items which are possible provisions under this standard. Some of these we have already touched on.

(a) **Warranties**. These are argued to be genuine provisions as on past experience it is probable, ie more likely than not, that some claims will emerge. The provision must be estimated, however, on the basis of the class as a whole and not on individual claims. There is a clear legal obligation in this case.

(b) **Major repairs**. In the past it was quite popular for companies to provide for expenditure on a major overhaul to be accrued gradually over the intervening years between overhauls. Under IAS 37 this is no longer possible as IAS 37 argues that this is a mere intention to carry out repairs, not an obligation. The entity can always sell the asset in the meantime. The only solution is to treat major assets such as aircraft, ships, furnaces etc as a series of smaller assets where each part is depreciated over shorter lives. Thus any major overhaul is a replacement and therefore capital rather than revenue expenditure.

(c) **Self insurance**. Historically, companies sometimes created a provision for self insurance based on the expected cost of making good fire damage etc instead of paying premiums to an insurance company. Under IAS 37 such a provision is not justifiable as the entity has no obligation until a fire or accident occurs. No obligation exists until that time.

(d) **Environmental contamination**. If the company has an environment policy such that other parties would expect the company to clean up any contamination or if the company has broken current environmental legislation then a provision for environmental damage must be made.

(e) **Decommissioning or abandonment costs**. When an oil company initially purchases an oilfield, it may be put under a legal obligation to decommission the site at the end of its life. Prior to IAS 37 most oil companies built up the provision gradually over the life of the field so that no one year would be unduly burdened with the cost.

Under IAS 37, however, a legal obligation exists as a result of the initial expenditure to prepare the field for oil extraction and therefore a liability exists immediately. This would appear to result in a large charge to profit and loss in the first year of operation of the field. However, IAS 16 *Property, Plant and Equipment* takes the view that the cost of purchasing the field in the first place is not only the cost of the field itself but also the costs of putting it right again. Thus all the costs of abandonment may be capitalised.

(f) **Restructuring**. This is considered in detail below.

2.6.1 Provisions for restructuring

One of the main purposes of IAS 37 was to target abuses of provisions for restructuring. Accordingly, IAS 37 lays down **strict criteria** to determine when such a provision can be made.

Key term

> IAS 37 defines a **restructuring** as:
>
> A programme that is planned and is controlled by management and materially changes either:
>
> - The scope of a business undertaken by an entity; or
> - The manner in which that business is conducted.

The IAS gives the following **examples** of events that may fall under the definition of restructuring.

- The **sale or termination** of a line of business
- The **closure of business locations** in a country or region or the **relocation** of business activities from one country region to another
- **Changes in management structure**, for example, the elimination of a layer of management
- **Fundamental reorganisations** that have a material effect on the **nature and focus** of the entity's operations

The question is whether or not an entity has an obligation – legal or constructive – at the year-end.

- An entity must have a **detailed formal plan** for the restructuring.
- It must have **raised a valid expectation** in those affected that it will carry out the restructuring by starting to implement that plan or announcing its main features to those affected by it.

Important

> **A mere management decision is not normally sufficient.** Management decisions may sometimes trigger off recognition, but only if earlier events such as negotiations with employee representatives and other interested parties have been concluded subject only to management approval.

Where the restructuring involves the **sale of an operation** then IAS 37 states that no obligation arises until the entity has entered into a **binding sale agreement**. This is because until this has occurred the entity will be able to change its mind and withdraw from the sale even if its intentions have been announced publicly.

2.6.2 Costs to be included within a restructuring provision

The IAS states that a restructuring provision should include only the **direct expenditures** arising from the restructuring.

- **Necessarily entailed** by the restructuring
- Not associated with the **ongoing activities** of the entity

The following costs should specifically **not** be included within a restructuring provision.

- **Retraining** or relocating continuing staff
- **Marketing**
- **Investment in new systems** and distribution networks

2.6.3 Disclosure

Disclosures for provisions fall into two parts.

- Disclosure of details of the **change in carrying value** of a provision from the beginning to the end of the year
- Disclosure of the **background** to the making of the provision and the uncertainties affecting its outcome

2.7 Contingent liabilities

FAST FORWARD
An entity should not recognise a contingent asset or liability, but they should be disclosed.

Now that you understand provisions, it will be easier to understand contingent assets and liabilities.

Key term

IAS 37 defines a **contingent liability** as:

- A possible obligation that arises from past events and whose existence will be confirmed only by the occurrence or non-occurrence of one or more uncertain future events not wholly within the entity's control; or
- A present obligation that arises from past events but is not recognised because:
  - It is not probable that a transfer of economic benefits will be required to settle the obligation; or
  - The amount of the obligation cannot be measured with sufficient reliability.

As a rule of thumb, probable means more than 50% likely. **If an obligation is probable, it is not a contingent liability** – instead, a **provision is needed**.

2.7.1 Treatment of contingent liabilities

Contingent liabilities **should not be recognised in financial statements** but they **should be disclosed**, unless the possibility of an outflow of resources is remote. The required disclosures are:

- A brief description of the nature of the contingent liability
- An estimate of its financial effect
- An indication of the uncertainties that exist in relation to the amount or timing of any outflow
- The possibility of any reimbursement

2.8 Contingent assets

Key term

IAS 37 defines a **contingent asset** as:

A possible asset that arises from past events and whose existence will be confirmed by the occurrence of one or more uncertain future events not wholly within the entity's control.

A contingent asset must not be recognised. Only when the realisation of the related economic benefits is **virtually certain** should recognition take place. At that point, **the asset is no longer a contingent asset!**

2.8.1 Disclosure: Contingent assets

Contingent assets must only be disclosed in the notes if an inflow of economic benefits is **probable**. In that case a brief description of the contingent asset should be provided along with an estimate of its likely financial effect.

2.8.2 'Let out'

IAS 37 permits reporting entities to avoid disclosure requirements relating to provisions, contingent liabilities and contingent assets if they would be expected to **seriously prejudice** the position of the entity in dispute with other parties. However, this 'let out' should only be employed in **extremely rare** cases. Details of the general nature of the provision/contingencies must still be provided, together with an explanation of why it has not been disclosed.

You must practise the questions below to get the hang of IAS 37. But first, study the flow chart, taken from IAS 37, which is a good summary of its requirements.

19: PROVISIONS, CONTINGENCIES AND EVENTS AFTER THE REPORTING PERIOD

Exam focus point

If you learn this flowchart you should be able to deal with most tasks you are likely to meet in an exam.

 Question

Recognise or not 1?

Warren Co gives warranties at the time of sale to purchasers of its products. Under the terms of the warranty the manufacturer undertakes to make good, by repair or replacement, manufacturing defects that become apparent within a period of three years from the date of the sale. Should a provision be recognised?

Answer

Warren Co **cannot avoid** the cost of repairing or replacing all items of product that manifest manufacturing defects in respect of which warranties are given before the year end, and a provision for the cost of this should therefore be made.

Warren Co is obliged to repair or replace items that fail within the entire warranty period. Therefore, in respect of **this year's sales**, the obligation provided for at the year end should be the cost of making good items for which defects have been notified but not yet processed, **plus** an estimate of costs in respect of the other items sold for which there is sufficient evidence that manufacturing defects **will** manifest themselves during their remaining periods of warranty cover.

Question: Recognise or not 2?

After a wedding in 20X8 ten people died, possibly as a result of food poisoning from products sold by Callow Co. Legal proceedings are started seeking damages from Callow but it disputes liability. Up to the date of approval of the financial statements for the year to 31 December 20X8, Callow's lawyers advise that it is probable that it will not be found liable. However, when Callow prepares the financial statements for the year to 31 December 20X9 its lawyers advise that, owing to developments in the case, it is probable that it will be found liable.

What is the required accounting treatment:

(a) At 31 December 20X8?
(b) At 31 December 20X9?

Answer

(a) *At 31 December 20X8*

On the basis of the evidence available when the financial statements were approved, there is no obligation as a result of past events. No provision is recognised. The matter is disclosed as a contingent liability unless the probability of any transfer of resources is regarded as remote.

(b) *At 31 December 20X9*

On the basis of the evidence available, there is a present obligation. A transfer of economic benefits in settlement is probable.

A provision is recognised for the best estimate of the amount needed to settle the present obligation.

2.9 IFRIC 1 Changes in existing decommissioning, restoration and similar liabilities

2.9.1 The issue

IFRIC 1 contains guidance on accounting for changes in decommissioning, restoration and similar liabilities that have previously been recognised both as part of the cost of an item of property, plant and equipment under IAS 16 and as a provision (liability) under IAS 37. An example would be a liability that was recognised by the operator of a nuclear power plant for costs that it expects to incur in the future when the plant is shut down (decommissioned). IFRIC 1 addresses subsequent changes to the amount of the liability that may arise from:

(a) A revision in the timing or amount of the estimated decommissioning or restoration costs; or
(b) A change in the current market-based discount rate

2.9.2 Required treatment

IAS 37 requires the amount recognised as a provision to be the best estimate of the expenditure required to settle the obligation at the end of the reporting period. This is measured at its **present value**, which **IFRIC 1 confirms should be measured using a current market-based discount rate**. IFRIC 1 deals with three kinds of change in an existing liability for such costs.

The two main kinds of change dealt with in IFRIC 1 are those that arise from:

(a) The revision of estimated outflows of resources embodying economic benefits. For example, the estimated costs of decommissioning a nuclear power plant may vary significantly both in timing and amount
(b) Revisions to the current market-based discount rate

Most entities account for their property, plant and equipment using the cost model. Where this is so, these changes are required to be capitalised as part of the cost of the item and depreciated prospectively over the remaining life of the item to which they relate. This is consistent with the treatment under IAS 16 of other changes in estimate relating to property, plant and equipment.

Where entities account for their property, plant and equipment using the fair value model, a change in the liability does not affect the valuation of the item for accounting purposes. Instead, it alters the revaluation surplus or deficit on the item, which is the difference between its valuation and what would be its carrying amount under the cost model. The effect of the change is treated consistently with other revaluation surpluses or deficits, being recognised in other comprehensive income. Any cumulative deficit in revaluation surplus is taken to profit or loss.

The third kind of change dealt with by IFRIC 1 is an increase in the liability that reflects the passage of time – also referred to as the **unwinding of the discount**. This is **recognised in profit or loss** as a finance cost as it occurs.

2.10 Section summary

- The objective of IAS 37 is to ensure that appropriate recognition criteria and measurement bases are applied to provisions and contingencies and that sufficient information is disclosed.
- The IAS seeks to ensure that provisions are **only recognised** when a **measurable obligation** exists. It includes detailed rules that can be used to ascertain when an obligation exists and how to measure the obligation.
- The standard attempts to **eliminate** the **'profit smoothing'** which has gone on before it was issued.

PART C ACCOUNTING AND REPORTING TECHNIQUES

Chapter roundup

- **IAS 10** should be familiar from your earlier studies, but it still could come up in part of a question.
- Under IAS 37, a **provision** should be recognised:
  - When an entity has a **present obligation**, legal or constructive
  - It is probable that a **transfer of economic benefits** will be required to settle it
  - A reliable estimate can be made of its amount
- An entity **should not recognise a contingent asset or liability**, but they **should be disclosed**.

Quick quiz

1. According to IAS 37 when, and only when, can a provision be recognised?
2. A provision can be made for future operating losses. True or false?
3. When should a contingent liability be recognised under IAS 37?

Answers to quick quiz

1 Three conditions are all met.
   - Present obligation
   - Probable transfer of economic benefits
   - Reliable estimate of value

2 False

3 Never. However, it should be disclosed in a note to the financial statements.

End of chapter question

Tine Foods (AIA May 2007)

(a) Explain how IAS 37 defines a provision and identify what distinguishes a provision from other liabilities. **(2 marks)**

(b) Summarise the rules in IAS 37 for recognising a provision. **(3 marks)**

(c) Tine Foods, a limited liability company, has been sued over its use of its 'Geordie' brand name. The case has been held and the claim was dismissed in January 20X7. However, the appellant has appealed – but the appeal has yet to be heard. In February 20X7 Tine Foods sold the brand name to a large multinational company. Tine Foods has granted a warranty to the multinational company with regard to the validity of the trademark and a contractual liability would be triggered in the event that the 'Geordie' brand name was to be cancelled.

Advise the directors of Tine Foods how they should report this item in the financial statements for its financial year ended 31 March 20X7? **(3 marks)**

(d) During the year ended 31 March 20X6 Tanfield Trucks purchased an interest in an associated company. In its financial statements for the year ended 31 March 20X6 Tanfield Trucks disclosed that following the acquisition of the associated company it would reorganise its distribution functions. It set up a provision for $500,000 on its statement of financial position, charging the amount as exceptional selling and distribution expenses for the year ended 31 March 20X6. The reorganisation was completed during the year ended 31 March 20X7. The costs paid for the reorganisation amounted to $460,000 with a further $34,000 incurred but not yet paid as at 31 March 20X7.

Advise the directors of Tanfield Trucks how they should report this item in the financial statements for the year ended 31 March 20X7? **(3 marks)**

(Total 11 marks)

PART C ACCOUNTING AND REPORTING TECHNIQUES

Related parties and share-based payment

Topic list	Syllabus reference
1 IAS 24 *Related Party Disclosures*	13.4
2 IFRS 2 *Share-Based Payment*	13.4

Introduction

Section 1 deals with related party disclosures, and Section 2 deals with IFRS 2 on share-based payment, a controversial area.

PART C ACCOUNTING AND REPORTING TECHNIQUES

1 IAS 24 *Related Party Disclosures*

FAST FORWARD

> IAS 24 is a primarily disclosure standard. It is concerned to improve the quality of information provided by financial statements and also to strengthen their stewardship roles. It was revised in November 2009.

In the absence of information to the contrary, it is assumed that a reporting entity has **independent discretionary power** over its resources and transactions and pursues its activities independently of the interests of its individual owners, managers and others. Transactions are presumed to have been undertaken on an **arm's length basis**, ie on terms such as could have obtained in a transaction with an external party, in which each side bargained knowledgeably and freely, unaffected by any relationship between them.

These assumptions may not be justified when **related party relationships** exist, because the requisite conditions for competitive, free market dealings may not be present. Whilst the parties may endeavour to achieve arm's length bargaining, the very nature of the relationship may preclude this occurring.

1.1 Objective of IAS 24

IAS 24 tackles the related parties issue by ensuring that financial statements contain the disclosures necessary to draw attention to the possibility that the reported financial position and results may have been affected by the existence of related parties and by material transactions with them. In other words, this is a standard which is concerned with **disclosure**.

1.2 Scope

The standard requires disclosure of related party transactions and outstanding balances in the **separate financial statements** of a parent, venturer or investor presented in accordance with IAS 27 *Separate Financial Statements* as well as in consolidated financial statements.

An entity's financial statements disclose related party transactions and outstanding balances with other entities in a group. **Intragroup** transactions and balances are **eliminated** in the preparation of consolidated financial statements.

1.3 Definitions

The following important definitions are given by the standard. Note that the definitions of **control** and **significant influence** are now the same as those given in IFRS 10 *Consolidated Financial Statements*, IFRS 11 *Joint Arrangements* and IAS 28 *Investments in Associates and Joint Ventures*.

Key terms

> **Related party.** A related party is a person or entity that is related to the entity that is preparing its financial statements ('the reporting entity')
>
> (a) **A person or a close member of that person's family is related to a reporting entity if that person:**
>
>   (i)   Has control or joint control over the reporting entity;
>
>   (ii) Has significant influence over the reporting entity; or
>
>   (iii) Is a member of the key management personnel of the reporting entity or of a parent of the reporting entity.
>
> (b) **An entity is related to a reporting entity if any of the following conditions applies:**
>
>   (i)   The entity and the reporting entity are members of the same group (which means that each parent, subsidiary and fellow subsidiary is related to the others).
>
>   (ii) One entity is an associate or joint venture of the other entity (or an associate or joint venture of a member of a group of which the other entity is a member).

> **Key terms cont'd**
>
> (iii) Both entities are joint ventures of the same third party.
>
> (iv) One entity is a joint venture of a third entity and the other entity is an associate of the third entity.
>
> (v) The entity is a post-employment benefit plan for the benefit of employees of either the reporting entity or an entity related to the reporting entity. If the reporting entity is itself such a plan, the sponsoring employers are also related to the reporting entity.
>
> (vi) The entity is controlled or jointly controlled by a person identified in (a).
>
> (vii) A person identified in (a) (i) has significant influence over the entity or is a member of the key management personnel of the entity (or of a parent of the entity).
>
> **Related party transaction.** A transfer of resources, services or obligations between a reporting entity and a related party, regardless of whether a price is charged.
>
> The terms **control, joint control and significant influence** are defined in IFRS 10, IFRS 11 and IAS 28 and are used in this standard with the meanings specified in those IFRSs.
>
> **Key management personnel** are those persons having authority and responsibility for planning, directing and controlling the activities of the entity, directly or indirectly, including any director (whether executive or otherwise) of that entity.
>
> **Close members of the family of an individual** are those family members who may be expected to influence, or be influenced by, that person in their dealings with the entity, and include:
>
> (a) That person's children and spouse or domestic partner;
> (b) Children of that person's spouse or domestic partner; and
> (c) Dependants of that person or that person's spouse or domestic partner.
>
> (IAS 24)

The most important point to remember here is that, when considering each possible related party relationship, attention must be paid to the **substance of the relationship, not merely the legal form**.

IAS 24 lists the following which are **not related parties**.

(a) **Two entities simply because they have a director or other member of key management personnel in common** or because a member of key management personnel of one entity has significant influence over the other entity.

(b) **Two venturers, simply because they share joint control over a joint venture.**

(c) (i) Providers of finance
    (ii) Trade unions
    (iii) Public utilities
    (iv) Government departments and agencies of a government that does not control, jointly control or significantly influence the reporting entity simply by virtue of their normal dealings with an entity.

(d) **A customer, supplier, franchisor, distributor, or general agent** with whom an entity transacts a significant volume of business, simply by virtue of the resulting economic dependence.

1.4 Disclosure

As noted above, IAS 24 is entirely concerned with disclosure and its provisions are meant to **supplement** those disclosure requirements required by national company legislation and other IAS (particularly *Presentation of Financial Statements* 1, 27 and 28 and IFRS 3 *Business Combinations*).

The standard lists some **examples** of transactions that are disclosed if they are with a related party:

- Purchases or sales of goods (finished or unfinished)
- Purchases or sales of property and other assets
- Rendering or receiving of services
- Leases
- Transfer of research and development
- Transfers under licence agreements
- Transfers under finance arrangements (including loans and equity contributions in cash or in kind)
- Provision of guarantees and collateral security
- Commitments to do something if a particular event occurs or does not occur in the future including executory contracts
- Settlement of liabilities on behalf of the entity or by the entity on behalf of that related party

Relationships between **parents and subsidiaries** must be **disclosed irrespective** of whether any **transactions** have **taken place between** the related parties. An entity must disclose the **name** of its **parent** and, if different, the **ultimate controlling party**. This will enable a reader of the financial statements to be able to form a view about the effects of a related party relationship on the reporting entity.

If neither the parent nor the ultimate controlling party produces financial statements available for public use, the name of the next most senior parent that does so shall also be disclosed.

An entity should disclose **key management personnel compensation** in **total** and for **each** of the following **categories**:

(a) **Short-term employee benefits** (eg wages, salaries, social security contributions, paid annual leave and paid sick-leave, profit sharing and bonuses and non-monetary benefits such as medical care, housing, cars and free or subsidised goods or services);

(b) **Post-employment benefits** (eg pensions, other retirement benefits, life insurance and medical care);

(c) **Other long-term benefits** (eg long-service leave, sabbatical leave, long-term disability benefits and, if they are not payable within 12 months after the end of the period, profit sharing, bonuses and deferred compensation);

(d) **Termination benefits; and**

(e) **Share based payments.**

Compensation includes amounts paid on behalf of a parent of the entity in respect of the entity.

Where **transactions have taken place** between related parties, the entity should disclose the **nature** of the related party relationships, as well as information about the **transactions and outstanding balances including commitments** necessary for an understanding of the potential effect of the relationship on the financial statements. As a minimum, disclosures must include:

(a) The **amount of the transactions**

(b) The **amount of outstanding balances including commitments**, and

    (i) Their terms and conditions, including whether they are secured, and the nature of the consideration to be provided in settlement

    (ii) Details of any guarantees given or received

(c) Provisions for **doubtful debts** related to the amount of outstanding balances

(d) The **expense** recognised during the period in respect of **bad or doubtful debts** due from related parties.

The above disclosures shall be made separately for **each** of the following categories:

(a) The parent
(b) Entities with joint control or significant influence over the entity
(c) Subsidiaries
(d) Associates
(e) Joint ventures in which the entity is a joint venturer
(f) Key management personnel of the entity or its parent
(g) Other related parties

Items of a similar nature may be **disclosed in aggregate unless** separate disclosure is necessary for an understanding of the effect on the financial statements.

Disclosures that related party transactions were made on terms equivalent to those that prevail in arm's length transactions should only be made if such disclosures can be substantiated.

1.4.1 Government-related entities

An entity is exempt from making disclosures in relation to the nature of relationships, transactions and outstanding balances with the following:

(a) A government that has control, joint control or significant influence over the reporting entity; and

(b) Another entity that is a related party because the same government has control, joint control or significant influence over both the reporting entity and the other entity.

Where an entity takes advantage of this exemption, it must disclose:

(a) The name of the government and the nature of its relationship with the reporting entity (control, joint control or significant influence)

(b) The following information in sufficient detail to enable an understanding of the effect of related party transactions on the entity's financial statements:

　(i) The nature and amount of each individually significant transaction; and

　(ii) For other transactions that are collectively but not individually significant, a qualitative or quantitative indication of their extent.

In order to determine whether a transaction is individually significant, the entity should consider whether it is:

(a) Significant in terms of size
(b) Carried out on non-market terms
(c) Outside normal day to day business operations such as the purchase and sale of businesses
(d) Disclosed to regulatory or supervisory authorities
(e) Reported to senior management
(f) Subject to shareholder approval

1.5 Section summary

IAS 24 is concerned with **disclosure**. You should learn the following.

- **Definitions**: these are very important
- Relationships covered
- Relationships that **are not** related parties
- The exemption for government-related entities
- **Disclosures**: again, very important, representing the whole purpose of the standard

PART C ACCOUNTING AND REPORTING TECHNIQUES

Question   Related parties

Fancy Feet Co is a UK company which supplies handmade leather shoes to a chain of high street shoe shops. The company is also the sole importer of some famous high quality Greek stoneware which is supplied to an upmarket shop in London's West End.

Fancy Feet Co was set up 30 years ago by Georgios Kostades who left Greece when he fell out with the military government. The company is owned and run by Mr Kostades and his three children.

The shoes are purchased from a French company, the shares of which are owned by the Kostades Family Trust (Monaco).

Required

Identify the financial accounting issues arising out of the above scenario.

Answer

Issues

(a) The basis on which Fancy Feet trades with the Greek supplier and the French company owned by the Kostades family trust.

(b) Whether the overseas companies trade on commercial terms with the UK company or do the foreign entities control the UK company.

(c) Who owns the Greek company: is this a related party under the provisions of IAS 24?

(d) Should the nature of trade suggest a related party controls Fancy Feet Co? Detailed disclosures will be required in the financial statements.

2 IFRS 2 *Share-based Payment*

> **FAST FORWARD**
>
> **Share-based payment** transactions should be recognised in the financial statements. You need to understand and be able to advise on:
>
> - Recognition
> - Measurement
> - Disclosure
>
> of both equity-settled and cash-settled transactions.

2.1 Background

Transactions whereby entities purchase goods or services from other parties, such as suppliers and employees, by **issuing shares or share options** to those other parties are **increasingly common.** Share schemes are a common feature of director and executive remuneration and in some countries the authorities may offer tax incentives to encourage more companies to offer shares to employees. Companies whose shares or share options are regarded as a valuable 'currency' commonly use share-based payment to obtain employee and professional services.

The increasing use of share-based payment has raised questions about the accounting treatment of such transactions in company financial statements.

Share options are often granted to employees at an exercise price that is equal to or higher than the market price of the shares at the date the option is granted. Consequently the options have no intrinsic value and so **no transaction is recorded in the financial statements.**

This leads to an **anomaly**: if a company pays its employees in cash, an expense is recognised in profit or loss, but if the payment is in share options, no expense is recognised.

2.1.1 Arguments against recognition of share-based payment in the financial statements

There are a number of arguments against recognition. The IASB has considered and rejected the arguments below.

(a) **No cost therefore no charge**

There is no cost to the entity because the granting of shares or options does not require the entity to sacrifice cash or other assets. Therefore a charge should not be recognised.

This argument is unsound because it ignores the fact that a transaction has occurred. The employees have provided valuable services to the entity in return for valuable shares or options.

(b) **Earnings per share is hit twice**

It is argued that the charge to profit or loss for the employee services consumed reduces the entity's earnings, while at the same time there is an increase in the number of shares issued.

However, the dual impact on earnings per share simply reflects the two economic events that have occurred.

(i) The entity has issued shares or options, thus increasing the denominator of the earnings per share calculation.

(ii) It has also consumed the resources it received for those shares or options, thus reducing the numerator.

(c) **Adverse economic consequences**

It could be argued that entities might be discouraged from introducing or continuing employee share plans if they were required to recognise them on the financial statements. However, if this happened, it might be because the requirement for entities to account properly for employee share plans had revealed the economic consequences of such plans.

A situation where entities are able to obtain and consume resources by issuing valuable shares or options without having to account for such transactions could be perceived as a **distortion**.

2.2 Objective and scope

IFRS 2 requires an entity to **reflect the effects of share-based payment transactions** in its profit or loss and financial position.

IFRS 2 applies to all share-based payment transactions. There are three types.

(a) **Equity-settled share-based payment transactions**, in which the entity receives goods or services in exchange for equity instruments of the entity (including shares or share options)

(b) **Cash-settled share-based payment transactions**, in which the entity receives goods or services in exchange for amounts of cash that are based on the price (or value) of the entity's shares or other equity instruments of the entity

(c) Transactions in which the entity receives or acquires goods or services and either the entity or the supplier has a **choice** as to whether the entity settles the transaction in cash (or other assets) or by issuing equity instruments

Certain transactions are **outside the scope** of the IFRS:

PART C ACCOUNTING AND REPORTING TECHNIQUES

(a) Transactions with employees and others in their capacity as a holder of equity instruments of the entity (for example, where an employee receives additional shares in a rights issue to all shareholders)

(b) The issue of equity instruments in exchange for control of another entity in a business combination

Key terms

> **Share-based payment transaction.** A transaction in which the entity receives goods or services as consideration for equity instruments of the entity (including shares or share options), or acquires goods or services by incurring liabilities to the supplier of those goods or services for amounts that are based on the price of the entity's shares or other equity instruments of the entity.
>
> **Share-based payment arrangement.** An agreement between the entity and another party (including an employee) to enter into a share-based payment transaction, which thereby entitles the other party to receive cash or other assets of the entity for amounts that are based on the price of the entity's shares or other equity instruments of the entity, or to receive equity instruments of the entity, provided the specified vesting conditions, if any, are met.
>
> **Equity instrument.** A contract that evidences a residual interest in the assets of an entity after deducting all of its liabilities.
>
> **Equity instrument granted.** The right (conditional or unconditional) to an equity instrument of the entity conferred by the entity on another party, under a share-based payment arrangement.
>
> **Share option.** A contract that gives the holder the right, but not the obligation, to subscribe to the entity's shares at a fixed or determinable price for a specified period of time.
>
> **Fair value.** The amount for which an asset could be exchanged, a liability settled, or an equity instrument granted could be exchanged, between knowledgeable, willing parties in an arm's length transaction.
>
> **Grant date.** The date at which the entity and another party (including an employee) agree to a share-based payment arrangement, being when the entity and the other party have a shared understanding of the terms and conditions of the arrangement. At grant date the entity confers on the other party (the counterparty) the right to cash, other assets, or equity instruments of the entity, provided the specified vesting conditions, if any, are met. If that agreement is subject to an approval process (for example, by shareholders), grant date is the date when that approval is obtained.
>
> **Intrinsic value.** The difference between the fair value of the shares to which the counterparty has the (conditional or unconditional) right to subscribe or which it has the right to receive, and the price (if any) the other party is (or will be) required to pay for those shares. For example, a share option with an exercise price of $15 on a share with a fair value of $20, has an intrinsic value of $5.
>
> **Measurement date.** The date at which the fair value of the equity instruments granted is measured. For transactions with employees and others providing similar services, the measurement date is grant date. For transactions with parties other than employees (and those providing similar services), the measurement date is the date the entity obtains the goods or the counterparty renders service.
>
> **Vest.** To become an entitlement. Under a share-based payment arrangement, a counterparty's right to receive cash, other assets, or equity instruments of the entity vests when the counterparty's entitlement is no longer conditional on the satisfaction of any vesting conditions.
>
> **Vesting conditions.** The conditions that determine whether the entity receives the services that entitle the counterparty to receive cash, other assets or equity instruments of the entity, under a share-based payment arrangement. Vesting conditions are either service conditions or performance conditions. Service conditions require the counterparty to complete a specified period of service, and specified performance targets to be met (such as a specified increase in the entity's profit over a specified period of time).
>
> **Vesting period.** The period during which all the specified vesting conditions of a share-based payment arrangement are to be satisfied.

Note that the definition of fair value within IFRS 2 is not in line with that provided in IFRS 13 *Fair Value Measurement*. Share-based payments is one of the few areas of accounting where fair value is relevant to which IFRS 13 does **not** apply.

2.3 Recognition: The basic principle

An entity should **recognise goods or services received or acquired in a share-based payment transaction when it obtains the goods or as the services are received.** Goods or services received or acquired in a share-based payment transaction **should be recognised as expenses unless they qualify for recognition as assets.** For example, services are normally recognised as expenses (because they are normally rendered immediately), while goods are recognised as assets.

If the goods or services were received or acquired in an **equity-settled** share-based payment transaction, the entity should recognise **a corresponding increase in equity** (reserves).

If the goods or services were received or acquired in a **cash-settled** share-based payment transaction, the entity should recognise a **liability**.

2.4 Equity-settled share-based payment transactions

2.4.1 Measurement

The issue here is how to measure the 'cost' of the goods and services received and the equity instruments (eg the share options) granted in return.

The general principle in IFRS 2 is that when an entity recognises the goods or services received and the corresponding increase in equity, it should measure these at the **fair value of the goods or services received**. Where the transaction is with **parties other than employees**, there is a rebuttable presumption that the fair value of the goods or services received can be estimated reliably.

If the fair value of the goods or services received cannot be measured reliably, the entity should measure their value by reference to the **fair value of the equity instruments granted**.

Where the transaction is with a party other than an employee, fair value should be measured at the date the entity obtains the goods or the counterparty renders service.

Where shares, share options or other equity instruments are granted to **employees** as part of their remuneration package, it is not normally possible to measure directly the services received. For this reason, the entity should measure the fair value of the employee services received by reference to the **fair value of the equity instruments granted**. The fair value of those equity instruments should be measured at **grant date**.

2.4.2 Determining the fair value of equity instruments granted

Where a transaction is measured by reference to the fair value of the equity instruments granted, fair value is based on **market prices** if available, taking into account the terms and conditions upon which those equity instruments were granted.

If market prices are not available, the entity should estimate the fair value of the equity instruments granted using a **valuation technique**. (These are beyond the scope of this exam.)

2.4.3 Recognition of transactions in which services are received

The issue here is **when** to recognise the transaction. When entitlements to equity instruments are granted, they may vest immediately, but often the counterparty has to meet specified conditions first. For example, an employee may have to complete a specified period of service. This means that the effect of the transaction normally has to be allocated over more than one accounting period.

If the equity instruments granted **vest immediately** (ie the counterparty is not required to complete a specified period of service before becoming unconditionally entitled to the equity instruments) it is presumed that the services have already been received (in the absence of evidence to the contrary). The entity should **recognise the services received in full**, with a corresponding increase in equity, **on the grant date**.

If the equity instruments granted do not vest until the counterparty completes a specified period of service, the entity should account for those services **as they are rendered** by the counterparty during the vesting period. For example, if an employee is granted share options on condition that he or she completes three years' service, then the services to be rendered by the employee as consideration for the share options will be received in the future, over that three-year vesting period.

The entity should recognise an amount for the goods or services received during the vesting period based on the **best available estimate** of the **number of equity instruments expected to vest**. It should **revise** that estimate if subsequent information indicates that the number of equity instruments expected to vest differs from previous estimates. On **vesting date**, the entity should revise the estimate to **equal the number of equity instruments that actually vest**.

Once the goods and services received and the corresponding increase in equity have been recognised, the entity should make no subsequent adjustment to total equity after vesting date.

2.5 Example: Equity-settled share-based payment transaction

On 1 January 20X1 an entity grants 100 share options to each of its 400 employees. Each grant is conditional upon the employee working for the entity until 31 December 20X3. The fair value of each share option is $20.

During 20X1 20 employees leave and the entity estimates that 20% of the 400 employees will leave during the three-year period.

During 20X2 a further 25 employees leave and the entity now estimates that 25% of the 400 employees will leave during the three-year period.

During 20X3 a further 10 employees leave.

Required

Calculate the remuneration expense that will be recognised in respect of the share-based payment transaction for each of the three years ended 31 December 20X3.

Solution

IFRS 2 requires the entity to recognise the remuneration expense, based on the fair value of the share options granted, as the services are received during the three-year vesting period.

In 20X1 and 20X2 the entity estimates the number of options expected to vest (by estimating the number of employees likely to leave) and bases the amount that it recognises for the year on this estimate.

In 20X3 it recognises an amount based on the number of options that actually vest. A total of 55 employees left during the three-year period and therefore 34,500 options (400 – 55 × 100) vested.

The amount recognised as an expense for each of the three years is calculated as follows:

	Cumulative expense at year-end $	Expense for year $
20X1 (end of first year) 40,000 × (100% - 20% expected to leave) × $20 × 1/3	213,333	213,333
20X2 (end of second year) 40,000 × (100% - 25% expected to leave) × $20 × 2/3	400,000	186,667
20X3 34,500 × $20	690,000	290,000

Question — Share-based payment

On 1 January 20X3 an entity grants 250 share options to each of its 200 employees. The only condition attached to the grant is that the employees should continue to work for the entity until 31 December 20X6. Five employees leave during the year.

The market price of each option was $12 at 1 January 20X3 and $15 at 31 December 20X3.

Required

Show how this transaction will be reflected in the financial statements for the year ended 31 December 20X3.

Answer

The remuneration expense for the year is based on the fair value of the options granted at the grant date (1 January 20X3). As five of the 200 employees left during the year it is reasonable to assume that 20 employees will leave during the four-year vesting period and that therefore 45,000 options (250 × 180) will actually vest.

Therefore the entity recognises a remuneration expense of $135,000 (45,000 × 12 × ¼) in profit or loss and a corresponding increase in equity of the same amount.

2.6 Cash-settled share-based payment transactions

Examples of this type of transaction include:

(a) **Share appreciation rights** granted to employees: the employees become entitled to a future cash payment (rather than an equity instrument), based on the increase in the entity's share price from a specified level over a specified period of time; or

(b) An entity might grant to its employees a right to receive a future cash payment by granting to them a **right to shares that are redeemable**

The basic principle is that the entity measures the goods or services acquired and the liability incurred at the **fair value of the liability**.

The entity should **remeasure** the fair value of the liability **at each reporting date** until the liability is settled **and at the date of settlement**. Any **changes** in fair value are recognised in **profit or loss** for the period.

The entity should recognise the services received, and a liability to pay for those services, **as the employees render service**. For example, if share appreciation rights do not vest until the employees have completed a specified period of service, the entity should recognise the services received and the related liability, over that period.

2.7 Example: Cash-settled share-based payment transaction

On 1 January 20X1 an entity grants 100 cash share appreciation rights (SARS) to each of its 500 employees, on condition that the employees continue to work for the entity until 31 December 20X3.

During 20X1 35 employees leave. The entity estimates that a further 60 will leave during 20X2 and 20X3.

During 20X2 40 employees leave and the entity estimates that a further 25 will leave during 20X3.

During 20X3 22 employees leave.

At 31 December 20X3 150 employees exercise their SARs. Another 140 employees exercise their SARs at 31 December 20X4 and the remaining 113 employees exercise their SARs at the end of 20X5.

The fair values of the SARs for each year in which a liability exists are shown below, together with the intrinsic values at the dates of exercise.

	Fair value $	Intrinsic value $
20X1	14.40	
20X2	15.50	
20X3	18.20	15.00
20X4	21.40	20.00
20X5		25.00

Required

Calculate the amount to be recognised in the statement of profit or loss and other comprehensive income for each of the five years ended 31 December 20X5 and the liability to be recognised in the statement of financial position at 31 December for each of the five years.

Solution

For the three years to the vesting date of 31 December 20X3 the expense is based on the entity's estimate of the number of SARSs that will actually vest (as for an equity-settled transaction). However, the fair value of the liability is **remeasured** at each year-end.

The intrinsic value of the SARs at the date of exercise is the amount of cash actually paid.

	Liability at year-end $		Expense for year $
20X1 Expected to vest (500 – 35 – 60):			
405 × 100 × $14.40 × 1/3	194,400		194,400
20X2 Expected to vest (500 – 35 – 40 – 25):			
400 × 100 × $15.50 × 2/3	413,333		218,933
20X3 Exercised:			
150 × 100 × $15.00		225,000	
Not yet exercised (500 – 35 – 40 – 22 – 150):			
253 × 100 × $18.20	460,460	47,127	
			272,127
20X4 Exercised:			
140 × 100 × $20.00		280,000	
Not yet exercised (253 – 140):			
113 × 100 × $21.40	241,820	(218,640)	
			61,360
20X5 Exercised:			
113 × 100 × $25.00		282,500	
	Nil	(241,820)	
			40,680
			787,500

20: RELATED PARTIES AND SHARE-BASED PAYMENT

Transactions in which either the entity or the other party has a choice of settling in cash or by issuing equity instruments:

(a) If the entity has incurred a liability to settle in cash or other assets, it should account for the transaction as a cash-settled share-based payment transaction

(b) If no such liability has been incurred, the entity should account for the transaction as an equity-settled share-based payment transaction.

2.8 Deferred tax implications

2.8.1 Issue

An entity may receive a tax deduction that differs from related cumulative remuneration expense, and may arise in a later accounting period.

> **Exam focus point**
>
> For example, an entity recognises an expense for share options granted under IFRS 2, but does not receive a tax deduction until the options are exercised and receives the tax deduction at the share price on the exercise date.

2.8.2 Measurement

The deferred tax asset temporary difference is measured as:

Carrying amount of share-based payment expense	0
Less: tax base of share-based payment expense (estimated amount tax authorities will permit as a deduction in future periods, based on year end information)	(X)
Temporary difference	(X)
Deferred tax asset at X%	X

If the amount of the tax deduction (or estimated future tax deduction) exceeds the amount of the related cumulative remuneration expense, this indicates that the tax deduction relates also to an equity item.

The excess is therefore recognised directly in equity.

2.8.3 Example: Deferred tax implications of share-based payment

On 1 January 20X2, Bruce granted 5,000 share options to an employee vesting two years later on 31 December 20X3. The fair value of each option measured at the grant date was $3.

Tax law in the jurisdiction in which the entity operates allows a tax deduction of the intrinsic value of the options on exercise. The intrinsic value of the share options was $1.20 at 31 December 20X2 and $3.40 at 31 December 20X3 on which date the options were exercised.

Assume a tax rate of 30%.

Required:

Show the deferred tax accounting treatment of the above transaction at 31 December 20X2, 31 December 20X3 (before exercise), and on exercise.

Solution

	31/12/20X2	31/12/20X3 before exercise
Carrying amount of share-based payment expense	0	0
Less: Tax base of share-based payment expense $(5{,}000 \times \$1.2 \times \tfrac{1}{2})/(5{,}000 \times \$3.40)$	(3,000)	(17,000)
Temporary difference	(3,000)	(17,000)
Deferred tax asset @ 30%	900	5,100
Deferred tax (Cr P/L) (5,100 – 900 – (Working) 600)	900	3,600
Deferred tax (Cr Equity) (Working)	0	600

On exercise, the deferred tax asset is replaced by a current tax one. The double entry is:

Debit deferred tax (P/L)	4,500	⎫
Debit deferred tax (equity)	600	⎬ reversal
Credit deferred tax asset	5,100	⎭
Debit current tax asset	5,100	
Credit current tax (P/L)	4,500	
Credit current tax (equity)	600	

Working

Accounting expense recognised $(5{,}000 \times \$3 \times \tfrac{1}{2})/(5{,}000 \times \$3)$	7,500	15,000
Tax deduction	(3,000)	(17,000)
Excess temporary difference	0	(2,000)
Excess deferred tax asset to equity @ 30%	0	600

2.9 Disclosures

IFRS 2 requires entities to disclose information that enables users of the financial statements to understand the **nature and extent** of share-based payment **arrangements that existed during the period**.

(a) A **description** of each type of share-based payment arrangement that existed at any time during the period, including the general terms and conditions of each arrangement;

(b) The **number and weighted average exercise prices** of share options for each of the following groups of options:

   (i) Outstanding at the beginning of the period
   (ii) Granted during the period
   (iii) Forfeited during the period
   (iv) Exercised during the period
   (v) Expired during the period
   (vi) Outstanding at the end of the period
   (vii) Exercisable at the end of the period

(c) For share options **exercised** during the period, the **weighted average share price** at the date of exercise

(d) For share options outstanding at the end of the period, the range of exercise prices and weighted average remaining contractual life

In addition, IFRS 2 requires disclosure of information that enables users of the financial statements to **understand how the fair value** of the goods or services received, or the fair value of the equity instruments granted, during the period **was determined**.

Entities should also disclose information that enables users of the financial statements to understand the effect of share-based payment transactions on the entity's **profit or loss for the period** and on its **financial position**.

(a) The **total expense recognised for the period** arising from share-based payment transactions, including separate disclosure of that portion of the total expense that arises from transactions accounted for as equity-settled share-based payment transactions;

(b) For **liabilities** arising from share-based payment transactions:

   (i) The **total carrying amount** at the end of the period

   (ii) The **total intrinsic value** at the end of the period of liabilities for which the counterparty's right to cash or other assets had vested by the end of the period

2.10 Section summary

IFRS 2 requires entities to **recognise** the goods or services received as a result of **share-based payment transactions.**

- Equity settled transactions: DEBIT Asset/Expense, CREDIT Equity
- Cash settled transactions: DEBIT Asset/Expense, CREDIT Liability
- Transactions are **recognised when goods/services are obtained/received** (usually over the performance period)
- Transactions are measured at fair value

PART C ACCOUNTING AND REPORTING TECHNIQUES

Chapter roundup

- **IAS 24** is primarily a disclosure standard. It is concerned to improve the quality of information provided by financial statements and also to strengthen their stewardship roles. It was revised in November 2009.
- **Share-based payment** transactions should be recognised in the financial statements. You need to understand and be able to advise on:
    - Recognition
    - Measurement
    - Disclosure

  of both equity-settled and cash-settled transactions.

Quick quiz

1. What is a related party transaction?
2. A managing director of a company is a related party. True/False?
3. What is a cash-settled share based payment transaction?
4. What is grant date?
5. If an entity has entered into an equity settled share-based payment transaction, what should it recognise in its financial statements?
6. Where an entity has granted share options to its employees in return for services, how is the transaction measured?

Answers to quick quiz

1 A transfer of resources, services or obligations between related parties, regardless of whether a price is charged.

2 True. A member of the key management personnel of an entity is a related party of that entity.

3 A transaction in which the entity receives goods or services in exchange for amounts of cash that are based on the price (or value) of the entity's shares or other equity instruments of the entity.

4 The date at which the entity and another party (including an employee) agree to a share based payment arrangement, being when the entity and the other party have a shared understanding of the terms and conditions of the arrangement.

5 The goods or services received and a corresponding increase in equity.

6 By reference to the fair value of the equity instruments granted, measured at grant date.

End of chapter question

Molar and Canal (AIA May 2011)

(a) Molar, a public limited company, is planning to rationalise its operations over the next three years. As part of the plan, Molar is considering changing a number of employee contracts so that settlement of the amounts payable will be by issuing shares, share options or by basing settlement on the company's share price. As this is a new method, the company's finance officer is seeking guidance on the implications of the new scheme for the company's financial statements. He believes that because there is no cash outflow no amount should be recognised in profit or loss. The following details relate to one suggested method of settlement.

On 1 June 2011 Molar will grant 250 share options to each of its 2,500 employees. All grants are equal and conditional upon the employee working for Molar until 31 May 2014. At the 1 June 2011 the fair value of each option is expected to be $30.

Molar's business plan for the period up to 31 May 2014 shows that it expects 60 employees will leave during the first year of the plan and that 25% of the remainder will leave before 31 May 2014. Of those expected to leave after the first year, it is estimated that two-thirds will leave during the second year of the plan and one-third in the final year.

Required

Advise Molar's finance director of the appropriate accounting treatment of the share options for each of the three years to 31 May 2014 if the company is correct in its estimates concerning the number of employees leaving its employment. **(10 marks)**

PART C ACCOUNTING AND REPORTING TECHNIQUES

(b) Canal, a public limited company, introduced a cash share appreciation rights (SAR) scheme on 1 June 2007. The scheme granted 200 SARs to each of Canal's 1,000 employees on condition they remain working for the company for the next three years ending on 31 May 2010. The following information relates to the scheme.

During the year ended 31 May:	Number of employees: Leaving during the year	Estimated to leave in future	Fair value of share at year end $	Cash per share actually paid $
2008	70	120	15	
2009	80	55	16	
2010	45		17	16.50
2011				18.00

At 31 May 2010, 300 employees exercised their SARs. The remaining employees exercised their SARs at 31 May 2011.

Required

Advise Canal of the amounts to be recognised in the company's financial statements for each of the four years ended 31 May 2011 and explore the difference between Canal's SAR scheme and the scheme Molar plans to introduce.

(10 marks)

(Total 20 marks)

Revenue recognition

Topic list	Syllabus reference
1 Revenue recognition	13.4
2 Off balance sheet finance	13.4
3 Substance over form	13.4
4 Common forms of off balance sheet finance	13.4

Introduction

IFRS 15 *Revenue from Contracts with Customers* is a new and detailed standard providing guidance on revenue recognition. The concept of substance over form is an important principle in determining how transactions are recognised in the financial statements.

PART C ACCOUNTING AND REPORTING TECHNIQUES

1 Revenue recognition

> **FAST FORWARD**
>
> Revenue recognition is straightforward in most business transactions, but some situations are more complicated.

1.1 Introduction

Revenue is a key performance measure used by companies and analysts. The amount of revenue recognised directly affects profit and key ratios such as profit margin and sales growth.

Recognising and measuring revenue appropriately requires the exercise of professional judgement and is crucial to ensuring that financial statements give a faithful representation of the underlying economic substance.

1.2 IFRS 15 *Revenue from Contracts with Customers*

> **FAST FORWARD**
>
> IFRS 15 *Revenue from Contracts with Customers* is concerned with the **recognition of revenues** arising from fairly common transactions.
>
> – The sale of goods
> – The rendering of services
> – The use by others of entity assets yielding interest, royalties and dividends
>
> Generally revenue is recognised when the entity has transferred promised goods or services to the customer. The standard sets out five steps for the recognition process.

Income, as defined by the IASB *Conceptual Framework* (see above), includes both revenues and gains. Revenue is income arising in the ordinary course of an entity's activities and it may be called different names, such as sales, fees, interest, dividends or royalties.

IFRS 15 *Revenue from Contracts with Customers* was issued in May 2014. It is the result of a joint IASB and FASB project on revenue recognition. It seeks to strike a balance between the IASB rules in IAS 18, which were felt to be too general, leading to a lot of diversity in practice, and the FASB regulations, which were too numerous.

IFRS 15 replaces both IAS 18 *Revenue* and IAS 11 *Construction Contracts*. It is effective for reporting periods beginning on or after 1 January 2018. Its core principle is that revenue is recognised to depict the transfer of goods or services to a customer in an amount that reflects the consideration to which the entity expects to be entitled in exchange for those goods or services.

Under IFRS 15 the transfer of goods and services is based upon the transfer of **control**, rather than the transfer of risks and rewards as in IAS 18. **Control of an asset** is described in the standard as the ability to direct the use of, and obtain substantially all of the remaining benefits from, the asset.

For straightforward retail transactions IFRS 15 will have little, if any, effect on the amount and timing of revenue recognition. For contracts such as long-term service contracts and multi-element arrangements it could result in changes either to the amount or to the timing of revenue recognised.

1.3 Scope

IFRS 15 applies to all contracts with customers except:

- Insurance contracts within the scope of IAS 4
- Financial instruments and other contractual rights and obligations within the scope of IFRS 9, IFRS 10, IFRS 11, IAS 27 or IAS 28.
- Non-monetary exchanges between entities in the same line of business

1.4 Definitions

The following definitions are given in the standard.

Key terms

> **Income** – Increases in economic benefits during the accounting period in the form of inflows or enhancements of assets or decreases of liabilities that result in an increase in equity, other than those relating to contributions from equity participants.
>
> **Revenue** – Income arising in the course of an entity's ordinary activities.
>
> **Contract** – An agreement between two or more parties that creates enforceable rights and obligations.
>
> **Contract asset** – An entity's right to consideration in exchange for goods or services that the entity has transferred to a customer when that right is conditioned on something other than the passage of time (for example the entity's future performance).
>
> **Receivable** – An entity's right to consideration that is unconditional – ie only the passage of time is required before payment is due.
>
> **Contract liability** – An entity's obligation to transfer goods or services to a customer for which the entity has received consideration (or the amount is due) from the customer.
>
> **Customer** – A party that has contracted with an entity to obtain goods or services that are an output of the entity's ordinary activities in exchange for consideration.
>
> **Performance obligation** – A promise in a contract with a customer to transfer to the customer either:
>
> (a) A good or service (or a bundle of goods or services) that is distinct; or
>
> (b) A series of distinct goods or services that are substantially the same ad that have the same pattern of transfer to the customer.
>
> **Stand-alone selling price** – The price at which an entity would sell a promised good or service separately to a customer.
>
> **Transaction price** – The amount of consideration to which an entity expects to be entitled in exchange for transferring promised goods or services to a customer, excluding amounts collected on behalf of third parties. (IFRS 15)

Revenue **does not include** sales taxes, value added taxes or goods and service taxes which are only collected for third parties, because these do not represent an economic benefit flowing to the entity.

1.5 Recognition and measurement of revenue

Under IFRS 15 revenue is recognised and measured using a five step model.

Step 1 **Identify the contract with the customer.**

A contract with a customer is within the scope of IFRS 15 only when:

(a) The parties have approved the contract and are committed to carrying it out.
(b) Each party's rights regarding the goods and services to be transferred can be identified.
(c) The payment terms for the goods and services can be identified
(d) The contract has commercial substance
(e) It is probable that the entity will collect the consideration to which it will be entitled.

The contract can be written, verbal or implied.

Step 2 **Identify the separate performance obligations.** The key point is distinct goods or services. A contract includes promises to provide goods or services to a customer. Those promises are called performance obligations. A company would account for a performance obligation separately only if the promised good or service is distinct. A good or service is distinct if it is sold separately or if it could be sold separately because it has a distinct function and a distinct profit margin. Factors for consideration as to whether an entity's promise to transfer the good or service to the customer is separately identifiable include, but are not limited to:

(a) The entity does not provide a significant service of integrating the good or service with other goods or services promised in the contract.

(b) The good or service does not significantly modify or customize another good or service promised in the contract.

(c) The good or service is not highly dependent on or highly interrelated with other goods or services promised in the contract.

Step 3 **Determine the transaction price**. The transaction price is the amount of consideration a company expects to be entitled to from the customer in exchange for transferring goods or services. The transaction price would reflect the company's probability-weighted estimate of **variable consideration** (including reasonable estimates of contingent amounts) in addition to the effects of the customer's credit risk and the time value of money (if material). Variable contingent amounts are only included where it is highly probable that there will not be a reversal of revenue when any uncertainty associated with the variable consideration is resolved. Examples of where a variable consideration can arise include: discounts, rebates, refunds, price concessions, credits and penalties.

Step 4 **Allocate the transaction price to the performance obligations**. Where a contract contains more than one distinct performance obligation a company allocates the transaction price to all separate performance obligations in proportion to the stand-alone selling price of the good or service underlying each performance obligation. If the good or service is not sold separately, the company would estimate its stand-alone selling price.

So, if any entity sells a bundle of goods and/or services which it also supplies unbundled, the separate performance obligations in the contract should be priced in the same proportion as the unbundled prices. This would apply to mobile phone contracts where the handset is supplied 'free'. The entity must look at the stand-alone price of such a handset and some of the consideration for the contract should be allocated to the handset.

Step 5 **Recognise revenue when (or as) a performance obligation is satisfied**. The entity satisfies a performance obligation by transferring **control** of a promised good or service to the customer. A performance obligation can be satisfied **at a point in time**, such as when goods are delivered to the customer, or **over time**. An obligation satisfied **over time** will meet one of the following criteria:

(a) The customer simultaneously receives and consumes the benefits as the performance takes place.

(b) The entity's performance creates or enhances an asset that the customer controls as the asset is created or enhanced.

(c) The entity's performance does not create an asset with an alternative use to the entity and the entity has an enforceable right to payment for performance completed to date.

The amount of revenue recognised is the amount allocated to that performance obligation in Step 4.

An entity must be able to **reasonably measure** the outcome of a performance obligation before the related revenue can be recognised. In some circumstances, such as in the early stages of a contract, it may not be possible to reasonably measure the outcome of a performance obligation, but the entity expects to recover the costs incurred. In these circumstances, revenue is recognised only to the extent of costs incurred.

1.5.1 Example: identifying the separate performance obligation

Office Solutions, a limited company, has developed a communications software package called CommSoft. Office Solutions has entered into a contract with Logisticity to supply the following:

(a) Licence to use CommSoft

(b) Installation service. This may require an upgrade to the computer operating system, but the software package does not need to be customized

(c) Technical support for three years

(d) Three years of updates for CommSoft

Office Solutions is not the only company able to install CommSoft, and the technical support can also be provided by other companies. The software can function without the updates and technical support.

Required

Explain whether the goods or services provided to Logisticity are distinct in accordance with IFRS 15 *Revenue from Contracts with Customers*.

Solution

CommSoft was delivered before the other goods or services and remains functional without the updates and the technical support. It may be concluded that Logisticity can benefit from each of the goods and services either on their own or together with the other goods and services that are readily available.

The promises to transfer each good and service to the customer are separately identifiable In particular, the installation service does not significantly modify the software itself and, as such, the software and the installation service are separate outputs promised by Office Solutions rather than inputs used to produce a combined output.

In conclusion, the goods and services are distinct and amount to four performance obligations in the contract under IFRS 15.

1.5.2 Example: determining the transaction price

Taplop supplies laptop computers to large businesses. On 1 July 20X5, Taplop entered into a contract with TrillCo, under which TrillCo was to purchase laptops at $500 per unit. The contract states that if TrillCo purchases more than 500 laptops in a year, the price per units is reduced retrospectively to $450 per unit. Taplop's year end is 30 June.

(a) As at 30 September 20X5, TrillCo had bought 70 laptops from Taplop. Taplop therefore estimated that TrillCo's purchases would not exceed 500 in the year to 30 June 20X6, and would therefore not be entitled to the volume discount.

(b) During the quarter ended 31 December 20X5, TrillCo expanded rapidly as a result of a substantial acquisition, and purchased an additional 250 laptops from Taplop. Taplop then estimated that TrillCo's purchases would exceed the threshold for the volume discount in the year to 30 June 20X6.

Required

Calculate the revenue Taplop would recognise in:

(a) The quarter ended 30 September 20X5
(b) The quarter ended 31 December 20X5

Your answer should apply the principles of IFRS 15 *Revenue from Contracts with Customers*.

Solution

(a) Applying the requirements of IFRS 15 to TrillCo's purchasing pattern at 30 September 20X5, Taplop should conclude that it was highly probable that a significant reversal in the cumulative amount of revenue recognised ($500 per laptop) would not occur when the uncertainty was resolved, that is when the total amount of purchases was known. Consequently, Taplop should recognise revenue of 70 × $500 = $35,000 for the first quarter ended 30 September 20X5.

(b) In the quarter ended 31 December 20X5, TrillCo's purchasing pattern changed such that it would be legitimate for Taplop to conclude that TrillCo's purchases would exceed the threshold for the volume discount in the year to 30 June 20X6, and therefore that it was appropriate to reduce the price to $450 per laptop. Taplop should therefore recognise revenue of $109,000 for the quarter ended 31 December 20X5. The amount is calculated as from $112,500 (250 laptops × $450) less the change in transaction price of $3,500 (70 laptops × $50 price reduction) for the reduction of the price of the laptops sold in the quarter ended 30 September 20X5.

1.6 Contract costs

The incremental costs of **obtaining** a contract (such as sales commission) are **recognised as an asset** if the entity expects to recover those costs.

Costs that would have been incurred regardless of whether the contract was obtained are recognised as an expense as incurred.

Costs incurred in **fulfilling** a contract, unless within the scope of another standard (such as IAS 2 *Inventories*, IAS 16 *Property, Plant and Equipment* or IAS 38 *Intangible Assets*) are recognised as an asset if they meet the following criteria:

(a) The costs relate directly to an identifiable contract (costs such as labour, materials, management costs);

(b) The costs generate or enhance resources of the entity that will be used in satisfying (or continuing to satisfy) performance obligations in the future; and

(c) The costs are expected to be recovered.

Costs recognised as assets are amortised on a systematic basis consistent with the transfer to the customer of the goods or services to which the asset relates.

1.7 Performance obligations satisfied over time

A performance obligation satisfied over time meets the criteria in Step 5 above and, if it entered into more than one accounting period, would previously have been described as a long-term contract.

In this type of contract an entity has an enforceable right to payment for performance completed to date. The standard describes this as an amount that approximates the selling price of the goods or services transferred to date (for example recovery of the costs incurred by the entity in satisfying the performance plus a reasonable profit margin).

Methods of measuring the amount of performance completed to date encompass **output methods** and **input methods**.

Output methods recognise revenue on the basis of the value to the **customer** of the goods or services transferred. They include surveys of performance completed, appraisal of units produced or delivered etc.

Input methods recognise revenue on the basis of the **entity's** inputs, such as labour hours, resources consumed, and costs incurred. If using a cost-based method, the costs incurred must contribute to the entity's progress in satisfying the performance obligation.

1.8 Performance obligations satisfied at a point in time

A performance obligation not satisfied over time will be satisfied at a point in time. This will be the point in time at which the customer obtains control of the promised asset and the entity satisfies a performance obligation.

Some indicators of the transfer of control are:

(a) The entity has a present right to payment for the asset.
(b) The customer has legal title to the asset.
(c) The entity has transferred physical possession of the asset.
(d) The significant risks and rewards of ownership have been transferred to the customer.
(e) The customer has accepted the asset.

1.9 Sale with a right of return

Where goods are sold with a right of return, an entity should not recognise revenue for goods that it expects to be returned. It can calculate the level of returns using the expected value method (the probability-weighted sum of amounts) or simply estimate the most likely amount. This will be shown as a refund liability and a deduction from revenue.

The entity also recognises an asset (adjusted against cost of sales) for its right to recover products from customers on settlement of the refund liability.

1.10 Warranties

If a customer has the option to purchase a warranty separately from the product to which it relates, it constitutes a distinct service and is accounted for as a separate performance obligation. This would apply to a warranty which provides the customer with a service in addition to the assurance that the product complies with agreed-upon specifications.

If the customer does not have the option to purchase the warranty separately, for instance if the warranty is required by law, that does not give rise to a performance obligation and the warranty is accounted for in accordance with IAS 37.

1.11 Principal versus agent

An entity must establish in any transaction whether it is acting as principal or agent.

It is a principal if it controls the promised good or service before it is transferred to the customer. When the performance obligation is satisfied, the entity recognises revenue in the gross amount of the consideration for those goods or services.

It is acting as an agent if its performance obligation is to arrange for the provision of goods or services by another party. Satisfaction of this performance obligation will give rise to the recognition of revenue in the amount of any fee or commission to which it expects to be entitled in exchange for arranging for the other party to provide its goods or services.

Indicators that an entity is an agent rather than a principal include the following:

(a) Another party is primarily responsible for fulfilling the contract.

(b) The entity does not have inventory risk before or after the goods have been ordered by a customer, during shipping or on return.

(c) The entity does not have discretion in establishing prices for the other party's goods or services and, therefore, the benefit that the entity can receive from those goods or services is limited.

(d) The entity's consideration is in the form of a commission.

(e) The entity is not exposed to credit risk for the amount receivable from a customer in exchange for the other party's goods or services.

1.11.1 Example: Principal versus agent

This example is taken from the standard.

An entity operates a website that enables customers to purchase goods from a range of suppliers. The suppliers deliver directly to the customers, who have paid in advance, and the entity receives a commission of 10% of the sales price.

The entity's website also processes payments from the customer to the supplier at prices set by the supplier. The entity has no further obligation to the customer after arranging for the products to be supplied.

Is the entity a principal or an agent?

Solution

The following points are relevant:

- Goods are supplied directly from the supplier to the customer, so the entity does not obtain control of the goods.
- The supplier is primarily responsible for fulfilling the contract.
- The entity's consideration is in the form of commission.
- The entity does not establish prices and bears no credit risk.

The entity would therefore conclude that it is acting as an agent and that the only revenue to be recognised is the amounts received as commission.

1.12 Options for additional goods or services

If an option in the contract grants the customer the right to acquire additional goods or services at a discount which can only be obtained by entering into the contract, that option gives rise to a performance obligation.

Revenue is recognised when the additional future goods or services are transferred, or when the option expires. Revenue will be based on the stand-alone selling price of the goods or services, taking account of the discount.

If the option granted to the customer does not offer a discount, it is treated as a marketing offer and no contract exists until the customer exercises the option to purchase.

1.13 Customers' unexercised rights

When a customer pays in advance for goods or services the prepayment gives rise to a contract liability, which is derecognised when the performance obligation is satisfied.

If, having made a non-refundable prepayment, the customer does not exercise their right to receive the good or service, the unexercised right is often referred to as breakage. A breakage amount can be recognised as revenue if the pattern of rights exercised by the customer gives rise to the expectation that the entity will be entitled to a breakage amount. If this does not apply, it can be recognised as revenue when the likelihood of the customer exercising its rights becomes remote.

1.14 Non-refundable upfront fees

A non-refundable upfront fee is often charged at the beginning of a contract, such as joining fees in health club membership contracts.

In many cases upfront fees do not relate to the transfer of any promised good or service but are simply advance payments for **future** goods or services. In this case revenue is recognised when the future goods or services are provided.

If the fee relates to a good or service the entity should evaluate whether or not it amounts to a separate performance obligation. This depends on whether it results in the transfer of an asset to the customer. The fee may relate to costs incurred in setting up a contract, but these setup activities may not result in the transfer of services to the customer.

1.15 Licensing

A licence establishes a customer's rights to the intellectual property of an entity. Intellectual property can include software, music, franchises, patents, trademarks and copyrights.

The promise to grant a licence may be accompanied by the promise to transfer other goods or services to the customer. If the promise to grant the licence is **not** distinct from the promised goods or services, this is treated as a single performance obligation.

If the promise to grant the licence **is** distinct, it will constitute a separate performance obligation. The entity must establish whether the performance obligation is satisfied 'at a point in time' or 'over time'.

In this respect the entity should consider whether the nature of the entity's promise in granting the licence to a customer is to provide the customer with either:

(a) A **right to access** the entity's intellectual property as it exists throughout the licence period; or

(b) A **right to use** the entity's intellectual property as it exists at the point in time at which the licence is granted.

A **right to access** exists where the entity can make changes to the intellectual property throughout the licence period, the customer is exposed to the effects of these changes and the changes do not constitute the transfer of a good or service to the customer. In this case the promise to grant a licence is treated as a performance obligation satisfied over time and the entity recognises revenue over time by measuring the progress towards complete satisfaction of that performance obligation.

Where this does not apply, the nature of the entity's promise is the **right to use** its intellectual property as it exists at the point in time at which the licence is granted. This means that the customer can direct the use of, and obtain substantially all of the remaining benefits from, the licence at the point at which it is transferred. The point at which revenue can be recognised may be later than the date on which the licence is granted if the customer does not have immediate access to the intellectual property, for instance if it has to wait to be granted an access code.

When **royalties**, based on sales or on usage, are promised by the customer in exchange for a licence of intellectual property, revenue can be recognised at the later of the following occurrences:

(a) The sale or usage occurs; and
(b) The performance obligation to which the royalty has been allocated has been satisfied.

1.16 Repurchase agreements

Under a repurchase agreement an entity sells an asset and promises, or has the option, to repurchase it. Repurchase agreements generally come in three forms:

(a) An entity has an obligation to repurchase the asset (a forward contract).
(b) An entity has the right to repurchase the asset (a call option).
(c) An entity must repurchase the asset if requested to do so by the customer (a put option).

In the case of a forward or a call option the customer does not obtain control of the asset, even if it has physical possession. The entity will account for the contract as:

(a) A lease in accordance with IFRS 16, if the repurchase price is below the original selling price; or
(b) A financing arrangement if the repurchase price is equal to or greater than the original selling price. In this case the entity will recognise both the asset and a corresponding liability.

If the entity is obliged to repurchase at the request of the customer (a put option), it must consider whether or not the customer is likely to exercise that option.

If the repurchase price is lower than the original selling price and it is considered that the customer does not therefore have significant economic incentive to exercise the option, the contract should be accounted for as an outright sale, with a right of return.

If the repurchase price is greater than or equal to the original selling price and is above the expected market value of the option, the contract is treated as a financing arrangement.

1.16.1 Example: Contract with a call option

This example is taken from the standard.

An entity enters into a contract with a customer for the sale of a tangible asset on 1 January 20X7 for $1 million. The contract includes a call option that gives the entity the right to repurchase the asset for $1.1 million on or before 31 December 20X7.

This means that the customer does not obtain control of the asset, because the repurchase option means that it is limited in its ability to use and obtain benefit from the asset.

Solution

As control has not been transferred, the entity accounts for the transaction as a **financing arrangement**, because the exercise price is above the original selling price. The entity continues to recognise the asset and recognises the cash received as a financial liability. The difference of $0.1 million is recognised as interest expense.

If on 31 December 20X7 the option lapses unexercised, the customer now obtains control of the asset. The entity will derecognise the asset and recognise revenue of $1.1 million (the $1 million already received plus the $0.1 million charged to interest).

1.16.2 Example: Contract with a put option

The same contract as above includes instead a put option that obliges the entity to repurchase the asset at the customer's request for $900,000 on or before 31 December 20X7, at which time the market value is expected to be $750,000.

Solution

In this case the customer has a significant economic incentive to exercise the put option because the repurchase price exceeds the market value at the repurchase date. This means that control does not pass to the customer. Since the customer will be exercising the put option, this limits its ability to use or obtain benefit from the asset.

In this situation the entity accounts for the transaction as a lease in accordance with IFRS 16. The asset has been leased to the customer for the period up to the repurchase and the difference of $100,000 will be accounted for as payments received under a lease.

1.17 Consignment arrangements

When a product is delivered to a customer under a consignment arrangement, the customer (dealer) does not obtain control of the product at that point in time, so no revenue is recognised upon delivery.

Indicators of a consignment arrangement include:

(a)   The product is controlled by the entity until a specified event occurs, such as the product is sold on, or a specified period expires.

(b)   The entity can require the return of the product, or transfer it to another party.

(c)   The customer (dealer) does not have an unconditional obligation to pay for the product

1.18 Bill-and-hold arrangements

Under a bill-and-hold arrangement goods are sold but remain in the possession of the seller for a specified period, perhaps because the customer lacks storage facilities.

An entity will need to determine at what point the customer obtains control of the product. For some contracts, control will not be transferred until the goods are delivered to the customer. For others, a customer may obtain control even though the goods remain in the entity's physical possession. In this case the entity would be providing custodial services to the customer over the customer's asset.

For a customer to have obtained control of a product in a bill and hold arrangement, the following criteria must all be met:

(a)   The reason for the bill-and-hold must be substantive (for example, requested by the customer).
(b)   The product must be separately identified as belonging to the customer.
(c)   The product must be ready for physical transfer to the customer.
(d)   The entity cannot have the ability to use the product or to transfer it to another customer.

1.18.1 Example: Bill and hold arrangement

This example is taken from the standard.

An entity enters into a contract with a customer on 1 January 20X8 for sale of a machine and spare parts. It takes two years to manufacture these and on 31 December 20X9 the customer pays for both the machine and the spare parts but only takes physical possession of the machine. The customer inspects and accepts the spare parts but requests that they continue to be stored at the entity's warehouse.

Solution

There are now three performance obligations – transfer of the machine, transfer of the spare parts and the custodial services. The transaction price is allocated to the three performance obligations and revenue is recognised when (or as) control passes to the customer.

The machine and the spare parts are both performance obligations satisfied at a point in time, and for both of them that point in time is 31 December 20X9. In the case of the spare parts, the customer has paid for them, the customer has legal title to them and the customer as control of them as they can remove them from storage at any time.

The custodial services are a performance obligation satisfied over time, so revenue will be recognised over the period during which the spare parts are stored.

1.19 Example: Applying the IFRS five-step model

On 1 January 20X4, Angelo enters into a 12-month 'pay monthly' contract for a mobile phone. The contract is with TeleSouth, and terms of the plan are:

(a) Angelo receives a free handset on 1 January 20X4

(b) Angelo pays a monthly fee of $200, which includes unlimited free minutes. Angelo is billed on the last day of the month

Customers may purchase the same handset from TeleSouth for $500 without the payment plan. They may also enter into the payment plan without the handset, in which case the plan costs them $175 per month.

The company's year-end is 31 July 20X4.

Required

Show how TeleSouth should recognise revenue from this plan in accordance with IFRS 15 *Revenue from Contracts with Customers.* Your answer should give journal entries:

(a) On 1 January 20X4
(b) On 31 January 20X4

Solution

IFRS 15 requires application of its five-step process:

(i) **Identify the contract with a customer.** A contract can be written, oral or implied by customary business practices.

(ii) **Identify the separate performance obligations in the contract.** If a promised good or service is not distinct, it can be combined with others.

(iii) **Determine the transaction price.** This is the amount to which the entity expects to be **'entitled'**. For variable consideration, the probability – weighted expected amount is used. The effect of any credit losses shown as a separate line item (just below revenue).

(iv) **Allocate the transaction price to the separate performance obligations in the contract.** For multiple deliverables, the transaction price is allocated to each separate performance obligation in proportion to the **stand-alone selling price** at contract inception of each performance obligation.

(v) **Recognise revenue when (or as) the entity satisfies a performance obligation,** that is when the entity **transfers** a promised good or service to a customer. The good or service is only considered as transferred when the customer obtains **control** of it.

Application of the five-step process to TeleSouth

(i) **Identify the contract with a customer.** This is clear. TeleSouth has a 12-month contract with Angelo.

(ii) **Identify the separate performance obligations in the contract.** In this case there are two distinct performance obligations:

(1) The obligation to deliver a handset
(2) The obligation to provide network services for 12 months

(The obligation to deliver a handset would not be a distinct performance obligation if the handset could not be sold separately, but it is in this case because the handsets are sold separately.)

(iii) **Determine the transaction price.** This is straightforward: it is $2,400, that is 12 months × the monthly fee of $200.

(iv) **Allocate the transaction price to the separate performance obligations in the contract.** The transaction price is allocated to each separate performance obligation in proportion to the **stand-alone selling price** at contract inception of each performance obligation, that is the stand-alone price of the handset ($500 and the stand-alone price of the network services ($175 × 12 = $2,100.00):

Performance obligation	Stand-alone selling price $	% of total	Revenue (=relative selling price = $2,400 × %) $
Handset	500.00	19.2%	460.80
Network services	2,100.00	80.8%	1,939.20
Total	2,600.00	100%	2,400.00

(v) **Recognise revenue when (or as) the entity satisfies a performance obligation,** that is when the entity **transfers** a promised good or service to a customer. This applies to each of the performance obligations:

(1) When TeleSouth gives a handset to Angelo, it needs to recognise the revenue of $460.80.

(2) When TeleSouth provides network services to Angelo, it needs to recognise the total revenue of $1,939.20. It's practical to do it once per month as the billing happens.

Journal entries

On 1 January 20X4

The entries in the books of TeleSouth will be:

DEBIT	Receivable (unbilled revenue)	$460.80	
CREDIT	Revenue		$460.80

Being recognition of revenue from the sale of the handset

On 31 January 20X4

The monthly payment from Angelo is split between amounts owing for network services and amounts owing for the handset.

DEBIT	Receivable (Angelo)	$200	
CREDIT	Revenue (1,939.20/12)		$161.60
CREDIT	Receivable (unbilled revenue)(460.80/12)		$38.40

Being recognition of revenue from monthly provision of network services and 'repayment' of handset

1.20 Presentation

Contracts with customers will be presented in an entity's statement of financial position as a contract liability, a contract asset or a receivable, depending on the relationship between the entity's performance and the customer's payment.

A **contract liability** is recognised and presented in the statement of financial position where a customer has paid an amount of consideration prior to the entity performing by transferring control of the related good or service to the customer.

When the entity has performed but the customer has not yet paid all of the related consideration, this will give rise to either a **contract asset** or a **receivable**. A contract asset is recognised when the entity's right to consideration is conditional on something other than the passage of time, for instance future performance. A receivable is recognised when the entity's right to consideration is unconditional except for the passage of time.

In practice, this aligns with the previous IAS 11 treatment. Where revenue has been invoiced a receivable is recognised. Where revenue has been earned but not invoiced, it is recognised as a contract asset.

1.21 Disclosure

The following amounts should be disclosed unless they have been presented separately in the financial statements in accordance with other standards:

(a) Revenue recognised from contracts with customers, disclosed separately from other sources of revenue

(b) Any impairment losses recognised (in accordance with IFRS 9) on any receivables or contract assets arising from an entity's contracts with customers, disclosed separately from other impairment losses

(c) The opening and closing balances of receivables, contract assets and contract liabilities from contracts with customers

(d) Revenue recognised in the reporting period that was included in the contract liability balance at the beginning of the period

(e) Revenue recognised in the reporting period from performance obligations satisfied in previous periods (such as changes in transaction price)

Other information that should be provided;

(a) An explanation of significant changes in the contract asset and liability balances during the reporting period

(b) Information regarding the entity's performance obligations, including when they are typically satisfied (upon delivery, upon shipment, as services are rendered etc.), significant payment terms (such as when payment is typically due) and details of any agency transactions, obligations for returns or refunds and warranties granted

(c) The aggregate amount of the transaction price allocated to the performance obligations that are not fully satisfied at the end of the reporting period and an explanation of when the entity expects to recognise these amounts as revenue

(d) Judgements, and changes in judgements, made in applying the standard that significantly affect the determination of the amount and timing of revenue from contracts with customers

(e) Assets recognised from the costs to obtain or fulfil a contract with a customer. This would include pre-contract costs and set-up costs. The method of amortisation should also be disclosed.

1.22 Contracts where performance obligations are satisfied over time

These contracts are generally construction contracts, and it is possible that you will see this term used as the old standard, IAS 11, used it.

A company is building a large tower block that will house offices, under a contract with an investment company. It will take three years to build the block and over that time it will obviously have to pay for building materials, wages of workers on the building, architects' fees and so on. It will receive periodic payments from the investment company at various predetermined stages of the construction. How does it decide, in each of the three years, **what to include as income and expenditure** for the contract in profit or loss?

Example: contract where performance obligations are satisfied over time

Suppose that a contract is started on 1 January 20X5, with an estimated completion date of 31 December 20X6. The final contract price is $1,500,000, and the contract is expected to be profitable. In the first year, to 31 December 20X5:

(a) Costs incurred amounted to $600,000.
(b) Half the work on the contract was completed.
(c) Certificates of work completed have been issued, to the value of $750,000.
(d) The customer has been invoiced for $800,000 to date and has settled $400,000 of this.

What is the contract profit in 20X5, and what entries would be made for the contract at 31 December 20X5?

Solution

This is a contract in which the performance obligation is satisfied **over time**. The entity is carrying out the work for the benefit of the customer rather than creating an asset for its own use and it has an enforceable right to payment for work completed to date. We can see this from the fact that certificates of work completed have been issued.

IFRS 15 states that the amount of payment that the entity is entitled to corresponds to the amount of performance completed to date, which approximates to the costs incurred in satisfying the performance obligation plus a reasonable profit margin.

In this case the contract is certified as 50% complete. At 31 December 20X5 the entity will recognise revenue of $750,000 and cost of sales of $600,000, leaving profit of $150,000. A **contract liability of $50,000** will be recognised as the difference between the amount recognised as revenue ($750,000) and the amount billed to the customer ($800,000). A receivable of $400,000 will be recognised as the difference between the amount invoiced to date and the amount settled by the customer.

Summary of accounting treatment

Statement of profit or loss

(a) **Revenue and costs**

   (i) Sales revenue and associated costs should be recorded in profit or loss as the contract activity progresses.

   (ii) Include an appropriate proportion of total contract value as sales revenue in profit or loss.

   (iii) The costs incurred in completing that amount of the performance obligation are matched with this sales revenue, resulting in the reporting of results which can be attributed to the proportion of work completed.

   (iv) Sales revenue is the value of work carried out to date.

(b) **Profit recognised in the contract**

   (i) It must reflect the proportion of work carried out.

   (ii) It should take into account any known inequalities in profitability in the various stages of a contract.

Statement of financial position

(a) **Contract asset** (presented separately under current assets)

	$
Revenue recognised to date	X
Less receivables (amounts invoiced)	(X)
Contract asset	X

(b) **Receivables**

Unpaid invoices	X

(c) **Contract liability**. Where the amount billed to the customer exceeds the revenue recognised to date, a contract liability will be presented separately under current liabilities.

Example

P Co has the following construction contract (performance obligations satisfied over time) in progress:

	$m
Total contract price	750
Costs incurred to date	225
Estimated costs to completion	340
Progress payments invoiced and received	290

Now we will calculate the amounts to be recognised for the contract in the statement of profit or loss and statement of financial position assuming the amount of performance obligation satisfied is calculated using the proportion of costs incurred method.

1 *Estimated profit*

	$m
Total contract price	750
Less costs incurred to date	(225)
Less estimated costs to completion	(340)
Estimated profit	185

If the contract was expected to be loss-making overall, the full extent of the loss should be recognised immediately.

2 *Percentage complete*

Costs to date / total estimated costs: 225 / (225 + 340) = 40%

3 *Statement of profit or loss*

	$m
Revenue (40% × $750)	300
Cost of sales	(225)
Profit (40% × 185)	75

4 *Statement of financial position*

	$m
Revenue recognised	300
Less receivable	(290)
Contract asset	10

As all amounts billed have been received, there is no receivable.

How would we account for this if it was a loss-making contract? We will reduce P Co's contract price to $550m.

PART C ACCOUNTING AND REPORTING TECHNIQUES

1 *Estimated loss*

	$m
Total contract price	550
Less costs incurred to date	(225)
Less estimated costs to completion	(340)
Estimated loss	(15)

The loss is recognised in full as a provision for an onerous contract.

2 *Percentage complete*

Costs to date/total estimated costs: 225/(225 + 340) = 40%

3 *Statement of profit or loss*

	$m
Revenue (40% × $550)	220
Cost of sales (balancing figure)	(235)
Loss	(15)

4 *Statement of financial position*

	$m
Revenue recognised	220
Less receivable	(290)
Contract liability	(70)
Provision for onerous contract	(15)

1.23 Likely impact on companies

Revenue is generally an entity's most important financial performance indicator, and one extensively scrutinised by analysts and investors. IFRS 15 is likely to impact on **the timing, measurement, recognition and disclosure of revenue**. These impacts will require adjustments **in policies, procedures, internal controls and systems.**

1.23.1 Timing of revenue

By far the most significant change in IFRS 15 is to the **pattern of revenue reporting. Even if the total revenue reported does not change,** the timing will change in many cases.

The example of TeleSouth, our fictitious company above, illustrates this point. Under IAS 18 *Revenue,* the old standard, TeleSouth would **not recognise any revenue from the sale of handset,** on the grounds that TeleSouth has given it to Angelo free. TeleSouth would view the free handset as a cost of acquiring a new customer, and the cost would be recognised in profit or loss immediately.

Revenue from the provision of network services would be recognised on a monthly basis as follows:

DEBIT	Receivable/Cash	$200	
CREDIT	Revenue		$200

TeleSouth's year-end is 31 July 20X4, which means that the contract falls into more than one accounting period. The impact of changing from IAS 18 to IFRS 15 for TeleSouth, for the year ended 31 July 20X4 is as follows:

Performance obligation	Under IAS 18	Under IFRS 15
	$	$
Handset	00.00	460.80
Network services: (200 × 6)/(161.60 × 6)	1,200.00	969.60
Total	1,200.00	1,430.40

The variation in timing has tax implications, and if the tax rate changes, may have an overall effect on profit.

1.23.2 Use of judgement

The standard will require entities to use more judgement and make more estimates than under IAS 18, which, as seen from the example above, is simpler, although less realistic.

1.23.3 Retrospective application

IFRS 15 must be applied retrospectively, that is as if it has always been in place. Companies will therefore need to re-perform any calculations performed under IAS 18 and adjust opening balances. This will be labour intensive for companies with a lot of long-term contracts, particularly in the construction industry.

Question — Recognition

Discuss under what circumstances, if any, revenue might be recognised at the following stages of a sale.

(a) Goods are acquired by the business which it confidently expects to resell very quickly.
(b) A customer places a firm order for goods.
(c) Goods are delivered to the customer.
(d) The customer is invoiced for goods.
(e) The customer pays for the goods.
(f) The customer's cheque in payment for the goods has been cleared by the bank.

Answer

(a) A sale must never be recognised before the goods have even been ordered by a customer. There is no certainty about the value of the sale, nor when it will take place, even if it is virtually certain that goods will be sold.

(b) A sale must never be recognised when the customer places an order. No performance obligation has been satisfied at that point. Even though the order will be for a specific quantity of goods at a specific price, control over the goods has not yet been transferred to the customer. The customer may cancel the order, the supplier might be unable to deliver the goods as ordered or it may be decided that the customer is not a good credit risk.

(c) A sale will be recognised when delivery of the goods is made only when:

 (i) The sale is for cash, and so the cash is received at the same time; or
 (ii) The sale is on credit and the customer accepts delivery (eg by signing a delivery note).

(d) The critical event for a credit sale is usually the despatch of an invoice to the customer. At that point the performance obligation has been satisfied. There is then a legally enforceable debt, payable on specified terms, for a completed sale transaction.

(e) The critical event for a cash sale is when delivery takes place and when cash is received; both take place at the same time.

It would be too cautious or 'prudent' to await cash payment for a credit sale transaction before recognising the sale, unless the customer is a high credit risk and there is a serious doubt about his ability or intention to pay.

(f) It would again be over-cautious to wait for clearance of the customer's cheques before recognising sales revenue. Such a precaution would only be justified in cases where there is a very high risk of the bank refusing to honour the cheque.

PART C   ACCOUNTING AND REPORTING TECHNIQUES

2 Off balance sheet finance

FAST FORWARD

> The subject of **off balance sheet finance** is a complex one which has plagued the accountancy profession. In practice, off balance sheet finance schemes are often very sophisticated and they are beyond the range of this syllabus.

Key term

> '**Off balance sheet finance**' is the funding or refinancing of a company's operations in such a way that, under legal requirements and existing accounting conventions, some or all of the finance may not be shown in its statement of financial position.

'Off balance sheet transactions' are transactions which meet the above objective. These transactions may involve the **removal of assets** from the statement of financial position, as well as liabilities, and they are likely to have a significant impact on the profit or loss.

2.1 Why off balance sheet finance exists

Why might company managers wish to enter into such transactions?

(a) In some countries, companies traditionally have a lower level of gearing than companies in other countries. Off balance sheet finance is used to **keep gearing low**, probably because of the views of some analysts and brokers.

(b) A company may need to keep its gearing down in order to stay within the terms of **loan covenants** imposed by lenders.

(c) A quoted company with high borrowings is often expected (by analysts and others) to declare a **rights issue** in order to reduce gearing. This has an adverse effect on a company's share price and so off balance sheet financing is used to reduce gearing **and** the expectation of a rights issue.

(d) Analysts' short term views are a problem for companies **developing assets** which are not producing income during the development stage. Such companies will match the borrowings associated with such developing assets, along with the assets themselves, outside the statement of financial position. They are brought back into statement of financial position once income is being generated by the assets. This process keeps return on capital employed higher than it would have been during the development stage.

(e) Groups of companies have excluded **subsidiaries** from consolidation in an off balance sheet transaction because they carry out completely different types of business and have different characteristics. The usual example is a leasing company (in say a retail group) which has a high level of gearing.

You can see from this brief list of reasons that the overriding motivation is to avoid **misinterpretation**. In other words, the company does not trust the analysts or other users to understand the reasons for a transaction and so avoids any effect such transactions might have by taking them 'off balance sheet'. Unfortunately, the position of the company is then misstated and the user of the financial statements is misled.

You must understand that not all forms of 'off balance sheet finance' are undertaken for cosmetic or accounting reasons. Some transactions are carried out to **limit or isolate risk**, to reduce interest costs and so on. In other words, these transactions are in the best interests of the company, not merely a cosmetic repackaging of figures which would normally appear in the statement of financial position.

2.2 The off balance sheet finance problem

The result of the use of increasingly sophisticated off balance sheet finance transactions is a situation where the users of financial statements do not have a proper or clear view of the **state of the company's affairs**. The disclosures required by national company law and accounting standards did not in the past provide sufficient rules for disclosure of off balance sheet finance transactions and so very little of the true nature of the transaction was exposed.

Whatever the purpose of such transactions, **insufficient disclosure** creates a problem. This problem has been debated over the years by the accountancy profession and other interested parties and some progress has been made (see the later sections of this chapter). Company collapses during recessions have often revealed much higher borrowings than originally thought, because part of the borrowing was not included in the statement of financial position.

The main argument used for disallowing off balance sheet finance is that the true **substance** of the transactions should be shown, not merely the **legal form**, particularly when it is exacerbated by poor disclosure.

3 Substance over form

> **Key term**
>
> **Substance over form.** The principle that transactions and other events are accounted for and presented in accordance with their economic substance and not merely their legal form.
>
> *(Conceptual Framework)*

This is a very important concept. It is used to **determine accounting treatment** in financial statements through accounting standards and so prevent off balance sheet transactions. The following paragraphs give examples of where the principle of substance over form is enforced in various accounting standards.

3.1 IFRS 16 *Leases*

IFRS 16 requires a lessee to recognise assets and liabilities for all leases with a term of more than 12 months unless the underlying asset is of low value. Prior to IFRS 16 leases could be designated by the lessee as 'operating leases' and no asset or liability would be recognised.

3.2 IAS 24 *Related Party Disclosures*

IAS 24 requires financial statements to disclose fully material transactions undertaken with a related party by the reporting entity, **regardless of any price charged** (see Chapter 20).

3.3 Consolidated financial statements

This is perhaps the most important area of off balance sheet finance which has been prevented by the application of the substance over form concept. The use of **quasi-subsidiaries** was very common in the 1980s. These may be defined as follows.

> **Key term**
>
> A **quasi-subsidiary** of a reporting entity is a company, trust, partnership or other vehicle that, though not fulfilling the definition of a subsidiary, is directly or indirectly controlled by the reporting entity and gives rise to benefits for that entity that are in substance no different from those that would arise were the vehicle a subsidiary.

The main off balance sheet transactions involving quasi-subsidiaries were as follows.

(a) **Sale of assets.** The sale of assets to a quasi-subsidiary was carried out to remove the associated borrowings from the statement of financial position and so reduce gearing, or perhaps so that the company could credit a profit in such a transaction. The asset could then be rented back to the vendor company under an operating lease (no capitalisation required by the lessee). This can no longer happen since the introduction of IFRS 16.

(b) **Purchase of companies or assets.** One reason for such a purchase through a quasi-subsidiary is if the acquired entity is expected to make losses in the near future. Post-acquisition losses can be avoided by postponing the date of acquisition to the date the holding company acquires the entity from the quasi-subsidiary.

(c) **Business activities conducted outside the group.** Such a subsidiary might have been excluded through a quasi-subsidiary or not consolidated under an excuse of 'dissimilar activities'. Exclusion from consolidation might be undertaken because the activities are high risk and have high gearing.

The current accounting standard applicable to accounting for subsidiaries within the group financial statements is IFRS 10 *Consolidated Financial Statements*. Prior to this, the applicable standard was IAS 27 *Consolidated and Separate Financial Statements*, issued initially in 1989 and revised in 2003 and 2008. This standard introduced a definition of a subsidiary based on **control** rather than just ownership rights, thus substantially reducing the effectiveness of this method of off-balance sheet finance. IAS 27 defined control of another entity as follows.

> **Key term**
>
> **Control** is the power to govern the financial and operating policies of an entity so as to obtain benefit from its activities. (IAS 27)

IAS 27 stated that control exists when:

(a) The parent has a **majority of the voting rights** in the subsidiary (possibly **by agreement** with other members); or

(b) The parent can appoint or remove a **majority of the** board of the subsidiary; or

(c) The parent can **direct the operating and financial policies** through a statute or agreement; or

(d) The parent can cast the **majority of votes** at a board meeting of directors (or equivalent).

The main effects of this definition on the use of quasi-subsidiaries were as follows.

(a) The use of 'voting rights' rather than 'equity shares' prevented the use of **company structures** which gave the benefits of ownership to one class of shareholder without the appearance of doing so, eg a company has 100 'A' shares with 10 votes each and 900 'B' shares with one vote each.

(b) The use of 'the right to appoint or remove a majority of the board' prevented control through **differential voting rights** at board meetings.

IAS 27 therefore **curtailed drastically** the use of quasi-subsidiaries for off balance sheet finance. More complex schemes are likely to be curtailed by the issue of IFRS 10 *Consolidated Financial Statements* which uses control as the single basis for consolidation (see Chapter 11), the IASB's *Conceptual Framework* and by various other standards (see below).

You may also hear the term **creative accounting** used in the context of reporting the substance of transactions. This can be defined simply as the manipulation of figures for a desired result. Remember, however, that it is very rare for a company, its directors or employees to manipulate results for the purpose of fraud. The major consideration is usually the effect the results will have on the company's share price. Some areas open to abuse (although some of these loopholes have been closed) are given below and you should by now understand how these can distort a company results.

(a) Income recognition and cut-off
(b) Manipulation of reserves
(c) Revaluations and depreciation
(d) Window dressing
(e) Changes in accounting policy

Creative accounting, off balance sheet finance and related matters (in particular how ratio analysis can be used to discover these practices) often come up in articles in the financial press. Find a library, preferably a good technical library, which can provide you with copies of back issues of such newspapers or journals and look for articles on creative accounting.

Question — Manipulation

One of the ways in which financial statements can be manipulated is through the use of extraordinary items.

True or false?

Answer

False, though true in the past. IAS 1 *Presentation of Financial Statements* outlaws extraordinary items.

4 Common forms of off balance sheet finance

FAST FORWARD

We will look at some of the **major types** of off balance sheet finance, including factoring, sale and leaseback and securitisation.

How does the theory of the *Conceptual Framework* **apply in practice**, to real transactions? The rest of this section looks at some complex transactions that occur frequently in practice. We will consider how the principles of the *Conceptual Framework* would be applied to these transactions.

- Factoring of receivables/debts (IFRS 15)
- Securitised assets (IFRS 9)
- Loan transfers (IFRS 9)

Exam focus point

These examples are taken from a UK Standard on reporting the substance of transactions, but that standard uses almost the same definitions for assets, liabilities, recognition, etc as the IASB *Conceptual Framework*, and so these notes are applicable internationally. Note also that, in all the cases discussed, there may be situations somewhere between the two extremes given in each.

4.1 Factoring of receivables/debts

Where debts or receivables are factored, the original supplier **sells the debts to the factor**. The sales price may be fixed at the outset or may be adjusted later. It is also common for the factor to offer a credit facility that allows the seller to draw upon a proportion of the amounts owed.

In order to determine the correct accounting treatment it is necessary to consider whether the significant risks and rewards of ownership of the debts have been passed on to the factor, or whether the factor is, in effect, providing a loan on the security of the debtors. If the seller has to **pay interest** on the difference between the amounts advanced to them and the amounts that the factor has received, and if the seller bears the **risks of non-payment** by the debtor, then the indications would be that the transaction is, in effect, a loan.

4.1.1 Summary of indications of appropriate treatment

The following is a summary of indicators of the appropriate treatment.

Indications the debts are *not an asset* of the seller	Indications that the debts are an *asset* of the seller
Transfer is for **a single non-returnable fixed sum**.	**Finance cost varies** with speed of collection of debts, eg: • By adjustment to consideration for original transfer; or • Subsequent transfers priced to recover costs of earlier transfers.
There is **no recourse** to the seller for losses.	There is **full recourse** to the seller for losses.
Factor is paid **all amounts** received from the factored debts (and no more). Seller has no rights to further sums from the factor.	Seller is required to **repay** amounts received from the factor on or before a set date, regardless of timing or amounts of collections from customers.

4.1.2 Required accounting

Where the seller has retained no significant risks and rewards of ownership relating to the debts and has no obligation to repay amounts received from the factors, the receivables should be derecognised from its statement of financial position and no liability shown in respect of the proceeds received from the factor. A profit or loss should be recognised, calculated as the difference between the carrying amount of the debts and the proceeds received.

Where the seller does retain the significant risks and rewards of ownership, a gross asset (equivalent in amount to the gross amount of the receivables) should be shown in the statement of financial position of the seller within assets, and a corresponding liability in respect of the proceeds received from the factor should be shown within liabilities. The interest element of the factor's charges should be recognised as it accrues and included in profit or loss with other interest charges. Other factoring costs should be similarly accrued and included in profit or loss within the appropriate caption.

4.2 Securitised assets

Securitisation is very common in the financial services industry, and the assets that are most commonly securitised are mortgages and credit card financial statements, although hire purchase loans, trade debts and even property and inventories are sometimes securitised. **Blocks of assets** are thus financed, rather than the company's general business.

The normal procedure is for the assets to be transferred by the person who held them (the originator) to a special purpose company (the issuer) in exchange for cash. The issuer will use the proceeds of an issue of debentures or loan notes to pay for the assets. The shares in the issuer are usually held by a third party so that it does not need to be consolidated. The issuer will usually have a very small share capital, and so most of the risk will be borne by the people who lent it the money through the debentures to pay for the assets. For this reason there is usually some form of insurance taken out on the assets to give some security for the lenders.

4.2.1 Summary of indications as to accounting treatment

The following is a summary of indications of the appropriate treatment.

	Indications that the securitised assets are *not assets* of the seller	Indications that the securitised assets are *assets* of the originator
Originator's individual financial statements	Transaction price is **arm's length price** for an outright sale.	Transaction price is **not arm's length price** for an outright sale.
	Transfer is for a **single, non-returnable fixed sum**.	Proceeds received are **returnable**, or there is a provision whereby the originator may keep the securitised assets on repayment of the loan notes or reacquire them.
	There is **no recourse** to the originator for losses.	There is or may be **full recourse** to the originator for losses, eg: • Originator's directors are unable or unwilling to state that it is not obliged to fund any losses • Noteholders have not agreed in writing that they will seek repayment only from funds generated by the securitised assets
Originator's consolidated financial statements	Issuer is owned by an **independent third party** that made a substantial capital investment, has control of the issuer, and has the benefits and risks of its net assets.	Issuer is a **subsidiary** or quasi-subsidiary of the originator.

4.2.2 Required accounting: Originator's financial statements

Where the originator has retained no significant risks and rewards of ownership relating to the securitised assets and has no obligation to repay the proceeds of the note issue, the asset should be derecognised from its statement of financial position, and no liability shown in respect of the proceeds of the note issue. A profit or loss should be recognised, calculated as the difference between the carrying amount of the assets and the proceeds received.

Where the originator has retained the significant risks and rewards of ownership, a gross asset (equal in amount to the gross amount of the securitised assets) should be shown on the statement of financial position of the originator within assets, and a corresponding liability in respect of the proceeds of the note issue shown within liabilities. No gain or loss should be recognised at the time the securitisation is entered into (unless adjustment to the carrying value of the asset independent of the securitisation is required).

4.2.3 Required accounting: issuer's financial statements

The requirements set out in the paragraphs above for the originator's individual financial statements also apply to the issuer's financial statements. In most cases the issuer will be required to show the gross amounts, in which case the provisions of Section 4.2.2 will apply.

4.3 Loan transfers

These are arrangements where a loan is transferred to a transferee from an original lender. This will usually be done by the **assignment of rights and obligations** by the lender, or the **creation of a new agreement** between the borrower and the transferee. The same principles apply to loan transfers as to debt factoring and securitised assets.

4.3.1 Summary of indications of appropriate treatment

Indications that the loan is *not* a *liability* of the lender	Indications the loan is a *liability* of the lender
Transfer is for a **single, non-returnable fixed sum**.	The proceeds received are **returnable** in the event of losses occurring on the loans.
There is **no recourse** to the lender for losses from any cause.	There is **full recourse** to the lender for losses.
Transferee is paid **all amounts received** from the loans (and no more), as and when received. Lender has no rights to further sums from the loans or the transferee.	Lender is required to **repay amounts received** from the transferee on or before a set date, regardless of the timing or amount of payments by the borrowers.

4.3.2 Required accounting

Where the lender has retained no significant risks and rewards of ownership relating to the loans and has no obligation to repay the transferee, the loans should be derecognised from its statement of financial position and no liability shown in respect of the amounts received from the transferee. A profit or loss may arise for the lender. Where the profit or loss is realised in cash it should be recognised, calculated as the difference between the carrying amount of the loans and the cash proceeds received. Where, however, the lender's profit or loss is not realised in cash and there are doubts as to its amount, full provision should be made for any expected loss but recognition of any gain, to the extent it is in doubt, should be deferred until cash has been received.

Where the lender has retained the significant risks and rewards of ownership, a gross asset (equivalent in amount to the gross amount of the loans) should be shown in the statement of financial position of the lender within assets, and a corresponding liability in respect of the amounts received from the transferee should be shown within creditors. No gain or loss should be recognised at the time of the transfer (unless adjustment to the carrying value of the loan independent of the transfer is required).

PART C ACCOUNTING AND REPORTING TECHNIQUES

Chapter roundup

- Revenue recognition is straightforward in most business transactions, but some situations are more complicated.

- IFRS 15 *Revenue from Contracts with Customers* is concerned with the **recognition of revenues** arising from fairly common transactions.
    - The sale of goods
    - The rendering of services
    - The use by others of entity assets yielding interest, royalties and dividends

    Generally revenue is recognised when the entity has transferred promised goods or services to the customer. The standard sets out five steps for the recognition process.

- The subject of **off balance sheet** finance is a complex one which has plagued the accountancy profession. In practice, off balance sheet finance schemes are often very sophisticated and they are beyond the range of this syllabus.

- We will look at some of the **major types** of off balance sheet finance, including factoring, sale and leaseback and securitisation.

Quick quiz

1. Revenue should include sales tax. True or false?
2. How is revenue from royalties recognised?
3. Why do entities want to use 'off balance sheet' finance?
4. What is a quasi-subsidiary?
5. What are the common features of transactions whose substance is not really apparent?
6. When should a transaction be recognised?

Answers to quick quiz

1. False

2. Royalty revenue is recognised on an accruals basis in accordance with the substance of the relevant agreement.

3. Often off-balance sheet finance is a method of removing assets and liabilities from the statement of financial position to present a better picture of financial position

4. An entity that does not fulfil the definition of a subsidiary but is directly or indirectly controlled by the reporting entity and gives rise to benefits that are in substance no different from those arising if it were a subsidiary.

5. (a) The legal title is separated from the significant risks and rewards of ownership
   (b) The transaction is linked to others so that the commercial effect cannot be understood without reference to the complete series.
   (c) The transaction includes one or more options under such terms that it is likely the option(s) will be exercised.

6. When it is probable that a future inflow or outflow of benefit to the entity will occur and the item can be measured in monetary terms with sufficient reliability.

End of chapter question

IFRS 15

Caravans Deluxe is a retailer of caravans, dormer vans and mobile homes, with a year end of 30 June 20X8. It is having trouble selling one model – the $30,000 Mini-Lux, and so is offering incentives for customers who buy this model before 31 May 20X7:

(a) Customers buying this model before 31 May 20X7 will receive a period of interest free credit, provided they pay a non-refundable deposit of $3,000, an instalment of $15,000 on 1 August 20X7 and the balance of $12,000 on 1 August 20X9.

(b) Equipment for the caravan, normally worth $1,500, is included free in the price of the caravan.

On 1 May 20X7, a customer agrees to buy a Mini-Lux caravan, paying the deposit of $3,000. Delivery is arranged for 1 August 20X7.

As the sale has now been made, the director of Caravans Deluxe wishes to recognise the full sale price of the caravan, $30,000, in the accounts for the year ended 30 June 20X7.

Required

Show how the IFRS 15 five-step plan is applied to this sale. Assume a 10% discount rate. Show the journal entries for this treatment.

PART C ACCOUNTING AND REPORTING TECHNIQUES

IFRS for SMEs

Topic list	Syllabus reference
1 Introduction	13.4
2 Who can use the IFRS for SMEs?	13.4
3 Structure of the IFRS for SMEs	13.4
4 Concepts and pervasive principles	13.4
5 Financial statements	13.4
6 Group financial statements	13.2, 13.3
7 Financial instruments	13.4
8 Assets	13.4
9 Liabilities	13.4
10 Other topics	13.4
11 Updating the IFRS for SMEs	13.4

Introduction

The IFRS for SMEs provides simplified accounting for eligible entities. Local legislative authorities can decide which entities can or must use the IFRS for SMEs within a given jurisdiction.

1 Introduction

> **FAST FORWARD**
>
> The IFRS for SMEs was developed to provide a simpler accounting regime within the IFRS framework for non-publicly listed entities. Other than an option to use IAS 39 in respect of financial instruments, it is a stand-alone standard.

1.1 Why was the IFRS for SMEs developed?

Full IFRS cover a wide range of accounting issues, and are specifically designed to meet the needs of investors in, and creditors of, publicly listed companies. The standards are often complex and have extensive disclosure requirements.

In making these standards more relevant to large listed companies, they have become less relevant to the needs of the users of small and medium-sized entities (SMEs). These users are more focused on cash flows, liquidity and solvency.

The IFRS for SMEs was therefore developed in order to provide a simpler accounting regime which:

- Is relevant to the needs of users of private entity accounts;
- Is understandable across borders; and
- Takes into account cost-benefit considerations.

One particular aim of the IASB in developing the IFRS for SMEs was to provide a standard for entities in countries that have no national GAAP. The IFRS for SMEs makes an international accounting framework accessible to entities that do not have the resources to adopt full IFRS.

1.2 Development of the IFRS for SMEs

The project to develop the IFRS for SMEs began 2003, and between this date and 2009, when the standard was finally issued, extensive deliberations and field testing took place. The IFRS for SMEs is based on full IFRS, however the IASB accepted that clear modifications to the recognition and measurement principles of full IFRS were required together with a significant reduction in disclosures. As a result, the volume of accounting guidance is reduced by more than 85% compared with full IFRS.

1.3 IFRS for SMEs vs full IFRS

Although the IFRS for SMEs is based on full IFRS, a number of aspects of full IFRS are omitted, whilst others are simplified:

- Certain topics which are not relevant to smaller and private entities are omitted completely (see below).
- Recognition and measurement rules are simplified.
- Where there is a policy choice in full IFRS, the IFRS for SMEs generally adopts the simpler option.
- Disclosure requirements are significantly reduced (from 3,000 disclosures in full IFRS to approximately 300).
- Much of the implementation guidance within full IFRS is omitted.

1.3.1 Omitted topics

Topics which are less relevant to non-publicly accountable entities have been omitted completely. These include:

- The accounting requirements for non-current assets held for sale (IFRS 5)
- Segment reporting (IFRS 8)
- Earnings per share (IAS 33)
- Interim financial reporting (IAS 34)
- Insurance contracts (IFRS 4*)
- Accounting and reporting by retirement benefit plans (IAS 26*)

22: IFRS FOR SMEs

Exam focus point

*IFRS 4 and IAS 26 are not within the Paper 13 syllabus.

1.4 A stand-alone standard

With one exception, the IFRS for SMEs is a stand-alone product which can be applied without reference to full IFRS. The exception relates to financial instruments, where there is the option to choose whether to apply the simplified recognition and measurement provisions of the IFRS for SMEs or the provisions of IAS 39 (until IFRS 9 replaces IAS 39). Where a company elects to use IAS 39 to account for financial instruments rather than the IFRS for SMEs, the extensive disclosure requirements of IFRS 7 **do not apply.**

Other than the option to use IAS 39, companies may not 'mix and match' the requirements of the IFRS for SMEs and full IFRS; they must apply one or the other in their entirety.

2 Who can use the IFRS for SMEs?

FAST FORWARD

The IFRS for SMEs defines those entities which are eligible to use it as entities which do not have public accountability and which publish general purpose financial statements.

2.1 Eligibility

Despite the name of the standard, eligibility to use the IFRS for SMEs is not dependent on the size of an entity. In the context of the standard, SMEs are defined as entities that:

- Do not have public accountability; and
- Publish general purpose financial statements for external users.

Subsidiaries of a parent company which uses full IFRS may use the IFRS for SMEs as long as they meet the definition given above. The ED states that a parent company may use the IFRS for SMEs in its own separate financial statements if it meets the criteria, even if certain subsidiaries do not.

2.1.1 Public accountability

An entity has public accountability if:

(1) Its debt or equity instruments are traded in a public market, or the entity is in the process of issuing debt or equity instruments which will be traded in a public market; or

(2) It holds assets in a fiduciary capacity for a broad group of outsiders as one of its primary businesses. The ED clarifies that this may be but will not necessarily be the case for banks, mutual funds etc.

2.1.2 General purpose financial statements

General purpose financial statements are financial statements which are directed towards the common needs of a wide range of users.

Question   Public accountability

Give examples of types of companies which are publicly accountable and therefore not permitted to use the IFRS for SMEs.

Answer

Companies may not use the IFRS for SMEs if they are publicly accountable. A company is publicly accountable if:

(1) Its debt or equity instruments are listed in a public market or are in the process of being listed eg in the UK, companies which are listed (or will be listed) on the London Stock Exchange (LSE) or Alternative Investment Market (AIM).

(2) It holds assets in a fiduciary capacity for a broad group of outsiders as one of its primary businesses. Banks, insurance entities, securities brokers and dealers and pension funds are all examples of companies which hold assets in a fiduciary capacity for a range of third parties. However it must also be considered (under the ED) whether these are primary businesses.

2.2 Application of the standard

The decision as to which entities are permitted or required to use the IFRS for SMEs is a matter for the relevant authorities in individual jurisdictions, and changes to local laws are likely to be required before the standard can be adopted in practice. Currently, some countries require the use of IFRS (including the IFRS for SMEs) for unlisted companies; others allow its use and some prohibit the use of IFRS.

Very few countries currently require the use of the IFRS for SMEs for unlisted companies; these include Antigua and Barbuda.

Countries which allow the use of the IFRS for SMEs for unlisted companies include Barbados, South Africa and the USA.

Countries which currently do not permit the use of IFRS for unlisted companies include India and Thailand.

2.3 Advantages of adopting the IFRS for SMEs

There are a number of potential advantages to companies of applying the IFRS for SMEs rather than local GAAP. Depending on the requirements of local GAAP, these may include:

- Improvements in the quality of financial reporting
- Less onerous reporting requirements than local GAAP

For the accounting boards of the countries themselves, use of the IFRS for SMEs may remove the need to maintain local GAAP.

In addition, some countries, for example Bahrain and Chile, require all companies to use IFRS in their financial reporting. In these countries the IFRS for SMEs provides a less onerous option than full IFRS.

The obvious downside of adopting a new GAAP, even where it is simplified, is the management of the transition and associated costs, including new software and training.

3 Structure of the IFRS for SMEs

FAST FORWARD The standard is organised into 35 sections, each dealing with a specific area of accounting.

The IFRS for SMEs is organised into sections, each relating to a specific area of accounting. It is written clearly and concisely and is significantly easier to read than full IFRS. The standard is accompanied by a glossary of terms, illustrative financial statements and a disclosure checklist.

The sections of the standard are as follows:

1	Small and medium-sized entities
2	Concepts and pervasive principles
3	Financial statement presentation
4	Statement of financial position
5	Statement of comprehensive income and income statement
6	Statement of changes in equity and statement of income and retained earnings
7	Statement of cash flows
8	Notes to the financial statements
9	Consolidated and separate financial statements
10	Accounting policies, estimates and errors
11	Basic financial instruments
12	Other financial instruments issues
13	Inventories
14	Investments in associates
15	Investments in joint ventures
16	Investment property
17	Property, plant and equipment
18	Intangible assets other than goodwill
19	Business combinations and goodwill
20	Leases
21	Provisions and contingencies
22	Liabilities and equity
23	Revenue
24	Government grants
25	Borrowing costs
26	Share-based payment
27	Impairment of assets
28	Employee benefits
29	Income tax
30	Foreign currency translation
31	Hyperinflation
32	Events after the end of the reporting period
33	Related party disclosures
34	Specialised activities
35	Transition to the IFRS for SMEs

Note that as the standard was issued in 2009, and has not yet been updated, certain terms do not correspond to those used in full IFRS. For example, IAS 1 has recently amended the name of the income statement to become statement of profit or loss and other comprehensive income, yet the IFRS for SMEs still uses the 'old' terms.

The remainder of this chapter groups related sections of the IFRS for SMEs in order to explain the accounting requirements of the standard. In particular we shall focus on **differences from full IFRS**. The content of the first section of the standard dealing with the definition of small and medium-sized entities was covered in Section 2 above. Section 34 Specialised activities concerns agriculture and extractive industries and is outside the scope of your syllabus.

4 Concepts and pervasive principles

> **FAST FORWARD**
>
> The IFRS for SMEs includes a section on concepts and pervasive principles which is an abbreviated form of the *Conceptual Framework*.

Section 2 of the IFRS for SMEs deals with concepts and pervasive principles. This section is based on the IASB's 2010 *Conceptual Framework*, and is therefore currently inconsistent with the 2018 version. It includes explanation of the qualitative characteristics of information, defines the elements of the financial statements and provides guidance on their recognition and measurement. In addition this section clarifies that the accruals basis of accounting should be used in preparing financial statements other than the statement of cash flows and that offsetting of assets and liabilities is not allowed other than where specifically required or permitted by the IFRS for SMEs.

4.1 Qualitative characteristics

The qualitative characteristics of financial information are listed as:

- Understandability
- Relevance
- Materiality
- Reliability
- Substance over form
- Prudence
- Completeness
- Comparability
- Timeliness

These characteristics are not identical to those within the *Conceptual Framework*, however they are very similar. The IFRS for SMEs requires that in applying the characteristics, a balance is achieved between benefit and cost.

Question — Qualitative characteristics

Explain what is meant by each of the characteristics of financial information listed in the IFRS for SMEs.

Answer

Understandability	Information should be presented so as to be understandable to users with a reasonable knowledge; information should not be omitted on the grounds that it may be difficult to understand.
Relevance	Information provided should be relevant to the decision-making needs of users.
Materiality	Information is material and so relevant if its omission or misstatement could influence the economic decisions of users.
Reliability	Information must be reliable; this is the case where it is free from material error and bias and represents faithfully what it purports to represent.
Substance over form	Transactions and events should be presented in accordance with their commercial substance and not merely their legal form.
Prudence	Prudence (a degree of caution) should be exercised when making judgements so that assets or income are not overstated and liabilities or expenses are not understated.
Completeness	The information in the financial statements should be complete within the boundaries of materiality and cost.
Comparability	Users must be able to compare the financial statements of an entity through time to identify trends and compare the financial statements of one entity with another. Therefore consistency must be applied in accounting treatment and accounting policies disclosed.
Timeliness	Information should be provided within the decision time frame of the users of the financial statements.

4.2 Elements of the financial statements, their recognition and measurement

The IFRS for SMEs defines assets, liabilities, equity, income and expenses in accordance with the 2010 *Conceptual Framework*.

Items are recognised when the definition of an element is met and:

(1) It is probable that any future economic benefit associated with the item will flow to or from the entity; and

(2) The item has a cost or value that can be measured reliably.

These recognition criteria are identical to those within full IFRS.

The measurement bases specified by the IFRS for SMEs are historical cost and fair value. In most cases the standard requires items to be measured at historical cost, however in some cases it requires revaluation to fair value where such information is readily available.

5 Financial statements

FAST FORWARD

> The IFRS for SMEs is generally consistent with IAS 1 in respect of requirements for the presentation of financial statements, although there is some relaxation of the full IFRS requirements.

Sections 3–8 of the IFRS for SMEs deal with the content and presentation of a set of financial statements. The requirements of these sections are generally consistent with those of IAS 1 *Presentation of Financial Statements*. Section 10 of the standard deals with accounting policies, estimates and errors; this section is generally consistent with IAS 8 *Accounting Policies, Changes in Accounting Estimates and Errors*.

5.1 Financial statement presentation

Section 3 of the IFRS for SMEs deals with fair presentation, compliance with the IFRS for SMEs, going concern, the frequency of reporting, consistency of presentation, the provision of comparative information, materiality and aggregation and a complete set of financial statements.

In respect of compliance with the IFRS for SMEs, Section 3 allows departure from the requirements of the standard only in very rare circumstances, in which case extra disclosures are required.

A complete set of financial statements as required by the IFRS for SMEs includes:

- A statement of financial position
- A statement of comprehensive income (one or two statements)
- A statement of changes in equity
- A statement of cash flows
- Notes to the accounts

Certain guidance contained within full IFRS is relaxed, in particular:

1. A third statement of financial position at the start of the earliest comparative period is not required when there is a retrospective restatement of items.

2. Where there is no other comprehensive income in any of the periods presented, an entity may present an income statement (statement of profit or loss) rather than a statement of comprehensive income (statement of profit or loss and other comprehensive income).

3. A single statement of income and retained earnings may be presented instead of a statement of comprehensive income and statement of changes in equity where the only changes to equity in a period arise from profit or loss, the payment of dividends and retrospective adjustments (see below).

4. The ED relaxes the requirement under full IFRS to disclose comparatives for the reconciliation of the opening and closing number of shares.

5.2 Statement of financial position

Guidance on the statement of financial position is generally consistent with that set out in IAS 1 with certain items that must be presented on the face of the main statement and others that may be presented instead in notes to the accounts.

5.3 Statement of comprehensive income and statement of changes in equity

The statement of comprehensive income for a company applying the IFRS for SMEs will include (where relevant) only three items of other comprehensive income:

- Some foreign exchange gains and losses
- Some actuarial gains and losses
- Some changes in fair value of hedging instruments

The ED states that items must be grouped on the basis of whether they are potentially reclassifiable to profit or loss. This updates the IFRS to bring it into line with IAS 1 (2011 amendment).

Otherwise, the guidance is consistent with IAS 1, with minimum disclosure requirements and analysis of expenses by either nature or function.

The statement of changes in equity is prepared and presented in line with the requirements of IAS 1.

5.4 Statement of income and retained earnings

Where a company has no changes to equity other than profit or loss, dividends and retrospective adjustments, it may present a statement of income and retained earnings rather than a statement of comprehensive income and statement of changes in equity.

5.4.1 Example: statement of income and retained earnings

The following example of a statement of income and retained earnings is taken from the illustrative financial statements provided as part of the IFRS for SMEs.

	$
Revenue	6,863,545
Cost of sales	(5,178,530)
Gross profit	1,685,015
Other income	88,850
Distribution costs	(175,550)
Administrative expenses	(810,230)
Other expenses	(106,763)
Finance costs	(26,366)
Profit before tax	654,956
Income tax expense	(270,250)
Profit for the year	384,706
Retained earnings at the start of the year	2,171,353
Dividends	(150,000)
Retained earnings at the end of the year	2,406,059

5.5 Statement of cash flows

All companies applying the IFRS for SMEs are required to prepare a statement of cash flows, with cash flows organised into operating, investing and financing amounts. Either the direct or indirect method may be applied.

5.6 Notes to the financial statements

Within the notes to the financial statements, a company must state that it has applied the IFRS for SMEs and disclose its accounting policies. Disclosure of significant judgements and sources of estimation uncertainly is also required.

5.7 Accounting policies, estimates and errors

> **FAST FORWARD**
>
> Where the IFRS for SMEs does not specifically address a transaction, the requirements of the IFRS for SMEs in relation to similar issues or the Concepts and pervasive principles section of the standard are considered.

Section 10 of the IFRS for SMEs specifies that the requirements of the standard should be applied where they specifically address a transaction. Where this is not the case, the following hierarchy should be applied in the development of accounting policies:

(1) The requirements of the IFRS for SMEs in relation to similar issues
(2) Guidance within the Concepts and pervasive principles section of the standard

Guidance within full IFRS may also be considered although this is not mandatory.

The treatment of changes to accounting policies, accounting estimates and errors is in line with that prescribed by IAS 8.

6 Group financial statements

> **FAST FORWARD**
>
> The IFRS for SMEs includes a different definition of control from IFRS 10, however consolidation procedures are largely the same.

Four sections of the IFRS for SMEs deal with group accounting issues: Section 9 deals with consolidated and separate financial statements; Sections 14 and 15 with investments in associates and joint ventures respectively and Section 19 with business combinations and goodwill.

Note that certain group issues dealt with in full IFRS are not referred to in the IFRS for SMEs. These include step acquisitions and the measurement period.

6.1 Consolidated financial statements

The IFRS for SMEs requires that consolidated financial statements are prepared where there is a parent-subsidiary relationship, except where:

- The parent itself is a subsidiary and its ultimate parent prepares consolidated accounts under either full IFRS or the IFRS for SMEs; or
- The subsidiary was acquired with the intention to dispose of it within 12 months.

In the latter case, the subsidiary is held at fair value with changes in fair value recognised in profit or loss unless fair value cannot be measured reliably in which case it is measured at cost less impairment.

6.1.1 Control

In common with IFRS 10 *Consolidated Financial Statements*, a parent-subsidiary relationship is established based on control. The definition of control presented within the IFRS for SMEs is based on IAS 27 (2009) *Consolidated and Separate Financial Statements* and so differs from that presented within the standard which replaced it, IFRS 10.

Key term

> **Control** is the power to govern the financial and operating policies of an entity so as to obtain benefits from its activities.

Control is presumed to exist where a parent owns directly, or indirectly, more than half of the voting power of an entity. It also exists where the parent does not have more than half of the voting power itself but does have:

- Power over more than half of the voting power by virtue of an agreement with other investors
- Power to govern the operating and financial policies of the entity under statute or an agreement
- Power to appoint or remove the majority of Board members or other controlling body
- Power to cast the majority of votes at meetings of the Board or other controlling body

The IFRS for SMEs also extends this definition to include special purpose entities (entities created to accomplish a narrow objective) which are controlled by a parent entity.

The ED clarifies that combined financial statements relate to all entities under common control rather than only those under common control by a single investor. The IFRS does not require preparation of combined financial statements.

6.1.2 Consolidation procedures

The consolidation procedures of the IFRS for SMEs are identical to those within IFRS 10, with one exception: where use of a uniform accounting date is impracticable, the IFRS for SMEs does not require that subsidiary accounts prepared to a date within three months of the parent's reporting date are used. The ED clarifies that, where use of a uniform accounting date is impracticable, the most recent accounts should be used and adjustments made for transactions occurring between the two dates.

6.2 Separate financial statements

The IFRS for SMEs does not require the presentation of separate financial statements for the parent company. Where they are prepared, the investment in a subsidiary, associate or joint venture is recognised either:

- At cost less impairment; or
- At fair value with changes in fair value recognised in profit or loss.

6.3 Investments in associates and joint ventures

FAST FORWARD Investments in associates and jointly controlled entities (JCEs) may be accounted for using the cost model, equity accounting or the fair value model.

The definition of significant influence contained within the IFRS for SMEs and applied to establish a parent-associate relationship is equal to that given in IAS 28 *Investments in Associates and Joint Ventures*.

The definition of joint control and types of joint arrangement differ, however to those given in IFRS 11 *Joint Arrangements*. The requirements of the IFRS for SMEs are based on the 'old' joint arrangement rules of IAS 31 *Interests in Joint Ventures*.

6.3.1 Joint ventures

Key term

The definition of **joint control** is provided as:

The contractually agreed sharing of control over an economic activity which exists only when the strategic financial and operating decisions relating to the activity require the unanimous consent of the parties sharing control.

This is a very similar definition to that within IFRS 11, however the new definition refers to 'relevant activities' rather than 'strategic financial and operating decisions', where relevant activities are those activities of the investee which significantly affect the investee's returns.

The IFRS for SMEs differs more significantly in how it classifies joint arrangements. These are:

- **Jointly controlled operations** (the venturers use their own assets and resources in a joint venture rather than establishing a separate entity; each takes a share of the profits)

- **Jointly controlled assets** (the venturers jointly control an asset dedicated to use in the joint venture eg an oil pipe; profits and expenses are shared)
- **Jointly controlled entities** (a separate entity is established for the purpose of the joint venture in which each venturer has an interest)

6.3.2 Accounting treatment

In respect of an interest in a **jointly controlled operation**, a venturer recognises in its own financial statements:

(a) The assets which it controls and liabilities which it incurs; and
(b) The expenses which it incurs and its share of income from the joint venture.

In respect of an interest in a **jointly controlled asset**, a venturer recognises in its own financial statements:

(a) Its share of the jointly controlled assets
(b) Any liabilities that it has incurred
(c) Its share of any jointly incurred liabilities
(d) Any income from the sale or use of its share of the output of the joint venture
(e) Its share of any expenses incurred by the joint venture
(f) Any expenses incurred in respect of its interest in the joint venture

The IFRS for SMEs requires that a **jointly controlled entity** is measured in the financial statements in the same way as an **associate**, using:

- The cost model (cost less accumulated impairment losses);
- The equity method as required by IAS 28; or
- The fair value model (fair value with gains and losses recognised in profit or loss).

One model is applied to all associates and one model to all JCEs.

Where a published price quotation is available, the fair value model must be used in preference to the cost model.

This is a simplification of the rules within IAS 28 where the equity method must be applied.

6.4 Business combinations and goodwill

FAST FORWARD

> Under the IFRS for SMEs, the NCI is not taken into account in the calculation of goodwill, acquisition costs form part of the cost of the combination and contingent consideration is only included where payment is probable and can be reliably measured.

The IFRS for SMEs requires the application of the purchase method to business combinations. This is very similar to the acquisition method required by IFRS 3 *Business Combinations* with the following notable exceptions:

(1) Contingent consideration is only included within the cost of the combination where it is probable and can be reliably measured.

(2) Directly attributable acquisition costs form part of the cost of the combination (and so increase goodwill).

(3) Goodwill is calculated as the difference between the cost of the combination and the share of the fair value of identifiable net assets acquired; the non-controlling interest is not included in the calculation.

(4) There is no option to measure the non-controlling interest at fair value at acquisition; it is always measured as a proportion of the net assets of the subsidiary. The ED clarifies that this means that any non-controlling interest in the acquiree is measured at the non-controlling interest's proportionate share of the recognised amounts of the acquiree's identifiable net assets.

(5) Goodwill is amortised over its useful life; if this cannot be estimated, it is presumed to be 10 years. The ED changes this to no more than 10 years.

Question — Goodwill

Potter Co is an unlisted entity which applies the IFRS for SMEs. On 1 September 20X2 Potter acquired 80% of the ordinary shares in Finch Co, paying $2 million immediately and agreeing to pay a further $2.12 million on 1 September 20X3 if Finch Co achieved a 5% growth in sales revenue in the year after acquisition. The cost of capital of Potter Co is 6%. On the date of acquisition, the fair value of the identifiable net assets in Finch Co was $1.8 million. Directly attributable costs of acquisition amounted to $50,000.

By the group year end of 28 February 20X3, Finch Co had achieved only a 2% growth in sales revenue on an annualised basis. The directors of Potter Co believed that further increase was unlikely given difficult trading conditions.

The directors of Potter Co have been unable to estimate a useful life for the goodwill arising in Finch Co.

At what amount is goodwill reported in the consolidated financial statement of position of Potter Co at 28 February 20X3?

Answer

- The contingent consideration in respect of the combination is unlikely to be received given the growth in sales revenue to date and difficult trading conditions. Therefore it is ignored in the calculation of goodwill.
- Acquisition costs are included as part of the cost of the combination.
- As the directors have been unable to estimate the useful life of goodwill, it is amortised over ten years:

	$
Cash consideration	2,000,000
Acquisition costs	50,000
	2,050,000
Share of FV of identifiable NAs acquired (80% × $1.8m)	(1,440,000)
Goodwill arising at acquisition	610,000
Amortisation $610,000/10 × 6/12	(30,500)
Carrying amount at 28 February 20X3	579,500

Tutorial note

If Potter applied full IFRS, the goodwill calculation would be as follows:

	$
Cash consideration	2,000,000
Deferred consideration (assuming FV = PV) 2,120,000/1.06	2,000,000
	4,000,000
NCI (assume measured as a proportion of net assets) 20% × $1.8m	360,000
	4,360,000
FV of identifiable NAs acquired	(1,800,000)
Goodwill arising at acquisition	2,560,000

This goodwill would not be amortised but instead tested for impairment at each period end.

7 Financial instruments

FAST FORWARD

The IFRS for SMEs contains two sections on accounting for financial instruments: basic financial instruments and other financial instruments. Basic financial instruments are normally measured at amortised cost and other financial instruments at fair value.

Sections 11 and 12 of the IFRS for SMEs deal with basic and other financial instruments respectively. Entities which adopt the IFRS for SMEs may elect to follow either the provisions of Sections 11 and 12, or IAS 39 *Financial Instruments: Recognition and Measurement*. Where IAS 39 is used, the disclosure requirements of Sections 11 and 12 apply rather than IFRS 7 *Financial Instruments: Disclosures*.

7.1 Basic and other financial instruments

The IFRS for SMEs defines basic and other financial instruments and provides examples of each. **Basic financial instruments** include:

- Cash
- Accounts receivable or payable
- Loans from banks and other third parties (ED: includes foreign currency loans and those with standard loan covenants)
- An investment in non-convertible preference shares and non-puttable ordinary shares or preference shares
- A commitment to receive a loan that cannot be settled net in cash
- Most debt instruments where returns to the holder are fixed or referenced to an observable interest rate

Other financial instruments include:

- An investment in another entity's equity instruments other than those listed above
- Options, rights, warrants, future and forward contracts and swaps
- Investments in convertible debt (because the return can vary with the market price of shares rather than just with interest rates)
- Commitments to receive a loan that can be settled net in cash

7.2 Initial measurement

7.2.1 Basic financial instruments

Basic financial instruments are initially measured at the **transaction price** (including transaction costs other than where the instrument is measured at fair value through profit or loss). However, where an arrangement constitutes a **financing transaction**, the instrument is measured at the present value of future payments discounted at a market rate of interest.

7.2.2 Example: initial measurement of basic financial instruments

- A long-term loan made to another entity (a financial asset) is measured at the present value of cash receivable.
- Amounts receivable from customers (financial assets) are recognised at the undiscounted amount receivable from the customer – normally the invoice price
- A cash purchase of another entity's shares (a financial asset) is recognised at the amount of cash paid to acquire the shares.
- A loan received from a bank (a financial liability) is measured at the present value of cash payable to the bank.
- Amounts owed to suppliers (financial liabilities) are recognised at the undiscounted amount owed to the supplier – normally the invoice price.

7.2.3 Other financial instruments

Other financial instruments are measured at fair value, which is normally the transaction price.

7.3 Subsequent measurement

7.3.1 Basic financial instruments

Basic financial instruments are measured at **amortised cost** using the **effective interest method**, with the following exceptions:

(1) Shares whose fair value can be measured reliably are measured at fair value, with changes recognised in profit or loss

(2) Shares whose fair value cannot be measured reliably are measured at cost less impairment

(3) Commitments to receive a loan that cannot be settled net in cash are measured at cost (which may be $nil) less impairment.

The ED clarifies that the best evidence of fair value may be a price in a binding sale agreement in an arm's length transaction.

7.3.2 Other financial instruments

Other financial instruments are measured at fair value with changes recognised in profit or loss. The ED clarifies that some changes in the value of hedging instruments are recognised initially in other comprehensive income. Where the fair value of equity instruments cannot be measured reliably, cost less impairment is required.

Question   Financial Instruments

On 1 January 20X0, Grey Co acquires a bond for $900,000, incurring transaction costs of $50,000. Interest of $40,000 is receivable annually in arrears from 31 December 20X0 to 31 December 20X4, and the bond will be redeemed for $1.1million on 31 December 20X4. The effective interest rate is 6.96%.

What amounts are recognised in the financial statements at 31 December in each of the years to redemption, assuming that Grey Co applies the IFRS for SMEs including the provisions in respect of financial instruments?

Answer

The bond is a basic financial instrument (financial asset) which is initially measured at $900,000 plus the transaction costs of $50,000:

Year	b/f	Interest income at 6.96%	Cash received	C/f
20X0	950,000	66,120	(40,000)	976,120
20X1	976,120	67,938	(40,000)	1,004,058
20X2	1,004,058	69,882	(40,000)	1,033,940
20X3	1,033,940	71,962	(40,000)	1,065,902
20X4	1,065,902	74,186	(1,140,088)	0

Extracts from the relevant financial statements are:

Statement of financial position at 31 December

	20X0	20X1	20X2	20X3	20X4
Financial asset	976,120	1,004,058	1,033,940	1,065,902	0

Statement of profit or loss and other comprehensive income for the year ended 31 December

	20X0	20X1	20X2	20X3	20X4
Interest receivable	66,120	67,938	69,882	71,962	74,186

7.4 Impairment testing

Basic instruments measured at amortised cost must be assessed for evidence of impairment at the end of each reporting period. Any impairment loss is recognised in profit or loss immediately. An impairment loss may be reversed if the loss is decreased due to an event after recognition of the impairment.

Entities should also apply this guidance on impairment testing to other financial instruments measured at cost less impairment.

7.5 Derecognition

For both basic and other financial instruments the following derecognition rules are applied:

- Financial assets are derecognised when contractual rights to cash flows expire, substantially all risks and rewards are transferred or control is transferred, even where some risks and rewards are retained.
- Financial liabilities are derecognised when the obligation is discharged, cancelled or expires.

7.6 Disclosure

The same disclosure requirements apply to both basic and other financial instruments:

- Carrying value of each category of financial asset/liability (FVTPL, cost less impairment, amortised cost)
- Details of debt instruments such as interest rate and maturity
- The basis for determining fair value where a financial instrument is measured at fair value
- Details of financial assets which have been transferred but not derecognised
- Details of collateral
- Defaults and breaches on loans payable
- Items of income, expense, gains and losses

In this area, the volume of disclosures is significantly less than that required by full IFRS.

8 Assets

FAST FORWARD

> The IFRS for SMEs requires that all PPE is held under the cost model and all investment property is held under the fair value model provided that fair value can be reliably measured without undue cost or effort.

The IFRS for SMEs deals with assets in sections on inventories, investment property, property, plant and equipment, intangible assets other than goodwill, leases, borrowing costs, and impairment of assets.

8.1 Inventories

The requirements of the IFRS for SMEs are consistent with the requirements of IAS 2 *Inventories* in respect of accounting for inventories. In particular:

- Inventories are measured at the lower of cost and net realisable value
- Cost is established using an actual cost basis, FIFO or weighted average cost.

8.2 Investment property

IAS 40 *Investment Property* allows entities to choose whether to apply the cost model or fair value model to their investment properties. The IFRS for SMEs removes this choice, requiring that where reliable measurement of a fair value is available, the fair value model is applied.

Therefore investment properties are carried at fair value in the statement of financial position with gains and losses recognised in profit or loss.

The standard does provide an exemption from the requirement to measure at fair value on the grounds of 'undue cost or effort'. If it is the case that establishing fair values would involve undue cost or effort, investment properties are accounted for in accordance with Section 17 on property, plant and equipment.

Unlike IAS 40, the IFRS for SMEs does not provide extensive guidance on transfers in and out of the investment property category.

8.3 Property, plant and equipment

Although the IFRS for SMEs bases Section 17 on IAS 16 *Property, Plant and Equipment*, there are a number of differences between the requirements of the two:

- As the IFRS for SMEs omits the topic of assets held for sale, these fall within the scope of Section 17.
- All property, plant and equipment is measured using the cost model; there is no option to revalue.
- A review of residual values, useful lives and depreciation methods is only required where there is a significant change in the asset or how it is used.
- Component depreciation of complex assets is only required where major parts of an asset have 'significantly different patterns of consumption of economic benefits'.

8.4 Intangible assets other than goodwill

FAST FORWARD

> The IFRS for SMEs does not permit internally generated development costs to be capitalised. All intangible assets must be amortised over a finite useful life.

Most of the requirements of the IFRS for SMEs mirror those contained within IAS 38 *Intangible Assets*. There are three notable exceptions:

(1) The IFRS for SMEs requires all internally generated intangible assets, including development costs, to be recognised in profit or loss. Capitalisation of these amounts is not permitted.

(2) The standard requires all intangible assets to be amortised over a finite life, which is assumed to be ten years unless an entity can estimate a different life reliably. The ED changes this to a maximum of ten years.

(3) The revaluation model is not available for intangible assets.

8.5 Leases

IFRS 16 has not amended the treatment of leases in the IFRS for SMEs. The requirements of the IFRS for SMEs are broadly in line with those of IAS 17 *Leases*, however, unlike IAS 17, the IFRS for SMEs does not require the straight-line method to be used for operating leases where payments to the lessor are structured to increase with general inflation.

8.5.1 Example: Operating leases

Reindeer Co leases office space from Moose Co for five years under an operating lease. The lease payments are structured to reflect an expected 10% general inflation rate over the term of the lease as follows:

Year 1 $100,000

Year 2 $110,000

Year 3 $121,000

Year 4 $133,000

Year 5 $146,000

A rent expense equal to the amounts shown above is recognised by Reindeer Co in the relevant year. If escalating payments are not structured to reflect general inflation, then an equal amount of $122,000 is recognised in profit or loss each year. This is calculated as the sum of the five payments divided by five years.

8.6 Borrowing costs

FAST FORWARD All borrowing costs are expensed as incurred under the IFRS for SMEs.

Under IAS 23 *Borrowing Costs*, all eligible borrowing costs incurred in relation to qualifying assets must be capitalised. The IFRS for SMEs, however, requires all borrowing costs to be expensed as incurred.

8.7 Impairment of assets

The IFRS for SMEs states that:

- **Inventories are impaired** when their selling price less costs to complete and sell is less than carrying value;
- **Other assets are impaired** when their recoverable amount is less than their carrying amount.

Guidance on when an impairment may have arisen and how recoverable amount is calculated is generally consistent with IAS 36 *Impairment of Assets*, although unlike full IFRS, the IFRS for SMEs has no requirement to test goodwill and intangible assets not available for use for impairment annually.

Like IAS 36, the IFRS for SMEs requires that goodwill is allocated to the CGUs that are expected to benefit from the synergies of the combination for the purpose of impairment testing. The IFRS for SMEs states that if an allocation is not possible:

- The acquired entity is tested as a whole for impairment where it has not been integrated into the existing business; or
- The entire group is tested where the acquired business has been integrated.

The issue of corporate assets is not dealt with in the IFRS for SMEs.

9 Liabilities

Section 21 of the IFRS for SMEs deals with provisions and contingencies and Section 22 deals with liabilities and equities.

9.1 Provisions and contingencies

The requirements of the IFRS for SMEs on the recognition and measurement of provisions and contingencies are consistent with IAS 37 *Provisions, Contingent Liabilities and Contingent Assets*. This section of the standard also includes an appendix of examples which are similar to those in the full standard.

9.2 Liabilities and equity

This section of the IFRS for SMEs is derived from:

- IAS 1 *Presentation of Financial Statements*
- IAS 32 *Financial Instruments: Presentation*
- IFRIC 2 *Members' Shares in Co-operative Entities and Similar Instruments*
- IFRIC 17 *Distributions of Non-cash Assets to Owners*

Guidance is provided for classifying financial instruments as either equity or liabilities in line with IAS 32, this guidance includes certain puttable instruments as equity.

9.2.1 Accounting for original issue of shares

Section 22 provides guidance on accounting for shares when first issued as follows:

- Amounts owed in respect of shares already issued are presented as an offset to equity rather than as an asset.

- Where cash is received prior to the issue of shares, an increase in equity is reported only where the cash is not repayable.

- An increase in equity is not reported where equity instruments have been subscribed for but not issued and payment has not been received.

- Equity instruments are measured at the fair value of cash or other resources received or receivable net of the direct costs of issue.

These principles are also extended to apply to the sale of options, rights and warrants.

9.2.2 Other issues

This Section of the IFRS for SMEs also:

- Clarifies that bonus issues do not result in any change to total equity.

- Requires a split-accounting approach to compound instruments (as required by IAS 32). The ED clarifies that the liability component is then accounted for in the same way as a similar standalone financial liability.

- Requires that the fair value of consideration provided for treasury shares (equity instruments that have been issued and subsequently reacquired by an entity) is deducted from equity.

- Requires that the fair value of distributions to owners are deducted from equity.

- Requires that the fair value of non-cash distributions declared are recognised as a liability with changes in fair value recognised in equity.

- Mirrors the requirements of IFRS 10 by requiring that changes in a parent's controlling interest in a subsidiary that do not result in a loss of control are treated as transactions with equity holders in their capacity as equity holders.

10 Other topics

The remaining sections of the IFRS for SMEs deal with revenue, government grants, share-based payment, employee benefits, income tax, foreign currency translation and hyperinflation, events after the end of the reporting period, related party disclosures and transition to the IFRS for SMEs.

10.1 Revenue

The guidance contained within Section 23 of the IFRS for SMEs is generally consistent with the current Standard IAS 18 *Revenue*. It also incorporates the current requirements based on IAS 11 *Construction Contracts*, IFRIC 13 *Customer Loyalty Programmes* and an example based on IFRIC 15 *Agreements for the Construction of Real Estate*.

This section of the standard is one of three with an appendix. The appendix contains similar examples of the application of the guidance on accounting for revenue to those contained in the appendix to IAS 18.

10.2 Government grants

> **FAST FORWARD**
>
> The IFRS for SMEs simplifies the accounting requirements in respect of government grants.

The IFRS for SMEs simplifies the IAS 20 *Accounting for Government Grants and Disclosure of Government Assistance* requirements with regard to accounting for government grants. In particular:

- Grants are measured at the fair value of the asset received or receivable
- Grants that do not impose future performance conditions are recognised in income when receivable
- Grants that do impose future performance conditions are recognised in income when the performance conditions are met
- Grants received before the revenue recognition criteria are satisfied are recognised as a liability

The IFRS for SMEs does not deal with the issues of government assistance, non-monetary government grants or the repayment of government grants.

10.3 Share-based payments

The accounting guidance provided in the IFRS for SMEs in respect of share-based payments is consistent with IFRS 2 *Share-based Payment*, albeit with simplified rules for measuring the fair value of equity instruments granted.

10.4 Employee benefits

> **FAST FORWARD**
>
> The measurement of a defined benefit pension scheme obligation is simplified if measurement using the projected unit credit method involves undue cost or effort.

The IFRS for SMEs, like IAS 19 *Employee Benefits*, provides guidance on accounting for short-term employee benefits, long-term benefits other than pensions, termination benefits and post-employment benefits. The prescribed accounting treatment for the first three types of benefit is consistent with IAS 19. In the case of post-employment benefits, and specifically defined benefit pension schemes, the accounting treatment is simplified.

In particular, in measurement of the defined benefit obligation, the projected unit credit method need only be used where it does not involve undue cost or effort. Otherwise, the measurement of the obligation can be simplified with factors such as estimated future salary increases and expected service of current employees ignored.

10.5 Income tax

> **FAST FORWARD**
>
> The IFRS for SMEs is based on IAS 12 with some simplifications. It requires a valuation allowance in respect of deferred tax assets. The ED makes substantial changes to this section of the IFRS, bringing it back into line with IAS 12 (see below).

Section 29 of the IFRS for SMEs is derived from IAS 12 *Income Taxes* but includes a number of simplifications, including reduced disclosures, and also reflects certain provisions of the 2009 exposure draft *Income Tax*, including tax basis and a 'valuation allowance'.

The guidance within Section 29 in respect of current tax mirrors that of IAS 12, although where the IFRS for SMEs specifically prohibits the discounting of current taxes, IAS 12 is silent.

The guidance on deferred tax differs in certain aspects from that within IAS 12, and the remainder of this section therefore focuses on deferred tax and those differences.

10.5.1 Definitions

Section 29 defines deferred tax assets and liabilities and temporary differences in the same way as IAS 12, however the **tax basis** (tax base) is determined based on **recovery through sale** at carrying amount whereas IAS 12 considers the expected manner of recovery or settlement (use, sale or a combination of both) in order to determine tax base. The ED removes the reference to recovery through sale, bringing the IFRS into line with IAS 12.

10.5.2 Recognition and measurement

The IFRS for SMEs requirements in respect of recognition and measurement differ from full IFRS in the following ways:

1. The IFRS for SMEs requires that deferred tax is provided for all temporary differences and the carry forward of unused tax losses with a few **exceptions** such as:

    - The initial recognition of goodwill; and
    - Temporary differences arising from permanent foreign investments in subsidiaries, branches, joint ventures and associates.

    In full IFRS the requirement is similar, although there is an additional exemption for the initial recognition of an asset or liability in a transaction that is not a business combination and affects neither accounting nor taxable profit at the time of the transaction. In addition the exception in IAS 12 relating to temporary differences in investments in subsidiaries, branches, joint ventures and associates relates to both foreign and domestic investments. The ED removes these distinctions, bringing the IFRS into line with IAS 12.

2. Under the IFRS for SMEs a deferred tax asset is recognised in full and then reduced by a **'valuation allowance'** so that the net carrying amount of the deferred tax asset is equal to the highest amount that is more likely than not to be recovered. IAS 12 does not include the concept of a 'valuation allowance', instead requiring that a deferred tax asset is only recognised to the extent that future taxable profits will be available to enable recovery of the deferred tax asset. Practically the net carrying amount of the asset is likely to be the same. The ED removes the concept of valuation allowance, and reverts to the language used in IAS 12.

3. In practice tax authorities will not always accept the amounts reported to them, resulting in an uncertain tax position. The IFRS for SMEs requires that all tax positions are measured using the **probability-weighted average amount of all possible outcomes**, assuming that the tax authorities will review the amounts reported and have full knowledge of all relevant information. There is no equivalent requirement in IAS 12, and no threshold is applied to this requirement in the IFRS for SMEs, making this area particularly contentious. This requirement is removed in the ED.

10.5.3 Omitted topics

The IFRS for SMEs does not deal with deferred tax in respect of:

- Assets carried at fair value. (The ED includes it.)
- The reassessment of unrecognised deferred tax assets. (The ED includes it.)
- Deferred tax arising from a business combination. (The ED includes it.)

10.6 Foreign currency translation and hyperinflation

Section 30 of the IFRS for SMEs deals with foreign currency translation. It provides guidance on determining functional currency, recording foreign currency transactions and translating foreign currency accounts into the presentation currency. Its requirements are similar to those of IAS 21 *The Effects of Changes in Foreign Exchange Rates*, although the IFRS for SMEs does not allow gains and losses of a net investment in a foreign entity that are initially recognised in other comprehensive income to be reclassified to profit or loss.

Section 31 deals with hyperinflation, and this is a simplified version of the guidance contained within IAS 29 *Financial Reporting in Hyperinflationary Economies.*

10.7 Events after the end of the reporting period

There are no differences between Section 32 of the IFRS for SMEs, which deals with events after the end of the reporting period and the requirements of IAS 10 *Events After the Reporting Period.*

10.8 Related party disclosures

IAS 24 *Related Party Disclosures* is concerned with defining a related party and prescribing the required disclosures in relation to them. Section 33 of the IFRS for SMEs reduces the disclosure requirements of full IFRS, in particular requiring disclosure of the compensation of key management personnel in aggregate only.

10.9 Transition to the IFRS for SMEs

The final section of the IFRS for SMEs is based on IFRS 1 *First-time Adoption of IFRS* and provides guidance for entities who are applying the IFRS for SMEs for the first time.

A number of exemptions are available within the full standard which may be applied when preparing a first set of financial statements under IFRS. The IFRS for SMEs includes all of these exemptions as well as a number of additional exemptions and relaxations. In total there are five mandatory exemptions and 12 optional exemptions. There is also a general exemption from retrospective application where this would be impracticable. In this instance 'impracticable' is defined as being 'when the entity cannot apply it after making every reasonable effort to do so'.

11 Updating the IFRS for SMEs

The IFRS for SMEs was issued in July 2009 and at that time the IASB expected to undertake a thorough review of the standard and experience in applying it after two years.

In May 2015, the IASB completed a comprehensive review of the IFRS for SMEs and made limited amendments to the standard.

The **majority** of the amendments **clarify existing requirements** of the IFRS for SMEs or add supporting guidance, and so **will not change the way entities account for certain transactions and events**. In many cases each amendment affects only a few words or sentences in the standard.

The two major exceptions are the following key changes:

(a) SMEs are now permitted to use a revaluation model for property, plant and equipment.

(b) The main recognition and measurement requirements for deferred income tax are aligned with full IFRS.

The IASB expects further revisions to the IFRS for SMEs to be limited to once every three years.

Chapter roundup

- The IFRS for SMEs was developed to provide a simpler accounting regime within the IFRS framework for non-publicly listed entities. Other than an option to use IAS 39 in respect of financial instruments, it is a stand-alone standard.

- The IFRS for SMEs defines those entities which are eligible to use it as entities which do not have public accountability and which publish general purpose financial statements.

- The standard is organised into 35 sections, each dealing with a specific area of accounting.

- The IFRS for SMEs includes a section on concepts and pervasive principles which is an abbreviated form of the *Conceptual Framework*.

- The IFRS for SMEs is generally consistent with IAS 1 in respect of requirements for the presentation of financial statements, although there is some relaxation of the full IFRS requirements.

- Where the IFRS for SMEs does not specifically address a transaction, the requirements of the IFRS for SMEs in relation to similar issues or the Concepts and pervasive principles section of the standard are considered.

- The IFRS for SMEs includes a different definition of control from IFRS 10, however consolidation procedures are largely the same.

- Investments in associates and JCEs may be accounted for using the cost model, equity accounting or the fair value model.

- Under the IFRS for SMEs, the NCI is not taken into account in the calculation of goodwill, acquisition costs form part of the cost of the combination and contingent consideration is only included where it is probable of payment and can be reliably measured.

- The IFRS for SMEs contains two sections on accounting for financial instruments: basic financial instruments and other financial instruments. Basic financial instruments are normally measured at amortised cost and other financial instruments at fair value.

- The IFRS for SMEs requires that all PPE is held under the cost model and all investment property is held under the fair value model provided that fair value can be reliably measured without undue cost or effort.

- The IFRS for SMEs does not permit internally generated development costs to be capitalised. All intangible assets must be amortised over a finite useful life.

- All borrowing costs are expensed as incurred under the IFRS for SMEs.

- The IFRS for SMEs simplifies the accounting requirements in respect of government grants.

- The measurement of a defined benefit pension scheme obligation is simplified if measurement using the projected unit credit method involves undue cost or effort.

- The IFRS for SMEs is based on IAS 12 with some simplifications. It requires a valuation allowance in respect of deferred tax assets. The ED makes substantial changes to this section of the IFRS, bringing it back into line with IAS 12.

Quick quiz

1. Which entities can use the IFRS for SMEs?
2. What topics are omitted from the IFRS for SMEs?
3. How many sections is the IFRS for SMEs split into?
4. Under what circumstances may an entity present a statement of income and retained earnings rather than a statement of comprehensive income and statement of changes in equity?
5. How does the cost of a business combination under the IFRS for SMEs differ from that under full IFRS?
6. How are basic financial instruments normally measured?
7. How are investment properties measured under the IFRS for SMEs?
8. What is the treatment of borrowing costs under the IFRS for SMEs?
9. How are the requirements of IAS 19 simplified in the IFRS for SMEs?
10. What is a valuation allowance in respect of deferred tax?

Answers to quick quiz

1. Those companies:
   - Which are not publicly accountable (ie not listed on a public market (or in the process of listing) and which do not hold assets for a wide range of third parties in a fiduciary capacity) and
   - Which prepare general purpose financial statements.

2. Complex topics which are not relevant to smaller private entities are omitted. These include segment reporting, interim reporting, earnings per share, assets held for sale and insurance contracts.

3. It is split into 35 sections.

4. When the only changes to equity are profit or loss, the payment of dividends and retrospective adjustments.

5. Acquisition costs form part of the cost of consideration whereas they must be expensed under full IFRS. In addition contingent consideration is only included where it will probably be paid; under full IFRS it is always included at fair value.

6. At amortised cost.

7. At fair value provided that it can be reliably measured and does not involve undue cost or effort.

8. All borrowing costs are expensed as incurred.

9. The projected unit credit method need not be applied if this results in undue cost or effort.

10. A valuation allowance is an amount that reduces a deferred tax asset to the highest amount that is more likely than not to be recovered.

End of chapter question

Tramwell

Tramwell Co is an unlisted, wholly owned subsidiary of Ramses Co. Ramses is listed on a national stock exchange, and is required to apply IFRS in preparing its financial statements.

Tramwell currently prepares its financial statements using local GAAP, however the Finance Director has heard that the IFRS for SMEs has recently been issued and is considering changing from local GAAP to the IFRS for SMEs.

The most recent statement of financial position of Tramwell, is given below:

	$'000	$'000
Non-current assets		
Property, plant and equipment		3,470
Investment properties		1,100
Development costs		220
		4,790
Current assets		
Inventories	321	
Financial assets (cost)	400	
Receivables	245	
Cash	63	
	1,029	
Current liabilities		
Current tax	114	
Payables	321	
	435	
Net current assets		594
Total assets less current liabilities		5,384

	$'000	$'000
Long-term liabilities		
Deferred tax		(256)
Bank loan		(400)
Net assets		4,728
Share capital		500
Retained earnings		2,668
Investment property reserve		360
Revaluation reserve		1,200
Equity and reserves		4,728

Required:

Prepare a briefing note for the Finance Director which includes advice on:

(a) Whether Tramwell can adopt the IFRS for SMEs in preparing its financial statements
(b) How accounting policies may change compared to local GAAP
(c) The practical aspects of adopting the IFRS for SMEs

Your advice should relate specifically to the circumstances of Tramwell.

Note. you are not required to address first-time adoption or the transition provisions of the IFRS for SMEs.

(Total 20 marks)

Ratio and trend analysis

Topic list	Syllabus reference
1 Sources of information and the role of regulation	13.2
2 The broad categories of ratios	13.2
3 Profitability and return on capital	13.2
4 Liquidity and working capital	13.2
5 Long-term solvency: Debt and gearing/leverage	13.2
6 Shareholders' investment ratios	13.2

Introduction

Ratio analysis is an important management tool to assess the performance of an entity over time, or to assess the performance of one or more entities.

PART C ACCOUNTING AND REPORTING TECHNIQUES

1 Sources of information and the role of regulation

The financial statements of a business are designed to provide users with information about its performance and financial position. The bare figures, however, are not particularly useful and it is only through **comparisons** (usually of ratios) that their significance can be established. Comparisons may be made with previous financial periods, with other similar businesses or with averages for the particular industry. The choice will depend on the purpose for which the comparison is being made and the information that is available.

Various groups are interested in the performance and financial position of a company:

(a) **Management** will use comparisons to ensure that the business is performing efficiently and according to plan

(b) **Employees**, trade unions and so on, to review future employment prospects

(c) **Government**, for statistical and tax-raising purposes

(d) Present and potential **investors** will assess the company with a view to judging whether it is a sound investment

(e) **Lenders** and **suppliers** will want to judge its creditworthiness

This text is concerned with financial rather than management accounting and the ratios discussed here are therefore likely to be calculated by external users. The following sources of information are readily available to external users.

- Published financial statements and interim statements
- Documents filed as required by company legislation
- Statistics published by the government
- Other published sources eg *Investors Chronicle*, *The Economist*, *Wall Street Journal*

1.1 Financial analysis

The **lack of detailed information** available to the outsider is a considerable disadvantage in undertaking ratio analysis. The first difficulty is that there may simply be insufficient data to calculate all of the required ratios. A second concerns the availability of a suitable 'yardstick' with which the calculated ratios may be compared.

1.1.1 Inter-temporal analysis

Looking first at inter-temporal or trend analysis (comparisons for the same business over time), some of the **problems** include the following.

- Changes in the nature of the business
- Unrealistic depreciation rates under historical cost accounting
- The changing value of the functional currency
- Changes in accounting policies

Other factors will include changes in government incentive packages, changes from purchasing equipment to leasing it, and so on.

1.1.2 Cross-sectoral analysis

When undertaking 'cross-sectoral' analysis (making comparisons with other companies) the position is even more difficult because of the problem of identifying companies that are comparable. **Comparability** between companies may be impaired due to the following reasons.

(a) Different degrees of diversification

(b) Different production and purchasing policies (if an investor was analysing the smaller car manufacturers, he would find that some of them buy in engines from one of the 'majors' whilst others develop and manufacture their own)

23: RATIO AND TREND ANALYSIS

(c) Different financing policies (eg leasing as opposed to buying)

(d) Different accounting policies (one of the most serious problems particularly in relation to non-current assets and inventory valuation)

(e) Different effects of government incentives

The major **intragroup comparison organisations** (whose results are intended for the use of participating companies and are not generally available) go to considerable length to adjust financial statements to comparable bases. The external user will rarely be in a position to make such adjustments. Although the position is improved by increases in disclosure requirements, direct comparisons between companies will inevitably, on occasion, continue to give rise to misleading results.

1.2 Social and political considerations

Social considerations tend to be short-lived or 'fashionable' and therefore each set of statements can be affected by a different movement or fad. In recent years, the social aspect much in evidence has been that of environmental issues. Companies have gone for a 'green' image, although this has been more in evidence in glossy pictures than in the financial statements themselves.

Political considerations may be more far reaching. The regulatory regime may be instituted by statutes, but often self-regulation is encouraged through bodies such as a stock exchange.

1.3 Multinational companies

Multinational companies have great difficulties sometimes because of the need to comply with **legislation** in a large number of countries. As well as different reporting requirements, different rules of incorporation exist, as well as different directors' rules, tax legislation and so on. Sometimes the local rules can be so harsh that companies will avoid them altogether. In California, for example, multinational companies with operations there are taxed on their **world wide** profits, not just their US profits. Local tax regimes may also require information about the group as a whole because of the impact of internal transfer pricing on tax.

Different local reporting requirements will also make **consolidation** more difficult. The results of subsidiaries must be translated not only to the company's functional currency but also using the accounting rules used by the parent. The requirement of IFRS is to use 'uniform accounting policies'.

2 The broad categories of ratios

FAST FORWARD

> Make sure that you can **define** all the ratios. Look out for variations in definitions of ratios which might appear in questions.

Exam focus point

> Questions are unlikely to be standard 'ratio calculation and comment' type of questions as these are examined at Paper 11. Instead, questions could examine the impact of a particular issue with group accounting; for example, the impact of reporting discontinued activities, disposing of an investment in a subsidiary or exchange gains/losses on the assessment of the group's overall performance. Questions could also (for example) ask for a comment on the impact on performance (group or individual company) of a change of accounting policy (see Chapter 18).

Ratio analysis involves **comparing one figure against another** to produce a ratio, and assessing whether the ratio indicates a weakness or strength in the company's affairs.

2.1 The broad categories of ratios

Broadly speaking, basic ratios can be grouped into five categories:

- Profitability and return
- Long-term solvency and stability
- Short-term solvency and liquidity

PART C ACCOUNTING AND REPORTING TECHNIQUES

- Efficiency (turnover ratios)
- Shareholders' investment ratios

Ratio analysis on its own is **not sufficient** for interpreting company financial statements; there are other items of information which should be looked at.

(a) The content of any **accompanying commentary** on the financial statements and other statements

(b) The age and nature of the **company's assets**

(c) Current and future **developments** in the company's markets, at home and overseas, recent acquisitions or disposals of subsidiaries by the parent

(d) Any other **noticeable features** of the financial statements, such as events after the reporting period, contingent liabilities, a qualified auditors' report, the company's taxation position

The following sections summarise what you already know about ratio analysis from your earlier studies. You should then perform the comprehensive questions given in this chapter. The following chapters look at more complex areas of analysis and interpretation, which build on the knowledge in this chapter.

3 Profitability and return on capital

One profit figure that should be calculated and compared over time is **PBIT, profit before interest and tax**, the amount of profit which the company earned before having to pay interest to the providers of loan capital. By providers of loan capital, we usually mean longer-term loan capital, such as debentures and medium-term bank loans, which will be shown in the statement of financial position as 'non-current liabilities'. Also, tax is affected by unusual variations which have a distorting effect.

Profit before interest and tax is therefore:

(a) The profit on operating activities before taxation, plus
(b) Interest charges on long-term loan capital.

Published financial statements do not always give sufficient detail on interest payable to determine how much is interest on long-term finance.

3.1 A warning about comments on profit margin and asset turnover

It might be tempting to think that a high profit margin is good, and a low asset turnover means sluggish trading. In broad terms, this is so. But there is **a trade-off** between profit margin and asset turnover, and you cannot look at one without allowing for the other.

(a) A high profit margin means a high profit per $1 of sales, but if this also means that sales prices are high, there is a strong possibility that sales turnover will be depressed, and so asset turnover lower.

(b) A high asset turnover means that the company is generating a lot of sales, but to do this it might have to keep its prices down and so accept a low profit margin per $1 of sales.

> **Knowledge brought forward from earlier studies**

> *Profitability*
>
> *Return on capital employed*
>
> $$\text{ROCE} = \frac{\text{PBIT}}{\text{Capital employed}} = \frac{\text{PBIT}}{\text{Total assets less current liabilities}}$$
>
> When **interpreting** ROCE look for the following.
>
> - How risky is the business?
> - How capital intensive is it?
> - What ROCE do similar businesses have?

The following **considerations** are important.
- Comparison from year to year
- Comparison to similar companies
- Comparison with current market borrowing rates

Problems: which items to consider to achieve comparability:

- Revaluation surplus – where one company adopts a revaluation policy and another doesn't, ROCE in the company which revalues will be depressed. The capital employed of this company can be normalised by deducting the revaluation reserve and recalculating ROCE based on the new amount.

- Choices, eg measurement of the non-controlling interest at fair value or as a proportion of net assets. Measurement at fair value will increase goodwill and so capital employed and in turn depress ROCE. This choice is made on an acquisition by acquisition basis, meaning that one company may have some 'full' goodwill and some 'partial' goodwill in their statement of financial position.

- Investments and related income – investments in associates and joint ventures which are equity accounted and the associated income are easily excluded from consolidated financial statements in order to make results comparable over time and from group to group.

Return on equity

$$ROE = \frac{\text{Profit after tax and pref div}}{\text{Ordinary share capital + reserves}} \%$$

This gives a more **restricted view** of capital than ROCE, but the same principles apply.

Secondary ratios

Profit margin × Asset turnover = ROCE

Profit margin

$$\text{Profit margin} = \frac{\text{PBIT}}{\text{Revenue}}\% \qquad \text{Gross profit margin} = \frac{\text{Gross profit}}{\text{Revenue}}\%$$

It is useful to compare profit margin to gross profit % to investigate movements which do not match. Take into account:

- Gross profit margin
    - Sales prices, sales volume and sales mix
    - Purchase prices and related costs (discount, carriage etc)
    - Production costs, both direct (materials, labour) and indirect (overheads both fixed and variable)
    - Inventory levels and inventory valuation, including errors, cut-off and stock-out costs

- Profit margin
    - Sales expenses in relation to sales levels
    - Administrative expenses, including salary levels
    - Distribution expenses in relation to sales levels

    Depreciation should be considered as a separate item for each expense category.

Asset turnover

$$\text{Asset turnover} = \frac{\text{Revenue}}{\text{Total assets less current liabilities}}$$

This measures the **efficiency** of the use of assets. Amend to just non-current assets for capital intensive businesses.

PART C ACCOUNTING AND REPORTING TECHNIQUES

4 Liquidity and working capital

Profitability is of course an important aspect of a company's performance and debt or gearing is another. Neither, however, addresses directly the key issue of liquidity in the **short term**.

Liquidity is the amount of cash a company can put its hands on quickly to settle its debts (and possibly to meet other unforeseen demands for cash payments too). Liquid funds consist of the following.

- Cash
- Short-term investments for which there is a ready market (as distinct from shares held in subsidiaries or associated companies)
- Fixed-term deposits with a bank (eg a six-month high-interest deposit)
- Trade receivables (because they will pay what they owe within a short period of time)
- Bills of exchange receivable (because these represent cash due to be received within a relatively short period of time)

A company can obtain liquid assets from sources other than sales, such as the issue of shares for cash, a new loan or the sale of non-current assets. But a company cannot rely on these at all times, and in general obtaining liquid funds depends on making sales and profits. Even so, **profits do not always lead to increases in liquidity**. This is mainly because funds generated from trading may be immediately invested in working capital or non-current assets, or paid out as dividends.

Efficiency ratios indicate how well a business is controlling aspects of its working capital.

Knowledge brought forward from earlier studies

Liquidity and working capital

Can a company meet its short-term debts?

Current ratio

$$\text{Current ratio} = \frac{\text{Current assets}}{\text{Current liabilities}}$$

Assume assets realised at book value ∴ theoretical. 2:1 acceptable? 1.5:1? It depends on the industry.

Quick ratio

$$\text{Quick ratio (acid test)} = \frac{\text{Current assets - Inventory}}{\text{Current liabilities}}$$

Eliminates illiquid and subjectively valued inventory. Care is needed: it could be high if **overtrading** with receivables, but no cash. Is 1:1 OK? Many supermarkets operate on 0.3.

Collection period

$$\text{Average collection period} = \frac{\text{Trade receivables}}{\text{Credit turnover}} \times 365$$

Is it **consistent** with quick/current ratio? If not, investigate.

Inventory turnover period

$$\text{Inventory turnover} = \frac{\text{Cost of sales}}{\text{Inventory}} \qquad \text{Inventory turnover period} = \frac{\text{Inventory}}{\text{Cost of sales}} \times 365$$

Higher the better? But remember:

- Lead times
- Seasonal fluctuations in orders
- Alternative uses of warehouse space
- Bulk buying discounts
- Likelihood of inventory perishing or becoming obsolete

Accounts payable payment period

$$\text{Accounts payable payment period} = \frac{\text{Trade payables}}{\text{Purchases}} \times 365$$

Use **cost of sales** if purchases are not disclosed.

Cash cycle

- Cash flow timing does not match sales/cost of sales timing as credit is taken
- Holding inventory delays the time between payments for goods and sales receipts

Reasons for changes in liquidity

- **Credit control** efficiency altered
- Altering **payment period** of creditors as a source of funding
- Reduce **inventory holdings** to maintain liquidity

5 Long-term solvency: Debt and gearing/leverage

Debt and gearing ratios are concerned with a company's **long-term stability**: how much the company owes in relation to its size, whether it is getting into heavier debt or improving its situation, and whether its debt burden seems heavy or light.

(a) When a company is heavily in debt, banks and other potential lenders may be unwilling to advance further funds.

(b) When a company is earning only a modest profit before interest and tax, and has a heavy debt burden, there will be very little profit left (if any) over for shareholders after the interest charges have been paid. And so if interest rates were to go up (on bank overdrafts and so on) or the company were to borrow even more, it might soon be incurring interest charges in excess of PBIT. This might eventually lead to the liquidation of the company.

Knowledge brought forward from earlier studies

Debt and gearing/leverage

Debt/equity

$$\text{Debt / equity ratio} = \frac{\text{Interest bearing net debt}}{\text{Equity}} \% \quad (>100\% = \text{high})$$

Or

$$\frac{\text{Interest bearing net debt}}{\text{Equity} + \text{interest bearing net debt}} \% \quad (>50\% = \text{high})$$

There is **no definitive answer**; elements included are subjective. The following should be considered

- Convertible loan stock must be split between debt and equity, however fixed interest is paid on the principal until such time as conversion arises. It may therefore be argued that inclusion of the whole amount as debt would give a better indication of gearing levels and capacity to take on more borrowings.
- Preferred shares should be accounted for as a liability where they are redeemable. Incorrect exclusion of these from debt will improve gearing.

> - Full goodwill based on measurement of the non-controlling interest at fair value will result in a more favourable gearing ratio than partial goodwill based on measurement of the non-controlling interest as a proportion of net assets.
> - The capitalisation of development expenditure will increase equity and so improves the gearing ratio. This is not an accounting choice, however it is fair to say that judgement is employed when applying the recognition criteria.
> - A policy of revaluing property will improve gearing by boosting equity. Where a revaluation exercise has been undertaken recently, the impact on gearing is particularly beneficial (assuming rising values).
>
> *Gearing/leverage*
>
> $$\text{Gearing ratio} = \frac{\text{Prior charge capital}}{\text{Total capital}} \qquad \text{Leverage} = \frac{\text{Total capital}}{\text{Prior charge capital}}$$
>
> *Interest cover*
>
> $$\text{Interest cover} = \frac{\text{PBIT (incl int receivable)}}{\text{Interest payable}}$$
>
> Is this a better way to **measure gearing** or **leverage**? Company must generate enough profit to cover interest. Is a figure of 3+ safe?

5.1 The implications of high or low gearing

Gearing or leverage is, amongst other things, an attempt to quantify the **degree of risk** involved in holding equity shares in a company, both in terms of the company's ability to remain in business and in terms of expected ordinary dividends from the company. The problem with a highly geared company is that, by definition, there is a lot of debt. Debt generally carries a fixed rate of interest (or fixed rate of dividend if in the form of preferred shares), hence there is a given (and large) amount to be paid out from profits to holders of debt before arriving at a residue available for distribution to the holders of equity.

The more highly geared the company, the greater the risk that little (if anything) will be available to distribute by way of dividend to the ordinary shareholders. The more highly geared the company, the greater the percentage change in profit available for ordinary shareholders for any given percentage change in profit before interest and tax. This means that there will be greater **volatility** of amounts available for ordinary shareholders, and presumably therefore greater volatility in dividends paid to those shareholders, where a company is highly geared. That is the risk. You may do extremely well or extremely badly without a particularly large movement in the PBIT of the company.

The risk of a company's ability to remain in business was referred to earlier. Gearing is relevant to this. A highly geared company has a large amount of interest to pay annually. If those borrowings are 'secured' in any way (and debentures in particular are often secured), then the holders of the debt are perfectly entitled to force the company to realise assets to pay their interest if funds are not available from other sources. Clearly, the more highly geared a company, the more likely this is to occur when and if profits fall. Note that problems related to '**off balance sheet**' **finance** hiding the level of gearing have gradually become rarer, due to standards such as IFRS 16 *Leases*.

Companies will only be able to increase their gearing if they have **suitable assets** to offer for security. Companies with assets which are depreciated rapidly or which are at high risk of obsolescence will be unable to offer sufficient security, eg computer software companies. On the other hand, a property company will have plenty of assets to offer as security whose value is fairly stable (but note the effect of a property slump).

Ideally, the following **gearing profiles** would apply, so that only certain types of company could have higher gearing.

Type of company	Assets	Profits
Highly geared companies	Holding value, long-term	Stable, steady trends
Low geared companies	Rapid depreciation/change	Erratic, volatile

5.2 The effect of GAAP on gearing/leverage

Variations in accounting policy can have a significant impact on gearing and it will be necessary to consider the individual policies of companies. The main areas which are likely to require consideration area as follows.

(a) Revaluation of non-current assets will have an impact on equity and it will be necessary to consider the frequency of such revaluations.

(b) The structure of group financial statements and methods of consolidation will also have a substantial impact on gearing. For example use of the full goodwill method will improve gearing by including the non-controlling interest within capital.

6 Shareholders' investment ratios

These are the ratios which help equity shareholders and other investors to assess the value and quality of an investment in the **ordinary shares** of a company.

The value of an investment in ordinary shares in a **listed company** is its market value, and so investment ratios must have regard not only to information in the company's financial statements, but also to the current share price.

Earnings per share is a valuable indicator of an ordinary share's performance and you should refer to Chapter 18 to revisit its calculation.

> **Knowledge brought forward from earlier studies**
>
> *Investors' ratios*
>
> Dividend yield
>
> $$\text{Dividend yield} = \frac{\text{Div per share}}{\text{Mid-market price}} \%$$
>
> - **Low yield**: perhaps the company retains a large proportion of profits to reinvest
> - **High yield**: this is a risky company or slow-growing
>
> Dividend cover
>
> $$\text{Dividend cover} = \frac{\text{EPS}}{\text{Dividend per share}}$$
>
> $$\text{Or } \frac{\text{Profit after tax and pref dividend}}{\text{Dividend per ordinary shares}}$$
>
> This shows **how safe the dividend is**, or the extent of profit retention. Variations are due to maintaining dividend when profits are declining.
>
> P/E ratio
>
> $$\text{P/E ratio} = \frac{\text{Mid-market price}}{\text{EPS}}$$
>
> The **higher the better** here: it reflects the confidence of the market. A rise in EPS may lead to an increase in P/E ratio (as further rises in EPS are anticipated in the future), but maybe not to same extent: look at the context of the market and industry norms.
>
> Earnings yield
>
> $$\text{Earnings yield} = \frac{\text{EPS}}{\text{Mid-market price}}$$
>
> This shows the dividend yield if there is no retention of profit. It allows you to compare companies with **different dividend payout policies**.

PART C ACCOUNTING AND REPORTING TECHNIQUES

> *Net assets per share*
>
> Net assets per share = $\dfrac{\text{Net assets}}{\text{No of shares}}$
>
> This is a **crude measure** of value of a company, liable to distortion.
>
> See also **EPS** and **dividend per share**

FAST FORWARD

Always remember that 'profit' and 'net assets' are fairly **arbitrary figures**, affected by different accounting policies and manipulation.

Financial analysis is a vital tool for **auditors**.

Question   Ratio analysis report

RST Co is considering purchasing an interest in its competitor XYZ Co. The managing director of RST Co has obtained the three most recent statement of profit or loss and other comprehensive income and statements of financial position of XYZ Co as shown below.

XYZ CO
STATEMENTS OF PROFIT OR LOSS AND OTHER COMPREHENSIVE INCOME FOR YEARS ENDED 31 DECEMBER

	20X6	20X7	20X8
	$'000	$'000	$'000
Revenue	18,000	18,900	19,845
Cost of sales	10,440	10,340	11,890
Gross profit	7,560	8,560	7,955
Distribution costs	1,565	1,670	1,405
Administrative expenses	1,409	1,503	1,591
Profit from operations	4,586	5,387	4,959
Interest payable on bank overdraft	104	215	450
Interest payable on 12% debentures	600	600	600
Profit before taxation	3,882	4,572	3,909
Income tax	1,380	2,000	1,838
Profit for the period	2,502	2,572	2,071

XYZ CO
STATEMENTS OF FINANCIAL POSITION AS AT 31 DECEMBER

	20X6		20X7		20X8	
	$'000	$'000	$'000	$'000	$'000	$'000
Assets						
Non-current assets						
Land and buildings	11,460		12,121		11,081	
Plant and machinery	8,896		9,020		9,130	
		20,356		21,141		20,211
Current assets						
Inventory	1,775		2,663		3,995	
Trade receivables	1,440		2,260		3,164	
Cash	50		53		55	
		3,265		4,976		7,214
		23,621		26,117		27,425

23: RATIO AND TREND ANALYSIS

	20X6		20X7		20X8	
	$'000	$'000	$'000	$'000	$'000	$'000
Equity and liabilities						
Equity						
Share capital	8,000		8,000		8,000	
Retained earnings	6,434		7,313		7,584	
		14,434		15,313		15,584
Non-current liabilities						
12% debentures 20Y1 – 20Y4		5,000		5,000		5,000
Current liabilities						
Trade payables	1,990		2,084		2,246	
Bank	1,300		2,300		3,400	
Taxation	897		1,420		1,195	
		4,187		5,804		6,841
		23,621		26,117		27,425

Required

Prepare a report for the managing director of RST Co commenting on the financial position and performance of XYZ Co and highlighting any areas that require further investigation.

(Marks will be awarded for ratios and other financial statistics where appropriate.)

Answer

To: MD of RST Co
From: An Accountant
Date: XX.XX.XX
Subject: *The financial position and performance of XYZ Co*

Introduction

This report has been prepared on the basis of the three most recent statements of profit or loss and other comprehensive income and statements of financial position of XYZ Co covering the years 20X6 to 20X8 inclusive. Ratio analysis used in this report is based on the calculations shown in the appendix attached.

Performance

Sales have increased at a steady 5% per annum over the three-year period.

In contrast, the gross profit percentage has increased from 42% in 20X6 to 45% in 20X7 before dropping back to 40% in 20X8. Similarly, operating profit as a percentage of sales was 26% in 20X6, 28.5% in 20X7 and 25% in 20X8. This may indicate some misallocation of costs between 20X7 and 20X8 and should be investigated or it may be indicative of a longer downward trend in profitability.

Return on capital employed, as one would expect, has shown a similar pattern with an increase in 20X7 with a subsequent fall in 20X8 to a level below that of 20X6.

Debt and liquidity

The debt ratio measures the ratio of a company's debt to its equity. Although we have no information as to the norm for the industry as a whole, the debt ratios appear reasonable. However, it should be noted that it has fallen slightly over the three-year period.

When reviewing XYZ Co's liquidity the situation has improved over the period. The current ratio measures a company's ability to meet its current liabilities out of current assets. A ratio of at least 1 should therefore be expected. XYZ Co did not meet this expectation in 20X6 and 20X7.

This ratio can be misleading as inventory is included in current assets. Because inventory can take some time to convert into liquid assets, a second ratio, the quick ratio, is calculated which excludes inventory. As can be seen, the quick ratio, although improving, is low and this shows that current liabilities cannot be met from current assets if inventory is excluded. As a major part of current liabilities is the bank overdraft, the company is obviously relying on the bank's continuing support with short-term funding. It would be useful to find out the terms of the bank funding and the projected cash flow requirements for future funding.

Efficiency ratios

The efficiency ratios, receivables ratio and inventory turnover, give a useful indication of how the company is managing its current assets.

As can be seen from the appendix the receivables collection period has increased over the three years from 29 days to 58 days. This may indicate that the company is failing to follow up its debts efficiently or that it has given increased credit terms to some or all of its customers.

Looking at inventory turnover, this has also risen from 62 days to 122 days. This may be an indication of over-stocking, stocking up on the expectation of a substantial sales increase or the holding of obsolete or slow-moving inventory items which should be written down. More investigation needs to be done on both receivables and inventory.

The financing of additional receivables and inventory has been achieved in the main through the bank overdraft as the trade payables figure has not increased significantly.

Conclusion

The review of the three year financial statements for XYZ Co has given rise to a number of queries which need to be resolved before a useful conclusion can be reached on the financial position and performance of XYZ Co. It may also be useful to compare XYZ Co's ratios to those of other companies in the same industry in order to obtain some idea of the industry norms.

APPENDIX TO MEMORANDUM

	20X6	20X7	20X8
% sales increase ((18,900/18,000) – 1) and (19,845(/18,900) – 1)		5%	5%
Gross profit % (7,560 as % of 18,000), (8,560 as % of 18,900) and (7,955 as % of 19,845)	42%	45%	40%
Operating profit % (4,586 as % of 18,000), (5,387 as % of 18,900) and (4,959 as % of 19,845)	25.5%	28.5%	25%

Return on capital employed

$$= \frac{\text{Profit before interest and tax}}{\text{Capital employed}} \times 100\%$$

	20X6	20X7	20X8
	$\frac{4{,}586 - 104}{14{,}434 + 5{,}000}$	$\frac{5{,}387 - 215}{15{,}313 + 5{,}000}$	$\frac{4{,}959 - 450}{15{,}584 + 5{,}000}$
	= 23%	= 25.5%	= 21.9%

Debt ratio

$$= \frac{\text{Debt}}{\text{Equity}} \times 100\%$$

	20X6	20X7	20X8
	$\frac{5{,}000}{14{,}434}$	$\frac{5{,}000}{15{,}313}$	$\frac{5{,}000}{15{,}584}$
	= 34.6%	= 32.7%	= 32.1%

Current ratio

$$= \frac{\text{Current assets}}{\text{Current liabilities}}$$

	20X6	20X7	20X8
	$\frac{3{,}265}{4{,}187}$	$\frac{4{,}976}{5{,}804}$	$\frac{7{,}214}{6{,}814}$
	= 0.78	= 0.86	= 1.06

Quick ratio

$$= \frac{\text{Current assets} - \text{inventory}}{\text{Current liabilities}}$$

	20X6	20X7	20X8
	$\frac{3{,}265 - 1{,}775}{4{,}187}$	$\frac{4{,}976 - 2{,}663}{5{,}804}$	$\frac{7{,}214 - 3{,}995}{6{,}814}$
	= 0.36	= 0.40	= 0.47

Receivables ratio

$$= \frac{\text{Trade receivables}}{\text{Sales}} \times 365 \text{ days}$$

	20X6	20X7	20X8
	$\frac{1{,}440}{18{,}000}$	$\frac{2{,}260}{18{,}900}$	$\frac{3{,}164}{19{,}845}$
	= 29.2 days	= 43.6 days	= 58.2 days

23: RATIO AND TREND ANALYSIS

	20X6	20X7	20X8
Inventory turnover			
$= \dfrac{\text{Inventory}}{\text{Cost of sales}} \times 365$ days	$\dfrac{1{,}775}{10{,}440}$ = 62 days	$\dfrac{2{,}663}{10{,}340}$ = 94 days	$\dfrac{3{,}995}{11{,}890}$ = 122.6 days

Question — Ratio analysis report 2

You are the management accountant of Fry Co. Laurie Co is a competitor in the same industry and it has been operating for 20 years. Summaries of Laurie Co's statements of profit or loss and other comprehensive income and statements of financial position for the previous three years are given below.

SUMMARISED STATEMENTS OF PROFIT OR LOSS AND OTHER COMPREHENSIVE INCOME FOR THE YEAR ENDED 31 DECEMBER

	20X6 $m	20X7 $m	20X8 $m
Revenue	840	981	913
Cost of sales	554	645	590
Gross profit	286	336	323
Selling, distribution and administration expenses	186	214	219
Profit before interest	100	122	104
Interest	6	15	19
Profit before taxation	94	107	85
Taxation	45	52	45
Profit after taxation	49	55	40
Dividends	24	24	24

SUMMARISED STATEMENTS OF FINANCIAL POSITION AS AT 31 DECEMBER

	20X6 $m	20X7 $m	20X8 $m
Assets			
Non-current assets			
Intangible assets	36	40	48
Tangible assets	176	206	216
	212	246	264
Current assets			
Inventories	237	303	294
Receivables	105	141	160
Bank	52	58	52
	606	748	770
Equity and liabilities			
Equity			
Ordinary share capital	100	100	100
Retained earnings	299	330	346
	399	430	446
Non-current liabilities			
Non-current loans	74	138	138
Current liabilities			
Trade payables	53	75	75
Other payables	80	105	111
	606	748	770

PART C ACCOUNTING AND REPORTING TECHNIQUES

You may assume that the index of retail prices has remained constant between 20X0 and 20X2.

Required

Write a report to the finance director of Fry Co:

(a) Assessing the performance of Laurie Co and showing any calculations in an appendix to this report.

(b) Recommending five areas which require further investigation, including reference to other pieces of information which would complement your analysis of the performance of Laurie Co.

Answer

(a) To: Finance Director
    From: Management accountant
    Subject: *Performance of Laurie Co 20X6 to 20X8*

An appendix is attached to this report which shows the ratios calculated as part of the performance review.

Profitability

The gross profit margin has remained relatively static over the three-year period, although it has risen by approximately 1% in 20X8. ROCE, while improving very slightly in 20X7 to 21.5% has dropped dramatically in 20X8 to 17.8%. The profit margin has also fallen in 20X8, in spite of the improvement in the gross profit margin. This marks a rise in expenses which suggests that they are not being well controlled. The utilisation of assets compared to the revenue generated has also declined reflecting the drop in trading activity between 20X7 and 20X8.

Trading levels

It is apparent that there was a dramatic increase in trading activity between 20X7 and 20X8, but then a significant fall in 20X8. Revenue rose by 17% ((981/840) – 1) in 20X7 but fell by 7% ((913/981) – 1) in 20X8. The reasons for this fluctuation are unclear. It may be the effect of some kind of one-off event, or it may be the effect of a change in product mix. Whatever the reason, it appears that improved credit terms granted to customers (receivables payment period up from 46 to 64 days) has not stopped the drop in sales.

Working capital

Both the current ratio and quick ratio demonstrate an adequate working capital situation, although the quick ratio has shown a slight decline. There has been an increased investment over the period in inventories and receivables which has been only partly financed by longer payment periods to trade payables and a rise in other payables (mainly between 20X6 and 20X7).

Capital structure

The level of gearing of the company increased when a further $64m was raised in long-term loans in 20X7 to add to the $74m already in the statement of financial position. Although this does not seem to be a particularly high level of gearing, the debt/equity ratio did rise from 18.5% to 32.0% in 20X7. The interest charge has risen to $19m from $6m in 20X6. The 20X7 charge was $15m, suggesting that either the interest rate on the loan is flexible, or that the full interest charge was not incurred in 20X7. The new long-term loan appears to have funded the expansion in both non-current and current assets in 20X7.

APPENDIX

Ratio	Working	20X6	20X7	20X8
Gross profit margin	(1)	34.0%	34.3%	35.4%
ROCE	(2)	21.1%	21.5%	17.8%
Profit margin	(3)	11.9%	12.4%	11.4%
Assets turnover	(4)	1.78	1.73	1.56
Gearing ratio	(5)	15.6%	24.3%	23.6%

Ratio	Working	20X6	20X7	20X8
Debt/equity ratio	(6)	18.5%	32.0%	30.9%
Interest cover	(7)	16.7	8.1	5.5
Current ratio	(8)	3.0	2.8	2.7
Quick ratio	(9)	1.2	1.1	1.1
Receivables payment period (days)	(10)	46	52	64
Inventory turnover period (days)	(11)	156	171	182
Payables turnover period	(12)	35	42	46

Workings (all in $m)

		20X6	20X7	20X8
1	Gross profit margin	$\dfrac{286}{840}$	$\dfrac{336}{981}$	$\dfrac{323}{913}$
2	ROCE*	$\dfrac{100}{473}$	$\dfrac{122}{568}$	$\dfrac{104}{584}$
3	Profit margin	$\dfrac{100}{840}$	$\dfrac{122}{981}$	$\dfrac{104}{913}$
4	Assets turnover	$\dfrac{840}{473}$	$\dfrac{981}{568}$	$\dfrac{913}{584}$
5	Gearing ratio	$\dfrac{74}{74 + 399}$	$\dfrac{138}{138+430}$	$\dfrac{138}{138+446}$
6	Debt/equity ratio	$\dfrac{74}{399}$	$\dfrac{138}{430}$	$\dfrac{138}{446}$
7	Interest cover	$\dfrac{100}{6}$	$\dfrac{122}{15}$	$\dfrac{104}{19}$
8	Current ratio	$\dfrac{394}{133}$	$\dfrac{502}{180}$	$\dfrac{506}{186}$
9	Quick ratio	$\dfrac{157}{133}$	$\dfrac{199}{180}$	$\dfrac{212}{186}$
10	Receivables payment period	$\dfrac{105}{840} \times 365$	$\dfrac{141}{981} \times 365$	$\dfrac{160}{913} \times 365$
11	Inventory turnover period	$\dfrac{237}{554} \times 365$	$\dfrac{303}{645} \times 365$	$\dfrac{294}{590} \times 365$
12	Payables payment period	$\dfrac{53}{554} \times 365$	$\dfrac{75}{645} \times 365$	$\dfrac{75}{590} \times 365$

*ROCE has been calculated here as:

$$\frac{\text{Profit before interest and taxation (PBIT)}}{\text{Capital employed}}$$

where capital employed = equity plus non-current liabilities. It is possible to calculate ROCE using profit after taxation and interest, but this admits variations and distortions into the ratio which are not affected by **trading** activity.

(b) Areas for further investigation include the following:

(i) *Non-current loan*

There is no indication as to why this loan was raised and how it was used to finance the business. Further details are needed of interest rate(s), security given and repayment dates.

(ii) *Trading activity*

The level of sales has fluctuated in quite a strange way and this requires further investigation and explanation. Factors to consider would include pricing policies, product mix, market share and any unique occurrence which would affect sales.

PART C ACCOUNTING AND REPORTING TECHNIQUES

(iii) *Further breakdown*

It would be useful to break down some of the information in the financial statements, perhaps into a management accounting format. Examples would include the following.

(1) Sales by segment, market or geographical area
(2) Cost of sales split, into raw materials, labour and overheads
(3) Inventory broken down into raw materials, work in progress and finished goods
(4) Expenses analysed between administrative expenses, sales and distribution costs

(iv) *Accounting policies*

Accounting policies may have a significant effect on certain items. In particular, it would be useful to know what the accounting policies are in relation to intangible assets (and what these assets consist of), and whether there has been any change in accounting policies.

(v) *Dividend policy*

The company has maintained the level of dividend paid to shareholders (although it has not been raised during the three-year period). Presumably the company would have been able to reduce the amount of long-term debt taken on if it had retained part or all of the dividend during this period. It would be interesting to examine the share price movement during the period and calculate the dividend cover.

Tutorial note. Other matters raised could have included:

1 Working capital problems, particularly inventory turnover and control over receivables

2 EPS (which cannot be calculated here as the number of shares is not given) and other related investor statistics, such as the P/E ratio.

Chapter roundup

- Make sure that you can **define** all the ratios. Look out for variations in definitions of ratios which might appear in questions.
- Always remember that 'profit' and 'net assets' are fairly **arbitrary figures**, affected by different accounting policies and manipulation.
- Financial analysis is a vital tool for **auditors**.

Quick quiz

1. What are the main sources of financial information available to the external users?
2. Apart from ratio analysis, what other information might be helpful in interpreting a company's financial statements?
3. In a period when profits are fluctuating, what effect does a company's level of gearing have on the profits available for ordinary shareholders?

Answers to quick quiz

1. Published financial statements and interim statements, filed documents, government statistics

2.
   - Other comments in the financial statements eg Directors' Report/Management Commentary/Business review
   - Age and nature of the assets
   - Current and future market developments
   - Recent acquisition or disposal of subsidiaries
   - Notes to the financial statements, auditors' report, events after the reporting period, etc.

3. Profits available for the shareholders will be highly volatile and in some years there may not be earnings cover for an ordinary dividend paid

End of chapter question

Curia (AIA May 2005)

A client of yours has applied for an executive post with Curia, a limited liability company. He is to be interviewed shortly and is keen to show a good knowledge of the company at the interview. The client has commissioned you to write a report on the recent performance of Curia.

You have obtained the following financial ratios which have been calculated from the financial statements of Curia for the three years ended 31 March 20X3, 20X4 and 20X5.

Financial year ended 31 March	20X3	20X4	20X5
Return on equity	10%	15%	13%
Net income to sales revenue	2.6%	4.3%	4.2%
Sales revenue to total assets	2.11	2.12	1.93
Gross profit to sales revenue	15%	18%	21%
Operating expenses to sales revenue	11%	12%	15%
Current/working capital ratio	1.33	1.42	1.30
Acid test ratio	0.96	1.03	0.95
Credit to customers (months)	1.7	1.5	1.2
Credit from suppliers (months)	1.5	1.5	1.3
Inventory turnover (months)	0.8	0.7	0.6
Earnings per share (cents per share)	14.3	25.2	23.4
Dividend per share (cents per share)	12.5	12.5	12.5
Net assets per share	1.50	1.63	1.74

Required

On the basis of the above information report to your client. Your report should include

- Reviews the performance of Curia as evidenced by the above ratios,
- Makes recommendations as to how the overall performance of Curia could be improved, and
- Indicates any limitations in your analysis.

(25 marks)

Answers to end of chapter questions

IASB

The purpose and status of the IASB's *Conceptual Framework* is included within it. Essentially, its purpose is to assist in the development of future IFRS and the review of existing IFRS and in promoting the harmonisation of regulations, accounting standards and procedures relating to the preparation of financial statements by providing a basis for reducing the number of alternative accounting treatments permitted by IFRS.

The following points may be made in favour of the *Conceptual Framework*.

(a) Its principles are being used in the formulation of standards, for example its definition of an asset and liability are consistent with new standards, such as IFRS 16 *Leases*. It must be noted, however, that the new definitions provided by the revised *Conceptual Framework* (2018) are now inconsistent with some of the older standards, such as the definition of a liability used in IAS 37 *Provisions, Contingent Liabilities and Contingent Assets*.

(b) The *Conceptual Framework* helps reduce scope for individual judgement and the potential subjectivity that this implies.

(c) Financial statements should be more comparable because, although alternative treatments will still be available, there will be a consistent and coherent framework on which to base one's choice of a particular alternative.

(d) The *Conceptual Framework* puts forward a consistent terminology and consistent objectives, for example in the definitions and the qualitative characteristics.

It could be argued that the *Conceptual Framework* is too theoretical. It is certainly general rather than particular. However, as has been seen with IFRS 15 and IFRS 16, the general principles can be applied to very specific issues in accounting standards. Moreover, in areas not at present covered by accounting standards, the statement can give general guidance. Nevertheless, in the short term, the principles in the *Conceptual Framework*, and the definitions provided, may conflict with some accounting standards which have already been issued before it was revised.

Polymer

POLYMER CO: STATEMENT OF PROFIT OR LOSS FOR THE YEAR ENDED 31 MAY 20X8

	$
Revenue	1,526,750
Cost of sales (W3)	(1,048,000)
Gross profit	478,750
Distribution costs (W4)	(124,300)
Administrative expenses (W5)	(216,200)
Finance costs (W6)	(18,400)
Profit before tax	119,850
Income tax expense	(40,000)
PROFIT FOR THE YEAR	79,850

POLYMER CO: STATEMENT OF FINANCIAL POSITION AS AT 31 MAY 20X8

	$
ASSETS	
Non-current assets	
Property, plant and equipment (W7)	452,250
Intangible assets	215,500
	667,750
Current assets	
Inventories (W8)	425,750
Receivables (W9)	171,880
Cash and cash equivalents	5,120
	602,750
Total assets	1,270,500

ANSWERS TO END OF CHAPTER QUESTIONS

	$
EQUITY AND LIABILITIES	
Equity	
Share capital	300,000
Share premium	100,000
Retained earnings (283,500 + 79,850)	363,350
General reserve	50,000
Revaluation surplus	50,000
	863,350
Non-current liabilities	
10% debentures	100,000
8.4% cumulative redeemable preference shares	100,000
	200,000
Current liabilities	
Trade and other payables (W10)	115,900
Bank overdraft	51,250
Current tax payable	40,000
	207,150
Total equity and liabilities	1,270,500

Workings

1 *Depreciation*

Cost of sales:	8% × 150,000 plant and equipment		12,000
Administration:	10% × 50,000 furniture and fixtures		5,000
	1/4 × 20% × (75,000 – 25,000) motor vehicles		2,500
			7,500
Distribution:	3/4 × 20% × (75,000 – 25,000) motor vehicles		7,500

2 *Depreciation (amortisation) of lease*

$75,000 × 1/50   1,500

3 *Cost of sales*

	$
Opening inventories (108,400 + 32,750 + 184,500)	325,650
Purchases	750,600
Carriage inwards	10,500
Manufacturing wages	250,000
Manufacturing overheads	125,000
Depreciation of plant (W1)	12,000
Closing inventories (W8)	(425,750)
	1,048,000

4 *Distribution costs*

	$
Per question	116,800
Depreciation (W1)	7,500
	124,300

5 *Administrative expenses*

		$
Per question		158,100
Legal expenses	54,100	
less: solicitors' fees capitalised	(5,000)	
		49,100
Depreciation (W1)		7,500
Amortisation of lease (W2)		1,500
		216,200

6 Finance costs

	$
Interest expense on loan notes ($100,000 × 10%)	10,000
Preference dividend	8,400
	18,400

7 Property, plant and equipment

	Freehold land $	Leasehold property $	Plant & Equipment $	Furniture & fixtures $	Motor vehicles $	Total $
Carrying amount per TB						
Cost or valuation	250,000	75,000	150,000	50,000	75,000	
Accumulated dep'n	–	(15,000)	(68,500)	(15,750)	(25,000)	
Net carrying amount	250,000	60,000	81,500	34,250	50,000	
Solicitor's fees	5,000					
Depreciation charge	–	(1,500)	(12,000)	(5,000)	(10,000)	
Carrying amount 31 May 20X8	255,000	58,500	69,500	29,250	40,000	452,250

8 Inventories

	$
Raw materials	112,600
Work in progress	37,800
Finished goods	275,350
	425,750

9 Receivables

	$
Trade receivables (177,630 – 5,750 allowance for receivables)	171,880

10 Trade and other payables

	$
Trade payables	97,500
Loan interest payable	10,000
Preference dividend payable	8,400
	115,900

Schrattenbach

Conventional financial statements do not highlight or specifically disclose this type of information. Disclosure is possible – but would probably be voluntary, depending upon the legal environment the company operates in. Any legal requirements would set the minimum disclosures required and it would be possible to exceed these requirements.

There are two possibilities for the disclosure of this type of information. The first is to disclose environmental and charitable information as appropriate throughout the corporate report eg (in the context of the UK) in the Directors Report, the Operating and Financial Review, the Business Review, accounting policies and the notes to the financial statements. The second is to collect all this information into a separate statement (or statements) highlighting the company's contribution to the environment and its charitable work.

The next decision is whether to quantify some or all of the information. The amounts involved in charitable work is likely to be straightforward to value and would most likely be cash flow donations. There may also be contributions in the form of know-how or other resources. The environmental information is likely to be more difficult to value.

ANSWERS TO END OF CHAPTER QUESTIONS

Practices in this area vary widely from company to company, and the managing director might wish to look at a number of corporate reports to get a feel for current practice. The company will have to decide how 'objective' the information disclosed should be. There may be a temptation to see this disclosure as public relations – but the danger is that information which is perceived to be unbalanced will be discounted by users. For example, if information on good environmental practice is to be disclosed, should information about negative environmental effects also be disclosed?

The managing director should also consider having any disclosures audited as this would enhance the credibility of the information presented.

Mancroft

Treatment of the sale of inventory

This transaction is known as 'window dressing'. It should not be shown as a sale; the sale must be cancelled and the inventory re-instated at $1m (cost) rather than $3m sales price.

The entries for the cancellation of the sale are:

DEBIT	Sales	$3m	
CREDIT	Cash (current liabilities)		$3m

For the cancellation of the purchase:

DEBIT	Cash (current assets)	$3m	
CREDIT	Purchases		$3m

The above entries have no effect on retained earnings, but the elimination of unrealised profit, reducing inventory from $3m to $1m, will affect it.

DEBIT	Closing inventory/cost of sales (Hungate's books): 3 – 1	$2m	
CREDIT	Inventory (current asset)		$2m

Ethical implications of sale of inventory

Members of the accounting profession enjoy a number of privileges. These include:

(a) Special status and respect within the community.

(b) Self-regulation, that is regulation by the accountants' professional body.

(c) An exclusive right to certain functions. For example, auditors must be members of certain professional bodies.

Like other professions, the accounting profession has **features that distinguish it** from non-professional jobs. The most important of these is specialist knowledge, but also recognition as being committed to the good of society, rather than just commercial gain.

To **earn this status and these privileges**, accountants should, as a minimum:

(a) Be committed to the fair presentation of financial statements.

(b) Show independence and objectivity in applying financial reporting standards.

(c) Be committed to an ethical approach to business, and apply this in the preparation of financial statements.

Ethical behaviour in the preparation of financial statements, and in other areas, is of **paramount importance**. This applies equally to preparers of financial statements, to auditors and to accountants giving advice to directors. Company accountants act unethically if they use 'creative' accounting in financial statements preparation to make the figures look better.

In treating the inventory as sold, Mancroft is indulging in '**window dressing**'. This is not a genuine sale; its purpose is purely **to show Mancroft's subsidiary Hungate in a better financial position** than is truly the case, in order to increase the likelihood of the sale of Hungate. The 'sale' of inventory would increase cash and retained earnings by $2m, boosting the appearance of both profitability and liquidity. This would **mislead a potential buyer**. Nor would this manipulation be a 'one-off'; if the subsidiary is not sold, the transaction would be carried out again in the interim financial statements. Neither the final financial statements for the year, nor the interim financial statements would give a fair presentation of the financial position and performance.

The treatment of the inventory is therefore **unethical**, and should be reversed when preparing the consolidated financial statements.

Small and medium-sized entities

Advantages

Although IFRS were originally designed to be suitable for all types of entity, they have become increasingly complex in recent years. It is often argued that they are now designed primarily to meet the information needs of **institutional investors in large listed entities**.

Shareholders of SMEs are often also directors. Therefore, through managing the company and maintaining the financial records, they are already aware of the company's financial performance and position and so do not need the level of detail in financial statements required by external institutional investors of larger companies.

The main external **users of SMEs tend to be lenders, trade suppliers and the tax authorities**. They have **different needs** from institutional investors and are more likely to focus on shorter-term cash flows, liquidity and solvency.

Full IFRS covers a wide range of issues, contain a sizeable amount of implementation guidance and include disclosure requirements appropriate for public companies. This can make them **too complex for users of SMEs to understand.**

Many SMEs now feel that following full IFRS places an unacceptable burden on preparers of SME financial statements – a burden that has been growing as IFRS become more detailed and more countries adopt them. The **cost of following full IFRS often appears to outweigh the benefits**.

The **disclosure** requirements of full IFRS are very **extensive** and as such, can result in **information overload** for the users of SME financial statements, reducing the understandability of financial statements.

Some IFRS still offer **choice of accounting treatments**, leading to **lack of comparability** between different companies adopting different accounting standards.

Disadvantages

If SMEs follow their own simplified IFRS, their financial statements will **no longer be comparable** with larger companies following full IFRS or SMEs choosing to follow full IFRS. This may make it harder to attract investors.

The changeover from full IFRS to the simplified IFRS for SMEs, will require training and possible changes in systems. This will place both a **time and cost** burden on the company.

Full IFRS is now well established and respected and act as a form of **quality control** on financial statements which comply with it. It could be argued therefore that financial statements which no longer comply with full IFRS will **lose their credibility**. This is often called the 'Big GAAP, Little GAAP divide'.

The new IFRS for SMEs proposes to **reduce disclosures** required by full IFRS. Omission of certain key information might actually make the financial statements **harder to understand**.

Conclusion

The advantages for SMEs of having a separate simplified IFRS outweigh the disadvantages. Now that the IASB has issued the IFRS for SMEs, both preparers and users of SME financial statements will benefit.

Answers to end of chapter questions

Akkeal

AKKEAL: CONSOLIDATED STATEMENT OF PROFIT OR LOSS FOR THE YEAR ENDED 31 MARCH 20X4

	$'000
Revenue (16,400 + 8,870 – 1,500 (W1))	23,770
Cost of sales (5,600 + 4,200 – 1,500 (W) + 25 (W1))	(8,325)
Gross profit	15,445
Operating expenses (5,780 + 3,370)	(9,150)
Dividends receivable (W3)	757
Investment income (233 + 97)	330
Finance cost (333 + 240)	(573)
Share of profit of Joint Venture (1,260 × 25%)	
Share of profit of Associate (2,290 × 30%)	687
Profit before tax	7,911
Income tax expense (1,800 + 500)	(2,300)
Profit for the period	5,511
Attributable to:	
Owners of the parent (Bal fig)	5,018
Non-controlling interest (W2)	493
	5,511
Earnings per share (in cents) (5,018 ÷ 20,000)	25.1

Earnings per share is based on group profit after tax, and non-controlling interest ($5,018,000) divided by 20,000,000 ordinary shares issued and ranking for dividends.

Workings:

1

	$'000
Intercompany sales	1,500
Mark-up	20.00%
Profit loading (1,500 × 20/120)	250
Proportion unsold	10.00%
Provision for unrealised profit	25

Here the provision should be made by Belloan

2

	$'000
Non-controlling interest	
Subsidiary's profit after tax	1,257
Provision for unrealised profit	(25)
	1,232
Non-controlling %	40%
Non-controlling interest	492.8

3 Dividends receivable

Akkeal plc	1,247	
Belloan plc	600	
less		
Belloan plc to Akkeal plc	(420)	60% of 700
Curtyn plc to Akkeal plc	(450)	30% of 1,500
Dojin plc to Akkeal plc	(220)	¼ of 880
	757	

ANSWERS TO END OF CHAPTER QUESTIONS

Insolo

Syllabus area: 13.2

This question tests the preparation of a consolidated statement of financial position for a vertical group.

Note. An alternative calculation of the goodwill and non-controlling interest in Transbuy is provided at the end of this Answer.

(a) **Calculation of goodwill**

In Vanior

Interest of holding company (1,350 as % of 2,250)	60%	
Consideration transferred (1,350 × $2.85)	3,847,500	(i)
Net assets acquired		
Reserves at acquisition	1,262,500	
Surplus on revaluation	400,000	
	1,662,500	
Ordinary share capital	2,250,000	
	3,912,500	
by	60%	
	2,347,500	(ii)
Goodwill (i less ii)	$1,500,000	

In Transbuy

		$
Insolo's interest in the consideration transferred by Vanior	Ords: (1,260 × $2.15 × 60%)	1,625,400
	Prefs: (60 × $1.25 × 60%)	45,000
		1,670,400
Insolo's effective interest in the fair value of identifiable NA acquired:	Ords: 60% × 70% × 2,462,857 (see below)	(1,034,400)
	Prefs: 60% × 20% × 300,000	(36,000)
Goodwill in respect of Transbuy		600,000
Impairment to date		(220,000)
Carrying amount of goodwill in Transbuy		380,000
Goodwill in respect of Vanior		1,500,000
Total carrying amount of goodwill		1,880,000
Transbuy: Identifiable net assets acquired		
Ordinary share capital		1,800,000
Reserves at acquisition		662,857
		2,462,857

(b) **INSOLO**
CONSOLIDATED STATEMENT OF FINANCIAL POSITION AS AT 31 OCTOBER 20X7

ASSETS
Non-current assets $
Intangible asset – goodwill (1,500 + 600 per (a) – 220) 1,880,000
Property, plant and equipment (W1) 12,805,600
Other non-current investments, at cost (W2) 73,800
14,759,400

ANSWERS TO END OF CHAPTER QUESTIONS

	$
Current assets	
Inventories, at cost (W3)	801,200
Trade receivables (W4)	1,152,630
Other receivables (W5)	137,590
Cash and cash equivalents	630,530
	2,721,950
Total assets	17,481,350
EQUITY AND LIABILITIES	
Equity	
Issued share capital:	
Ordinary shares of $1	2,000,000
Preference shares of $1	400,000
Retained earnings (W7)	8,054,167
	10,454,167
Non-controlling interest (W8)	4,165,693
	14,619,860
Non-current liabilities (W6)	1,240,800
	1,240,800
Current liabilities	
Trade payables (539.08 + 345.62 + 412.09 − 94.4 (W4))	1,202,390
Other payables (66.9 + 18.7 + 14.5)	100,100
Current taxation (164.2 + 88.6 + 65.4)	318,200
	1,620,690
Total equity	14,619,860
Total liabilities	2,861,490
Total equity and liabilities	17,481,350

Other workings

1   *Property, Plant and Equipment*

	$
In Insolo	4,568,900
In Vanior	3,556,000
In Transbuy	4,280,700
Surplus on revaluation	400,000
	12,805,600

2   *Non-current Asset Investments*

The non-current asset investments consist of

	Insolo $	Vanior $	Transbuy $
In Transbuy			
Ordinary shares	3,847,500		
In Transbuy			
Ordinary shares	–	2,709,000	
Preference shares	–	75,000	
	3,847,500	2,784,000	
So, other investments =	22,000	17,600	34,200
	3,869,500	2,801,600	34,200

So, consolidated non-current asset investments:

	$
Insolo	22,000
Vanior	17,600
Transbuy	34,200
	73,800

ANSWERS TO END OF CHAPTER QUESTIONS

3   *Inventories*

This is the total for the group companies less the total unrealised profit.

Insolo	440,000
Vanior	186,500
Transbuy	230,800
Unrealised profit (100 – 68.2) + (80 – 55.7)	(56,100)
	801,200

4   *Trade Receivables*

This is the total for the group companies less the total intercompany indebtedness.

Insolo	539,080
Vanior	306,750
Transbuy	401,200
Intragroup (41.2 + 53.2)	(94,400)
	1,152,630

5   *Other Receivables*

This is the total for the group companies.

Ie	Insolo	87,090
	Vanior	34,000
	Transbuy	16,500
		137,590

6   *Non-current Liabilities*

This is the total for the companies in the group less intragroup loans.

Ie	Insolo	500,000
	Vanior	420,000
	Transbuy	320,800
		1,240,800

7   *Retained Earnings*

Retained profits at consolidation:

	Insolo	Vanior	Transbuy
	$	$	$
Per statement of financial position	6,071,090	3,748,230	2,258,140
Goodwill written off		(220,000)	
Surplus on revaluation		400,000	
Unrealised profit in inventory (W3)	(31,800)	(24,300)	
	6,039,290	3,903,930	2,258,140
Retained profits as at acquisition:			
per statements of financial position		1,262,500	662,857
surplus on revaluation		400,000	
		1,662,500	662,857
Post-acquisition retained profits		2,241,430	1,595,283
Interest of holding company		60%	70%
		1,344,858	1,116,698
Share of sub-subsidiary			60%
			670,019
Hence, to non-controlling interest			446,679

So, group retained profits

Holding company		6,039,290	
Subsidiaries	1,344,858		
	670,019		
		2,014,877	
		8,054,167	

ANSWERS TO END OF CHAPTER QUESTIONS

8 Non-controlling Interest

	Vanior $	Transbuy $
Ordinary share capital	2,250,000	1,800,000
Reserves at consolidation (W7)	3,903,930	2,258,140
	6,153,930	4,058,140
Less Vanior investment in Transbuy (W2)	2,784,000	–
	3,369,930	4,058,140
	× 40%	× (100% – (60% × 70%))
	1,347,972	2,353,721
Pref share capital – Vanior = 100%, Transbuy = (100% – (60% × 20%)) × 300,000	200,000	264,000
	1,547,972	2,617,721
		4,165,693

AN ALTERNATIVE CALCULATION OF THE GOODWILL AND NON-CONTROLLING INTEREST IN TRANSBUY

GOODWILL

Interest of holding co	Ord. (1,260 as % of 1,800)		70%	
	Pref. (60 as % of 300)		20%	
Consideration transferred	(1,260 × $2.15) + (60 × $1.25)		2,784,000	(i)
Net assets acquired				
Reserves at acquisition			662,857	
Ordinary share capital			1,800,000	
			2,462,857	
		by	70%	
			1,724,000	
Preference shares			300,000	
		by	20%	
			60,000	
			1,784,000	(ii)
Goodwill	(i – ii)		$1,000,000	
Goodwill in respect of Vanior (unchanged)			$1,500,000	
Impairment			($220,000)	
Total carrying amount of goodwill			$2,280,000	

Higher by 400,000 (2,280,000 – 1,880,000)

NON-CONTROLLING INTEREST

	Vanior	Transbuy
Ordinary share capital	2,250,000	1,800,000
Reserves at consolidation	3,903,930	2,258,140
	6,153,930	4,058,140
Non-controlling interest (W7)	40%	30%
	2,461,572	1,217,442
Preference shares	200,000	300,000
Non-controlling interest	100%	80%
	200,000	240,000
Total non-controlling interest is	2,461,572	
	1,217,442	
	200,000	
	240,000	
Extra non-controlling interest in sub-subsidiary (1,116,698 × 40%) (W7)	446,679	
	$4,565,693	

Total non-controlling interest
Higher by 400,000 (4,565,693 – 4,165,693)

Mozart, Constanza and Salzburg

Syllabus area: 13.2

This question tests the application of knowledge and understanding of group financial statements. This case study required the preparation of a consolidated statement of financial position for a group where a controlling interest in a subsidiary has been disposed of but the former subsidiary has been retained as a joint venture. The question also tests the calculation of profit or loss on the disposal of a block of shares and its different treatments in the financial statements of the parent and the group financial statements.

(a) Interest of holding company in Salzburg

- before disposal   60.0% for   6 months
- after disposal   25.0% for   6 months

Interest sold   35.0%

(i) **Calculation of holding company profit/(loss) on disposal**

	$
Fair value of consideration received (2 × 525,000)	1,050,000
Carrying value of investment sold (35/60 × (60% × 1,500,000 × 2.20))	(1,155,000)
	(105,000)
Income tax relief thereon at 30%	31,500
Holding company's loss on sale	**(73,500)**

(ii) **Calculation of group profit/loss on disposal**

	$
Fair value of consideration received (as above)	1,050,000
Fair value of interest retained = proportion of net assets (25% × 2,230,245 (see below))	557,561
	1,607,561
Net assets at date control lost (60% × 2,230,245) (see below)	(1,338,147)
Goodwill at date control lost	–
Group profit on sale	**269,414**

Net assets at date control lost	$	$
Share capital		1,500,000
Reserves at year-end		986,000
Profit after tax for the year	511,511	
Proportion of year	½	
		(255,755)
		2,230,245

(b) **Mozart**

CONSOLIDATED STATEMENT OF FINANCIAL POSITION AS AT 31 DECEMBER 20X5

	$
Assets	
Non-current assets	
Intangible assets (W1)	207,000
Property, plant and equipment (5,548,450 + 3,370,400)	8,918,850
	621,500
	9,747,350
Current assets (1,133,000 + 724,000)	1,857,000
Total assets	1,604,350

ANSWERS TO END OF CHAPTER QUESTIONS

Equity

Ordinary shares of $1	5,000,000
Retained earnings (W3)	3,969,500
	8,969,500
Non-controlling interests (40% × 3,660,000)	1,464,000
	10,433,500

Liabilities

Current liabilities (767,950 – 31,500 tax relief + 434,400)	1,170,850
	11,604,350

Workings

1 **Intangible assets**

	$
Calculation of goodwill in Constanza	
Consideration transferred	1,680,000
Non-controlling interests (40% × 2,455,000)	982,000
	2,662,000
Net assets acquired	
Subsidiary's share capital at acquisition	2,000,000
Subsidiary's reserves at acquisition	455,000
	2,455,000
Goodwill	207,000
Calculation of goodwill in Salzburg	
Consideration transferred ((60% × 1,500,000) × $2.20	1,980,000
Non-controlling interests (40% × 2,285,000 (see below))	914,000
	2,894,000
Net assets acquired	
Subsidiary's share capital at acquisition	1,500,000
Subsidiary's reserves at acquisition	785,000
	2,285,000
Goodwill	609,000
Less Impairment to date	(609,000)
Carrying amount	Nil

2 **Investment in Joint Venture**

	$
Fair value of investment retained on date control lost	557,561
Share of post-disposal earnings (511,511 × 6/12 × 25%)	63,939
	621,500

3 **Group Retained Earnings**

	Mozart	Constanza	Salzburg 25%	Salzburg 35% sold
	$	$	$	$
Per question/at date of disposal	4,573,500	1,660,000	986,000	730,245
Less: proceeds of disposal	(1,050,000)			
Group profit on disposal (part (a))	269,414			
Tax relief on disposal (part (a))	31,500			
Retained earnings at acquisition		(455,000)	(785,000)	(785,000)
		1,205,000	201,000	(54,755)
Constanza: share of post-acqn. earnings (1,205,000 × 60%)	723,000			
Salzburg: share of post-acqn. earnings (201,000 × 25%)	50,250			
Salzburg: share of post-acqn losses ((54,755) × 35%)	(19,164)			
Goodwill impairment	(609,000)			
	3,969,500			

Eufonion

Syllabus areas 13.4 and 13.1 (part d).

This is a largely discursive question focusing on functional currencies. The small numerical part is not difficult, but other areas need careful consideration. Part (d) may prove difficult – but it is included in the Basis for Conclusions in the standard.

(a) The currency of the primary economic environment in which the entity operates generating and expending cash will normally be its functional currency. The entity should consider:

- The currency which mainly influences its selling prices for goods and services, and
- The currency which mainly influences its labour, materials and other costs of providing its goods and services,
- The currency which funds the entity's financing activities
- The currency in which the funds from operating activities are normally retained.

If the functional currency is not obvious from the above, management should use its judgement to decide which currency most faithfully represents the economic effects of its transactions and conditions.

(b) All items in the statement of financial position would be translated at the closing rate of €1 = $1.38074 (1/0.72425).

	€m	Factor	$m
ASSETS			
Non-current assets			
Property, plant and equipment	420	1.38074	580
Current assets			
Inventories	26	1.38074	36
Trade and other receivables	42	1.38074	58
Cash and cash equivalents	8	1.38074	11
	76		105
Total assets	496		685
EQUITY AND LIABILITIES			
Equity			
Share capital	200	1.38074	276
Retained earnings	107	1.38074	148
	307		424
Non-current liabilities	85	1.38074	117
Current liabilities			
Trade and other payables	63	1.38074	87
Current taxation	41	1.38074	57
	104		144
Total liabilities	189		261
Total equity and liabilities	496		685

(c) As far as the statement of profit or loss is concerned income and expenses should be translated using exchange rates as at the date of the transactions. If exchange rates have not fluctuated significantly the company may be able to use the average rate as an approximation for the actual rates.

Assets and liabilities should be translated using the closing rate as at the end of the reporting period. IAS 21 does not offer any guidance as to how equity items should be translated. The exposure draft proposed using the closing rate for equity items other than 'those resulting from income and expenditure recognised in the period'. However, IAS 21 is silent. The directors could follow the proposals in the exposure draft. Other authorities recommend using historical rates for equity items.

ANSWERS TO END OF CHAPTER QUESTIONS

All exchange differences resulting from the translation from the functional currency to the presentation currency should be separately disclosed in equity.

The directors should also disclose in the financial statements

- That the presentation currency is different from the functional currency
- What the functional currency is
- The reason for using a different presentation currency.

(d) There are strong arguments in favour of allowing a reporting entity to present its financial statements in a currency other than its functional currency.

- It is consistent with the increasing globalisation of economic activity and the capital market.
- It is consistent with removing restrictions in order to increase the efficiency of the international capital markets.
- Many reporting entities do not have a single functional currency, and it may not be clear which one should be the presentation currency.
- Some jurisdictions may require the presentation of financial statements in the local currency which might not be the same as the functional currency. This would mean reporting entities preparing two sets of financial statements for legal rather than economic reasons.
- A company may raise capital in a variety of markets – and therefore should have the right to report to markets in the appropriate currency.
- Management may not use one single currency in managing the activities of a global group – control and monitoring may be done in different currencies as appropriate.

Arguments against include:

- The functional currency is the currency of the primary economic environment in which the reporting entity operates. This should therefore be the currency which most usefully reflects the economic effects of transactions and events on the entity.
- If an entity has a number of functional currencies the functional currency in which top management controls and monitors performance should be the currency used for the financial statements.
- Presentation of the financial statements in more than one currency may be confusing for users. It might be better to present in the functional currency – but, if helpful, present convenience translations outside the scope of international standards.

Porter

PORTER GROUP
STATEMENT OF CASH FLOWS FOR THE YEAR ENDED 31 MAY 20X6

	$m	$m
Cash flows from Operating Activities		
Profit before taxation	112	
Adjustments for:		
Depreciation	44	
Impairment losses on goodwill (W2)	3	
Foreign exchange loss (W8)	2	
Investment income – share of profit of associate	(12)	
Investment income – gains on financial assets measured at fair value	(6)	
Interest expense	16	
	159	
Increase in trade receivables (132 – 112 – 16)	(4)	
Decrease in inventories (154 – 168 – 20)	34	
Decrease in trade payables (110 – 98 – 12 – (W8) 17 PPE payable)	(17)	
Cash generated from operations	172	
Interest paid (W7)	(12)	
Income taxes paid (W6)	(37)	
Net cash from operating activities		123
Cash flows from investing activities		
Acquisition of subsidiary, net of cash acquired (26 – 8)	(18)	
Purchase of property, plant and equipment (W1)	(25)	
Purchase of financial assets (W4)	(10)	
Dividend received from associate (W3)	11	
Net cash used in investing activities		(42)
Cash flows from financing activities		
Proceeds from issue of share capital	18	
(332 + 212 – 300 – 172 – (80 × 60%/2 × $2.25))		
Proceeds from non-current borrowings (380 – 320)	60	
Dividend paid	(45)	
Dividends paid to non-controlling interests (W5)	(4)	
Net cash from financing activities		29
Net decrease in cash and cash equivalents		110
Cash and cash equivalents at the beginning of the year		48
Cash and cash equivalents at the end of the year		158

Workings

1   Additions to property, plant and equipment

PROPERTY, PLANT AND EQUIPMENT

	$m		$m
b/d	812		
Revaluation	58	Depreciation	44
Acquisition of subsidiary	92		
Additions on credit (W8)	15		
∴ Additions for cash	25	c/d	958
	1,002		1,002

ANSWERS TO END OF CHAPTER QUESTIONS

2 *Impairment losses on goodwill*

GOODWILL

	$m		$m
b/d	10		
Acq'n of subsidiary		∴ Impairment losses	3
[(80 × 60%/2 × 2.25) + 26 − (120 × 60%)]	8		
		c/d	15
	18		18

3 *Dividends received from associate*

INVESTMENT IN ASSOCIATE

	$m		$m
b/d	39		
P/L	12	∴ Dividends received	11
OCI	8		
		c/d	48
	59		59

4 *Purchase of financial assets*

FINANCIAL ASSETS MEASURED AT FAIR VALUE

	$m		$m
b/d	0		
P/L	6		
∴ Additions	10		
		c/d	16
	16		16

5 *Dividends paid to non-controlling interests*

NON-CONTROLLING INTERESTS

	$m		$m
		b/d	28
∴ Dividends paid	4	TCI	12
c/d	84	Acquisition of subsidiary (120 × 40%)	48
			88
	88		

6 *Income taxes paid*

INCOME TAX PAYABLE

	$m		$m
		b/d (deferred tax)	26
		b/d (current tax)	22
		P/L	34
∴ Income taxes paid	37	OCI	17
c/d (deferred tax)	38	Acquisition of subsidiary	4
c/d (current tax)	28		
	103		103

7 *Interest paid*

INTEREST PAYABLE

	$m		$m
		b/d	4
		P/L	16
∴ Interest paid	12		
c/d	8		
	20		20

8 *Foreign currency transaction*

			$m	$m
Transactions recorded on:				
(1) 5 March	DEBIT Property, plant and equipment (102m/6.8)		15	
	CREDIT Payables			15
(2) 31 May	Payable = 102m/6.0 = $17m			
	DEBIT P/L (Admin expenses)		2	
	CREDIT Payables (17 – 15)			2

Tollirene

Report

To: Chief Executive Officer
From:
Date:
Subject: Impact of International Standards on Tollirene

IFRS 1 applies to the first financial statements produced using IFRS. In the case of Tollirene that will be both the interim financial statements and the full financial statements for the year ended 31 December 20X5.

The standard allows for what essentially is a form of 'fresh start' accounting. An opening Statement of financial position will be prepared as at the start of the period covered by the financial statements and this defines the date of transition to IFRS. In the case of Tollirene this will be 1 January 20X4. The opening statement of financial position will:

- Recognise all assets and liabilities required by IFRS,
- Not recognise any assets and liabilities not permitted by IFRS,
- If necessary, reclassify any items into the appropriate type of asset, liability or component of equity required by IFRS and
- Measure each asset, liability and component of equity using IFRS.

When it comes to measuring the opening assets and liabilities there are a number of exemptions which Tollirene may elect to use. These will allow Tollirene to avoid having to apply certain requirements of certain IFRS retrospectively, and include:

- Business combinations, allowing Tollirene not to have to apply IFRS 3 *Business Combinations* retrospectively.

- Fair value or revaluation as deemed cost, allowing Tollirene to measure an item of property, plant and equipment in the opening statement of financial position at fair value or using a previous revaluation.

- Cumulative translation differences, allowing Tollirene to value cumulative translation differences for all foreign operations at zero as at the date of transition to IFRS.

- Compound financial instruments, which would permit Tollirene not to split a compound financial instrument at inception into separate liability and equity components as required by IAS 32.

- Assets and liabilities of subsidiaries, associates and joint ventures, which covers the valuation of assets and liabilities in the separate financial statements of a subsidiary, associate or joint venture which adopts IFRS at a later date than its parent or *vice versa*.

There is supplementary implementation guidance which gives examples of the implementation of each of the above.

IFRS 1 makes it clear that the estimates used by Tollirene to prepare its opening IFRS statement of financial position should be consistent with the estimates made for the same date under local GAAP unless there is objective evidence that the estimates were in error. So any information received about

ANSWERS TO END OF CHAPTER QUESTIONS

those estimates after the date of transition to IFRS should be treated as a non-adjusting event under IAS 10 and reported in the statement of profit or loss and other comprehensive income for the year ended 31 December 20X4.

After establishing its opening IFRS statement of financial position [ie as at 1 January 20X4] Tollirene will present its financial statements for the year ended 31 December 20X5 along with comparative figures for the year ended 31 December 20X4 under IFRS. It will also present a statement of financial position at 1 January 20X4 (the date of transition to IFRS). These financial statements will also need to include a number of reconciliations required by IFRS 1. Tollirene will need to include the following reconciliations:

(1) A reconciliation of equity as at 1 January 20X4 [the date of transition to IFRS] reported under local GAAP with the figure reported under IFRS.

(2) A similar reconciliation of equity as at 31 December 20X4 reported under local GAAP with the figure reported under IFRS.

(3) A reconciliation of the total comprehensive income reported for the year ended 31 December 20X4 using local GAAP with the total comprehensive income reported for the same period using IFRS.

The implementation guidance gives an example of how Tollirene might present these reconciliations. These adopt a columnar approach. The reconciliation of equity takes the form of a summarised statement of financial position with three columns of figures. In the first column Tollirene would present its local GAAP figures. The third column gives the equivalent figures using IFRS. The middle column identifies the effect of transition to IFRS. Each difference in the figures is explained in a supporting note. The reconciliation of total comprehensive income adopts a similar layout using a summarised statement of profit or loss and other comprehensive income with three columns and supportive notes.

As all the companies in the Tollirene group have adopted IFRS at the same time the above process will be repeated in each of the group companies.

Tollirene might also find it has to publish quarterly reports under the proposed EU Transparency Directive. Depending on when this is implemented, the financial information contained in the first quarter's report and all other interim reports will also have to be based on IFRS.

Summary

- The above shows that the most demanding accounting year for Tollirene will be the current year ie the year ending on December 20X4, when it will need to prepare two sets of financial statements using local GAAP and IFRS respectively.

- If all the companies in the Tollirene group intend converting to IFRS they should continue preparing their 20X3 financial statements using local GAAP. However, Tollirene as the listed holding company should include additional information about the groups plans to convert to IFRS in its Annual Report for 20X3.

- During 20X4 all the companies in the group will need to prepare two sets of financial statements, one using local GAAP and one using IFRS and IFRS 1. The local GAAP financial statements will be published in the Annual Report for 20X4. The IFRS financial statements will enable Tollirene to prepare a set of consolidated financial statements using IFRS and this will allow it to quantify the effect of the transition to IFRS in its Annual Report for 20X4.

- During 20X5 all the companies in the group will prepare their financial statements using IAS/IFRS. This will enable Tollirene to publish its interim financial statements and its Annual Report for 20X5 in accordance with IFRS and IFRS 1.

Please do not hesitate to contact me if I can be of any further help.

> **Tutorial note**: This question was originally set when many EU companies would have been preparing to report under IFRS for the first time. However, the method of making the transition from previous (local) GAAP to IFRS remains the same and the advice given in the answer is still relevant.
>
> It should also be noted that the EU Transparency Directive took effect in January 2007 and therefore quarterly reporting is now relevant to all EU listed entities.

NCH

Syllabus area: 13.4

This is a detailed question on knowledge and understanding of IAS 36 *Impairment of Assets* and its application to a case study about a cash generating unit.

(a)

Year ended 31 March …	20X7	20X8	20X9
Real cost of capital	8.15%	8.15%	9.20%
Discount factor	0.924641701	0.854962276	0.782932487
Calculation of value in use	20X7	20X8	20X9
Units sold	1,500,000	500,000	500,000
Selling price	17.80	17.80	17.80
Income generated	26,700,000	8,900,000	8,900,000
Scrap proceeds			1,000,000
	26,700,000	8,900,000	9,900,000
Discount factor	0.9246	0.8550	0.7829
PV	24,687,933	7,609,164	7,751,032
Net present value	€40,048,129		

Summary of values
- Carrying amount €132,350,000
- Value in use €40,048,129
- Net realisable value €115,294,500

(b) The carrying value should be changed to the unit's fair value less costs of disposal of €115,294,500. This will result in an impairment loss of €17,055,500 [€132,350,000 less €115,144,500]. The impairment loss should be recognised in profit or loss in the year in which the impairment arises – here, in the year ending 31 March 20X6.

(c) (i) The impairment loss would be recognised in the Revaluation Reserve up to the amount of any previous recognised revaluation gain. Any excess impairment would be charged to profit or loss.

(ii) If the impairment loss cannot be allocated to a particular non-current asset it should be apportioned within the cash generating unit in a way which reduces the most subjective values first, ie

(1) To reduce any goodwill in the cash generating unit;

(2) Any excess should be charged to other assets of the cash generating unit on a pro rata basis.

In making the allocation the carrying amount of an individual asset should not be reduced below the highest of:

- The asset's net selling price (if determinable);
- The asset's value in use (if determinable); and
- Zero.

If the above restricts the amount of the impairment loss allocated to a particular asset the excess should be allocated to other assets on a *pro rata* basis.

Grimsel

Syllabus area: 13.4

This question covers various aspects of accounting for non-current assets. Topics covered include component depreciation, treatment of decommissioning costs, reversal of impairments, calculation of goodwill and the treatment of negative goodwill.

(a) Component depreciation is where various components of a long-lived asset may be depreciated over the appropriate lives for those components rather than the (longer) economic life of the asset. For example, a building may include heating equipment and roofing and these may be depreciated over the appropriate lives for those components. Those lives may be different from each other and shorter than the economic life of the building as a whole. IFRS requires a component approach to depreciation.

(b) If Trin decommissions its machinery and plant, there will be substantial costs incurred. However, it is not legally liable to decommission. It could leave the machinery and plant in place – but this would reduce the value of the premises. Because there is no legal obligation (and presumably no constructive obligation) the decommissioning costs should not be recognised until they are incurred. It would not be possible to make a provision for decommissioning costs.

IAS 37 *Provisions, Contingent Liabilities and Contingent Assets* requires a provision to be recognised only if (1) there is a present obligation as a result of a past event (2) it is probable that an outflow of resources will be required, and (3) a reliable estimate can be made of the outflow. The first condition is not met here.

(c)

	$	
Depreciation for 20X7	15,250	ie 122,000 divided by 8
This would give a carrying value of	106,750	122,000 less 15,250
Estimate of recoverable amount	125,000	

Carrying value as it would have been had the previous impairments not been recognised

	$
Cost	240,000
Accumulated depreciation (5/12 of cost)	100,000
	140,000

This is the maximum carrying value that can be reported as at 31 October 20X7 and thus limits the amount of the impairment that can be reversed.

Statement of profit or loss and other comprehensive income

So depreciation charge for 20X7 is (140,000 c/f – 122,000 b/f)   (18,000) ie a negative charge to depreciation

Statement of financial position

and the asset is reported as	$
Cost	240,000
Accumulated depreciation	100,000
Carrying amount	140,000

As this asset's recoverable amount of $125,000 is less than its depreciated historical cost, the asset would be written down to $125,000. So the net write off for 20X7 would be a negative charge to depreciation of $3,000 and the asset would be reported as its recoverable amount of $125,000.

(d) **Calculation of goodwill**

	$'000
Property, plant and equipment	8,000
Inventory	2,000
Receivables	3,710
Cash	430
Deferred tax balance	2,200
Patents	1,000
Customer list	1,500
Current liabilities	(3,775)
Non-current liabilities	(12,500)
	2,565
Amount paid	2,000
Gain on bargain purchase	(565)

(e) There is a presumption that in an arm's length transaction negative goodwill should not arise. The first thing to do, therefore, is to ensure that all assets and liabilities have been identified – in particular, all intangible assets. Second, the valuations attached to all assets and liabilities should be reviewed to ensure that they are appropriate ie at fair values. If negative goodwill remains it should be treated as a bargain purchase and reported as part of profit or loss for the year.

Financial instruments

(a) Not all of the costs involved are costs of making the issue. The following costs should be written off to profit or loss as incurred:

- Feasibility study $6,480
- Management time negotiating the issue $8,500

The following costs are issue costs and should be written off against reserves:

- Publicity and printing costs $11,500
- Legal fees and costs $23,400

If there is a share premium account, the issue costs should be written off against this. Otherwise they should be written off against another reserve eg retained earnings.

(b) The finance charge reported in the statement of profit or loss and other comprehensive income for Years 1 to 4 will be $900,000 each year. If the issuer elects to redeem the bonds at the start of the fifth year, there will be a loss on the exercise of the option of $2,500,000. This will be reported in the statement of profit or loss and other comprehensive income for Year 5.

(c) The cash flow model is:

Year	Balance b/f	Finance cost at 11.37351% of b/f	Cash paid at % of nominal amount	Balance c/f
	$	$	$	$
1	800,000	90,988	44,000 (5.5%)	846,988
2	846,988	96,332	48,000 (6.0%)	895,320
3	895,320	101,829	52,000 (6.5%)	945,150
4	945,150	107,497	56,000 (7.0%)	996,646
5	996,646	113,354	60,000 (7.5%)	1,050,000

If the interest is not paid until after the financial year end, the financial statements will include the following figures for the first two years:

ANSWERS TO END OF CHAPTER QUESTIONS

Statement of profit or loss and other comprehensive income	Year 1	Year 2
Interest payable	90,988	96,332
Statement of financial position	Year 1	Year 2
Accrued interest	44,000	48,000
Loans	846,988	895,320

Trench Quarries

This question concerns accounting for leases under IFRS 16 *Leases*.

(a) (i) IFRS 16 distinguishes between the inception date (when leases are classified) and the lease term commencement date (when recognition takes place) so Trench Quarries could make an initial calculation of the asset and liability at inception but may not recognise these in the financial statements until the commencement date, if later.

> **Tutorial note**: these amounts may in some circumstances be revised.

The inception date is the earlier of the date of the lease agreement and the date of commitment of the parties to its principal provisions, which is 1 October 2009. The lease term commencement date is the date on which Trench Quarries is entitled to exercise its right to use the machine and is the date of initial recognition of the assets, liabilities, income and expenses related to the lease in its financial statements. This is also 1 October 2009. Therefore, despite the postponement of the lease rental payments the asset and liability should be recognised from 1 October 2009.

Trench Quarries should recognise a right–of-use asset and a liability in its statement of financial position at the commencement of the lease term (1 October 2009). The measurement of the right-of-use asset is the sum of the present value of the lease payments (8.1m) and the initial direct costs (0.2m), making the right-of-use asset total $8.3 million. This amount will be depreciated over the lease term of 5 years.

Interest will accrue from 1 October 2009 using the interest rate implicit in the lease. The rental payments from 1 January 2010 must be apportioned as to the payment of this accrued interest and repayment of the lease liability.

(b) IFRS 16 defines a lease as a contract that conveys to the customer ('lessee') the right to use an asset for a period of time in exchange for consideration. A company assesses whether a contract contains a lease on the basis of whether the customer has the right to control the use of an identified asset for a period of time.

IFRS 16 eliminates the IAS 17 classification of leases as either operating leases or finance leases for a lessee. Instead all leases are accounted for in a similar way to finance leases under IAS 17.

The most significant effect of the new requirements in IFRS 16 will be an increase in leased assets and financial liabilities. Accordingly, for companies with material off balance sheet leases, there will be a change to key financial metrics derived from the company's assets and liabilities (for example, leverage ratios).

For companies with material off balance leases, IFRS 16 changes the nature of expenses related to those leases. IFRS 16 replaces the typical straight-line operating lease expense for those leases with a depreciation charge for lease assets (included within operating costs) and an interest expense on lease liabilities (included within finance costs). This change aligns the lease expense treatment for all leases. Although the depreciation charge is typically even, the interest expense reduces over the life of the lease as lease payments are made. This results in a reducing total expense as an individual lease matures. The difference in the expense profile between IFRS 16 and IAS 17 is expected to be insignificant for many companies holding a portfolio of leases that start and end in different reporting periods.

Leasing provides an important and flexible source of financing for many companies. However, the old lease accounting Standard (IAS 17 *Leases*) made it difficult for investors and others to get an accurate picture of a company's lease assets and liabilities, particularly for industries such as the airline, retail and transport sectors.

Listed companies using IFRS Standards or US GAAP are estimated to have around US$3.3 trillion of lease commitments; over 85% of which do not appear on their balance sheets.

This somewhat arbitrary distinction made it difficult for investors to compare companies. It also meant that investors and others had to estimate the effects of a company's off balance sheet lease obligations, which in practice often led to overestimating the liabilities arising from those obligations. IFRS 16 solves this problem by requiring all leases to be reported on a company's balance sheet as assets and liabilities.

The new standard provides increased transparency on companies' lease assets and liabilities, and will also improve comparability between companies that lease and those that borrow to buy.

Employee benefits

A question on a defined benefit employee compensation scheme.

Syllabus reference: 13.4

(i) **Present value of obligation**

	20X8 $K	20X9 $K
Present value of obligation at start of year	20,000	23,000
Interest cost thereon at 8%	1,600	1,840
Current service cost	1,250	1,430
Benefits paid	(987)	(1,100)
Actuarial gain/(loss)	1,137	330
Present value of obligation at end of the year	23,000	25,500

(ii) **Market value of plan assets**

	20X8 $K	20X9 $K
Market value of plan assets at start of year	20,000	21,500
Expected return thereon at 8%	1,600	1,720
Contributions	1,000	1,100
Benefits paid	(987)	(1,100)
Remeasurement of plan assets	(113)	(920)
Market value of plan assets at end of the year	21,500	22,300

(iii) **Amounts recognised in statement of profit or loss and other comprehensive income:**

	20X8 $K	20X9 $K
Recognised in profit or loss:		
Current service cost	(1,250)	(1,430)
Net interest cost on defined benefit liability (asset)	0	(120)
Recognised in other comprehensive income		
Actuarial gain on defined benefit obligation	1,137	330
Remeasurement of plan assets	(113)	(920)

ANSWERS TO END OF CHAPTER QUESTIONS

DT

Calculation of deferred tax liability

	Carrying amount $m	Tax base $m	Temporary differences $m
Goodwill (Note 1)	14	–	–
Subsidiary (Note 1)	76	60	16
Inventories (Note 2)	24	30	(6)
Property, plant and equipment (Note 3)	2,600	1,920	680
Other temporary differences			90
Property sold – tax due 30.11.20X4 (165/0.3)		–	550
Liability for health care benefits	100		(100)
Unrelieved tax losses (Note 4)			(100)
Temporary differences			1,130
Deferred tax liability (Note 1)	16 at 25%		4.0
Deferred tax asset (note 2)	(6) at 25%		(1.5)
Deferred tax asset (100 + 100)	(200) at 30%		(60.0)
Deferred tax liability (bal fig)	1,320 at 30%		396.0
Total differences	1,130		338.5
Less: Opening deferred tax liability			(280)
Addition to goodwill re deferred tax attributable to subsidiary (Note 1)			(4)
Deferred tax expense for the year			54.5

Notes

1. As no deduction is available for the cost of goodwill in the subsidiary's tax jurisdiction, then the tax base of goodwill is zero. Paragraph 15a of IAS 12, states that DT should not recognise a deferred tax liability in respect of taxable temporary differences arising from the initial recognition of goodwill. Goodwill will be increased by the amount of the deferred tax liability in respect of the remaining taxable temporary differences in the subsidiary, ie 25% × $16m = $4m.

2. Unrealised group profit eliminated on consolidation is 20% × $30m = $6m. Deferred tax is provided for at the receiving company's rate of tax (ie at 25%).

3. The tax that would arise if the properties were disposed of at their revalued amounts which was provided at the beginning of the year will be included in the temporary difference arising on the property, plant and equipment at 30 November 20X1.

4. DT has unrelieved tax losses of ($34m + $56m)/0.3 ie $300m. This will be available for offset against current year's profits ($110m) and against profits for the year ending 30 November 20X2 ($100m). Because of the uncertainty about the availability of taxable profits in 20X3, no deferred tax asset can be recognised for any losses which may be offset against this amount. Therefore a deferred tax asset may be recognised for the losses to be offset against taxable profits in 20X2. That is $100m × 30% ie $30m.

Comment

The deferred tax liability of DT will rise in total by $335.5 million ($338.5m – $3m), thus reducing net assets, distributable profits, and post tax earnings. The profit for the period will be reduced by $54.5 million which would probably be substantially more under IAS 12 than the old method of accounting for deferred tax. A prior period adjustment will occur of $280m – $3m as IFRS are being applied for the first time (IFRS 1) ie $277m. The borrowing position of the company may be affected and the directors may decide to cut dividend payments. However, the amount of any unprovided deferred tax, analysed into its major components, was required to be disclosed under the previous standard used. IAS 12 brings this liability onto the statement of financial position but because the bulk of the liability has already been disclosed the impact on the share price should be minimal.

Bartolo

(a) The increase in profit attributable to ordinary equity holders on conversion of potential ordinary shares is:

	Increase in earnings $	Increase in no. of ord. shares	Earnings per incremental share Cents
Number of shares resulting from options	nil	460,000	nil
Deemed to be issued at full market price (460,000 × 0.85/0.99)		(394,949)	
Deemed issued for no consideration		65,051	
Convertible preference shares (800,000 × 6.8%) and (800,000 × 1.25)	54,400	1,000,000	5.44
Convertible bonds (5,500,000 × 12% × (100% − 30% tax) and (5,500,000 × 2.5)	462,000	13,750,000	3.36

The larger the earnings per incremental share the smaller dilutive effect.

So now consider in descending order of dilutive effect.

Calculation of dilutive or antidilutive effect of potential ordinary shares

	Profit: continuing operations $	Ordinary shares	Per share Cents	
Profit from continuing operations	880,000	20,000,000	4.40	
Options	nil	65,051		
	880,000	20,065,051	4.39	dilutive
12% convertible bonds	462,000	13,750,000		
	1,342,000	33,815,051	3.97	dilutive
6.8% convertible preference shares	54,400	1,000,000		
	1,396,400	34,815,051	4.01	antidilutive

The antidilutive effect of the convertible preference shares is ignored.

So, the diluted EPS figure is 3.97 cents.

(b) **Theoretical ex-rights fair value per share**

Initial holding of shares	10	at $1.40 per share	14.0
Rights issue	1	at $1.15 per share	1.15
	11		15.15

Therefore, theoretical ex-rights fair value per share is $1.38 ie 15.15 divided by 11.00

Calculation of adjustment factor for bonus element

Fair value per share before exercise of rights	1.40
Theoretical ex-rights fair value per share	1.38
Adjustment factor	1.014492754

ANSWERS TO END OF CHAPTER QUESTIONS

Weighted average number of shares in issue

First 3 months:			
Shares in issue		25,000,000	
Adjustment factor		1.014492754	
		25,362,318.84	
Weighting		¼	6,340,580
Last 9 months:			
Shares in issue		27,500,000	
Weighting		¾	
			20,625,000
			26,965,580

Calculation of EPS

This year
Profit on ordinary activities after taxation	3,100,000	
Weighted average number of shares in issue	26,965,580	
So, EPS	11.50	cents

Recalculation of previous year's EPS
Profit on ordinary activities after taxation	2,200,000	
Number of shares in issue (after bonus element)	25,362,319	
So, restated EPS	8.67	cents

or

Previous year's EPS	8.80	cents	x	
Adjustment to number of shares for bonus element	1.014492754		Y	
So, restated EPS	8.67	cents	x/y	

(c) **Current year's EPS**

Profit before taxation ($)	2,276,850	
Taxation	(1,350,000)	
Transfer from deferred taxation	227,600	
Profit after tax ($)	1,154,450	
So EPS =	23.1	cents
(ie 1,154,450 / 5,000,000)		

Previous year's EPS (restated for comparatives)

As previously stated	22.2	cents
Old number of shares in issue	4,000,000	
New number of shares in issue	5,000,000	

Restated EPS = previous EPS times old no. of shares divided by new no. of shares

22.2 times 4,000,000 / 5,000,000

=	17.8	cents

Tine Foods

This question explores a number of aspects of accounting and reporting techniques.

(a) IAS 37 defines a provision as 'a liability of uncertain timing or amount'. What distinguishes a provision from other liabilities is the uncertainty of the liability.

(b) A provision should be recognised when, and only when:

   (i) An entity has a present obligation (legal or constructive) as a result of a past event;

   (ii) It is probable (ie more likely than not) that an outflow of resources embodying economic benefits will be required to settle the obligation; and

   (iii) A reliable estimate can be made of the amount of the obligation. The standard notes that it is only in extremely rare cases that a reliable estimate will not be possible.

(c) Under IAS 37 there is a potential liability depending on the outcome of the appeal – although the probability of the appeal succeeding may be regarded as low given the circumstances. This should therefore be reported as a contingent liability, with the potential amount disclosed. The company might prefer not to disclose an amount on the grounds that it is not possible to estimate it with sufficient reliability. However, the company has just sold the brand name and should be aware of its liability under that contract if the brand name is cancelled. It should also be possible to estimate any further legal costs and damages should the appeal be successful.

(d) Charge to profit or loss would be $494,000 as reorganisation costs; the provision is no longer needed so $500,000 would be written back to profit or loss – making a net addition to profit (reduction in loss) of $6,000. The accrued reorganisation costs would appear as a current liability in the statement of financial position.

Molar and Canal

This question involves IFRS 2 share based payment schemes and is relevant to Section 13.4 of the syllabus.

> **Tutorial note:** this question concerns share-based payment schemes. The starting point with such a question is to identify the type of scheme being examined.

(i) Advice to finance director:

This is an equity-settled share-based payment transaction. In other words, Molar has received employee services in exchange for equity instruments of the company. It is an increasingly common method of settling amounts owed for the payment of goods or services. If Molar had paid for the employees services in cash the amount would be recognised in profit or loss. The finance director is quite typical of those who believe that, as there is no cash outflow, there should not be any charge to profit or loss. However, this would ignore the fact that Molar has entered into a transaction and to ignore it would result in financial statements which did not reflect all economic transactions of the company.

The basic principle behind IFRS 2 *Share-based Payment* is that all transactions are measured at fair value. The fair value of transactions with employees is measured by reference to the fair value of the equity instruments at the grant date, that is, the date that Molar and the employees agree to the arrangement: 1 June 2011.

Molar should recognise a remuneration expense as employees provide their services over the three year vesting period. As employees will leave the scheme at various points during the three years, the number of options that are likely to vest at the end must be recalculated each year.

The accounting entry each year is:
Dr Expense in profit or loss
Cr Other component of equity

The amount to be recognised as an expense each year would be found by calculating the accumulated expense at the end of each year of the scheme and measuring the change, as follows:

- *Year to 31 May 2012*

    Number of employees likely to remain in the scheme as at 31 May 2012:

    2,500 (as at 1 June 2011) – 60 (expected to leave during first year) – 610 (25% of those expected to leave before 31 May 2014; ie 2,500 – 60 = 2,440) = 1,830.

    Expense recognised: 1,830 × 250 (no. of share options) × $30 (fair value at grant date × 1/3 (one year of scheme) = $4.575m

- *Year to 31 May 2013*

    Number of employees likely to remain in the scheme as at 31 May 2013:

    2,440 (as at 1 June 2012) – 407 (2/3 of those expected to leave during second year, that is 610 × 2/3) = 2,033.

    Accumulated expense as at 31 May 2013:

    2,033 × 250 (no. of share options) × $30 (fair value at grant date) × 2/3 (two years of scheme) = $10.165m

    Expense recognised: $10.165 – $4.575 = $5.590m

- *Year to 31 May 2014*

    Number of employees likely to be in the scheme as at 31 May 2014; that is, on vesting day:

    2,033 (as at 1 June 2013) – 203 (1/3 of those expected to leave during final year, that is 610 × 1/3) = 1,830.

    Accumulated expense as at 31 May 2014:

    1,830 × 250 (no. of share options) × $30 (fair value at grant date) × 3/3 (three years of scheme) = $13.725m

    Expense recognised: $13.725m – $10.165 = $3.560m

(ii) Advice to Canal:

This is a cash-settled share-based payment transaction. Canal has acquired employees' services in exchange for amounts of cash measured by reference to the company's share price. They are known as 'share appreciation rights' (SARs). Under the scheme Canal's employees will become entitled to future cash payments based on the increase in the company's share price over a specified period of time, that is, three years. Unlike Molar's equity settled scheme, SARs are measured at the fair value of the **liability**; that is, the liability to transfer cash. The liability is therefore re-measured at each year end. This is unlike an equity settled scheme where fair value is measured at the grant date and remains constant.

Any changes in the fair value of the liability are recognised in profit or loss. Similar to Molar's equity settled scheme, the cost of employees' services are recognised over the period such services are provided but unlike an equity settled scheme, the credit is to liabilities that is, the accounting entry each period is:

Dr Expense in profit or loss
Cr Liabilities

The amount to be recognised as an expense each year would be found by calculating the accumulated liability at the end of each year of the scheme and measuring the change, as follows:

- *Year to 31 May 2008*

    Number of SARs likely to vest: 1,000 – 190 = 810.

    Expense for the year and liability as at year end: 810 (employees) × 200 (SARs) × $15 × 1/3 = $0.810m

- *Year to 31 May 2009*

    Number of SARs likely to vest: 1,000 – 70 (left during 2008) – 135 = 795.

    Liability as at year end: 795 (employees) × 200 (SARs) × $16 × 2/3 = $1.696m

    Expense for the year: $1.696m - $0.810m = $0.886m

- *Year to 31 May 2010*

    Liability at year end for SARs not exercised: $1.717m

    1,000 – 195 (left to date) – 300 (exercised during year): 505 (employees) × 200 (SARs) × $17 =

                                             Expense

    SARs actually exercised during the year: 300 (employees) × 200 (SARs) × $16.50 $0.990m

    Expense for the year: $1.717m - $1.696m = $0.0.021m $0.021m

                                             $1.011m

- *Year to 31 May 2011*

    Final cash settlement: 505 (employees) × 200 (SARs) × $18 = $1.818m

    Expense for year: $1.818m (final cash settlement) – $1.717m (liability b/f) = $0.101m

IFRS 15

Syllabus area: 13.4

The director wishes to recognise the sale as early as possible. However, following IFRS 15 *Revenue from contracts with customers*, revenue from the sale should only be recognised when the performance obligations in the contract have been satisfied.

Performance obligations in the contract

The contract contains a promise to deliver the caravan and a promise to deliver additional goods free of charge. These are distinct promises and therefore the contract contains two performance obligations.

Transaction price

The transaction price is made up of three elements.

A significant financing component must be considered where consideration is received more than 12 months before or after the date on which revenue is recognised (being the delivery date, 1 August 20X7). Therefore the payment on 1 August 20X9 must be discounted to present value at 1 August 20X7.

ANSWERS TO END OF CHAPTER QUESTIONS

	K
Deposit	3,000
Payment on 1.8.X7 (the delivery date)	15,000
Payment on 1.8.X9 ($12,000/ 1.1^2)	9,917
	27,917

Allocation to performance obligations

The transaction price is allocated based on standalone selling prices:

Caravan	30,000/31,500 × $30,000	= $28,571
Free equipment	1,500/31,500 × $30,000	= $1,489

Recognition of revenue

The two performance obligations are satisfied simultaneously on 1 August 20X7, and therefore all revenue is recognised on this date.

Journal entries are as follows:

1 May 20X7

The receipt of cash in the form of the $,3000 deposit is recognised on receipt as a contract liability (deferred income) in the statement of financial position by:

DEBIT	Bank	$3,000	
CREDIT	Contract liability (deferred income)		$3,000

1 August 20X7

Revenue is recognised together with payment of the first $15,000. The contract liability is transferred to be revenue:

DEBIT	Bank	$15,000	
DEBIT	Contract liability	$3,000	
DEBIT	Receivable	$9,917	
CREDIT	Revenue		$27,917

Tramwell

Briefing Note

To: Finance Director
From: Accountant
Re: IFRS for SMEs

The purpose of this briefing note is to address the following issues:

(1) Whether Tramwell is eligible to adopt the IFRS for SMEs
(2) How the accounting policies of Tramwell may change under the IFRS for SMEs
(3) The practical considerations of adopting the IFRS for SMEs

Eligibility to adopt

The IFRS for SMEs can be applied by those entities which:

(a) Do not have public accountability;
(b) Publish general purpose financial statements for external users; and
(c) Are permitted to by the legislative authorities of the jurisdiction in which they operate.

An entity with public accountability is an entity whose debt or equity instruments are traded or will be traded in a public market, or an entity which holds assets in a fiduciary capacity for a broad range of third parties. Although Tramwell's parent company Ramses is listed (and so its debt or equity instruments are publicly traded), Tramwell itself is not. The IFRS for SMEs stipulates that in this situation, provided that the subsidiary itself is not publicly accountable, it may apply the standard. The second part of the definition of public accountability refers to holding assets in a fiduciary capacity for third parties as a primary part of the business. It is clear from Tramwell's statement of financial position that Tramwell's business is not primarily concerned with holding assets for others. Therefore Tramwell does not have public accountability.

It is also apparent that Tramwell does publish general purpose financial statements, which are presumed to be for external users. Therefore the second condition is met.

Tramwell therefore meets the eligibility criteria stipulated within the IFRS for SMEs. However, it may only apply the standard if the legislative authorities of the country in which it operates permits application.

Accounting policies

A review of Tramwell's statement of financial position (SOFP) reveals a number of areas in which accounting policies would change on adoption of the IFRS for SMEs:

- The revaluation reserve in Tramwell's SOFP suggests that Tramwell adopts a policy of revaluing its property, plant and equipment (PPE). This option is not allowed under the IFRS for SMEs and the cost model must instead be applied. PPE is therefore measured at cost less depreciation and any impairment losses. In respect of PPE, you should also note that the IFRS for SMEs requires a review of residual values, useful lives and depreciation methods only where there is a significant change in an asset or how it is used.

- It is unclear whether items of PPE are self-constructed or adapted after purchase for use by Tramwell. Where this is the case and borrowing costs are incurred in order to meet construction or adaption costs, the IFRS for SMEs is clear that these costs must be recognised in profit or loss and may not be capitalised.

- In respect of investment properties, the IFRS for SMEs requires measurement at fair value, unless this involves undue cost or effort. It appears that investment properties are currently measured at fair value under local GAAP, however the existence of an investment property reserve suggests that fair value gains and losses are currently recognised in equity. Under the IFRS for SMEs these must be recognised in profit or loss, meaning that the profits of Tramwell may become more volatile.

- Tramwell's SOFP includes capitalised development costs of $220,000. The IFRS for SMEs requires that all internally generated intangible assets, including development costs are recognised immediately in profit or loss. If Tramwell is engaged in a number of ongoing development costs, this will result in lower profits after adoption of the IFRS for SMEs.

- Tramwell has recognised $400,000 financial assets at cost. It is unclear what type of financial assets these are. Under the IFRS for SMEs, financial instruments are classified as either 'basic' or 'other'. Basic financial instruments are generally measured at amortised cost using the effective interest method and other financial instruments at fair value with changes recognised in profit or loss. Clarification is required before further advice can be given in this area.

- Long term liabilities includes deferred tax. The IFRS for SMEs requires that provision is made for deferred tax on all temporary differences with limited exceptions. Where there is an uncertain tax position, the standard requires the provision is measured using the probability-weighted average amount of all possible outcomes. If this is not required under local GAAP it may result in additional work for the finance team, and different measurement of the liability.

- The IFRS for SMEs includes illustrative financial statements where a suggested format for the statement of financial position is provided. This shows all assets in the 'top half' of the SOFP and all equity, reserves and liabilities in the 'bottom half'. Although the standard does not prescribe this format or sequence of items, it is the format usually adopted by companies applying IFRS therefore Tramwell may wish to change to such a format on adoption of the IFRS for SMEs.

Practical considerations

If Tramwell adopts the IFRS for SMEs, it must consider a number of practical issues as well as the impact on amounts reported in the financial statements.

In the first case, IFRS for SMEs accounting software will be required. This may involve a significant capital outlay. In addition, accounting staff will need to be trained in its operation. Accounting staff will also need

ANSWERS TO END OF CHAPTER QUESTIONS

training in the requirements of the IFRS for SMEs, and as the standard evolves and is updated, staff knowledge will need to be updated.

Tramwell should also consider whether the IFRS for SMEs is a widely accepted financial reporting framework in the business environment in which it operates. For example, local finance providers may require additional disclosures and statements which may result in a cost-benefit test not being met.

Tramwell's results are consolidated into the Ramses group accounts. As accounting policy differs in some instances between full IFRS and the IFRS for SMEs, the need for GAAP adjustments on consolidation is not removed.

If local tax law is based on accounting treatment, taxable income and therefore taxes payable could change under the IFRS for SMEs. Other items affected by profits and where policy review may therefore be needed include:

- Distributable reserves and potential dividends
- Management compensation

Curia

The following suggested solution is indicative only.

REPORT
FROM:
TO:
DATE:
SUBJECT: Financial performance of Curia

The following report is based on a series of financial ratios calculated from the financial statements of Curia for the financial years 20X3, 20X4 and 20X5.

The overall performance of Curia as evidenced by its return on equity has fluctuated. There was a significant improvement from 20X3 to 20X4 due to significant improvements in profitability on trading (net income to sales revenue) and a marginal improvement in assets utilisation (sales revenue to total assets).

That improvement in overall efficiency was not maintained in 20X5 and return on equity declined to 13%. This time the decrease was due to a significant decline in assets utilisation which is now at its lowest for the three-year period. There was an accompanying decline in profitability on trading but this may be marginal.

Earnings per share have followed a similar pattern to return on equity. There was a very significant rise in earnings per share for 20X4 – but this was followed by a decline of approximately 10% in 20X5. Dividends per share, however, have been constant over the three-year period suggesting that there may have been relative increases in profits retained within the company in 20X4 and 20X5.

Changes in the profitability on trading over the three-year period seem to be attributable to steadily increasing margins on sales (gross profit to sales revenue). However, progress here seems to have been offset by increases in operating expenses (operating expenses to sales revenue) – particularly in 20X5.

Control of working capital seems efficient. There has been no significant trend in the current and acid test ratios and, while it is not known what business sector Curia operates in, these ratios seem to have been stable for the past three years. All components of working capital seem to be being managed more efficiently with falling trends in the period of credit taken by customers and from suppliers, and increasingly efficient turnover of inventory.

The fall in efficiency in the use of assets to generate sales (sales revenue to total assets) and the increasing net assets per share would therefore appear to signify increasing investment in non-current assets. It may be that some of the inefficiency in the use of these non-current assets may be temporary and may disappear once the assets become fully utilised for a full financial year.

ANSWERS TO END OF CHAPTER QUESTIONS

Recommendations for improving the performance of Curia.

The overall performance of Curia could be improved by:

- Better control of operating expenses. Reducing operating expenses would increase profitability on sales and hence overall return on equity.

- Careful monitoring of non-current assets utilisation. Increasing sales revenue to non-current assets would increase sales revenue to total assets and hence overall return on equity.

Limitations

- It has been assumed that all the data is comparable ie that similar accounting policies have been used over the three years.

- It has only been possible to look at trends within Curia over the past three years. It would be useful to compare Curia's performance with its competitors – particularly the leading firms in the same industry sector with a view to knowing what is achievable.

- It would be useful to know more about the sector Curia operates in and general economic conditions. This would help identify what changes are attributable to changes in sector performance and general economic conditions and changes attributable to good or bad management.

- The available information is very limited. It would be useful to have additional information about the quality of Curia's management, its risk exposure and the prospects for the industry sector.

ANSWERS TO END OF CHAPTER QUESTIONS

Exam question bank

Question 1 – AIA May 2017

Prent, a public limited company manufactures electronics. The statements of financial position of the members of the Prent Group as at 31 March 2017 were as follows:

	Prent $m	Malt $m	Dolt $m
Investment in Malt	48		
Investment in Dolt	214		
Property, plant and equipment	1,188	150	180
	1,450	150	180
Current assets	260	30	52
	1,710	180	232
Equity			
Share capital	600	24	80
Retained earnings	1,006	124	140
	1,606	148	220
Current liabilities	104	32	12
	1,710	180	232

(i) Prent purchased 80% of Malt on 31 March 2012 for $160m when Malt had retained earnings of $84m. The fair value of the non-controlling interest was $36m.

Prent sold half of its investment in Malt for $112m on 31 March 2016 when Malt's retained earnings were $108m. The proceeds of disposal were debited to cash and credited to investment in Malt. The estimated fair value of the remaining 40% holding in Malt at the date of disposal was $120m.

Prent accounts for its remaining investment in Malt on the basis that it has a significant influence over Malt's management.

(ii) Prent purchased 60% of Dolt on 31 March 2013 at a cost of $160m. On that date Dolt's retained earnings were $70m and the fair value of its non-controlling interest was $116m.

Prent made a further payment of $40m for an additional 15% of Dolt on 31 March 2014. At that date, Dolt's retained earnings were $124m.

(iii) Prent shows its investments at their fair value in its statement of financial position.

(iv) Prent's maintenance staff carried out an extensive refurbishment of Dolt's property during the year. The work cost Prent $5m and was invoiced to Dolt at $8m. Dolt has capitalised the $8m. No additional depreciation has been charged on this amount.

(v) An impairment adjustment of $40m is to be made to the goodwill on the acquisition of Dolt.

Required

(a) Prepare the consolidated statement of financial position for the Prent Group as at 31 March 2017.

(35 marks)

(b) Prent's external auditor investigated the relationship between Prent and Malt at an early stage in the year ended 31 March 2017 and was satisfied that Prent could exercise a significant influence. There have been no further investigations or discussions of that matter since.

The relationship between Prent and Malt has changed during the final few months of the year ended 31 March 2017. Prent's board has found it increasingly difficult to exercise any control over Malt. Despite that, Prent intends to treat Malt as an associate.

Advise Prent's board on the ethical implications of their proposed treatment of this investment.

(5 marks)

(Total 40 marks)

Question 2

Nedell Corp, a multinational diversified company, is preparing its financial statements for the year ended 31 October 20X6. A number of issues have arisen and the company has asked you for advice.

(a) During its financial year ended on 31 October 20X6 Nedell Corp sold a commercial building to one of its directors, A J Parrish. The sale of the property was approved by the board of directors but A J Parrish did not participate in the discussions and did not vote on the decision. In order to keep the transaction at arm's length, the selling price of $1.5 million was a valuation determined by a firm of independent valuers. The sale agreement also includes a provision that if the building is given planning permission for alternative use and is sold at a profit within 20 years any surplus attributable to the granting of planning permission will be payable to Nedell Corp. The property is let out to a tenant at a commercial rent.

Required

Advise how the sale should be dealt with in the financial statements for the year ended 31 October 20X6. **(5 marks)**

(b) Nedell Corp has entered into an agreement to dispose of its activities in Brazil. Competition and monopoly legislation requires the disposal to be scrutinised by a regulatory body. It is expected that the sale will shortly be given clearance and that the disposal will be completed within the next six months.

Required

Advise how this matter should be reported in Nedell Corp's financial statements. **(5 marks)**

(c) Nedell Corp includes in land and buildings a property which it thinks might now meet the criteria for an investment property. If it does, Nedell Corp would like to continue reporting it in land and buildings at cost less depreciation.

Required

What are the criteria for an investment property under IAS 40, and will it be possible to continue reporting the property at cost less depreciation? **(6 marks)**

(d) Nedell Corp has a number of associates and joint ventures which are reported in accordance with IAS 28 *Investments in Associates and Joint Ventures*. Nedell Corp had significant trading transactions with these companies during the year ended 31 October 20X6 but these will be eliminated upon consolidation.

Required

Other than reporting the associates and joint ventures in accordance with IAS 28, are there any additional disclosure requirements? **(4 marks)**

(Total 20 marks)

Question 3 – AIA Nov 2014

Ardew is a public limited company and has produced the following draft group financial statements:

Ardew Group
Statement of comprehensive income for the year ended 31 October 2014

	$m
Revenue	270.0
Cost of sales	198.1
Gross profit	71.9
Other income	15.6
Operating expenses	(57.2)
Finance costs	(3.8)
Operating profit	26.5
Gain in fair value of investment property	6.6
Share of profit after tax of associate	3.8
Profit before tax	36.9
Income tax expense	(6.9)
Profit for the year	30.0
Other comprehensive income after tax	
Items that will not be reclassified to profit or loss:	
Remeasurement deficit on defined benefit plan	(3.8)
Fair value gain on investment in equity instruments	1.3
Loss on revaluation of owner-occupied property	(4.4)
Other comprehensive income for the year after tax	(6.9)
Total comprehensive income for the year	23.1
Profit for the year attributable to:	
Owners of the parent	23.8
Non-controlling interest	6.2
	30.0
Total comprehensive income for the year attributable to:	
Owners of the parent	16.9
Non-controlling interest	6.2
	23.1

Ardew Group
Statement of changes in equity for the year ended 31 October 2014

	Share capital $m	Retained earnings $m	Revaluation surplus (PPE) $m	Investments in equity instruments $m	Total $m	Non-controlling interest $m	Total equity $m
Balance as at 1 November 2013	171.9	202.5	10.0	2.5	386.9	22.5	409.4
Issue of share capital	10.6				10.6		10.6
Dividends paid		(3.1)			(3.1)	(8.1)	(11.2)
Acquisitions						12.5	12.5
Total comprehensive income for the year		20.0	(4.4)	1.3	16.9	6.2	23.1
Balance as at 31 October 2014	182.5	219.4	5.6	3.8	411.3	33.1	444.4

Ardew Group
Statement of financial position as at 31 October 2014

	2014 $m	2013 $m
ASSETS		
Non-current assets		
Property, plant and equipment	204.4	158.8
Investment property	5.0	3.8
Intangible assets	53.1	45.0
Goodwill	30.0	42.5
Investment in associate	33.8	–
Investments in equity instruments	58.8	56.2
	385.1	306.3
Current assets		
Inventories	65.6	80.0
Trade receivables	38.7	70.6
Cash and cash equivalents	145.0	89.4
	249.3	240.0
TOTAL ASSETS	634.4	546.3
EQUITY AND LIABILITIES		
Equity		
Equity attributable to owners of the parent		
Share capital	182.5	171.9
Retained earnings	219.4	202.5
Other components of equity	9.4	12.5
	411.3	386.9
Non-controlling interest	33.1	22.5
Total equity	444.4	409.4
Liabilities		
Non-current liabilities		
Long-term debt	41.9	44.4
Deferred tax	21.9	25.6
Defined benefit pension liability	15.6	13.8
	79.4	83.8
Current liabilities		
Trade payables	90.0	34.3
Current income tax payable	20.6	18.8
	110.6	53.1
Total liabilities	190.0	136.9
TOTAL EQUITY AND LIABILITIES	634.4	546.3

The following information is relevant to the financial statements of the Ardew Group:

(i) Ardew gained control over Palan by acquiring 60% of Palan's equity shares in two stages as follows:

	Holding %	Consideration $m
1 November 2012	10	2.5
1 January 2014	50	18.8

On 1 January 2014, the fair value of Ardew's 10% holding was $3.1 million and the fair value of the non-controlling interest was $12.5 million. The purchase consideration at 1 January 2014 comprised cash $10 million and shares of $8.8 million.

The fair value of Palan's identifiable net assets, excluding deferred tax, at 1 January 2014 was $28.1 million as follows:

	$m
Property plant and equipment	9.4
Intangible assets	11.2
Trade receivables	3.1
Cash	4.4
	28.1

Palan's tax rate is 30% and the tax base of the identifiable net assets was $25 million.

Impairment testing relating to all subsidiaries' goodwill was carried out by Ardew at 31 October 2014. Any impairment relates solely to wholly-owned subsidiaries and has been accounted for in the above draft financial statements.

(ii) On 1 November 2013 Ardew paid $5 million to acquire patents concerning a research project aimed at developing a new production process. The item was recognised as an intangible asset. During the year the following further expenditures were incurred. Ardew adopted the provisions of IAS 38 concerning the recognition of intangible assets.

	$m
Evaluation of research findings	1.0
Final selection of new process	0.3
Construction and testing of new process	2.5
Initial marketing costs	0.6

There were no other additions to intangible assets other than those on the acquisition of Palan.

(iii) During the year, fair value movements related to Ardew's defined pension liability were as follows:

	$m
Current service cost	6.3
Enhancements to scheme's benefits	1.2
Net interest receivable by scheme	5.0

Remeasurement gains and losses are recognised in accordance with IAS 19 *Employment Benefits* as amended with effect from 1 January 2013.

(iv) Property, plant and equipment depreciation for the year was $16.9 million. In addition, in order to enhance future group cash flows, Ardew exchanged surplus land with a carrying value of $6.2 million for land with a fair value of $2.5 million plus cash of $9.4 million.

(v) During the year, in the ordinary course of business, land with a cost of $6 million was acquired by Ardew exclusively for development and resale in the near future. Ardew accounted for this as investment property under IAS 40. The closing balance sheet figures for inventory and investment property were correct.

(vi) During the year Ardew purchased 15% of the equity shares of Koje and was able to exert significant influence over the company. Koje did not pay any dividends during the year.

Required

(a) Prepare the consolidated statement of cash flows for the Ardew Group for the year ended 31 October 2014 using the indirect method in accordance with IAS 7 *Statements of Cash Flows*.
(35 marks)

(b) Ardew is a property developer and has built up a substantial portfolio of prime development land which has yet to be developed. Ardew is presently negotiating to raise a five-year loan based upon the value of the land portfolio. The proceeds will be received in the year to 31 October 2015 and repayments will begin in the following year. Ardew's directors wish to account for the proceeds as operating cash flows on the basis that without the loan the land could not be developed and as such are operating in nature. Ardew's directors receive a bonus if operating cash flows exceed a certain target.

Advise Ardew's directors on the nature of any ethical implications concerning their proposed treatment of the loan proceeds.
(5 marks)

(Total 40 marks)

EXAM QUESTION BANK

Question 4 – AIA May 2015

(a) Fere, a public limited company, is considering whether to adopt a revaluation policy under IAS 16 *Property, Plant and Equipment* in the financial statements for the year ended 30 April 2015. The directors require advice on the accounting implications of such an adoption and have provided the following information concerning one of the entity's assets.

The asset was purchased on 1 May 2009 at a cost of $10 million. During the purchase period, Fere incurred additional administration and general overheads of $100,000. The asset has a life of ten years and a residual value of $nil. Depreciation is provided on a straight-line basis. On 30 April 2012, the asset was revalued to $3.5 million. On 30 April 2015 the asset was revalued to $5 million.

The directors would choose to deal with depreciation by eliminating it against the asset's gross carrying value as allowed by IAS 16.

Upon each revaluation the useful life of the asset did not change.

Required

(i) Advise the directors of the accounting entries necessary had Fere adopted a revaluation policy from 30 April 2012 and of whether any adjustments to prior years would be necessary at 30 April 2015 to comply with IAS 8 *Accounting Policies, Changes in Accounting Estimates and Errors*. **(6 marks)**

(ii) Fere's directors understand that, if a revaluation policy is adopted, the international accounting standard IFRS 13 *Fair Value Measurement* provides guidance on the measurement of the fair value of assets such as property, plant and equipment. However, they are unsure of the extent of the changes IFRS 13 has introduced.

Required

Advise the directors of the main measurement changes IFRS 13 has introduced which will be relevant if they were to adopt a revaluation policy for property, plant and equipment under IAS 16. **(4 marks)**

(b) Fere's directors are considering whether to lease items of property, plant and equipment and have heard that the IASB has recently published IFRS 16 *Leases*. They require advice concerning the reasons for the change and their likely practical impacts. Fere has a number of leases which were accounted for as operating leases under IAS 17

Required

(i) Advise Fere's directors of the reasons behind the IASB's introduction of IFRS 16 and of the likely effect of IFRS 16 on Fere's income statement and statement of financial position. **(4 marks)**

(ii) At the start of the year, Fere hired a machine under a four year lease. The expected useful life of the machine is five years. A deposit of $700,000 was payable on the commencement of the lease on 1 January 20X6. The present value of the future lease payments was $1,871,100. A further three instalments of $700,000 are payable annually in advance. The interest rate implicit in the lease is 6%.

Required

Advise Fere's directors of the amounts to be included in its income statement and statement of financial position for Year 1 under IFRS 16. **(6 marks)**

(Total 20 marks)

Question 5 – AIA Nov 2016

(a) Atab, a public limited company, is preparing group financial statements for the year ended 31 October 2016. The entity has two investments as follows:

   (i) Atab owns 100% of the equity of Begi. The equity was originally acquired for $7.5 million when the fair value of Begi's identifiable net assets was $4.5 million. On 31 October 2016 Atab sold 60% of the equity to Cogni for $2 million. On disposal the carrying value of Begi's net assets in Atab's group financial statements was $1.8 million and the fair value of Atab's remaining 40% interest in Begi was $1.2 million. As a result of the sale, Atab and Cogni have joint control over Begi.

   Atab has attempted to follow IAS 28 *Investments in Associates and Joint Ventures*, and has used the equity method to account for the initial carrying value of the joint venture at cost; ie $3 million, being 40% of the original cost. Atab has recognised a loss on disposal of $2.5 million.

   (ii) Atab gained significant influence over Blo by acquiring 25% of Blo's equity shares on 1 November 2015 for $5.1 million. Directly attributable costs were $400,000. The fair value of Blo's identifiable net assets on 1 November 2015 was $16 million.

   On 31 October 2016, Atab acquired an additional investment of 20% in Blo at a cost of $6.8 million and incurred directly attributable costs of $200,000. Atab retained significant influence over Blo. In the year to 31 October 2016 Blo's retained earnings increased by $13.5 million and on that date an item of plant and equipment in Blo's financial statements increased in value by $3.5 million.

   Required

   Advise Atab on how the above investments should be accounted for in its group statement of financial position as at 31 October 2016. You should show the amount to be disclosed for goodwill relating to (ii).

   Note. Marks for individual sections are shown above.

   (12 marks)

(b) Alac is considering forming an investee for the purpose of developing a new health drink. Two entities, Bin and Cons, have approached Alac each with a view to entering into separate contractual arrangements with Alac concerning the product. The details are as follows:

   Bin is proposing an arrangement whereby Bin will develop the drink and obtain regulatory approval for it. Alac would be responsible for manufacturing and marketing the drink once regulatory approval has been received. Both parties would have unilateral ability to make all decisions concerning their own activity.

   Cons is proposing an arrangement identical to Bin's with the exception that both Alac and Cons will jointly make decisions over both activities.

   Required

   Advise Alac on whether, under each proposal, joint control exists in accordance with IFRS 11 *Joint Arrangements*. **(4 marks)**

(c) Exten and Gect have established a joint venture sharing profits in the ratio 60:40 respectively. Exten has contributed inventory with a historical cost of $3.4 million to the venture and has estimated its net realisable value at either $3.7 million or $3 million. Exten is now preparing its group financial statements and has included $3.4 million in revenue.

   Required

   Advise Exten on how to account for the above transaction should the inventory be valued at (i) $3.7 million and (ii) $3 million. **(4 marks)**

   (Total 20 marks)

Question 6 – AIA May 2015

Radmin, a public limited company, owns and operates a number of department stores around the world. The group's statements of comprehensive income for the year ended 30 April 2015 were as follows:

	Radmin $m	Ture $m	Ream $m
Revenue	520	292	137
Cost of sales	416	143	98
Gross profit	104	149	39
Other income	20	13	8
Administrative costs	(59)	(72)	(22)
Finance costs	(14)	(20)	(14)
Profit before tax	51	70	11
Income tax expense	(17)	(23)	(4)
PROFIT FOR THE YEAR	34	47	7
Other comprehensive income:			
Items that will not be reclassified to profit or loss (net of tax)			
Gain on revaluation of property, plant and equipment	21	4	–
Re measurements of defined benefit pension plans	6	–	–
nvestments in equity instruments	10	–	–
Other comprehensive income for the year, net of tax	37	4	3
TOTAL COMPREHENSIVE INCOME FOR THE YEAR	71	51	10

The following information is relevant to the preparation of the Radmin Group's statement of comprehensive income:

(i) Radmin gained control of Ture, a public limited company, by acquiring 75% of Ture's equity interests on 1 May 2013. The purchase consideration comprised cash $195 million plus a further payment of $4 million contingent upon Ture attaining certain performance targets by 2016. The current indications are that these targets will be achieved. Acquisition fees of $7 million have been capitalised by Radmin.

At the date of acquisition, the fair value of Ture's identifiable net assets was $209 million and the fair value of the non-controlling interests was $70 million at that date. For all acquisitions, it is group policy to measure non-controlling interests at fair value as at the date of acquisition.

Ture's share capital, retained earnings and other components of equity were $72 million, $110 million and $13 million respectively at the date of acquisition. The excess of the fair value of the identifiable net assets at acquisition is due to an increase in administrative plant and equipment unique to Ture's department stores. These assets are depreciated on a straight-line basis and have a seven-year remaining life at the date of acquisition.

Goodwill in Ture was impairment tested on 30 April 2015 and was found to have lost 10% of its original value.

(ii) Radmin acquired 100% of the equity interests of Ream, a public limited company, on 1 May 2012 for a cash consideration of $110 million. At the date of acquisition, the fair value of Ream's identifiable net assets was $70 million. There has been no impairment to goodwill since the date of acquisition.

On 30 April 2015, Radmin disposed of all of the equity for $160 million. At the date of disposal, the carrying value of Ream's identifiable net assets of $108 million was deemed to be their fair value.

(iii) During the year, Radmin sold inventory to both Ture and Ream with a sale price of $16 million and $4 million respectively. At the year-end all of the goods sold to Ream had been sold to third parties and a quarter of the goods sold to Ture remained unsold. Radmin sells all goods at a margin of 25%.

(iv) During the year, Radmin acquired $20 million investments in equity instruments which were subsequently designated as measured at fair value through other comprehensive income. At the year end, the fair value of these instruments was $25 million. Radmin estimated that, if the investment was to be sold, sale costs would be $1 million and has therefore included a gain of $4 million in other comprehensive income.

Radmin expects to receive dividends from this investment and has therefore included an estimated amount of $2 million in other income. The investee has not yet declared the amount of any dividend.

Radmin has adopted IFRS 9 *Financial Instruments*.

(v) On 1 May 2013 Radmin purchased an item of property, plant and equipment for $20 million. The item has nil residual value and is being depreciated over ten years on a straight-line basis. The item was revalued to $22 million and $13.6 million on 30 April 2014 and 30 April 2015 respectively. Depreciation has been charged for the year and company policy is to include the whole of any revaluation gains and losses in other comprehensive income. The company does not make any transfers for excess depreciation following revaluation.

(vi) After preparing the above statements, Radmin discovered that contributions of $2 million paid into its defined benefit pension plan had been included in the above figure for finance costs.

(vii) Ignore any taxation effects relevant to the above adjustments.

(viii) Ignore any discounting implications concerning the deferred purchase consideration referred to in note (i).

Required

(a) Prepare the consolidated statement of profit or loss and comprehensive income for the year ended 30 April 2015 for the Radmin Group. **(35 marks)**

(b) Radmin is considering the purchase of a debt instrument with five years remaining to maturity. The company's policy is to hold such instruments to maturity in order to benefit from principal repayments and interest on that principal. Following Radmin's adoption of IFRS 9, the directors wish to account for the instrument using fair value as they believe this will have a greater short-term impact on the income statement than if the instrument was accounted for using amortised cost. They believe that having the ability to manage earnings this way is essential if they are to effectively discharge their responsibilities to shareholders. They also believe that shareholders would not object so long as the accounting practice used is within IFRS guidelines.

Required

Advise Radmin's directors of the nature of and motivations for this type of earnings management and whether 'earnings management', in the manner proposed, is ethically acceptable. **(5 marks)**

(Total 40 marks)

Question 7 – AIA Nov 2012

Tree is a public limited company operating in the manufacturing sector. Draft statements of financial position for companies within the group as at 31 October 2012 are as follows:

	Tree $m	Leaf $m	Roots Krons m
Assets			
Non-current assets:			
Property, plant and equipment	308	92	317
Investment in Leaf	94	-	-
Investment in Roots	38	-	-
Financial instruments	13	6	42
	453	98	359
Current assets:			
Inventories	56	43	174
Trade receivables	27	37	80
Cash and cash equivalents	15	3	21
	98	83	275
TOTAL ASSETS	551	181	634
Equity and liabilities			
Equity:			
Share capital	132	31	167
Retained earnings	213	47	250
Other components of equity	5	3	
Total equity	350	81	417
Liabilities:			
Non-current liabilities	48	35	133
Current liabilities	153	65	84
Total liabilities	201	100	217
TOTAL EQUITY AND LIABILITIES	551	181	634

The following information is relevant to the group financial statements of Tree:

(i) On 1 November 2011, Tree acquired 60% of Leaf's equity interests. Leaf is a public limited company. The purchase consideration comprised cash of $78 million which included transactions costs of $5 million. The fair value of Leaf's identifiable net assets was $100 million. This figure did not include the fair value of a trade name which Leaf's directors have not included in the company's financial statements. The directors believed the trade name could be sold separately for its fair value of $6 million. This fair value remained unchanged at 31 October 2012. The retained earnings of Leaf were $41 million and other components of equity were $2 million at the date of acquisition. Any remaining excess of fair value over the carrying value of Leaf's net assets is attributable to land.

Tree uses the 'full goodwill method' and for this purpose has calculated that the fair value of the non-controlling interest in Leaf was $38 million at the date of acquisition. No issues of ordinary shares have been made since the 1 November 2011 and goodwill has not been impaired since that date.

On 31 October 2012, Tree acquired a further 10% of Leaf's equity interests. The fair value of the consideration paid was $16 million.

(ii) Tree acquired 80% of the equity interest of Roots on 1 November 2011 when Roots' retained earnings were 183 million Krons and the fair value of Roots identifiable net assets was 412 million Krons. Any remaining excess of fair value over the carrying value of Roots' net assets is attributable to land. The functional currency of Roots is the Kron.

Tree uses the 'full goodwill method' and for this purpose the fair value of the non-controlling interest in Roots was 105 million Krons. No issues of ordinary shares have been made since the 1 November 2011 and goodwill has not been impaired since that date.

Exchange rates relevant to the consolidation of Roots are as follows:

	Krons to $
1 November 2011	10
31 October 2012	8
Average for the year ended 31 October 2012	9

(iii) On 31 October 2012 Tree purchased a warehouse for $15 million from Dande. Dande has the choice of how to settle the purchase price. The choice is either to receive a cash payment equivalent to four million shares in Tree in nine months' time or the receipt of five million shares in Tree in one year's time. The fair value of the two choices is $13 million and $17 million respectively.

As part of the deal, Tree also acquired highly specialised inventory which was housed in the warehouse. Dande agreed to accept two million shares in Tree as payment for the inventory and presented Tree with a purchase invoice for $5 million. Due to the nature of the inventory its fair value cannot be measured reliably. At 31 October 2012 the value of each Tree share was $3.

Neither aspect of this event has been taken into account in preparing Tree's financial statements as at 31 October 2012.

(iv) Tree's financial instruments comprise an investment bought on 1 November 2011 for $12 million plus transaction costs of $1 million. The asset was designated as at fair value through profit and loss. On 31 October 2012 the fair value of the asset had risen to $15 million. Tree wishes to adopt IFRS 9 *Financial Instruments* to account for the investment.

Required

(a) Prepare the Tree Group Statement of Financial Position as at 31 October 2012 in accordance with International Financial Reporting Standards (IFRS). Ignore any deferred taxation implications. **(34 marks)**

(b) The acquisition of the warehouse and highly specialised inventory on 31 October 2012 has proved so successful that Tree is now considering the acquisition of a controlling interest in Dande. Tree's directors believe the acquisition would give the group ready access to a highly skilled and motivated workforce that would otherwise take a number of years to train in the handling of the specialised inventory. The directors also believe that the unique nature of the workforce would allow Tree to recognise it as an asset on the consolidated statement of financial position should the acquisition eventually take place. The directors also believe that the recognition of the asset would have the advantage of strengthening the group's balance sheet.

Required

Advise Tree's directors whether the proposed accounting treatment of the workforce would be acceptable under IFRS and discuss any possible ethical issues that might arise.

(6 marks)

(Total 40 marks)

Question 8 – AIA Nov 2012

Bing is a public limited company and operates in the aerospace industry.

(a) Bing, together with two other public limited companies Ollis and Roy, have established a fourth entity Doe for the purpose of building a new type of passenger aircraft. Ownership and responsibilities with respect to Doe are as follows:

Company	Ownership of Doe	Responsibility
Bing	49%	To build the body of the aircraft
Ollis	32%	To build the aircraft engines
Roy	19%	To design and build the aircraft flight control systems and mechanics.

Bing and Ollis have entered into a contractual arrangement whereby all budgeting, capital expenditure, treasury management, dividend policy, production, marketing, sales and human resource decisions they take in connection with the activities of Doe require the unanimous consent of Bing and Ollis. Roy is not represented on Doe's board of directors although Roy does participate in Doe's policy-making processes.

Required

Advise each company on how to account for their respective interest in Doe. **(8 marks)**

(b) Bing, together with Ong and Luft, established a jointly controlled entity Thansa. Each company contributed $10 million in cash in exchange for one-third of the equity of Thansa. Thansa then used $24 million of the contributed cash to acquire a manufacturing plant from Bing. It was agreed between all parties that $24 million represented the plant's fair value. The plant was carried in Bing's financial statements at $15 million.

Required

Prepare journal entries to contrast the treatments if Bing were to account for the transaction using (i) proportional consolidation and (ii) equity accounting. **(8 marks)**

(c) On 1 November 2011 Bing entered into a joint venture arrangement with Carav under which both companies acquired and controlled 50% of the equity of a jointly controlled entity Deecee. Deecee's statement of financial position on 1 November 2011 showed a portfolio of debt instruments with a combined asset value of $10 million. The debt matures in five years time and carries an interest rate of 10%. Deecee does not expect any debts to default during the year to 31 October 2012 but expects 20% to default in the following year. If this happens, the rate of return on the debt would be approximately 7.3%. Bing and Carav have unanimously decided neither to restructure this debt nor to introduce any other impairment tests.

Required

Calculate the debt asset figure that will appear in Deecee's statements of financial position as at 31 October 2012 and 31 October 2013 if Bing and Carav account for the asset in Deecee's financial statements using the expected loss model in IFRS 9 *Financial Instruments*. **(2 marks)**

(Total 18 marks)

Question 9 – AIA May 2013

Denmarc, a public limited company, is a pharmaceutical manufacturer. The entity's draft statements of financial position as at 30 April 2013 are as follows:

	Denmarc $m	Kenz $m	Zenu $m
Assets			
Non-current assets			
Property, plant and equipment	673	1,053	806
Investment in subsidiaries	1,669		
Financial assets	140	13	27
	2,482	1,066	833
Current assets	1,294	1,015	455
TOTAL ASSETS	3,776	2,081	1,288
Equity and liabilities			
Equity			
Share capital	1,456	783	507
Retained earnings	1,386	575	220
Other components of equity	78	48	59
Total equity	2,920	1,406	786
Liabilities			
Non-current liabilities	592	420	95
Current liabilities	264	255	407
Total liabilities	856	675	502
TOTAL EQUITY AND LIABILITIES	3,776	2,081	1,288

The following information is relevant to the preparation of the group financial statements of Denmarc:

(i) On 1 May 2012, Denmarc paid $780 million cash to acquire a controlling interest in Kenz, a public limited company, by acquiring 67% of the entity's share capital. The following financial data refers to Kenz at acquisition:

	$m
• Fair value of identifiable net assets	1,216
• Retained earnings	389
• Other components of equity	34
• Fair value of non-controlling interest	514

Denmarc wishes to use the 'full goodwill' method in the preparation of its group financial statements. Any excess in fair value is due to non-depreciable land.

On 30 April 2013, Denmarc paid $184 million cash to acquire a further 11% interest in the share capital of Kenz. There have been no other events affecting the share capital of Kenz.

Following the further acquisition on 30 April 2013, goodwill was tested for impairment. The recoverable amount of Kenz was $1,430 million. No adjustment for this has yet been made in any of the above financial statements.

EXAM QUESTION BANK

(ii) On 1 May 2012 Denmarc acquired 100% of the equity interest of Zenu, a limited company. Denmarc has calculated the total consideration transferred to be $705 million, as follows:

	$m
Cash	643
Carrying value of non-depreciable land transferred to:	
Zenu	24
Former owners of Zenu	26
Acquisition costs	12
	705

Both parcels of land had a fair value of $35 million at the date of acquisition. The sale price of $35 million in respect of the land transferred to the former owners of Zenu has been debited to trade receivables and credited to retained earnings. No other entries have been made in the financial statements concerning either parcel of land.

As part of the above arrangement, Denmarc also agreed to pay a further $40 million cash to the former owners of Zenu contingent upon the approval of a licence for a new medicine. There was no significant difference in the fair value of this obligation at 30 April 2013.

At the date of acquisition, Zenu's retained earnings were $117 million, other components of equity were $55 million and share capital was $507 million. The fair value of Zenu's identifiable net assets was not significantly different to carrying value. No goodwill impairment was necessary as at 30 April 2013.

(iii) Included in Denmarc's property, plant and equipment is a research plant with a carrying value of $50 million. Denmarc is required by legislation to dismantle the plant at the end of its useful life and has therefore built up a dismantling provision of $10 million in its financial statements. On 30 April 2013 another pharmaceutical company offered to buy the plant for $47 million. The offer includes taking over responsibility for the dismantling of the plant. Denmarc has estimated that the present value of the estimated cash flows from the plant's continued use by the group is $55 million.

(iv) Included in the financial assets of Denmarc is a portfolio of 5% loans. The portfolio's effective rate of interest is 10%. Denmarc has adopted IFRS 9 *Financial Instruments* and the portfolio is included at its amortised cost carrying value of $118 million. On 30 April 2013 Denmarc granted a concession to the borrowers which requires an immediate payment of $14 million followed by two payments of $50 million at the end of each of the next two years. The effective interest rate under the concession is 9.3% and the current market interest rate is 10.7%.

(v) In an attempt to boost sales of one of its new products, on 1 May 2012 Denmarc appointed 100 employees on fixed three-year contracts. The starting salary for each employee is $200,000 per annum. It is estimated that salaries will rise by 8% per annum. Denmarc agreed to pay each employee a retirement benefit of 10% of final salary per annum for each year of the contractual period. Denmarc's entity-specific credit risk is 7%. The yield on AA-rated corporate bonds of a term and currency consistent with the obligation is 5%. No entries have been made in the financial statements apart from the recording of salary payments for the current year.

Required

(a) Prepare the Denmarc group statement of financial position as at 30 April 2013 in accordance with International Financial Reporting Standards (IFRS). **(35 marks)**

(b) The directors of Denmarc have been discussing the financial asset referred to in note (iv) above and now plan to value the loan at its fair value in next year's financial statements. They believe future market interest rates are set to fall and that the resulting increase in the loan's fair value will have two beneficial impacts: (1) any increase will be included in profits which will enhance the group's performance figures and (2) parts or all of the asset could be sold if necessary to fund future capital expenditure.

EXAM QUESTION BANK

Required

Advise the directors of Denmarc on whether their future plan to value the loan at fair value is both ethically acceptable and available under IFRS. **(5 marks)**

(Total 40 marks)

Question 10 – AIA May 2014

(a) The functional currency of Arenta, a public limited company, is the Dollar ($). Two years ago, Arenta established a European-based subsidiary Rima that produces and sells electronic equipment throughout Europe. The sale prices for Rima's goods, labour and materials are determined in Euros (€). Rima has often considered exporting outside Europe but believes that the external market forces and government regulations around the world are too restrictive to make this feasible. Rima is financed predominantly by an inter-company loan from Arenta denominated in dollars and regularly transfers cash flows from its operations to Arenta.

The directors of Arenta are not sure how to determine Rima's functional currency for the purpose of producing its consolidated financial statements.

Required

Advise Arenta's directors of Rima's functional currency. Explain your advice. **(5 marks)**

(b) Rima has produced the following draft financial statements for the year ended 30 April 2014.

Statement of financial position	€m	€m
Non-current assets		831
Current assets		
Inventories	514	
Trade receivables	237	
		751
		1,582
Equity share capital (€1 shares)		267
Retained earnings		776
		1,043
Non-current liabilities		304
Current liabilities		235
		1,582

Statement of profit or loss	
Profit before tax	443
Tax	200
Profit after tax	243

(i) Rima was incorporated during May 2012 when Arenta subscribed $70 million for 100% of the equity share capital. No dividends were paid during the year.

(ii) All transactions occurred evenly throughout the year.

(iii) Exchange rates: €:$
- On incorporation 4:1
- 30 April 2013 3.5:1
- Average for the year ended 30 April 2014: 3:1
- 30 April 2014 2:1

Required

Translate the above financial statements of Rima for the purpose of the consolidation exercise for the year ended 30 April 2014 showing and describing all movements in the group's equity and retained earnings as a result of the translation exercise. **(10 marks)**

(c) The IASB believes that the purpose of the statement of profit or loss and other comprehensive income is to provide information about the financial performance of an entity that is useful to a wide range of users in making economic decisions. For this purpose, all changes in net assets are regarded as 'performance' in its widest sense. Many entities have responded to this wide definition of performance, by disclosing non-GAAP key performance indicators.

Required

Advise Arenta's directors of how any exchange gains/losses, calculated in (b), will be accounted for and disclosed in the group statement of profit or loss and other comprehensive income and of the impact this will have on the group's non-GAAP key performance indicators (KPIs). **(5 marks)**

(Total 20 marks)

Question 11 – AIA May 2014

(a) Several years ago Ezmee, a public limited company, acquired 25% of the equity shares of one of its main competitors, Stoe. The purchase consideration was $4 million. The other 75% of shares have been held ever since by a single investor so that Ezmee had no influence over Stoe's operating activities. Ezmee accounts for such investments at fair value through other comprehensive income.

On 30 April 2013, Ezmee acquired a further 45% of Stoe for $13 million cash and gained control. At that date the carrying value of Ezmee's initial investment in Stoe was $5 million and the fair value of Stoe's identifiable net assets was $25 million. It has been estimated that, due to the entity gaining control, Stoe had to pay a premium of 8% to acquire the additional 45% shareholding.

Ezmee includes non-controlling interest in its consolidated financial statements at fair value.

Required

Advise the Ezmee's directors of the figures to be included in the entity's consolidated financial statements for goodwill and non-controlling interest and explain how the initial holding of 25% should be accounted for as at 30 April 2013. **(10 marks)**

(b) When measuring the fair values of Stoe's identifiable net assets at 30 April 2013 a number of provisional figures were used. During the year ended 30 April 2014 the following information became available:

– At 30 April 2013 Stoe held a passive investment at a fair value of $2 million in Pan, a mining company. During February 2014, as a result of Pan's discovery of a new deposit of minerals, the fair value of Stoe's investment increased to $3 million.

– Stoe owned a property which was surplus to requirements as at 30 April 2013. Stoe was actively looking for a buyer at that date and included the property in the financial statements at a carrying value of $1 million. Stoe eventually disposed of the property in July 2013 for $1.4 million.

– At 30 April 2013 Stoe had six months outstanding on a contract to service equipment. On gaining control, Ezmee assumed responsibility for the service contract. The customer had paid an annual fee of $2.4 million and Stoe therefore carried deferred revenue of $1.2 million in its year end financial statements. During June 2013 it was finally agreed that companies similar to Stoe would incur costs of $0.9 million to fulfill the contract and would expect to earn a profit mark-up for that effort of 20%.

– At the date Ezmee gained control of Stoe, one of Stoe's identifiable net assets was a brand name, Diga. As Ezmee owned a similar product, it did not intend to market Diga post-control. Ezmee discontinued sales of the Diga product thereby enhancing sales of its own product and the value of its own brand name. As the future cash flows from sales of Diga were expected to be nil, Ezmee included it as an intangible asset in Stoe's identifiable net assets at a fair value of zero. During the following year it became known to Ezmee that other companies within the industry would have been willing to acquire the name Diga for $1 million at 30 April 2013 and to continue to sell the product.

Required

Advise Ezmee's directors of the effect, if any, the above information will have on the remeasurement of goodwill as at 30 April 2013. Explain your advice. **(10 marks)**

(Total 20 marks)

Question 12 – AIA Nov 2013

Gico plc is an audio equipment manufacturer. The company has grown its business by developing new products and expanding overseas. Gico has investments in Redit and Seph. All three are public limited companies. The following financial statements relate to the three companies as at 31 October 2013:

	Gico $m	Redit $m	Seph $m
Assets			
Non-current assets			
Property, plant and equipment	302	162	48
Investment in Redit	149		
Investment in Seph	51		
Financial assets	24	16	38
Joint operation	15		
	541	178	86
Current assets	17	19	32
TOTAL ASSETS	558	197	118
Equity and liabilities			
Equity			
Ordinary share capital	68	54	5
Retained earnings	190	72	65
Other components of equity	30	-	-
Total equity	288	126	70
Liabilities			
Non-current liabilities	143	55	37
Current liabilities	127	16	11
Total liabilities	270	71	48
TOTAL EQUITY AND LIABILITIES	558	197	118

The following information is relevant to the preparation of the group financial statements of Gico:

(i) Gico acquired 80% of Redit's ordinary share capital on 1 November 2011, at which time the fair value of the identifiable net assets of Redit were $162 million and retained earnings of Redit were $43 million.

Group policy is to measure non-controlling interest at fair value. At 1 November 2011 this amounted to $41 million.

The purchase consideration at 1 November 2011 comprised cash of $135 million. Professional fees of $1 million relating to the acquisition were debited to the Investment in Redit account. Gico also agreed to pay a further sum to the former owners of Redit if earnings were above an agreed target by 31 March 2014. The fair value of this sum was $5 million. Gico accounted for its investment in Redit as at fair value through profit or loss. No impairment losses were required for recognised goodwill.

The excess of the fair value of Redit's net assets is due to non-depreciable land.

(ii) Gico acquired holdings in Seph in two steps as follow:

Date of investment	% ordinary shares acquired	Cash consideration $m
1 November 2011	25%	15
31 July 2013	35%	29

Other relevant information concerning the financial statements of Seph as at the date of the above two investments was as follows:

	Retained earnings $m	Fair value of identifiable net assets $m	Fair value of Gico's investment in Seph $m	Fair value of non-controlling interest $m
1 November 2011	42	52		
31 July 2013	56	68	21	33

Notes

Gico's investment on 1 November 2011 gave the company significant influence over Seph. The investment on 31 July 2013 gave Gico control over Seph.

Gico accounted for the investment in Seph in its own financial statements as at fair value through profit or loss.

The difference between the fair value of Seph's identifiable net assets and their carrying value relates to land which is not depreciated.

Group policy is to measure non-controlling interest at fair value. An impairment review at 31 October 2013 found that no impairment losses were necessary for recognised goodwill.

(iii) On 1 November 2011 Gico contributed 30% towards the $50 million construction cost of an audio research facility. The facility was completed on 1 November 2012 and is expected to have a useful life of 15 years. Gico accounts for this investment as a jointly controlled operation but so far has only accounted for its share of the construction costs in its financial statements.

During the year ended 31 October 2013 the facility sold goods with a direct cost of $40 million for $70 million.

The facility's executive team are to be paid a lump sum benefit on termination of service equal to 1% of final salary for each year of service. Their combined salaries in the year ended 31 October 2013 amounted to $1.3 million. The present value of this obligation was estimated to be $1 million as at the year end. The facility's other operating overheads during the year amounted to $10 million.

(iv) Gico purchased production equipment for $27 million on 1 November 2010. In addition, during the year ended 31 October 2011, direct costs attributable to bringing the equipment to a working condition and testing that it was functioning properly were $5 million and net proceeds from selling prototypes produced during the testing phase were $2 million. The equipment began full production on 1 November 2011. The equipment's expected useful life is 10 years.

On 31 October 2012 the equipment was revalued to $32 million. Useful life was reassessed to ten years at the same date.

On 31 October 2013 changes in Gico's technological environment were noticed. An impairment review suggested that the equipment's recoverable amount was $21 million.

Depreciation for the year ended 31 October 2013 has been based upon the equipment's revalued amount. No other adjustments have been made in the financial statements for this year.

(v) Gico's financial assets include a debt instrument purchased for its fair value of $20 million on 1 November 2012. The instrument has a principal amount of $25 million. Fixed interest at 4.7% is paid annually and has been included in profit or loss. The instrument's effective rate of interest is 10%.

Required

(a) Prepare the Gico Group's consolidated statement of financial position as at 31 October 2013 in accordance with International Financial Reporting Standards. **(35 marks)**

(b) On 5 November 2013 Gico sold an under-utilised production facility to a bank for $43 million. The sale gives Gico an option to repurchase the facility within one year at a premium of 10%. Gico would exercise the option and repurchase the facility if market conditions showed additional capacity was necessary. The asset's carrying value on 5 November 2013 was $30 million. Gico is planning further expansion and has recognised the transaction as a sale and used the proceeds to reduce its short-term borrowings in order to make the entity look more liquid to potential lenders.

Required

Advise the directors of Gico whether recording the above transaction as a sale is acceptable under IFRS and whether the treatment breaches their ethical responsibilities to stakeholders.

(5 marks)

(Total 40 marks)

Question 13 – AIA Nov 2013

(a) Bilko plc is a real estate company and has a number of joint arrangements with other entities. The directors are concerned about the impact IFRS 11 *Joint Arrangements* will have on the entity's financial reporting. The following summarises the contractual circumstances concerning two of these arrangements:

(i) Bilko and two other entities, Verv and Loit, have 50%, 30% and 20% respectively of the voting rights in an arrangement to acquire and operate a hotel. The contractual arrangement specifies that at least 75% of the voting rights are required to make decisions about the relevant financial and operating activities of the hotel. **(4 marks)**

(ii) Bilko has an arrangement with Dusti (the 'parties') to acquire and operate an industrial estate. The estate is established as a separate vehicle, IndusNE. Both parties must agree on all activities relevant to the estate. These activities include rental of units, maintenance of equipment and marketing of the estate. The legal form of IndusNE establishes that it is the estate, and not the parties, that has rights to the assets, and obligations for the liabilities, relating to the arrangement. The arrangement stipulates the following:

- IndusNE owns the industrial estate and neither party has rights to the estate.
- Neither party is responsible for IndusNE's debts. If IndusNE cannot settle its debts, their contribution is limited to the amount of any unpaid capital.
- Both parties have the right to sell their interests in IndusNE.
- The profit from operating the industrial estate is divided between both parties in accordance with their interests in IndusNE. **(8 marks)**

Required

Advise Bilko's directors how the above two arrangements should be classified under FRS 11 *Joint Arrangements*.

Note. Mark allocation is shown above.

(b) Bilko acquired 40% of the voting rights over the activities of a shopping mall on 1 November 2012 for $60 million. The shopping mall is a separate vehicle trading under the name Cum2us. On the same date, Bilko entered into a contractual arrangement with Rang plc to jointly control the financial and operating policies of Cum2us. This arrangement gave Bilko and Rang rights to the net assets of the shopping mall. During the year ended 31 October Cum2us made a profit before tax of $34 million, income tax was $9 million and dividends paid amounted to $6 million.

Required

Advise Bilko on how Cum2us would be accounted for in both its individual and consolidated financial statements for the year ended 31 October 2013 if the company was to adopt IFRS 11 *Joint Arrangements*. **(8 marks)**

(Total 20 marks)

Question 14 – AIA Nov 2013

Ravar, a public limited company, operates through a number of foreign subsidiaries. One of its subsidiaries, Krow, operates as an autonomous subsidiary. Krow's functional currency is the Zlotty (Zy). Krow has produced the following draft financial statements for the year ended 31 October 2013:

KROW
STATEMENT OF FINANCIAL POSITION AS AT 31 OCTOBER 2013

	Zy (m)	Zy (m)
Non-current assets		
Property, plant and equipment		83
Current assets		
Inventories	141	
Trade receivables	78	
Cash and cash equivalents	34	
		253
Total assets		336
Equity		
Share capital		23
Retained earnings		239
		262
Current liabilities		74
		336

STATEMENT OF PROFIT OR LOSS AND OTHER COMPREHENSIVE INCOME FOR THE YEAR ENDED 31 OCTOBER 2013

	Zy (m)
Revenue	1,651
Cost of sales	1,318
Gross profit	333
Expenses	99
Profit before tax	234
Income tax expense	80
Profit after tax	154

The following information is relevant to Ravar's investment in Krow:

(i) Krow paid dividends of Zy64 million on 18 July 2013.

(ii) Ravar gained control of Krow on 31 October 2010 by acquiring 75% of its share capital for a cash consideration of $14.3 million. At that date, Krow's retained earnings were Zy49 million.

Group policy is to measure non-controlling interest at the date control is gained at fair value. The fair value of non-controlling interest in Krow at 31 October 2010 was $4.6 million. The fair value of Krow's identifiable net assets was not significantly different to carrying value at the date control was gained.

(iii) Goodwill is reviewed for impairment each year. These showed no impairment loss provisions have been necessary to date.

(iv) Exchange rates

	Zy to $
31 October 2010	4.51
31 October 2011	4.26
31 October 2012	4.05
31 October 2013	3.75
18 July 2013	3.96
Average for year to 31 October 2013	3.80

Required

(a) Advise Ravar's directors of the translated figures that would be included in Ravar's consolidated financial statements for the year ended 31 October 2013 with reference to Krow's:

(i) Statement of financial position
(ii) Statement of profit or loss and other comprehensive income
(iii) Goodwill
(iv) Retained earnings
(v) Non-controlling interest
(vi) Total foreign currency translation difference for the year. **(16 marks)**

(b) On 1 November 2013, Ravar accepted in principle an unexpected offer for the sale of half its holding in Krow. It is expected the sale will be finalised before the next reporting date; although, as the offer was unexpected, actions to complete the sale have yet to be taken substantially. Ravar believes that acceptance of the offer clearly shows it no longer intends to recover its investment principally through use of the asset and that Krow's results should therefore be presented in accordance with IFRS 5 *Non-current Assets Held for Sale and Discontinued Operations*.

Required

Advise Ravar whether the provisions of IFRS 5 should be applied to the results of Krow in the financial statements for the year ended 31 October 2014. **(4 marks)**

(Total 20 marks)

Question 15 – AIA May 2015

(a) Dyer is a private company. The directors are reviewing certain events which have occurred during the entity's year ended 30 April 2015 and require advice on their accounting treatment.

On 1 March 2015, the directors discussed the finance director's (FD) proposal to obtain a listing on a recognised stock market. They were advised that one way of achieving this is for a listed company to acquire Dyer by means of a share exchange, Terco, a listed company, had been identified by the FD as a potential acquirer. The FD believed that the terms of the acquisition would be unanimously accepted by Dyer's shareholders and would result in Terco issuing four of its own shares in exchange for one share in Dyer.

The relevant summarised statements of financial position as at 1 March 2015 were as follows:

	Terco $m	Dyer $m
Assets		
Non-current	14.25	28.00
Current	5.35	4.00
	19.60	32.00
Equity and liabilities		
Ordinary shares	4.00	10.00
Retained earnings	9.00	7.00
	13.00	17.00
Liabilities	6.60	15.00
	19.60	32.00

The following information is relevant to the above financial statements:

(1) The par value of Terco's and Dyer's ordinary shares was $2 and $10 respectively.

(2) An agreed reliable estimate of the fair value of Dyer's ordinary shares was $30.

(3) It was agreed that land owned by Terco had a fair value $0.5 million higher than its carrying value.

Required

(i) Prepare a consolidated statement of financial position as if the proposed share exchange had gone ahead on 1 March 2015. **(8 marks)**

(ii) The directors have heard that publication of IFRS 11 *Joint Arrangements* raised questions concerning whether 'proportionate consolidation' was still allowable under IFRS. The directors are considering their future business model should they become a listed company and require advice upon whether this method of consolidation would still be available for two types of arrangement: joint operations and joint ventures. Their preferred model would be to contract for rights to share and operate future assets with another party.

Required

Advise Dyer's directors of how the provisions of IFRS 11 concerning the use of proportionate consolidation for the above two types of arrangement would impact on the accounting for their preferred model. **(8 marks)**

(b) Abli, a public limited company which is a group parent entity, is considering the publication of key performance indicators (KPI) and requires advice on the following matters:

(i) Abli had one million ordinary shares in issue during the year and three million convertible bonds. Each block of 100 convertible bonds is convertible into 4 ordinary shares. The finance charge for the year relating to these bonds is $3 million and the related current and deferred tax is $1 million. The group profit attributable to ordinary shareholders of Abli is $27.81 million.

Required

Advise Abli on the amounts to be included in its group income statement for basic and diluted earnings per share. **(4 marks)**

(ii) Abli's management have heard that many companies now publish non-GAAP KPIs in addition to those required by IFRS. The management wish to publish earnings per share (EPS) figures based upon earnings before interest, tax, depreciation and amortisation (EBITDA).

Required

Advise Abli's management whether the practice of reporting an EPS figure based upon EBITDA is ethically acceptable and to what extent it complies with IAS 33 *Earnings Per Share*. **(4 marks)**

(Total 24 marks)

Question 16 – AIA Nov 2014

(a) Denz is a public limited company. The company employs fifty people and has an annual turnover of $50 million. Denz's business model is to invest in small private fast growing companies with the aim of disposing of the investment at such time in the future when sale profits can be maximised.

On 1 November 2013 Denz gained control of Zin Limited, an unlisted company, by acquiring 75% of Zin's equity. The fair value of Zin's identifiable net assets was $3 million. Denz paid $3.34 million immediately and agreed to pay a further $3.54 million in one year's time if Zin's sales volumes increased by more than 20% over the year. Accounting and legal fees concerning the acquisition were paid by Denz and amounted to $83,000. Denz estimates its cost of capital at 5%.

The group year end is 31 October 2014. By that date, Zin's sales volume had increased by 12%. Zin believed that future growth in sales volumes would stabilise at 15% per annum due to a competitor entering the market. Due to the increased competition, Zin estimated that goodwill would have a useful life of six years. Zin measures goodwill using the 'full' goodwill approach.

Required

(i) Advise Denz of the goodwill amount to be included in its group statement of financial position for the year ended 31 October 2014 with respect to its investment in Zin. **(5 marks)**

(ii) The directors of Denz are considering a delisting of the entity so that its equity or debt would no longer be available to the public; although the entity would still prepare general purpose financial statements.

Advise Denz how your advice in (i) above would have changed had Denz been an unlisted company upon the acquisition of Zin. **(7 marks)**

(b) Deliberations by the directors of Denz concerning whether or not to delist the entity have reached a stalemate. The directors cannot agree on the benefits of adopting the IFRS for SMEs. They also require clarity on the impact of the IFRS for SMEs on one of the entity's main assets, investment properties. Denz currently measures investment property at cost under IAS 40 *Investment Property*. Denz owns an investment property which comprises land and buildings. The land could be sold for redevelopment and the best price it could obtain for doing so is $9 million; although currently Denz has no intention of selling. A reliable market value of the land and buildings as a going concern is $5 million.

Required

(i) Advise the directors of Denz on the benefits to the entity of adopting the IFRS for SMEs.
(5 marks)

(ii) Advise Denz on the impact of adoption on the entity's financial statements with respect to its investment property. **(3 marks)**

(Total 20 marks)

Question 17 – May 2017

Wilton was listed on the stock exchange on 1 May 2016. During the year ended 30 April 2017 the company appointed a number of non-executive directors and established an audit committee. The convener of the audit committee has raised the following issues for discussion with the finance director.

(a) Wilton makes and sells food products. The finance director is concerned that the requirements of IFRS 8 *Operating Segments* will put Wilton at a competitive disadvantage because other manufacturers may discover that Wilton's seafood division is very profitable.

The following analysis relates to the year ended 30 April 2017:

	Revenue	Profit	Net assets
	$m	$m	$m
Fresh foods, excluding seafood	100	10	18
Fresh seafood	40	8	9
Tinned vegetables	150	110	23
Frozen vegetables	160	87	26
	450	215	76

The production director has suggested that Wilton could simply claim that it has a single segment, namely food, and that no further analysis is required.

Required

(i) Explain whether it would be acceptable to restrict segmental information on the basis that a full report would harm Wilton's competitive position. **(4 marks)**

(ii) Explain the minimum segmental reporting requirements for Wilton. **(6 marks)**

(10 marks)

(b) As at 1 May 2016 the present value of the obligation arising from Wilton's defined benefit pension plan was $650m. At that date the fair value of the plan's assets was $635m.

The discount rate at the start of the year was 7.8%. By the end of the year it had risen to 11.5%.

The following figures were recorded during the year ended 30 April 2017:

	$m
Current service cost	124
Benefits paid	128
Contributions received	70

On 30 April 2017 the present value of the plan's obligation was $730m and the fair value of the plan's assets was $645m.

Required

(i) Calculate the figures that will appear with respect to pensions in Wilton's financial statements for the year ended 30 April 2017. **(5 marks)**

(ii) Evaluate the suggestion that the estimate for the value of the plan's obligations is too uncertain to be reflected in the financial statements. **(5 marks)**

(10 marks)

(Total 20 marks)

Question 18 – AIA May 2015

(a) Quest, a public limited company, intends to dispose of a group of assets together with a number of associated liabilities. The entity's year end is 30 April. On 1 May 2014 the assets and liabilities associated with this disposal were as follows:

	$m
Goodwill allocated to the disposal group	2.55
Property, plant and equipment (PPE) at a revalued amount	7.82
Property, plant and equipment at cost	9.69
Inventory	4.08
Investment in equity instruments	3.06
	27.20
Liabilities associated with above assets	(4.20)
Other group liabilities to be paid out of disposal proceeds	(8.00)

On 31 October 2014, the disposal group was classified as held-for-sale in accordance with IFRS 5 *Non-current Assets Held for Sale and Discontinued Operations*. At that date it was found that goodwill had not been impaired, the revalued amount for PPE carried at a valuation was $7 million, depreciation on PPE carried at cost during the period was $1 million, there was no change necessary to inventory valuation or the amount for liabilities and the fair value of investments in equity instruments was $2.6 million. The fair value of the disposal group at that date was $15 million.

Required

Advise Quest of the accounting treatment of the above disposal group if Quest was to produce group financial statements as at 31 October 2014. **(12 marks)**

(b) Quest's directors understand that IFRS 5 *Non-current Assets Held for Sale and Discontinued Operations* requires that for an asset to be classified as held for sale it must be available for immediate sale. The entity has committed to a plan to sell a building used as its headquarters. The entity will either move temporarily into alternative accommodation or will wait until construction of a new building is complete.

Required

Advise Quest's directors whether, and if so under what circumstances, the above commitment will qualify the building as being for 'immediate sale' under IFRS 5. **(4 marks)**

(c) Quest's directors are considering a first investment in Tinu, an overseas group entity. Tinu is domiciled in a country which requires IFRS in an entity's financial reporting. However, the directors have heard that international investors need to be cautious when assessing such an entity's financial performance due to (1) the possible impact of changes to International Generally Accepted Accounting Principles (GAAP) and (2) an entity's choice of practices concerning the presentation of information in its financial statements.

Required

Advise Quest's directors how their assessment of Tinu's performance may be affected by the two issues mentioned above. **(4 marks)**

(Total 20 marks)

Question 19 – AIA Nov 2014

(a) Paxdal, a public limited company whose functional currency is the dollar ($), acquired 100% of the equity share capital of Dia upon its incorporation many years ago. The functional currency of Dia, a foreign entity, is the boli (β). The equity shares were acquired when the exchange rate was $1= β2. Paxdal is consolidating the financial statements of the subsidiary for the year ended 31 October 2014 at which point the exchange rate was $1= β4 (2013 comparative $1= β3). The weighted average exchange rate for the year was $1= β3.5. Dia is domiciled and trades in a country whose economic environment provides strong indicators of the existence of hyperinflation.

Dia has produced the following draft financial statements for use by Paxdal in the consolidation exercise:

DIA
STATEMENT OF INCOME FOR THE YEAR ENDED 31 OCTOBER 2014

	βm
Sales	52.50
Cost of sales	(49.79)
Depreciation	(0.75)
Finance charge	(0.53)
Profit before tax	1.43
Income tax	(0.69)
Profit after tax	0.74

STATEMENT OF FINANCIAL POSITION AS AT 31 OCTOBER 2014

		2014	2013
		βm	βm
Property, plant and equipment		8.25	9.00
Inventories		4.50	4.07
Trade receivables		6.00	7.20
Cash and cash equivalents		0.90	0.30
	Total assets	19.65	20.57
Trade payables		5.76	6.80
Taxation		0.69	1.31
Non-current liabilities		5.40	5.40
	Total liabilities	11.85	13.51
Share capital		1.50	1.50
Retained earnings		6.30	5.56
	Total equity	7.80	7.06

EXAM QUESTION BANK

Required

Prepare translated financial statements for Dia for use by Paxdal in its consolidation exercise. Your statement of financial position should show comparative figures. **(12 marks)**

(b) Paxdal is known mainly as a highly successful retailer of mobile technology which it distributes through a chain of High Street shops; whereas Dia develops and manufactures devices which allow people to control appliances in the home by using their smartphones. The directors of Paxdal wish to exclude Dia from Paxdal's consolidated financial statements on the grounds that, not only are Dia's activities too dissimilar but Dia is the only entity within the group to have suffered hyperinflation and that to include the financial results of Dia would mislead users and thereby reduce the usefulness of the group statements.

Required

Advise the directors whether the option to exclude Dia is available to them under IFRS. **(4 marks)**

(c) Paxdal's directors have been advocates of historical cost accounting for many years. They are concerned about the positive progress being made towards the much wider use of fair values in financial reporting and argue that historical cost accounting provides objective, verifiable and reliable information which is more useful to users as it is free from bias and is better at restricting managers' ability to manipulate financial reports.

Required

Advise the directors on the benefits that users of Paxdal's financial statements would gain from Paxdal's use of fair value reporting. **(4 marks)**

(Total 20 marks)

Question 20 – AIA Nov 2014

Mendez, a public limited company, is preparing group financial statements for the year ended 31 October 2014. The entity is seeking advice on a number of matters concerning the non-current assets section of the statement of financial position.

(a) Mendez holds less than a majority of the voting rights in a number of investments, as follows:

(i) 46% of the voting rights of Gon. The remaining 54% of Gon's voting shares is held by widely dispersed independent shareholders. The largest remaining holding by any one shareholder is 1.3%. There is no history of any remaining shareholders acting jointly at the entity's annual general meetings.

(ii) 45% of the voting rights of Ena. The remaining 55% of Ena's voting rights is held by five shareholders. Two of the remaining shareholders hold 26% each. At a recent AGM these two shareholders combined to vote against a policy change proposed by Mendez. The other three remaining shareholders hold 1% each of the voting rights.

Required

Advise Mendez on how the investments in Gon and Ena should be accounted for in its group financial statements. **(5 marks)**

(b) During the year Mendez acquired Orca, a company engaged in oil and gas technology. Mendez is concerned about two issues involved in the acquisition:

(i) A significant factor in the decision to acquire Orca was the reputation of the company's research staff, many of whom are internationally renowned in the field.

(ii) Orca has a five-year contract to supply goods to a customer, Jorz. Orca's directors believe that Jorz will renew the agreement at the end of the contract. Orca could not sell the contract without selling the business as a whole.

Required

Advise Mendez on whether the above two items could be identified as assets in the group statement of financial position. **(4 marks)**

(c) At 31 October 2014, Mendez employees are working on four research and development projects. The following information refers to each of these projects:

	1 $000	2 $000	3 $000	4 $000
Expenditure incurred during the year:				
Salaries and wages	156	52	75	91
Indirect overheads	-	8	13	5
Direct overheads	29	10	39	8
Staff training costs	5	-	-	-
Patents	-	-	5	-
Market analysis	5	-	26	-
Carrying value as at 1 November 2013	-	-	1,170	728
	195	70	1,328	832

Project notes

(1) This two-year project involves the testing of a new oil product. Mendez believes the entity has the technical ability and resources to complete the project before selling it. Market analysis costs were incurred early in the R&D phase and established that there will be a ready market for the product.

(2) Costs refer to an online product database commercially launched some years ago and fully amortised in the previous accounting period. The costs were incurred to ensure that the asset retained its functional capacity to service higher volumes of user contacts.

(3) These costs refer to a project designed to make fuel use more efficient in jet engines. A prototype of the system was successfully tested last year and, as a result, Mendez had expected the project to be highly profitable. However, development is well behind schedule this year due to a large number of research and development staff leaving their employment to work for a competitor. The staff have not yet been replaced and Mendez now believes that the competitor has gained significant ground in developing a competing technology.

(4) Commercial production began at the start of the year. The asset's recoverable amount is $1.5 million and Mendez expects revenues will be received over an indefinite period.

Required

Advise Mendez on how each project should be accounted for in the financial statements for the year ended 31 October 2014 and of the amount to be included in the group statement of financial position at that date. **(11 marks)**

(Total 20 marks)

Question 21 – AIA May 2017

Millennium manufactures steel. The company has a single large site that is situated in a region where there is a great deal of heavy industry.

Millennium's site is divided into several plants, each of which has a defined role. The plants trade with one another, but also with external customers. For example, Millennium's rolling mill makes steel plates from steel supplied by the Millennium's steel works, which operates the furnaces that make the steel. The rolling mill sells 90% of its output to Millennium's pipeworks and the remaining 10% is sold to external customers.

The rolling mill's assets have the following carrying values:

	$m
Land	25
Buildings	50
Rolling plant	45
	120

Millennium's board believes that it could sell the rolling mill in its entirety for $80m. They believe that the future cash flows from the mill have a net present value of $55m.

The land occupied by the rolling mill has a fair value of $30m.

If Millennium combines the rolling mill with the pipeworks then the total carrying value of the assets is $280m, with a combined potential sales value of $300m and a combined net present value of $420m.

Required

(a) Advise whether the rolling mill's assets are impaired. **(4 marks)**

(b) Calculate the carrying values of the rolling mill's assets, assuming that they are impaired. **(4 marks)**

(c) Critically evaluate the proposition that a good accountant must understand the reporting entity's business. **(12 marks)**

(Total 20 marks)

Question 22 – AIA May 2010

Harden, a public listed company, builds steel frames for large construction projects. The company focuses mainly on commercial buildings and on the overseas oil and gas industry. A new CEO is proposing to change the company's business plan as follows:

(i) Owing to variability in the quality of steel used in the past, 90% of steel will be purchased from one supplier, Brace Inc. The CEO realises this is a high risk strategy and will result in dependence on Brace's reliability but industry specialists have confirmed that Brace, having been in business for over 100 years, is thought of as the market leader in terms of its high dependability for both supply and quality.

(ii) To achieve greater control over trading, there will be more intragroup trading; to such an extent that at the year end, 75% of Harden's trade receivables will be owed by subsidiaries and 15% by associated companies.

(iii) Owing to difficult trading conditions in the property market, surplus properties will be offered first to key members of the management team. One such property is under consideration by the wife of a member of the Harden Executive board. She plans to purchase an apartment from a group company ultimately owned by Harden. The purchase will be made at full market value via an open bidding/tendering process managed by independent property consultants. Her son is also considering the purchase of a similar property.

(iv) Key management personnel will be encouraged to maintain interests in companies in the same industry to provide networking opportunities. As a result, one of Harden's directors is considering the purchase of a proportion of the equity of Gritdelv, a small entity engaged in research into steel structures. The director does not intend to take a seat on Gritdelv's board of directors.

Required

Evaluate the impact IAS 24 *Related Party Disclosures* will have on the treatment of the above events in Harden's consolidated financial statements. **(20 marks)**

Question 23 – AIA Nov 2012

Expan, a public limited company, organises its business into two operating segments: (1) supermarkets and convenience stores and (2) property investment. The following summary has been taken from Expan's most recent draft statement of income. The presentation is based on the directors' belief that certain items recognised in reported profit before tax can vary significantly from year to year and therefore create a volatility in reported earnings which does not reflect Expan's underlying performance. The directors believe that the 'underlying profit before tax' and the 'underlying basic earnings per share' present a clearer and more consistent presentation of the underlying performance of Expan's ongoing business to shareholders.

EXAM QUESTION BANK

EXPAN GROUP
EXTRACTS FROM DRAFT GROUP STATEMENT OF INCOME FOR THE YEAR ENDED 31 OCTOBER 2012

	Notes	2012 $m	2011 $m
Profit before tax		24	23
Analysed as:			
Underlying profit before tax		19	18
Profit on disposal of properties		3	1
Investment property fair value movements		1	5
Financing fair value movements	1	1	(1)
		24	23
Income tax expense		6	5
Profit for the year attributable to ordinary shareholders		18	18
Earnings per share	2	cents	cents
Basic		32.14	33.33
Underlying basic		23.21	24.07

Notes

(1) Fair value gains and losses on non-derivative financial assets and liabilities carried at amortised cost.

(2) Basic earnings per share is calculated by dividing the earnings attributable to ordinary shareholders by the weighted average number of ordinary shares in issue during the year.

Required

Advise the directors of Expan on how the following transactions should be dealt with in the entity's financial statements for the year ended 31 October 2012.

(a) (i) On 1 November 2011 Expan introduced a customer loyalty programme for customers purchasing a specialised range of goods. The loyalty points have no expiry date and each point may be exchanged for goods valued at $1. During the year 4 million points were granted on sales of $40m but owing to customers' unfamiliarity with the scheme only 20% of points had been redeemed by 31 October 2012.

However, the directors believe that 75% of the remaining points will be redeemed in the following year and that the remainder will never be redeemed. Expan's directors have not made any adjustments in the financial statements in connection with the new loyalty scheme. The directors believe none are necessary as the scheme closely resembles a 'money off' voucher scheme currently in use. **(5 marks)**

(ii) Expan purchased a 5% non-derivative financial asset in Nap on 1 November 2010 for $10 million. The asset had a term of five years and a maturity value of $13 million. Expan has measured these assets at amortised cost using the effective interest method. The effective interest rate on the asset is 10%.

On 31 October 2012 Nap went into liquidation. All interest had been paid until that date. Expan learned that Nap would not be able to pay any further interest and would receive only $6.5 million on the original maturity date. Nap has written off the difference between the asset's carrying value and its new maturity value to finance costs.

The discount factor for a sum of $1 received in three years' time at 10% is 0.751.

(6 marks)

EXAM QUESTION BANK

(b) Recalculate Expan's basic and underlying basic earnings per share figures for the year ended 31 October 2012, following any profit adjustments that are necessary as a result of your answer to part (a). **(3 marks)**

(c) A number of accounting firms believe that since the introduction of IFRS, many entities have adopted a number of different ways of presenting the earnings that directors believe are sustainable and more transparently and accurately reflect the entity's underlying* financial performance. Although Expan has drawn up the entity's draft statement of income in a manner which reflects this belief by presenting 'underlying profit before tax' and 'underlying earnings per share', the directors are still unsure whether they are violating IFRS.

*The word 'underlying' refers to a financial reporting metric that does not have an agreed definition but is commonly used by entities to represent performance attributable to continuing operations, that is, before adjustments for, for example, gains or losses from disposal of properties, investment property fair value movements, impairment of goodwill, IAS 19 pension financing gains or losses and any other items that are material and infrequent in nature.

Required

Advise Expan's directors whether the reporting of underlying figures is acceptable practice within the context of IFRS. **(6 marks)**

(Total 20 marks)

Question 24 – AIA Nov 2012

Pera, a public limited company, operates in the mining industry.

(a) (i) During the year ended 31 October 2012 Pera sold inventory to Otion a subsidiary for $20 million. The subsidiary sold 75% of this inventory to external parties before the 31 October 2012 and fully expects the remaining inventory to be sold within the first few months of the following year. Pera made a profit of 30% on the selling price. Both Pera and the subsidiary are subject to the same tax jurisdiction and pay tax on profits of 30%. **(2 marks)**

(ii) Pera also controls an overseas subsidiary Kram which, in the year ended 31 October 2012, made a loss adjusted for tax purposes of $10 million. The loss may only be relieved by carrying it forward to be offset against Kram's future taxable profits. Kram expects profits to grow over the forthcoming year. In Kram's jurisdiction taxable profits are subject to tax at 20%. **(2 marks)**

(iii) On 1 November 2011 Pera paid $20 million cash to acquire 100% of the equity of a competitor Ember. The fair value of Ember's identifiable net assets was $16 million. The tax base of the net assets was $14 million. Ember has not identified any deferred tax asset as part of its identifiable net assets.

Required

Advise Pera on how the above transactions will affect the deferred tax amounts recognised in Pera's group financial statements for the year ended 31 October 2012. **(2 marks)**

(b) Pera exerts control over an operating subsidiary Santi. Pera also holds 15% of the equity of another entity Compu. The 15% holding in Compu will allow Santi access to highly specialised mining technology owned by Compu and provided to Santi for use free of charge. This commitment will begin in December 2012. So that Pera can monitor the use of the technology Pera participates in Compu's operating and financial policy decisions.

The Pera directors are unsure about whether a related party situation exists between the three companies.

Required

Advise Pera's directors how the above transaction should be dealt with in the Pera group financial statements for the year ended 31 October 2012 and explain the purpose of any disclosure requirements. **(7 marks)**

(c) Pera is considering the introduction of interim financial reporting during the year ended 31 October 2013. The first report would be for the six months to 30 April 2013. In planning for the introduction of interim reporting Pera wishes to be advised of the appropriate accounting treatment for the following event.

Pera is planning the major overhaul and restructuring of a distribution facility. Work is scheduled to begin in August 2013 although contracts will not be issued until May 2013; at which date Pera is planning to inform the workforce of the plan. The overhaul will take four months and cost $5 million. As a result of the reorganisation retraining costs of $1 million are likely to be incurred in October 2013.

The workforce will receive a year-end bonus of 10% of wages based on profits over the year. Owing to the seasonal nature of work at the distribution facility most of the profits are earned in the second half of the year. It is not possible to measure the monthly profits with any accuracy.

The distribution facility is planning to develop a new computer based distribution system. It is planned to spend $2 million on 1 November 2012 to carry out basic research into the system's feasibility. It is intended that feasibility will be established by 1 May 2013 at which point a further $3 million will be spent to develop the system. Pera plans to have the system fully commissioned by October 2013.

Required

Advise Pera's directors on the appropriate accounting treatment of the above transactions if the entity were to introduce interim financial reporting on 30 April 2013. **(7 marks)**

(Total 20 marks)

Question 25 – AIA Nov 2012

(a) Globalisation involves the close integration of national economies and removal of any obstacles to free trade. Thus, globalisation requires the further integration of world capital markets. The result of such integration is that entities that were once dependent on domestic financial markets for debt and equity capital now have access to financial markets outside of their national borders. To aid the preparers and users of the financial statements of these entities, International Financial Reporting Standards (IFRSs) attempt to ensure consistency in the interpretation and application of generally accepted accounting principles (GAAP) from country to country. However, the transition to IFRS often involves significant changes to an entity's financial reporting as IFRSs often introduce new accounting practices that were not required by the entity's domestic GAAP.

Required

Appraise the challenges faced by an entity adopting IFRS for its financial reporting and discuss how amendments to its accounting practices and the availability of alternatives in IFRS could lead to inconsistency between entities in their financial reporting. **(9 marks)**

(b) A public limited company Recto has chosen to adopt IFRS and has a date of transition of 1 November 2012. On 1 November 2010 Recto acquired manufacturing property with an expected remaining useful life of 50 years for $12 million and accounted for it at cost. The property is depreciated systematically over 50 years. Under domestic GAAP the property was revalued to $14 million on 1 November 2011 with any consequent adjustment being recognised in equity. Following initial recognition the property was measured at fair value less subsequent depreciation and any impairment losses.

Upon transition to IFRS and in accordance with IAS 16 *Property, Plant and Equipment*, Recto's directors selected the cost model as the appropriate accounting policy for measurement of the manufacturing property. However, they are unsure which figure to use in the financial statements. The market value of the property at 1 November 2012 is $15 million.

Required

Advise Recto's directors on the options available concerning the initial measurement of the manufacturing property at the date of transition to IFRS and show by use of journal entries the necessary financial statement adjustments which will have to be made under each option.

(11 marks)

(Total 20 marks)

Question 26 – AIA May 2013

Olco, a public limited company, owns and manages hotels. The company uses leasing as a way to finance the business and is seeking advice on how to account for these transactions. The directors have also asked for advice on the impact of IFRS 16 *Leases* and the extent to which Olco's accounting practices will need to change following the adoption of IFRS 16.

(i) Olco leases laptops and tablets from an IT supplier for use by management in hotels. The list price of these items is between $200 and $500 and Olco rents machines for a three year period, at the end of which they are returned to the IT supplier for recycling or disposal. Up until last year, Olco applied IAS 17 and categorised these leases as operating leases.

(ii) Olco operates a hotel transport service and is considering the acquisition of a fleet of vehicles. The directors are uncertain about the impact the method of acquisition might have on the company's gearing as shown on its balance sheet. The acquisition alternatives are either to lease the fleet or to buy it via a loan. The fleet would cost $1 million if purchased. Forecasts show the purchase would increase operating profit by 12% per annum. Current operating profit is $400,000, share capital is $2 million and the current debt/equity gearing ratio is 0.5:1.

Olco would negotiate a four-year lease. The annual lease payments would be $286,000 payable in advance. Olco's cost of borrowing is 15% and the rate implicit in the lease would be 9.7%.

The following discount factors are relevant:

Year	Annuity at 15%
1	0.870
2	1.626
3	2.283
4	2.855

Required

Prepare a report for the directors of Olco to advise them on the following:

(a) How the lease of laptops and tablets in (i) will be accounted for under IFRS 16 **(5 marks)**

(b) The impact on the company's gearing and return on capital employed if the fleet of vehicles in (ii) is acquired both by purchase and leasing, and **(9 marks)**

(c) The reasons why the IASB issued IFRS 16 *Leases* and what impact the changes in IFRS 16 changes would have on Olco's accounting. **(6 marks)**

(Total 20 marks)

Question 27 – AIA May 2013

Mondo, a public limited company, is a manufacturer and trades through three distinct business segments which operate in different parts of the world. Operating results are regularly reviewed by the company's chief operating decision maker (CODM). The directors are seeking advice on how the principles and requirements of IFRS 8 *Operating Segments* should apply to the group. The following information has been extracted from the company's records:

Segment	Number of employees	Turnover External $m	Turnover Internal $m	Profit/(loss) before common costs $m	Net assets before common items Assets $m	Net assets before common items Liabilities $m
Tuedo	100	360	20	(26)	510	350
Wedon	200	500	10	176	1,300	480
Thurso	300	840	–	100	3,400	2,300

Common costs include central head office service costs of $17 million, property management costs of $30 million and post-employment service costs of $20 million. Mondo has confirmed that these costs are included in the CODM review but is unsure of how to allocate them to segments.

The Tuedo segment comprises a subsidiary which was recently acquired by Mondo. In return for a guaranteed contract for the sale of goods to Tuedo's former owners, Mondo did not take over Tuedo's post-employment benefit obligations upon acquisition. Tuedo's turnover figure includes sales of $200 million to Tuedo's former owners. All current Tuedo employees belong to a defined contribution scheme. All Wedon and Thurso employees are members of a defined benefit scheme.

The average age of property, plant and equipment in the three segments is: Tuedo 5 years, Wedon 10 years and Thurso 15 years. Property management costs accrue in close proportion to the age of the assets.

Most strategic management decisions are made centrally by head office staff. Mondo estimates that staff time spent on decision making and general management duties is in proportion to the turnover of each segment.

The CODM is provided with amounts for all assets and liabilities, apart from the head office, as part of his review. The head office was valued at $20 million. This was purchased with a 6% loan for the same amount. Neither the loan nor the asset is included in the above asset and liability figures. Loan interest is not included in the segment profit or loss figures although Mondo has indicated that it is a cost reviewed by the CODM.

Mondo attributes $420 million of its external sales and $300 million of its non-current assets to its country of domicile. $260 million of Mondo's external sales are attributed to one foreign country.

Required

Advise the directors of Mondo on how the principles and requirements of IFRS 8 *Operating Segments* would apply to the information given above. In particular, Mondo requires advice on the:

- Allocation of Mondo's common costs, assets and liabilities
- Recognition and reporting of the company's reportable segments
- Reporting of information about Mondo's geographical areas of trading and major customers.

(20 marks)

Question 28 – AIA May 2013

Financial reporting is constantly changing to meet the practical needs of the evolving business environment in which it operates. One of these changes is the on-going move towards the use of fair value measurements; a change made more urgent by the global financial crisis which emphasised the importance of having common fair value measurement and disclosure requirements – with identical wording – in IFRSs and US GAAP. This evolution has been criticised by the advocates of historical cost who believe there are unresolved issues concerning fair value's reliability and measurement and concerning the current practical use and disclosure of fair value in financial statements. They argue that historic cost provides users with a more useful measure.

In May 2011 the IASB published IFRS 13 *Fair Value Measurement*. The IFRS establishes a single source of guidance for fair value measurements under IFRS where that is required by other standards. Its stated objectives are to define fair value, establish a single framework for measuring fair value and require disclosures about fair value measurements. The CEO of Seph, a public limited company, has studied IFRS

13 and is concerned about the changes IFRS 13 will bring to the group's financial reporting practices with respect to the entity's assets and liabilities.

Required

(a) Advise the CEO of Seph of the main changes introduced by IFRS 13. The CEO is particularly interested in changes to the definition of fair value, measurement and valuation techniques and disclosures. **(8 marks)**

(b) Seph has assumed responsibility for a decommissioning liability in a business combination. This involves the dismantling of an offshore oil platform in 10 years' time. Seph would be contractually allowed to transfer the liability to a third party but, due to its unique nature, a quoted price is not available for the amount Seph would be willing to pay to complete the transfer.

Seph assesses long-term liabilities of this nature on a cost-plus basis by taking into account the future cash outflows that a market participant would be expected to incur to fulfil the obligation. Based upon its experience of fulfilling obligations of this type and on its knowledge of the market, Seph has provided the following data relevant to the measurement of the dismantling obligation:

(i) Labour costs have been estimated on the basis of current market rates, adjusted for expected increases. There is a 30% probability they will amount to $20 million, a 40% probability they will amount to $25 million and a 30% probability they will amount to $35 million.

(ii) Industry practice is to allocate overheads and plant operating costs at 90% of expected labour costs.

(iii) The profit mark-up that a third-party contractor would typically require for undertaking the dismantling and assuming the risk associated with the obligation is 20%

(iv) The compensation that a contractor would typically require for the risk that actual cash flows may differ from those expected is 5% of cash flows after inflation.

(v) Based on market and economic forecasts the rate of inflation is estimated to be 4.5% over the ten-year period. The inflation factor to reflect this is 1.553.

(vi) The risk-free rate of interest for a bond maturing in ten years' time is 6%. Seph has estimated that a rate of 3% is appropriate to reflect its own credit risk and risk of non-performance.

The following present value discount factors are relevant:

Period (years)	3%	6%	9%
10	0.744	0.558	0.422

Required

Advise Seph of the amount to be included in the entity's statement of financial position to reflect the above dismantling obligation. Explain the background to the calculations. **(12 marks)**

(Total 20 marks)

Question 29 – AIA Nov 2015

(a) Employee benefits form a significant part of Bee's costs. Bee is a public limited company. The entity has recently appointed a new finance director (FD) who is seeking advice on how this type of cost should be accounted for in the entity's financial statements. The following employee benefit transactions relate to Bee's financial statements for the year ended 31 October 2015.

(i) As part of the entity's terms of employment, Bee began a defined benefit scheme for the FD's benefit. The following information relates to this scheme:

	$'000
As at 1 November 2014	
Fair value of scheme assets	256
Defined benefit obligation	266
Past service cost	20
For the year ended 31 October 2015	
Gross service cost	115
Present value of FD's contributions	106
Remeasurement loss	17
Actual contribution by Bee to the scheme	100

The appropriate discount rate as at 1 November 2014 was 10%

The actual contribution by Bee to the scheme has been included in profit or loss.

Required

Provide calculations to advise Bee on the treatment of the above transactions in the entity's statement of comprehensive income for the year ended 31 October 2015. **(4 marks)**

(ii) On 1 November 2012 Bee granted 5,000 share options to each of its 15 main sales staff. Vesting is conditional upon the member of staff working for Bee for the next three years. Bee estimated that the fair value of each option was $20.

During the first year, two staff members left and at the year end Bee estimated that a further four would leave before the end of the vesting period.

During the second year, one further staff member left and Bee estimated that a further two would leave before the end of the vesting period.

During the third and final year of the scheme, no members of staff left.

Required

Provide calculations to advise Bee on the treatment of the above transaction in the entity's financial statements for the year ended 31 October 2015. **(4 marks)**

(iii) On 1 October 2015, Bee announced a plan to close a manufacturing plant on 31 March 2016 and to terminate the employment of all employees at the plant. Bee requires the employees to stay in service until closure of the plant to complete existing orders. The termination plan is as follows: each employee who remains in service until the factory closes will receive a cash payment of $10,000 payable in the following month. Any employee leaving before the factory closes will receive a cash payment of $6,000.

On 1 October 2015, 1,000 employees were in service at the factory. At that time, Bee estimated that 100 employees would leave before the factory closes on 31 March 2016.

At 31 October 2015, none of the employees had left service at the factory.

Required

Provide calculations to advise Bee on the treatment of the above transaction in the entity's financial statements for the year ended 31 October 2015. **(4 marks)**

(b) Sac, a public limited company, is a subsidiary of Bee. Sac has awarded equity shares it holds in Bee to its employees in exchange for services performed. Sac has an obligation as a principal to settle the award with its employees.

Bee's new FD is of the opinion that the group financial statements should simply reflect economic reality and, as such, the award should not be recognised as it is ultimately a cost to the shareholders and not to the entity.

Required

Advise the FD on whether his opinion complies with IASB thinking on the matter and on how this transaction would be accounted for in (i) the Bee group consolidated financial statements, (ii) the separate financial statements of Bee, and (iii) the separate financial statements of Sac. **(8 marks)**

(Total 20 marks)

Question 30 – AIA May 2014

(a) The Sideel group operates in the oil industry. Occasionally the group's activities cause contamination of rivers and land. The group rectifies this contamination only if it is a legal requirement of the country in which it occurs. This corporate attitude to the environment has been widely criticised. Many commentators have observed that Sideel demonstrates little concern for the impact that the group's business model may have on the environment. As a result of the group's environmental stance Sideel has never produced an environmental report. The group has three long-term contracts to operate in three countries where contamination has become an issue during the year ended 30 April 2014:

Country 1: No law exists requiring clean up of contamination. Industry experts have estimated the costs of clean up to be $13 million.

Country 2: A law requiring clean up exists and the cost has been estimated by industry experts at $10 million.

Country 3: A law requiring clean up of land already contaminated has been passed but it will not come into force until 1 May 2014. The cost of clean up is estimated to be $15 million.

Required

(i) Advise Sideel's directors on how the group should account for the above three events in the group financial statements for the year ended 30 April 2014. You must explain your advice.
(6 marks)

(ii) Advise Sideel's directors on the benefits to the group of producing a social and environmental report. **(11 marks)**

(b) At 30 April 2014 Sideel is being sued by a customer for damages of $100 million relating to a claim that one of its products was not fit for purpose. The customer has begun legal proceedings although Sideel is disputing any liability for the damage. Sideel's legal team has estimated that Sideel has a 30% chance of losing the case. The team has also estimated that, given the circumstances, there is a 10% chance that actual outflows, if any, will differ from those expected.

Required

Advise Sideel on how the above event would be accounted for in its financial statements for the year ended 30 April 2014. **(3 marks)**

(Total 20 marks)

Question 31

(a) Krz, a public limited company, sells vehicles in three different markets. At various stages in its history, the entity has transacted in all three markets and retains the ability to do so at any time. Krz currently holds one thousand identical vehicles and is reviewing their fair value in accordance with IFRS 13 *Fair Value Measurement*. The following information relates to transactions in the vehicles in the respective markets:

	America	Europe	Asia
Total market volume	20%	70%	10%
Volume of market achieved by Krz	55%	30%	15%
	$'000	$'000	$'000
Price per vehicle	60	50	56
Transaction costs per vehicle (eg commissions)	6	2	1
Costs to transport each vehicle to the market	2	2	2

Required

Advise Krz, showing relevant calculations, how the fair value of the vehicles should be determined.

(8 marks)

(b) On 30 April 2014 Krz owned a vehicle showroom which it rented to Buz and on which Buz owed rent of $1 million. Krz employs professional valuers and the showroom was carried in Krz's financial statements at its fair value of $20 million. On 5 May 2014, before the financial statements were authorised for issue, Buz unexpectedly announced its insolvency and informed Krz that it would be seeking to write off the full amount of its debt.

Required

Advise Krz how the above events should be accounted for in its financial statements for the year ended 30 April 2014. **(5 marks)**

(c) Krz purchased an asset for $10 million on 1 May 2011. Depreciation is calculated on a straight-line basis over the asset's useful life of five years. The local tax jurisdiction allows a tax allowance on such assets over four years on a straight-line basis but does not allow the tax base of such assets to be adjusted for revaluations. On 1 May 2013 the business use of the asset was reviewed. The asset's depreciation method and useful life remained unchanged but the carrying value of the asset was increased to its fair value of $9 million.

Krz is unsure of the financial reporting implications of the revaluation.

The tax rate for all years is 30%.

Required

Advise Krz of the effect of the revaluation on the deferred tax figures carried in its financial statements for the year ended 30 April 2014. **(7 marks)**

(Total 20 marks)

Question 32 – AIA Nov 2013

Ding is a public limited company. The company has decided to adopt IFRS for the first time in its financial statements for the year ended 31 October 2013. The directors have asked for advice on how to calculate the deferred tax liability under IAS 12 *Income Taxes*.

(a) The company's statement of financial position for the year ended 31 October 2012 shows a deferred tax liability of $10 million. The following information has been provided by the directors and is relevant to the calculation of deferred tax for the year ended 31 October 2013:

(i) On 31 October 2013, a foreign subsidiary was acquired for $153 million. The subsidiary's identifiable net assets (excluding deferred tax) had a carrying value of $129 million. There was no significant difference between the carrying value and fair value of net assets on acquisition. The subsidiary's net assets had a tax base of $102 million on acquisition. In the subsidiary's tax jurisdiction, goodwill is not allowed as a deduction for tax purposes.

Immediately following acquisition, Ding supplied the subsidiary with inventory amounting to $50 million at a margin of 20%. None of the inventory had been sold by the end of the year.

The tax rate relevant to the subsidiary's profit is 25%.

(ii) The carrying value of property, plant and equipment (excluding that relating to the subsidiary) was $30 million at 1 November 2012 and their tax base was $24 million. During the year, depreciation and capital allowances for tax purposes amounted to $10 million and $12 million respectively. On 31 October 2013 the assets were revalued to $50 million.

(iii) Ding operates a scheme to provide employees with a range of benefits related to health care. Benefits are tax deductible when paid. No benefits were paid during the year. The liability for future benefits at 31 October 2013 amounted to $70 million. The tax base of these benefits was zero.

(iv) Other taxable temporary differences amounted to $120 million as at 31 October 2013. In Ding's tax jurisdiction, income tax is assumed to be 30% for the foreseeable future.

(v) Ding's directors have calculated that the deferred tax liability on 31 October 2012 under IAS 12 would be $12 million.

Required

Advise the directors of Ding on how the above will affect the calculation of the group's deferred tax liability as at 31 October 2013 and deferred tax expense for the year ended 31 October 2013. **(16 marks)**

(b) Ding's directors believe that as deferred tax assets or liabilities represent taxes that will be recovered or paid some time in the future, statement of financial position amounts should be shown at their present value. They have also heard that IAS 12 is inconsistent with the IASB's *Conceptual Framework*.

Required

Advise Ding's directors on whether IAS 12 allows discount rates to be applied to deferred tax assets or liabilities and explain the inconsistency referred to above. **(4 marks)**

(Total 20 marks)

Question 33

You work for Eurotoc, a limited liability company, which seeks growth through acquisitions. You are a member of a team which is investigating the possible purchase of Choggerell, a limited liability company which manufactures a product which is complementary to the products currently being sold by Eurotoc.

Your team leader wants you to prepare a report for the team evaluating the recent performance of Choggerell and the quality of its management, and has given you the following financial information which has been derived from the financial statements of Choggerell for the three years ended 31 March 20X6, 20X7 and 20X8.

Financial year ended 31 March	20X6	20X7	20X8
Revenue (€million)	2,243	2,355	2,237
Cash and cash equivalents (€million)	(50)	81	(97)
Return on equity	13%	22%	19%
Sales revenue to total assets	2.66	2.66	2.01
Cost of sales to sales revenue	85%	82%	79%
Operating expenses to sales revenue	11%	12%	15%
Net income to sales revenue	2.6%	4.3%	4.2%
Current/Working Capital ratio (to 1)	1.12	1.44	1.06
Acid test ratio (to 1)	0.80	1.03	0.74
Inventory turnover (months)	0.6	0.7	1.0
Credit to customers (months)	1.3	1.5	1.7
Credit from suppliers (months)	1.5	1.5	2.0
Net assets per share (cents per share)	0.86	0.92	0.97
Dividend per share (cents per share)	10.0	14.0	14.0
Earnings per share (in cents)	11.5	20.1	18.7

Required

Use the above information to prepare a report for your team leader which:

- Reviews the performance of Choggerell as evidenced by the above ratios,
- Makes recommendations as to how the overall performance of Choggerell could be improved, and
- Indicates any limitations in your analysis.

(20 marks)

Question 34 – AIA May 2017

Poole is a quoted company, with a 31 December year end. The company entered into a 15-year lease on its office premises on 1 January 2014. The lease has a break point that permits either party to cancel the lease on 1 January 2019, but it is regarded as unlikely that the break clause will be invoked by either party.

The annual lease payment is $500,000, payable annually in advance.

The lease falls within the definition of an operating lease under the provisions of IAS 17 *Leases*. Poole is considering implementing IFRS 16 *Leases* early when it prepares its financial statements for the year ended 31 December 2017.

The interest rate implicit in the lease is unavailable, Poole's marginal borrowing rate is 8%.

The following discount factors relate to the present value of an 8% annuity:

Periods	
1	0.926
2	1.783
3	2.577
4	3.312
5	3.993
6	4.623
7	5.206
8	5.747
9	6.247
10	6.710
11	7.139
12	7.536
13	7.904
14	8.244
15	8.559

Required

(a) Advise how the lease would be accounted for under IFRS 16 *Leases*. Your advice should cover the treatment of this lease in the financial statements for the year ended 31 December 2017. **(8 marks)**

(b) Explore the effect of the early implementation of IFRS 16 *Leases* on the interpretation of Poole's performance and financial position. **(4 marks)**

(c) Evaluate the difficulties associated with determining the interest rate implicit in a lease. **(4 marks)**

(d) Evaluate the ethical issues arising from the election to implement IFRS before their effective date. **(4 marks)**

(Total 20 marks)

Question 35 – AIA May 2016

(a) The draft income statement of the Verti Group as at 30 April 2016 shows profit attributable to ordinary shareholders of the parent entity of $12 million and a loss from discontinued operations attributable to the parent entity of $8 million.

Verti has 4 million ordinary equity shares outstanding with a market value of $80 each. There are 400,000 ordinary share options outstanding with an exercise price of $60 each.

Verti has in issue 1.6 million convertible preference shares with a par value of $100 each. The preference shares are entitled to a cumulative dividend of $0.10 per share. Each preference share will convert into 2 ordinary shares.

Verti has $200 million 6% convertible bonds in issue. Each $1,000 bond is convertible into 20 ordinary shares. Interest expense is not affected by amortisation of premium or discount.

The relevant tax rate is 30%.

Required

Advise Verti of the basic and diluted earnings per share figures to be disclosed in the group income statement for the year ended 30 April 2016. **(12 marks)**

(b) Verti operates in the telecommunications industry. The entity's directors are supportive of the International Standards Board's (IASB) attempts to publish Generally Accepted Accounting Principles (GAAP) which govern how entities define their periodic earnings. They believe that GAAP helps to ensure a level of reliability and consistency across firms and over time. The directors have now become concerned about the development of non-GAAP earnings performance measures disclosed by a large number of the entity's competitors in their financial reporting and require advice on whether Verti is at a competitive disadvantage by not disclosing such information.

Required

Advise Verti's directors on whether the disclosure of non-GAAP (also known as 'pro-forma') earnings measures is likely to add valuable information to the entity's annual reporting or whether it would be seen as an example of the entity indulging in earnings management. **(4 marks)**

(c) Verti's directors are keen to develop the entity's engagement with capital providers and have been informed of a development in corporate reporting known as The International Integrated Reporting Framework. They were previously unaware of the existence of the framework and would like advice on what impact it may have on the entity's annual reporting, which presently focusses primarily on traditional concepts of historical performance.

Required

Advise Verti's directors on the possible impact of the above 'framework' on the annual reporting of the group as far as its engagement with capital providers and its focus on historical performance are concerned. **(4 marks)**

(Total 20 marks)

Exam answer bank

EXAM ANSWER BANK

Question 1

Syllabus section: 13.2

This question draws on material covered in Chapter 8 of the AIA text. It focuses on the ability to make the entries and calculations associated with accounting for piecemeal acquisitions and also the disposal of shares, leading to the designation of a subsidiary as an associate. The question also addresses the ethical issues associated with the classification of an investment as an associate in circumstances where that classification may be inappropriate.

(a) Malt workings

W1
Goodwill calculation
Fair value of investment consideration	160.0
Fair value of non-controlling interest	36.0
Net assets	(108.0)
Goodwill	88.0

W2
No gain or loss on disposal has been shown in the parent's financial statements.
NCI as at date of disposal
Fair value as at date of acquisition	36.0
NCI share of post-acquisition profits (108 – 84)*20%	4.8
	40.8

W3
Consideration received	112.0	Malt's net assets at disposal	132.0
Fair value of investment retained	120.0	Unimpaired goodwill (W1)	88.0
		NCI as at disposal (W2)	(40.8)
	232.0		179.2

Difference – gain on disposal   52.8

W4
Investment in associate
Fair value	120.0
Group share of post-acquisition earnings (W12)	6.4
	126.4

Dolt workings

W5
Investment
Fair value of 60% at date of acquisition of control	160.0
Further investment	40.0
Fair value of controlling interest	200.0
Further capital gain – to be eliminated as a consolidation adjustment	14.0
	214.0

W6
Goodwill calculation
Fair value of investment consideration	160.0
Fair value of non-controlling interest	116.0
Fair value of net assets	(150.0)
Impairment	(40.0)
Goodwill	86.0

W7
Non-controlling interest at 31 March 2014 before further acquisition

Fair value of NCI at acquisition	116.0
NCI share of post-acquisition earnings 40% × (124.0 – 70.0)	21.6
	137.6

W8
Non-controlling interest at 31 March 2014 after further acquisition

Fair value of NCI at acquisition	116.0
NCI share of post-acquisition earnings 25% × (124.0 – 70.0)	13.5
	129.5

W9

Decrease in non-controlling interest	8.1
Cost of additional investment	(40.0)
Loss – taken to retained earnings	(31.9)

W10
Non-controlling interest

As at 31 March 2014	129.5
NCI share of post-acquisition earnings	4.0
Goodwill impairment	(10.0)
	123.5

W11
Property, plant and equipment

Prent	1,188.0
Dolt	180.0
Adjustment for profit element of addition	(3.0)
	1,365.0

W12
Retained earnings

Prent	1,006.0
Malt	
Group share of Malt's profits while a subsidiary 80% × (108 – 84)	19.2
Group share of Malt's profits while an associate 40% × (124 – 108)	6.4
Equity adjustment on disposal	52.8
	1,084.4
Dolt	
Gain on investment in Dolt	(14.0)
Adjustment on additional investment	(31.9)
Group share of post-acquisition earnings 1 April 2013–31 March 2014 (60% × (124.0 – 70.0))	32.4
Group share of post-acquisition earnings 1 April 2014–31 March 2017 (75% × (140.0 – 124.0))	12.0
Property	(3.0)
Impairment of goodwill	(30.0)
	1,049.9

PRENT GROUP
CONSOLIDATED STATEMENT OF FINANCIAL POSITION
AS AT 31 DECEMBER 20X9

	$m
Investment in associate	126.4
Goodwill on acquisition	86.0
Property, plant and equipment	1,365.0
	1,577.4
Current assets	312.0
	1,889.4
Share capital	600.0
Retained earnings	1,049.9
	1,649.9
NCI	123.5
Current liabilities	116.0
	1,889.4

(b)

> **Tutorial Note:** Ethical arguments are best approached by applying the IFAC Code of Ethics. Otherwise, moral dilemmas can require the application of personal values, which may be difficult to describe and justify effectively during the examination.

The question here is whether it would be acceptable for Prent's board to exploit an oversight by the external auditor in order to misclassify the investment in Malt as an associate. Malt's retained earnings have grown quite rapidly, which means that misclassifying the company as an associate would have the effect of increasing group earnings.

Prent's directors would be acting against the IFAC Code of Ethics for Professional Accountants. Exploiting someone else's error for personal gain would be a failure of integrity. There would also be a clear lack of professional behaviour because this case has all the hallmarks of an accounting scandal, of a nature that would bring the profession into disrepute.

Question 2

A question of miscellaneous mini case studies involving knowledge and application of IAS 24 *Related Party Disclosures*, IFRS 5 *Non-current Assets Held for Sale and Discontinued Operations*, IAS 40 *Investment Property* and IAS 28 *Investments in Associates and Joint Ventures*.

(a) IAS 24 *Related Party Disclosures* includes within its definition of a related party: a party that has significant influence over an entity and members of the key management personnel of a company. It requires disclosure of the nature of any related party relationship as well as any information about the transactions and outstanding balances.

A director is a related party and so details of the transaction will have to be disclosed in the financial statements. The information to be disclosed will include all of the factual information given in the question.

(b) Applying IFRS 5 *Non-current Assets Held for Sale and Discontinued Operations*, the Brazilian activities should be classified as held-for-sale (para 6). Accordingly, the company should disclose separately in the statement of financial position the assets and liabilities of the Brazilian activities.

IFRS 5 includes in its definition of a discontinued operation, a business that is classified as held-for-sale and represents a separate major line of business or geographical area of operations (paragraph 32). The results of the Brazilian activities should be disclosed separately in the statement of profit or loss and other comprehensive income (paragraph 33(a)). The company should also include in the notes an analysis of revenue, costs, and tax from the discontinued operations and the net cash flows attributable to the operating, investing and financing activities of the discontinued operations (paragraph 33).

EXAM ANSWER BANK

(c) According to IAS 40 *Investment Property* an investment property is property (any combination of land and buildings) held to earn rentals or for capital appreciation or both rather than being used in the production and supply of goods and services or held for sale in the ordinary course of business. It would not be possible to continue disclosing the proposed investment property in land and buildings – it would have to be separately disclosed as an investment property. IAS 40 (paragraph 30) allows investment properties to be measured after recognition using either the cost model or the fair value model. So Nedell can adopt the accounting policy of measuring it at cost less depreciation, **but only** if it applies the same policy to all other investment properties it owns.

(d) IAS 24 *Related Party Disclosures* requires disclosure of the nature of any related party relationship as well as any information about the transactions and outstanding balances. The associates and joint ventures are related parties so even though the transactions have been eliminated as part of the consolidation process, details of the transactions will have to be disclosed.

Question 3

(a) This question is drawn from syllabus section 13.2 and requires the preparation of a group statement of cash flows. It mainly requires application of knowledge from the BPP Study Text Chapter 10 *Group Statements of Cash Flows*. The necessary adjustments require knowledge of topics from other chapters as follows:

6 Revision of basic groups re treatment of associate and calculation of goodwill
8 Changes in group structures re step acquisition
12 Non-current assets: tangible assets
13 Non-current assets: intangible assets
14 Financial instruments
16 Employee benefits
17 Taxation

ARDEW GROUP
CONSOLIDATED STATEMENT OF CASH FLOWS FOR THE YEAR ENDED 31 OCTOBER 2014

	w	$m	$m
Cash flows from operating activities			
Profit before tax	Q	36.9	
Add: adjustments to profit before tax:			
Impairment of goodwill	5	19.7	
Depreciation	2	16.9	
Amortisation of intangible assets	4	10.6	
Profit on disposal of land	2a	(5.7)	
Gain in fair value of investment property	3	(6.6)	
Gain on revaluation of equity instrument	7	(0.6)	
Share of profit after tax of associate	6	(3.8)	
Finance costs	Q	3.8	
Defined benefit pension plan net expense	17	2.5	
Contributions to defined benefit pension plan	17	(4.5)	
		69.2	
Decrease in trade receivables	9	35.0	
Decrease in inventories	8	20.4	
Increase in trade payables	18	55.7	
Cash generated from operations		180.3	
Finance costs	Q	(3.8)	
Income tax paid	16	(10.3)	
Net cash inflow from operating activities			166.2

EXAM ANSWER BANK

	w	$m	$m
Cash flows from investing activities			
Purchase of property, plant and equipment	2	(61.2)	
Proceeds from sale of surplus land	2a	9.4	
Acquisition of intangible assets	4	(7.5)	
Purchase of investment property	3	(0.6)	
Purchase of investment in associate	6	(30.0)	
Purchase on investments in equity instruments	7	(3.2)	
Net purchase of subsidiary	1	(5.6)	
Net cash outflow from investing activities			(98.7)
Cash flows from financing activities			
Proceeds from issue of share capital	11	1.8	
Dividends paid	12	(3.1)	
Dividends paid to non-controlling interests	14*	(8.1)	
Repayment of long-term debt	15	(2.5)	
Net cash outflow from financing activities			(11.9)
Net increase in cash and cash equivalents	10		55.6
Cash and cash equivalents at 1 November 2013	Q		89.4
Cash and cash equivalents at 31 October 2014	Q		145.0

Workings

> **Tutorial note:** Your first step in answering a group cash flow statement question should be to prepare a draft group cash flow statement in accordance with the presentation and disclosure requirements of IAS 1 and IAS 7. Pay particular attention to the question's requirements as to whether a direct or indirect presentation is required! Leave plenty of room between the main headings so you can fill in the blanks as you go through the question later.

The Ardew question involves the gaining of control over another company, Palan, by way of a step acquisition. In addition, questions concerning the preparation of a group cash flow statement will nearly always involve the gaining of control over a subsidiary **during the current year** (as this is arguably the most complex aspect of preparing a cash flow statement for a group). It is therefore always a good idea to continue your answer by next recreating the journal entries that would have been prepared to account for the acquisition **at the date control was gained**. We usually need to do this so we can see whether there has been any impairment to goodwill.

Legend: Q = figure taken directly from question, * = figure taken from question but also showing cross-reference to the double-entry necessary.

1   *Original journal entries to record the acquisition of Palan*

	w	Dr $m	Cr $m
FV of Palan's identifiable net assets:			
PPE	2*	9.4	
Intangible assets	4*	11.2	
Trade receivables	9*	3.1	
Cash acquired	Q	4.4	
	Q	28.1	
FV Consideration:			
Share capital	11*		8.8
Cash paid	Q		10.0

EXAM ANSWER BANK

> **Tutorial note:** net cash purchase of subsidiary is therefore $5.6m ($10.0m – $4.4m)

FV Non-controlling interest	14*	12.5
FV of previously held 10% equity investment	7*	3.1
Deferred tax [$28.1m (Q) – $25m (Q: tax base) × 30%]	16	0.9
Goodwill (balance)	5	7.2
		35.3
		35.3

> **Tutorial note:** having completed w1 above, the best way to tackle a cash flow question like this is to open T-accounts for each balance sheet item. Having done this, you should then answer the question systematically as follows:
>
> (i) Enter figures into the T-accounts for the opening and closing balances as shown in the question's balance sheet;
>
> (ii) Enter figures into the T-accounts from the opening acquisition journal entries (w1 above);
>
> (iii) Work systematically through the notes in the question making appropriate entries into the T-accounts you have opened; and
>
> (iv) Balance off the T-accounts to find the balancing figures. These balancing figures will provide most of the figures you will need to prepare the cash flow statement. You can now finally enter these figures into your draft cash flow statement under the appropriate headings.

The T-account workings below also include all equity items for the sake of explanation and completeness. However, under exam conditions, you should not have to prepare these as all movements in these items are shown for you in the Statement of changes in equity provided in the question.

2   Property Plant and Equipment (PPE)

		Dr	Cr
Opening balance 1 Nov 2013		158.8	
Closing balance 31 Oct 2014			204.4
From acquisition of Palan	1	9.4	
Depreciation	Q		16.9
Loss on revaluation of owner-occupied property	13*		4.4
Carrying value of surplus land exchanged	2a		6.2
FV of land acquired in exchange	2a	2.5	
Purchase of PPE (balance)		61.2	
		231.9	231.9

2a   PPE: Disposal account

		Dr	Cr
Carrying value of surplus land exchanged	2	6.2	
FV of land acquired in exchange	2a		2.5
Cash received	Q		9.4
Profit on exchange of land (balance)		5.7	
		11.9	11.9

> **Tutorial note:** as the exchange of land will 'enhance future group cash flows', the transaction has commercial substance and as such, under IAS 16, must be measured at fair value.

3   Investment Property (IP)

		Dr	Cr
Opening balance 1 Nov 2013		3.8	
Closing balance 31 Oct 2014			5.0
To correct treatment of land acquisition	8*		6.0

> **Tutorial note:** property acquired exclusively for sale in the near future or for development and sale is not investment property and must be accounted for under IAS 2 *Inventories*.

Gain in FV on revaluation of IP	Q	6.6	
Purchase of IP (balance)		0.6	
		11.0	11.0

4 Intangible Assets

Opening balance 1 Nov 2013		45.0	
Closing balance 31 Oct 2014			53.1
From acquisition of Palan	1	11.2	
Purchase of patents	Q	5.0	
Construction and testing of new process	Q	2.5	

> **Tutorial note:** following IAS 38 Ardew will have expensed costs concerning evaluation of research and selection of new process as they refer to research expenditure. In addition IAS 38 does not allow the capitalisation of marketing costs. So only development cost will have been capitalised ($2.5m). Total purchase of intangibles = $7.5m.

Amortisation (balance)			10.6
		63.7	63.7

5 Goodwill

		Dr	Cr
Opening balance 1 November 2013	Q	42.5	
On acquisition of Palan (above)	1	7.2	
Closing balance as at 31 October 2014	Q		30.0
Impairment (balance)			19.7
		49.7	49.7

> **Tutorial note:** all of the above goodwill impairment is treated as having been written off to profit or loss as the question tells us that it related to 100% owned subsidiaries. If it related to partially owned subsidiaries the question would have to give information concerning the size of the NCI holding so that the impairment adjustment could be split between NCI and the parent.

6 Investment in associate (Koje)

> **Tutorial note:** although Ardew only acquired 15% Ardew can exert significant influence therefore Koje is an associate.

Opening balance 1 Nov 2013		–	
Closing balance 31 Oct 2014			33.8
Share of profit after tax of associate	Q	3.8	
Purchase of associate (balance)		30.0	
		33.8	33.8

7 Investment in equity instruments

Opening balance 1 Nov 2013		56.2	
Closing balance 31 Oct 2014			58.8
Acquisition of Palan (FV of 10% Palan when control gained)	1*		3.1
Revaluation gain (re 10% in Palan when control gained $3.1m – $2.5m per Q)			0.6

EXAM ANSWER BANK

> **Tutorial note:** the above gain will have been included in profit or loss so it needs to be adjusted in the CFS

Fair value gains in OCI (net)	13*	1.3	
Adj for def tax on above FV gain (ie grossed up at $1.9m x 30%)	16	0.6	
Additions (balance)		3.2	
		61.9	61.9

8   *Inventories*

Opening balance 1 Nov 2013		80.0	
Closing balance 31 Oct 2014			65.6
To correct treatment of land acquisition	3*	6.0	
Decrease in inventory (balance)			20.4
		86.0	86.0

9   *Trade Receivables (TR)*

Opening balance 1 Nov 2013		70.6	
Closing balance 31 Oct 2014			38.7
From acquisition of Palan	1	3.1	
Decrease in TR (balance)			35.0
		73.7	73.7

10   *Cash and Cash Equivalents (CCE)*

Opening balance 1 Nov 2013		89.4	
Closing balance 31 Oct 2014			145.0
Net increase in CCE (balance)		55.6	
		155.0	155.0

11   *Share Capital (SC)*

		Dr	Cr
Opening balance 1 Nov 2013			171.9
Closing balance 31 Oct 2014		182.5	
Re acquisition of Palan	1		8.8
Proceeds from issue of SC (balance)			1.8
		182.5	182.5

12   *Retained Earnings*

Opening balance 1 Nov 2013			202.5
Closing balance 31 Oct 2014		219.4	
Profit before tax	Q		36.9
Income tax expense	16*	6.9	
Remeasurement deficit on pension plan	17*	3.8	
NCI share of profit for the year	14*	6.2	
Dividends paid	Q	3.1	
		239.4	239.4

13   *Other components of equity* (RS = revenue surplus IEI = Investment in equity instruments)

Opening balance 1 Nov 2013 [RS 10+IEI 2.5]			12.5
Closing balance 31 Oct 2014 [RS 5.6 + IEI 3.8]		9.4	
Loss on revaluation of owner-occupied property	2*	4.4	
Fair value gains in OCI (net)	7*		1.3
		13.8	13.8

14 Non-controlling Interest

Opening balance 1 Nov 2013		22.5
Closing balance 31 Oct 2014	33.1	
From acquisition of Palan 1		12.5
NCI share of profit for the year 12*		6.2
Dividends paid (balance per question)	8.1	
	41.2	41.2

15 Long-term Debt (LTD)

Opening balance 1 Nov 2013		44.4
Closing balance 31 Oct 2014	41.9	
Repayment of LTD (balance)	2.5	
	44.4	44.4

16 Taxation

Deferred tax:	Opening balance 1 Nov 2013		25.6
:	Closing balance 31 Oct 2014	21.9	
Current tax:	Opening balance 1 Nov 2013		18.8
:	Closing balance 31 Oct 2014	20.6	
From acquisition of Palan 1			0.9
Def tax on FV gain on inv in equity inst 7			0.6
Income tax expense 12*			6.9
Income taxes paid (balance)		10.3	
		52.8	52.8

17 Defined benefit pension liability

Opening balance 1 Nov 2013	Q		13.8
Closing balance 31 Oct 2014	Q	15.6	
Remeasurement deficit in OCI	12*		3.8
Current service costs*	Q		6.3
Enhancement to scheme benefits*	Q		1.2
Net interest receivable by scheme*	Q	5.0	
Contributions paid into scheme (balance)		4.5	
		25.1	25.1

Tutorial note: The revised IAS 19 requires that enhanced benefits (ie past service costs) are written off immediately to profit or loss. * refers to other non-cash flows which must be adjusted on the cash flow statement (ie 6.3 + 1.2 – 5.0 = $2.5m).

18 Trade Payables (TP)

Opening balance 1 Nov 2013		34.3
Closing balance 31 Oct 2014	90.0	
Increase in TP (balance)		55.7
	90.0	90.0

(b) This question concerns IAS 7's requirements concerning the classification of cash flows and the related ethical responsibilities of directors. It is drawn from syllabus sections 13.1 and 13.2 and is covered by the BPP text at chapters:

4 Ethics and regulation of corporate reporting
10 Group statements of cash flows

Advice to directors of Ardew

Re Classification of operating cash flows

The first point to make to the directors is that due to the way their bonuses are calculated they would appear to have a vested interest in classifying cash flows as operating in nature. Any

EXAM ANSWER BANK

suggestion by them to classify cash flows in this manner would therefore immediately arouse suspicion.

IAS 7 *Statement of Cash Flows* is not totally rigid in its requirements and allows some flexibility in cash flow classification and presentation. This is so that entities can choose a way of classifying that provides as much clarity and useful information as possible to users. For example, in the above statement of cash flows, dividends paid by Ardew are shown as financing cash flows as they are deemed to be part of the cost of obtaining entity finance. Alternatively, they could have been classified as operating cash flows on the basis that such classification would allow users to more clearly assess the extent to which profits cover dividends. Also, the use of the indirect method (as adopted by Ardew) to present net cash flow from operating activities, rather than the allowed alternative – the direct method, presents information concerning the makeup of operating cash flows with much greater clarity. The overriding criterion is that information must be presented fairly and, despite the flexibility IAS 7 allows in pursuit of this, it is quite clear that loan proceeds are not operational in nature and presenting them as such would not achieve a fair presentation.

The directors must adopt an ethical approach when presenting information and must not be governed by self-interest. Using accounting techniques and approaches in the interest of making the figures look good, for whatever reason, would constitute acting unethically and the directors must be cautioned against it. If the directors have any concerns about this they can be directed towards the IFAC 2013 Handbook of the Code of Ethics for Professional Accountants.

The interest of the entity and its stakeholders must come first. The directors should therefore be advised that any loan proceeds must be presented as cash flows from financing.

Question 4

Part (a) concerns the adoption by an entity of the revaluation model for property, plant and equipment under IAS 16 and the impact of IAS 8 *Accounting Policies, Changes in Accounting Estimates and Errors*. It also requires a discussion of the fair value measurements changes under IFRS 13. It is drawn from syllabus sections 13.1 and 13.4 and requires application of knowledge from the BPP Study Text Chapters 12 *Tangible non-current assets and inventory* and 18 *Reporting financial performance*.

(a) **Tutorial Note:** Under IAS 16 administration and general overheads cannot be capitalised.

(i)

	$m	
Cost 1 May 2009	10.0	
		Company policy would be to
Depn to 30 April 2012 (3yrs × $1m)	3.0	eliminate depn against gross CV
Carrying value 30 April 2012	7.0	
		This defecit would be written off
Revaluation deficit 30 April 2012	3.5	to profit or loss.
CV 1 May 2012	3.5	
		Company policy would be to
Depn to 30 April 2015 (3 yrs × $0.5m)	1.5	eliminate depn against gross CV
CV at 30 April 2015	2.0	
Revaluation surplus*	3.0	
	5.0	

* $1m of the surplus would be credited to the revaluation surplus in OCI representing the difference between the NBV that would have resulted had the asset been held on a cost basis ($4m) and the NBV on a revalued basis ($5m). The remaining $2m would be taken through profit or loss.

Although the adoption of a revaluation policy by Frere and changing from a cost model would be a change in accounting policy, it is **not** dealt with as a prior year adjustment under IAS 8 *Accounting Policies, Changes in Accounting Estimates and Errors*. Therefore comparatives would not have to be amended.

(ii) Using the cost model under IAS 16 requires a consideration of exactly which costs are to be capitalised. Using the revaluation model means this will no longer be necessary as costs such as borrowing, transportation and other directly attributable costs are not part of the measure of an asset's fair value.

The FV of an asset is to be a market-based and non entity-specific exit price (IFRS 13.B2). So Fere would only be allowed to use entity-specific prices in very restricted circumstances; ie when observable market prices are not available. These would be 'valuation techniques' such as present values.

The market-based nature of the price means it takes into account current market conditions when measuring the asset. So, for instance, if Fere held an item of PPE, the price will be the amount the asset **could** be sold for. Due to the market-based nature, the measure of the asset must take into account the characteristics of that item and the assumptions made by market participants. It is assumed that transactions will take place in the **principal market** in which an orderly transaction for the asset would take place or, in its absence, the **most advantageous** market.

The principal market is the market with the greatest liquidity (in terms of volume and level of activity for that asset). If there is no principal market, the price in the most advantageous market would be used; ie the market in which Fere could achieve the most beneficial price; eg by maximising the amount received. If market activity is in decline, then IFRS 13 recognises that valuation techniques as mentioned above may have to be used to measure FV; although in such a case it would have to be determined whether this still represented an orderly sale (eg a forced sale would have to be accounted for outside the FV requirements). Although the price may have to be adjusted if costs are incurred to transport an asset to the principal (or most advantageous) market, transaction costs would not be included in fair value because such costs are not a characteristic of the asset or liability.

(b) Part (b) requires a discussion of the reasons behind the introduction of IFRS 16. It is drawn from syllabus sections 13.1 and 13.4 and requires application of knowledge from the BPP Study Text Chapter 15 *Leasing contracts*.

(i) *Reason for changes*

The IASB believes that the accounting rules under IAS 17 did not reflect the definitions or recognition criteria in the *Conceptual Framework* in that most leases, whether finance or operating in nature, contain an unavoidable liability (an obligation) and an asset providing rights to control and obtain the potential economic benefits embodied in the asset. Therefore the old rules, under which operating leases do not appear on balance sheets, did not reflect the *Conceptual Framework's* requirements for transparency and full disclosure.

Effect of IFRS 16 on Recognition of Leases

The new approach eliminates the operating lease accounting model under IAS 17 *Leases* and replace it with a 'right-of-use' model, in which a lessee would recognise an asset representing its right to use the leased item during the lease term as well as a liability for the lessee's obligations to pay rentals. This would apply to all leases except those of up to 12 months.

In the SoFP, a lessee would report an asset and a lease liability at the discounted amount of lease payments to be made during the lease term.

In the income statement, the presentation of lease-related expenses would depend on the nature of the asset and the extent to which the lessee consumes that asset; as follows.

- If the lessee is expected to consume more than an insignificant portion of the leased asset, the lessee would account for the lease similarly to a finance lease in the existing IAS 17. This means that for the substantial majority of leases of PPE (eg aircraft, ships, mining equipment, cars, trucks), a lessee, in the income statement, would report amortisation of the asset separately from interest on the lease liability over the lease term.

- If the lessee is paying only for use of the leased asset (and is not expected to consume more than an insignificant portion of that asset), the lessee would account for the lease in the income statement similarly to an operating lease in IAS 17. This means that for the substantial majority of leases of property (ie land and/or a building), although it would report assets and liabilities on a discounted basis on the balance sheet, a lessee, in the income statement, would report a lease expense on a straight-line basis over the lease term.

(ii) Right of use asset and lease liability

On initial recognition, the lease liability would be measured as:

	$
PV of future cash flows	1,871,100
Interest at 6% (6% × $1,871,100)	112,266 (SPL)
Balance of the lease liability at end Year 1	1,983,366

The right of use asset is initially recognised as the lease liability plus the deposit paid = $1,983,366 + $700,000 = $2,683,366.

The asset is depreciated over four years, which is the shorter of the lease term and its useful life. Depreciation for the year is therefore $670,842.

The carrying amount of the asset at the end of Year 1 is $2,012,524.

The lease liability and the carrying amount of the right of use asset will be recognised in the statement of financial position.

The finance charge (interest) and depreciation will be in the statement of profit or loss.

Question 5

Syllabus section: 13.2

This question concerns IFRS 11 *Joint Arrangements* and their accounting using the equity method as set out in IAS 28 *Investments in Associates and Joint Ventures*. Part (a) concerns a subsidiary which becomes a joint venture, part (b) concerns the identification of joint control in a joint arrangement, (c) concerns the accounting treatment of gains, losses and revenue in a joint venture.

(a) (i)
> **Tutorial note:** Atab's accounting is incorrect. Under IFRS 10, if a parent loses control of an entity, the retained interest must be measured at its fair value and this fair value becomes the cost on initial recognition of an investment in an associate or joint venture (IFRS 10.25). Therefore Atab's use of historic cost of $3m (and therefore its subsequent measurement of a loss on disposal of $2.5m) is incorrect.

Correct measurement of gain/loss on disposal of 60% of Begi's shares

		$m
Fair value of consideration		7.5
Fair value of Begi's identifiable net assets		4.5
Goodwill on acquisition		3.0
Carrying value of Begi's net assets		1.8
		4.8
Less: sale proceeds of 60%	2.0	
fair value of remaining 40% of Begi	1.2	
		3.2
Loss on disposal of 60% of Begi		1.6

Atab's original (incorrect) accounting will have been as follows in the consolidated accounts:

DR cash	2.0	
DR Joint Venture	3.0	
DR Retained earnings	2.5	
CR Net assets		7.5

The correct accounting treatment is shown above. To correct the consolidated accounts Atab must therefore:

DR Net assets	2.7	
CR Joint Venture		1.8
CR Retained earnings		0.9

(ii) **Tutorial note:** When an investor increases its ownership in an existing joint venture or associate (and control is not acquired) there is no significant change in the nature and economic circumstances of the investment. Therefore there is no justification for re-measurement of the existing interest at the time of the increase (as there would be if **control** was acquired).

The cost of an investment in an associate or joint venture (and each additional acquisition) is allocated between net assets and goodwill for the purpose of disclosure. However, this does not result in any revaluation of the existing and recognised share of net assets (IAS 28.32).

For the purpose of calculating the goodwill to be disclosed in the notes, we must calculate the fair value of the associate's net assets at the year end.

FV of Blo's net assets at 31 October 2016

	$m
FV of INAs at 1 Nov 2015	16.0
Increase in Blo's retained earnings	13.5
Increase in fair value of plant and equipment	3.5
	33.0

	% held	Carrying value of investment (inc costs IAS 28) $m	Share of net assets $m	Goodwill included in investment (balance) $m
Original investment	25	5.5	4.0 (16m × 25%)	1.5
Additional investment	20	7.0	6.6 (33m × 20%)	0.4
Share of Blo's profit for the year (25% × $13.5m)		3.4	3.4	—
		15.9	14.0	1.9

(b) Bin

'Relevant activities' are the activities of the investee that significantly affect the investee's returns (IFRS 10.10). As each party is able to unilaterally direct their own activity, no joint control exists because Alac and Bin do not collectively direct the relevant activities of the arrangement.

Cons

Because both Alac and Cons make all decisions together throughout the arrangement's life, it is unnecessary to determine which party significantly affects the returns of the arrangement. They are all directed in the same manner. Alac and Cons have joint control over the arrangement.

EXAM ANSWER BANK

(c) As this is a joint venture, the inclusion of $3.4m in revenue is unacceptable under IFRS 15 *Revenue from Contracts with Customers*. Under IAS 28 (2011) *Investments in Associates and Joint Ventures*, the consolidated statement of comprehensive income should include the group share of the JV's profit or loss as a one-line entry. When a joint venturer contributes assets to a JV any gain or loss is recognised to the extent that it reflects the substance of the transaction. As a result:

(i) Only the gain attributable to the interests of the other joint venturers should be recognised in the financial statements. Exten would make a gain of $300,000 but only 40% can be considered as realised; ie that proportion attributable to Gect. Exten should therefore include a gain of $120,000 in 'profit or loss attributable to joint ventures'.

(ii) A loss of $400,000 would be made on the inventory. The full amount should be recognised when the transaction shows evidence that the NRV of the asset is less than cost. If it is probable that the loss will be incurred, prudence requires that Exten recognises the full loss in 'profit or loss attributable to joint ventures'.

Tutorial Note: this shows that an asymmetric treatment of gains and losses still exists in corporate reporting.

Question 6

(a) This part of the question is drawn from syllabus section 13.2 and requires the preparation of a group statement of comprehensive income. It mainly requires application of knowledge from the BPP Study Text Part B 'Business combinations and group financial statements' and in particular Chapters 6–8.

The necessary adjustments require knowledge of topics from other chapters as follows:

2	Presentation of published financial statements
12	Tangible non-current assets and inventory
14	Financial instruments
16	Employee benefits
21	Revenue recognition

(b) This part involves a discussion of earnings management and requires advice to be given concerning its ethical implications. It is drawn from syllabus section 13.1 and requires application of knowledge from BPP Study Text Part A 'Contemporary issues' Chapter 4 *Ethics and regulation of corporate financial reporting* and Part C 'Accounting and Reporting Techniques' Chapter 14 *Financial instruments*.

RADMIN GROUP
STATEMENT OF PROFIT OR LOSS AND COMPREHENSIVE INCOME FOR THE YEAR ENDED 30 APRIL 2015

	w	$m
Revenue	1	796
Cost of sales	1	546
Gross profit		250
Other income	1	31
Administrative costs	1	(146)
Finance costs	1	(32)
Profit before tax		103
Income tax expense	1	(40)
Profit for the year from continuing operations		63
Profit for the year from discontinued operations		19
		82

EXAM ANSWER BANK

	W	$m
Other comprehensive income		
Items that will not be reclassified to profit or loss (net of tax)		
Gain on revaluation of property, plant and equipment	1	27
Remeasurements of defined benefit pension plans	1	4
Investments in equity instruments	1	11
Gain on revaluation of PPE in discontinued operation	1	3
Other comprehensive income for the year, net of tax		45
Total comprehensive income for the year		127
Profit for the year attributable to:		
Owners of the parent from continuing operations	9	52
Owners of the parent from discontinued operations	1	19
Non-controlling interest	9	11
		82
Total comprehensive income for the year attributable to:		
Owners of the parent from continuing operations	9	112
Owners of the parent from discontinued operation	9	3
Non-controlling interest	9	12
		127

Workings

> **Tutorial notes:**
>
> Note that Radmin has adopted IFRS 9 *Financial Instruments*. The caption in the question 'Investment in equity instruments' under the heading 'Items that will not be reclassified to profit or loss' is as a result of this adoption. The caption would have been 'Available-for-sale financial instruments' and shown under the heading 'items that may be reclassified to profit or loss' had IFRS 9 not been adopted.
>
> Note that Ream is disposed of on 30 April and is therefore a discontinued operation under IFRS 5.
>
> The workings below are shown in pro forma style. This is often an efficient way to work through a consolidated statement of income question as it helps to focus on the structure of what you are preparing and provides figures for use in the 'attributable profit' calculations.
>
> Legend: Q = figures taken from question.
> OCI = other comprehensive income
> ITWNBRTPL = items that will not be reclassified to profit or loss.

	W	Radmin $m	Ture $m	Adj $m	Con St of income $m	Ream $m
CONTINUING OPERATIONS						
Revenue						
Per question	Q	520	292			137
Inter-company sales	5			(16)	796	
Cost of sales						
Per question	Q	(416)	(143)			(98)
Inter-company sales	5			16		
Inter-company profit	5	(1)				
Impairment adjustment	7	(2)			(546)	
Gross profit		101	149		250	39
Other income						
Per question	Q	20	13			8
Dividend adjustment	6	(2)			31	

EXAM ANSWER BANK

	W	Radmin	Ture	Adj	Con St of income	Ream
Administrative costs						
Per question	Q	(59)	(72)			(22)
Acquisition fees w/b	TN2	(7)				
Goodwill impairment Ture	2	(6)				
Additional depreciation Ture	4		(2)			
					(146)	
Finance costs						
Per question	Q	(14)	(20)			(14)
Contribution adjustment	8	2			(32)	
Profit before tax		35	68		103	11
Income tax expense						
Per question	Q	(17)	(23)		(40)	(4)
Profit for the year from continuing operations		18			63	
DISCONTINUED OPERATIONS	3					
Profit for the year from discontinued operations					19	
					82	
OCI						
ITWNBRTPL						
Gain on property revaluation						
Per question	Q	21	4			
Impairment adjustment	7	2			27	
From discontinued operation	Q					3
Remeasurements of defined pension plans						
Per question	Q	6				
Contribution adjustment	8	(2)			4	
Investments in equity instruments						
Per question	Q	10				
Sale cost adjustment	6	1			11	
OCI for the year		38	4		42	3
TCI for the year		75	49		124	10

2   Goodwill in Ture

> **Tutorial Note:** candidates sometimes believe that because the question involves an income statement, it is not necessary to calculate goodwill. This is a mistake. Goodwill needs to be calculated to see whether, and by how much, it has been impaired. An impairment write-off will affect the income statement.

Under IFRS 3, acquisition costs (such as legal, accounting and valuation fees) must be expensed and cannot be capitalised. $7m needs to be deducted as an expense (it is assumed in the answer below, that fees had not been capitalised in purchase consideration. However, net purchase consideration of £188m is equally acceptable). The standard also requires that contingent consideration (in this case a cash liability of $4m) is recorded at fair value. Any subsequent change in the contingent obligation is accounted for according to whether additional information reflects conditions at the date of acquisition (in which case goodwill and the liability are adjusted) or not (in which case goodwill is not adjusted but the liability is). In this question, there is no change to be accounted for as the entity believes that performance targets in 2016 will be met.

		$m
FV of consideration for 75% of Ture	Q	195
Contingent consideration	Q	4
FV of NCI	Q	70
		269
FV of identifiable net assets at acquisition	Q	209
Goodwill		60
Impairment (10%)		6

3 Disposal of investment in Ream

> **Tutorial Note:** There is no NCI in Ream. Therefore, the calculation of the disposal gain/loss is relatively straight-forward.

		$m	$m
Goodwill in Ream at date of acquisition:			
FV of consideration transferred	Q	110	
FV of Identifiable net assets at date of acquisition	Q	70	
Goodwill		40	
Gain/loss on disposal of Ream:			
FV of consideration received			160
Less: consolidated carrying value when control lost:			
FV of Ream's net assets (ie carrying value)		108	
Goodwill at acquisition as above (note: no impairment)		40	
			148
Gain on disposal			12
Profit for the year		1	7
			19

4 Depreciation of plant and equipment

	$m	$m
FV of Ture's identifiable net assets at acquisition (INA)		209
Carrying value of INA at acquisition:		
Share capital	72	
Retained earnings	110	
Other components of equity	13	
		195
Increase in FV of INA at acquisition		14
Additional depreciation required ($14m / 7 years)		2

5 Inter company sales

Revenue adjustment: Ture $16m + Ream $4m = $20m
Inter-company profit adjustment: Ture $16m × 1/4 × 25% = $1m

6 Investment in equity instruments

> **Tutorial Note:** Radmin has adopted IFRS 9 so, after initial recognition, investments in equity instruments that are designated as measured at fair value through other comprehensive income should be measured at fair value, with no deduction for sale costs. Dividends from such investments should be recognised in profit or loss when the right to receive payment is established.

As a result, in this case, there must be an adjustment for $1m sale costs and, as a right to receive payment has not been established, an adjustment for $2m dividends.

7   *Revaluation of PPE*

> **Tutorial Note:** In 2015 there has been a downward revaluation of the PPE. Under IAS 16's revaluation model, decreases must be written off to profit and loss with the exception that, if there has been a previous revaluation surplus, the decrease must first be written off against that surplus (in OCI*).

Note. In this question we do not have to account for any transfers for excess depreciation following revaluation as the company has a policy of **not** making such transfers.

*If this had been an impairment loss, then under IAS 36 this amount would be charged to profit and loss

First we must work out what the company **has** done.

	$m
As at 30 April 2014:	
Revaluation of PPE on 30 April 2014	22.0
Initial carrying value at 30 April 2014 [20 – depn 2 (20/10)]	18.0
Surplus included in other components of equity	4.0
As at 30 April 2015:	
Initial carrying value of PPE at 30 April 2015 [22 – depn (22/9)]	19.6
Revaluation at 30 April 2015	13.6
Decrease	6.0

The question tells us that the whole of the revaluation loss (of $6m) has been included in OCI. This is incorrect. Only $4m can be dealt with this way as it reverses the previous revaluation increase. The remaining $2m must be written off in profit or loss.

8   *Contributions to defined benefit pension plan*

> **Tutorial Note:** The only figures that should be included in profit or loss with respect to defined benefit plans (IAS 19) are the value of current service costs and net interest. Assuming, the carrying values of plan assets and liabilities are correct (there is nothing in the question to suggest otherwise), the $2m contribution should be taken out of finance costs and adjusted against the figure for 'remeasurements of defined benefit plans'.

9   *Profit attributable*

> **Tutorial Note:** it is acceptable in exam answers to calculate the profits attributable to NCI and find the profits attributable to owners as a balancing figure.

Profit for the attributable to NCI 25% × $45m (W1)	11.25
Profit for the year attributable to owners of parent (balancing figure)	51.75
	63.00
TCI for the year attributable to NCI 25% × $49 (W1)	12.25
TCI for the year attributable to owners of parent (balancing figure)	114.75*
	127.00

(* includes $3m from discontinued operation)

(b) *Nature of a motivation for 'earnings management' (EM)*

It may be argued that EM is used by managers for altruistic reasons; eg to smooth out performance thereby providing shareholders with a more predictable income stream or to reduce a user's incorrect perception of risk. However, EM is usually associated with the manipulation of financial reports in order to deliberately mislead shareholders and other stakeholders about an entity's performance. There could be a number of motivations for this. The directors may be attempting to benefit personally from the manipulation; eg due to a link between the performance of the entity and their remuneration; or they may perhaps be trying to influence the decision-making of stakeholders; eg shareholders and lenders making investment decisions, suppliers and customers making contractual decisions and regulators making policy decisions.

The proposed manipulation

The proposal uses accounting techniques that are included in the guidelines to IFRS 9. However, in the circumstances concerning the debt instrument, the proposed technique is incorrect. As Radmin's business model is to hold the financial asset to maturity so as to benefit from principal and interest on that principal, IFRS 9 would require that amortised cost is used. Fair value can only be used when the entity's business model is to hold such instruments to benefit from changes in their fair value. This would not normally apply to debt assets held to maturity.

Ethical acceptability

When making decisions about financial reporting practices, Radmin's directors should always bear in mind that they have an overriding responsibility to fairly report the entity's performance. This is because the IASB's *Conceptual Framework* states that the objective of such financial statements is to assist investors, lenders and other creditors in their decision-making activities. By fairly stating performance, the information is more reliable for and relevant to that purpose. Fair information also enhances the predictive quality of the information. The directors need to consider that auditors will be aware that managers may wish to indulge in EM and will design tests to detect it.

The directors have an ethical and a social responsibility to avoid misleading the stakeholders. This is often in conflict with the directors' desire to ensure survival of the entity in the short-term – as with Radmin's proposed choice of accounting technique which would enhance earnings in the short-term. However, it is clearly an ethically unacceptable position if the result is to damage Radmin's prospects in the long-term.

Stakeholders should be able to rely on the directors' ethical integrity and should be able to expect them to demonstrate the IFAC ethical values of honesty, trustworthiness and lack of bias. It is not clear why Radmin's directors wish to 'manage earnings' in this way but they clearly have a dilemma between managing earnings so as to effectively discharge their responsibilities for the benefit of the shareholders whilst at the same time providing those very same shareholders with misleading information.

Question 7

(a) **This question concerns the preparation of a consolidated statement of financial position and is relevant to syllabus section 13.2. It involves a consideration of:**

IFRS 3 (Revised) *Business Combinations*

IAS 38 *Intangible Assets*

IAS 21 *The Effects of Changes in Foreign Exchange Rates*

IFRS 2 *Share-based Payment*

IFRS 9 *Financial Instruments*

EXAM ANSWER BANK

TREE PLC

CONSOLIDATED STATEMENT OF FINANCIAL POSITION AS AT 31 OCTOBER 2012

	w	$m
Assets:		
Non-current assets:		
Property, plant and equipment	7	488.37
Goodwill	1	14.13
Intangible asset	8	6.00
Financial instruments	10	26.25
		534.75

	w	$m
Current assets		
Inventories	11	126.75
Trade receivables	12	74.00
Cash and cash equivalents	13	20.63
		221.38
Total assets		756.13
Equity and Liabilities		
Equity:		
Share capital	6	132.00
Retained earnings	3	219.55
Other components of equity	5	18.24
Non-controlling interest	4	45.21
Total equity		415.00
Liabilities:		
Non-current liabilities	14	99.63
Current liabilities	15	241.50
Total liabilities		341.13
Total equity and liabilities		756.13

Workings

> **Tutorial note:** the solutions and workings shown below are shown, as far as is possible, in double entry form. This will be of help to students by showing the workings in more detail.

1 *Goodwill in Leaf on acquisition of 60% on 1 Nov 2011*

> **Tutorial note:** IFRS 3 (revised) disallows the inclusion of transaction costs in the fair value of consideration. These must therefore be adjusted against retained earnings (w3)

	w	Dr	Cr
Fair value of consideration paid (less transaction costs of $5m)	Q(i)	73	
Fair value of NCI	4	38	
Net assets at carrying value at date of acquisition represented by equity at date of acquisition:			
Equity	Q		31
Retained earnings	3		41
Other components of equity	5		2
			74
Increase in value of land (100 – 74)	7		26

EXAM ANSWER BANK

> **Tutorial note:** both IFRS 3 and IAS 38 regard an intangible asset as recognisable upon acquisition if it is separable or it arises from contractual or other legal rights.

Intangible asset: trade name	8	6
Fair value of recognisable net assets on acquisition		106
Balance: goodwill		5

Goodwill in Roots

Fair value of consideration paid on acquisition	Q(i)	38.00
Fair value of NCI on acquisition (see w9) ($^{105 \text{ Krons}}/_{10}$)	4	10.50

Fair value of identifiable net assets at acquisition as represented by equity: (see w9)		
Equity share capital		16.70
Retained earnings		18.30
Other components of equity		6.20
		41.20

Exchange difference on translation at 31 Oct 2012 (see w9) accounted for:		
Other components of equity: exchange reserve	5	1.46
NCI	4	0.37
Balance: goodwill		9.13

Total goodwill (5.00 + 9.13) = 14.13

2 *Adjustment between owners*

> **Tutorial note:** Tree's original interest was 60% in Leaf. As the increase of 10% on 31 October 2012 is therefore in a holding which was previously a controlling interest, there is no re-measurement to fair value and no gain or loss is taken to profit or loss. The increase of 10% is therefore accounted for as simply representing a transaction between owners.

		Dr	Cr
Fair value of consideration paid	Q(i)	16.0	
Transfer to equity from NCI	4		10.2
Balance: movement in equity (negative)	5		5.8

3 *Retained earnings*

		Dr	Cr
• Tree	Q		213.00
Transaction costs: Re acquisition of Leaf (78 – 73)	Q(i)	5.00	
Re financial instruments	10	1.00	
Fair value gain on financial instruments	10		3.00
• Leaf			
As at 31 Oct 2012	Q		47.00
As at 1 Nov 2011	1	41.00	
NCI share of increase over year ($6m × 40%)	4	2.40	
• Roots			
Post acquisition earnings (7.44 [see w9] × 80%)			5.95
Total retained earnings: balance		219.55	

EXAM ANSWER BANK

4 **Non-controlling interest**

		Dr	Cr
• Leaf			
Fair value at 1 Nov 2011	1		38.00
NCI share of increase in earnings over year ($6m × 40%)	3		2.40
NCI share of increase in other components of equity ($1m × 40%)	5		0.40
			40.80
Transfer to equity ($40.8m × 10/40)	2	10.20	
Balance: NCI in Leaf as at 31 Oct 2012		30.60	

Tutorial note: the total increase in NCI over the year 2.80 (2.40 + 0.40) could have been calculated by using net assets figures:

Fair value of net assets as at 1 Nov 2011 (w1)	106
Fair value of net assets as at 31 Oct 2012 ($81m [per balance sheet] + 26 land + 6 trade name)	113
Increase in fair value of net assets	7
NCI share of increase $7m × 40% = $2.8	

		Dr	Cr
• Roots			
Fair value at 1 Nov 2011	1		10.50
NCI share of increase in earnings over year ($7.44m [w9] × 20%)			1.49
			11.99
Exchange difference on translation of goodwill	1		0.37
Exchange difference on translation of financial statements	9		2.25
			14.61
Balance: NCI in Roots as at 31 October 2012		14.61	

Total non-controlling interest (14.61 + 30.60) = 45.21

5 **Other components of equity**

		Dr	Cr
• Tree	Q		5.00
Share-based payment: property	16		2.00
: inventory	16		6.00
• Leaf			
As at 31 Oct 2012			3.00
As at 1 Nov 2011	1	2.00	
NCI share of increase over the year ($1m × 40%)	4	0.40	
• Adjustment between owners: balance	2	5.80	
• Roots exchange reserve on translation of goodwill	1		1.46
Exchange difference on translation of financial statements	9		8.98
Total other components of equity: balance		18.24	

6 **Equity**

		Dr	Cr
Tree	Q		132.00

7 Property, plant and equipment

		Dr	Cr
Increase in value of land in Leaf	1	26.00	
Roots (w9)		47.37	
Tree	Q	308.00	
Leaf	Q	92.00	
Share-based payment: warehouse	16	15.00	
Total property, plant and equipment		**488.37**	

8 Intangible assets

		Dr	Cr
Trade name	1	6.00	

9 Translation of Roots

> **Tutorial note:** The first step with a question concerning an overseas subsidiary is to determine the subsidiary's functional currency. If the subsidiary acts as if it were an extension of the parent then its functional currency will be that of the parent and the translation rules will follow those for a single company; ie any exchange differences should be recognised in profit or loss. If the subsidiary acts as if it were an independent business separate from the parent then exchange differences impact upon the entity's net investment and exchange differences are recognised in other comprehensive income.
>
> In this question you are told that the functional currency of Roots is the Kron therefore the subsidiary is an independent business and all assets and liabilities are translated at the closing rate.
>
> The next step is to translate the subsidiary's balance sheet as at 31 October 2012. Note this must first be amended for any fair value adjustments as shown below.

Fair value adjustment:	Krons m		
Fair value of identifiable net assets at acquisition	412		
Retained earnings at acquisition	(183)		
Equity share capital at acquisition	(167)		
	62		

	Krons m	rate	$m
Property, plant and equipment	317	8	39.62
Fair value adjustments (see above)	62	8	7.75
			47.37
Financial instruments	42	8	5.25
Inventories	174	8	21.75
Trade receivables	80	8	10.00
Cash and cash equivalents	21	8	2.63
	696		87.00
Equity share capital	167	10	16.70
Retained earnings at acquisition	183	10	18.30
Post acquisition profits (250m – 183m)	67	9	7.44
Other components of equity: fair value adjustment	62	10	6.20
Non-current liabilities	133	8	16.63
Current liabilities	84	8	10.50
	696		75.77
Exchange difference			11.23
			87.00

The exchange difference will be recorded in:

Other components of equity: exchange reserve (80%)	8.98
NCI (20%)	2.25

EXAM ANSWER BANK

> **Tutorial note:** the next step is to measure goodwill as at the date of acquisition in Krons and to translate using the rate on consolidation.

	Krons m	rate	$m
Fair value of consideration ($38m × 10)	380	10	38.00
Fair value of NCI	105	10	10.50
	485		48.50
Less fair value of identifiable net assets acquired	412	10	41.20
Goodwill	73		7.30

> **Tutorial note:** IAS 21 requires that any goodwill arising on the acquisition of a foreign subsidiary should be treated as an asset of the subsidiary and translated at the closing rate for consolidation. This will result in an exchange difference which will be accounted for as shown below.

Goodwill as at 1 Nov 2011 (73 Krons m /8)	9.13
Goodwill as at 31 Oct 2012 (see above)	7.30
Exchange difference	1.83
This will be recorded in:	
Other components of equity exchange reserve (80%)	1.46
NCI (20%)	0.37

10 *Financial instruments*

		Dr	Cr
Roots (w9)		5.25	
Tree			

> **Tutorial note:** As Tree has designated the asset as at fair value through profit or loss the transaction costs must be expensed

Financial instruments	Q	13.00	
Retained earnings: transaction costs	3		1.00
Retained earnings: fair value gain at 31 Oct 2012	3	3.00	
Leaf		6.00	
Total financial instruments: balance	Q		**26.25**

11 *Inventories*

		Dr	Cr
Roots (w9)		21.75	
Share-based payment	16	6.00	
Tree	Q	56.00	
Leaf	Q	43.00	
Total inventories		**126.75**	

12 *Trade receivables*

		Dr	Cr
Roots (w9)		10.00	
Tree	Q	27.00	
Leaf	Q	37.00	
Total trade receivables		**74.00**	

EXAM ANSWER BANK

13 *Cash and cash equivalents*

		Dr	Cr
Roots (w9)		2.63	
Tree	Q	15.00	
Leaf	Q	3.00	
Total cash and cash equivalents		**20.63**	

14 *Non-current liabilities*

		Dr	Cr
Roots (w9)			16.63
Tree	Q		48.00
Leaf	Q		35.00
Total non-current liabilities			**99.63**

15 *Current liabilities*

		Dr	Cr
Roots (w9)			10.50
Share-based payment	16		13.00
Tree	Q		153.00
Leaf	Q		65.00
Total current liabilities			**241.50**

16 *Share-based payments*

> **Tutorial note:**
>
> - Purchase of warehouse. Under IFRS 2, accounting for a transaction that can be settled for cash or shares is dependent upon which party has the choice of settlement and the extent to which a liability exists. As Dande has the choice, Tree is deemed to have issued a compound financial instrument. The fair value of the warehouse can be measured reliably so the equity element is determined as the difference between the fair value of the property and the fair value of the debt (cash payment due).

		Dr	Cr
PPE	7		15.00
Current liabilities	15	13.00	
Equity: other components (15 – 13)	5	2.00	

> - Acquisition of highly specialised inventory. As the fair value of the inventory cannot be determined reliably, the invoice value of $5 million must be being used simply for cosmetic purposes. The fair value of Tree's shares must be used to calculate the inventory figure.

		Dr	Cr
Equity: other components (2m shares × $3)	5	6.00	
Inventory	11		6.00

(b) **This part of the question requires consideration of a proposed accounting treatment for intangible assets and its ethical implications. It is relevant to sections 13.1 and 13.3 of the syllabus.**

> **Tutorial note:** questions of this nature should be approached in a methodical manner as follows:
> 1 Set out the key facts as briefly as possible.
> 2 Identify the alternative courses of action available to the entity/individual.
> 3 Consider whether ethical guidelines have been observed.
> 4 Recommend a course of action.

IFRS 3 would deal with the requirement for Tree to recognise, separately from goodwill, the identifiable assets acquired should the entity acquire Dande. Any intangible assets not so recognised would be subsumed into goodwill on acquisition and would not be recognised separately on the statement of financial position.

A particular example of such an intangible asset is a workforce already assembled at the date of acquisition. Although individual members of the workforce may have employment contracts with the entity, an assembled workforce, as a whole, does not. Therefore the 'asset' does not arise from contractual or legal rights. Neither is it separable. Nor can it be sold, transferred or leased out without causing major disruption to the entity's business. An assembled workforce is not therefore an identifiable asset recognisable on acquisition.

IFRS 3 states that the value of the 'unique nature of the workforce' – such as its intellectual capital – is in effect already recognised because that uniqueness is part of the fair value of the entity's technologies, processes, contracts and relationships; which may be recognised if they are separable. The value of having a workforce in place on the date Tree acquires Dande, so that operations can continue without having to train the workforce in the handling of the specialised inventory, is not therefore recognisable.

The IFAC Code of Ethics requires that accountants act with integrity when presenting financial information. As IFRS 3 would disallow the proposed accounting treatment, the recognition of the workforce as an asset so that the directors' objective of strengthening the group balance sheet would be achieved would amount to an unethical practice.

There is very definitely a potential ethical issue here. To avoid such an issue arising, the directors of Tree should ensure that if Dande is acquired the requirements of IFRS 3 are followed as outlined above.

Question 8

This question concerns the accounting for interest in joint ventures. It is relevant to syllabus sections 13.2, 13.3 and 13.4. It involves knowledge and application of the requirements of:

IFRS 11 *Joint Arrangments*

IFRS 9 *Financial Instruments*

(a) Under IFRS 11 a joint venture is a contractual arrangement whereby two or more parties have joint control and have rights to the net assets of the arrangement. Joint control is the contractually agreed sharing of control and exists only when the activity's strategic operating and financial decisions require the unanimous consent of the parties sharing control.

Quite clearly, as Bing and Ollis control 81% of Doe's equity the two companies share control. As any strategic decisions concerning Doe must be made by the two companies acting in unison, Doe should be accounted for as a joint venture in each of the individual company's financial statements. Doe is therefore a joint venture under IFRS 11.

IFRS 11 requires that venturers account for their interest using the equity method according to IAS 28. Bing and Ollis must therefore use the equity method.

Roy does not have joint control of Doe due to the terms of the contractual agreement between Bing and Ollis and must therefore account for its 19% interest either as a financial asset within the scope of IFRS 9 or as an associate within the scope of IAS 28. Under IAS 28 a holding of less than 20% of the voting power of Doe would be presumed not to give rise to significant influence, and thereby associate status, unless it can be clearly demonstrated that there is in fact significant influence. Although Roy is not represented on Doe's board of directors, Roy does participate in policy-making processes and also provides essential technical information and expertise. Under IAS 28 Roy would therefore account for Doe as an associate.

(b)

	Proportionate consolidation		Equity accounting	
	Dr $m	Cr $m	Dr $m	Cr $m
Net cash from Thansa (24m – 10)	14		14	
Share of Thansa cash [(30 – 24)/3]	2			
Gain in sale of plant:				
Fair value 24				
Carrying value 15				
Gain 9 × 2/3		6		6

Tutorial note: the above entry is similar in concept to the entry made in consolidated accounts to eliminate inter-company profit. Bing cannot make a profit with itself and so its share of the profit must be eliminated.

Share of Thansa manufacturing plant
[(1/3 × 24) carrying value to Thansa – eliminated profit 3]   5

Tutorial note: the above entry reflects the fact that Bing still controls 1/3 of the plant at its carrying value to Bing; ie 1/3 × 15.

PPE manufacturing plant (derecognition of plant)		15		15
Investment in Thansa (associated company)			7	
	21	21	21	21

(c)

	Expected loss model $m
Debt Instruments	
As at 1 November 2011	10.000
Finance income at 10%	
Finance income at 7.3%	0.730
Cash received	(1.000)
As at 31 October 2012	9.730
Finance income at 10%	
Finance income at 7.3%	0.710
Cash received ($10m × 10% × 80%)	(0.800)
Loss (balance)	
As at 31 October 2013	9.640

* 10m × 80%

Question 9

(a) This question is drawn from syllabus section 13.2 and requires the preparation of a group statement of financial position. It requires application of knowledge from the BPP Study Text chapters as follows:

- 2 Presentation of published financial statements
- 6 Revision of basic groups
- 7 Complex groups
- 8 Changes in group structures
- 12 Tangible non-current assets and inventory
- 14 Financial instruments
- 16 Employee benefits

DENMARC PLC

GROUP STATEMENT OF FINANCIAL POSITION AS AT 30 APRIL 2013

	W	$m
Assets		
Non-current assets		
Property, plant and equipment	6	2,563
Goodwill [14 + 39]	2 + 3	53
Financial assets	10	163
		2,779
Current assets	8	2,729
TOTAL ASSETS		5,508
Equity and liabilities		
Equity		
Attributable to owners of the parent		
Share capital	Q	1,456
Retained earnings	4	1,504
Other components of equity	7	100
		3,060
Non-controlling interest	5	373
Total equity		3,433
Liabilities		
Non-current liabilities	11	1,109
Current liabilities	9	966
Total liabilities		2,075
TOTAL EQUITY AND LIABILITIES		5,508

Workings

Note. In order to present workings more clearly, wherever possible workings are shown in double-entry format.

> **Tutorial note:** it is usually best to begin a question of this type by calculating the various indirect company holdings to calculate effective percentage controlled. However, there is no such problem with this question.

1   *Goodwill in Kenz on acquisition at 1 May 2012*

> **Tutorial note:** goodwill is calculated as at the date a controlling interest is gained. As control was achieved on 1 May 2012, the further investment on 30 April 2013 does not affect the calculation. Note Denmarc is using the 'full' goodwill method.

EXAM ANSWER BANK

	W	Dr $m	Cr $m
FV of consideration for 67% investment	Q	780	
FV of NCI	5	514	
FV of identifiable net assets at acquisition			
Share capital	Q		783
Retained earnings	Q		389
Other components of equity	Q		34
Balance being increase in non-depreciable land	6		10
	Q		1,216
Goodwill on acquisition (balance)			78
		1,294	1,294

2 *Impairment of Kenz goodwill at 30 April 2013*

		Dr $m	Cr $m
Goodwill on acquisition (as above)		78	
Impairment test			
Goodwill at acquisition	78		
Net assets per SoFP at 30 April 2013	1,406		
Increase in value of land	10		
	1,494		
Recoverable amount per question	1,430		
Impairment	64		

> **Tutorial note:** The impairment must be allocated between the Group and NCI. IAS 36 requires allocation to be made on the basis of allocation used for profit or loss but, in this question, there would be a debate about whether that means 'during the year' on the basis that impairment probably arose 'during the year' (and the allocation should be 67/33) or whether it means when impairment is calculated; ie immediately following the further investment (and the allocation would be 78/22). This solution uses the latter approach but the former would be equally acceptable.

Impairment is therefore allocated: Retained earnings (78%)	4		50
NCI (22%)	5		14
Balance: Kenz goodwill as at 30 April 2013			14

3 *Goodwill in Zenu on acquisition 1 May 2012*

	W	Dr $m	Cr $m
FV of consideration for 100% investment	Q	705	

> **Tutorial note:** normally if the consideration transferred includes assets whose carrying value differs from fair value they are re-measured and any gain/loss is taken to profit or loss. However if the asset remains within the combined entity after acquisition because it was transferred to the acquiree rather than to its former owners, they remain under the control of the acquirer and therefore remain at their existing carrying amounts. So land transferred to Zenu's former owners must be transferred back into PPE (IFRS 3.38).

Carrying value of land transferred back into PPE	6		24

> **Tutorial note:** Zenu has credited sales proceeds to retained earnings, so the gain on the transfer of land to its former owners is accounted for by transferring the carrying value of the land at acquisition to retained earnings.

EXAM ANSWER BANK

		4		26

Tutorial note: the FV of the land transferred to former owners must be included as part of the consideration so it must be transferred from trade receivables.

FV of land transferred from trade receivables	8	35

Tutorial note: acquisition costs are not part of the consideration transferred for the acquisition of Zenu and must be expensed to profit or loss.

Acquisition costs expensed	4	12

Tutorial note: the contingent consideration is a non-financial liability and must be accounted for under IAS 37.

Contingent consideration	9		40
FV of identifiable net asset at acquisition:			
Share capital	Q		507
Retained earnings	Q		117
Other components of equity	Q		55
Balance being goodwill on acquisition of Zenu			39
		780	780

4   *Retained earnings*

		Dr $m	Cr $m
Denmarc			
Per question	Q		1,386
Impairment loss on research plant	6	3	
Impairments loss on financial asset	10	17	
Current service cost of retirement benefits	11	2	
Kenz			
Increase in retained earnings over the year [575 – 389]	Q		186
Increase attributable to NCI [186 × 33%]	5	61	
Goodwill impairment attributable to group	2	50	
Zenu			
Increase over the year [220 – 117]			103
Acquisition costs written off	3	12	
Carrying value of land transferred to former owners	3	26	
Group balance as at 30 April 2013		1,504	

5   *Kenz Non-controlling interest*

	Dr $m	Cr $m

Tutorial note: the calculation of NCI must take into account the increase in the investment in Kenz at 30 April 2013. As it is an increase in an interest which is itself already a 'controlling' interest, it will involve only a transfer between NCI and equity.

		Dr $m	Cr $m
FV of NCI at 1 May 2012	1		514
Increase in net assets over the year attributable to NCI			
Share capital	Q		-
Retained earnings	4		61
Other components of equity	7		5
			580
FV of consideration for further 11% investment	Q	184	
Balance c/d as at 30 April 2013 [580 × 22/33]		387	
Balance being positive movement in equity	7	9	
		580	580
Balance b/d			387
Goodwill impairment	2	14	
Balance as at 30 April 2013		373	

6 *Property, plant and equipment*

		Dr $m	Cr $m
Denmarc	Q	673	
Kenz	Q	1,053	
Zenu	Q	806	
Increase in FV of land: Kenz	1	10	
Transfer of CV of land in Zenu	3	24	
Impairment test of research plant in Denmarc			
FV of plant 47			
Value in use of plant [55 – 10] 45			
Recoverable amount (higher of the above two) 47			
CV of plant 50			
Impairment loss	4		3
Balance as at 30 April 2013			2,563

7 *Other components of equity*

		Dr $m	Cr $m
Denmarc	Q		78
Kenz			
Increase over the year [48 – 34]	Q		14
Increase attributable to NCI [14 × 33%]	5	5	
Positive movement in equity re further investment	5		9
Zenu			
Increase over the year [59 – 55]	Q		4
Balance as at 30 April 2013		100	

8 *Current assets*

		Dr $m	Cr $m
Denmarc	Q	1,294	
Kenz	Q	1,015	
Transfer of FV of land transferred to former owners	3		35
Zenu	Q	455	
Balance as at 30 April 2013			2,729

9   Current liabilities

		Dr $m	Cr $m
Denmarc	Q		264
Kenz	Q		255
FV of contingent consideration	3		40
Zenu	Q		407
Balance as at 30 April 2013		966	

10 Financial assets

			Dr $m	Cr $m
Present value of: immediate payment 14 × 1.0	14			
: payment 30 April 2014 50 × 1/1.1	46			
: payment 30 April 2015 50 × 1/(1.1)2	41			
	101			
Carrying value as at 30 April 2013	118			
Impairment loss		4		17
Denmarc		Q	140	
Kenz		Q	13	
Zenu		Q	27	
Balance as at 30 April 2013				163

11 Non-current liabilities

		Dr $m	Cr $m

Retirement benefit obligation

> **Tutorial note:** the discount rate used to calculate long-term employee benefit obligations must reflect 'high quality corporate bonds with the same currency and term as the obligation' (IAS 19.78).

Final salary obligation = 100 × $200,000 × 1.082 = $23,332,800
Value of Year 1 service cost = $23,332,800 × 10% = $2.33m

PV of this service cost = $2.33m × 1/1.052 = $2.11m	4	2
Denmarc	Q	592
Kenz	Q	420
Zenu	Q	95
Balance as at 30 April 2013	1,109	

(b) **This part is taken from syllabus section 13.1 and requires discussion and application of knowledge concerning the ethical issues involved when a company chooses an accounting policy for financial assets which has the aim of enhancing the group's performance rather than reporting in an unbiased manner. Reference is to BPP Text Chapters 4 & 14.**

The plan to replace IAS 39 with IFRS 9 *Financial Instruments* was introduced after it became clear to the IASB that accounting for financial instruments was both overly complex technically and potentially misleading to both preparers and analysts in that the presentation of fair value gains and losses did not clearly reflect their true substance. Also the ability for entities to reclassify between types of financial instruments meant that accounting changes could be made for cosmetic reasons rather than for sound business reasons. As a leading accounting practitioner recently commented, in '…highly adverse economic conditions … growth and ethical business conduct can sometimes appear to be competing priorities'. (Stulb, D. in International Accountant, July/August 2012. Issue 65, AIA.)

Directors generally have a duty to aim to make a profit for their shareholders. Hence Denmarc's directors' keenness to enhance the company's performance measures. Their plan to choose an accounting policy which has the effect of increasing profits could also be driven by management salary and bonus structures. However, this is inappropriate stewardship and would be classed as poor corporate governance. The directors must always be aware of the fact that investors and analysts will rely on the accounting information produced in the financial statements to make investment decisions. The information should therefore reflect the true substance of transactions and be as reliable as possible.

So, whatever the reason for choosing one accounting practice over another, the directors should be guided in their choice of appropriate action. To help them, codes of ethics such as the IFAC Code of Ethics are available. This code is particularly targeted at accountants but its requirements are generally applicable to business managers. It states that accountants must display **integrity** (in that they should be honest in all business relationships) in their dealings with external parties and that they should be **objective** (in that they should not allow bias, conflict of interest or undue influence of others to override their business judgements).

Denmarc's directors could also be helped in their decision by the discussion and explanation sections of IFRSs – in this case IFRS 9 *Financial Instruments*, which states that loans are to be measured at amortised cost if:

(i) The **business model** is to collect the contractual cash flows of the loan rather than to benefit from changes in the loan's fair value; and

(ii) The contractual cash flows are of principal and interest on principal.

Although Denmarc is considering the fair value of the loans from a liquidity perspective, in that they could be sold and the proceeds used to fund future capital expenditure, the concession negotiated with the borrowers quite clearly shows the entity's objective is to hold the asset and to collect contractual cash flows, albeit in a different manner to that first envisaged. Some part disposals of the portfolio would not contradict that objective and the fair value approach would not be available to the directors. However, if disposals became more frequent or perhaps if Denmarc made a firm decision to dispose of the whole portfolio in one transaction, the entity would again have to consider whether the amortised cost approach was appropriate.

Question 10

This question involves the translation of a subsidiary's financial statements for the purpose of a consolidation exercise. It is taken from section 13.2 of the syllabus and is covered in BPP Study Text chapter:

9   Foreign currency translation

(a) Rima's functional currency (FC) will be the currency of the primary economic environment in which the entity operates; ie the one in which it primarily generates and expends cash (IAS 21.9). However, it is not obvious from the question whether this is the $ or the €. As there is a lack of clarity, Arenta's directors must use their judgement to determine the FC that most faithfully represents the economic effects of the subsidiary's underlying business circumstances.

Arenta's directors should first give priority to the primary indicators of business circumstances before, if necessary, considering other factors (IAS 21.12). IAS 21 requires the directors to consider two primary factors:

– The currency that mainly influences sales prices for goods and services (ie usually the currency in which sales prices for goods and services are denominated and settled); and

– The currency of the country whose competitive forces and regulations mainly determine the sale prices of its goods and services.

As Rima produces and sells its goods throughout Europe, the € clearly influences the sale prices of its electronic equipment and also its labour and materials. Also, as external market forces and government regulations are too restrictive to foster external exports, Rima's business circumstances are subject only to restrictions from within Europe.

Other factors (ie the currency in which funds from financing activities are generated and the currency in which receipts from operating activities are usually retained [IAS 21.10]) are only to be considered if the FC is not obvious. In this case Rima's FC is obviously the € so other factors do not have to be considered by the directors.

EXAM ANSWER BANK

> **Tutorial note:** if Rima was, for instance, purchasing the electronic equipment in dollars rather than producing it in Europe so that its operating costs were mainly in dollars, its FC would no longer be obvious. In this case, the other factors would have to be considered.

(b)

> **Tutorial note:** as Rima's FC is different to the parent company Arenta, its financial statements must be translated to the currency of Arenta; ie dollars. Rima is acting in a semi-autonomous way so any change in the exchange rate will have little or no effect on the group's cash flows. Instead, any change in exchange rates will affect Arenta's net investment and the translation is carried out from this perspective.

It is recommended that the translation exercise is carried out in the sequence shown.

Workings

1   Translate Rima's SoFP as at 30 April 2014

> **Tutorial note:** Arenta acquired 100% of Rima's shares on incorporation therefore the post acquisition retained earnings can be found by deducting the translated share capital figure (effectively the cost to Arenta of the subscribed shares) from the translated shareholders' equity figure.

		€ : $	$m
Non-current assets	(€831)	2 : 1	415.5
Inventories	(€514)	2 : 1	257.0
Trade receivables	(€237)	2 : 1	118.5
Non-current liabilities	(€304)	2 : 1	(152.0)
Current liabilities	(€235)	2 : 1	(117.5)
Translated shareholders' equity as at end of year			521.5
Equity share capital	(historical cost)		70.0
Retained earnings	(balance)		451.5
			521.5

2   Translate Rima's SoPL

			$m
Profit after tax	(€243)	3 : 1	81.0

3   Translate Rima's shareholders' equity at start of year

		$m
Shareholders' equity at end of year (in euros)	Q	1,043.0
Retained profit after tax (in euros)		243.0
Shareholders' equity at start of year (in euros)		800.0
		$m
Translated opening shareholders' equity	3.5 : 1	228.6

4   Calculate the exchange difference

		$m
Shareholders' equity (in dollars): at end of year	W1	521.5
at start of year	W3	228.6
Movement in equity		292.9
Retained profit after tax	W2	81.0
Exchange gain for the year		211.9

(c) IAS 1 requires that exchange differences on translating foreign operations are included in other comprehensive income. Due to a 2012 amendment to IAS 1, items of other comprehensive income must be grouped into those that will and those that will not be subsequently reclassified into profit or loss. Consequently, the exchange gain of $211.9m will be disclosed under the former group as IAS 21 requires such a reclassification for translation gains or losses upon subsequent disposal of a foreign subsidiary.

Investors commonly analyse an entity's performance by using non-GAAP KPIs such as EBITDA (earnings before interest tax depreciation and amortisation) or 'underlying profits' (EBITDA adjusted for other non-cash movements). EBITDA and 'underlying' figures can be used to analyse and compare profitability between companies and industries because they eliminate the effects of financing and accounting decisions and, with underlyings, non-cash adjustments such as gains and losses due to fair value adjustments and foreign subsidiary translation. It is common therefore for translation gains and losses to have no impact on such KPIs. However, they are non-GAAP metrics and as a result allow a greater amount of discretion as to what is (and is not) included in their calculation. This means that companies often change the items included in their calculation from one reporting period to the next. Such flexibility will therefore be afforded to Arenta's directors. However, when considering such changes, the directors must always remember their overriding ethical and accounting responsibilities to act in the best interests of the entity's stakeholders.

Question 11

(a) This question involves a step acquisition in which the initial holding was held as a passive investment – due to the holding company being unable to exert significant influence. It therefore involves consideration of IFRS 3 *Business Combinations* and IFRS 9 *Financial Instruments*. It is drawn from syllabus sections 13.3 and 13.4 and is covered by BPP Study Text chapters:

8   Changes in group structures
14   Financial instruments

> **Tutorial note:** Ezmee's initial holding of 25% must be measured at its FV at 30 April 2013 (we know that its carrying value is $5m but we need to see if this is different to its FV). We are not told what the FV is and so must use the cost of the further acquisition of 45% as a guide. However, the cost includes a premium of 8% because Ezmee is buying a controlling interest. If we are to use the cost as a guide to the price of the initial investment, the premium must be adjusted.

Cost of 45% investment without the premium loading:
$13m (per Q) × 100/108 = $12.04m

	$m
FV of the initial holding of 25%:	
FV of 100% holding using the above figure $12.04 × 100/45 = $26.76	
FV of 25% holding therefore = $26.76 × 25%	6.69

> **Tutorial note:** alternatively this could be calculated as 12.04 × 25/45 = 6.69.

Carrying value of initial investment of 25% (per Q)	5.00
Gain transferred to profit or loss	1.69

As the initial investment is carried at FV through other comprehensive income Ezmee will have previously included gains of $1m (carrying value 5 – original cost 4) in other comprehensive income. Under IFRS 9 these previous gains of $1m must also be transferred to profit or loss.

Calculation of goodwill

FV of non-controlling interest $26.76 (see above) × 30%	8.03
FV of consideration (6.69 [see above] + 13)	19.69
	27.72
FV of Stoe's identifiable net assets (per Q)	25.00
Goodwill	2.72

(b) **This question concerns the amounts used to measure identifiable net assets when measuring goodwill on acquisition. It is drawn from syllabus sections 13.3 and 13.4 and is covered by BPP Study Text chapters:**

13   Intangible non-current assets

Under IFRS 3 the measurement period within which adjustments can be made to provisional amounts used in the measurement of goodwill cannot exceed one year.

Investment in Pan

The facts concerning the new mining deposits came to light within the one year remeasurement period allowed by IFRS 3. However, the increase in fair value is the result of circumstances arising in February 2014 and do not reflect circumstances at 30 April 2013. No change will therefore be allowed to the measurement of goodwill.

Property

As the property was surplus to requirements, Stoe would have included it in the financial statements at its expected net realisable value $1m. The disposal at $1.4m in July 2013 is likely to reflect the fair value at 30 April 2013 and goodwill will therefore be adjusted by the increase of $0.4m.

Deferred revenue

IFRS 3 requires that items are included in the calculation of goodwill at their fair value. The fair value of a liability is defined in IFRS 13 as the price that would be paid to transfer a liability in an orderly transaction between market participants at the measurement date (IFRS 13 App.A). The deferred revenue represents an upfront payment for a service that has not yet been provided by Stoe but for which responsibility has been assumed by Ezmee. Its fair value must therefore be used in the calculation of goodwill. Fair value is $0.9m [incurred cost] × 1.2 [profit loading] = $1.08m. Goodwill must therefore be adjusted by the decrease in liabilities of $0.12m.

Intangible asset Diga

IFRS 3 requires an acquirer to recognise an identifiable asset such as Diga at its fair value determined in accordance with its use by other market participants (IFRS 3 B43). Ezmee's future intentions not to use the asset should only be reflected in determining its fair value if that is what other market participants would do. However, during the year ended 30 April 2014 it became known that other companies within the industry would have acquired the brand name and would have sold the product. Therefore IFRS 3 would require a value of $1m to be attributed to the brand name for the purpose of measuring goodwill.

Adjustments should be made as follows:

	$m
Goodwill (as in (a) above)	2.72
Investment in Pan	–
Property	(0.40)
Deferred revenue	(0.12)
Intangible asset Diga	(1.00)
Revised goodwill figure as at 30 April 2013	1.20

EXAM ANSWER BANK

Question 12

This question is drawn from syllabus section 13.2 and requires the preparation of a group statement of financial position. It requires application of knowledge from the BPP Study Text chapters as follows:

2	Presentation of published financial statements
6	Revision of basic groups
7	Complex groups
8	Changes in group structures
12	Tangible non-current assets and inventory
14	Financial instruments
16	Employee benefits

(a) GICO PLC

GROUP STATEMENT OF FINANCIAL POSITION AS AT 31 OCTOBER 2013

	W	$m
Assets		
Non-current assets		
Property, plant and equipment	7	590.2
Goodwill [19 + 15]	1+2	34.0
Financial assets	13	78.8
		703.0
Current assets	9	89.0
TOTAL ASSETS		792.0
Equity and liabilities		
Equity		
Attributable to owners of the parent		
Ordinary share capital	Q	68.0
Retained earnings	4	206.3
Other components of equity	12	25.0
		299.3
Non-controlling interest	5	83.4
Total equity		382.7
Liabilities		
Non-current liabilities	10	235.3
Current liabilities	6	174.0
Total liabilities		409.3
TOTAL EQUITY AND LIABILITIES		792.0

Workings

Note. In order to present workings more clearly, wherever possible workings are shown in double-entry format.

> **Tutorial note:** it is always best to begin a question of this type by calculating the various indirect company holdings to calculate effective percentage controlled. However, there is no such problem with this question.

EXAM ANSWER BANK

1 **Goodwill in Redit on acquisition at 31 October 2013**

> **Tutorial note:** goodwill is calculated as at the date a controlling interest is gained. This was on 1 November 2011. Any subsequent increase in the fair value of this investment (under IFRS 9) in a parent's individual statements must therefore be reversed for consolidation purposes. This shows that it is always wise to analyse the make-up of any SoFP 'investment in' figure before proceeding to calculate goodwill. Note also, as group policy is to measure non-controlling interest at fair value, Gico is using the 'full' goodwill method.
>
> | Analysis of Investment in Redit | $ |
> |---|---|
> | Cash consideration for 80% (see w below) | 135 |
> | Professional fees (these must be expensed against retained earnings. IFRS 3 does not allow them to be included in goodwill. (see w4) | 1 |
> | Fair value increase [balance] (reversed against retained earnings for consolidation purposes. see w4). **Note.** if Gico had chosen to account as at FVTOCI the reversal would have been against 'other components of equity'. | 13 |
> | | 149 |
>
> The following workings are provided in double-entry fashion in the hope they will be easier for students to follow. (* = figure from question)

	w	Dr $m	Cr $m
FV of consideration for Gico's 80% investment	Q	135	
Contingent consideration	6	5	
FV of NCI	5*	41	
FV of identifiable net assets at acquisition			
Share capital	Q		54
Retained earnings	4*		43
Balance being increase in non-depreciable land	7		65
Fair value	Q		162
Goodwill on acquisition (balance)			19
		181	181

2 **Goodwill in Seph**

> **Tutorial note:** Analysis of Investment in Seph
>
> | | | |
> |---|---|---|
> | Cost of acquisition of associated company 1 Nov 2011 | 3* | 15 |
> | Investment to gain control 31 July 2013 (see w below) | * | 29 |
> | Fair value increase [balance] (reversed against retained earnings for consolidation purposes. See w4). Note: if Gico had chosen to account as at FVTOCI the reversal would have been against 'other components of equity' | | 7 |
> | | | 51 |

	w	Dr	Cr
FV of consideration for Gico's 35% investment on 31.7.2013	*	29	
FV of Gico's previously held (ie 25%) equity at date control obtained (ie 31.07.2013)	3*	21	
FV of NCI at date control obtained	5	33	
FV of Seph's identifiable net assets at date control obtained:			
Share capital	Q		5
Retained earnings	4*		56
FV PPE adjustment (land) [balance]	7		7
	Q		68
Goodwill on control being obtained (balance)			15
		83	83

EXAM ANSWER BANK

3   *Profit on derecognition of Seph as an associated company*

> **Tutorial note:**
>
> Under IFRS 3 if an acquirer holds a non-controlling interest equity investment in the acquiree immediately before obtaining control, the acquirer remeasures that previously held equity investment at its acquisition-date fair value and recognises any resulting gain or loss in profit or loss [IFRS 3.42]

		Dr	Cr
FV of 25% investment at date control obtained (ie date Seph ceased to be an associated company)	2*		21.0
Cost of 25% investment	2*	15.0	
Gico's share of retained earnings whilst Seph was an associated company [56 – 42] × 25%	4	3.5	

> **Tutorial note:** the total of the above two figures is effectively the carrying value of Seph as an associated company in the group SoFP.

Profit on derecognition (balance)	4	2.5	

4   *Retained earnings*

		Dr $m	Cr $m
Gico			
Per SoFP as at 31 October 2013	Q		190.0
Professional fees re acquisition of Redit	Q	1.0	
Reversal of fair value adjustment Redit (see W1)		13.0	
Reversal of FV adjustment Seph (see W2)		7.0	
Group share of Seph's retained earnings whilst an associated company	3		3.5
Profit on derecognition of Seph as an associated company	3		2.5
Impairment loss	11	2.8	
Adjustment re financial asset	13		0.8
Group figure (balance)		173.0	
Profit of jointly controlled operation	8		4.7
Group figure		4.7	
Redit			
Per SoFP as at 31 October 2013	Q		72.0
Retained earnings at acq.	1	43.0	
NCI share of post acq. profits ([72 – 43] × 20%)	5	5.8	
Group share of post acq profits [72 – 43] × 80% (ie balance)		23.2	
Seph			
Per SoFP as at 31 October 2013	Q		65.0
Retained earnings as at date control obtained	2	56.0	
NCI share of post control profits [65-56] × 40%	5	3.6	
Group share of post control profits [65-56] × 60% (balance)		5.4	
Total			206.3

5 Non-controlling interest

Redit		
Fair value at 1 November 2011	1*	41.0
NCI share of post acq. profits	4	5.8
Seph		
FV at date control obtained (ie 31.07.2013)	2	33.0
Share of post acq. retained earnings	4	3.6
		83.4

6 Current liabilities

Gico	Q	127.0
Contingent consideration	1	5.0
Joint operation cost of goods	8	12.0
Joint operation overheads	8	3.0
Redit	Q	16.0
Seph	Q	11.0
		174.0

7 Property plant and equipment

		Dr	Cr
Gico as at 31 October 2013	Q	302.0	
Joint operation	8	14.0	
Impairment loss	11		7.8
Redit as at 31 October 2013	Q	162.0	
Increase in value of land on acquisition	1	65.0	
Seph as at 31 October 2013	Q	48.0	
Increase in value of land on acquisition	2	7.0	
Balance			590.2

8 Jointly controlled operation

> **Tutorial note:** Gico accounts for this as a jointly controlled operation and must therefore apply IFRS 11 *Joint Arrangements*. A JCO involves the use of assets of the venturer (Gico) rather than the establishment of a separate entity. IFRS 11 requires Gico to recognise the assets that it controls, liabilities and expenses that it incurs and its share of the income from the sale of goods by the facility.

		Dr	Cr
Investment in joint operation	Q	15	
Depreciation ($15m × 1/15) [calculated from date of completion]	below		1
PPE (balance)	7		14
Profit in JCO:			
Revenue ($70m × 30%)	9		21.0
Cost of sales ($40m × 30%)	6	12.0	
Depreciation	above	1.0	
Overhead expenses ($10m × 30%)	6	3.0	
	10	0.3	
Retained earnings (balance) (21 – 16.3)	4	4.7	

9 Current assets

Joint operation	8	21.0
Gico	Q	17.0
Redit	Q	19.0
Seph	Q	32.0
		89.0

EXAM ANSWER BANK

10	Non-current liabilities		
	Jointly controlled operation: post retirement benefit	8	0.3
	Gico	Q	143.0
	Redit	Q	55.0
	Seph	Q	37.0
			235.3

11 Impairment of equipment

> **Tutorial note:** under IAS 16, when an asset has been revalued any impairment loss is charged to revaluation reserve (via other comprehensive income) to the extent of the previous revaluation. Any further loss is charged to profit or loss. Note that Gico has not chosen to make a transfer from revaluation surplus to retained earnings for the excess depreciation charged during the year.

		$m	$m
Cost of equipment 1 November 2010:			
Purchase cost		27.0	
Direct costs of bringing to a working condition		5.0	
Net proceeds from selling prototypes		(2.0)	
Carrying value at 31 October 2011 [no depreciation as not complete]		30.0	
Depreciation [30 × 1/10]		3.0	
Carrying value at 31 October 2012 before revaluation		27.0	
Revaluation		5.0	
Carrying value at 31 October 2012 after revaluation		32.0	
Depreciation [32 × 1/10]		3.2	
Carrying at 31 October 2013 value before impairment		28.8	
Recoverable amount at 31 October 2013		21.0	
Impairment		7.8	
The impairment is accounted for as follows:			
Other components of equity (ie revaluation reserve)	12		5.0
Retained earnings (profit or loss)	4		2.8
PPE	7	7.8	

12	Other components of equity			
	Impairment loss	11	5.0	
	Gico	Q		30.0
	Balance		25.0	

13 Financial assets

> **Tutorial note:** the purchase on 1 November 2012 must be dealt with using amortised cost under IFRS 9.

		$m
The correct treatment is as follows:		
Fair value at 1 November 2012	Q	20.0
Profit or loss: interest income at 10%		2.0
Interest received during the year [25 × 4.7%]		(1.2)
Amortised cost at 31 October 2013		20.8

> **Tutorial note:** Gico has included $20m in financial assets but has incorrectly included interest received in profit or loss. So the entry to adjust the financial statements is as follows:
>
> Dr   Financial instruments   0.8
> Cr   Retained earnings   0.8

Adjustment to Retained earnings (2 – 1.2)	4	0.8
Gico	Q	24.0
Redit	Q	16.0
Seph	Q	38.0
		78.8

(b) This question is drawn from syllabus sections 13.1 and 13.4 and requires the presentation of advice concerning the ethical responsibilities of accountants concerning the presentation of information. It requires application of knowledge from the BPP Study Text chapters as follows:

4   Ethics and regulation of corporate financial reporting
21 Revenue recognition

IFRS 15 would not allow the recognition of the sale of the production facility as a sale as control of the asset has not been transferred substantially to the bank. The premium of 10% Gico will pay if the asset is repurchased is therefore effectively interest on a loan. The entries to record the sale on 5 November 2013 must therefore be reversed; ie the entries will be as follows ($m):

Dr	PPE	30	
Dr	Retained earnings	13	
Cr	Liabilities		43

'Ethics is a system of principles, which affect how people live their lives and make decisions' (Faherty, A. (2012) 'Ethical Dilemmas for Accountants', *International Accountant*, September/October 2012, Issue 66, pp 22–25). This also applies to accountants in business who have an ethical responsibility to ensure that information does not mislead stakeholders. Quite clearly the sale transaction is motivated by Gico's attempt to mask its liquidity problems. Without the sale, Gico's negative working capital would have been much worse ($85m at 31 October 2013 – see statement of financial position above).

It is sometimes not obvious what a decision should be as many decisions do not result in the breaking of rules. However, in this case it is fairly obvious that Gico is breaching the provisions of IFRS 15. The financial statements would thus lack credibility and may not, as a result, provide useful information to decision-makers – the *Conceptual Framework*'s prime objective of financial reporting. To an accountant, providing useful information, and thereby acting in the public interest, should be a main ethical responsibility. By recognising the transaction as a sale, the accountant would not be faithfully representing the substance of the transaction.

Question 13

This question is drawn from syllabus sections 13.1 and 13.3. It requires application of knowledge from the BPP Study Text Chapter 6 Revision of basic groups; specifically with reference to IFRS 11 *Joint Arrangements*.

(a) (i) Bilko does not control the arrangement although it can block any decisions made by the venturers. As 75% of voting rights must be controlled for any decisions to become binding, Bilko cannot control the arrangement with Loit. For control to be exercised Bilko needs the agreement of Verv. Under IFRS 11 Bilko and Verv would therefore be seen to have joint control and the arrangement would be accounted for either as a joint operation or a joint venture depending on the provisions of the contract.

(ii) Bilko and Dusti must unanimously agree on decisions concerning the estate. They therefore have joint control of the arrangement.

The estate is established as a separate vehicle and as such could be classified either as a joint operation or a joint venture.

As a separate vehicle owning the estate, IndusNE must be considered in its own right; that is, the assets and liabilities of the arrangement are assets and liabilities of IndusNE and not of the parties. On this basis, there are no other facts or circumstances that indicate that the parties have rights to substantially all the economic benefits related to the arrangement's assets or that they have any obligations for the arrangement's liabilities other than an obligation to pay unpaid capital should IndusNE be unable to pay its debts.

The conclusion is that Bilko has an interest in the net assets of IndusNE (rather than rights to the assets and obligations for the liabilities, relating to the arrangement – which would classify a joint operation) and as such must account for the investment as a joint venture using the equity method. One of IFRS 11's aims is to eliminate the previously existing possible difference in how like investments were accounted for in the consolidated financial statements. Under IAS 31 it was possible for joint ventures to be accounted for using proportional consolidation whereas under IAS 28 associated companies, which are essentially similar vehicles to joint ventures (the difference being the notion of control versus significant interest) are accounted for under the equity method.

(b) It is clear from the question that Cum2us satisfies the criteria to be classified as a joint venture under IFRS 11; ie the entity is a separate vehicle under joint control and the parties do not have rights to its assets nor obligations for its liabilities, relating to the arrangement; ie the parties do not have different interests in specific assets, liabilities, revenues and expenses. This means that, being a joint venture as opposed to a joint operation, the investment must be accounted for using the equity method.

In Bilko's individual statement of financial position the investment in Cum2us will be recorded at its cost of $60 million. This amount will permanently remain in Bilko's individual SoFP at $60 million unless there has been an impairment in its value (or the entity elects to measure the investment at fair value under IFRS 9). There is no such indication in the question.

The only amount to record in Bilko's income statement is the dividend it has received from Cum2us of $2.4 million ($6m × 40%). This will be shown as 'income from investment in joint venture'.

In Bilko's consolidated financial statements, the Bilko group's share of Cum2us's net profit after tax $10m ($34m – $9m × 40%) will be shown as 'income from investment in joint venture' in the income statement. In the statement of financial position, the asset 'investment in joint venture' will be included at $67.4m ($60m + $10m – $2.4m).

Question 14

This question is taken from syllabus section 13.2. The question requires application of knowledge from the following BPP Study Text chapters:

9   Foreign currency translation

18 Reporting financial performance; with particular reference to IFRS 5 *Non-current Assets Held for Sale and Discontinued Operations.*

(a)

> **Tutorial note:** Krow uses a different functional currency to that of its parent Ravar. This means that despite being controlled by Ravar, Krow conducts financial activities in its own currency and is therefore independent of Ravar. In fact, the question tells us that Krow is autonomous. Changes in currency exchange rates will therefore have little or no effect on the present and future cash flows from operations of either company. Rather, any changes will affect Ravar's net investment in Krow and not Krow's individual monetary and non-monetary items. It is therefore appropriate to translate Krow's financial statements using the closing rate approach; ie 'closing rate' reflects the net investment at the reporting date.
>
> An important point to note is that we are translating from Zy into $ so we **divide** by the exchange rate!

EXAM ANSWER BANK

(i) *Translation of Krow – statement of financial position*

	Zy(m)	Rate	$m
PPE	83	3.75	22.13
Inventories	141	3.75	37.60
Trade receivables	78	3.75	20.80
Cash and cash equivalents	34	3.75	9.07
	336		89.60
Share capital	23	4.51	5.10
Retained earnings:			
Pre-control	49	4.51	10.86
Post-control [Zy239m – Zy49m]	190	bal	53.91
			69.87
Current liabilities	74	3.75	19.73
	336		89.60

(ii) *Translation of Krow – statement of profit or loss and other comprehensive income*

	Zy(m)	Rate	$m
Revenue	1,651	3.80	434.47
Costs of sales	1,318	3.80	346.84
Gross profit	333		87.63
Expenses	99	3.80	26.05
Profit before tax	234		61.58
Income tax expense	80	3.80	21.05
Profit after tax	154		40.53

(iii) *Goodwill in Krow at 31 Oct 2010*

	Zy(m)	Zy(m)	rate	$m
FV of consideration transferred [$14.3m × 4.51]		64.49		
FV of NCI [$4.6m × 4.51]		20.75		
Less: FV of identifiable net assets:				
Share capital	23.00			
Retained earnings	49.00			
		(72.00)		
Goodwill at 31 Oct 2010		13.24	4.51	2.94
Exchange gain for year 2010–2011	bal			0.17
Goodwill at 31 Oct 2011		13.24	4.26	3.11
Exchange gain for year 2011–2012	bal			0.16
Goodwill at 31 Oct 2012		13.24	4.05	3.27
Exchange gain for year 2012–2013	bal			0.26
Goodwill at 31 Oct 2013		13.24	3.75	3.53

Tutorial note: goodwill remains unchanged in Zy as there has been no impairment

(iv) *Group retained earnings re Krow*

Share post control [$53.91 × 75%]	40.43
Share of goodwill exchange differences [(0.17 + 0.16 + 0.26) × 75%]	0.44

(v) *Non-controlling interest*

At date control gained (Q)	4.60
Share of retained earnings post-control [$53.91 (wi) × 25%]	13.48
Share of goodwill exchange differences [(0.17 + 0.16 + 0.26) (wiii) × 25%]	0.15
	18.23

(vi) *Exchange differences for the year ended 31 Oct 2013*

Statement of profit or loss and other comprehensive income
Other comprehensive income

			$m
• On translation of Krow's net assets			
Closing net assets at closing rate (wi)			69.87

Less: opening net assets at opening rate:

	Zy(m)		
Net assets at 31 Oct 2013 (Q)	262		
Less profit for the year after tax (Q)	(154)		
Add dividends paid (Q)	64		
	172	@4.05	42.47
			27.40

Less: translated retained profit for the year		
[$40.53 (wii) – $16.17 [(dividends paid) Zy64m/3.96]		24.36
		3.04
• On goodwill (wiii)		0.26
Exchange gain for the year		3.30

> **Tutorial note:** the above calculation may be explained as follows: closing net assets = opening net assets + retained profit. If we adjust (translate) all three components of the equation by the appropriate exchange rates, we are left with a balancing figure which is in effect the exchange gain/loss caused by the translation of those net assets.

The foreign currency translation difference of $3.3m will be described in OCI as an item that 'may be reclassified subsequently to profit or loss' under IAS 1.

(b) Ravar is disposing of a controlling interest in Krow whilst retaining an interest; which may, subsequent to the sale, be accounted for either as an associated company or a trade investment (this depends on whether Ravar retains significant influence or not). From the point control is lost, Krow should cease to be accounted for as a subsidiary (ie on a line-by-line basis). However, up to that point, the accounting for Krow will depend upon whether it can be judged that the assets are 'held for sale'.

Under IFRS 5, Ravar would classify Krow as being a disposal group held for sale if its carrying amount will be recovered principally through sale in a single transaction rather than through use. IFRS 5 lays down the following conditions:

(1) The asset is available for immediate sale in its present condition and sale is highly probable.

(2) The asset is currently actively marketed at a price that is reasonable in relation to its fair value.

(3) The sale is expected to be completed within a year of the date of classification.

(4) It is unlikely that the plan to sell the asset will be significantly amended or withdrawn and actions have been substantially taken to complete the sale.

(5) Management is committed to the sale plan.

Not all the conditions laid down in IFRS 5 appear to have yet been met; ie in particular, condition 4 (in that actions have not yet been taken substantially) and condition 5 (in that the offer has only been accepted in principle).

On balance, it could be concluded therefore that until conditions 4 and 5 are satisfied or the sale actually takes place (whichever comes first) there should be no change to the accounting for Krow and it should be fully consolidated on a line-by-line basis.

EXAM ANSWER BANK

Question 15

Part (a) concerns a reverse acquisition whereby a listed company acquires shares in a private company in such a way that the private company becomes the acquirer under IFRS 3 *Business Combinations*. It also requires a discussion of the (arguable) demise of proportionate consolidation. It is drawn from syllabus sections 13.1 and 13.3 and requires application of knowledge from the BPP Study Text Chapter 6 *Revision of basic groups*.

(a)

> **Tutorial note:** the first step in a question of this nature is to work out the respective share holdings.

(i) Terco would issue 4m new shares. That is, Dyer has 1m shares in issue ($10m equity ÷ $10 par value) × 4 Terco shares = 4m new shares.

As a result of the share issue and exchange, shareholdings in Terco would be as follows:

2m shares (Equity $4m ÷ $2 par value) owned by Terco's original shareholders	33.3%
4m shares owned by previous shareholders in Dyer	66.7%

> **Tutorial note:** This would concern a 'reverse acquisition' as shareholders of Dyer would have achieved control of Terco. It is called a 'reverse acquisition' because although Terco is the legal acquirer, from an IFRS 3 perspective control is in the hands of the legal acquiree Dyer and the group (and thereby preparation of group statements) must be viewed from Dyer's perspective; ie 'the reverse is true' – Dyer is the parent entity.

> **Tutorial note:** this creates an odd scenario because Dyer has not actually transferred any form of consideration for the 'acquisition'. The question is therefore 'How should we calculate goodwill?' In this situation, IFRS 3 tells us that this 'theoretical' consideration is equal to the market value of the shares which Dyer would have had to issue to the shareholders of Terco for them to own 33.3% (see above) in the new group.

There are 1m shares in Dyer, therefore Dyer would have had to issue a further 500,000 shares for Terco's shareholders to own 33.3% of the new group (remember Dyer is the parent entity so the shares of the new group would reflect Dyer's balance sheet; ie 1m shares). The theoretical consideration is therefore 500,000 × $30 (market value of Dyer's shares) = $15m.

W1 Goodwill

	$m	$m
Cost of theoretical consideration (see above)		15.00
Net assets of 'acquired' Terco		
Share capital	4.00	
Retained earnings	9.00	
FV adjustment for land	0.50	
		13.50
Goodwill		1.50

> **Tutorial note:** there is no NCI as 100% of Dyer's shares were exchanged.

EXAM ANSWER BANK

DYER GROUP STATEMENT OF FINANCIAL POSITION AS AT
1 MARCH 2015

Assets	$m
Non-current [14.25 + 28 + 0.50]	42.75
Current [5.35 + 4]	9.35
Goodwill (above)	1.50
	53.60
Equity and liabilities	
Ordinary shares [10 + 5 (500,000 × $10)]	15.00
Share premium [500,000 × $20]	10.00
Retained earnings*	7.00
Liabilities [6.60 + 15.00]	21.60
	53.60

*Note that no post acquisition earnings as consolidated as at date of acquisition

(ii) If the arrangement's contractual terms provide Dyer (and at least one other party) with rights to the **net assets** of the arrangement; ie a separate vehicle is established and it is that vehicle which has rights to the individual assets and liabilities, then a joint venture has been established and under IFRS 11 *Joint Arrangements* proportionate consolidation is not allowed. The JV must be accounted for using the equity model under IAS 28 *Associates and Joint Ventures*. Dyer's preferred model, whereby the entity would contract for rights to share and operate future assets with another party would not therefore be a JV.

However, if under the arrangement Dyer adopts its preferred model and, together with other parties, is provided with rights to the assets and obligations for the liabilities of the arrangement, a joint operation (JO) is established.

The accounting for a JO **may** be similar to that for a JV under the now replaced IAS 31 *Interests in Joint Ventures*. If the parties have rights to a **specific percentage** of **all** those assets and obligations, there would be no difference between the accounting for a JO under IFRS 11 and using the proportionate consolidation model previously allowed under IAS 31. However, it is possible that the parties may have differing rights and percentages to different assets and or different obligations for different liabilities. In this case, the financial statements would not reflect IAS 31's proportionate consolidation method which consolidated a 'blended' percentage of all assets and liabilities. In this case, Dyer would consolidate the JO using the percentages of assets and liabilities it had rights and obligations over and not by using the percentage of the equity owned in the JO.

(b) Part (b) concerns the calculation of basic and diluted earnings per share when a group has convertible bonds in issue. It also requires discussion of issues surrounding an entity's publication of KPIs. It is drawn from syllabus sections 13.2 and 13.4 and requires application of knowledge from the BPP Study Text Chapter 18 *Reporting financial performance*.

(i)

	Per share $
Basic earnings per share $27.81 ÷ 1m	27.81
Diluted eps:	
Adjusted profit attributable to Abli's equity ($27.81m + $3m − $1m)	$29.81m
Number of shares to issue if bonds converted (3m ÷ 100 × 4)	120,000
Total shares in issue if bonds converted (1m + 120,000)	1.12m
Diluted eps ($29.81m ÷ 1.12m)	26.62

(ii) The reporting of an eps figure based upon EBITDA has its roots in 'impression management'. This is the practice whereby entities attempt to control the impressions of corporate performance made by financial statement users by, for instance, reporting a non-GAAP eps figure which shows the entity in a better light than that shown by the GAAP-based eps figure (as required by IAS 33 *Earnings Per Share*). It is now common practice for entities to report 'pro-forma' earnings along with GAAP-based figures. It could be that management are acting altruistically and are keen to provide users with more accurate and/or more useful information. This is a virtuous act and can be seen to be ethically acceptable. However, their motivation may be to deliberately make the entity look more profitable because, for instance, their remuneration may be linked to eps growth. If so, the practice cannot be ethically acceptable.

IAS 33 would allow Abli to present an eps figure based on EBITDA. However, there are certain rules which must be adhered to:

1. The weighted average number of shares used in the denominator must be the same as that required by IAS 33.

2. A reconciliation must be provided between the numerator (ie earnings) used in the EBITDA eps calculation and the line item (ie the profit figure appearing in the group income statement) used in the IAS 33 eps calculation.

The EBITDA figure must be shown in the notes and not in the income statement.

Question 16

This question concerns the IASB's stand-alone standard (SAS) *IFRS for SMEs* and involves the application of knowledge concerning (a) the differences between accounting practices using full IFRS and those using the SAS and (b) the applicability and usefulness of the SAS in a corporate reporting context. It is relevant to syllabus sections 13.1, 13.2 and 13.3 and is covered by BPP Paper 13 Study Text chapters:

6   Revision of basic groups
7   Complex groups
22 IFRS for SMEs

(a) (i) As Denz is a PLC it must use full IFRS in its financial statements. In this respect, goodwill in Zin would be calculated as follows:

	$m
FV of consideration transferred for 75% investment	3.34
Contingent consideration	3.37
This is estimated using present values ($3.54m/1.05)	
FV of NCI	0.75
Denz uses the full goodwill method. As FV is not given, it must be estimated (using a proportion of net assets approach) $3m × 25%	
	7.46
FV of identifiable net assets	3.00
Goodwill	4.46

If Denz believes that the information concerning Zin's sales targets is reliable and, as a result, contingent consideration will not have to be paid a case could be made for an adjustment to the goodwill on acquisition by excluding the consideration. Following this approach, which is equally acceptable, the goodwill figure as at 31 October 2014 would be $1.09m.

(ii) Had Denz not been a PLC upon the acquisition of Zin then it would not have had public accountability. Also, the entity's business model does not involve the holding of assets in a fiduciary capacity for a broad group of outsiders. This, together with the absence of public accountability, means that Denz would have had the option of adopting the IFRS for SMEs in its financial statements. This would have the following impacts:

- Contingent consideration is only included where it is probable and can be reliably measured: this is not the case here.

- Acquisition costs form part of the cost of acquisition and so increase goodwill.

- NCI is not included in the calculation of goodwill: goodwill is the difference between the cost of the combination and Denz's share of the FV of Zin's identifiable net assets.

- Goodwill is amortised over its useful life, or if this cannot be estimated, 10 years.

Goodwill would have been calculated as follows:

FV of consideration transferred for 75% investment	3.34
Acquisition costs (not allowed under full IFRS)	0.83
	4.17
Denz's share of Zin's identifiable net assets ($3m × 75%)	2.25
	1.92
Goodwill amortisation (1/6)	0.32
Goodwill	1.60

(b) (i) Denz has a turnover of $50m and employs 50 people. It would therefore probably satisfy local criteria as to the size of an SME; although the IFRS for SMEs does not identify SMEs on the basis of size but on the basis of whether they are publicly accountable or not. The main benefit to Denz would therefore be to reduce the cost burden of reporting, which is often much heavier for smaller entities. The cost burden of adopting full IFRS may not be justifiable on the grounds of providing useful information to the users of Denz's financial statements. Much of the present financial reporting framework is based upon the needs of larger entities so full-IFRS based statutory financial statements would be less relevant to the users of Denz's financial statements.

A narrower range of decisions will be made by users based on Denz's financial statements. For instance, as an SME and with a business model which is mainly based on one income stream, Denz is likely to have fewer complex transactions and therefore will have a reduced need for complex analysis by users. The full IFRS disclosure requirements would be inappropriate and for this reason the IFRS for SMEs has much fewer disclosure requirements. Full-IFRS disclosures are more relevant to investment decisions in capital markets and are therefore mainly irrelevant to an unlisted SME. This will result in significant cost savings for Denz.

The IFRS for SMEs is based on the principles contained in the full IFRS programme. Therefore it will be quite straight forward for Denz to adopt new practices if it ever decided to gain a new listing in future.

(ii) The IFRS for SMEs requires that Denz uses fair value to measure investment properties. Fair value generally refers to the property's market value. Market value would be the best possible price reasonably obtainable by the seller. Therefore with the land and buildings cost could not be used. The best possible price is $9m. This should be used to value the land and a value of zero given to the buildings. Gains and losses on adoption would be recognised in profit or loss.

Question 17

Syllabus section: 13.4

This material is covered in Chapter 18 of the AIA text. The question deals with the issues associated with segmental reporting and the implications of protecting commercial sensitivity.

(a)

> **Tutorial Note:** There can be valid commercial considerations associated with protecting business information, but those must be balanced against the need to inform shareholders. The first part of this question requires the expression of an opinion, which must be supported.
>
> A further opinion is required in (b) (ii).
>
> There is no need to agree with the direction taken in the Model Answer, provided the arguments that are offered are properly supported.

(i) Quoted companies must keep their shareholders informed, even if it is costly to do so because of commercial sensitivity. There would be no point in having accounting standards if their requirements can be set aside on the basis that the directors would prefer not to make those disclosures.

The history of segmental reporting has been about change and development in the regulations in order to force companies to publish useful segmental reports. Segmental reports have generally been less helpful than they could have been because directors often aim to meet the minimum reporting requirements set out in terms of the letter of the rules.

(ii) The fact that each of the four elements listed in the analysis being studied by management is an operating division suggests that each has its own separate risk characteristics. A divisional structure implies autonomy and an element of each division having its own risk characteristics.

The analysis being studied by management suggests that each of the four elements is studied separately. IFRS 8 *Operating Segments* states that the fact management tracks the performance of each segment means that all must be disclosed in the segmental information.

The fact that seafood is relatively small may have been sufficient justification to merge it with fresh food, but seafood exceeds the 10% threshold in terms of net assets, which would make it a reportable segment.

The remaining segments all look substantial and it may be necessary for Wilton to break the totals down even further if there are reportable segments within, say, frozen vegetables.

(b) (i)

	$m
Present value of plan obligation at 1 May 2016	650.0
Interest cost	50.7
Current service cost	124.0
Benefits paid	(128.0)
Actuarial (gain)/loss on obligation (balancing figure)	33.3
Present value of plan obligation at 30 April 2017	730.0

	$m
Fair value of assets at 1 May 2016	635.0
Expected return on plan assets	73.0
Contributions received	70.0
Benefits paid	(128.0)
Actuarial gain/(loss) on obligation (balancing figure)	(5.0)
Fair value of assets at 30 April 2017	645.0

(ii) The figures are highly subjective and it could be argued that there is too much doubt as to their accuracy for reporting purposes. The company needs to predict a host of factors into the long-term future, including the longevity of staff, salary levels at the date of retirement and returns on investments, which will almost certainly span a range and will include art and property, which may not have readily observable market prices.

Conversely, there is an actuarial profession that exists to advise members on the management of pension schemes. Those experts are, necessarily, required to make the assumptions described above in order to maintain the solvency of pension schemes. While those predictions will always have a margin for error, they are regarded as sufficiently defensible to make substantial decisions concerning investments, pension holidays and the like. Pension commitments also feature in corporate acquisitions.

Question 18

(a) Parts (a) and (b) concern the accounting for a disposal group and an asset under IFRS 5 *Non-current Assets Held for Sale and Discontinued Operations*. They are drawn from syllabus sections 13.2 and 13.3 and require application of knowledge from the BPP Study Text Chapter 18 *Reporting financial performance*.

TNs:

Immediately before classification as held for sale, the carrying value of the net assets of a disposal group (DG) must be accounted for using the normal group policies for the individual assets and liabilities of the disposal group.

Upon classification as a DG any impairment loss must be allocated, first to any goodwill in the DG and then to other non-current assets (but only those included in the measurement rules of IFRS 5 – which excludes inventory as it's a CA and not an NCA and, specifically, Investments in equity instruments as they're accounted for under IFRS 9). Allocation is on a pro rata basis.

	As at 1 May 2014 $m	CV upon class^n as held for sale 31 Oct 2014 $m	Alloc^n of imp loss $m	CV in group accounts after class^n as held for sale $m
Goodwill	2.55	2.55[1]	(2.55)	-
PPE revalued	7.82	7.00[2]	(1.41)[7]	5.59
PPE cost	9.69	8.69[3]	(1.76)[8]	6.93
Inventory	4.08	4.08[4]	-	4.08
Inv in equity instruments	3.06	2.60[5]	-	2.60
Liabilities assoc with above	(4.20)	(4.20)[4]		(4.20)
Other liabilities	(8.00)	–[6]		
		20.72		
FV of DG		15.00		
Impairment loss		5.72	5.72	15.00

No depreciation will be charged on PPE from the date classified as held for sale.

[1] No impairment to goodwill

[2] Revalued PPE must be stated at its revalued CV and the impairment loss will be included in profit or loss.

[3] Normal depreciation will be charged for the period up to classification as held for sale.

[4] No change per question

[5] Investment in equity instrument must be stated at FV with the loss shown in other comprehensive income.

[6] These liabilities are not to be assumed by the purchaser of the DG and are to be settled from the proceeds from disposal and so are not part of the DG's net assets.

[7] $7 \div 15.69 \, (7 + 8.69) \times 5.72$

[8] $8.69 \div 15.69 \times 5.72$

(b) Temporary accommodation

If the time taken to vacate the building and move into temporary accommodation is usual and customary for such assets then at the date the entity becomes committed to the plan, it qualifies as being available for immediate sale. IFRS 5 also requires that the sale is highly probable. If vacation would not be complete within one year of the commitment date then the building would not be available for immediate sale unless there are events beyond Quest's control which would extend the date thus.

Wait until construction of a new building is complete

Quest would wait until the new building is complete before vacating its current HQ and transferring it to the buyer. This would demonstrate that the HQ is not available for immediate sale and would not become so until construction of the new building was complete. This would apply even if a firm commitment to transfer the current building to a future buyer has been made.

(c) Part (c) concerns the difficulties of international financial analysis. It is drawn from syllabus sections 13.2 and requires application of knowledge from the BPP Study Text Chapter 23 *Ratio and trend analysis*.

Changes to GAAP

If the IASB has issued new standards or interpretations or the country in which Tinu is domiciled requires new measures by statute (ie changes to GAAP), there is usually flexibility (albeit restricted) concerning the period over which Tinu may adopt the new pronouncements. Tinu's directors may make a decision concerning whether to adopt the new GAAP based upon its effect on financial performance. The directors may then have difficulty in assessing Tinu's real performance. There may also be an issue concerning the comparability of Tinu's performance with other entities.

Choice of practices concerning presentation

The IASB requires a minimum layout in financial statements, mainly under IAS 1 *Presentation of Financial Statements*. This means in practice that Tinu's directors could produce financial statements following any format or layout it wishes so long as it complies with the 'minimum' requirement. This extends to the titles of financial statements which can be anything the entity wishes so long as the meaning is clear and reflects the purpose of the statement. The 'minimum' requirement also often allows entities to choose between different formats; eg the statement of other comprehensive income can be a separate statement or can be linked to the profit or loss statement; also, detail can often be shown on the face of a statement or in the notes to the accounts. When entities are allowed this freedom they will often choose a presentation policy which serves the purpose of best impressing investors. Quest would need to be wary of this when analysing Tinu's performance. It may be the case that Quest may have to recreate Tinu's accounts into a more recognisable form. Tinu may follow IFRS but this does not mean that differences in GAAP and presentation practice have been eliminated.

Question 19

This question involves (a) the translation of a subsidiary's hyperinflationary functional currency to a non-hyperinflationary presentation currency, (b) the potential to exclude subsidiaries from consolidation and (c) the use of fair value reporting. The question is drawn from syllabus sections 13.1 and 13.2 and is covered in BPP Study Text chapters:

6 Revision of basic groups
9 Foreign currency translation

(a) Tutorial note: IAS 21 *The Effects of Changes in Foreign Exchange* Rates allows an entity to present its financial statements in any currency. If the functional currency (FC) differs to the presentation currency (PC) a translation is required. A group may contain many individual entities with different FCs so each set of financial statements must be expressed in the common PC so that a common set of group accounts may be prepared. When a hyperinflationary FC is translated into a non-hyperinflationary PC, the basic procedure is (IAS 21.42):

(i) the entity should restate its financial statements in accordance with IAS 29 *Financial Reporting in Hyperinflationary Economics*.

(ii) all amounts are translated at the closing rate, except that

(iii) comparative amounts are those that were presented as current year amounts in the relevant prior year financial statements (ie not adjusted for subsequent changes in price levels or exchange rates).

As there is no mention to the contrary in the question we can ignore step (i).

DIA
STATEMENT OF INCOME FOR THE YEAR ENDED 31 OCTOBER 2014

		$m
Sales	52.50/4	13.13
Cost of sales	49.79/4	(12.45)
Depreciation	0.75/4	(0.19)
Finance charge	0.53/4	(0.13)
Profit before tax		0.36
Income tax	0.69/4	(0.17)
Profit after tax		0.19

DIA
STATEMENT OF FINANCIAL POSITION AS AT 31 OCTOBER 2014

		2014		2013
		$m		$m
Property, plant and equipment	8.25/4	2.06	9.00/3	3.00
Inventories	4.50/4	1.13	4.07/3	1.36
Trade receivables	6.00/4	1.50	7.20/3	2.40
Cash and cash equivalents	0.90/4	0.22	0.30/3	0.10
Total assets		4.91		6.86
Trade payables	5.76/4	1.44	6.80/3	2.27
Taxation	0.69/4	0.17	1.31/3	0.44
Non-current liabilities	5.40/4	1.35	5.40/3	1.80
Total liabilities		2.96		4.51
Share capital	1.50/4	0.38	1.50/3	0.50
Retained earnings	W1	1.57	5.56/3	1.85
Total equity		1.95		2.35

W1: 2014 retained earnings

Balance brought forward from 2013		1.85
Profit after tax for the year		0.19
Exchange difference (loss):		
Op ret earnings at op rate (5.56/3)	1.85	
Op ret earnings at cl rate (5.56/4)	1.39	(0.46)
		1.58 (rounding)

(b) IFRS 10 *Consolidated Financial Statements* provides guidance on the procedures to be applied when preparing the combined financial statements of a parent and its subsidiaries.

The rules on exclusion are strict as this is a common method used by entities to manipulate their group financial statements. Dia is quite highly geared (ie non-current liabilities are approx. 27.5% of total assets) and if Paxdal could exclude the subsidiary from its group statements, group gearing would be improved. This is one way of removing liabilities from the balance sheet and is therefore not allowed by IFRS. It is also highly unethical.

Some commentators would agree with Paxdal's directors and would argue that Dia should be excluded on the grounds of dissimilar activities; ie inclusion would result in misleading results. IFRS 10 firmly rejects this argument. The IASB argues that exclusion is not justified on the basis that more relevant results can be provided about subsidiaries by firstly including them in the group statements and then providing additional information about "dissimilar" activities under IFRS 8 *Operating Segments*.

Hence IFRS 10 requires that consolidated financial statements are prepared to include ALL subsidiaries, both foreign and domestic, other than:

- Those held for sale under IFRS 5
- Those which cannot be controlled due to long-term restrictions imposed eg by the country's government.

EXAM ANSWER BANK

As none of the above applies to Paxdal's case, Dia must be included in the consolidation exercise.

(c) Historical cost accounting (HCA) has been used for centuries and is easily understood. However, HCA has distinct disadvantages when inflation is rising. The *Conceptual Framework* includes current value as one of its measurement bases, of which fair value is one way of measuring current value. Fair value (FV) reporting (as advocated by IFRS 13 *Fair Value Measurement*) has distinct benefits which would help to overcome these disadvantages. They can be summarised as follows:

Paxdal operates through a chain of High Street shops. If these shops are owned by Paxdal, the use of the cost model under IAS 16 *Property, Plant and Equipment* could seriously understate their value. Such an understatement could produce misleading information to users who may be trying to assess the entity's current and 'real' gearing and earning power potential. The depression of asset value could make Paxdal vulnerable to a takeover. Also, as retail fashions change, the equipment in the shops may become quickly out-of-date and may need replacing at shorter intervals.

The use of FVs has the potential to protect the entity from a takeover and to flag up the need to make provisions for replacement in earlier years.

The same thinking could also apply to Dia's manufacturing and distribution equipment. The mobile smartphone technology field changes rapidly and it is very possible that manufacturing and distribution equipment and networks may have to be updated at frequent intervals.

The technology industry has particular problems when it comes to valuing closing inventory. Technology changes rapidly and any new designs or products coming to the market tend to be marketed at high prices which eventually reduce as the technology becomes more available to buyers. So a company using the standard approach of FIFO may have closing inventory at lower prices than those included in cost of sales. This has the potential to overstate cost of sales and thereby lead to relatively lower profits. This may be the case with Paxdal as it is a highly successful retailer so it is assumed the entity is rarely left with large amounts of old higher priced stock.

Under IFRS entities are now permitted to revalue non-current assets such as property, plant and equipment and to use fair values for items such as investment property and financial instruments. Such developments, and the use of FVs in acquisition accounting to measure goodwill, are becoming more accepted by investors and users who argue that HCA is out-of-date and not relevant to their decision making. It is argued that FV information, based on active market prices, is the best available measure of the future economic benefits (eg cash flows) which an asset can be expected to generate.

Question 20

This is a multi-part question and concerns the accounting for non-current assets.

Part (a) is drawn from syllabus section 13.3 and involves the identification of control when dealing with investments where less than a majority of the investee's voting shares are held by the investor. It is covered by BPP Study Text Chapter 6.

Part (b) is drawn from syllabus section 13.4 and requires a discussion concerning the recognition of intangible assets upon an acquisition. The topic is covered by BPP Study Text Chapter 13.

Part (c) is drawn from syllabus section 13.4 and requires calculation and discussion of the amount to be capitalised for R&D expenditure. The topic is covered by BPP Study Text Chapter 13.

(a) Despite holding less than 50% of the voting rights, Mendez might have power to control the investees if its rights are sufficient to give it power when it has the practical ability to direct the investee's activities unilaterally. This is known as *de facto* control (IFRS 10. para B41). Mendez must consider all the facts and circumstances, including:

- The size of its holding relevant to the size and dispersion of other holdings;
- The likely impact of any potential voting rights held by Mendez;
- Any rights arising from other contractual arrangements; and
- Any additional facts and circumstances concerning the directing by Mendez of an investee's activities; such as Mendez's voting patterns at AGMs.

Having considered the above, if it is still not clear that Mendez has power, then Mendez would not control the investee (IFRS 10. para B46)

(i) Mendez would have power to control Gon due to its dominant voting interest. This is based on the fact that it has a 46% interest whereas no other shareholder holds more than 1.3% of the voting shares. The other shareholders are widely dispersed. A large number of them would have to act in unison to outvote Mendez and there is no history of this. Therefore Mendez has de facto control and Gon would be consolidated as a subsidiary.

(ii) Mendez would **not** have power over Ena. The two remaining shareholders with large holdings of 26% each could easily combine to outvote Mendez – as they did when voting against Mendez's proposed change of policy. The size of Mendez's holding and its size relative to other shareholders would not give it power.

(b) Both the research staff and the customer contract are intangible in nature (ie 'an identifiable non-monetary without physical substance') and would be accounted for under IAS 38. IAS 38 defines an asset as 'a resource controlled by an entity from which future economic benefits are expected to flow to the entity' (IAS 38.8).

(i) Orca's research staff would obviously be thought as 'assets' by Mendez as they were a significant factor in the entity's decision to buy the company. However, they could not be recognised as assets in Mendez's group financial statements because they would not meet IAS 38's recognition criteria; namely, in the absence of any other legal rights it would not be possible to show that Mendez could control the economic benefits embodied in the staff; as they could easily leave employment and work elsewhere for another company.

(ii) An intangible asset needs to be identifiable so that it can be distinguished from goodwill. The two elements of identifiability are separability or the existence of contractual or other legal rights. The supply agreement between Orca and Jorz is not separable but it does meet the contractual/legal right criterion for identification as an intangible asset.

It is unlikely that an active market exists for this type of intangible asset. In its absence, the fair value would be measured on a basis that reflects the amounts Mendez would have paid in an arm's length transaction between knowledgeable willing parties (IAS 38.40).

(c) IAS 38 requires that research costs are written off. Development costs are capitalised if, and only if, Mendez can demonstrate all of the following IAS 38.57):

- Technical feasibility of completing the project;
- Its intention to complete the project and its ability to use or sell it;
- How the project will generate future economic benefits;
- The availability of adequate technical, financial and other resources to complete the project; and
- Its ability to reliably measure the project's attributable costs.

The following table applies the above principles to the scenario.

Project		1	2 *	3 **	4 ***
		$'000	$'000	$'000	$'000
Salaries and wages		156	–	–	–
Indirect overheads	Specifically disallowed by IAS 38	–	–	–	–
Direct overheads		29	–	–	–
Staff training costs	Specifically disallowed by IAS 38	–	–	–	–
Patent		–	–	–	–
Market analysis	Effectively disallowed by IAS 38 as it refers to gaining knowledge and is therefore a research cost.	–	–	–	–
Carrying value at 1 November 2013		–	–	–	728
Carrying value at 31 October 2014		185	–	–	728

Notes

Project 1: Qualifies as development expenditure and must be capitalised. However, staff training and market analysis must be expensed.

Project2: Costs incurred in ensuring the database is up-to-date and retains functional capacity would be deemed to be part of a routine process. As it does not involve innovations to the database or new technology, the costs do not meet the definition of 'research' or 'developments' and must be written off as an expense.

Project 3: Although the project was previously capitalised, the IAS 38 criteria for recognition (see above) now no longer apply as Mendez does not appear to have the technical resources to complete the project. The ability to generate future economic benefits must also be called into question. The costs should therefore be written off.

Project 4: Costs incurred after commercial production begins must be written off as they would not pass the recognition criteria to be capitalised. As the asset has an indefinite life it is not amortised but tested for impairment. As recoverable amount ($1.5m) is greater than carrying value ($0.728m) there is no impairment and it will be carried in the SoFP at $0.728m.

Question 21

Syllabus section: 13.4

The question deals with the issues associated with accounting for impairment of cash generating units, and the wider issue of the roles and responsibilities of the accountant.

(a)

> **Tutorial Note:** Questions about impairment often hinge on the identification of cash generating units.

The first question is whether we should be considering the rolling mill in isolation. Arguably, we could argue that the rolling mill is part of the steelmaking site. The site, overall, is not impaired because it has a recoverable amount of $420m, considerably higher than the carrying value of $280m.

The rolling mill is a cash generating unit. We know that because the output from the mill could be sold separately. It makes little difference that the bulk of the output is actually sold to another division of Millennium.

The rolling mill is impaired because the recoverable amount is $80m, which is less than the carrying amount of $120m.

(b) The impairment loss is $120m – 80m = $40m. This is divided as follows:

	Carrying value $m	Proportion	Allocation of impairment loss $m	Adjusted carrying value $m
Land	25	0	(5)	30
Buildings	50	53%	24	26
Rolling plant	45	47%	21	24
	120	100%	40	80

(c)

> **Tutorial Note:** It may be necessary to take a wider view of the accountant's role and the background to the preparation of financial statements. It would be difficult, if not impossible, to prepare a set of financial statements without having a full understanding of the business and its strategy. The first two parts of this question offered a hint because the accountant must understand the steel-making business in order to establish how cash generating units are to be identified.

Preparing a set of financial statements requires a sound understanding of the company and its business model. For example, Millennium's accountant needs to understand the steel industry in order to appreciate how to go about valuing the underlying assets. The market for heavy engineering plant and equipment will be very different from that used by, say, an electronics manufacturer. Similarly, it will require an understanding of the business in order to establish whether or not there is a need to conduct an impairment review. Millennium's accountants must have understood that there is a disruption in the market for rolled steel that has affected the recoverable amount of that division's assets. Equally, the accountants need to understand the business and the industry in order to identify cash generating units. Hypothetically, the rolling mill could have had no external sales and the accountants would have had to have reached a decision as to whether the company could sell rolled steel as a separate product.

The need for an understanding of the business extends to almost every area in which it is necessary to apply professional judgement. For example, deciding whether the entity is a going concern requires a knowledge of the issues that might undermine going concern.

There will also be a need to understand the business from an advisory perspective. For example, will a business proposal increase or decrease reported profits? The accountant will have to understand the business issues in order to advise on how they will affect the impressions being communicated to the shareholders.

Question 22

This question concerns the treatment of related party transactions under IAS 24 *Related Party Disclosures*.

(i) IAS 24 states that a supplier is not necessarily a related party merely by virtue of the resulting economic dependence.

> **Tutorial note:** others would include:
> - Two entities 'simply' because they have a director or other member of key management personnel in common, notwithstanding parts (d) and (f) in the definition of 'related party';
> - Two venturers simply because they share control over a joint venture;
> - Providers of finance, trade unions, public utilities, and government departments and agencies, simply by virtue of their normal dealings with an entity (even though they may affect the freedom of action of an entity or participate in its decision-making process);
> - A customer, franchisor, distributor or general agent with whom the entity transacts a significant volume of business, merely by virtue of the resulting economic dependence.

If the standard did not contain these exclusions, many entities that would normally be regarded as unrelated could potentially fall within the detailed definition of a related party, resulting in a plethora of financial statement disclosures. Effective control is a deciding issue in determining whether a party is related to another; so, for example, a small food manufacturer selling over 75% of its output to a high street supermarket could be said to be under the effective control of that customer.

For exclusion to be effective, the party should be considered as related to the reporting entity only as a result of the relationship noted above. So, if there are other reasons why Brace Inc would be considered a related party, the exclusion would not apply. So, if Brace Inc only supplies steel to Harden and there is no other relationship, it is not considered a related party. If, however, Brace Inc is also an associate of Harden, the exclusion does not apply and the two are considered related parties, in which case transactions relating to the supply of steel must be disclosed if material.

(ii) IAS 24 states that 'intragroup related party transactions and outstanding balances are eliminated in the preparation of consolidated financial statements of the group'. This is more than just a statement about a consolidation procedure. Presumably it means that disclosure of such balances is not required in Harden's consolidated financial statements since, so far as those financial statements are concerned, such items do not exist.

> **Tutorial note:** The standard explicitly requires disclosure of related party transactions and outstanding balances in the separate financial statements of a parent, venturer or investor presented in accordance with IAS 27 (2011) *Separate Financial Statements*.
>
> Also, all entities within a group that prepare their financial statements under IFRS have to disclose related party transactions and outstanding balances with other entities in the group in their financial statements.

Under IAS 28 (2011) *Investments in Associates and Joint Ventures*, balances with associated companies are not eliminated but separately disclosed.

(iii) Although the purchase will be made at full market value via an open bidding/tendering process, the fact that the wife's proposed purchase would be by a close member of the family (ie wife) of an individual who is a member of Harden's key management personnel, means that this is a related party transaction and must be disclosed.

For this purpose, 'close members of the family of an individual' are defined as 'those family members who may be expected to influence, or be influenced by, that individual in their dealings with the entity'. The standard goes on to state that they may include:

- The individual's domestic partner and children;
- Children of the individual's domestic partner; and
- Dependants of the individual or the individual's domestic partner.

The son would therefore also count as a related party. A number of commentators believe that these should not necessarily be the only family members that fall within the definition. Other family members such as parents, brothers and sisters could also be included, particularly where they have been influenced by or had influence over the individual in their dealings with the entity.

(iv) The director of Harden is a member of its key management personnel. If he/she purchases a controlling interest in Gritdelv, that entity will become a related party of Harden.

If the director only purchases say a 25% interest in Gritdelv, but this gave him/her significant influence over Gritdelv, it would still be a related party of Harden.

It would only be if the director's interest in Gritdelv was such that it did not give him/her significant influence, or could not be said to have significant voting power, that Gritdelv would not be a related party of Harden.

Question 23

This question concerns the assessment of an entity's financial performance; in particular: the recent and growing use of 'underlying profit' presentations and the related earnings per share figures as key performance indicators in the income statement: and, the ethical issues that arise. It is therefore relevant to syllabus sections 13.1 and 13.4.

(a) This part will involve consideration of:
IFRS 15
IAS 1 *Presentation of Financial Statements*

(i) Under IFRS 15 the awarding of points to customers is a performance obligation. Expan should allocate the transaction price of $40m to the product and the points on a relative stand-alone basis. The stand-alone selling price of the goods is $40m, as the price is the same regardless of whether the customer accepts the points. The stand-alone price of the points is $3.2m((20% + (80% × 75%)) × $4m).

The consideration of $40m should be allocated as follows:

	$'000	
Product	37,037	$40m × $40m/$43.2m
Points	2,963	$40m × $3.2m/$43.2m
	40,000	

Since 20% of the points had been redeemed by 31 October 2012, revenue of $592,600 (20% × $2,963k) should be recognised for the points and $37,037,000 for the products. The contract liability will be $2,370,400 ($2,963,000 − $592,600).

(ii) **This part concerns impairment of a financial asset and involves consideration of: IFRS 9 *Financial Instruments*.**

The liquidation of Nap means that expected credit loss on the financial asset has now increased and so an impairment loss must be measured based on the difference between the asset's carrying amount and its recoverable amount – the present value of the asset's estimated future cash flows discounted at the asset's original effective rate of interest. Expan has incorrectly calculated impairment as the difference between the asset's carrying value and new maturity value. An adjustment to finance costs is therefore necessary.

- Expan's original calculation will have been as follows:

	$m
Initial cost on 1 Nov 2010	10.00
Interest at 10%	1.00
Cash at 5%	(0.50)
Carrying value at 31 Oct 2011	10.50
Interest at 10%	1.05
Cash at 5%	(0.50)
Carrying value before impairment at 31 Oct 2012	11.05

Expan will therefore have written off $4.55m ($11.05 − $6.5m) to finance costs.

- The correct treatment should have been to use present values (amortised cost) as follows:

	$m
Carrying value before impairment	11.05
Recoverable amount using effective interest rate ($6.5m × 0.751)	4.88
Correct impairment	6.17

The adjustment to finance costs is therefore as follows:

	Dr $m	Cr $m
Finance costs in income statement ($6.17m − $4.55m)	1.62	
Financial asset		1.62

(b) Weighted average number of shares in issue = 56m as follows:

2012: Basic $18m/32.14p

or

2012: Underlying basic $18m − ($3m + $1m + $1m)/23.21p

Recalculation of eps for year ended 31 Oct 2012:	Basic $m	Underlying $m
Draft profit attributable to ordinary shareholders	18.00	13.00
See (a) (i) above	(2.37)	(2.37)
See (a) (ii) above	(1.62)	(1.62)
Adjusted profit figures	14.01	9.01
Weighted average number of shares (see above)	56m	56m
New eps figures	25.02	16.09

(c) **This part requires a discussion of current developments, in particular whether the *Conceptual Framework*'s objective of useful information is violated by the inclusion of information not subject to current IFRS.**

The *Conceptual Framework* states quite categorically that the objective of financial information is the provision of information which is useful to investors, lenders and other creditors, who are considered the primary users of published financial statements. Although 'underlying' profit and 'underlying' earnings per share is not defined by IFRS and therefore may not be directly comparable with the similarly adjusted figures of other companies, there is a growing belief in business that without such adjustments an entity's true potential and sustainable earnings figures can be hidden from view.

This is partly due to current value accounting (such as the use of fair values), which, due to the recent economic crisis, has forced entities to take significant write-downs in asset values. The impact of these write-downs on statutory profit has led to many entities reporting what they believe are 'sustainable' performance figures.

Of course, there is the possibility that underlying profit as a key indicator of corporate performance may mislead investors. Expan's original draft accounts show earnings per share and profit before tax figures little changed from 2011. As shown above this is due to errors in accounting which, when amended, show significant decreases in both indicators. There is no indication that a desire to present similar indicators to 2011 is what drove Expan to use the incorrect accounting treatments in 2012 but it does highlight the risk of allowing entities the freedom, unrestrained by IFRS, to present information in this way.

An additional problem is that if underlying figures become a prime focus of analysts, shareholders and management, the lack of guidance gives rise to a potential for a lack of consistency in reporting. The lack of an agreed definition gives rise to problems for auditors who will become concerned about inconsistent profit adjustments leading to differences in the amount of disclosure and the impact on the Framework's requirement for comparability across entities.

However, it is incumbent upon directors to act in an ethical manner when producing financial statements. Underlying profit is an important development in the key indicators used to report corporate performance as it provides potentially useful information on the 'normalised' profit of the entity. However, it should not receive greater priority than any other KPI which comments on results and like any other emerging approach to reporting performance, it is critically important that it is transparent and consistently applied year-to-year across both the entity and industry sector.

Question 24

(a) **This part of the question concerns the accounting for deferred taxation in the context of consolidated accounts. It is therefore relevant to syllabus sections 13.2. It requires a consideration of:**

IAS 12 *Income Taxes*

(i) As Otion has 25% of the inventory still unsold at the year end there will be a provision for unrealised profit of $1.5m ($20m × 30% × 25%) in the group financial statements. However, the fact that Pera has already suffered income tax on the profit gives rise to a timing difference for deferred tax purposes. In the following year when the remaining inventory is sold the provision for unrealised profit will be released but will not be taxed. This gives rise to a deferred tax asset of $0.45m ($1.5m × 30%).

The deferred tax asset is recognised to the extent that it is recoverable. That is, it is more likely than not that sufficient tax profits will arise from which the reversal of the timing difference can be deducted. In this case Otion fully expects the inventory to be sold in the following year and so the asset would be recognised and carried forward on that basis.

(ii) Kram's unrelieved tax loss gives rise to a timing difference because although the loss is recognised in the group financial statements, it can not yet be recognised for tax purposes as it can only be relieved by carrying it forward to be offset against Kram's future profits. Kram expects profits to grow over the forthcoming year so it will generate sufficient profits for the purpose of offsetting this tax loss. A deferred tax asset in the group financial statements will therefore be recognised at $2.5m ($10m × 25%).

As with Otion, the deferred tax asset is recognised to the extent that it is recoverable.

(iii) As the group deferred tax position is viewed from the perspective of the group as a whole, the fair value adjustment made for the purpose of consolidating the financial statements of Ember will affect the deferred tax charge for the year. Ember has not recognised a deferred tax asset as part of its calculation of identifiable net assets. So a provision should be made for the difference between the fair value of identifiable net assets acquired and their carrying value; that is $0.6m [($16m – $14m) × 30%].

(b) **This part of the question involves a consideration of whether related party transactions exist for the purpose of reporting the results of the Pera group. It therefore is relevant to syllabus section 13.2. It involves:**

IAS 24 *Related Party Disclosures*

Santi is a subsidiary of Pera. Whether a related party situation exists with Compu depends upon the nature of the dealings between the entities. A holding of less than 20% of an entity is assumed not to result in significant influence unless it can be shown otherwise. Pera can participate in Compu's operating and financing policies. Therefore Compu will be deemed to be an associate of Pera.

Under IAS 24 (2011) Compu and Santi are related parties as Pera has control over Santi and exerts significant influence over Compu.

Tutorial note: control has to exist in Santi and/or Compu for them to be related. If Pera had simply exerted significant influence over both then they would not have been related.

A related party transaction is defined as a 'transfer of resources, services or obligations between related parties, regardless of whether a price is charged' (IAS 24.9 [2011]). The IFRS therefore applies to gifts of assets. Although the mining technology is to be provided free of charge the fair market value of the transaction will therefore have to be disclosed.

An issue arises because the commitment to use the technology will not become firm until December 2012 after the year end. However, IAS 24.21 (2011) specifically includes 'commitments to do something if a particular event occurs' as an example of a qualifying related party transaction. This is a new requirement introduced by IAS 24 (2011).

Upon adopting IAS 24 (2011) Pera would be required to disclose comparative commitments at the end of the previous reporting period. Also, although IAS 24 (2011) does not refer specifically to materiality (as it is covered by IAS 1), the general concept of materiality would have to be applied. The commitment is likely to be material as it refers to 'highly specialised mining technology'. The presence of such a commitment is likely to be of significant interest to investors.

Pera's (and the individual entities') financial statements would be more difficult to understand if related party transactions were to be excluded. In extreme cases, transactions such as the transfer of technology free of charge may be part of a deliberate strategy aimed at manipulating the profitability of entities. If this was to be so then the financial statements would not be showing a true and fair view in that they would not be free from bias and would not therefore be providing useful information to the user.

(c) **This part of the question concerns planning for the introduction of interim financial reporting. It is relevant to syllabus section 13.4. It involves application of the proposals in:**

IAS 34 *Interim Financial Reporting*
IAS 37 *Provisions, Contingent Liabilities and Contingent Assets*
IAS 38 *Intangible Assets*

IAS 34 is not a mandatory standard in that it only provides guidelines for those entities wishing to introduce interim financial reporting. There are sections dealing with minimum components, scope, form and content and explanatory notes. A large part however deals with recognition and measurement principles and provides guideline as to their practical application.

The main principle in IAS 34 is that an entity should adopt the same recognition and measurement principles as it does in its annual financial statements. So, for example, the interim report should not contain provisions for items for which there is no present obligation – just as it would in its annual financial statements. This may of course result in the need to re-measure items in the following interim reports or at the year end. The nature and amount of any significant re-measurements should be reported.

The $5 million cost of the distribution facility overhaul in August 2013 must not therefore be anticipated in the 30 April 2013 interim financial report unless there exists a legal or constructive obligation (IAS 37) at that date. This is unlikely as contracts have not yet been issued and won't be until May 2013; at which time the workforce will be informed.

Similarly, the interim report should not contain an accrual for the year end bonus. Payments are dependent on profits which are seasonal and cannot be measured reliably. Also, there is no constructive obligation to pay bonuses as they are dependent on profits.

IAS 38 requires that costs incurred to generate non-monetary intangible assets, development costs, are expensed unless they form part of an identifiable intangible asset. Under IAS 38 the $2m to be incurred on 1 November 2012 would therefore be classed as a research cost and must be expensed as an identifiable asset is not yet in existence. Once expensed, those costs cannot be subsequently capitalised once development of the system takes place and must therefore remain as expensed items. IAS 34 requires similar treatment in interim financial reports. It would therefore be inappropriate in the interim financial report to 'defer' the initial research costs in the expectation that it will eventually form part of an identifiable intangible asset.

Question 25

(a) **This part of the question specifically concerns the regulation of corporate financial reporting and the implications of changing to IFRS for corporate accounting systems and financial statements. It is therefore relevant to syllabus section 13.1**

Any entity adopting IFRS for its financial reporting faces significant changes as domestic GAAP and IFRS GAAP often differ substantially. This was particularly evident in the case of IAS 39 *Financial Instruments: Recognition and Measurement,* which is why it has been replaced with IFRS 9. This criticism has been levelled against IFRS generally as IFRS tends to introduce far more recognition, measurement and disclosure requirements than required by a country's domestic GAAP. Complexity of this nature can therefore lead to inconsistency in the interpretation of the financial statements.

The presentation of financial statements is governed by IAS 1 (revised 2011) which has retained the 'one or two statement' approach to reporting comprehensive income at the option of the entity. To reduce the degree of change necessary, the choice of which to adopt may therefore be made on the basis of which approach corresponds more closely to that required by domestic GAAP. Alternative forms of presentation may therefore lead to inconsistencies in interpretation of performance.

IFRSs are principle-based. It is often claimed that IFRSs provide insufficient guidance on the application of principles. An entity may therefore interpret the principles in an IFRS in different ways, especially in connection with concepts such as 'reliable measurement' and 'probable cash flows'.

Certain IFRS allow alternative accounting practices. For example, IAS 40 *Investment Property* and IAS 16 *Property, Plant and Equipment* both allow a choice of two measurement methods to be used. An entity may again choose a method which corresponds with domestic GAAP which may thereby lead to a lack of comparability between different entities in different countries and inconsistency. The lack of any substantial industry guidance in these areas results in the need to use judgement in the selection of accounting practices.

If the entity in question is adopting IFRS for the first time it will have to consider the requirements of IFRS 1 *First Time Adoption of IFRS* which at the time of adoption allows a number of exemptions from the requirements of IFRS. For example, IFRS 1 permits a first-time adopter not to restate business combinations prior to its date of transition to IFRS. The entity could for example carry forward amortised figures for goodwill. The amortisation method is not allowed by IFRS 3.

Another source of inconsistency between entities could be the IASB's allowance of early-adoption of IFRS. For example any entities adopting IFRS 9 early may have produced figures that were incomparable and inconsistent with entities who decided to use IAS 39 and leave adoption of IFRS 9 until the effective date; although IAS 8 *Accounting Policies, Changes in Accounting Estimates and Errors* does require an entity to report the possible future impact of such an early adoption.

(b) **This part of the question concerns the accounting options available for property, plant and equipment upon transition to IFRS. It is relevant to syllabus section 13.4. It involves the application of requirement from**

IFRS 1 *First-time Adoption of IFRS*
IAS 16 *Property, Plant and Equipment*

Recto may elect to measure the manufacturing property at fair value at the date of transition and use that fair value as the property's deemed cost and then account for the asset prospectively under IAS 16's cost approach or the entity may elect to adopt IAS 16 retrospectively. Alternatively Recto may elect to use previous domestic GAAP if the approach used is comparable to current IFRS requirements – in this case, the appropriate IFRS is IAS 16. Recto has elected to use IAS 16's cost model. There are therefore three options available to Recto upon transition to IFRS on 1 November 2012 to measure cost:

1. Adopt fair value at 1 November 2012 as deemed cost
2. Apply IAS 16's cost approach retrospectively
3. Use domestic GAAP as the basis of cost if acceptable

No adjustments would be necessary under the last option which uses written down revaluations as the carrying amounts under domestic GAAP have been measured using an approach acceptable under IAS 16. That is, the manufacturing property is depreciated systematically over its estimated useful life and the revaluation is measured at fair value less subsequent depreciation and impairment losses.

Options 1 and 2 will require adjustments as follows:

Tutorial note: although not strictly required in answer to the question, to make the adjustments clear, it is best to start such a question with a view of what the brought forward figures would be as at 1 November 2012 under domestic GAAP. The following show the journal entries by way of T accounts to make the entries' impact clearer.

	1 Fair value as deemed cost		2 Applying IAS 16's cost approach	
	Dr	Cr	Dr	Cr
• Manufacturing asset				
As at 1 Nov 2012 under domestic GAAP	14.000		14.000	
1 Nov 2012 acc depn written back		0.286		
Retained earnings [2]	1.286			
1 Nov 2012 initial revaluation surplus w/b				2.000
Balance c/d		15.000		12.000

EXAM ANSWER BANK

	1 Fair value as deemed cost		2 Applying IAS 16's cost approach	
	Dr	Cr	Dr	Cr
• Accumulated depreciation				
As at 1 Nov 2012 under domestic GAAP ($14m × 1/49)		0.286		0.286
1 Nov 2012 To asset account	0.286			
1 Nov 2012 Retained earnings w/b			0.286	
1 Nov 2012 Rev surplus Cost based depn w/b				0.240
1 Nov 2012 Ret earnings Cost based depn 2011				0.240
• Revaluation surplus				
As at 1 Nov 2012 under domestic GAAP[1]		2.240		2.240
1 Nov 2012 Trf to retained earnings	2.240			
1 Nov 2012 Revaluation w/b			2.000	
1 Nov 2012 Excess depn w/b			0.240	
• Retained earnings				
1 Nov 2012 increase in FV of asset		1.286		
1 Nov 2012 revaluation surplus trf		2.240		
1 Nov 2012 acc depn Cost based depn 2011			0.240	
1 Nov 2012 acc depn w/b				0.286

[1]
Asset cost	12.000
Depreciation year 1 ($12m /50)	0.240
	11.760
Revaluation	14.000
Revaluation surplus	2.240

[1]
Asset cost	12.000
Depreciation year 1 ($12m /50)	0.240
	11.760
Revaluation	14.000
Revaluation surplus	2.240

[2] Any gains or losses on adjustment when adopting IFRS 1 must be accounted for in retained earnings.

> **Tutorial note:** the above adjustments may also be shown in journal entry form as follows:

Note. Carrying value under domestic GAAP:

As at 1 Nov 2011: $12m × 49/50 $11.760m
As at 1 Nov 2012: $14m × 48/49 $13.714m

1   Using fair values at 1 Nov 2012 as deemed cost

	Dr $m	Cr $m
PPE: manufacturing property at NBV ($15m – $13.714m)	1.286	
Retained earnings		1.286

Being adjustment of carrying value to fair value at 1 Nov 2012

Revaluation surplus ($14m – $11.760m)	2.240	
Retained earnings		2.240

Being reversal of initial revaluation at 1 Nov 2011

2   Applying IAS 16 cost approach retrospectively

Revaluation surplus (as in note [1] above)	2.240
Manufacturing property ($14m – $12m)	2.000
Accumulated depreciation: depn for 2011 ($12m/50)	0.240
Being reversal of revaluation adjustment at 1 Nov 2011	
Accumulated depreciation ($14m × 1/49)	0.286
Retained earnings	0.286
Being reversal of depreciation based on initial revaluation at 1 Nov 2011	
Accumulated depreciation	0.240
Retained earnings	0.240
Being cost based depreciation for y/e 31 Oct 2012	

Question 26

This question concerns IFRS 16 *Leases*. It requires a report to be prepared showing how to account for a sale and leaseback, the impact of leases on gearing ratios and discussion of the impact of the new standard.

It is applicable to syllabus sections 13.1, 13.2 and 13.4. The appropriate BPP Study Text chapters are:

Chapter 15 *Leasing contracts*

Chapter 23 *Ratio and trend analysis*

(i)   IFRS 16 *Leases* contains an exemption for low value items. Personal computers and tablets are given as an example of low value items in IFRS 16. They meet the criteria for the exemption because Olco can benefit from use of the assets on their own or together with other resources that are readily available (eg publicly available software).

Rather than applying the usual accounting treatment of recognising right-of-use assets and lease liabilities, Loco can recognise the lease payments in the contract on a straight-line basis over the lease term of three years. (Another systematic basis would also be allowed if it were more representative of the pattern of the consumption of benefits but in this case a straight line basis would seem to be most appropriate.)

Deferred income balance (SoFP)		40.0
Leased assets	110.7	
Lease obligation		110.7
($27m annual rent × 4.100 [discount factor])		
During the year ended 30 April 2013		
Lease obligation: rental payments	27.0	
Cash		27.0
Finance cost: profit or loss	7.75	
Lease obligation		7.75
($110.7 × 7%)		
Depreciation: profit or loss	22.14	
Lease asset accumulated depreciation		22.14
($110.7/5)		

(ii)

Accounting entries	$m
Opening obligation	1.000
Rental (paid in advance)	(0.286)
Obligation during the year	0.714
Interest at 9.7%	0.069
Closing obligation	0.783

Tutorial note: note use of implicit rate of interest above and not Olco's borrowing cost.

Accounting entries

	Current $000	Buy $000	Lease $000
Operating profit (+ 12% increase)	400	448	448
Finance charge	–	(150)*	(69)**
Depreciation	–	(250)	(250)
Rental			
Adjusted profit	400	48	129

*$1m × 15%
**See calculation above

	Current $000	Buy $000	Lease $000
Share capital	2,000	2,000	2,000
Long term debt	1,000	1,000	1,000
Loan to purchase assets		1,000	
Lease obligation			783
Capital employed	3,000	4,000	3,783
Gearing ratios	0.5:1	1:1	0.89:1
ROCE	13.3%	1.2%	3.4%

IAS 17 was introduced to counteract off-balance sheet financing by requiring the capitalisation of finance leases. These finance leases affect gearing and ROCE. As shown above, the use of operating leasing rather than finance leasing has a beneficial impact on ROCE. The attractiveness can be seen in the above ratios which show 5.4% ROCE when using operating leasing and 3.4% when using finance leasing. The use of IAS 17 can therefore affect key accounting ratios of a company. Operating leases are not capitalised and continue to act as a form of off-balance sheet finance. The impact of a leasing decision on a company's financial ratios can therefore be significant.

(iii) Problems with IAS 17 Leases

IAS 17 allows different accounting treatments for operating and finance leases. It is generally thought that IFRS should not allow multiple treatments in any circumstance; but IAS 17 has been criticised on a number of specific points:

1 the classification of operating and finance leases can sometimes be arbitrary (eg over the definition of 'substantially all' as mentioned in (ii) above). This can result in what appear to be similar transactions being accounted for differently; this, it is argued, leads to lack of transparency.

2 The above difference in accounting treatment makes it possible for directors to structure lease contracts so as to achieve a desired result rather than a substantive one.

3 Many analysts and other users of financial statements believe that any lease contract which exists at a balance sheet date gives rise to assets and liabilities – and that this thinking is consistent with the definitions of assets and liabilities contained in the IASB's *Conceptual Framework*. They should therefore appear on that balance sheet. Analysts routinely make adjustments for such items when making investment decisions.

IFRS 16 changes and impact on Olco

IFRS 16 fundamentally changes the accounting for leases. All leases will be recognised on the balance sheet at lease commencement – this is the 'right-of-use model'. Olco would not have to distinguish between operating and finance leases and would recognise an asset for the right to use the asset (eg the fleet of vehicles) and a liability to make rental payments. In the circumstances this would not change the company's current accounting.

However, the proposal contains a key factor which, when measuring Olco's lease asset and lease liability, may have an impact depending on the lease contract terms: the lease term would be the non-cancellable lease period plus any renewal periods for which there is a significant economic incentive for Olco to exercise the renewal option. This may apply for instance to the unique hotel.

Question 27

This question requires the application of knowledge to a scenario concerning segmental reporting and the writing of a report to advise a company's directors. The main issues are to do with the inclusion/exclusion of common costs and assets and liabilities in the segment report and the identification of segments for reporting purposes. The question is drawn from syllabus section 13.4. The relevant BPP Study Text chapter is:

Chapter 18 *Reporting financial performance*

Allocation of common costs, assets and liabilities

Measurement

There is the potential for a mismatch between the internal information presented to a chief operating decision maker (CODM) for decision making and that presented externally in a company's IFRS-compliant financial statements. There is no requirement in IFRS 8 that the two are similar. Rather, IFRS 8 requires the amounts reported in the segmental reports to be on the same basis as those used by the CODM. It appears that Mondo complies with that requirement. Any significant differences must be reconciled; eg where segment assets are reported, between reported assets and the entity's assets as reported in the statement of financial position.

The IFRS prohibits the segmental reporting of any items unless that measure is used by the CODM for determining resource allocation and for assessing performance. However, the IFRS does not prescribe the reporting treatment of common costs and common assets. Instead – and as such reporting could have a significant effect on segment analysis – the IFRS requires that the allocation is made on a reasonable basis. In this respect:

- *Central head office service costs*: would best be allocated on the basis of turnover as head office staff spend time on strategic duties in proportion to the turnover of each segment.

- *Property management costs*: would be best allocated on the basis of the age of properties as such costs accrue in close proportion to that age.

- *Post employment service costs*: would be best allocated on the basis of pensionable employees in each segment.

- *Loan interest*: IFRS 8 does not require symmetry between revenues and expenses included in segment results and the assets and liabilities allocated to segments. The IFRS simply requires disclosure of the nature and effect of any asymmetrical allocations. Another example would be where depreciation of the head office is included in segment results but the depreciated asset is excluded. In the absence of any indication of how best to allocate interest costs, they have been allocated on the same basis as central head office costs.

Allocation

	Basis	Tuedo $m	Wedon $m	Thurso $m
Profit/(loss)		(26)	176	100
Central head office costs (eg Tuedo $380m/$1,730m × $17m)	Turnover	(4)	(5)	(8)
Property management costs (eg Wedon 10yrs/30yrs × $30m)	Age of property	(5)	(10)	(15)
Post-employment service costs (eg Thurso 300/500 × $20m)	Pensionable employees	–	(8)	(12)
Loan interest (eg Tuedo $380m/$1,730m × [$20m × 6%])	Turnover	(0.3)	(0.3)	(0.6)
Adjusted profit/(loss)		(35.3)	152.7	64.4

Recognition and reporting of reportable segments

Qualitative criteria

All three segments meet IFRS 8's qualitative criteria for an operating segment. These are that:

- It engages in a business activity from which it earns revenues and incurs expenses;
- Its operating results are regularly reviewed by a chief operating decision maker with respect to making decisions about resource allocation and performance; **and**
- Discrete financial information is available for the segment (IFRS 8.5)

Quantitative criteria

Once the segments have been identified as above, the IFRS requires the application of quantitative criteria to determine whether each segment should be reported separately. If **any** of the following apply then the segment is reported separately (IFRS 8.13):

- Reported revenue is 10% or more of the combined (internal and external) revenue of all operating segments; or
- The segment's reported profit or loss, in absolute terms, is 10% or more of the greater of:
    (i) The combined profit of all operating segments that did not report a loss; or
    (ii) The combined loss of all operating segments that reported a loss; or
- Its assets are 10% or more of the combined assets of all operating segments.

Applying the above quantitative criteria to:	Tuedo	Wedon	Thurso
Reported revenue	√	√	√
Combined profit	√	√	√

Note: combined profit = $217.1m [10% = $21.7m] and combined loss = $35.3m [10% = $3.53m]. so $21.7m is the benchmark

| Combined assets | x | √ | √ |

As only one of the criteria has to be satisfied, all segments count to be reported separately

Reporting of information about geographical areas of trading and major customers.

Geographical areas

IFRS 8 requires revenues from external customers and non-current assets (excluding financial assets, deferred tax assets, post-employment benefit assets and rights arising under insurance contracts) to be classified into those attributed to Mondo's own country of domicile and those attributed to all foreign countries (IFRS 8.33).

Therefore, Mondo must disclose the following information:

	External sales $m	Non-current assets*
Attributed to:		
Country of domicile	420	300
All foreign countries	1,310	4,910
	1,730	5,210

*assuming there are none of the assets mentioned above.

In addition, if revenues from external customers or assets attributed to an individual foreign country are material, separate disclosure of that country's revenues or assets is required (IFRS 8.33). The IFRS does not define what is meant by 'material' but given that 10% is used for other purposes, it is reasonable to assume the same percentage can be used for this purpose. Mondo sells $260m of goods to one country. As this is 15% of external sales, Mondo should disclose the name of the country and the amounts involved.

Reporting of information about major customers

IFRS 8 would require Mondo to give information showing the extent of its reliance on major customers (IFRS 8.34). Mondo sold $200m of goods to Tuedo's former owners. As this is more than 10% of total sales, Mondo should disclose:

- The fact
- The amount involved
- The reportable segment involved; ie Tuedo.

Note. Mondo does not have to disclose the name of the customer – although several companies do so!

Question 28

This question concerns the application of fair values. IFRS 13 *Fair Value Measurements* became effective from 1 January 2013, so part (a) requires the provision of advice to a PLC and a discussion about the likely changes that will be seen in the reporting of assets and liabilities in financial statements and is drawn from syllabus section 13.1. Application of fair value is covered throughout the BPP Study Text but is covered in most detail in Chapter 6 *Revision of basic groups*. Part (b) requires application of IFRS 13 to a scenario involving the measurement of a dismantling obligation assumed in a business combination. It is drawn from syllabus sections 13.2 and 13.3.

(a) **Definition of fair value**

IFRS 13 defines fair value (FV) as 'the price that would be received to sell an asset or paid to transfer a liability in an orderly transaction between market participants at the measurement date' (IFRS 13 Appendix A). This is sometimes referred to as 'exit price' – as in US GAAP. With the publication of IFRS 13, FV definition, its measurement and disclosure requirements are now aligned between IFRS and US GAAP.

The previous definition used throughout IFRS was 'the amount for which an asset could be exchanged, or a liability settled, between knowledgeable, willing parties in an arm's length transaction. This produced difficulties for an entity such as Seph when deciding on FV in that 'exchange' could imply exit or entry price, 'settled' implies the liability is extinguished – when in fact it may still exist, albeit transferred, and 'arm's length transaction' has been replaced by 'market participants' to focus measurement more specifically on an independent market-based price.

Measurement of fair value

The FV of an asset or liability is to be a market-based and non entity-specific exit price (IFRS 13.B2). So Seph would only be allowed to use entity-specific prices in very restricted circumstances – as explained below in 'valuation techniques'.

The market-based nature of the price means it takes into account current market conditions when measuring those assets and liabilities. So, for instance, if Seph held a financial asset, the price will be the amount the asset **could** be sold for or, if Seph held an issued bond, the price would be the amount Seph **could** pay to transfer it to someone else.

Due to the market-based nature, the measure of the item (asset or liability) must take into account the characteristics of that item and the assumptions made by market participants. It is assumed that transactions will take place in the **principal market** in which an orderly transaction for the item would take place or, in its absence, the most **advantageous** market.

The principal market is the market with the greatest liquidity (in terms of volume and level of activity for that item). If there is no principal market, the price in the most advantageous market would be used; ie the market in which Seph could achieve the most beneficial price; eg by maximising the amount received or minimising the amount paid. If market activity is in decline, then IFRS 13 recognises that valuation techniques (see below) may have to be used to measure FV; although in such a case it would have to be determined whether this still represented an orderly sale (eg a forced sale would have to be accounted for outside the FV requirements). Although the price may have to be adjusted if costs are incurred to transport an asset to the principal (or most advantageous) market, transaction costs would not be included in fair value because such costs are not a characteristic of the asset or liability.

Non-financial assets

The fair value measurement will consider the use to which the asset can be put. The measurement takes into account the ability of a market participant to generate economic benefits by using the asset in its highest and best use. Unless market factors dictate otherwise, the IFRS envisages that Seph's current use of a non-financial asset reflects its highest and best use. In doing so, Seph must consider whether the asset is used in combination with other assets or on a stand-alone basis and whether the use of the asset is physically possible, legally permissible and financially feasible.

Valuation techniques

When transactions are directly observable in a market, the determination of FV is relatively straightforward, but when they are not, a valuation technique is used. IFRS 13 describes three such valuation techniques:

- The **market approach** uses prices and other relevant information generated by market transactions involving identical or comparable assets or liabilities,

- The **income approach** converts future amounts (eg cash flows or income or expenses) to a single current amount (using present value techniques), and

- The **cost approach** determines a value which reflects the amount that would be required currently to replace the service capacity of an asset (also known as current replacement costs).

The technique chosen should be consistently applied to maximise the use of relevant observable inputs and minimise unobservable inputs. There are three levels of inputs as follows:

Level 1   These are fully observable (eg unadjusted quoted prices in an active market for identical assets and liabilities that Seph can access at the measurement date).

Level 2   These are directly or indirectly observable but exclude level 1 inputs; eg quoted prices for **similar** assets in active markets, prices for similar or identical assets in non-active markets or quoted rates used for valuation purposes.

Level 3   These are unobservable inputs; eg Seph's own assumptions about selling prices.

Disclosures

IFRS 13 requires a number of quantitative and qualitative disclosures about FV measurements. Many are related to the three-level hierarchy shown above on the basis of their input to the valuation techniques adopted. This requirement already exists for financial instruments under IFRS 7, but is extended to other assets and liabilities (within its scope) by IFRS 13.

Disclosure requirements may also depend upon whether the FV measurement is **recurring** (other IFRSs require or permit FV in the SoFP at the end of each reporting period) or non-recurring (other IFRSs require or permit in the SoFP in particular circumstances); eg if an entity is using recurring FV measurements using level 3 unobservable inputs, it must disclose the impact of those measurements on profit or loss or other comprehensive income.

(b) **Background**

The fair value (FV) of a liability is determined on the assumption that the liability would be transferred on the measurement date but would remain outstanding; ie it is a transfer value and not an extinguishment/settlement cost. The FV of the obligation must take into account non-performance risk (the risk that Seph will not fulfil its obligation) and Seph's own credit risk. As a level 1 (observable) price is not available to Seph to assess the liability's transfer value, the entity must measure its FV from the perspective of a market participant that owes the liability, using a valuation technique (IFRS 13.40).

Seph is contractually allowed to transfer the obligation to a market participant but, even if it had not been, IFRS 13 does not allow a separate input into the valuation exercise to reflect this. The effect of the restriction would be either implicitly or explicitly included in other inputs into the FV price (IFRS 13.45–46).

Seph assesses long-term liabilities on a cost-plus basis – hence the need for the calculations to include separately, the return for the undertaking and the risk premium. If the assessment had been on a fixed-fee basis, for example, these two inputs would have been indistinguishable.

Calculation		$m
Expected labour cost	$20m × 30% + $25m × 40% + $35m × 30%	26.50
Overheads	$26.50 × 90%	23.90
		50.40
Contractor's profit mark-up	+ 20%	10.08
		60.48
Inflation	×	1.553
		93.93
Market risk premium	+ 5%	4.70
		98.63
Discount rate 9%	×	0.422
PV of expected cash flows using discount rate of 9%		41.62

Question 29

This question concerns employee benefits. IFRS devotes considerable attention to them in two standards – IFRS 2 *Share-based Payment* and IAS 19 *Employee Benefits* – which applies to all other employee benefits. Part (a) of the question requires calculations of (i) the amounts to be included in the statement of comprehensive income (SOCI) re a defined benefit scheme, (ii) and (iii) the amounts to be included in the SOCI and statement of financial position re share-based payments and termination benefits respectively. Part (b) requires a discussion of the controversies related to IFRS2 and recognition of an appropriate accounting treatment. Questions cover syllabus sections 13.1 and 13.4.

(i)

Impact of transactions on statement of comprehensive income (SOCI)	$'000
Actual contribution by Bee to the scheme	–

> **Tutorial note:** Under IAS 19 contributions to defined benefit schemes are a movement between line items in the statement of financial position; ie the reduction in cash for Bee is reflected by an increase in the scheme assets. Hence there is no effect on the SOCI.

Net service cost (115 – 106)		9

> **Tutorial note:** the present value of employees' contributions attributable to the period, reduce the cost of the benefits to the entity (IAS 19.92)

Net interest cost [10% × (266 – 256)]		1
Past service cost		20

> **Tutorial note:** past service costs would have been included in the net scheme obligation as at 1 November 2014 so there is no need to charge an interest cost on them for the current year.

To be recognised in profit or loss		30
Remeasurement loss		
To be recognised in other comprehensive income under the title 'Items that will not be reclassified to profit or loss'.		17

(ii)

	Calculation of cumulative liability	Cum. liability $'000	Expense for the year $'000
Year 1	5,000 options × 9 × $20 × 1/3	300,000	300,000
Year 2	5,000 options × 10 × $20 × 2/3	666,667	366,667
Year 3	5,000 options × 12 × $20	1,200,000	533,333

(iii)

> **Tutorial notes:**
>
> The number of staff members who leave during Years 1 and 2 are not relevant to the calculation of the cumulative liability as it is based upon the number who Bee **expects** to stay for the whole vesting period. However, they are taken into account in estimating the number of options that will finally vest at the end of Year 3.
>
> Total expected cash flows are $9.6m [(1,000 × $6K + 900 × $4K (10 – 6)]
>
> IAS 19 requires that termination benefits, paid regardless of whether the employee stays and renders service, should be provided for as a liability immediately. This should be at the earlier of when the plan is announced and when the entity recognises the relevant restructuring costs. In this question we assume that is 1 October 2015.

Liability to recognise at 31 Oct 2015: 1,000 employees × $6,000   6.0m

> **Tutorial note:** Under IAS 19 that part of the termination plan which relates to benefits received as a result of providing service must be recognised incrementally as short-term benefits (because they are payable within 12 months). No discounting is required.

Liability to recognise at 31 Oct 2015:
900 emp'ees × incremental benefit $4,000 (10 – 6) / 6 months   0.6m
                                                                      6.6m

The FD's opinion on share-based payment (SBP)

SBP is a very controversial subject as it usually involves the issue of shares and option to employees, most commonly senior management, as remuneration. It is usually undertaken by entities in an attempt to align the employees' economic interests with those of the shareholders.

Usually, the SBP does not entail a cash cost to the entity. However, there is a cost to shareholders (as identified by the FD) through dilution of their shareholdings. There developed a consensus amongst investors therefore that such awards (which amount to remuneration for the employee) should be recognised in the financial statements. Despite a great deal of opposition particularly in the USA, the IASB eventually published IFRS 2 *Share-based Payment* in February 2004. IFRS 2 supports the views of investors. The FD's view therefore does not comply with current IASB thinking.

Treatment in the Bee Group financial statements

The award would be accounted for as an equity-settled transaction; ie the cost would be recognised in the group SOCI and in the group SOFP as a movement in equity. This is because the parent **group** receives services as consideration for its own equity.

Treatment in the separate financial statements of Bee

Bee **as a separate entity** does not receive the services of Sac's employees nor does it have an obligation to settle the transaction. It is not therefore within the scope of IFRS 2 and would not be accounted for.

Treatment in the separate financial statements of Sac.

The award is accounted for as a cash-settled transaction because Sac has the obligation to settle the award with assets (ie equity held in Bee) rather than with Sac's own equity.

> **Tutorial note:** Sac is granting the award as a principal (ie not as an agent of Bee). If Sac was granting the award under instructions from Bee (ie as an agent) it is likely that it would be accounted for as an equity-settled transaction.

Question 30

This question concerns environmental and social reporting involving financial reporting and narrative reporting. It is taken from sections 13.1 and 13.4 of the syllabus and is covered in BPP Study Text chapters:

3   Environmental and social reporting
19 Provisions, contingencies and events after the reporting period

(a) (i) Under IAS 37, an entity must recognise a provision if, and only if:

- The amount can be measured reliably
- Cash outflow is probable, and
- A present obligation (legal or constructive) exists which has arisen as a result of a past obligating event.

As industry experts have estimated the clean up costs, it can be assumed that the first criterion is satisfied in all three situations.

In **country 1** no law exists which would require Sideel to rectify any contamination. Also, Sideel's environmental stance would suggest that a constructive obligation does not exist as the entity only rectifies contamination if it has a legal obligation to do so. A provision would therefore be inappropriate.

In **country 2** a law exists requiring a clean up by Sideel. The second two criteria are satisfied and therefore a provision of $10 million is required adjusted, if appropriate, to reflect the time value of money.

Although in many cases it will be impossible to be virtually certain of the enactment of a law until it is actually enacted (IAS 37.22), as a date has been set for enactment by **country 3** it is virtually certain that a law will be enacted which will require clean up of the land already contaminated. The virtual certainty of the new law being enacted means that a cash outflow is probable and that Sideel has a present legal obligation as a result of the past contamination. A provision of $15 million is required adjusted, if appropriate, to reflect the time value of money.

(ii) The benefits to Sideel of producing a separate social and environmental report (SER) concern stakeholder communication and in particular its impact on any stakeholder wishing to make an overall assessment of the group's performance. The process by which an SER is produced would also help to identify inefficiencies in its management systems. These benefits can be outlined as follows:

- Sideel's market share in the oil industry could be increased if it is seen to be a more attractive supplier than its competitors. The publication of more detailed performance information would increase customer confidence. An SER would be attractive to customers as those customers themselves are under increasing pressure by their own stakeholders to deal only with 'environmentally friendly' suppliers. There would be a competitive advantage from disclosure.

- Investors are becoming increasingly concerned about risks to the sustainability of operations in the oil industry. A report produced with sufficient and high quality information about mitigation of those risks by Sideel would make the group more attractive to investors.

- There is a growing international demand for transparency in the reporting of sustainability. If Sideel wishes to continue the development of operations internationally it will have to improve its corporate image. An SER would be just the vehicle to help achieve this.

- Sideel has a very poor reputation as a corporate citizen. Production of a social and environmental report would help foster better relations with local communities and foster better community support for its activities.

- Sideel's environmental stance is bound to annoy regulators. By producing an SER and perhaps identifying ways in which its environmental performance may be improved, the entity's relationship with regulators would be improved.

- The process by which an SER is produced would help Sideel to identify inefficiencies in its operations and thereby improve its management information system. This would have the additional benefit of helping to identify opportunities to reduce costs and use of resources.

(b) Under IAS 37 a contingent liability is a possible obligation or a present obligation that is not recognised. A present obligation would not be recognised if either it is not probable that an outflow of resources will be required to settle it or because the amount of the obligation cannot be measured with sufficient reliability. A contingent liability is disclosed unless the chance of occurrence is remote.

Sideel has a possible obligation only and, as it is not remote (say less than a 5% chance of occurrence), under IAS 37 the amount should be disclosed in the notes to the accounts.

Question 31

(a) **This question involves the determination of the fair value of an asset. It requires a decision as to the entity's principal market. It refers to syllabus section 13.4 and is drawn from BPP Study Text chapter:**

11   Interim reporting, first-time adoption and fair values

IFRS 13's fair value measurement assumes that the transaction to sell the vehicles will take place in Krz's principal market [PM] or (in its absence) in the most advantageous market for that asset. (IFRS 13.16).

While the perspective of the entity is considered when determining the PM, the decision is based upon overall market volume or level of activity for the asset in question. It is not based upon the volume or level of activity of Krz's own transactions in that market. Applying these criteria, the PM is clearly Europe as it has a greater volume of activity for the vehicles in question (70%). This is despite Krz selling more of its vehicles in America and despite its most advantageous market (because of the higher net profit of $53K [see below]) being Asia.

	America $000	Europe $000	Asia $000
Price per vehicle	60	50	56
Transaction costs per vehicle (eg commissions)	6	2	1
Costs to transport each vehicle to the market	2	2	2
Net profit	52	46	53

An entity may have more than one PM for identical assets if for example different units *within* the entity have different exit strategies for the assets. However, this does not appear to be relevant to this question. Therefore, if FV is to be measured on the basis of one principal market it would not be appropriate to value identical assets at different FVs because Krz's management intend to sell them in three different markets. Nor would it be appropriate to use a FV averaged over the three markets. Rather, the vehicles should be measured on the basis of the FV in the market determined to be the entity's PM; ie Europe.

IFRS 13 is clear that transaction costs are not to be included in the determination of fair value (IFRS 13.25–26). The FV of the vehicles will therefore be $48,000 × 1,000 = $48m.

(b) **This question involves accounting for events after the reporting period and concerns the valuation of investment property at fair value and the tenant's insolvency. It refers to syllabus section 13.4 and is drawn from BPP Study Text chapter:**

19   Provisions, contingencies and events after the reporting period

The vehicle showroom would be shown in Krz's SoFP as an investment property. The fair value of investment property reflects, amongst other things, the quality and reliability of the tenant's covenants to meet the rental payments due.

IAS 40 *Investment Property* would require that Krz recognise the property's market conditions when assessing its FV at the 30 April 2014. This would not normally involve hindsight. The insolvency of Buz would not normally therefore be an adjusting event to the carrying value of the showroom. Unless there are circumstances to the contrary (which does not appear to be the case in this question) the showroom property would still hold a value in the market. IAS 10 states quite clearly that a decline in the market value of investments after the reporting period and before the date on which the financial statements are authorised for issue, is a non-adjusting event as the condition does not normally relate to conditions existing at the end of the reporting period (IAS 10.11–12,22). The showroom would continue to be carried on the SoFP at $20m.

However, the event will be an adjusting one in relation to the amount due from Buz at 30 April 2014. The financial statement should therefore be amended by the write off of the $1m owing by Buz.

(c) **This question involves accounting for deferred tax when an asset has been revalued to fair value. It refers to syllabus section 13.4 and is drawn from BPP Study Text chapter:**

17   Taxation

Year ended	Carrying amount of asset in SoFP $m	Tax base of asset $m	Temp timing diff $m	D tax liability @30% $m	Movement in D tax liability $m	D tax charge in SoPL and OCI $m	D tax impact on revaluation reserve $m
30.4.2012[1]	8.00	7.50	0.50	0.15	0.15	0.15	–
30.4.2013	6.00	5.00	1.00	0.30	0.15	0.15	
30.4.2014[2]	9.00	2.50	6.50	1.95	1.65	0.15	1.50

Tutorial note: remaining years for information							
30.4.2015	4.50	–	4.50	1.35	(0.60)	(0.60)	(0.75)
30.4.2016	–	–	–	–	(1.35)	(1.35)	(0.75)

[1] Carrying amount depreciation based on $10m/5 years
Tax base allowance based on $10m/4 years

[2] As at 30 April 2014 the asset will be revalued from $4m to $9m. Therefore $5m in fair value gain will be transferred to revaluation reserve (via SoPL&OCI). The deferred tax impact on the fair value gain will be $5m × 30% = $1.5m.

Question 32

This question is draw from syllabus sections 13.1 and 13.4. It requires knowledge and application from BPP Study Text chapters:

1 Current thought and practice
11 Interim reporting, first-time adoption and fair value (re IFRS 1 *First-time Adoption of IFRS*)
17 Taxation

(a)

> **Tutorial note:** as Ding has adopted IFRS for the first time, we should first calculate what the deferred tax liability would be under IFRS.

	Note	SoFP carrying value $m	Tax Base $m	Temporary differences $m
Goodwill ($153m – $129m)	1	24	–	–
PPE	2	50	12	38
Health care benefits		(70)	–	(70)
Other temporary differences			–	120
				88
The above differences are provided for at Ding's tax rate of 30%				**26.4**
Subsidiary's net assets		129	102	27
Inter-company unrealised profit ($50m × 20%)	3	40	50	(10)
				17
The above differences are provided for at the subsidiary's tax rate of 25%				**5.1**
Total deferred tax liability of the Ding Group as at 31 Oct 2013				**31.5**
Less opening liability per IAS 12 (given in question)				12.0
Increase in deferred tax liability				19.5
The increase in the liability will be accounted for as follows:				
Dr Goodwill (on acquisition of subsidiary) [$27 × 25%]				6.75
Dr Revaluation reserve (and reported in OCI) [$30m × 30%]				9.00
Dr Taxation in profit or loss (balance)				3.75
				19.50

Notes

1. In the subsidiary's tax jurisdiction, goodwill is not allowed as a deduction for tax purposes. Its tax base is therefore zero. Theoretically, goodwill therefore gives rise to a temporary difference that would result in a deferred tax liability as it is an asset with a carrying value in the group accounts and a zero tax based. However, IAS 12 specifically excludes a deferred tax liability being recognised for goodwill.

2. When PPE is revalued within the financial statements, the revaluation surplus is recorded in equity and reported in other comprehensive income. Whilst the carrying value increases, the tax base remains the same and so a temporary difference arises. Tax will become payable on the surplus when the PPE is sold. Since the surplus has been recognised within equity, the tax charge on the surplus is also charged to equity.

	Carrying value (cost – accumulated depreciation) $m	Tax base (cost – accumulated capital allowances) $m	Temporary difference $m
Opening balance at 1 Nov 2012	30	24	6
Depreciation/capital allowances	(10)	(12)	2
Revaluation	30	–	30
Closing balances	50	12	38

3. When inventories are sold between group companies and remain in inventory of the buying company at the year end an adjustment is made to remove the unrealised profit from the group accounts. This adjustment reduces inventory to its original cost to the group. However, the inventory's tax base is based on the subsidiary's individual financial statements and so will be higher; ie at the transfer price. To this extent a deferred tax asset will arise. Recognition of this asset and the reduction in the tax expense of the group ensures that the tax already charged to Ding is not reflected in the group income statement but will be matched against the future period when the inventory is finally sold. The unrealised profit is included as a liability at the receiving company's tax rate.

(b) IAS 12 requires that deferred tax assets and liabilities should be measured using the tax rates that are expected to apply when the asset/liability is recovered/settled. Normally, current rates are used in the calculation on the basis that estimates of future rates may be too unreliable and that current rates are a reasonable estimate of future rates. As deferred tax assets/liabilities represent events that will take place in the future, it is reasonable to expect that they would be discounted to present values using rates which reflect the time value of money – this is an approach used for other types of liabilities; eg rectification costs under IAS 37. However, IAS 12 does not allow the discounting of deferred tax amounts on practical grounds; ie the liability reflects many different timing differences and calculating a present value for each would be too difficult.

IAS 12's statement of financial position approach (ie deferred tax is calculated using differences between statement of financial position carrying values and tax bases) does not appear to be consistent with the *Conceptual Framework's* recognition criteria, as it is not clear whether the resultant deferred tax asset or liability satisfies its definition of an asset or a liability. Meeting the definition of one of the elements of the financial statement is one of the recognition criteria in the *Conceptual Framework*. It is applied to satisfy matching criteria (eg Ding has recognised a deferred tax liability of $9m to reflect the future tax payable when the revaluation gain of $30m is realised). However, as there is not a present obligation to sell the asset, there is not a present obligation to pay tax. The deferred tax liability therefore does not satisfy the *Conceptual Framework's* definition of a liability. IAS 12 is therefore inconsistent with the *Conceptual Framework*.

EXAM ANSWER BANK

Question 33

A time series analysis of the results of a potential takeover target using financial ratios.

Syllabus section: 13.2

The following suggested solution is indicative only.

REPORT

FROM:
TO:
DATE:

SUBJECT: Financial performance of Choggerell

The following report is based on a series of financial ratios calculated from the financial statements of Choggerell for the financial years 20X6, 20X7 and 20X8.

The overall performance of Choggerell as evidenced by its return on equity has fluctuated. There was a significant improvement from 20X6 (13%) to 20X7 (22%) due to improvements in profitability on trading (net income to sales revenue).

That improvement in overall efficiency was not maintained in 20X8 and return on equity declined to 19%. This time the decrease was due to a significant decline in asset utilisation which at 2.01 is now at its lowest for the three year period. Profitability on trading was maintained – although there was a marginal decline.

Earnings per share have followed a similar pattern to return on equity. There was a very significant rise in earnings per share for 20X7 – but this was followed by a small decline in 20X8. Dividends per share, however, have been maintained in 20X8 after a significant increase in 20X7.

Changes in the profitability on trading over the three year period seem to be attributable to steadily increasing margins on sales (decreasing cost of sales relative to sales). However, progress here seems to have been offset by increases in operating expenses (operating expenses to sales revenue).

Control of working capital does not seem to have been optimal. The current and acid test ratios have fluctuated but were the lowest for the three years in 20X8. Inventory turnover has been falling for the past three years and the period of credit taken by customers has increased significantly. This suggests possible liquidity problems and there seems to have been a significant overdraft at the end of 20X6 and 20X8. The period of credit taken from suppliers has increased significantly in 20X8 and is now an average of two months which may invite pressure from suppliers for faster payment.

The fall in efficiency in the use of assets to generate sales (sales revenue to total assets) and the increasing net assets per share would therefore appear to be a result of increasing non-current assets and possible poor working capital management.

Recommendations for improving the performance of Choggerell

The overall performance of Choggerell could be improved by:

- Better control of operating expenses. Reducing operating expenses would increase profitability on sales and hence overall return on equity.

- Careful monitoring of non-current asset utilisation. Increasing sales revenue to non-current assets would increase sales revenue to total assets and hence overall return on equity.

- Careful cash flow management to avoid widely fluctuating cash balances and the reliance on bank overdrafts.

EXAM ANSWER BANK

Limitations

- It has been assumed that all the data is comparable ie that similar accounting policies have been used over the three years.

- It has only been possible to look at trends within Choggerell over the past three years. It would be useful to compare Choggerell's performance with its competitors – particularly the leading firms in the same industry sector with a view to knowing what is achievable.

- It would be useful to know more about the sector Choggerell operates in and general economic conditions. This would help identify what changes are attributable to changes in sector performance and general economic conditions and what are attributable to good or bad management.

- The available information is very limited. It would be useful to have additional information about the quality of Choggerell's management, its risk exposure and the prospects for the industry sector.

Question 34

This question draws on Section 13.1 Contemporary Issues. This material is covered in Chapter 15 of the BPP Study Text. The question deals with the implications of the changes to lease accounting, as set out in IFRS 16. Candidates are required to compare the new rules to those of IAS 17.

(a)

> **Tutorial Note:** This question requires an understanding of the implications of IFRS 16, which is not yet in force. IFRS 16 applies to accounting periods beginning on or after 1 January 2019. It is important to stay up to date with current developments. The IASB website is an excellent source.

On 31 December 2017, the lease will have 11 years to run. There is a break point in the contract as at 1 January 2019, but it seems likely that the lease will run to its agreed term.

If IFRS 16 is to be implemented early for the year ended 31 December 2017 then we should focus on the position as at 1 January 2017, when the lease had 12 years to run.

We do not know the fair value of the asset or the interest rate implicit in the lease, so we use Poole's marginal borrowing rate to give a net present value of the lease liability.

At 1 January 2017, there will be an immediate payment of $500,000, followed by an eleven year annuity, with the next payment due on 1 January 2018. The value of the asset and liability were $500,000 + $500,000 × 7.139 = $4,069,500.

The financial statements will show a finance charge for the year of 7% × ($4,069,500 – 500,000) = $249,865 and a closing current liability of $500,000 and a non-current liability of $500,000 × 7.139 = $3,569,500.

(b)

> **Tutorial Note:** The new standard cannot affect the actual financial position, but it can change the manner in which it is reported and understood by users of the financial statements.

Under IAS 17 *Leases* Poole's classification of the lease as an operating lease is probably justifiable. The risks and rewards of ownership are likely to remain with the lessor and so Poole has not been required to capitalise the lease.

Under IAS 17 the lease payments would simply be written off as an expense as and when paid. The impact of an early adoption of IFRS 16 is that the payments will have to be split between interest and capital. There will also be an amortisation of the right of use that would be capitalised as an asset. The overall impact on reported profit may be very small, but there could be some changes to the recognition pattern from year to year, with more interest being charged in early years.

The early adoption will also increase Poole's gearing because of the lease liability. That is probably the most significant implication.

(c)

> **Tutorial Note:** It is important to be aware of the estimates and assumptions required by different accounting standards. It may be that the accounting entries are relatively straightforward and that the principal issues arising from implementation are the responsibility of other professionals.

Determining the interest rate implicit in the lease would require an appreciation of the fair value of the asset and the asset's expected life in order to determine the rate that is effectively being charged by the lessor. Property values can vary significantly and valuations have proved controversial in the past. The lack of an open and observable market makes it difficult to ensure that the valuation has been conducted accurately.

The estimation of an interest rate may require insights and understandings that the lessor regards as confidential. Divulging that information could have an impact on the lessor's relationship with the lessee and could make the lease payments appear to be poor value.

(d) Early adoption could be viewed as a demonstration of integrity and professional competence on the part of the preparer. The publication of a new IFRS is frequently motivated by concerns that there has been malpractice in a particular area. The new standard should have the effect of improving the quality of the information in the financial statements. It is probable that early adoption will enhance the transparency and accountability of the company, which is clearly an ethical and professional act. It is also likely that early adoption will be perceived as an indication of openness and integrity by the board.

There is a danger that the early adoption might confuse readers of the financial statements, who do not realise that the entity's financial statements are not prepared on the same basis as before and are not directly comparable with similar companies that have not adopted early.

Question 35

(a) **This question is drawn from part 13.4 of the syllabus and concerns the calculation of group basic and diluted earnings per share. It requires application of knowledge from BPP Study Text Chapter 19.**

> **Tutorial note:** The earnings figure on which basic eps is calculated should be the consolidated net profit or loss for the year after tax, non-controlling interests and after adjusting for returns to preference shareholders if necessary (ie if not already included in the income statement). For diluted eps, IAS 33 *Earnings per Share* requires that we start with the basic earnings figure and reflect any changes that would arise if the potential shares outstanding in the period were actually issued. (IAS 33.33).
>
> Potential ordinary shares are only to be treated as dilutive if their conversion to ordinary shares would **decrease** eps (or increase loss per share) from **continuing** operations. In other words, the earnings used in the calculation should be those **before** any profit or loss from discontinued operations.

Step 1: *Judging the cumulative impact of potential shares*

> **Tutorial note:** Where an entity has a variety of **potential** ordinary shares, in deciding whether they are dilutive (ie are included in the calculation) or antidilutive (ie ignored in the calculation), each item must be considered in sequence from the most to the least dilutive. Only those items which produce a cumulative dilution are included in the calculation. We must therefore perform a calculation to show which is the most and which is the least dilutive.

EXAM ANSWER BANK

	Increase in earnings $m	Increase in number of ordinary shares m	Earnings per incremental share $
Options			
Increase in earnings	nil		
Increase in shares			
400,000 × ($80 − $60)/$80		0.1	nil
Convertible preference shares			
Increase in earnings			
(1.6m × $0.1)	0.16		
Increase in ordinary shares			
(1.6m × 2)		3.2	0.05
6% convertible bonds			
Increase in earnings			
(200m × 6% × (1 − 0.3 tax))	8.4		
Increase in shares			
(200,000 × 20)		4.0	2.1

The order in which to include the dilutive instruments is therefore:

1. Most dilutive: options
2. convertible preference shares
3. Least dilutive: convertible bonds

Step 2: *calculation of basic and diluted eps*

	Profit from continuing operations attributable to ordinary equity shareholders of parent entity $m	Ordinary shares m	Per share $	
As per draft accounts				
($12m + $8m)	20.0	4.0	5	
Options	–	0.1		
	20.0	4.1	4.88	dilutive
Convertible pref shares	0.16	3.2		
	20.16	7.3	2.76	dilutive
Convertible bonds	8.40	4.0		
	28.56	11.3	2.53	dilutive
Basic group eps			**$5.0**	
Diluted group eps			**$2.53**	

(b) This question is drawn from syllabus section 13.2 and concerns whether or not non-GAAP performance KPIs provide valuable information. It is covered by BPP Study Text Part A 'Contemporary issues' and Part C: Chapter 19 *Reporting financial performance.*

Entities in industries such as telecommunications often have numerous and complex income streams. A one-size-fits-all GAAP approach therefore seems an inappropriate way for management to report performance. For that reason, demand has grown for custom-made performance measures which supplement (rather than replace) the GAAP earnings measure disclosed by management. Typically, a non-GAAP measure would exclude non-cash (eg fair value adjustments) and one-off (eg restructuring provisions) items.

This is not a new phenomenon and has been discussed by regulators (eg the US SEC and UK FRC) for decades; often with dire warnings of the potential confusion for users. The information is not only published in regulated statements but in narrative reports and press briefings. The confusion arises because it is often difficult to discern the motives behind the non-GAAP measures. On the one hand the exclusion of unusual items may actually improve transparency by, for example, making it easier for Verti and its competitors to compare across firms and over time. The non-GAAP information may also be used to provide a link between information in the regulated statements and the actual performance calculations on which users such as investors often typically rely. On the other hand, allowing management free-rein over what to publish gives them the opportunity to indulge in earnings management, which is both inappropriate and unethical. It is no coincidence that, typically, the excluded items will be expenses.

In entities such as telecom companies, there is clearly a place for the non-GAAP reporting of those KPIs used by management, possibly in private, to direct and manage the entity. However, there is also a place for regulated information to avoid management acting opportunistically. This is an example of the classic conflict between relevance and reliability.

As investors are likely to concentrate on the (usually) higher non-GAAP KPI of an entity, it is entirely possible that an entity such as Verti, not indulging in non-GAAP reporting, would lose competitive advantage. Perhaps the way forward is for regulators to insist on the publication of reconciliations between non-GAAP and regulated KPIs.

(c) **This question is drawn from syllabus section 13.1** (as updated for 2016) **and concerns the International Integrated Reporting Council's (IIRC) framework for corporate reporting.** (It is not yet covered by BPP Study Texts but should be for the updated 2016 syllabus.)

It is argued that capital providers are interested in so much more than simply financial returns on their investment. An integrated report (IR) would set out how Verti's strategy, governance, performance and prospects leads to the creation of value. It will be very different from the entity's present traditional corporate reporting which concentrates primarily on financial performance. The aim of the IR would be to explain to Verti's capital providers how the entity creates value over time. The term 'capital providers' is very wide and would include employees, customers, suppliers, business partners, local communities, legislators, regulators and policymakers; as well as the traditional providers of financial capital.

Verti's historically-based financial statements would still be essential, particularly for compliance purposes, but they are unlikely to provide meaningful information regarding business value. It is argued that users and capital providers need a more forward-looking focus which attempts to present a fuller, more holistic view of the entity's activities. To achieve this, the framework will encourage Verti to prepare a report that shows the entity's performance against targets and strategies, explains how the various capitals are employed and affected by those activities and presents a more long-term view of the entity's organisation and activities.

It is often said that the compliance-led approach under IFRS is 'boilerplate' in execution and that an IR will provide information more business relevant than at present. An IR would not **replace** Verti's present form of reporting but would pull together information already produced to explain, and help users to assess, the key drivers of value creation. Information not material to this assessment would not be reported. It is possible that the IR could be prepared in response to the IASB's non-mandatory IFRS Practice Statement *Management Commentary* (issued in December 2010) which is a non-binding framework for the presentation of narrative reporting to accompany financial statements prepared under IFRS. The IR could be published either as a stand-alone document or included in the entity's financial statements.

The report would include traditional performance information but would also include the following key components: organisational overview and the external environment under which the entity operates, governance structure, business model, risks and opportunities, strategy and resource allocation, achievement of key objectives and outlook and challenges.

Entities such as Verti struggle to communicate value through traditional reporting. The IR could prove to be a useful tool for an entity wishing to shift its reporting focus from traditional annual performance to long-term stakeholder value creation. The IR would be useful to companies such as Verti who wish to develop their engagement with capital providers by developing their narrative reporting around their business model to explain how the business has been developed.

Mock exam 1 questions and answers

MODULE E

PAPER 13 - FINANCIAL ACCOUNTING 3

MONDAY 27th NOVEMBER 2017

Time allowed - 3 hours

SECTION A
This question is compulsory

SECTION B
Any THREE questions to be answered

(FOUR questions in all)

Clear workings should be submitted with all your answers.
All calculations should be made to the nearest $ (or $000) as appropriate.

You are allowed an additional 15 minutes reading time before the exam begins, during which you should read the question paper and, if you wish, make notes on the question paper. You are **not** allowed to open the exam script booklet and start writing or use your calculator during the reading time.

Tutorial note: Please note that this paper has not been amended in line with subsequent changes to IFRS.

Section A

This question is compulsory and must be attempted

1 Holld

Holld is a quoted company that manufactures household goods. Holld has investments in Targ and Voce. The statements of financial position of Holld, Targ, Voce and Assk as at 30 September 2017 are shown below.

	Holld $m	Targ $m	Voce $m	Assk $m
Investment in Targ	1,780			
Investment in Voce	370			
Investment in Assk			50	
Property, plant and equipment	1,000	2,000	500	380
	3,150	2,000	550	380
Current assets	260	120	90	50
	3,410	2,120	640	430
Equity				
Share capital	2,100	1,600	200	120
Retained earnings	1,200	500	400	280
	3,300	2,100	600	400
Current liabilities	110	20	40	30
	3,410	2,120	640	430

(i) Holld purchased 80% of Targ's issued equity on 1 October 2010 for $1,980m. At that time, Targ's retained earnings were $200 million. The non-controlling interest in Targ was valued at its share of the company's net assets.

Holld sold a 10% holding in Targ to a third party on 1 October 2016 in return for a cash payment of $200 million. At that date Targ's retained earnings were $450m. Holld debited the cash received to bank and credited Investment in Targ. No other entries were made.

(ii) Holld purchased 70% of Voce on 30 September 2012 at a cost of $370m. On that date Voce's retained earnings were $70m. The non-controlling interest in Voce was valued at its share of the company's net assets.

(iii) Voce acquired 30% of Assk on 30 September 2013. At that date, the company's retained earnings were $80m. Voce has demonstrated that it has the ability to exert significant influence over Assk.

Required

(a) Prepare the consolidated statement of financial position for the Holld Group as at 30 September 2017. **(35 marks)**

(b) Discuss your treatment of Voce's investment in Assk in the Holld Group consolidated financial statements. **(5 marks)**

(Total 40 marks)

Section B

Attempt ANY THREE questions

2 Wax

The directors of Wax have asked for your advice on the use of fair values in the preparation of their financial statements.

The company owns a piece of land in the town where its head office is located. That land was purchased by Wax for $50,000 in 1970, when the company's founder wished to celebrate the company's first ten years in business. The land was landscaped and set aside as a public park for all of the townspeople to enjoy.

Since 1970 Wax has become a public company and has been quoted on the stock exchange. Despite that, it still retains the piece of land.

Wax's directors have been debating the application of fair value accounting to the land.

- Similar plots of land in similar locations can be purchased on the open market for $2 million.
- When Wax was negotiating a bank loan recently, the bank offered to accept the land as collateral against which to secure the full value of the loan, which was for $5 million.
- A local property expert believes that the land could be sold on the open market for $6 million.
- Wax's board believes that if the company spent $10 million on development, the land could be converted to a shopping centre worth $30 million.

Wax's directors have found the concept of fair values difficult ever since IFRS 2 *Share-based Payment* required Wax to recognise the fair value of the instruments issued under the company's executive share options scheme.

Required

(a) Discuss the difficulties associated with determining the fair value of this land to Wax, taking account of the requirements of IFRS 13 *Fair Value Measurement*. **(10 marks)**

(b) Discuss the difficulties associated with determining the fair value of executive share options under IFRS 2. **(10 marks)**

(Total 20 marks)

3 Oliver

Oliver is a qualified accountant who is employed by Zanger, an unquoted company that manufactures electronic components. Zanger operates from a single, large factory that is the largest employer in Corrtown.

Oliver is assisting with the preparation of Zanger's annual report for the year ended 30 September 2017. The company has had a difficult year and it has sustained large losses that have pushed its gearing ratio close to the upper limit imposed by a debt covenant. If the debt covenant is breached then the bank will be entitled to foreclose on the loan, which will put Zanger out of business.

Oliver has conducted an impairment review of the equipment in Zanger's factory. In his opinion, the equipment is impaired and an adjustment should be made. He reported his findings to Zanger's Finance Director, who congratulated him for his thoroughness, but then asked him to destroy all working papers relating to the impairment review and to delete any files on his laptop. The Finance Director said that the impairment adjustment would put Zanger in breach of its debt covenant and would cause the bank to put the company out of business.

The Finance Director reminded Oliver that the local economy in Corrtown relies on Zanger. Apart from those employed in Zanger's factory, many others work for small business that provide Zanger with goods and services. Local retailers depend on Zanger's employees to remain viable. Those who own their own homes will be unable to pay their mortgages and house prices will slump, creating massive financial difficulties.

Required

(a) Evaluate the ethical dilemma faced by Oliver and advise him on how he should respond to the Finance Director's request. **(12 marks)**

(b) Critically analyse the assertion that it is often difficult for accountants to identify the public interest. **(8 marks)**

(Total 20 marks)

4 Papa Drey

Papa Drey supplies the confectionary industry with high quality ingredients. Demand can be seasonal and sales are often heavier in the last few months of the year.

In March 2017 Papa Drey purchased 5,000 tonnes of premium cocoa beans for $7,500,000, with the intention of keeping those beans until they could be sold to a manufacturer in December 2017.

Papa Drey's finance director was worried that cocoa prices might fall before the beans could be sold on the open market, so she entered into a forward contract to sell the beans for $8,000,000 on 1 December 2017.

At Papa Drey's year end of 30 September 2017, the market price of cocoa was $1,400 per tonne for immediate delivery and $1,560 per tonne for delivery on 1 December 2017.

On 1 December 2017, Papa Drey sold the cocoa at its market price of $1,555 per tonne.

Required

(a) Advise the Board of Papa Drey on whether hedge accounting would be appropriate for the above arrangements. **(7 marks)**

(b) Evaluate the effects that hedge accounting would have on the interpretation of Papa Drey's financial statements. **(4 marks)**

(c) Assuming that hedge accounting is to be applied, recommend the journal entries that would be required in Papa Drey's bookkeeping records during each of the years ended 30 September 2017 and 2018. **(9 marks)**

(Total 20 marks)

5 Tronto

Tronto has recently acquired its first subsidiary company, Lantak. The two companies' statements of financial position as at 30 September 2017 were as follows:

	Tronto	Lantak
	$'000	$'000
Property, plant and equipment	570	100
Current assets	444	130
	1,014	230
Share capital ($1 shares, fully paid)	240	120
Retained earnings	690	90
	930	210
Current liabilities	84	20
	1,014	230

Throughout the month of September 2017, Tronto's share price was selling for approximately $6.20 and Lantak's was selling for approximately $2.20.

Tronto's Board announced an offer on 30 September 2017. It offered to exchange one fully paid share in Tronto for every two shares in Lantak. This offer was open until the end of October 2017 and was conditional upon Tronto obtaining at least 80% of Lantak's issued shares.

Tronto's share price rose to $6.50 on the day that the offer was announced and Lantak's rose to $3.20. Both share prices remained steady throughout October 2017.

Tronto acquired 90% of Lantak's shares on 31 October 2017. New shares were issued, with administrative and other costs of $4,000.

Tronto's share price fell to $6.30 by 6 November 2017.

Required

(a) Prepare the financial statements for Tronto as at 6 November 2017, assuming that there have been no further transactions in addition to those shown above. You are NOT required to prepare consolidated financial statements for the Tronto Group. **(7 marks)**

(b) Justify your valuation of the purchase consideration in Tronto's books. **(7 marks)**

(c) Advise Tronto on the difference that would have arisen if it had exchanged one share in Tronto for every four shares in Lantak. Assume that all of the other facts are unchanged. **(6 marks)**

(Total 20 marks)

[End of question paper]

MODEL ANSWERS

MODULE E

PAPER 13 - FINANCIAL ACCOUNTING 3

MONDAY 27th NOVEMBER 2017

Valid alternative points, whether or not they are shown in the Model Answers, will be given credit where appropriate.

1 Holld

This question draws on material from Section 13.2 of the syllabus The Financial Statements of Groups. This material is covered in Chapters 7 and 8 of the AIA text. It focuses on the adjustments required by reductions in the shareholding in a subsidiary and in accounting for a subsidiary having an associate.

(a) *Workings*

> **Tutorial note:** In a complicated consolidation question, it is usually easier to deal with each group member separately.

Workings relating to Targ

> **Tutorial note:** The key to accounting for a partial disposal, where control is retained, is to present it almost as a transaction between the parent company and the NCI in the subsidiary.

Goodwill on initial acquisition of Targ	
Consideration	1,980
Share of net assets acquired	
share capital = 80% × 1,600	1,280
Retained earnings = 80% × 200	160
	1,440
Goodwill	540
NCI before disposal	
share capital = 20% × 1,600	320
retained earnings = 20% × 450	90
	410
NCI after disposal	
share capital = 30% × 1,600	480
retained earnings = 30% × 450	135
	615

MOCK EXAM 1 ANSWERS

NCI increase =	205	
Equity adjustment = 200 – 205	(5)	
Closing NCI		
share capital = 30% × 1,600	480	
retained earnings = 30% × 500	150	
	630	

Workings relating to Voce

> **Tutorial note:** When a subsidiary has an associate then the NCI is entitled to a share of the associate's net assets.

Goodwill on acquisition of Voce		
Consideration	370	
Share of net assets acquired		
share capital = 70% × 200	140	
retained earnings = 70% × 70	49	
	189	
Goodwill	181	
Investment in Assk		
Consideration	50	
Group share of post-acquisition profit = 30% × (280 – 80)	60	
Investment in associate	110	
NCI = 30% × 30% × (280 – 80) =	18	

Workings for combined figures to appear in the consolidated statement of financial position

Retained earnings		
Holld		1,200
Targ		
Up to disposal	200	
Post disposal	35	
Adjustment	(5)	
		230
Voce		
Group share of post acq	231	
Associate	42	
		273
		1,703
NCI		
Targ		
2,100 × 30%		630
Voce		
600 × 30%		180
Associate		18
		828

MOCK EXAM 1 ANSWERS

Solution
Holld Group
Consolidated statement of financial position
As at 30 September 2017

	$m
Goodwill	721
Property, plant and equipment	3,500
Investment in associate	110
Current assets	470
	4,801
Share capital	2,100
Retained earnings	1,703
	3,803
NCI	828
	4,631
Current liabilities	170
	4,801

(b) First of all, we need to establish the relationship between Assk and Voce. Voce has a 30% shareholding, which we would normally assume to mean that Voce has significant influence. That makes Assk Voce's associate.

Next, we have to consider the Assk's place within the Holld Group. Holld has a controlling interest in Voce, which means that Holld has the same degree of significant influence over Assk as Voce does. That suggests that Holld should treat Voce as an associate under the requirements of IAS 28 *Investments in Associates*.

The entries for accounting for Assk are the same as in any other vertical consolidation. We calculate the proportion of all equity and other balances that are attributable to Holld, allowing for all NCI in the intermediate levels. So, we take the NCI in Voce into account when calculating the figures.

> **Additional areas where credit might be given, note this is not an exhaustive list:**
>
> - Credit will be awarded for any further arguments that address the question of Assk's status as an associate of Holld and of the values attributed to that group member in the consolidated financial statements.

2 Wax

This question draws on Section 13.4 of the syllabus Accounting and reporting techniques. This material is covered in Chapters 11 and 20 of the AIA text. It requires candidates to consider the difficulties associated with accounting for fair values.

(a) The basic problem is that Wax has permitted the land to be used as a public park for more than 40 years. Presumably, it yields little economic value to the company, other than as a source of positive publicity. As a public park it does not, in itself, yield any revenues and so the land's fair value would be close to zero as long as it remains in that role.

MOCK EXAM 1 ANSWERS

Presumably, the land remains Wax's property and must be available for redevelopment for business purposes, otherwise the bank would be unwilling to accept it as collateral. The valuation is probably on the conservative side because lenders are usually keen to value assets on the understanding that they can be realised quickly at that price.

IFRS 13 asks for the fair value to be determined in terms of the principal market for that asset. We have at least two possibilities because similar plots can be purchased for $2 million, but a higher value has been suggested for this specific property. Presumably, the $2 million valuation is for plots of a similar size in either the same or a similar town. The principal market for Wax's land should be the market for this specific plot, taking into account such factors as proximity to transport links, suitability for development and so on.

There is the further question of whether the value of the land should take into account the possibility of redevelopment as a retail site. IFRS 13 requires that it be valued at its highest and best use. Spending $10 million on the land would increase its value to $30 million, which suggests that it could be valued at the $20 million net. The only real condition would be that this basis would depend on the land being suitable for such development and there would have to be a realistic belief that redevelopment would be permissible.

> **Tutorial note:** Fair values can often only be fully understood when put in the particular context in which the question has been raised.

> **Additional areas where credit might be given, note this is not an exhaustive list:**
> - Credit will be awarded for any valid discussion that relates to the requirement. Candidates could, for example, discuss the disparity between the various values attached to the land according to the scenario. There could also be issues concerning the objectivity of specific values (eg sales of similar plots in the area have observable selling prices whereas valuation reports are matters of opinion).

(b) IFRS 2 requires that shares issued as payment should be valued in terms of the fair value of the goods or services received. Unfortunately, when the shares are used to reward employees as a part of a remuneration scheme then there is no realistic way to measure the value of the services received in return for the shares. The skills applied by the directors cannot be evaluated apart from the assets and other resources that they use to generate wealth. There is no objective way to measure the value of the work done by the directors, even by looking at the going rates offered for similar work by other companies.

The requirements of IFRS 2 impose a duty to report an estimated value, even though that estimate may be unreliable and open to challenge. The financial statements must, however, still present fairly.

The biggest problem with determining the fair value of executive share options (ESOPs) is that they tend to have a number of specific features that means they differ from the options that are commonly traded on the open market. For example, there is usually a vesting period during which the right to the ESOPs might lapse. For example, a director may lose all rights to ESOPs that have been granted but not yet vested in the event of termination of employment. Further complications include the possibility that an ESOP can often only be exercised on a specific date at the end of the vesting period, which makes them even less comparable to traded options.

There are valuation models that can be used to give at least a defensible valuation for an option. For example, the Black Scholes model is frequently applied in order to estimate the value of the options. Unfortunately, there is no objective basis on which to evaluate the accuracy of the resulting prices. Indeed, IFRS 2 sets out a number of bases that are to be applied in the event that there is no directly comparable market price.

> **Tutorial note:** The basis for a critique of any accounting standard boils down to basic questions, such as the potential conflict between relevance and reliability.

> **Additional areas where credit might be given, note this is not an exhaustive list:**
> - Credit will be granted for additional points or expansion. For example, the applicability of Black Scholes to ESOPs is open to doubt because the conditions attached to ESOPs differ materially from those attached to traded options. There could also be motivational issues, such as board members being keen to undervalue ESOPs for the sake of making their remuneration appear less generous.

3 Oliver

This question draws on Section 13.1 of the syllabus Contemporary Issues. This material is covered in Chapter 4 of the AIA text. It requires candidates to consider the ethical implications of financial reporting by addressing an ethical dilemma.

(a) The basic ethical dilemma is that Oliver has a duty to the users of the financial statements to report truthfully. However, that duty is in conflict with the fact that a truthful report will lead to the company's failure and the associated impact on the company's employees and the economy of the town in which the company is based. It could be argued that the interests of the employees and the bank are in conflict. If Oliver makes an honest report then the bank will be able to act to withdraw its funds from Zanger while it still can. But a dishonest report will enable Zanger to keep its staff in full employment.

The dilemma is complicated by the fact that the accounting issues that will affect the outcome are a matter of professional judgement. In the event that the impairment problem comes to light, Oliver and the remainder of Zanger's management team could easily deny that they had been aware of the matter.

Oliver has a clear ethical duty to act with integrity, which requires behaviour that is straightforward and honest. The fact that he has been instructed to destroy documents that would otherwise incriminate him and his colleagues clarifies the extent of the dishonesty that is being considered. He should also act with objectivity, which means that the accounting treatment of the asset in question should be considered without regard to the implications of that decision.

Oliver could risk bringing the accountancy profession into disrepute, because he is a qualified accountant and must demonstrate professional behaviour. At best, he will appear negligent if problems arise with the financial statements and, at worst, he will appear fraudulent if the circumstances come to light.

It could be argued that Oliver's dilemma is less complicated than it appears. He could prepare the financial statements correctly and then ask the bank to consider a sympathetic response to the breach of the debt covenant. It is not necessarily a foregone conclusion that the funding will be withdrawn and the bank may be keen to support Zanger rather than go through the disruption of foreclosure proceedings.

> **Tutorial note:** There is no ethical dilemma unless there are two or more conflicting interests. There are alternative approaches to resolving ethical dilemmas, but focussing on the Fundamental Principles set out in the IESBA Handbook will always be applicable.

> **Additional areas where credit might be given, note this is not an exhaustive list:**
> - Credit will be awarded for any valid approach to the identification of the ethical dilemma and its resolution. In particular, the IESBA Code implied by the suggested answer is clearly a valid starting point for evaluating ethical dilemmas, but there are other ways in which ethical behaviour can be identified and supported.

(b) There is no single "public interest" that can be measured or evaluated in the light of different decisions. Society has a variety of needs and those needs may come into conflict. There can be pressing needs at a local level that undoubtedly impact upon the public interest, but they may affect society as a whole in a different manner. For example, keeping these employees in secure jobs is in the public interest. Unfortunately, publishing misleading figures and undermining confidence in the professionalism of accountants is against the wider public interest.

The concern is that there may be conflicting effects that make it difficult to tell whether the public interest has suffered any net gain or loss. For example, suppose Zanger dismissed Oliver and published misleading financial statements. Oliver might feel that it would be against the public interest to remain silent and to leave the bank ignorant of the breach of the breached debt covenant. Having said that, any report will put him in breach of the duty of confidence, which would undermine the accountancy profession's credibility and would harm the public interest in the process. Also, if Oliver makes his concerns known then he will risk undermining the reputation of accountants and the accountancy profession simply by drawing attention to an "accounting scandal".

Protecting the public interest may be further complicated by the fact that it is not always clear how interested parties will be affected. For example, misleading the bank about the debt covenant will not necessarily expose it to loss. The bank will almost certainly have other safeguards in place to protect it against default and so the technical breach of the gearing limit may not create any specific risk. Having said that, the discovery of this breach could undermine the banking industry's confidence in accounting numbers and that could damage the wider public interest by making it more difficult for companies to obtain credit.

Overall, deciding how best to protect the public interest often requires a very delicate balance.

> **Tutorial note:** It is important to understand the role that financial accounting might play within society.

> **Additional areas where credit might be given, note this is not an exhaustive list:**
> - Credit will be awarded for any relevant expansion of the arguments concerning the public interest. Candidates may offer further practical or hypothetical illustrations.

4 Papa Drey

This question draws on Section 13.4 Accounting and Reporting Techniques. This material is covered in Chapter 14 of the AIA text. The question deals with the issues associated with accounting for a fair value hedge.

(a) The first question is whether Papa Drey wishes to apply hedge accounting. Strictly, hedge accounting is mandatory when all of the conditions apply, but one key condition is that the hedge relationship has to be documented at the outset. If the board chooses not to designate a hedging relationship then hedge accounting is not applicable.

There are conditions that must be met before hedge accounting can be applied. There must be an eligible hedging instrument and an eligible hedged item or items. This condition appears to have been satisfied because the hedging instrument will fix the selling price of the commodity and Papa Drey has an asset whose value is being hedged.

As noted above, Papa Drey must have documented the hedging relationship. We do not know whether that is the case, but the finance director's intention was that the forward contract would hedge the cocoa beans and so it would have been a simple matter to designate this relationship.

MOCK EXAM 1 ANSWERS

There are also effectiveness criteria that must be considered. The first is that there must be an inverse economic relationship. In this case, if the value of the cocoa beans falls below $8 million the forward contract will become more valuable. The hedge relationship will be effective.

> **Tutorial note:** The decision to apply hedge accounting is effectively a matter of accounting choice.

> **Additional areas where credit might be given, note this is not an exhaustive list:**
> - Credit will also be awarded for the arguments against the applicability of hedge accounting. Arguments based on IAS 39 will also be accepted.

(b) Without hedge accounting, the company would be faced with the potential need to report a loss on any decrease in value of the cocoa beans. That would decrease profits for the year ended 30 September 2017. The gain on the forward contract would be recognised in other comprehensive income and carried forward in reserves, so it would do nothing to offset the loss on the cocoa. The profit on the instrument would then be realised when the cocoa was sold in the year ended 30 September 2018.

Hedge accounting will have the effect of reducing the volatility in Papa Drey's reported profits. The readers of the financial statements will have a more realistic understanding of the impact of movements on commodity prices.

> **Tutorial note:** It is very difficult to understand accounting standards without first appreciating what impact they will have on the interpretation of the resulting financial statements.

> **Additional areas where credit might be given, note this is not an exhaustive list:**
> - Credit will also be awarded for any discussion of the reported profit. Candidates might also elaborate on risk and volatility issues.

(c) The inventory cost $7,500,000. On 30 September 2017 the inventory had a net realisable value of $1,400 × 5,000 = $7,000,000, so there was a loss of $500,000.

The gain on the forward contract at 30 September 2017 = $8,000,000 − (1,560 × 5,000) = $200,000.

The settlement of the forward contract will yield a cash receipt of $8,000,000 − (1,555 × 5,000) = $225,000.

The financial asset will have increased by $25,000

	$	$
Year ended 30 September 2017		
Loss on cocoa		
Statement of profit or loss	500,000	
Inventory		500,000
Gain on forward		
Financial asset	200,000	
Statement of profit or loss		200,000
Year ended 30 September 2018		
Sale of cocoa		
Bank	7,775,000	
Statement of profit or loss – Revenue		7,775,000
Statement of profit or loss – Cost of sales	7,000,000	
Inventory		7,000,000
Financial asset	25,000	
Statement of profit or loss		25,000
Bank	225,000	
Financial asset		225,000

> **Tutorial note:** Totalling the various debits and credits that will be taken to the statement of profit or loss gives us ($500,000) + 200,000 + 7,775,000 − 7,000,000 + 25,000 = $500,000. That is a reassuring double check, because the cocoa beans originally cost $7,500,000 and were to be sold at a price that had been fixed at $8,000,000.
>
> Notice that the forward contract is settled with cash, with the amount and direction of the cash settlement depending on the difference between the contract and market prices. Papa Drey would not literally deliver the 5,000 tonnes of cocoa beans to the counterparty.

5 Tronto

This question draws on Section 13.3 Business Combinations. This material is covered in Chapter 6 of the AIA text. The question deals with the issues associated with the parent's separate financial statements.

(a) *Workings*

Shares issued = 90% × 120,000/2 = 54,000
Fair value = 54,000 × $6.50 = $351,000
Share capital = $240,000 + 54,000 = $294,000
Share premium = $351,000 − 54,000 − 4,000 = $293,000

Tronto
Statement of Financial Position
As at 7 November 2017

	$'000
Property, plant and equipment	570
Investment in Lantak	351
Current assets	440
	1,361
Share capital ($1 shares, fully paid)	294
Share premium	293
Retained earnings	690
	1,277
Current liabilities	84
	1,361

Presentation

> **Tutorial note:** Take care to read the requirements. A common error is to offer group financial statements, even though those have not been requested.

(b) IFRS 3 requires that the consideration should reflect the fair value as at the date of acquisition. In this case, it is complicated by the fact that the price was lower before the exchange was announced. That suggests that the fair value of Tronto's shares was $6.20 and that the $6.50 reflects the company's value after it has acquired its interest in Lantak. The decrease in the share price immediately after acquisition further suggests that the share price had been artificially boosted beyond its intrinsic value because of the speculation surrounding the negotiations.

Despite these concerns, the market price as at the date of the acquisition was used as the fair value because it is an objective and relevant measure. The danger is that basing the calculation on a different date could adjust the share price for factors that have nothing to do with the acquisition and could simply introduce a spurious element into the calculation. The question of what constitutes the fair value of a share will always be complicated when the share price is volatile. The fact that the price has remained constant at a certain level in the past does not mean that price movement is a temporary deviation from an underlying intrinsic value.

> **Additional areas where credit might be given, note this is not an exhaustive list:**
> - Credit will also be awarded for any wider discussion of the values. There are potential discussions to be had of the other figures that have been listed in the scenario.

(c) If the number of shares was halved then this would be a bargain purchase. The fair value of the shares issued would be $351,000/2 = $175,500. The book value of the net assets acquired would be 90% × $210,000 = $189,000. The fact that Lantak's shares are trading at a premium over their nominal value suggests that the book value of the assets is more likely to be understated than overstated.

If this is a bargain purchase then Tronto will have to ensure that it has correctly identified all of the liabilities due by Lantak and that all of the assets have been valued in a realistic manner. The expectation in IFRS 3 is that any bargain element is likely to imply an error in the calculations underpinning the goodwill figure.

If there is a bargain element then it will result in negative goodwill on the acquisition. That should be eliminated by debiting goodwill and crediting profit for the year.

> **Additional areas where credit might be given, note this is not an exhaustive list:**
> - Credit will be awarded for any further discussion, particularly of the evaluation of whether this really is a bargain purchase.

Mock exam 2 questions and answers

MODULE E

PAPER 13 - FINANCIAL ACCOUNTING 3

MONDAY 21st MAY 2018

Time allowed - 3 hours

SECTION A
This question is compulsory

SECTION B
Any THREE questions to be answered

(FOUR questions in all)

Clear workings should be submitted with all your answers.
All calculations should be made to the nearest $ (or $000) as appropriate.

You are allowed an additional 15 minutes reading time before the exam begins, during which you should read the question paper and, if you wish, make notes on the question paper. You are **not** allowed to open the exam script booklet and start writing or use your calculator during the reading time.

Tutorial note: Please note that this paper has not been amended in line with subsequent changes to IFRS.

Section A

Question ONE is compulsory and must be attempted.

1 Arvo

Arvo is a quoted company that has grown significantly in recent years due to its acquisition strategy. The individual statements of financial position for the members of the Arvo group are shown below as at 31 March 2018:

	Arvo $m	Becco $m	Como $m	Disueri $m
ASSETS				
Non-current assets				
Property, plant and equipment	165	36	30	40
Investments (at fair value):				
Becco	90	–	–	–
Como	–	24	–	–
Disueri	15	–	–	–
	270	60	30	40
Current assets	70	20	15	15
Total assets	340	80	45	55
EQUITY AND LIABILITIES				
Equity				
Share capital – $1 equity shares	50	10	5	5
Retained earnings	95	25	15	12
Other components of equity	40	10	–	5
Total equity	185	45	20	22
Non-current liabilities	100	20	15	16
Current liabilities	55	15	10	17
Total equity and liabilities	340	80	45	55

The following information is relevant:

1 Arvo acquired 90% of the equity shares in Becco on 1 April 2016 for $72 million in cash. The fair value of Becco's net assets at 1 April 2016 was $50 million, which included retained earnings of $18 million and other components of equity of $2 million. The difference between the fair value of the net assets acquired and the book value relates to leasehold property which had a remaining useful life of 20 years at 1 April 2016.

It is group policy to measure the non-controlling interest at fair value at the date of acquisition. The fair value of the 10% non-controlling interest in Becco was $8 million at 1 April 2016.

2 On 1 April 2017, Becco acquired an 80% stake in Como for $20 million. The fair value of the net assets acquired was $20 million, which included retained earnings of $10 million (Como had no other components of equity). The difference between the fair value of the net assets acquired and the book value relates to non-depreciable land. The fair value of the non-controlling interest was valued at $5 per share at the date of acquisition.

3 Arvo acquired 10% of the equity in Disueri on 1 April 2017 for $2 million. On 31 March 2018, Arvo acquired an additional 50% stake in Disueri for $12.5 million. At 31 March 2018, the fair value of Disueri's net assets were equal to their book values and no fair value adjustments were required. The fair value of the 40% non-controlling interest in Disueri on 31 March 2018 was $10 million.

4   It is group policy to record all investments at fair value through other comprehensive income in accordance with IFRS 9 *Financial Instruments*. The investments shown in the above statements of financial position were correctly recorded at fair value at 31 March 2018, and the resulting fair value gain has been included in other comprehensive income.

On 31 March 2018, the fair value of each $1 equity share was:

	Market value per $1 equity share $
Becco	10
Como	6
Disueri	5

5   During the year ended 31 March 2018, Como sold goods for $10 million and $5 million to Arvo and Becco respectively at a 25% mark up. As at 31 March 2018, half of these goods remained unsold and have been included in the closing inventory of Arvo and Becco.

6   On 2 January 2018, Como acquired inventory from an overseas supplier for €5 million and the invoice remained unpaid at the year end. Como had correctly recorded the transaction on 2 January 2018, but no further entries have been made.

The following exchange rates are relevant:

02.01.2018	€1 = $1.20
31.03.2018	€1 = $1.30

7   On 1 April 2017, Arvo issued 20 million $1 zero coupon redeemable bonds at par value and included the $20 million cash raised in non-current liabilities. The bonds are redeemable in five years' time at a 20% premium.

Issue costs of $1 million were incurred and these have been written off to profit or loss in the year. No further entries have been made in the year in respect of these bonds. The effective rate of interest for the bonds has been calculated at 4.8% per annum.

8   An impairment review was conducted on 31 March 2018, and it was decided that the goodwill arising in Becco and Como should be impaired by $10 million and $2 million respectively. The goodwill created on the acquisition of Disueri remains unchanged.

Required

(a) Prepare the consolidated statement of financial position for the Arvo group as at 31 March 2018.

All calculations should be shown to the nearest $0.1 million. Ignore any deferred tax consequences of consolidation. **(35 marks)**

(b) Having reviewed the above consolidated statement of financial position for the year ended 31 March 2018, Arvo's directors are concerned that the group appears close to current borrowing covenant limits. The managing director has read that IAS 32 *Financial Instruments: Presentation* permits the offsetting of financial assets and liabilities (ie presented as a single amount), and has instructed you to debit non-current liabilities and credit consolidated goodwill with $30 million. He proposes that this adjustment is appropriate in the group accounts since the investments in Como and Disueri were both financed by borrowings in the year.

Advise Arvo's managing director on the ethical implications of the proposed reclassification of non-current liabilities in the financial statements for the year ended 31 March 2018.

(5 marks)

(Total 40 marks)

SECTION B

Attempt any THREE questions

2 Fusaro

Fusaro is a quoted company specialising in digital software solutions. In the year ended 31 March 2018, the directors have entered into several transactions for the first time. The directors are unsure of the accounting treatment of these items, including any deferred tax consequences, and require your advice on the following:

(1) Fusaro granted 1,000 $1 equity share options to each of its 100 staff on 1 April 2017. The share options vest in three years' time, on 31 March 2020, provided that the employees still work for the company. The fair value of each share option at 1 April 2017 is $6 per share.

On 1 April 2017, the directors anticipated that 25% of the relevant employees would leave the company within the three-year vesting period, and would forfeit their rights to the share options. At 31 March 2018, the directors reassessed the expected number of leavers and revised their assumption to 20%.

In the country that Fusaro operates tax relief is given on the intrinsic value of the shares at the date of exercise. At 31 March 2018, the intrinsic value of the share options was calculated at $9 per share. **(7 marks)**

(2) On 1 April 2017, Fusaro introduced a new retirement benefit scheme. Under the terms of the scheme, Fusaro will contribute 7% of the total remuneration expense into the pension scheme on behalf of its employees. Fusaro's obligations are limited to its annual contribution to the fund each year, and the employees pension will be solely dependent on the performance of pension fund.

Total staff remuneration for the year ended 31 March 2018 was $5 million, and Fusaro had paid $200,000 into the pension fund by 31 March 2018.

Tax relief on pension contributions are deductible on a cash basis. **(5 marks)**

(3) On 1 July 2017, Fusaro acquired 100% of the equity share capital of Garda, for $2 million. The investment was held at cost in Fusaro's own single company financial statements as permitted under IFRS 3 *Business Combinations*.

For the purposes of the consolidated financial statements, Fusaro performed a fair value exercise and determined that the fair value of Garda's identifiable net assets was $1.5 million on 1 July 2017. This fair value included customer contracts with a fair value of $0.5 million, which were not recognised in Garda's own financial statements. The tax base of the identifiable net assets acquired was equal to their accounting values, with the exception of the customer contracts, whose tax base was nil. No entries have been made for the deferred tax on the fair value adjustment at the date of acquisition.

The customer contracts were deemed to have a useful life of five years at 1 July 2017. **(8 marks)**

Assume a tax rate of 20% applies throughout.

Required

Advise the directors on the accounting treatment, including any deferred tax consequences, of items (1) – (3) above in Fusaro's consolidated statements for the year ended 31 March 2018.

(Total 20 marks)

3 Iseo

IFRS 16 *Leases* will replace IAS 17 *Leases* for accounting periods commencing on or after 1 January 2019 (although early adoption is permitted). Under IFRS 16 *Leases*, the inconsistencies in the treatment of operating leases and finance leases have been removed and replaced by a single lessee accounting model. It is anticipated that IFRS 16 *Leases* will have a significant impact on the reported earnings, assets and liabilities, and cash flows of lessees.

Iseo is currently considering the impact IFRS 16 *Leases* will have on its own financial statements. Iseo plans to enter into a three-year lease on a machine with a market value of $5,000,000. Under the terms of the lease, Iseo will pay three annual instalments of $1,000,000 per annum in advance commencing on 1 January 2019. At the end of the lease term, the machine will be returned to the lessor. It is highly likely that Iseo will then lease a new machine on similar terms as the directors prefer to lease machinery as it is needed rather than buying it outright.

Previously under IAS 17 *Leases*, the lease would be classified as an operating lease and the annual lease payment of $1,000,000 would have been expensed to profit or loss each year.

The rate of interest implicit in the lease is estimated at 10% per annum.

Required

(a) Advise the Iseo's directors on the accounting treatment of the proposed lease in the three years ended 31 December 2021 under IFRS 16 *Leases*. (You should consider the accounting treatment in the statement of profit or loss, statement of financial position and the statement of cash flows).

(12 marks)

(b) Discuss the main implications of adopting IFRS 16 *Leases* in terms of changes to reported earnings, asset and liabilities, and cash flows for Iseo. Where possible, use your answer to part (a) to demonstrate your point. **(8 marks)**

(Total 20 marks)

4 Liscia

Liscia is a manufacturer and supplier of transit vans used for business purposes. The directors of Liscia are currently preparing the accounts for the year ended 31 March 2018, and require your advice on the following matters:

(1) On 1 October 2017 Liscia entered into a 12-month contract with Marcio, a new customer, to supply vans at $10,000 each. Under the terms of the contract, if Marcio purchases more than 1,000 vans in the year, the purchase price of each van will be retrospectively reduced to $9,500 per van. Liscia invoices Marcio on a quarterly basis starting on 31 December 2017 and Marcio is required to settle the invoice in full in 30 days. Following successful credit checks the contract was issued and signed by both parties.

In the quarter ended 31 December 2017, Marcio purchased 100 vans. At this point Liscia estimated that it was unlikely that Marcio would buy 1,000 vans in the year to qualify for the volume discount. In the quarter ended 31 March 2018, Marcio purchased 600 vans and placed a firm order for delivery of a further 500 vans in the quarter ended 30 June 2018. **(6 marks)**

(2) On 1 April 2017, Liscia issued 20,000 $1,000 2% convertible bonds at par. Each $1,000 bond is convertible in three years' time into 500 $1 equity shares at the option of the bond holder. The market rate of interest for similar $1,000 bonds without conversion rights is 5%. Liscia incurred issue costs of $1 million. The effective rate of interest for the liability component of the convertible bonds is 6.8% due to the allocation of the issue costs.

The following discount factors are applicable:

Year	2%	5%	6.8%
1	0.980	0.952	0.936
2	0.961	0.907	0.877
3	0.942	0.864	0.821

(8 marks)

(3) On 1 February 2018, Liscia signed a contract to buy a machine from an overseas supplier for 10 million dinars on 31 July 2018. The machine is custom built, based on Liscia's specifications, and will be ready for delivery and installation on 31 July 2018. To hedge against adverse foreign currency movements, Liscia enters into a forward contract to buy 10 million dinars on 31 July 2018 at an exchange rate of $1 to 2.5 Dinars. The directors wish to use hedge accounting in accordance with IFRS 9 *Financial Instruments*.

The spot rates and forward exchange rates are:

	Spot rate	Forward contract for delivery on 31.7.18
01.02.2018	$1 : 2.45D	$1 : 2.50D
31.03.2018	$1 : 2.20D	$1 : 2.25D

(6 marks)

Required

Advise the directors of the correct accounting treatment of the above transactions for the year ended 31 March 2018.

(Total 20 marks)

5 Orta

The Orta group consists of Orta and its one subsidiary Piatto.

Orta acquired 80% of the equity share capital of Piatto for $800,000 on its incorporation in 2006. It is group policy to value the non-controlling interest at fair value at the date of acquisition. The fair value of each $1 share in Piatto at incorporation was $1 per share.

An extract from Orta's consolidated statement of changes in equity for the year ended 31 March 2017 showed the following:

	Share capital $'000	Retained earnings $'000	Non-controlling interest $'000	Total $'000
At 31.3.2017	5,000	28,000	2,200	35,200

You have also been provided with the following information taken from the individual statements of financial position for Orta and Piatto as at 31 March 2018:

	Orta $'000	Piatto $'000
Share capital – $1 equity shares	5,000	1,000
Retained earnings		
– At 1.4.17	20,000	10,000
– Profit for the year ended 31 March 2018	5,000	2,000
Dividends (paid 31 December 2017)	(3,000)	(500)
Retained earnings at 31.3.18	22,000	11,500
Total equity	27,000	12,500

The following information is relevant for the year ended 31 March 2018:

1. On 1 October 2017, Orta disposed of 200,000 shares in Piatto for $2,100,000. No entries have been made in respect of this disposal in Orta's own individual financial statements.

2. Both Orta and Piatto paid dividends on 31 December 2017.

3. Assume profit accrues evenly throughout the year.

Required

(a) Prepare the consolidated statement of changes in equity for the Orta Group for the year ended 31 March 2018. **(10 marks)**

Orta's finance director, Teo Xie, has recently returned from a conference sponsored by the International Integrated Reporting Council on integrated reporting. Having heard how favourably external stakeholders respond to integrated reporting information, Teo now wishes to adopt integrated reporting at the earliest opportunity. He believes that the publication of an integrated report would give stakeholders a better understanding of Orta's ability to create value sustainably, which would help attract further investment and strengthen its competitive advantage.

The finance director's proposal has not been well received by the rest of the Orta's directors who are concerned that the costs of adopting integrated reporting far outweigh the benefits provided to external stakeholders.

(b) Discuss the key principles of integrated reporting and consider how the costs of adopting integrated reporting for Orta may outweigh the benefits provided to external stakeholders.

(10 marks)

(Total 20 marks)

[End of question paper]

MOCK EXAM 2 QUESTIONS

MODEL ANSWERS

MODULE E

PROFESSIONAL EXAMINATION 2

PAPER 13 - FINANCIAL ACCOUNTING 3

MONDAY 21st MAY 2018

Valid alternative points, whether or not they are shown in the Model Answers, will be given credit where appropriate.

1 Arvo

Part (a) requires the preparation of the consolidated statement of financial position which includes a vertical group structure and an acquisition of a subsidiary in stages (Syllabus section 13.2 and 13.3). The question also examines functional currency transactions and zero-coupon bonds (Syllabus section 13.4).

The following chapters of the BPP Paper 13 Study Text are relevant:

Chapter 6	Revision of basic groups
Chapter 7	Complex groups
Chapter 8	Changes in group structures
Chapter 9	Foreign currency translation
Chapter 14	Financial instruments

Consolidated statement of financial position for the year ended 31 March 2018.

	$m
ASSETS	
Non-current assets	
Property, plant and equipment 165 + 36 + 30 + 40 + 18 (W2c) + 5 (W3c)	294.0
Goodwill 20 (W2b) + 3 (W3b) + 3 (W4b)	26.0
	320.0
Current assets 70 + 20 + 15 + 15 – 1.5 (W8)	118.5
Total assets	438.5
EQUITY AND LIABILITIES	
Equity	
Share capital – $1 equity shares	50.0
Retained earnings (W5)	91.4
Other components of equity (W6)	25.6
	167.0
Non-controlling interest (W7)	23.1
	190.1
Non-current liabilities 100 + 20 + 15 + 16 – 1 (W10) + 0.9 (W10)	150.9
Current liabilities 55 + 15 + 10 + 17 + 0.5 (W9)	97.5
Total equity and liabilities	438.5

W1 Group structure

01.04.2016
RE = $18m
OCE = $2m

Arvo

90%

Becco   Disueri

01.04.2017   01.04.2017   31.03.2018
RE = $10m   10%   + 50% = 60%
OCE = $0m   80%
                                                  RE = $12m
                                                  OCE = $5m

Como

Como Effective interest = 90% × 80% = 72%
Como NCI = 28%

> **Tutorial note:**
>
> **Becco & Como**
>
> Arvo must consolidate any entity that it controls, either directly (Becco) or indirectly (Como). Como's assets and liabilities are consolidated on a line by line basis since Arvo controls these. When recognising Arvo's share of post-acquisition reserves, Arvo's 72% effective interest must be used (with the remaining 28% being allocated to Como's non-controlling interest).
>
> **Disueri**
>
> Disueri should be recognised in the consolidated statement of financial position from date control is achieved ie 31.03.2018.

W2 Acquisition of Becco

(a) **Restate fair value of investment to original cost**

	$m
Investment per Arvo's statement of financial position	90.0
Original cost (per question)	72.0
Increase in fair value (included in OCE)	18.0

Adjustment	Dr $m	Cr $m
Arvo's OCE	18.0	
Investment in Becco		18.0

> **Tutorial note:**
>
> **Investment in Becco**
>
> The investment in Becco is currently stated at fair value in Arvo's own financial statements. On consolidation this uplift in fair value is removed in order to restate the investment to its original cost, ie the consideration paid in the goodwill working in W2(b).

(b) **Goodwill**

	$m	$m
Consideration paid (original cost)		72.0
Non-controlling interest (fair value)		8.0
Fair value of net assets acquired at 01.04.2016		
Share capital	10.0	
Retained earnings (per question)	18.0	
Other components of equity (per question)	2.0	
Fair value adjustment – leasehold property (balance)	20.0	
Fair value of net assets at acquisition (per question)	50.0	(50.0)
Goodwill at 01.04.2016		30.0
Impairment		(10.0)
Goodwill at 31.03.2018		20.0

(c) **Fair value adjustment**

	At 01.04.2016 $m	Movement $m	At 31.03.2018 $m
Leasehold property	20.0	(2.0)	18.0

Fair value amortisation: $20m/20 years × 2 years = $2m

W3 Acquisition of Como

(a) **Restate fair value of investment to original cost**

	$m
Investment per Becco's statement of financial position	24.0
Original cost (per question)	20.0
Increase in fair value (included in OCE)	4.0

Adjustment	Dr $m	Cr $m
Becco's OCE	4.0	
Investment in Como		4.0

> **Tutorial note:**
>
> **Investment in Como**
>
> The investment in Como is currently stated at fair value in Arvo's own financial statements. On consolidation this uplift in fair value is removed in order to restate the investment to its original cost, ie the consideration paid in the goodwill working in W3(b).

MOCK EXAM 2 ANSWERS

(b) **Goodwill**

	$m	$m
Consideration paid (original cost) $20m × 90%		18.0
Non-controlling interest (fair value)		7.0
5m shares × 28% (effective interest) × $5 (fair value at acquisition)		
Fair value of net assets acquired at 01.04.2017		
Share capital	5.0	
Retained earnings (per question)	10.0	
Other components of equity (per question)	–	
Fair value adjustment – land (balance)	5.0	
Fair value of net assets at acquisition (per question)	20.0	(20.0)
Goodwill at 01.04.2017		5.0
Impairment		(2.0)
Goodwill at 31.03.2018		3.0

> **Tutorial note:**
>
> **Como's goodwill**
>
> The consolidation is prepared from Arvo's point of view. Therefore, since Arvo owns 90% of Becco, it should recognise only 90% of the consideration paid by Becco to acquire Como in the goodwill working.
>
> The remaining 10% of the consideration paid by Becco, will be adjusted for in Becco's non-controlling interest working (W7).

(c) **Fair value adjustment**

	At 01.04.2017 $m	Movement $m	At 31.03.2018 $m
Land (non-depreciable)	5.0	–	5.0

W4 Acquisition of Disueri

(a) **Restate original 10% holding to fair value when control is achieved on 31.03.2018**

- Normally, the carrying amount of the original 10% investment would be uplifted to fair value at the date control was achieved. However, this is not necessary since the original 10% investment has already been restated to fair value on 31.03.2018 in accordance with group policy.

- Fair value of the original 10% stake is $2.5 million (5m shares × 10% × $5) at 31.03.2018.

(b) **Goodwill**

	$m	$m
Fair value of original 10% holding (as above)		2.5
Consideration paid for additional 50% shareholding (per question)		12.5
Non-controlling interest (fair value)		10.0
Fair value of net assets acquired at 31.03.2018		
Share capital	5.0	
Retained earnings (as per statement of financial position)	12.0	
Other components of equity (as per statement of financial position)	5.0	
Fair value adjustment (per question)	–	
Fair value of net assets at acquisition (per question)	22.0	(22.0)
Goodwill at 31.03.2018		3.0

W5 Retained earnings

	Arvo $m	Becco $m	Como $m	Disueri $m
Per question	95.0	25.0	15.0	12.0
Fair value amortisation (W2c)		(2.0)		
Unrealised profit (W8)			(1.5)	
Foreign exchange loss (W9)			(0.5)	
Redeemable bonds (W10)				
Issue costs	1.0			
Finance costs	(0.9)			
At acquisition (W1)		(18.0)	(10.0)	(12.0)
		5.0	3.0	–
Group % retained earnings:				
Becco: 90% × 5m	4.5			
Como: 72% × 3m	2.2			
Group % goodwill impairment:				
Becco: 90% × 10m	(9.0)			
Como: 72% × 2m	(1.4)			
	91.4			

W6 Other components of equity

	Arvo $m	Becco $m	Como $m	Disueri $m
Per question	40.0	10.0	–	5.0
Cancel fair value uplift				
• Becco shares (W2a)	(18.0)			
• Como shares (W3a)		(4.0)		
At acquisition (W1)		(2.0)	–	(5.0)
		4.0	–	–
Group % post acquisition:				
Becco: 90% × 4m	3.6			
	25.7			

W7 Non-controlling interest

	Becco $m	Como $m	Disueri $m
NCI at acquisition (from goodwill W2b/3b/4b)	8.0	7.0	10.0
NCI % retained earnings (W5)			
Becco: 10% × 5m	0.5		
Como: 28% × 3m (W5)		0.8	
NCI % other components of equity (W6)			
Becco: 10% × 4m	0.4		
NCI % goodwill impairment:			
Becco: 10% × 10m	(1.0)		
Como: 28% × 2m		(0.6)	
Less: Becco's NCI's % cost of Como:			
$20m × 10%	(2.0)		
	5.9	7.2	10.0

Total NCI: 5.9 + 7.2 + 10.0 = $23.1m

W8 Unrealised profit

	$m
Como → Arvo: $10m × 25/125 × ½	1.0
Como → Becco: $5m × 25/125 × ½	0.5
Total unrealised profit	1.5

	Dr $m	Cr $m
Como's retained earnings (W5)	1.5	
Inventory (current assets)		1.5

W9 Foreign transaction

	$m
02.01.2018 – Record at spot rate: €5m × $1.20	6.0
31.03.2018 – Translate at year-end closing rate: €5m × $1.30	6.5
Foreign exchange loss	0.5

	Dr $m	Cr $m
Como's P/L (retained earnings)	0.5	
Como's current liabilities		0.5

W10 Zero coupon bonds

Issue costs should have been deducted from opening liability balance and not debited to profit or loss.

Correction:	Dr $m	Cr $m
Non-current liabilities	1.0	
Arvo's retained earnings (W5)		1.0

Recognise finance costs in profit or loss at the effective rate of interest of 4.8%

	$m
01.04.2017 Cash raised	20.0
Less: issue costs	(1.0)
	19.0
31.03.2018 Finance costs: $19m × 4.8%	0.9
At 31.03.2018	19.9

	Dr $m	Cr $m
Arvo's retained earnings (W5)	0.9	
Non-current liabilities		0.9

Additional areas where credit might be given, note this is not an exhaustive list:
- Own figure rules apply throughout.
- Candidates will obtain marks for workings even if the figures are not transferred onto the consolidated statement of financial position.

Part (b) covers the ethical and professional issues relating to the reclassification of long term liabilities (Syllabus section 13.1).

The following chapters in the BPP Paper 13 Study Text are relevant:

Chapter 4: Ethics and regulation of corporate financial reporting
Chapter 14: Financial instruments

The managing director's proposal to offset borrowings against consolidated goodwill appears to be an attempt at 'window dressing' the financial statements in order to ensure that borrowing covenants have not been breached.

The managing director points to the offsetting provisions of IAS 32 *Financial Instruments: Presentation*, however his argument is fundamentally flawed.

Firstly, consolidated goodwill does not meet the definition of a financial asset in accordance with the IAS 32 *Financial Instruments: Presentation* (which includes cash; equity instruments of another entity and contractual rights to receive cash or other financial assets from another entity). The provisions of IAS 32 *Financial Instruments: Presentation* therefore would not apply to this transaction.

Secondly, even if goodwill had met the criteria for a financial asset, the offsetting provisions are only permitted in limited circumstances, when:

- A legal enforceable right exists to set off the financial asset and financial liability; and
- The entity intends to settle on a net basis, or to settle the financial asset and liability simultaneously.

Since the proposed accounting treatment is in contravention of IFRS requirements the managing director's request cannot be actioned in the financial statements.

Directors have a responsibility to behave ethically at all times, particularly when preparing the financial statements. Directors are responsible for ensuring that the financial statements have been fairly presented, prepared in accordance with relevant IFRS and that adequate disclosure had been made. In accordance with IAS 1 *Presentation of Financial Statements* fair presentation requires faithful representation of transactions and other events. Clearly this is not the case since the managing director is attempting to hide the full extent of the borrowings by the group to avoid potential financial repercussions for exceeding borrowing covenants.

The directors must act ethically and in the best interests of the company and its stakeholders. Therefore, full amount of borrowings should be presented under non-current liabilities and adequate disclosures should be made in accordance with the economic substance of the transaction.

> Additional areas where credit might be given, note this is not an exhaustive list:
> - Relevant additional references from *The Conceptual Framework for Financial Reporting* or other relevant IFRSs.
> - Additional discussion on ethical and professional issues raised in the scenario.

2 Fusaro

This question examines the accounting treatment and deferred tax consequences of a number of transactions including equity settled share based payments, a defined contribution retirement scheme, and the acquisition of a subsidiary incorporating fair value adjustments.

The following chapters in the BPP Paper 13 Study Text are relevant:

Chapter 16: Employee benefits
Chapter 17: Taxation
Chapter 20: Related parties and share based payment

MOCK EXAM 2 ANSWERS

Advice to the directors of Fusaro

(1) Share options

In accordance with IFRS 2 *Share-based Payments* this is an equity settled transaction.

The share options should be recognised at fair value at the date of grant of $6, over the vesting period of three years.

Fusaro should recognise the share based payment expense based on the best available estimate of the number of share options that are expected to vest. The initial leavers estimate of 25% is not relevant, and the calculations for the year ended 31 March 2018 should be based on the revised 20% estimate determined at the year end.

The share based payment expense/equity reserve for the year ended 31 March 2018 is calculated as follows:

	$
2018: 1,000 options × (100 × 80%) × $6 × 1/3	160,000

Since the tax relief on the share based payment is not deductible until the share options are exercised, this creates a deferred tax asset as at 31 March 2018.

Tax relief is based on the intrinsic value of the share options (which represents the difference between the market value of the share at exercise less the exercise price). Since the share options vest over time the tax base of the share based payment at 31 March 2018 is calculated as follows:

	$
2018: 1,000 options × (100 × 80%) × $9 × 1/3	240,000

This generates a deferred tax asset of $48,000 ($240,000 × 20%) at 31 March 2018.

The deferred tax is credited to the profit or loss account unless the expected tax deduction exceeds the cumulative share based payment expense recognised to date. Here the deferred tax credit on the excess tax deduction is recognised directly in equity.

At 31 March 2018, the expected tax deduction exceeds the share based payment expense by $80,000 ($240,000 – $160,000). Therefore, a tax credit of $32,000 ($160,000 × 20%) should be recognised in profit or loss and a tax credit of $16,000 ($80,000 × 20%) recognised in equity.

Tutorial note (double entry not required)	Dr $	Cr $
Recognition of share based payment expense in P/L		
Share based payment expense (P/L)	160,000	
Equity reserve (SOFP)		160,000
Recognition of deferred tax on share based payments		
Deferred tax asset (SOFP)	48,000	
Tax (P/L)		32,000
Tax (Equity)		16,000

(2) Retirement benefit scheme

This is a defined contribution scheme since Fusaro's only obligation is to make a fixed contribution into the scheme each year. The pension risk (risk of variable returns) lies with the employee, since the pensions are not guaranteed and are based on the future performance of the pension fund.

Fusaro should account for the contributions made to the pension fund on an accruals basis. Therefore, an expense of $350,000 ($5m × 7%) should be recognised in profit or loss in the year ended 31 March 2018. Since Fusaro has only paid $200,000 into the fund by the year-end, it should accrue for the unpaid contributions of $150,000 in the statement of financial position.

As tax relief for pension contributions is obtained on a cash basis, the corresponding tax base relating to the pension accrual is nil. A deductible temporary difference of $150,000 arises at the year end, which represents a deferred tax asset of $30,000. Since the pension contributions are expensed to profit or loss, the deferred tax credit will also be recognised in profit or loss.

Tutorial note (double entry not required)	Dr $	Cr $
Recognition of defined contribution expense		
Profit or loss	350,000	
Cash (paid in year)		200,000
Accrual (SOFP)		150,000
Recognition of deferred tax asset		
Deferred tax asset (SOFP)	30,000	
Tax (P/L)		30,000

(3) **Acquisition of Garda**

In Fusaro's own single company financial statements, the investment in shares represents a financial asset in accordance with IFRS 9 *Financial Instruments*. Since the asset is held on a cost basis, no timing difference occurs since the tax base of the investment is also cost.

In the consolidated financial statements Garda will be recognised in the group accounts from 1 July 2017. Nine months of Garda's income and expenses will be consolidated in the statement of profit or loss and other comprehensive income and Garda's assets and liabilities on hand at the year end will be included in the group statement of financial position.

In addition, goodwill will be calculated at 1 July 2017. Goodwill is the difference between the fair value of the consideration paid less the fair value of all identifiable assets and liabilities at the date of acquisition. IFRS 3 *Business Combinations* requires all identifiable assets to be recognised at the date of acquisition provided a fair value can be obtained. Therefore, whilst the customer contracts would not be recognised in the individual accounts of Garda, they would be recognised in the consolidated financial statements and would form part of the initial goodwill combination.

No deferred tax will arise where the tax base of the identifiable assets is equal to the accounting base. However, since the tax base of the customer contracts is nil, this will create a taxable temporary difference of $0.5 million, which will generate a deferred tax liability of $100,000 ($0.5m × 20%) at the date of acquisition which will be included in the goodwill calculation as follows:

		$
Consideration paid		2,000,000
Fair value of identifiable net assets (including customer contracts)	1,500,000	
Deferred tax on customer contracts	(100,000)	
		(1,400,000)
Goodwill		600,000

In accordance with IAS 12 *Income Taxes* no deferred tax is recognised on the goodwill asset of $600,000, since goodwill in the consolidated financial statements is not a taxable asset. Subsequently, the goodwill asset will be subject to an annual impairment test each year.

Amortisation of $75,000 ($500,000/5 years × 9/12) will be charged to the consolidated profit or loss in respect of the customer contracts. The customer contracts will be shown in the consolidated statement of financial position at $425,000 ($500,000 – $75,000). The year-end deferred tax liability in respect of this intangible asset is now $85,000 ($425,000 × 20%) and the deferred tax liability is reduced by $15,000 ($100,000 – $85,000). As the amortisation on the intangible asset has been expensed to profit or loss, the reduction in the deferred tax liability will be credited to tax in profit and loss.

MOCK EXAM 2 ANSWERS

> Additional areas where credit might be given, note this is not an exhaustive list:
> - The use of own figures applies throughout. Mark for deferred tax calculations will be awarded based on students' own figures.
> - Further relevant discussion points relevant to the scenario.

3 Iseo

This question examines the accounting treatment and implications of adopting IFRS 16 Leases for the first time (syllabus area 13.4).

The following chapter in the BPP Paper 13 Study Text is relevant:

Chapter 15:   Leasing contracts

Part (a)

Accounting treatment under IFRS 16 *Leases*.

On 1 January 2019, Iseo will need to recognise a lease liability and a right of use asset in respect of the lease of the new machine.

The lease liability is calculated as the present value of the lease payments not paid on 1 January 2019 of $1,735,000 (as shown below):

Lease payments	*Instalment* $	*10% discount factor*	*Present value* $
01.01.2019 (not applicable as paid)	–		–
01.01.2020	1,000,000	0.909	909,000
01.01.2021	1,000,000	0.826	826,000
Present value of lease payments not paid			1,735,000

A right of use asset is recognised at $2,735,000, which is equal to the lease liability of $1,735,000 plus the first instalment of $1,000,000 paid on 1 January 2019.

The right of use asset will be depreciated over the shorter of the lease term or the useful life of the asset. As the asset is returned to the lessor at the end of the lease, the right of use asset will be depreciated over the three-year lease term, at $911,667 per annum.

The lease liability will be held on an amortised cost basis, and a finance cost at 10% will be allocated to profit or loss each year as follows:

Year ended 31.12	Lease liability at 1.1 $	Instalment $	Sub-total At 1.1 $	Finance cost @ 10% $	Lease liability at 31.12 $
2019	–	–	1,735,000	173,500	1,908,500
2020	1,908,500	(1,000,000)	908,500	*91,500	1,000,000
2021	1,000,000	(1,000,000)	–		

*rounding

Therefore, Iseo will record a finance charge of $173,500 and $91,500 in its profit and loss account in the years ended 31 December 2019 and 2020 respectively. As the lease liability is repaid in full on 1 January 2021, there is no finance charge in the 2021 profit or loss account.

The lease liability should be classified between current and non-current liabilities as follows:

	2019 $	2020 $	2021 $
Total lease liability	1,908,500	1,000,000	–
Current liability (due within one year)	1,000,000	1,000,000	–
Non-current liability (due after more than one year)	908,500	–	–

In the statement of cash flows, the annual payment of $1,000,000 will be allocated between operating and financing cash flows.

The finance cost paid will be classified as an operating cash out flow. Since the lease instalments are paid in advance, the first instalment is non-interest bearing. Interest is therefore paid in the following year as part of the next instalment.

The capital repayment element will be included as a financing cash outflow.

	2019 $	2020 $	2021 $
Cash flows from operating activities			
Finance costs	–	(173,500)	(91,500)
Cash flows from financing activities			
Finance lease (capital repayment)	(1,000,000)	**(826,500)	***(908,500)

**2020: 1,000,000 – 173,500 = 826,500
***2021: 1,000,000 – 91,500 = 908,500

Part (b)

Main implications of adopting IFRS 16 *Leases*
Reported earnings

The pattern of recognising expenses in profit or loss will change as shown below:

Under IFRS 16:	2019 $	2020 $	2021 $
Depreciation	911,667	911,667	911,666
Finance costs	173,500	91,500	–
Total expenses	1,085,167	1,003,167	911,666
Under IAS 17:			
Operating lease expense	1,000,000	1,000,000	1,000,000

Lease expenses under IFRS 16 *Leases* will generally be higher in the early years of the lease and lower in the later years of the lease. This is due to the recognition of depreciation and finance costs instead of a constant lease rental charge.

This change in reported earnings may impact on key performance ratios such as earnings per share, which would be lower than usual in the early years of the lease, and on interest cover due to the higher level of finance costs being recognised. The fall in reported profits could also negatively impact profit based remuneration schemes and debt covenants.

The change would however positively impact EBITDA (earnings before interest, tax, depreciation, and amortisation) and operating profit.

Recognition of assets and liabilities

Under IFRS 16 *Leases* Iseo will report higher assets and liabilities than under IAS 17 *Leases*. This is because under IAS 17 *Leases* the rental payment is expensed directly to profit and loss each year, and therefore no asset or finance lease liability is recognised in the statement of financial position.

Under IFRS 16:	2019 $	2020 $	2021 $
Right of use asset	2,735,000	2,735,000	2,735,000
Depreciation	(911,667)	(1,823,334)	(2,735,000)
	1,823,333	911,667	–
Finance lease liability (total)	1,908,500	1,000,000	–

The recognition of new assets and liabilities is particularly relevant to entities such as Iseo, whose leasing commitments were previously 'off balance sheet.'

There is a mis-match between the value of right of use asset and the corresponding lease liability. The lease liability exceeds the right of use assets carrying amount by $85,167 ($1,908,500 – $1,823,333) in 2019 and by $88,333 in 2020, which overall reduces Iseo's net assets in the period.

The finance lease liability will be classified as a financial liability and will therefore impact Iseo's overall borrowing levels, key solvency ratios such as gearing and its debt covenants. Care must be taken to ensure that Iseo does not accidentally breach existing loan covenants due the recognition of the lease liability and where necessary loan covenants may require renegotiating.

Reclassification of cash flows

The adoption of IFRS 16 *Leases* will have no impact on overall net cash flows since Iseo will continue to pay out $1,000,000 per year. Instead, there will be a change in the classification of cash flows. Under IAS 17 *Leases* the lease rental would have been treated as a $1,000,000 cash outflow under operating activities. Under IFRS 16 *Leases* operating cash flows will increase which will be accompanied by an equal corresponding decrease in financing cash flows as shown in part (a).

> **Additional areas where credit might be given, note this is not an exhaustive list:**
> - The use of own figures applies throughout. Marks for part (b) will be based on figures calculated in part (a).
> - Marks will be given for alternative calculations or disclosures presented.

4 Liscia

This question examines revenue recognition with variable consideration, the treatment of convertible bonds including the allocation of issue costs, and cash flow hedge accounting (syllabus area 13.4).

The following chapters from the BPP Paper 13 Study Text are relevant:

Chapter 14: Financial instruments
Chapter 21: Revenue recognition

Revenue recognition – sale of vans

The contract with Marcio will be accounted for in accordance with IFRS 15 *Revenue from Contracts with Customers* five step model.

A written contract exists between Liscia and Marcio which has commercial substance from which each party's rights and payment terms can be identified. The successful credit checks would suggest that it is probable that Liscia will be able to collect the amounts due from Marcio (step 1).

Under the terms of the contract Liscia's single performance obligation can be easily identified. Liscia is obliged to provide vans to Marcio over the 12-month contract term (step 2).

Liscia must then determine the transaction price (step 3). The transaction price is the amount of consideration that Liscia expects to be entitled to in exchange for transferring vans to Marcio.

In the quarter ended 31 December 2017, Marcio's buying patterns to date indicated that the volume discount would not apply and therefore Liscia should recognise revenue of $1,000,000 (100 × $1,000). In the quarter ended 31 March 2018, the purchase of an additional 600 vans and the firm order of a further 500 vans, provides sufficient evidence that Marcio qualifies for the volume discount and that this will need to be applied retrospectively to reduce the purchase price to $9,500 per van. In the quarter ended 31 March 2018, Liscia should recognise revenue of $5,650,000 [(600 × $9,500) – (100 × $500)], which represents the revenue from the quarter 2 sales less the $500 reduction for quarter 1 sales.

As a single performance obligation exists there is no requirement to allocate the transaction price to the separate performance obligations (step 4).

Liscia will recognise the revenue as the performance obligation is satisfied (step 5). Liscia will satisfy its performance obligation when Marcio receives control of the vans (this is normally at the point of delivery). In the year ended 31 March 2018, Liscia will recognise total revenue of $6,650,000 (700 × $9,500) as shown above. Revenue relating to the firm order of 500 vans will be recognised in the quarter ended 30 June 2018 when the vans are made available to Marcio.

$20 million convertible bonds

The convertible bonds will be accounted for as a compound instrument in accordance with IAS 32 *Financial Instruments: Presentation*. A compound instrument contains two components: a financial liability component (a contractual obligation to deliver cash to another entity) and an option over the entity's shares (the equity component). For Liscia, the economic effect of issuing the convertible bonds is substantially the same as simultaneously issuing a debt instrument and an option to the bond holders to acquire equity shares in three years' time.

IAS 32 *Financial Instruments: Presentation* requires the debt and equity components to be presented separately in the statement of financial position to reflect the economic substance of the arrangement and in accordance with the definitions of financial liabilities and equity instruments.

The $20 million cash raised will be separated into the debt and equity components on 1 April 2017. The fair value of the financial liability is established first and this is usually done using a discounted cash flow approach. The relevant discount rate is 5% ie the market rate of interest for similar bonds without conversion rights. The equity component represents the residual value after deducting the fair value of the liability from the $20 million cash proceeds raised.

	Cash flow $	5% Discount factor	Present value $	$
Cash raised				20,000,000
Less:				
Financial liability component				
(Coupon interest $20m × 2% = $400,000 pa)				
31.03.2018 Interest paid	400,000	0.952	380,800	
31.03.2019 Interest paid	400,000	0.907	362,800	
31.03.2020 Interest paid	400,000	0.864	345,600	
31.03.2020 Principal	20,000,000	0.864	17,280,000	
				18,369,200
Equity component (balance)				1,630,800

The issue costs of $1 million are then allocated against the initial value of the debt and equity components on a pro-rata basis as follows:

	Total $	Financial liability $	Debt $
Initial debt/equity split	20,000,000	18,369,200	1,630,800
Issue costs	(1,000,000)	(918,460)	(81,540)
	19,000,000	17,450,740	1,549,260

$1,000,000 × 18,369,200/20,000,000 = $918,460
$1,000,000 × 1,630,800/20,000,000 = $81,540

On 1 April 2017, the financial liability component will be recorded at $17,450,740 and the equity component at $1,549,260. The value of the equity component will remain fixed at $1,549,260 for the three years until conversion. The financial liability component will subsequently be held on an amortised cost basis at the revised effective rate of interest of 6.8% due to the allocation of the issue costs above.

	At 01.04.2017 $	Finance cost at 6.8% $	Interest paid $	At 31.03.2018 $
Financial liability	17,450,740	1,186,650	(400,000)	18,237,390

Finance costs of $1,186,650 will be expensed to profit or loss in the year. The financial liability will be carried at $18,237,390 in the statement of financial position at 31 March 2018

Forward contract

The forward contract is a derivative contract in accordance with IFRS 9 *Financial Instruments* which Liscia should recognise in its financial statements from 1 February 2018 when it became party to the contractual provisions of the contract.

As at the 1 February 2018 the fair value of the forward contract is nil. As 31 March 2018 the derivative is restated to fair value as follows

		$
Fair value at 31.03.2018	10,000,000 Dinars/2.25	4,444,444
Fair value at 01.02.2018	10,000,000 Dinars/2.50	4,000,000
Gain on forward contract		444,444

Liscia will recognise a financial asset of $444,444 at 31 March 2018. The fair value gain would normally be credited to profit or loss immediately unless the conditions for hedge accounting have been met in accordance with IFRS 9 *Financial Instruments*.

The following conditions must be satisfied for hedge accounting to apply:

(a) The hedging relationship must consist of relevant hedging instruments and eligible hedged items. A forward foreign currency contract would qualify as a relevant hedging instrument and the future purchase of the machine would qualify as a highly probable forecast transaction.

(b) The hedge must be properly documented at inception, including details of the hedged item and the hedging instrument, the type of hedge and how the hedge effectiveness will be calculated. It is unclear from the scenario presented whether the relevant documentation has been prepared and this requires further investigation.

(c) The hedge effectiveness requirements are met. In summary, this requires ensuring that there is an economic relationship between the hedged item and the hedging instrument; the effect of credit risk does not dominate changes in value and the hedge ratio of the hedging relationship falls within acceptable parameters (IFRS 9 *Financial Instruments*, para. 6.4.1).

> **Tutorial note:**
>
> Candidates are expected to have a general awareness of the IFRS 9 *Financial Instruments* hedging criteria and how it may apply to the scenario.

On the basis that the above criteria have been met, Liscia would account for this transaction as a cash flow hedge. This is because Liscia is hedging the risk in the changes of future cash flows in respect of a highly probable forecast transaction (the purchase of a machine in dinars on 31 July 2018).

The cash flow hedge will be accounted for as follows:

The portion of the gain on the forward contract that is deemed to be effective is recognised in other comprehensive income and in a corresponding cash flow hedge reserve in the statement of financial position. Any excess gain will be credited to profit or loss account immediately.

MOCK EXAM 2 ANSWERS

The effective portion is measured by comparing the gain to the unrecognised movement in the value of the asset calculated at the relevant spot rate as shown below:

		$
Value of asset at 31.03.2018	10,000,000 Dinars/2.20	4,545,455
Value of asset at 01.02.2018	10,000,000 Dinars/2.45	4,081,632
Increase in cost of the asset (unrecognised)		463,823

Since the gain on the forward is less that the increase in the cost of the asset at 31 March 2018, the hedge is deemed to be fully effective at this point and full gain of $444,444 is recognised in other comprehensive income.

Tutorial note (double entry not required)

	Dr $	Cr $
Cash flow hedge		
Financial asset	444,444	
Other comprehensive income/cash flow reserve		444,444

Additional areas where credit might be given, note this is not an exhaustive list:
- The use of own figures applies throughout.
- Credit will be given for all reasonable assumptions made.
- Marks will be awarded for any other relevant discussion points made.

5 Orta

Part (a) required the preparation of the consolidated statement of changes in equity which included a disposal of shares in subsidiary where control was retained (syllabus areas 13.2 and 13.3). The question required the application of knowledge to key consolidation workings eg group retained earnings, non-controlling interest in profit and loss and in the statement of financial position.

The following chapters of the BPP Paper 13 Study Text are relevant:

Chapter 2: Presentation of published financial statements
Chapter 6: Revision of basic groups
Chapter 8: Changes in group compositions

Consolidated statement of changes in equity for the year ended 31 March 2017

	Share capital $'000	Retained earnings $'000	Non-controlling interest $'000	Total $'000
At 01.04.2017 (per question)	5,000	28,000	2,200	35,200
Total comprehensive income (W2)		6,100	600	6,700
Adjustment to parent's equity (W4)/(W6)		(300)	2,400	2,100
Dividends paid (W3)		(3,000)	(200)	(3,200)
At 31.03.2017 (W5)/(W6)	5,000	30,800	5,000	40,800

MOCK EXAM 2 ANSWERS

W1 Group structure

Retained earnings: nil (incorporation)	Retained earnings at 01.10.2017:
	To 01.04.2017 10,000
	6m to 30.09.2017
	(2,000 × 6/12) 1,000
	11,000

W2 Total comprehensive income

	Orta	Piatto	Consolidated
	$'000	$'000	$'000
Profit for the year	5,000	2,000	7,000
Less: intra-company dividend (W3)	(300)	–	(300)
	4,700	2,000	6,700
Attributable to:			
Owners of the parent (balance)			6,100
Non-controlling interest			600
(2,000 × 20% × 6/12) + (2,000 × 40% × 6/12)			
			6,700

W3 Intra-company dividends

Piatto paid a dividend of $500,000 million on 31 December 2017 (after the part disposal of shares). Orta's share of divided of $300,000 (60% × $500,000) is eliminated in TCI. The non-controlling interest share of $200,000 (40% × $500,000) is shown in the consolidated statement of changes in equity.

W4 Part disposal: adjustment to parent's equity

	$'000
Proceeds	2,100
Increase in non-controlling interest (W5)	2,400
Adjustment to parent's equity	(300)

W5 Proof of group retained earnings at 31.03.2018 (not required)

	Orta	Piatto 80% to 1.10.17	Piatto 60% from 1.10.17
	$'000	$'000	$'000
Retained earnings at year end/disposal date (W1)	22,000	11,000	11,500
Adjustment to parent's equity (W6)	(300)		
Pre-acquisition retained earnings		–	(11,000)
		11,000	500
Group share:	8,800		
80% × 11,000	300		
60% × 500	30,800		

W6 Proof of non-controlling interest at 31.03.2018 (not required)

	$'000
At acquisition (1,000,000 × 20% × $1)	200
NCI % post acquisition profit to 01.10.2017: 11,000 × 20%	2,200
20% NCI at 01.10.2017	2,400
Increase in NCI (balance)	2,400
40% NCI at 01.10.2017 (2,400 × 40%/20%)	4,800
NCI% post acquisition profit from 01.10.2017: 500 × 40%	200
40% NCI at 31.03.2017	5,000

W7 Proof of group retained earnings at 31.03.2017 (per question)

	Orta	Piatto 80%
	$'000	$'000
Retained earnings at 31.03.2017 (from question)	20,000	10,000
Pre-acquisition retained earnings (W1)		–
		10,000
Group share:		
80% × 10,000	8,000	
	28,000	

W8 Proof of non-controlling interest at 31.03.2017 (per question)

	$'000
NCI at acquisition (1,000,000 × 20% × $1)	200
NCI % post acquisition profits (10,000 × 20%)	2,000
	2,200

> **Additional areas where credit might be given, note this is not an exhaustive list:**
> - The use of own figures applies throughout.
> - Credit will be given for alternative workings presented.
> - Marks will be awarded for relevant workings even if these have not been included on the face of statement of changes in equity.

Part (b) examined the key principles of integrated reporting and a discussion of whether the costs of preparation outweigh the benefits provided to external stakeholders.

The following chapter in the BPP Paper 13 Study Text is relevant:

Chapter 3: Environmental and social reporting

Integrated reporting provides a holistic view of how an entity creates value over time, by considering its use of its non-financial resources in addition to its financial capital. According to the International Integrated Reporting Council's (IIRC) Framework, the stated aims of the Integrated Report are to:

- Improve the quality of the information available to providers of finance to enable a more efficient and productive allocation of capital;

- Promote a more cohesive and efficient approach to corporate reporting that draws on a full range of factors that affect an entity's ability to create value over time;

- Enhance accountability and stewardship of the capitals available to an entity;

- Support integrated thinking, decision making and actions that focus on the creation of value in the short, medium and long term.

The resources available to an entity are referred to as 'capitals' which are used to assess value creation. Increases or decreases in these capitals are used to determine the amount of value created or exhausted in the period. The IIRC have identified six capitals which the entity might have access to:

- Financial capital: the funds available to an entity obtained either through financing eg debt or equity, or due to operating or investing activities.
- Manufactured capital: the manufactured physical objects available for use in the production and supply of goods and services eg buildings, plant and equipment.
- Intellectual capital: knowledge based intangibles and intellectual property eg licences, trademarks, patents etc.
- Human capital: the competencies, capabilities and expertise of employees.
- Social and relationship capital: relationships with stakeholders including local communities and customers.
- Natural capital: natural resources such as land, water, minerals and forests.

The capitals are interrelated, which requires management to balance short-term objectives eg profit maximisation, with long-term strategic goals. It is envisaged that such a holistic view of the entity's performance will encourage better decision making whereby decisions are not made in isolation.

It is expected that integrated reporting will benefit management and external stakeholders alike, by encouraging better decision making and by providing more relevant information on how an entity creates value over time.

Orta will need to weigh up the benefits of introducing integrated reporting with the associated costs, which include:

- Staff time/costs: The process of capturing and collating data is likely to require a significant amount of time and effort. Orta may need to employ additional staff to assist with the preparation of the integrated report or redeploy staff from other activities. In addition, staff training costs may be significant as it is likely that all staff, including the directors, will require training on this new holistic approach to corporate reporting in addition to more generic training on data capture and monitoring.
- IT systems: Orta may need to invest in IT systems capable of capturing and monitoring non-financial key performance information. IT costs may be significant due to the broad range of business activity which needs to be collected and monitored.
- Consultancy costs: It is unlikely that Orta's directors currently have the necessary expertise to produce the integrated report initially and may need to make use of external specialists in integrated reporting which may prove costly in the short term.
- Loss of competitive advantage: There is a risk that Orta may unintentionally disclose more information about its operational performance than intended which could be exploited by competitors.
- Dissemination costs: the additional costs associated with the production and distribution of the integrated report, including any additional website costs, will need to be considered.

Ultimately, it is up to the directors of Orta to decide whether integrated reporting is right for them. However, the positive evidence disseminated at the recent IIRC's conference on integrated reporting may suggest that for many companies the benefits of preparing the integrated report far outweigh the costs of its preparation.

> **Additional areas where credit might be given, note this is not an exhaustive list:**
> - Marks will be awarded for any other relevant points made regarding the key principles of integrated reporting including additional costs and benefits not specifically mentioned in the solution above.

MOCK EXAM 2 ANSWERS

Index

> Note: **Key Terms** and their page references are given in **bold**

Accounting concepts, 4
Accounting policies, 73, 460
Accounting profit, 422
Accounting records, 29
Accounting standards, 4
Accounting Standards Board (ASB), 284
Accrual basis of accounting, 456
Acquiree, 107
Acquirer, 107
Active market, 275
Actuarial gains and losses, 401
Advantages of global harmonisation, 20
Amortised cost, 353
Analysis of exchange differences, 219
Antidilution, 475
Asset, 18, 284, 400
Asset ceiling, 400
Asset turnover, 580
Assets held for sale, 464
Associate, 106, 109, 110, 442
Associates and joint ventures, 245

Barriers to harmonisation, 19
Basis of provision of deferred tax, 434
Benefits of cash flow information, 236
Big GAAP/little GAAP, 93
Bonus issues, 199
Borrowing costs, 291
BS 7750 Environmental Management System, 54
Business combination, 107

Capital reductions, 199
Capitalisation/bonus issue, 477
Carrying amount, 286, 294, 307
Cash, 236
Cash equivalents, 236
Cash flow hedge, 362
Cash flows, 234, **236**
Cash generating unit, 299
CERES Principles, 53
Change in accounting estimate, 460
Change in functional currency, 222
Changes in accounting policy, 73, 74
Changes in direct ownership, 200
Changes in equity, 40

Close members of the family of an individual, 509
Closing rate, 210
Comparative accounting systems, 19
Comparative information, 458
Competence, 77
Component of an entity, 466
Compound financial instruments, 345
Conceptual Framework, 13, 14, 341
Conceptual nature of employee benefit costs, 398
Confidentiality, 77
Conflict of interest, 80
Consistency of presentation, 456
Consolidated financial statements, 106
Consolidated income statement, 137
Consolidated Statement Of Financial Position, 138
Consolidating sub-subsidiaries, 156
Constructive obligation, 406, 495
Contingent asset, 500
Contingent consideration, 107
Contingent liability, 500
Contingent rights and obligations, 342
Contingent share agreement, 475
Contingently issuable ordinary shares, 475
Contract, 341, 527
Contract asset, 527
Contract liability, 527
Control, 106, 544, 559
Conversion, 208
Cost, 285, 307
Costs to sell, 465
Cross-sectional analysis, 578
Current asset, 34
Current cost, 19
Current liability, 34
Current service cost, 401
Current tax, 422
Customer, 527

Date of effective control, 160
Date of transition to IFRS, 269
Debt ratios, 583
Deductible temporary differences, 424, 431, 441
Deemed cost, 269
Deferral method, 434

INDEX

Deferred tax, 424
Deferred tax assets, 424
Deferred tax liabilities, 424
Deferred taxation and business combinations, 439
Deficit or surplus, 400
Defined benefit liability, 409
Defined benefit plans, 400, 404, 405
Defined contribution plans, 400, 404, 405
Demographic assumptions, 408
Depreciation, 268
Derivative, 341
Derivative instruments, 340
Determining functional currency, 212
Diluted eps, 479
Dilution, 475
Dilutive potential ordinary shares, 483
Direct holdings in sub-subsidiaries, 168
Direct method, 238
Disclosure of financial instruments, 368
Discontinued operation, 465
Discount rate, 408
Disposal group, 463
Disposal of foreign entity, 222
Disposals, 180
Dividend in specie, 200, 202
Divisionalisation, 202
Due care, 77

Eco-audit, 54
Eco-labelling, 54
Economic life, 381
Economies ceasing to be hyperinflation economies, 227
ED Recognition of deferred tax assets for unrealised losses, 446
ED2015/8: Application of Materiality to Financial Statements, 457
Effect of GAAP on gearing, 585
Effective date of disposal, 181
Effective interest method, 353
Effective interest rate, 353
Elements of financial statements, 18
Embedded derivative, 367
Employee benefits, 399
Entity, 341
Entry price, 275
Environmental audit, 53
Environmental Impact Assessments (EIAs), 54
Environmental Quality Management (EQM), 54
Environmental SWOT analysis, 54
Equity, 18
Equity instrument, 341, 514

Equity instrument granted, 514
Equity method, 109, 136, **107**
Ethical framework, 77
European Commission (EC), 5, 21
Exchange difference, 210
Exchange differences, 211
Exchange rate, 210
Exemption from preparing group accounts, 115
Exit price, 275
Expenses, 18

Fair presentation and compliance with IASs, 455
Fair value, 107, 128, 269, 285, 307, 312, 341, 382, 401, 465, 514
Fair value adjustments, 129
Fair value hedge, 362
Finance lease, 381, 384
Finance lease transactions, 245
Financial Accounting Standards Board (FASB), 14, 284
Financial analysis, 578
Financial asset, 341
Financial assumptions, 408
Financial instrument, 341
Financial liability, 341
Financing activities, 236, 237
First IFRS financial statements, 269
Fixed assets, 285
Fixed production overheads, 313
Foreign associates, 223
Foreign currency, 210, 268
Foreign operation, 212
Forgivable loans, 290
Framework for the preparation and presentation of financial statements, 16
Functional currency, 210
Fundamental principles, 76
Funds flows, 234

Generally Accepted Accounting Principles (GAAP), 6, 14
Going concern, 456
Goodwill, 136, 330, **331**
Goodwill and fair value adjustments, 221
Government grants, 290
Grant date, 514
Grants related to assets, 290
Grants related to income, 290
Gross investment in the lease, 382
Group, 106
Guaranteed residual value, 382

INDEX

Harmonisation and international differences, 19
Hedge effectiveness, 359
Hedge of a net investment in a foreign operation, 362
Hedged item, 359
Hedging, 359
Hedging instrument, 359
Held for sale, 464
Historical cost, 19
HKFRS 10, 107, 115
HKFRS 11, 142, 143, 144
Hyperinflation, 223

IAS 1 (revised) *Presentation of financial statements*, 29
IAS 1 Presentation of financial statements, 347
IAS 2 *Inventories*, 312
IAS 7 Statements of Cash Flows, 235
IAS 8 *Accounting Policies, Changes in Accounting Estimates and Errors*, 133, 423, 460
IAS 10 *Events After the Reporting Period*, 494
IAS 16 *Property, Plant and Equipment*, 285
IAS 17 *Leases*, 543
IAS 18 *Revenue*, 554, 557, 572
IAS 19 *Employee Benefits*, 398
IAS 21 *The Effects of Changes in Foreign Exchange Rates*, 210
IAS 22 *Business Combinations*, 442
IAS 23 *Borrowing Costs*, 291
IAS 24 *Related Party Disclosures*, 508, 543
IAS 25 *Accounting for Investments*, 109
IAS 27 *Consolidated AND SEPARATE financial statements*, 115
IAS 28 *Investments in Associates*, 135
IAS 29 *Financial Reporting in Hyperinflationary Economies*, 222
IAS 33 *Earnings Per Share*, 475
IAS 34 *Interim Financial Reporting*, 264
IAS 37 *Provisions, Contingent Liabilities and Contingent Assets*, 494
IAS 39, 349
IASB
    structure, 12
IASC Framework, 16
IFAC Code of Ethics, 76
IFRIC 1, 502
IFRIC 1 Changes in existing decommissioning, restoration and similar liabilities, 502
IFRS 1 *First Time Adoption of International Financial Reporting Standards*, 269
IFRS 3 *Business Combinations*, 126, 320, 331, 442
IFRS 5 *Non-Current Assets Held for Sale and Discontinued Operations*, 294, 463
IFRS 9 *Financial Instruments*, 340
IFRS 15, 527
IFRS 15 *Revenue from Contracts with Customers*, 526, 548
IFRS for small and medium-sized entities, 94
IFRS Practice Statement Management Commentary, 487
Impaired asset, 294
Impairment, 294
Implications of high or low gearing, 584
Impracticable, 461
Inception of the lease, 381
Income, 18, 527
Incremental costs, 381
Independent, 77
Indirect method, 238
Indirect versus direct, 238
Initial direct costs, 381
Inputs, 275
Insurance benefits, 404
Intangible asset, 320
Intangible non-current asset, 331
Integrated reporting, 60
Interest, dividends, losses and gains, 346
Interest cost, 401
Interest rate implicit in the lease, 381, 384
Interim financial report, 264
Interim period, 264
International Accounting Standards, 4
International Accounting Standards Committee (IASC), 4, 6
International Ethics Standards Board for Accountants (IESBA), 76
International Federation of Accountants (IFAC), 5
International Integrated Reporting Council, 60
Inter-temporal analysis, 578
Intrinsic value, 514
Inventories, 312
Investing activities, 236, 237
Investment, 110
Investment Entities, 115
Investment property, 307

Joint arrangement, 106
Joint control, 107, 560
Joint operation, 107
Joint venture, 107, 109, 442

Key management personnel, 509

INDEX

Lease, 378, 384
Lease term, 381, 385
Lessee's incremental borrowing rate, 384
Lessee's incremental borrowing rate of interest, 382
Lessee's incremental borrowing rate of interest, 382
Leverage, 584
Liability, 18, 495
Liability method, 434
Limited liability, 28
Liquidity, 582
Loan transfers, 547

Management Commentary, 487
Market participants, 275
Material, 457, 460
Material, 460
Materiality, 457
Measurement, 19
Measurement date, 514
Measurement of revenue, 527
Measuring unit current at the balance sheet date, 224
Minimum lease payments, 381, 384
Minority interests, 158, 160
Mintzberg, 64
Monetary items, 210
Most advantageous market, 275
Multi-employer plans, 400, 404
Multinational companies, 579

Nature of profit, 74
Net defined benefit liability, 400
Net interest on the net defined benefit liability, 401
Net investment in a foreign operation, 212
Net investment in the lease, 382
Net realisable value, 312, 314
New top holding company, 200
Non-cancellable lease, 381
Non-controlling interest, 107, 220, 244
Non-controlling interests, 303
Non-current asset, 285

Off balance sheet finance, 542
Offsetting a financial asset and a financial liability, 347

Onerous contract, 498
Opening IFRS statement of financial position, 269
Operating activities, 236, 237
Operating cycle, 34
Operating lease, 381, 384
Operating segment, 469
Options, 481, 487
Options, warrants and their equivalents, 475
Ordinary share, 475
Organisation for Economic Co-operation and Development (OECD), 5
Originating timing differences, 426
Other comprehensive income, 38
Other long-term employee benefits, 399
Owner-occupied property, 307

Parent, 106
Past service cost, 401
PBIT, profit before interest and tax, 580
Pension schemes, 403
Performance obligation, 527
Permanent differences, 426
Piecemeal acquisitions, 190
Plan assets, 400
Post-employment benefit plans, 399
Post-employment benefits, 399
Potential ordinary share, 475
Power, 106, 108
Practice Statement: Application of Materiality to Financial Statements, 457
Present value, 19
Present value of a defined benefit, 400
Presentation and disclosure of taxation, 437
Presentation currency, 210
Presentation of accounting policies, 459
Presentation of financial instruments, 343
Previous GAAP, 269
Principal market, 275
Prior period errors, 460
Professional behaviour, 77
Profit margin, 580
Profit smoothing, 495
Profitability, 580
Progress with harmonisation, 21
Property, plant and equipment, 285
Prospective application, 461
Provisions, 495
Purchased goodwill, 331
Purpose of financial statements, 454

Qualifying asset, 291
Qualifying insurance policy, 400
Quasi-subsidiary, 543

Ratios, 579
Realisable (settlement) value, 19
Realisable value, 19
Receivable, 527
Recognition, 18, 292
Recoverable amount, 295, 465
Recoverable amount of an asset, 295
Related party, 508
Related party transaction, 508, 509
Relevant activities, 106
Remeasurements of the net defined benefit liability, 401
Reporting date, 270
Reporting period, 30
Residual value, 285
Responsibility for financial statements, 454
Restructuring, 498, **499**
Retrospective application, 460
Retrospective restatement, 460
Return on plan assets, 401
Revalued assets, 429
Revenue, 527
Reversal of an impairment loss, 305
Reverse acquisitions, 133, 134
Right-of-use asset, 384
Rights issue, 478

Sale and leaseback transactions, 391
Sare split/reverse share split, 477
Seasonal fluctuations, 75
Securitised assets, 546
Segment reporting, 469
Service cost, 401
Settlement, 401, 412
Settlement value, 19
Share option, 514
Share-based payment arrangement, 514
Share-based payment transaction, 514
Shareholders' investment ratios, 585
Short-term employee benefits, 399, 402
Significant influence, 106, 109, **509**
Small Business Enterprise and Employment Act, 94
Social and political considerations, 579
Spot exchange rate, 210

SSAP 1, 543
Stand-alone selling price, 527
State plans, 404
Statement of comprehensive income, 35
Statement of financial position, 31
Statement of principles, 284
Subsidiaries, 111
Subsidiary, 106, 110
Subsidiary moved along, 201
Subsidiary moved down, 201
Substance over form, 543
Sub-subsidiaries, 155
Supplier audits, 54

Tax, 268
Tax base, 424, 425, 439
Tax expense (tax income), 422
Tax planning opportunities, 433
Taxable profit (tax loss), 422
Taxable temporary differences, 424, 427, 441
Temporary differences, 424
Termination benefits, 399, 417
Timing differences, 428
Transaction costs, 275
Transaction price, 527
Translation, 209
Treasury shares, 346
Trend analysis, 578
True and fair view, 6

UK GAAP (Davies, Paterson & Wilson, Ernst & Young, 4th edition)., 15
Unearned finance income, 382
Unguaranteed residual value, 382
United Nations (UN), 5
Unprofessional behaviour, 80
Useful life, 382

Value in use, 295, 465
Value of purchased goodwill, 331
Variable lease payments, 382
Variable production overheads, 313
Vest, 514
Vesting conditions, 514
Vesting period, 514

Window dressing, 75
Working capital, 34

INDEX

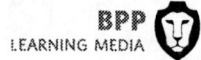